T0368445

SOLDIER:
A Memoir
VOLUME II

NEAL GRIFFIN

authorHOUSE®

AuthorHouse™
1663 Liberty Drive
Bloomington, IN 47403
www.authorhouse.com
Phone: 1 (800) 839-8640

Published by AuthorHouse 08/22/2016

ISBN: 978-1-5246-2514-6 (sc)
ISBN: 978-1-5246-2515-3 (hc)
ISBN: 978-1-5246-2513-9 (e)

Library of Congress Control Number: 2016913571

Print information available on the last page.

ACKNOWLEDGMENT

Special thanks to Kate Page Korp for her warmhearted review and wealth of positive suggestions. She donated endless hours editing the draft to make it readable and coherent. Her kind support and encouragement gave me the confidence to share my story openly. I am blessed and forever grateful for her friendship.

CONTENTS

Chapter 1   Vietnam 1
Chapter 2   Back to Germany 149
Chapter 3   Transition to Rotary Wing and Mohawk 216
Chapter 4   Korea 312
Chapter 5   Artillery Officer Advanced Course 493
Chapter 6   Fort Huachuca 513
Epilogue 703

CHAPTER 1

Vietnam

Though many dangers, toils and snares I have already come,
Tis grace has brought me safely thus far,
Tis grace that will lead me home.

M y tour in Vietnam started the 1st of August, 1967, when I kissed my wife, Claudia, good-bye in Fort Lewis, Washington. I held her tightly, savoring her soft body. After letting her go, I got on the army bus that would take me to the airfield. As the bus pulled away, she waved until I was out of sight. She then got into our Volkswagen and started the long drive back to Fayetteville, North Carolina.

The bus was full of soldiers on the way to Vietnam. As I walked down the aisle, looking for a seat, I saw Darrel sitting near the rear of the bus. I took the empty seat beside him and waved to Claudia. I watched her waving back until the bus turned, and she disappeared.

Darrel said, "I'm glad you're here. It's a long trip without company."

At the airfield, we boarded a civilian 707, one of the fleet of 707s the air force leased to shuttle troops back and forth to Vietnam. A soldier occupied every seat. Some were heading over for the second time, and some, like me, were going for the first time.

It was the second time for Darrel. He'd been an enlisted man in a transportation unit on his first tour. Now he was going back as a first lieutenant after going to transportation OCS and flight school. We talked for a while about what we had done while on leave and then settled down in our own thoughts.

I reclined my seat and let my mind roam. At last, I was on the way to war. It excited me and, at the same time, caused me apprehension. This could be a one-way trip. The army had prepared me for the job I was going to do. I trusted that God would be by my side, and as long as I relied on him, I would be fine. If I didn't make it back, I would have died doing the job I loved for the country I loved. As a soldier, I had given the army a signed blank check, so to speak. So far, my time in the army had been fun. Now it would be time to do the job for which I had been training for eleven years. It was like going to school, and at last, I would graduate.

I thought about Claudia. She had a long drive ahead of her, but I had faith in her ability and felt sure she would make it home okay. The night before, I had laid out her route on a map and identified where she had to stop each night. I had also told her to stay only in recognized hotels, such as the Holiday Inn. I didn't want to worry about her, since it would be at least a month before I would know how her trip went.

It was a long flight to Vietnam. We stopped in Tokyo to refuel and then landed in Cam Ranh Bay, Vietnam, around 1300. Cam Ranh Bay was a sprawling air force and navy base that housed one of the two reception centers in Vietnam. The other one was at Bien Hoa, near Saigon. There was no terminal, and buses picked us up at the apron where the aircraft parked. The 707 spent minimal time on the ground, and the buses that came for us unloaded soldiers who were headed home. Ground crews were quickly refueling and servicing the aircraft. We left the aircraft silently, while the soldiers heading home were shouting and obviously joyful. After we emptied the aircraft, they boarded. The apron was in range of Vietcong mortars and rockets, so no one wanted to give them time to set up and fire.

As the bus pulled off the apron and onto the service road, I saw two small doves sitting on a limb in a bush beside an old bomb crater. The bush was leafless, as were all the trees and vegetation. Bomb blasts and artillery and small-arms fire had destroyed all except that which was slowly growing. I thought it was ironic that doves, a symbol of peace, were there to welcome me to war. Or were they God's symbol to me that he was by my side?

The buses took us to an array of large tents. A wall of sandbags rose halfway up the sides of the tents. A stench hung over the area. I later found out that it was the stench that comes from cleaning latrines by burning excrement.

The tents housed the reception center that would process us. There, we had our records checked, indoctrination classes on Vietnam, and assignments issued. They assigned Darrel and me to the 220th Aviation Battalion. The headquarters were in Tuy Hoa, with the companies based in the outlying provinces. When we finished processing, it was evening, and a sergeant took us to a tent for the night. After Darrel and I ate at the officers' field mess, I headed to my tent to write Claudia a letter. Darrel put on some civilian clothes, and I asked him where he was going. He said he was going to party and wanted to know if I wanted to come. I said, "Damn, Darrel, it's our first night in Vietnam, and you are already going out to party?"

He answered, "Don't forget! I've been here before, and I know where to go and what to do." With that, he left, and I wrote to Claudia and went to sleep.

The next morning, Darrel showed the effects of his partying. We ate breakfast and reported to the personnel company. The sergeant who finished processing us said a helicopter would pick us up at 1000 to take us to Tuy Hoa. He pointed out the helipad and told us to be there at ten minutes to ten.

We watched a UH-1 helicopter, or Huey, approach and land in a swirl of dust. The crew chief jumped out with his helmet on and approached us, asking, "Are you the two officers going to the 220th?"

We said yes over the roar of the helicopter, and he said, "Jump aboard." We grabbed our duffel bags and threw them onto the Huey. No sooner had we sat down than the pilot applied power, and we began to lift off. Before we could get our seat belts fastened, the Huey was flying south along Highway 1 to Tuy Hoa. I later learned that it was best to fly over safe areas whenever possible, in the event you had to ditch the aircraft. Highway 1 was safe along the coast and provided a suitable emergency landing site for a helicopter.

The flight to Tuy Hoa took about an hour. A jeep met us at the flight operations lounge and took us to the battalion headquarters. The driver dropped us off at a tent with a sign labeling it the administration office. Inside, we reported to the S1, a captain, who welcomed us to the 220th and told us we were going to the 219th Aerial Recon and Surveillance Company in Pleiku. The company had further assigned us to the First Platoon, located in Qui Nhon, north of Tuy Hoa. A Huey would take us there tomorrow. First, we had to attend some indoctrination classes that afternoon. After looking at our records and having us sign in, he directed us to the S4 section to draw our field equipment, an M16, and a .45 automatic.

After we drew our field equipment and weapons, he assigned us BOQ (bachelor officer quarters) rooms for the night. Plywood partitions created the rooms in a large tent. Each room contained a GI cot and a wall locker where we could secure our equipment. The weapons we kept with us, although we had no ammo. We stored our gear, had lunch, and attended orientation classes on Vietnam. After the classes and evening meal, I was ready for bed. Darrel was dressing to go out.

"You sure you don't want to go with me?" he asked. "Tuy Hoa has some great bars and beautiful women."

"No, thanks, Darrel," I answered. "I'm hitting the sack."

It took awhile for me to go to sleep. My mind was jumping from thought to thought and did not want to calm down. I thought about Claudia and the kids, flying, and ammo, and I wondered when we would get to fire our weapons and zero them. From far off, I could hear the *thump-thump* of artillery fire. I must have been asleep when Darrel came in, because he woke me up momentarily.

I slept lightly and woke up at 0530. I was ready to get going. After shaving, I asked Darrel if he was going to breakfast. He mumbled a no and asked me to wake him in time to catch our flight to Qui Nhon.

I studied Qui Nhon from the air as the Huey taking us there entered a downwind for landing. It was a large port city. The airfield and most of the city lay between a mountain west of the city and the sea to the east. This view would quickly become as familiar as the back of my hand. The winds were mostly out of the north and northwest, and with the mountain on the west side of the airfield, the usual approach to the Qui Nhon airfield was a right downwind for runway thirty-six.

The Huey sat down on the helipad and let us out in front of base operations. A jeep was waiting, and when we got off the Huey, the driver approached us, asking, "Are you the new pilots for First Platoon of the 219th?"

"We are," I answered.

He replied, "Welcome to the First Platoon, sir. I'll take you to platoon headquarters and Captain Tom, the platoon leader." He helped us put our bags on the jeep, and we drove about a hundred yards to a Quonset hut that had a big sign in front: Headhunters, First Platoon. I could see OV-1 Bird Dogs in the two rows of revetments in front of the Quonset hut. A pilot was conducting a preflight on one. He saw us, waved, and continued his preflight.

Captain Tom was standing behind a counter in the rear of the Quonset hut. The hut served as the flight operations and platoon headquarters office. On the wall behind the counter was a 1:50,000 scale map of Qui Nhon province covered by acetate.

Walking up to Captain Tom, I saluted and said, "Lieutenant Griffin reporting for duty, sir."

I think this surprised as well as impressed Captain Tom and surprised Darrel. Captain Tom returned my salute and shook my hand, saying, "Glad you're finally here." Darrel followed my example.

Captain Tom stood about six feet tall and had a medium build, a lightly freckled face, and reddish hair. He wasted no time and started briefing us on our mission, Qui Nhon Province, the status of the platoon, and the company, located at Camp Holloway in Pleiku. He spoke with authority and expertise gained during the almost two years he had been doing aerial reconnaissance. Since he was a bachelor and loved the job he was doing, when his first tour was up, he'd extended for another year. During the briefing, two of the platoon pilots, a W-2 Henry and a Captain Malady, completed their reconnaissance missions and came in to prepare their reports.

After introductions, Captain Tom turned us over to Captain Malady, his platoon operations officer. He would get us settled in the BOQ and scheduled for in-country training flights. It had been more than a month since Darrel and I had touched the controls of an aircraft. We would have to refresh our flying skills by flying ten hours with an instructor pilot. That would qualify us to fly a combat mission.

We talked with Warrant Officer Henry while Captain Malady completed his recon report. WO Henry was a new pilot, having arrived in the country two months ago. He spoke highly of the platoon and Captain Tom. While we were waiting, he helped us carry our gear out to the platoon jeep.

Captain Malady drove us the half mile around the north end of the runway to our BOQ hooch. All the platoon officers slept in the same

Quonset hut. Plywood walls partitioned the hut to form individual cubicles. It was not much but was a lot better than I'd expected. I noted three large fuel storage tanks sitting about fifty yards from the BOQ. That worried me the entire time I was at Qui Nhon. Although they had berms around them, the berms didn't look high enough to contain the fuel if the Vietcong (VC) decided to blow them.

After we put our gear in the BOQ, Captain Malady took us to the post exchange, mess hall, and officers' club. Those were the most important places and provided most everything we would need to live while there. After that, he took us back to the flight line and briefed us on the Bird Dogs assigned to the platoon.

Then he showed us the preflight checks. Each plane had two 2.75 rocket tube launchers on each wing. The planes only had basic instruments, as they had in flight school. He told us to only trust the airspeed, turn and ball, engine rpm, power, fuel flow, and flap gauges. All flying was conducted strictly on visual flight rules since no one had calibrated the instruments in two or three years.

Five of the seven planes assigned to the platoon were D models, which meant they had a constant-speed variable-pitch propeller. This propeller automatically varied its pitch depending on what it needed to maintain the speed set by the power setting. It saved the pilot from having to constantly adjust power during turns, climbs, and descents. It worked like cruise control on modern cars. The other two were G models with fixed-pitch propellers. The pilot had to add or decrease power constantly to maintain airspeed during maneuvers.

That evening, we met the remaining three pilots assigned to the platoon, who were glad to see us. With us aboard, each would only have to fly one or two missions a day instead of the three or four they were flying now.

Darrel and I spent the next two days getting checked out. We flew training missions morning and afternoon. The emphasis was on touch-and-go landings. The Bird Dog is a tail dragger, which means it has a tail wheel instead of tricycle gear. The tail wheel makes the Bird Dog susceptible to ground loops in crosswind landings, especially if the pilot gets careless. The crosswind can catch the tail and spin the plane around, usually flipping the plane onto its side and causing extensive damage to the aircraft.

After six hours of takeoffs and landings, I was proficient enough to fly safely. Captain Malady spent the next four hours showing me the boundaries of Binh Dinh Province and our mission area. He showed me all the army airfields and dirt strips within the province. It was good to know these locations if an emergency occurred, forcing one to land. After we reviewed visual reconnaissance procedures, we entered a free-fire zone north of Qui Nhon, and I practiced firing the 2.75 rockets mounted on the Bird Dog. After that, he cleared me to fly combat missions as a high aircraft chasing one of the experienced pilots. I would do this for four or five flights before flying on my own. The checkout was thorough, and I felt confident about my ability to begin flying missions.

Flying a high aircraft provides extra training. The high aircraft flies at 1,500 feet AGL and watches the mission aircraft flying along at treetop level. Doing this, I could mentally note the various roads and landmarks, mark them on my map, note the communications between the mission pilot and supported units, and follow the various support missions in progress. At 1,500 feet AGL, I could see more and picture what it was going to look like navigating at treetop level. I got to see how one used the 2.75 rocked to mark targets for gunships and air force FACs, vector medivacs, and help infantry units find themselves in the triple-canopy jungle. After the fourth mission as high aircraft, I entered platoon flight operations to complete my report and saw my name on the mission board for a 1000 coastal reconnaissance mission.

Seeing my name thrilled me. I was bursting with excitement. I was going to fly a combat mission on my own. At last, training was over, and I had to perform. It was the first time I would fly an airplane for a purpose other than training. I felt an awesome responsibility. Captain Tom walked up to me and asked, "You got any questions on you mission tomorrow?"

"Not right now, sir," I answered.

The navy conducted a recon of the coastal area once a week to ensure they were prepared for naval actions along the coast. I was flying Lieutenant Commander Wilson on this week's recon. It was an easy mission for a new pilot: all I had to do was fly the coast north to Chu Lai and back. Lieutenant Commander Wilson had been flying this mission for more than a year, and I would be able to learn from him. That night, I slept soundly after going over the flight in my mind before drifting off to sleep.

Lieutenant Commander Wilson did not look like a navy guy with his jungle uniform and big mustache. He had started the preflight by the time I arrived, and he took stock of me as I introduced myself. He knew that I was a green pilot and that this was my first mission, but he did not show any concern as we finished the preflight. He joked easily and quickly briefed me on a couple areas he wanted to take a close look at.

Fifteen minutes later, we were airborne at six hundred feet, headed north. Once we got clear of the city, we turned to the east and headed for the coastline. I kept smiling to myself in disbelief that I was flying toward the coast of Vietnam in the middle of a war. I felt like a kid, enjoying a first-time experience of something that was dangerous yet feeling no fear.

When we reached the coast, I turned north, and our recon started. The coast of Vietnam from Nha Trang north is beautiful and totally different from the Florida coast. Small mountains jut into the dark blue sea, which turns green when small beaches interrupt the mountains. I knew the fishing would be good. Then my mind returned to our mission, and I started looking for signs of activity along the shore. The evidence of past battles was present here and there. The gutted ruins of a village appeared occasionally as the mountains flowed into rice paddies that extended almost to the small beaches. Trench lines along hilltops and areas pockmarked with bomb craters marked previously contested areas, but neither of us saw any sign of new activity.

I could see Chu Lai up ahead, when Lieutenant Commander Wilson spoke over the intercom. "I've seen enough. We can go home now."

Turning south, I felt a little let down. *That's all? No enemy sightings. No real war experience. Just a sightseeing flight along the coast, and now it's over for today.* I decided to at least vary my flight home. I asked Lieutenant Commander Wilson if he had any objections to flying about a half mile inland on the return flight. He said no problem, and I flew inland about a mile and paralleled the coast back to Qui Nhon. Again, we saw nothing new, but it was good recon technique practice for me. I did feel a little disappointed that we saw no action.

About five miles north of the airfield, I called for landing. The tower responded with landing instructions: "Enter a right downwind for runway thirty-six. Barometer thirty-[point-two zero. Winds two hundred ninety at eight knots. Report downwind."

I answered, "Roger. Report downwind." For the first time on the flight, my heartrate quickened, and I felt a twinge of stress. I had to land with a ten-degree, eight-knot crosswind in an aircraft that was unforgiving in crosswind landings. I had to do this right! This increased tension became the usual routine for each mission. It did not matter how difficult the mission or how many times the enemy shot at or hit me. My real panic started when I got landing instructions and had to land in a crosswind. Simply put, my fear of a ground loop turned the landing into the most stressful phase of the flight. When it was over and I was taxiing to the ramp, only then could I begin to relax and say the mission was complete. I left Vietnam with 799 combat support flight hours, in which I landed the Bird Dog more than a thousand times. I can honestly say the landing terrified me the most each time.

After each mission, the pilot completed a recon report of sightings and locations except for the coastal recon. The navy observer, because of the naval-specific information, did that report, while the pilot added any army-specific info. Army doctrine called for an observer on every flight, but most of the time, it was just the pilot. On any mission, one could expect to fly recon at treetop level, listen to two radios, mark targets for the air force FAC, adjust artillery fire, and vector in gunships and medical evacuation. That was what I did day after day, depending on the particular mission.

Because of the missions' repetitious nature, I am not going to describe every mission. Many were actually boring except for the fun derived from flying over mountains, triple-canopy trees, and grass-covered valleys at treetop level. From here on, I am going to focus on those that were uniquely different or had a significant impact on me.

The first night after reporting in to the First Platoon, I wrote Claudia a letter to the address in North Carolina. If it got there before she left for Germany, she would have my address, and I would start getting mail. Our plan was for her to stay with her mom in Germany while I was in Vietnam. Then I would ask for a direct assignment to Germany after my tour in Vietnam. If the letter did not get there before she left, then she would have to send my letters to the replacement company listed on my orders, and it would be weeks before my mail caught up to me.

I was surprised and happy when I got three letters from her the third week in August. She had received my letter at the North Carolina address. When I read about what she had done, it upset me a little. Instead of moving to Germany, she had decided to move to Atlanta, Georgia, because that was where her friend Marcy was staying while her husband, Dale, was in Vietnam. Claudia thought it would be better to have someone she knew living nearby while I was gone. I felt that Marcy would not be a good influence on Claudia, but there was no way I could broach the subject purely on my suspicions. I would just have to trust Claudia, which I did. I guess the problems Claudia and I had in our marriage worried me and caused the pain I felt sometimes during these long separations.

The most important occasion each day is mail call. A letter is a symbol that someone cares one way or another, and most of the time, it does not matter which. War does not take away problems between individuals. It will not strengthen a weak union or improve a good one. War interrupts and tests relationships, and many times, it destroys them. Letters become the vessels crossing the distance between war and home and bringing a cargo of news bursting with love, anger, mistrust, tenderness, sadness, facts, hellos and good-byes, and pleas for understanding. In war, every participant attends mail call with expectations. Even if there is no letter coming, few soldiers miss mail call.

I was determined to be the best aerial reconnaissance pilot in Vietnam. I did not want marital problems distracting me. To be the best, I knew I had to master reconnaissance techniques and develop my skills as a pilot. I read all the reconnaissance reports and studied photos of the various enemy positions so I would quickly recognize them from the air. When one of my peers returned from a mission, I discussed it with him to gain insight from what he saw and did. Every time I had the opportunity, I practiced my flying skills.

I decided not to waste the time it took to fly back to Qui Nhon after each mission. We usually climbed to 1,500 feet to avoid small-arms fire on the way back to Qui Nhon. I took advantage of that time by simulating an emergency and practiced flying the aircraft under that condition. For example, I would pretend I had no aileron control and would fly the aircraft back using just the rudder to turn the aircraft and keep it on course. The next time, I would simulate the loss of my vertical stabilizers and fly the aircraft using trim tab to climb or descend. I would fly without using the rudder by using engine torque to turn the aircraft. Whatever I could imagine, I did it to hone my skills.

Even in war, army units have to meet regulatory requirements. Army regulations require aviators to attend a monthly safety briefing. To meet the monthly safety briefing requirement and complete administrative actions, the 219th staged what was called a monthly fly-in. On that day, the 219th aviators based at Qui Nhon and Kontum would stand down and fly to Camp Holloway the night before the meeting. This brought all the officers together once a month and allowed the commander an opportunity to interact with his officers without having to fly to each location.

The fly-in also provided an opportunity to catch up on aircraft maintenance. Army aircraft undergo a detailed maintenance inspection at every twenty-five and every one hundred hours of operation. At every twenty-five hours, the crew chief performs a maintenance inspection at his level. The company maintenance platoon does the one-hundred-hour inspection and all the maintenance on the aircraft above crew chief level. That meant that periodically, we had to stand down a pilot so he could fly an aircraft to Camp Holloway for the maintenance. We saved hours of downtime by flying those aircraft needing maintenance to Camp Holloway on the fly-ins. While the aviators attended the safety meeting, the maintenance platoon completed the hundred-hour inspections and worked on the airplanes. They had the airplanes ready when it was time for us to return to our areas.

By the time of the fly-in for September, the monsoon season had started for the eastern half of Vietnam. Every day was cloudy and rainy, which grounded most flights since we could only fly under visual flight rules. Even on days with partial clearing, we had to be careful to avoid instrument flight conditions. The weather had a habit of turning nasty at a moment's notice and encasing you in clouds. None of the flight instruments in the airplanes worked, so getting caught in instrument flight conditions could be disastrous. The monsoon conditions extended westward to a line formed by the rising terrain at the An Khe Pass. There, the terrain rose two thousand feet to the plateau of central Vietnam.

The afternoon before the September fly-in, I flew the plane with Darrel in the backseat to Camp Holloway. After takeoff, I found a hole in the clouds and climbed to four thousand feet. At that altitude, I could see over the clouds and the plateau to the west. The sky was solid clouds all the way to the An Khe Pass, except for the hole I used to climb up above the clouds. After I reached four thousand feet, it was a simple forty-minute flight to Camp Holloway.

That night, the company commander had officers' call in the officers' club. The officers' call evolved into a rip-roaring party, and since no one had to fly the next day, we got bombed. I had a great time listening to the many war stories that abounded that night. Most of them were hilarious, while some had less-than-desirable endings. That was the night I met a captain nicknamed Wild Bill. I would see him one more time at another fly-in, at which we would share an incident.

Most of us stumbled out of bed just in time to make the 0800 company formation. With hangovers pounding, we stood in the hot sun through roll call, an awards ceremony, and a pep talk from the CO. After that, we moved to the officers' club for the safety meeting. After the safety briefing, the operations officer discussed recon reports and how he wanted us to complete them to help him in turning them into a monthly summary. It was lunchtime when the meetings were over.

After lunch, Darrel and I moved down to the maintenance platoon to see if our plane was ready. It was, and we did a thorough preflight. It was important to inspect thoroughly an airplane after it came out of maintenance, because occasionally, the maintenance people had bolts and nuts left over. You wanted to find out where the hardware went while you were still on the ground.

Since I had flown there, Darrel was flying back to Qui Nhon. I climbed into the rear seat, and as I buckled my seat belt, I noticed that the removable control stick was not in its storage position. Since many aircraft were missing them, I didn't think anything about it. The removable control stick locks into a receptacle on the floor of the aircraft and allows a pilot in the rear seat to fly the plane. Instructor pilots mainly use the stick when checking out new pilots or giving the required ninety-day check rides.

After takeoff, Darrel climbed to four thousand feet and headed east. We could see the stacks of clouds beginning at the An Khe Pass and socking in the eastern coast of Vietnam. The weather report for Qui Nhon called for rain showers with broken cloud cover up to four thousand feet.

That meant we would have to find a hole in the clouds so we could let down and land.

As we crossed the An Khe Pass, I noticed Darrel rubbing his forehead and eyes. At the same time, the nose of the aircraft drifted left of course.

"Darrel, what's wrong?" I asked.

He was slow to respond, as if confused. "I don't know, Neal. My head started hurting after we reached altitude, and now my vision is blurry."

That got my attention right away. "You mean you can't see?"

"No. My vision is all blurry. You are going to have to help me fly the plane," he replied brokenly, as if under stress, still rubbing his forehead.

My heartrate increased a bit as I tried to grasp what was happening. I looked at the mount where the missing stick should have been and cursed. If I got back, I was going to ensure that every plane had a stick. *Calm down, Neal,* I told myself. "Okay, Darrel, we're drifting off course and starting to descend, so turn the nose right until I tell you to stop, and put some back pressure on the stick."

When the nose pointed at Qui Nhon again, I told Darrel to stop the right turn but hold the back pressure. I did not want to chance entering the thick bank of clouds below us. I unstrapped my rifle and tried to fit it in the stick mount on the floor, but it wouldn't work. I had rudder pedals up, but without a stick, I could not fly the airplane from the rear seat. I mentally ran through how we would land the airplane with Darrel blind and me directing him. It did not come out pretty. I thought about turning back to Camp Holloway, but the problem was the same. We had to land, and Qui Nhon would be better since the hospital was right on the airfield. "Darrel, can you see any better?"

He was still rubbing his forehead and shaking his head. "No, it's still blurry, and my head hurts."

Now I could see a good-sized hole in the cloud bank about five miles north of Qui Nhon. We had to descend now, because there was no telling how long it would stay open. "Okay, Darrel, we are going to start a descent. There's a large break in the clouds a couple of miles ahead and to the left. Turn left, and lower the nose."

I couldn't believe the situation we were in. It frightened me. Landing a Bird Dog is difficult enough, but doing it blind with someone coaching you would be almost impossible. I could not let Darrel know I was terrified, because I was sure he was too, and we both needed to be as calm as possible to make this work. "Okay, Darrel, stop turning, and lower the nose a little more."

We were in the hole and descended about a thousand feet, when suddenly, Darrel said, "Neal, I think I can see again, and the pain in my head is easing."

I thought he must have had some sinus blockage if losing altitude was relieving the problem. "Darrel, can you see, or do you just think you can see?"

He replied in a relieved tone, "No, I can see now. I'm okay now."

"Thank God," I answered. "You scared the shit out of me."

"What do you think I did to myself?"

We were under the clouds at a thousand feet, and Darrel contacted the Qui Nhon tower for landing. I was happy to be on the ground again. After we reported the incident, all planes had sticks in the mounts. The flight surgeon's diagnosis was blocked sinuses above his eyes, which caused the pain and somehow blurred his vision. He was not sure why the blurred vision occurred. Obviously, Darrel had a mild sinus infection, and he'd climbed too fast after we left Camp Holloway, which had caused his sinuses to block. We learned a lesson from that flight.

The monsoon rains played havoc with recon flights. Most of the time, we hung around the platoon operations, waiting for a break in the rain clouds. When we had enough visibility and altitude, one of us would take off and see how far we could make it. Using this technique, we managed to get a flight or two in each day. Of course, the Vietcong and North Vietnamese Army (NVA) were aware of our situation and took advantage of it to move, resupply, prepare fighting positions, and, undetected, conduct surprise attacks on outposts.

We could easily detect their movement once we were in the air. They could not see the trails they left when moving in the rain-soaked grass. Dry grass keeps its position, while wet grass bends in the direction of the object moving through it. That made their movement easy to spot.

One morning, Darrel and I were in platoon operations, when the overcast broke up into larger cumulus clouds, and the rain stopped. We had about five miles' visibility, so Darrel and I decided to fly into the free-fire zone north of Qui Nhon to see what was going on. None of us had been able to fly for three days, and no doubt the Vietcong and NVA were taking advantage of their ability to move freely.

I flew the first mission with Darrel in the rear observer seat. We covered half the area, when it started to rain again, with visibility dropping to about a mile. We decided to get back to Qui Nhon before it closed in to where we could not land.

We were on the ground for about an hour, when the weather broke again. This time, Darrel flew, and I took the backseat. We were working the canals along the coast, looking for boat movement and personnel, when we spotted a VC courier in a small boat. He was wearing a backpack with an AK-47 slung across it. We startled him as we passed overhead at twenty feet. Darrel yelled, "Neal, get your rifle ready!" as he made a steep turn to get back to the VC's location.

I unslung my M-16, charged it, and put the muzzle out the side window as Darrel maneuvered the Bird Dog around. The VC had jumped from the small skiff and was trudging through the narrow irrigation ditch toward a berm that would provide him cover. "Get ready, Neal," Darrel said as he positioned the aircraft so I could see the VC out of the left window. We approached him at twenty feet above the ground, and at about a hundred yards, I squeeze off three rounds. They hit the ditch left and about twenty yards ahead of the fleeing VC. I had fired directly at him the first time. Now at forty yards, I fired behind him, and the rounds struck the water to his rear and then struck him, driving him down into the water. By then, we'd soared past him, and Darrel started a steep turn so we could see if he was still moving. He was not. Only an arm and the top of the backpack were visible as he floated in the water. Around him, the water was turning red.

Darrel was shouting, "Great shot, Neal!" and I was getting sick, shocked at what I had just done. At the time, we were hunting the enemy, and when we found him, we engaged and destroyed him. He was in the free-fire zone, and our orders were to engage all targets in that area. That was the justification for what we had done. When we returned to base and reported the incident, everybody congratulated us.

I do not know how Darrel felt about it. We never talked about it, and I never asked Darrel. But the more I thought about it, the more it tormented me. I did not have to kill him. Although he was the enemy, he was running from us, not firing at us. Some would say what we did probably saved the lives of friendly soldiers, which might true. However, I could not forgive myself and have never forgiven myself for that act. While flying back, it was hard for me to thank God for keeping us safe during the flight. While I would be responsible for the deaths of many more enemy soldiers, those deaths did not affect me, because those men were trying to kill me. But this single incident would continue to torment me over the years until enough time passed to dim my memory of it.

The effect it had on me would change the way I conducted myself during other missions. By the second week in October, the weather was starting to clear. We were starting to see more movement in the free-fire area north of Qui Nhon. One morning, a few minutes after I had taken off on a recon mission, I received a call from the sector headquarters liaison NCO. "Headhunter 19, this is Alfa Control. Over."

I wondered what they wanted as I answered, "Alfa Control, this is Headhunter 19. Over."

"Headhunter 19, go to map coordinates 346756 and check road running north into free-fire zone. An ARVN outpost can see individuals moving north along road. We have no report of friendlies operating in that area."

"Roger, Alfa Control," I answered as I turned the Bird Bog to the north. I pulled out my map and quickly found the road. It ran north from Qui Nhon, past an Army of Vietnam (ARVN) observation post, and into the free-fire zone. Once, it had been the major artery to many villages in the free-fire zone. Because of Vietcong and North Vietnamese Army presence in the area, the Army of the Republic of Vietnam had cordoned the area and declared it a free-fire zone. Periodically, they conducted search-and-destroy operations throughout the area based on intelligence that we often provided. All Vietnamese knew the area was a free-fire zone and off limits. That was why the ARVN considered all personnel in the area to be enemies and attacked them when they were found.

It took about five minutes to reach the road entering the free-fire zone. At first, I saw nothing, but after flying the road for about five miles, I could see seven figures with rucksacks walking north on the road. They wore black pajama-like clothes. I could see no weapons, and as I flew over them, they looked up at me. Seeing their faces, I could tell that five of the seven were female, and two were children, according to their height and size.

I turned and flew back over them about fifty feet to verify my identification. They all looked at me, and I thought I could see fear on their faces. They started moving faster as I flew past and turned to go back over them. "Alfa Control, this is Headhunter 19. Over."

"Headhunter 19, this is Alfa Control. What do you have for me?"

"Okay, there are seven personnel—five females and two children—moving on the road about six miles northeast of the ARVN outpost. All are dressed in black with rucksacks and no weapons."

"Roger, Headhunter 19. Wait out."

While I waited for him to get back to me, I climbed to a thousand feet to get a better view of the surrounding area. I didn't want to let my focus on the females on the road distract me from the possibility of other threats to me in the form of an automatic-weapon position or an antiaircraft weapon. Keeping the individuals on the road in sight, I flew a recon of the area surrounding the road out to a couple of miles. The women kept walking in the same direction.

"Headhunter 19, this is Alfa Control. The sector commander's orders are to destroy the group. Can you attack them with your rockets or vector a gunship into the area?"

The sector commander he was referring to was an ARVN major general and the military commander for Qui Nhon Province. "Hey, Alfa Control, these are women and children. I don't intend to attack them. Think we ought to send a truck out with infantry to secure them."

There was silence for a few minutes, and then I heard, "Headhunter 19, the sector commander orders you to take them out now. They are taking in supplies to the VC in the area."

"Roger, Alfa Control, but I am not going to kill women and children. You need to think of some other course of action."

"Headhunter 19, may I remind you the sector commander gave you a direct order? You know the consequences of disobeying a direct order in combat."

I had not thought of that. They could court-martial me for disobeying a direct order, but I could not destroy them. The memory of the courier I had killed made it impossible. Many times, the VC and NVA forced

17

innocent civilians into service. The way these people were reacting to my threat suggested to me that they were not combatants or dedicated VCs. Someone had forced them to walk down this road in hopes that some American like me would not attack them. I had to do something that would result in their capture. It had to be something that would relieve them of any retribution if they survived. I thought maybe if I could get them to go back, I could get them close enough to the ARVN outpost four miles from there. There, the soldiers could deal with them. I decided to try to herd them back the way they'd come.

I turned the Bird Dog, dropped down to about fifteen feet off the ground, and flew toward them on the left side of the road. I could see them out my right window, and they could clearly see me. I slowed down to slow-flight speed to give me more time over them. They must have sensed something was about to happen, because they stopped and watched me closely. I did not point the nose of the plane at them, so I suspect they knew I was not going to attack them with my rockets.

As I passed about ten feet to the side of them, I could see the frightened expressions on their faces. At my closest point to them, I motioned emphatically with my finger and arm for them to go back. After I passed them, I added power and began a turning climb to see how they had reacted to my signal. They were standing there as if trying to decide what to do. Then they continued the way they had been going, so I made another low, slow pass, motioning for them to turn back.

They continued down the road, ignoring my signal again. *Okay*, I said to myself, *I am going to get their attention*. Flying low and slow in the direction they were walking, I took a frag grenade from my bag and pulled the pin. Holding the handle, I flew over them, and about fifty meters past them, I dropped the grenade. I banked quickly to see their reaction.

The exploding grenade stopped them. I could see their arms waving as if they were discussing what to do. Again, I flew over them, motioning for them to turn back. They stopped again, and I could tell they understood what I wanted them to do. However, after some discussion, they continued. I decided a stronger warning was in order.

This time, I decided to use a rocket, which makes a hell of a noise when fired, and the explosion is much larger than that of a grenade. I circled to their rear and started flying toward them at fifty feet. When I was over them, I fired a high-explosive rocket at the road about a hundred meters ahead of them. I was so close that I barely cleared the rocket exploding in the roadbed. The blast of the rocket convinced them to turn around and walk back toward the ARVN outpost. I herded them back to the ARVN outpost by slowly circling them. Each time I flew by them, I motioned for them to keep going. Once, they stopped as if they were going to turn around, but after I dropped another grenade, I had no further trouble with them.

I called Alfa Control and told him what I was doing. He was not happy that I did not attack and destroy them. He asked me to report when the soldiers at the outpost had them in custody. It took an hour and a half for the women to make it to the outpost. When I saw the ARVN take them in the outpost, I called Alfa Control to report that they were in custody. I hoped my refusal to obey a direct order would blow over without further incident.

After reporting to Alfa Control, I turned toward Qui Nhon. I was getting low on fuel and would not be able to fly my original mission without refueling. After landing, while the crew chief refueled my aircraft, I reported to Captain Tom and briefed him on what had happened with Alfa Control. He told me not to worry about it. He would take care of it if anything came down. That was a relief, and I felt better knowing I had his support. I took off again and completed my original mission: a recon of the An Khe area northeast of Pleiku. I never heard anything further about the incident. I hoped the women survived.

By October of 1967, I had transitioned into a skilled aerial reconnaissance pilot. I had mastered flying the Bird Dog to include crosswind landings. I have to clarify that. Crosswind landings still made me nervous, and unfortunately, I never could overcome the twinge of anxiety when flying a Bird Dog and entering the traffic pattern for landing. After a while, I decided that it was good to feel that way. It would keep me from becoming complacent. Complacency in the cockpit is a big factor in many aviation accidents.

On October 19, the South Vietnamese Army moved out on a search-and-destroy mission in an area fifteen kilometers north of Qui Nhon. The units included combined South Vietnamese Regional Forces and South Vietnamese Popular Forces. American army advisers were among the units. We were providing aerial support for the operation. Captain Tom scheduled the missions so that there would always be one aircraft supporting the units.

On the morning of October 20, I relieved Headhunter 12 at 1000. I contacted Panther 2A, the call sign of the army adviser to the Popular Force company I was supporting. After setting up communications, I began a visual reconnaissance ahead of the Popular Force company that was advancing toward the small hamlet of Dinh Than. In this form of recon, I would fly fifty feet above the ground, looking for bunkers, fighting positions, or any sign that would give the company advanced notice of contact. This support was different from the usual recon. Usually, I would mark my findings on a map, so after the flight, I could prepare a detailed report. Analysts would consolidate this report with others from across Vietnam and develop an intelligence picture of Vietnam.

After about two hours of my tedious flying without sighting any sign of enemy forces, Captain Tom called me on platoon FM to tell me that I had to stay on the mission until around 1500. He recommended using An Khe to refuel and reload rockets since it was closer than Qui Nhon.

The Popular Forces were now about a kilometer from Dinh Than and entering the rice paddies that extended up to the edge of the village. The open, flat terrain there provided no cover except for the berms that divided the rice fields into smaller fields and enabled the farmers to flood the fields. Trails lined the berms, which were about two or three feet high in places. If enemy forces were present, they would use the berms as cover and as a place to set up fighting positions, such as bunkers, so that was where I focused my recon. I started flying back and forth along the berms ahead of the advancing forces, looking closely for any sign of enemy activity.

As the point unit got to within two hundred meters of the village, I climbed up to two hundred feet so I would have a better view of the village. I had seen nothing out of the ordinary in the rice fields and berms. The village was in a contested area and deserted. The residents had left earlier because anyone in the village would be a Vietcong suspect. The regional forces would interrogate them and possibly take them prisoner.

I was on the north side of the village, when Panther 2A called. His voiced was strained and tense as he spoke. "Headhunter 19, we're under heavy automatic-weapons and machine-gun fire. We have wounded and need medevac." I heard the weapons firing and small explosions in the background when he transmitted. It was a blow in the stomach to me because I had obviously missed something, and now wounded or dead men were the result.

"Roger, Panther 2A," I answered as I banked the aircraft in a steep turn to get back over the area so I could see what was happening. As I flew over the rice paddy the lead unit was crossing, I could see six soldiers on the ground about thirty meters from the last berm on the edge of the village. The first burst of fire had wounded six soldiers and pinned the rest of the lead unit down. I could see the forces pinned down behind the berms to the rear of the wounded soldiers. Three of the six soldiers were rolling as if in pain, while the other three lay still.

"Panther 2A, can you get to the wounded?" I asked.

"No, Headhunter 19. The fire is so heavy we can't get to them. The heaviest fire is coming from where the two berms meet in front of the downed troops. We can't put medevac in, because it's too hot. Can you call in artillery?"

"No way, 2A. The wounded are too close to the target. I still don't see the guns. They must be firing from a well-camouflaged bunker."

As I flew directly over the spot he described, I could see smoke from the firing weapons but not the weapons. They had to be in a bunker not visible from the air.

"Panther 2A, I am going to try something to distract them while your guys see if they can reach the wounded. I am going to make a low pass straight into the berm to see if that will draw their fire from the wounded. You copy?"

"Roger, Headhunter 19. Copy that. We will have our men ready to go."

I banked, flew about a mile south of the firefight, and dropped down to what I estimated to be twenty feet above the ground. I lined up and flew straight at the spot where I had seen the smoke from the firing weapons. I lowered fifteen degrees of flaps to slow my speed down. I hoped the enemy force would start firing at me and give the Popular Forces an opportunity to recover their wounded. I was heartbroken that I had missed sighting the firing position.

As I drew closer, I could see tracers from the enemy machine guns arching up toward me. I immediately put in right rudder, and the nose of the aircraft turned to the right. I applied left aileron, and instead of flying straight ahead, I was sliding straight ahead, because I was cross-controlling the aircraft. I was praying the instructors who'd trained the gunners firing at me had taught them to lead the nose of the aircraft. If so, they would try to lead the nose of the aircraft, but because of the cross controls I was applying, the aircraft was not going in the direction the nose pointed. It was sliding in a direction about ten degrees to the left of the nose.

I heard 2A call out, "Headhunter 19, be aware you are under heavy fire."

"Roger, 2A. Can you get to the wounded?" I could see the tracers zipping across my nose. I felt myself tense up, expecting any second to feel the rounds rip into the Bird Dog. As I passed overhead, I saw several soldiers jump up from behind a berm and run for the wounded. However, I could not see if they made it to the wounded. Then I crossed over the spot marked by the smoke from the weapons firing at me.

As I crossed over the smoke, I heard 2A say, "That almost worked, Headhunter, but they couldn't get the wounded. The fire is too heavy, and we can't chance losing more troops. Can you attack it with your rockets?"

"I don't know, 2A. The wounded are too close. I could hit them with a rocket attack." What 2A didn't know was that we had no real sights for firing our rockets. During training, each pilot used a different-colored grease pencil to put a mark on the windshield. He would use that mark as an aiming point to sight and fire the rockets in that aircraft. Since we usually used the rockets to mark a position for gunships or FACs, the accuracy wasn't a big problem. We could compensate for accuracy by using the rocket's impact to point out the target. But to attack a bunker, especially with wounded troops lying within thirty meters of the bunker, I needed pinpoint accuracy, which was impossible with grease-mark sights.

"We've got to do something, Headhunter. We are going to lose those wounded if we don't get them out."

I could feel the pressure of being the only one able to do something but not knowing what to do. *Okay*, I thought, *if we don't do something, they'll die. If I attack with my rockets, I might kill them or I might hit the bunker if I am lucky.* Obviously, I had to attack the bunker. I switched to Guard frequency and called, "Any gunships in vicinity of An Khe, come up on

Headhunter frequency, please." I repeated the call once more but got no response, so it was up to me now.

"Panther 2A, this is Headhunter 19. I am going to make another low pass to see if I can pinpoint the bunker. If I can, I will come around and try to take it out with my rockets. Give me all the covering fire you can."

I heard 2A say, "Roger," as I banked the aircraft and set up another low pass. My plan was hopefully to see the bunker and not just the smoke from the firing weapons. That would help me line the aircraft up more accurately when I made the firing pass. This time, I was about a kilometer out when I started my approach. I was about ten feet above the ground, which was a little scary because there was no room for errors on my part. It also put me in the direct fire of the enemy, who could see that I was going to make another pass. I put in left rudder and right aileron this time, hoping to once again fool the enemy gunners. It seemed like eternity flying the kilometer to the target. I could hear 2A warning about being under heavy fire and see the tracers zipping by the front of the aircraft. A line of tracers would go to the left of the aircraft and then to the right as the enemy gunners desperately searched for the right lead. I heard 2A say, "Break it off; the fire is too heavy," but I ignored everything and concentrated on finding the bunker. I saw the wounded go past and then the berm and smoke but no real feature that I could say was the bunker. All I had was the spot where the smoke from the weapons was the thickest.

"Okay, 2A, I don't see the bunker. I see the spot where the smoke is thickest from the machine guns firing. I will try to hit that spot with a rocket."

"Headhunter, recommend you not make another pass. You are a sitting duck."

"Roger, 2A. Understand."

I banked around again to set up my approach. This time, I was going straight in with no cross controls. To hit the spot where I thought the bunker might be, the aircraft had to be straight and level when I fired for the rocket to run straight. I was going to start the rocket run at a hundred feet above, in a shallow dive straight for the spot where I thought the bunker might be. I decided I would wait until I saw the wounded start moving under the nose of the aircraft before I fired. I hoped this would keep them safe from the possibility of the rocket going short and hitting

23

them. At the same time, I had to be far enough from the target for the rocket to arm itself.

Climbing to a hundred feet above the ground, I lined the aircraft up on the target. Taking a deep breath, I started the run toward the target. I centered the ball in the turn indicator and armed my high-explosive rockets, ignoring everything except keeping my grease mark lined up on the target and the ball centered as I flew toward the target. Again, the tracers came for me. It seemed I could have reached out and touched them. I was tensing and forcing myself to keep flying toward the spot on the ground, as if I were going to crash into it. As the first wounded soldier passed under my nose, I fired my right wing's HE rocket.

The rocket soared ahead of me in a plume of smoke, and I pulled back on the stick and applied full power to the engine. I could feel the aircraft start to respond to my controls as I flew into the black cloud of the exploding rocket. For a second that seemed like an eternity, all I could see was a grayish cloud of dirt and debris surrounding me. Then I felt the concussion tossing the aircraft about. Then I was past the berm and climbing through fifty feet. My heart was pounding, and sweat soaked my Nomex flight suit. As I climbed out in a slow turn, I could see troops from the Popular Forces charging toward the berm. Running beyond the berm, I could see what looked like six or seven Vietcong heading for the north side of the village.

Quickly, I called 2A and told him of the Vietcong. "Roger, Headhunter," he answered. Excitedly, he said, "Man, you creamed that bunker. You put that rocket dead in the firing port. Request you bring in the medevac for the wounded."

"Roger, 2A." I switched the VHF and called the medevac helicopter standing by. I vectored them into the rice paddy where the wounded were waiting.

"Panther 2A, request you pop smoke. Do you have medevac in sight?"

I watched a green smoke grenade detonate near the wounded, and medevac headed for it. Within ten minutes, the wounded were on their way to the field hospital at Qui Nhon. Meanwhile, Popular Force units destroyed the fleeing Vietcong. Now it became a routine mission again. Panther 2A told me that they were halting for about an hour to regroup. I told him I was going to An Khe to refuel and replace the rocket I had fired.

Thirty minutes later, I was back over the area. When I let 2A know, he responded, "Roger, Headhunter. Your rocket destroyed a well-disguised bunker. We found the remnants of a machine gun and four bodies. Good job."

"Thanks for the update, 2A," I answered with a feeling of satisfaction and pride. It made me feel better knowing the bunker had been so well camouflaged that anyone could have missed seeing it. I had learned a lot in the past three hours, and I did recon differently for the rest of the mission. When there was even a remote possibility of an area holding enemy forces, I adjusted artillery way before arrival of the lead units of the Popular Force. I finally contacted some gunships and used them several time to do recon by fire. The Popular Force company had no further contact with enemy forces that day.

It was getting late, and I was tired when I heard, "Headhunter 19, this is Headhunter 17. What's your position? Over."

I was glad to hear Headhunter 17 call. It meant he was en route to relieve me, and about now, I needed relief. I had been flying combat support for more than six hours. I was out of rockets and running low on fuel. The only break had been three hours ago, when I had taken fifteen minutes to land at the Eleventh Cavalry's LZ near An Khe to refuel, reload rockets, and take a piss. The last two hours had drained the energy from me and used up most of my adrenaline.

"Headhunter 17, this is Headhunter 19. I am near coordinates ND 650342. I am in a shallow climbing turn to the west. Let me know when you have me in sight."

"Roger, Headhunter 19. I'm on a heading of three hundred degrees at twelve hundred AGL. About two minutes from your location."

I applied full throttle and started my climb. At the same time, I called Panther 2A and told him that Headhunter 17 was relieving me and that I would brief Headhunter 17 and have him make contact as soon as he arrived on location.

"Headhunter 19, this is Headhunter 17. I've got you in sight. I am at your nine o'clock at a half mile." Glancing over my left wing, I saw Headhunter 17 starting a right turn to keep separation. I gave him the frequencies for the artillery, gunships, and medevac. I briefed him on the Popular Force company's location, their direction of movement, and what support I had been providing. I told him to contact Panther 2A and turned the mission over to him.

I continued my climb to 1,500 feet to avoid small-arms fire on the way back to Qui Nhon and turned to a heading of one hundred. Taking a deep breath, I popped the windows open. My Nomex flight suit was soaking wet, and while opening the windows only let in the hot, moist air of Vietnam, it did provide a small breeze that created a sensation of being cool.

As was my ritual after each action, I thanked God for delivering me safely through the mission and for giving me the courage to do my job. Then I asked him to forgive me for killing the four men who'd died at my hands that day. Then, with nothing to do but fly the aircraft, realization slowly sank in. Normally, I would practice emergency procedures when returning from a mission, but I needed a break this time. I needed some time to come down from the high I was on. I let my mind drift away from reality until it became a kaleidoscope of thoughts. Slowly, I started to unwind as I began to fragment and fuse the emotions of the previous six hours with the past events in my life.

I had often heard the saying "Flying is hours and hours of boredom interrupted by minutes of sheer terror." Now I knew what it meant. After almost three months of flying recon and combat support missions, I had not experienced one hostile action toward me. Today the five minutes of terror during my attack on the bunker had interrupted that boredom. In my mind, I could still see the tracers zipping by me as I lined up to attack the Vietcong bunker. I still do not know why they did not hit me. They certainly shared the same space with me. I do not know if other men ever question their courage. I know I questioned mine constantly. That day, I had experienced numbing fear that had tested my courage and ability. I had risen to the task, but I dreaded the idea of ever again having to feel such fear.

Now, with that mission over, feeling reasonably safe, I felt a sense of pride in myself and a need to somehow share the feelings from that day's actions. My past achievements paled in comparison to that day. None had raised my self-esteem and confidence like my performance that day. Most of all, I wanted to share this experience with someone I loved.

I thought of Claudia and wondered what she would think if somehow I could tell her. I knew she would not fully understand what I was feeling, but she would be proud of me, though probably bored at another war story. She was used to me succeeding in everything I did. She wouldn't understand, even if she was aware of the doubts I often felt.

I have seldom been able to share my fears or doubts with anyone, including her. I did not want to admit fear or weakness. Or maybe my teenage life, which had damaged my self-esteem, had taught me to be responsible for myself and resilient to survive. I think my life would have been much easier had I been able to more openly share my feelings. I have never told Claudia or anybody else about the events of October 20, 1967.

It had been three weeks since the last letter from Claudia. That in itself was not unusual, because oftentimes, you could go a week without a letter and then get ten in one day. I still fumed over her first letter in August, in which she'd told me that Marcy Smith had convinced her to move to Atlanta instead of going back to Germany, as we had planned. The news had upset me and caused some feelings that I did not need.

Marcy's husband, Dale, was stationed at a base near Saigon, about two hundred miles south of me. I'd immediately liked Dale when I met him and Marcy during flight school. He was a country boy with a big smile, a comic, and a dedicated officer. I did not like Marcy. There was something about her body language and the subtle hints in her conversations that always left me with the opinion that she was a promiscuous woman.

When Claudia met her at our flight school graduation ball, they'd hit if off right away, so I never said anything to Claudia about what I thought of Marcy. Besides, the plan was for Claudia stay with her mother in Germany while I was in Vietnam, and that would solve the problem. Then, when my mail finally caught up to me and I got the letter saying Marcy had convinced her to move to Atlanta while Dale and I were in Vietnam, I felt Claudia had betrayed me. Looking west, I could see the An Khe Pass. Suddenly, I realized where my thoughts were going, and right now, I did not want to go there.

Looking east, I could see the ocean about ten miles away. Flying coastal recon missions on the east coast of Vietnam fascinated me. There was something soothing and comforting in its beauty. Pristine beaches of white sand were divided by small mountains that speared the sea with jutting rocks. The deep waters were hues of dark blue up to the shoreline. How different they were from the beaches at Jacksonville Beach. I knew the fishing would be excellent in the deep water so close to shore. I wondered what my childhood friends Bob, Don, and Tom would think of these beaches.

What would they think of me? I was almost two years their junior. Our friendship had been one of constant competition. We constantly challenged one another, but despite how hard I tried, I could never equal their skills at fishing and hunting and their success with the girls. I wanted to match their skills, and it frustrated me that I could not. Plus, being younger, I was often the target of their friendly jokes.

So how would they see me today? I had long ago convinced myself that I was now superior in skills and abilities that they did not have. The competition that had been so important when I was a kid was now no longer an issue. Maturity had replaced it. The competition had been the game we played to hone our skills. Their skills were better then and would always appear to be better because they were older and had been playing the game longer; I would never catch up to them in years. I knew now that the competition was over, and it was not important anymore. We were friends. But they would probably never know what had taken place today or how, in my mind, I'd finally topped them in a different game.

I knew my father would be proud of me. I held him responsible for most of my emotional quirks. Yet he would be the only one with whom I would feel comfortable talking about what had happened that day. What I had done was part of the life of which he dreamed. The army had barred his enlistment in World War II because he worked in a shipyard, and they considered his job essential to the war effort. It hurt him to not be able to fight in the war. I sometimes wondered if his sense of failure somehow led to his alcoholism.

The kaleidoscope in my head kept spinning, and suddenly, I thought of Kate. It had been several years since Kate had come to mind. I tried to picture what she would be doing today, but I could not. I could only remember our last night together. We'd parked on a road off Penman Road and started some heavy petting, when I heard her say, "Neal, you can do anything you want to." I don't know if it surprised her when I did nothing. I knew she meant I could make love to her. I did not. It is hard to explain today why I did not, but I was not ready for sex. I had no idea what to do, and I did not want to leave her with the memory of a onetime experience with a boy who would not have the opportunity to learn and perfect his love of her. I wondered if she ever thought of me. I have always felt that many of my achievements were due to the influence Kate had on me.

In high school, she believed in me so much. When I told her of some of my wild dreams, she always cautioned me that dreams were okay, but if they were to bear fruit, you had to first build a foundation for them. Long ago, I had promised myself that I would never do anything that would make me unworthy of that belief.

I thought, *Kate, I gave a good account of myself today, and though you will never know, you can always be proud of me. I pray you have soared past the moon I once gave you and have gathered the stars to your bosom and are holding them tightly.*

The sound of the Qui Nhon airfield tower giving another aircraft landing instructions jarred me back to reality. Now it was time to put my mind back into real life. "Qui Nhon Tower, this is Headhunter 19, six miles north for landing."

"Roger, Headhunter 19. Enter left downwind for runway thirty-six. Winds variable from two hundred seventy to two hundred ninety degrees, gusting to thirteen knots. Barometer 31.89. Report downwind."

Oh shit, I thought. *The wind is almost a ninety-degree crosswind at maximum allowable speed.* Fifteen knots at ninety degrees was maximum crosswind. A crosswind at that speed and direction made it difficult to control the aircraft and land without ground looping. As usual, I started sweating again. Entering downwind, I could feel the effects of the wind whipping around the mountain to the west of the airfield. I had to use right aileron and almost all the left rudder available to hold the proper downwind track.

I reported entering downwind, and the tower answered, "Roger, Headhunter 19. Cleared for landing report final."

As I turned final, I had to reverse the controls to left aileron and right rudder. Before I could do that, I had drifted right of the centerline and had to turn slightly to the left to line up. It took all the left aileron and right rudder to keep it on the centerline as I descended to the runway. I reported final, and the tower started broadcasting wind speed every ten seconds to aid in controlling the aircraft. I was using full left stick and right rudder to stay lined up as I approached the threshold to round out. I moved the stick to the rear to round out, and two seconds later, the left gear and tail wheel contacted the runway with a plop. I held the right gear off the runway until my speed dropped off to thirty knots, and then I slowly moved the stick to the right and eased off the rudder to let the right gear contact the runway. On rollout, the tower cleared me to our revetment area, and I taxied to the parking ramp, soaked in sweat.

Captain Tom and Captain Malady were standing at the door to the Quonset hut to greet me. Captain Tom said, "Great job, Neal. According to sector headquarters, you saved the day for the Popular Forces unit. What happened?"

I explained what I had done, hoping Captain Tom was not going to be angry about the way I had endangered the aircraft. The battalion and company commanders were constantly reminding us that we were reconnaissance pilots and not attack aircraft. Captain Tom said, "You handled it just the way I would have." His words were a relief, and I felt good about the credit he gave me.

It took awhile for me to complete my recon report. All I said about the attack on the bunker was that I fired one HE rocket at the bunker, which allowed the recovery of the wounded soldiers.

After completing my report, the three of us went to the officers' club for dinner and drinks.

After a dinner of beef fried rice cooked the Vietnamese way and three beers, my exhaustion took hold. Back at the BOQ, I checked for mail and found none. I started to write Claudia a letter but decided I was too exhausted, so I hit the sack.

The next day, I got a letter from Claudia saying she had changed her mind and was moving to Germany. Staying in Atlanta had not worked out the way she'd thought it would. She did not think Marcy was the friend she wanted. She would write again when she had an address in Germany. I felt a little sense of relief but still did not understand what was going on or what Claudia was thinking. I had to put it out of my mind and hope for the best. I could not let it distract me from the job I had to do.

It was the third week in November before I got another letter from Claudia. She and the kids were fine. They had first stayed with her mother in Munich after she returned to Germany, but that had become difficult with Michele going all the way across Munich to the American school at McGraw Casern. She wrote that she had found a little apartment about a mile from the casern and had waited to write until she had the apartment, so she could give me an address that would not change.

I missed Claudia and the kids beyond what words can describe. For me, most days usually ended after dinner. We seldom flew a night mission, and there were no TV sets to sit around. I did not drink much other than an occasional beer and did not venture downtown, as a lot of the guys did. The army considered Qui Nhon pacified and a safe area. There were seldom any war-associated problems in the town, and several restaurants and bars were on limits for the soldiers. Some of our crew chiefs had girlfriends and spent most nights in town. I was always in the BOQ after dinner, either writing a letter or reading a book. Sometimes the nights were long and lonely with just me and my thoughts.

By day, I controlled my mind and focused it on the mission, but the long nights allowed my mind to roam the memories that formed my life. I relived the good memories and endured the bad while trying to gain some clue as to how I could improve relations with Claudia. I tried to understand the negative feelings I had slowly developed about her and why I'd gotten them.

Some of what I felt was jealously, or maybe it was distrust. I think my lack of self-esteem was the strongest when it involved relations with Claudia. My sense was that we had married too young. She seemed hungry now for the life marriage had caused her to miss. Now two kids and a husband who was gone for long periods of time tied her down. I knew she had to be as lonely as I was, but I did not know for sure why I felt uneasy about how she would handle that loneliness.

Growing up, I'd had no example of what a happy home or a loving marriage was like. In my mind, I was a good husband. I provided her with an admirable standard of living; I was attentive, romantic, and a good lover. I supported her wishes, encouraged her undertakings, and always wanted her company. Most of all, I wanted her to be proud of me and want to be with me. Despite trying not to, I always reacted angrily to any rejection on her part. In my anger, I discarded any valid reason for her rejection. That rejection translated, to me, to her not wanting me because

I was not good enough. The following argument always left us angry with each other.

While we had tender moments, the many fights and arguments overshadowed them. Sadly, I failed to see that I was mostly the problem. I knew we were drifting apart, but try as I might, I could not see that I was the problem, and therefore, I did not know what to fix, even if I wanted to. I often felt as if we were two people who loved each other but did not like each other. But no matter how hard I tried to deny it, I believed she was searching for something that I was not providing. So openly, I loved her dearly, but inside, there was a hurt that would not go away. I did not know it at the time, but it would take another ten years of hurt, anger, and betrayal before I was smart enough to understand fully the emotions that drove me. After that, we began to make the changes that let us find the loving relationship we'd always wanted.

On one of these nights, I began to think about where we could meet for my midtour rest and relaxation (R&R) leave. Mine would be coming up in January or February. I thought it would be wonderful to meet for our anniversary, which was February 27. I wrote to her and asked about where she would like to meet. I liked the idea of meeting in Bangkok. Bangkok was an R&R town with a military support unit and would be an easy flight for me. When I got the next letter from her, I learned she was thrilled about this possibility. In fact, she had checked with a German tour agency and found that it had three tours going to Bangkok each month. The February tour arrived on February 21 and left March 14. That settled it. We made plans to meet on February 25.

The idea of meeting so soon excited both of us. The following letters were sweet and kept me updated on our plan. Claudia reserved a flight early because she got a discount for making reservations so far in advance. The tour cost $200, which included the flight and hotel and two side tours from Bangkok. It was a good deal by any measure. I applied for my midtour R&R leave and had it approved for February 25 through March 4. We were all set, excited and happy about seeing each other.

The war hummed on while I waited for February 25. Like the rest of the pilots, I flew two missions a day. The missions varied, including support of infantry troops, area recon, route recon, and special missions. One day I was flying cover for a Special Forces team operating in triple-canopy jungle. My only contact was by radio and occasional smoke grenade. From fifty feet above the treetops, the canopy looked like an overgrown lawn that needed mowing. It stretched in a twenty-mile-wide band for about fifty miles north and south. Of course, I could see nothing below the triple canopy, and the Special Forces team could not see much beyond the trail on which they were moving.

They were on the way to a Montagnard village. Intelligence confirmed the Montagnards from this village were working with the VC and NVA. This was unusual since the Montagnards were the native people of Vietnam and considered themselves independent of the Vietnamese people, North or South Vietnamese. Thus, the VC and NVA were forcing them to work against their will. SF was leading a friendly unit composed of Montagnards fighting for South Vietnam. Their mission was to convince the Montagnards from the village to switch sides.

Earlier, the SF team had given me the coordinates of the village, and I had been trying desperately to find it through the triple canopy. Finally, on one of my low passes, I noticed a small veil of smoke hanging in the trees. I decided the smoke was from the charcoal fires the Montagnards used for cooking.

"Demon 23, this is Headhunter 19. Over."

"HH 19, this is Demon 23. Over."

"Roger, Demon 23. I think I have located the village. There's a smoke plume I can see through the trees that might be from charcoal fires. Can you hear the plane from your current location?"

"Roger, HH 19. We hear you fairly loud north of us."

"Okay, Demon 23, I am going to fly over the smoke and give you a mark."

"Roger, HH 19. Waiting for your mark."

I banked the Bird Dog and lined up on the spot where I saw the smoke. As I got close to the smoke, I started seeing what looked like sticks flying up through the canopy. When I was over the smoke, I announced, "Demon 23, mark!"

"Roger, HH 19. You sound close. We are going to mark our position with smoke and let you give us a heading and distance to the village."

"Roger, Demon 23. I'm turning south, looking for your smoke." The smoke would mark their location under the triple-canopy jungle.

When I saw and identified the color of their smoke, I called Demon 23 and told him that I marked green smoke. He confirmed green smoke, and from there, I flew directly to the smoke from the village. By noting the compass direction and timing how long it took me to fly the distance at my airspeed of 120 knots, I could give them the direction and estimated distance to the village. They did not tell me the color of the smoke grenade, in order to prevent an enemy listening to our transmissions from igniting the same color. That would cause more confusion in an already confusing situation. If I identified a color different from the one they ignited, we would know that an enemy was listening to us and that I was over the wrong location.

It took me two minutes to fly to the smoke on a heading of ten degrees. That put them about three miles from the village, which was closer than their estimate of five miles based on just the sounds of my aircraft. Knowing a more accurate distance gave them a better feel for when to shift from a march formation into a skirmish formation.

"Demon 23, got you three miles from the smoke on a heading of ten degrees."

"Roger, HH 19. Can you see anything under the canopy?"

"Negative, Demon 23. All I can see is what looks like short sticks flying up through the canopy."

"That's good information, HH 19. The Montagnards are shooting at you with crossbows. Those sticks are the arrows. That means they probably don't have weapons other than the crossbows. We will let you know when we get there."

"Roger, Demon 23. I'm overhead, so let me know if you need anything."

I continued to circle the area, searching for any possible movement I could see through the triple-canopy jungle. One time, I passed over a bunch of monkeys swinging among the tops of the trees. It took a second or two for my mind to register what I was seeing. By then, I was past them, and I never saw them again.

After about an hour with only an occasional communications check to make sure we could still communicate with one another, Demon 23 called and said, "HH 19, we're in the village. No contact made. It appears the Montagnards fled the village when we got too close. We're okay and don't need any further support, so you can return to base. Thanks for a great job."

"Roger, Demon 23. I'm returning to base. Out." My mission was over, and I turned toward Qui Nhon and climbed to 1,500 feet.

On the way back, I practiced flying without using the stick. To turn, I used the left or right rudder to force the nose in the direction I wanted to go. I used elevator trim to hold altitude. It added about ten minutes to my flight back, but I thought the training was worth it. It prepared me to fly without the stick if I had damage to my ailerons or vertical stabilizer. Of course, landing would be another problem, but there was no way I could practice that. I would have to take my chances with landing.

A week later, an SF sergeant pulled up to the operations hut. He dropped off three of the crossbows the Montagnards had used to shoot at me that day. I took them home with me as souvenirs.

In December, the monsoons began to shift from along the coast to the highlands. With the improved weather came an increase in flights. One morning, I found myself flying an artillery support mission. The Fifty-Second Artillery Group, based north of Qui Nhon, asked for support because their assigned OV-1 was down for maintenance. The mission called for me to pick up an artillery observer at a remote landing strip about forty miles north of Qui Nhon. We considered the remote strip safe for occasional use since the VC and NVA had no idea when we would use it.

Arriving at the strip, I could see a jeep parked at the north end. Dropping down to about fifty feet, I did a low recon of the strip to check it for any obstacles to landing there. As I flew over the end, the lieutenant standing by the jeep waved. I climbed back up to landing altitude and banked around for my downwind. The strip looked short—about 1,200 feet, I guessed. The wind was blowing down the runway, which would help in landing. I turned final, dropped full flaps, and added power. The full flaps slowed me down below normal landing speed, and I added power to compensate for the lost airspeed. I descended on my glide path in a perfect short-field approach and touched down on the end of the runway. I marveled at how easy it was now, when it had been so difficult in flight school.

As soon as my rollout speed allowed, I turned around and taxied backed to the end of the runway. I turned around, facing down the runway

35

into the wind so that I was ready for an immediate takeoff if there were trouble. The jeep followed me and pulled up beside the aircraft. I motioned for the lieutenant to get out and get in the backseat. I felt uneasy sitting on the strip and wanted to get off as soon as possible.

I slid my seat forward as far as it would go and opened the door for the lieutenant to get in. As he approached the aircraft, I motioned for him to be careful of the turning propeller. As unbelievable as it might seem, several people have walked into a turning propeller without thinking. The lieutenant crawled into the backseat. He had flown observer before and was familiar with the backseat.

After he got his shoulder harness and seat belt buckled, he put on the observer's helmet, plugged the microphone jack into the communications panel, and keyed the mike. "Can you hear me, sir?"

"Got you loud and clear," I answered. "I'm Lieutenant Griffin. Let me give you a quick briefing, and we'll get out of here. First and most importantly, if you get sick and need to upchuck, use the shell canister stuck in the side pocket. If you don't and get my plane dirty, it'll cost you twenty dollars for the crew chief to clean it. Second, I'll fly the aircraft, and you tell me where to go. In case of an emergency, I'll let you know what we are going to do. Tighten your seat belt and harness up as tight as you can. The only time we will think about using the parachutes is in case we catch on fire. In that event, I will pull my seat forward and open the door for you to get out. Don't hesitate, because I will only give you a couple of seconds before I shove my seat backward and go. Once I shove my seat back, you won't be able to exit. Keep a lookout for other aircraft. Sometimes there is a crowd up here, and we do not want a midair collision. Any questions?"

"No, sir. I'm Second Lieutenant Bill Johnston. I have flown a couple missions with our pilot. He's given me the same briefing."

"Okay. Let's get on the way. Are you ready?" I asked. He said yes, I applied takeoff power, and we started rolling.

I used most of the runway in taking off and was barely airborne when we crossed the end of the strip. The O1-D—with its variable-speed prop, two people aboard, all the grenades and ammo, and four rockets—was two hundred pounds over the recommended gross weight. In the hot, humid air, the density altitude was high, making takeoff speed much higher. I made a mental note that next time I did something like this, I would ask for the bird with the fixed-pitch prop.

As I gained airspeed and climbed out, I asked my observer what area we would be firing into. He told me to turn southwest to a heading of 210. Our mission for today was to register the 155-millimeter and eight-inch batteries.

A registration is an important procedure for artillery units. In a registration, the observer adjusts one gun until he hits the target. The target is usually an object identifiable on a map road intersection, from which the observer can get precise coordinates. The artillery FDC element can then plot the target on their firing chart and compare the firing data that hit the target with the firing data they used. That corrects the firing data for the effects of interior and exterior ballistics, weather, and positional errors. The results of registrations are usually accurate up to about twenty-four hours. I had done hundreds of registrations during my days as FDC chief. I had never done one as an air observer.

The FDC chose that day's registration. It was an intersection formed by a large and small river joining. Clearly identifiable on the ground and on the map, it was a perfect registration point. When the lieutenant told me the site, I recognized it from the many recons I had done along the large river.

I turned directly toward the intersection as the lieutenant set up communications with the battalion FDC. Hearing his transmissions brought memories of my artillery days. I was still proficient in gunnery techniques and was a little excited. Although I had called in artillery many times to attack targets, this was a registration mission and a first for me in combat.

After I arrived at the river intersection, I flew past it a mile or so and circled. I was looking for the track that gave us the best view of the target but kept us out of the trajectory of the artillery rounds. Nothing can spoil your day more than getting clobbered by a 155-millimeter or eight-inch round. Once I found a track with the best view of the target, I turned directly toward the target to identify the direction we would fly to make corrections and pass to the FDC. The proper technique for aerial adjustment of artillery is to fly a figure-eight pattern clear of the gun-to-target trajectory. The observer makes all changes along the fixed azimuth.

The FDC plots the azimuth on the target grid. This becomes the reference for making corrections as the observer sees them.

Once I was set up, I told the lieutenant to begin anytime he was ready. The lieutenant turned his selector to FM and started the fire mission. "Big Daddy 15, this is HH 19. Fire mission. Over."

"HH 19, this is Big Daddy 15. Fire mission. Over."

"This is HH 19. Coordinates 68543278, azimuth forty-five, registration. Will adjust. Over." In a fire mission, personnel repeat each command to ensure accuracy. This prevents firing on the wrong target, which, of course, could cause a problem.

"This is Big Daddy 15. Fire mission. Coordinates 68543278, azimuth forty-five, registration. Will adjust. Wait." The *wait* meant they would develop firing data, pass it to the gun, and let us know when the gun fired.

I started the lazy-eight patterns while we waited. "HH 19, this is Big Daddy. Shot. Time of flight nineteen seconds."

The lieutenant answered, "This is HH 19. Shot. Time of flight nineteen seconds. Wait." While he did that, I banked the aircraft around so we were on our azimuth and looking at the target. It would take nineteen seconds for the round to hit the target from the time the gun fired it. Knowing this helps the pilot line the aircraft up on the azimuth to view the round's impact.

Five seconds after I had the aircraft lined up, the round impacted the edge of the main river with an eruption of mud and water. A 155-millimeter is a big round and makes a hell of a crater. The eight-inch is even bigger. The lieutenant, looking through his binoculars, gave his first adjustment. "Big Daddy 15, this is HH 19. Right eighty. Drop two hundred. Over."

"HH 19, this is Big Daddy 15. Right eighty. Drop two hundred. Wait."

I extended my inbound leg to better synchronize my turns so I could be inbound on the azimuth at the right time.

"HH 19, this is Big Daddy. Shot. Over."

"Big Daddy 15, this is HH 19. Shot. Wait." We waited, and then the lieutenant said, "Big Daddy 15, this is HH 19. Right twenty. Add one hundred. Over."

"HH 19, this is Big Daddy 15. Right twenty. Add one hundred. Wait."

We continued this procedure of bracketing the target until a round hit the middle of the intersection. When the lieutenant reported this, Big

Daddy gave us an end-of-mission confirmation for that battery and told us to stand by for the next mission. In the middle of a turn, I smelled the odor of vomit. Turning around, I saw the lieutenant with his head in the shell canister. I'd expected this. The backseat of the Bird Dog magnifies the effects of banking left and right and can make most observers upchuck. The lieutenant worsened the sensation by using the binoculars. I pushed the mike button. "Are you okay?"

He did not answer me. He just shook his head. He did not look good, but there was nothing I could do to relieve his discomfort. When Big Daddy 15 called, telling us they were ready for the next mission, the lieutenant just shook his head. He was fortunate that I was an experienced forward observer. Getting airsick is forgivable, but not completing the mission is unacceptable.

I took over and adjusted the second 155 battery and the eight-inch battery while the lieutenant suffered. Seeing the craters formed from the first registration and knowing the corrections needed to move them onto the target allowed me to make corrections without using the binoculars. When I reported that the eight-inch round had fallen in the middle of the river intersection, Big Daddy 15 gave us an end-of-mission call and released us to return to base.

On the way back, the lieutenant did not get better, but he did manage to call his unit and tell them to send the jeep for him. However, when we arrived at the landing strip, there was no jeep, so I did another low pass to ensure the area was clear of any bad guys. I was going to circle while we waited for the jeep as an extra precaution against any danger that I did not see, but the lieutenant did not look as if he wanted to fly much longer, so I chanced it and landed.

When I slowed enough to turn around, I taxied back to the departure end of the strip so I would be ready for a quick takeoff. I let the lieutenant out and watched him take a deep breath. He looked at me and shook his head. "Sorry, sir. I have never been that sick before. I was thinking of applying for flight school, but I think I will pass now. I hope we can keep this between us."

I handed him the shell canister, which, by its weight, I could tell was full of vomit. "No problem," I answered. "We did the mission, and that's what counts."

He took the canister, set it on the ground, and adjusted his field belt. We both turned at the sound of the jeep racing down the side of the dirt strip. "Thank you, sir," he said as he turned and walked toward the jeep. Before he got to it, I was applying full power and starting my takeoff roll. I did not know it then, but whoever had picked the river intersection as a registration point had made a wise decision.

I was back in the platoon operations hut, completing my recon report, when Captain Tom walked in and asked, "Neal, how did it go?"

I told him about the mission and said I'd enjoyed doing a little artillery work again. He smiled and said, "That's great. How would you like to do some more artillery work?"

"I'd like to. It was a break from daily recon missions," I answered.

"Good. A long-range reconnaissance patrol has been tracking an NVA regiment for two days. It looks like the regiment is going to cross the Hann River and move into the Bon Son area. The sector commander has ordered the regiment attacked. The LRRP"—or long-range reconnaissance patrol—"has recommended an artillery or air strike. Since the regiment will be most vulnerable while crossing the river and in good range of the Fifty-Second Artillery BDE, the sector commander wants to hit it with artillery first. I was going to take the mission, but you are better qualified to handle the artillery in case there's a repeat of the observer getting sick. It's a night mission. Are you up to flying a night mission tonight?"

"Hell yeah," I said. At the same time, a little twinge of apprehension came over me. It would be my first night mission since flight school. I told myself to calm down. After all, a night mission is the same as a day mission, except it is dark. "What time?" I asked.

Captain Thomson walked over to the map. "You pick up the observer at the Fifty-Second's airstrip at twenty hundred hours. Now, the strip is only twelve hundred feet long. It's like the one you used today, except it's on the edge of town and secure. The only problem will be power lines. They cross the approach path about a hundred yards south of the touchdown spot. So make sure you keep a steep approach going in. There's no lighting around the field, so you won't be able to see the wires. They will have a jeep parked at each end of the runway with the headlights on and shining down the runway. Once you touch down, the drivers will put the lights on dim to protect your night vision. Any questions?"

I thought for a few minutes while studying the map and asking myself why the hell I'd opened my big mouth. "Yes, sir. How do I contact the LRRPs?"

"Don't worry about it. The LRRPs have our FM number and will call you when they are ready to attack. Remember, they are very close to the NVA unit and must maintain radio silence as much as possible."

"How about my observer?" I asked.

"He's supposed to be an experienced captain. But you never know until you get there."

After Captain Tom left, I continued to study the map until I had all the major ground features memorized. Flying the first mission in that area earlier helped. When I was satisfied that I could picture the landing strip and its location in my mind, I headed to the BOQ to take a nap.

I ate dinner in the officers' mess and returned to the platoon operations hut. I would leave at 1930 to pick up the captain at 2000. I replaced the batteries in my flashlight and folded my map so that it showed just the area in which we would be flying. I did a thorough preflight of the aircraft and made sure all lights were working. By 1900, I was ready to go. The crew chief and maintenance sergeant came in the operations hut, and we sat around talking while I waited for takeoff time.

Both of them had extended for a second tour of duty to work for Captain Tom. That spoke well of his leadership. They both had girlfriends in Qui Nhon and usually spent the night in town with them. They were happy with their job. Here, they did not have to contend with the usual army harassment, inspections, and formations found in the stateside units. Here, they kept the airplanes flying on schedule and considered each aircraft their personal property. The pilot who stupidly damaged one suffered their wrath.

At 1925, I climbed into the cockpit, started the engine, and did a thorough run-up. I did not want an engine problem tonight. I started my takeoff roll exactly at 1930. The night air was calm as I climbed out to 1,500 feet and turned toward Bon Son. Reaching 1,500 feet, I looked around to orient myself. I could see the lights of Bon Son to the north and An Khe to the west. The lights of many hamlets dotted the landscape, mixed with the light traffic on Highway 1. To the east, I could see the light of an occasional boat. The scene was reminiscent of what I had seen while flying night training missions in rural Alabama.

I arrived at the airstrip a few minutes before 2000. It was dark, but visibility was good, and since I knew where the strip was supposed to be, I had no trouble finding it. I could not see the power lines, and keeping that in mind, I made a pass over the runway to let the observer know I was there. As I climbed up to downwind altitude, the trucks on each end of the runway turned on their lights. This made the runway look even shorter than 1,200 feet.

I started my approach with a little knot in my stomach. On the downwind leg, I descended to about six hundred feet to shorten and steepen my final approach. I wanted to make sure I missed the power lines. Turning base, I still could not see the lines, nor could I see them between my touchdown point and me when I turned to final, so I figured I would be clear of them. Fortunately, the short-field landing that morning had been good training for that night. On short final, I turned my landing light on, dropped full flaps, and added power to slow my descent. I touched down with a bounce about a quarter of the way down the strip. It was not a smooth landing, but I did not hit the power lines, and since it was my first night landing in seven months, I was happy.

As I turned around, the trucks turned on their parking lights, and I taxied to the end of the strip. I could see my observer standing there. I turned around for takeoff and opened the door so he could get in. It wasn't the captain I was expecting. He introduced himself as Lieutenant Brown. I introduced myself and gave him my standard briefing as he buckled his seat belt.

When I asked him what our mission was, he said all the S3 had told him was that we were supporting an LRRP. That disappointed me because I had counted on him knowing more than I did, but that was not the case. He had no idea how to locate our area of interest. All I knew was that the LRRP expected the NVA regiment to start crossing the Hann River somewhere south of Bon Son. I had no way to contact the LRRP; I had to wait until they contacted me. I opened my map and, using my flashlight, looked at the Hann River. It flowed north past Bon Son and turned northeast into the sea. Two smaller rivers flowed into it about ten miles apart. I had labeled the southernmost intersection RP 203, noting it as the registration point we'd used that morning. I decided I would fly a tract five miles on the west side of the river south for thirty miles and then five miles east of the rivers on the north tract. That should keep me within radio range of the LRRP, whenever they decided to contact me. Carl von Clausewitz, the German military theorist, cautioned about the fog of war, and this was clearly an example of it.

Satisfied that I had a plan, I held the brakes on the aircraft and advanced the throttle to full power. The engine screamed, I released the brakes, and we jumped forward on our takeoff roll. As we climbed, I entered a slow turn to the south on a course that set me up to fly the racetrack course I had decided to use. I leveled off at 1,500 feet on my southbound leg. The observer set up communications with Big Daddy 15, and we settled in to wait on a call from the LRRP. While visibility was good enough for us to make out the ribbon of water that was the Hann River, we could not see any details of it. Far to the west of us, a base camp must have been under attack, because we could see the flash of explosions and tracers arching back and forth. It went on for about an hour before the firefight subsided.

I was starting to think about my fuel and how much longer I could stay airborne, when a whisper broke the silence on the radio: "Headhunter 19, this is Stalker 5. Over."

I answered, "Stalker 5, Headhunter 19. Over."

"Roger, HH 19. Request fire mission."

"Roger, Stalker 5. Go ahead."

While I was talking to Stalker 5, the lieutenant contacted Big Daddy 15 and told them to stand by.

"Headhunter 19, this is Stalker 5. Coordinates 674382, azimuth sixty-one. NVA units crossing river. Will adjust. Over."

The observer was about to pass the fire mission to Big Daddy 15, when I told to him to wait. I was looking at my map, and the coordinates marked a spot about fifty meters north of the registration point I'd fired on that day. We did not need to adjust the fire, as the bursting radius of a 155 was more than fifty meters. Because we had accurate firing data from the earlier registration, all we had to do was make a small shift and fire for effect. I called, "Stalker 5, this is Headhunter 19. How close are you to the target?"

"Roger, HH 19. We are about six hundred meters overlooking the target."

"Roger, Stalker 5. The target is nearly on the registration point we fired about eight hours ago. No need to adjust. We are going to fire for effect. You guys hunker down just in case the rounds come close to your location."

"Roger, HH 19. Go for it."

The lieutenant called, "Big Daddy 15, this is Headhunter 19. Fire mission from RP 203. Azimuth 6,340. Add five zero. North Vietnam Army units crossing river. Request battalion fire for effect."

Big Daddy 15 answered, repeated the fire request, and gave us a wait. A battalion fire for effect would have six eight-inch howitzers and twelve 155-millimeter howitzers firing on the target at one time. That would cause one hell of an effect.

"Headhunter 19, this is Big Daddy 15. Shot. Time to target eighteen seconds. Over."

"This is Headhunter 19. Shot. Roger. Break, Stalker 5. Rounds on the way; fourteen seconds to impact. Hunker down. Over."

By this time, we were flying south to stay out of the trajectory area, and I did a steep turn so we could see the impact. Just as I leveled, the rounds impacted on top of the registration point to at least three hundred meters north, right, and left of the target coordinates. From two miles away, the concussion from all the high-explosive rounds going off bounced the Bird Dog around like a kite in a storm.

I was praying that Stalker 5 was where he said he was. I was saying silently, *Come on, Stalker 5. Come on. Call.*

Then I heard Stalker 5 say, "Oh my God, it's carnage," as if he were talking to himself. Then he said to me, "Headhunter 19, repeat fire for effect. Over."

"Roger, Stalker 5. Repeat fire for effect."

The lieutenant relayed the request to Big Daddy 15. I felt relived. It had worried me that Stalker 5 might have been too close to the target. His asking for a repeat told me that I had guessed it right; the rounds were hitting the target.

Big Daddy 15 gave us another shot, and I relayed it to Stalker 5. The explosions covered a box five hundred meters long and two hundred meters wide around the target. Considering that the kill distance of each round was more than fifty meters and that the LRRP had described the target as a battalion-sized unit bunched up to cross the river, I could only believe that we had destroyed the battalion or at least most of it.

This time, I couldn't wait. "Stalker 5, what's it look like?"

"Roger, Headhunter 19. Wait until some of the smoke clears."

We waited for about five minutes before he said, "Headhunter 19, end of mission. The best count we can confirm with our night-vision device is sixty-two bodies. With so much destruction and so many bodies and body parts flung about, there's no telling how many KIAs they are. No movement at all. After the first barrage slaughtered them, the survivors seemed disoriented and confused as to what to do. Then the second barrage wiped them out. We will file a more detailed recon report after looking at it in the daylight. We are going to move now and hunker down for tonight. So thank you for a job well done, and good night."

"Roger, Stalker 5. Good luck." They had to move because any surviving NVA would figure out that an LRRP had tracked them and would be looking for the LRRP. The lieutenant gave Big Daddy 15 the end-of-mission call with a firm sixty-two KIA and estimated destruction of the NVA battalion. I headed back to the airstrip to drop off the lieutenant. I made the same approach as I had earlier and made a smooth landing in the still night air. We shook hands, and the lieutenant got out of the aircraft. He was smiling and said, "Thanks, Lieutenant Griffin. That was the best mission I've ever been on."

"Take care," I answered. "Call us if you need support again." I shut the door; adjusted my seat; and, holding the brakes, advanced the power to take off. Releasing the brakes, I surged forward and was quickly airborne. I felt none of the remorse I had experienced in killing the Vietcong courier in the free-fire zone—it was not the same. We had attacked a military unit that, if not destroyed, would have attacked US forces sometime in the future. I had at last used all my years of training in artillery against an enemy with devastating results. Thanking God for his grace, I looked out over the night-cloaked landscape of Vietnam and felt blessed.

Landing at Qui Nhon was a pleasure. The runway was five thousand feet long, was fully lit, and had no power lines to dodge. Captain Tom, the crew chief, and the maintenance sergeant were waiting for me as I taxied into the revetment area. Captain Tom was eager to hear my report, and while the crew chief put the aircraft away, I debriefed him on the flight. He was happy about our success in supporting the LRRP. He took pride in his platoon, and under his leadership, it had always carried out its mission.

Lying in bed and waiting for sleep, I replayed the events of the day. It fascinated me how all the players had acted their parts, not knowing what the result of their actions would be. I had flown the registration mission. The LRRP had found and tracked the NVA regiment. The NVA commander had decided to cross the river fifty meters from an artillery registration point. Captain Tom had decided to let me fly the mission because of my earlier flight. My artillery expertise had enabled me to recognize that we could fire for effect and surprise the NVA. That expertise existed because I'd decided to join the paratroopers in September 1956. I was a recon pilot in the First Platoon because of my decision to go to OCS and then to flight school. I thought about how cool it would be to one day paint a picture that captured each major decision point that guided my journey through life.

On December 1, Captain Tom held a platoon formation and told the platoon that effective the eighth, he was moving to Kontum to take command of the Second Platoon. Captain Dawson, the current platoon leader, was leaving on the ninth. Captain Tom looked at Darrel and me and said, "I only agreed to move on the condition that you two go with me. I know you two do not want to live under the thumb of the company, so pack your bags."

There was a general expression of "Oh no, you can't leave us!" from the platoon ranks. He went on to explain that the First Platoon would move back to the 219th at Camp Holloway and support Binh Dinh Province from there. That was a shock to the enlisted men who had girlfriends in Qui Nhon. Darrel and I were happy about going with Captain Tom.

Flying recon in Binh Dinh had become boring. Most of the action had moved into the highlands. American forces had pretty much pacified the coastal plains that made up much of Binh Dinh Province.

The NVA unit we'd destroyed crossing the river to reestablish a presence in Dinh Binh was a severe loss to its commander, so to say the least, Darrel and I were thrilled about going to Kontum with Captain Tom. There was some jealously among the other pilots, but they took it good-naturedly.

On December 6, Captain Thompson handed me orders promoting me to captain. I was elated. I'd been commissioned a second lieutenant on July 6, 1965, and now, twenty-seven months later, I was a captain. It meant more responsibility but also a $200-per-month pay raise. I would not see the raise, because the army automatically deposited all of my pay except for thirty-five dollars a month into Claudia's and my joint checking account with the Bank of America. But I would have fun writing her about my promotion. I knew she would be proud of me.

That evening, we celebrated my promotion at the officers' club. I spent all of my thirty-five dollars buying drinks. That was a lot at fifty cents a shot. That night, I decided that as a captain, I was going to need a little more money each month, so I decided that I would change my allotment to keep the $200 a month. That night, I wrote to Claudia about my move to Kontum and my promotion. I did not say anything about changing my allotment, because it would give me money to buy her some gifts with which I could surprise her. I had noticed some beautiful diamond and sapphire rings in the PX, but with thirty-five dollars a month, I could not afford them. However, with $200, I could.

We had a platoon party on the night before we left for Kontum. Captain Tom had rounded up a box of steaks and some chicken legs for the grill. I provided ten cases of beer for my promotion. We rearranged the platoon operations hut to create a dance floor, and the maintenance sergeant borrowed enough folding chairs to provide seats. One of the crew chiefs hooked up his stereo, and we had good country music to dance to. The enlisted men had invited their girlfriends, who brought some of their girlfriends to the party. The girlfriends brought some delicious Vietnamese dishes to go with the meat.

Although the early mood was one of sadness over the platoon—as well as some relations—breaking up, it turned out to be a great party. I was helping Captain Tom grill, drinking beer, and listening to the music. After the time it took to down a couple of beers, I took a tray of cooked steaks and chicken legs inside to the food line. I expected everybody to be dancing and having fun, but I found most of the young women lined up on one side of the room, while the guys hung out on the other side. The young women were in traditional Vietnamese dress and attractive. The party was dead unless someone ignited it.

I remembered the advice Thomas had given me about party behavior when I was a rookie in the Eleventh Airborne Division: "Anytime you're at a party where everybody is standing around slyly eyeing each other, move out and ask the prettiest girl you see to dance. She may not accept, but you break the ice. If she dances with you, and most times she will, the other young women will think you're hot and want you to ask them to dance. The guys will be jealous because they all wanted to ask the woman you asked. Since most of them are better looking than you and can dance better, they'll start asking young women to dance, and the party will liven up." However, he cautioned about not asking the prettiest woman if you were trying to get laid. "In that case, you should ask the least attractive."

There was an attractive woman standing with two or three other women. She stood out because she looked a little older than the rest. With Thomas's words on my mind, I said, "Come on, guys," and I walked up to the older woman and said, "Hi. I am Neal. Would you like to dance?"

In perfect English, she answered, "Yes, I would," and she extended her hand for me to lead her to the dance floor.

We started dancing to a rock-and-roll song, and when it ended, a slow song started. I took her hand, and we started dancing to it. By then, there were several couples dancing. I looked at her and asked, "Where did you learn to speak such perfect English?"

"In school," she answered. "I am a teacher now, and I teach English. So I have improved." We talked a lot that evening about Vietnam and her family. She would not reveal much about herself other than that she was a teacher. She wanted to know about me and my family and where I came from in the States.

The food was great, the company was good, and the night passed quickly. Around 2300, all the women started leaving, and the teacher said good night to me and left. The maintenance sergeant drove them home in the platoon jeep, and Captain Tom, Lieutenant Stevens, and I cleaned up the mess from the party. I was just finishing, when the maintenance sergeant stuck his head in the door and said, "Captain Griffin, may I speak with you a minute?"

"Sure," I said, and I walked outside.

"The teacher asked me to tell you that she knows you are leaving tomorrow, but she would like for you to come spend the night with her if you want to."

Gee, I thought, *what an invitation. Why didn't I get invitations like this when I was single?* Shaking my head gently, I replied, "Tell her I am flattered, and there is nothing more I would rather do right now than accept her offer. But I'm faithful to my wife. Sorry. Tell her I will forever keep her memory in my heart."

The sergeant responded, "Okay, sir. I'll tell her." As he drove away, I could not help but think about Thomas and how his advice usually worked.

The next morning, W-3 Johnston picked us up in the company's Beaver and flew us to Kontum. Kontum was different from Qui Nhon. It was located about fifty miles north of Pleiku in the central highlands, in a bend of the Dak Bla River and surrounded by mountains and mountain passes. Three valleys running generally north–south essentially divided Kontum Province into three main areas. The center valley was the most settled, with Highway 14 running through its center north from Pleiku, through Kontum to Dak To, and then north through rugged mountains to Da Nang. At the northern end of Kontum Province, Highway 14 rose into a four-thousand-foot mountain pass. Mountains on either side reached higher, with one estimated at 10,500 feet.

In this area, the NVA controlled Highway 14. At the top of the pass, antiaircraft positions sat alongside the highway. Whenever we approached the pass, we could see NVA running to the gun positions. The platoon had reported this many times, but for some reason or another, higher headquarters had never attacked the positions. Maybe their location between the mountains made it too risky for any tactical value. No friendly traffic ever went this far north on Highway 14.

The western valley ran north from the Pleiku plains parallel to the Cambodian and Laotian borders, joining the center valley north of Dak To. Pilots called it the Play Trap, which sounded like its Vietnamese name. Because of its closeness to the border, there was more NVA activity in the Play Trap. The Dak Hodrol, a stream, flowed southwesterly through the valley until it met the Se San River. The Se San flowed westerly through Cambodia until it joined the Mekong River. A dirt road ran along the banks of the river.

The third and smallest of the valleys ran northeast out of Pleiku past Kontum and then turned east toward the coast. Highway 19A split off Highway 19, which ran between Qui Nhon and Pleiku, and ran into Kontum and then east back to Highway 1. There was little evidence of war in this valley, although Highway 19A was in disrepair and grown over in several areas. A large, old French plantation sat beside the highway about halfway between Kontum and Pleiku. Although we reconned the valley every day, there were seldom any sightings of the enemy—or friendlies, for that matter.

The mountainous terrain required aerial reconnaissance techniques different from those used in flatlands. Mountains and NVA concentrations increased the danger to pilots while flying reconnaissance missions.

Chief Johnston landed the Beaver and taxied to the east end of the airfield and into a row of revetments. The Second Platoon operations hut sat in the middle of a row of revetments. Captain Rater, the acting platoon leader, was standing in front of the hut, waiting to greet us. Chief Johnston turned the Beaver around and stopped. He left the engine running while we got out. Captain Tom, who knew Rater, introduced Darrel and me while two crew chiefs grabbed our bags out of the Beaver and loaded them onto a jeep. Captain Tom told Darrel and me to go to the BOQ and get settled in. He was going to Pleiku with the chief to talk with the company commander.

Darrel and I crawled into the jeep with our baggage, and Captain Rater drove us to the MACV (Military Assistance Command, Vietnam) compound. The compound was laid out in a square on the northwest side of Kontum City. The compound housed Second Platoon personnel, logistics and maintenance support personnel for MACV headquarters, Special Forces team B24, and the Forty-Third signal compound. The structures were old French buildings left over from the Indochina War.

A line of trenches and bunkers encased the compound. Interlocking lines of barbed wire and mines outside the trenches and bunkers surrounded the compound. The lines were more than two hundred yards deep in some places. The SF team, B24, was the only combat unit on the compound; therefore, the pilots, mechanics, clerks, cooks, and radio operators billeted there were responsible for defending the compound if attacked. Team B24 defended the north side of the compound. The remaining personnel provided security for the other three sides. The compound commander divided those personnel into three teams under the command of officers. Each team had a side to defend in case of attack. I commanded the team defending the south side. Each night, twenty soldiers, divided into three four-hour shifts, guarded the compound.

The French had built a tennis court on the west side of the compound. Placed outside the bunker and trench line but inside the barbed wire and mines, it served as a helipad. Sitting on the west side of the tennis court was the communications tower that housed the radios and antennae linking the compound to the outside world and to the higher command elements to the south, in Saigon.

The rear row of buildings served as the BOQ. Darrel and I had the first room on the south end. The room had two wall lockers, a small table with two chairs, and two GI cots double bunked. I looked at Darrel and said, "Since I outrank you, I will take the bottom bunk." Jokingly, I continued, "That will provide me more protection from mortar and artillery rounds."

Darrel's response was "Thanks a lot."

While we were unpacking our equipment, a couple warrant officers came by to meet us. They started explaining how different the flying here was and said one was consistently engaging NVA targets. As I listened, I could not help but think that little was said about reconnaissance and intelligence collected. They had the attitude that they were here to provide fire support for the ground troops. After Darrel and I unpacked, they showed us around the compound, and we had lunch. The two WOs disappeared after lunch, and Darrel and I waited in our BOQ for someone from the platoon to show up.

Captain Rater knocked on the door about 1300 and told us to get our flight gear and get in the jeep; he had scheduled us for area orientation flights at 1400. He drove us back to the flight line, and we entered the operations hut, which had an arrangement similar to the one in Qui Nhon. A big map of the province hung on the rear wall, with a counter in front. A desk and two wall lockers behind the counter served as the operations officer and platoon leader's desk

A W-2 and a lieutenant were waiting for us when we arrived. Captain Rater introduced us. Using the map, he gave us an overview briefing of Kontum Province. He spent about thirty minutes discussing the dangers of

51

flying recon in mountainous terrain and pointed out several known NVA antiaircraft positions. He lingered on the various locations where platoon pilots had attacked NVA forces and told us the number they had killed. We discussed the method and agencies to contact to get clearance to fire on targets. When he ran out of subjects, he asked us if we had any questions, and of course, we did not. Darrel and I wanted to fly.

WO Benet was flying me, so I followed him to the revetment holding our aircraft, and we did a preflight. Benet had another month to go before his tour was up, at which point he would return to the States. He had flown his whole tour there in Kontum Province and knew it well.

With me in the backseat, we took off on runway thirty-two. As we climbed out, I could see the rifle range on the right about three hundred yards off the end of the runway. *Great,* I thought. *A place to zero my M16.* Benet turned to a southwesterly course and entered a valley. As I listened to him explain where we were going, I studied the terrain passing by our flight path.

The mountains forming the valley we were over were about five to six thousand feet high and covered with lush forests and grasses. The Montagnards had cleared plots by burning areas so they could plant crops. A clearly visible trail ran along the ridge formed by the mountaintops. Occasionally, the trail divided into several and worked down the sides of the mountains, disappearing into dark green forests and reappearing here and there as they meandered to the valley floor.

The valley floor had a few open areas that might have been for crops at one time but now looked overgrown and untended. A stream flowed through the valley and almost split the valley evenly. I made a mental note that there were no good places to land in case of an emergency. The mountains and valleys had a serene beauty, and other than the trails, they seemed uninhabited and remote. Benet was explaining that we were en route to an SF team whose base sat on a plateau named Plateau GI. The base was also a good place to take a break, eat lunch, refuel, and reload rockets. He explained that we flew daily recon missions for them, and often, we were the only support they had when weather socked them in and other planes could not get in. I could see what he was talking about as the valley became narrower and narrower and the clouds came closer to the mountain peaks.

After we flew about thirty miles into the valley, there was barely enough room to do a 360-degree turn, and the clouds covered the tops of the mountains. I was unsure of Benet's flying skills, and we were running out of airspace, which was making me a little nervous. Then Benet banked toward an opening that suddenly appeared between the mountains. At five thousand feet, we were just below the clouds as we flew through the pass. The terrain quickly dropped away about a thousand feet and flattened out to form a large plateau. It seemed as if some giant had leveled the mountains and hills to create a grass-covered plain.

A red dirt landing strip sat in the center of the plateau, with a dirt road to a fortified firebase a quarter mile away. Benet explained that once you reached the opening, you could call the SF team on their FM frequency. If, for some reason, you could not contact them by radio, you should make a low pass over the firebase to let the SF team know you were there. If it was safe to land, they would pop a green smoke grenade, which would signal that it was safe to land and give you wind direction, and they would send a jeep down for you. If the base was under attack, they would pop red smoke, warning you not to land.

Benet overflew the runway and continued toward the triangle-shaped firebase. As flew, he called the SF team on the FM radio. They answered as he made a low pass and told them he was taking a new pilot on an orientation flight and would not be landing unless they needed something. The voice on the radio said they needed nothing today; everything was quiet. He wanted to know when they would get to meet the new pilots. Benet told them as soon as they started flying missions. Then we turned and headed back through the pass into the valley.

Halfway out of the valley, the elevation dropped down to around three thousand feet. Benet banked right and turned to the southwest. He told me we were headed to the Play Trap.

As we crossed into the Play Trap, he stayed at an altitude of two thousand feet—no sense in getting shot at on an orientation flight! Bomb craters pockmarked the valley floor, while bunker complexes and trenches, tactically located to provide observation of the valley, were visible on most of the mountaintops. The valley provided a natural avenue of approach to any force with plans to attack Pleiku. Because of that, the Second Platoon conducted two or three recons of the Play Trap each day to prevent a surprise attack.

We flew the valley until we reached the Se San River where it flowed into Cambodia. This was the southern boundary of our area. From two thousand feet, the valley seemed empty of life. Turning back to the north, Benet climbed up over the mountains separating the Play Trap from the center valley. The Fourth Infantry Division's area of operations included the Play Trap and these mountains north to Dak To. Here and there, in no specific scheme, I could see bunker complexes and trench lines dotting the mountaintops. Bomb craters polka-dotted most, depicting the fury of past battles.

We had flown for about ten minutes, when a transmission on Guard channel blurted out, "Attention, all aircraft. Attention, all aircraft. This is Pleiku air traffic control with an Arc-glide warning. Avoid the area sixty miles north of Pleiku on the Pleiku VOR radial 310 for the next fifteen minutes. I repeat: avoid the area sixty miles north of Pleiku on the Pleiku VOR radial 310 for the next fifteen minutes. All aircraft flying in that area must leave it immediately."

By then, both Benet and I were studying our maps. *Arc-glide* was the code word for a B-52 strike, and we sure as hell did not want to be near that area when those bombs started exploding. I estimated that we were either dead in the middle of the strike area or damn near it. Benet agreed with me and turned due east to take us out of the area. We were both guessing. We did not have a VOR in the Bird Dog, but we could project the 310-degree azimuth out of Pleiku. By comparing that to where we were, we could see that we were close to the target area.

After flying about two miles east, Benet turned on a heading of 310. I was not comfortable with that and told him, "Hey, Chief, I think you need to go east three or four more miles to make sure we are clear."

He answered with excitement in his voice, "We need to stay close because the strike will disorient any NVA left alive, and they'll be an easy target for us."

I said, "I agree with you, but if the strike destroys us, it will not matter how many it leaves alive."

A series of huge explosions a quarter mile wide coming straight at us interrupted our debate. "Shit," Benet said as he banked hard to the right and dove to increase airspeed. I could see the carpet of explosions coming straight at us as we slowly cleared to the east. As the carpet of explosions moved by us, a wave of extreme turbulence rolled over us, tossing us as if the Bird Dog were a feather in a tornado. I held on and braced myself as Benet fought for control of the aircraft. As quickly as it had hit, it ended, and we returned to normal flight.

During the battering, we lost about five hundred feet of altitude. Now we were about two hundred feet above the mountaintops, in smoke and dust thrown up by the severe concussion of the exploding five-hundred-pound bombs. The carpet of explosions was now a mile to the south of us. Benet banked the aircraft back to the west, and we began a recon of the target area.

The bombs had destroyed a swath about a half mile wide through the mountaintops. The blasts had piled dirt and debris across the area. Benet flew back and forth across the swath as we looked for any sign of life. His quick banks to the left and then to the right nauseated me after about ten minutes. Finally, I said, "Hey, Chief, you're killing me with all these erratic turns. Let's climb up to five hundred feet so we can see without so many turns." He looked back at me as if I were kidding. I guess he saw that I wasn't, so he started a climbing turn to five hundred feet. The more stable flight calmed my stomach.

We reconned for twenty or thirty minutes more without seeing anything except bomb craters. My stomach was churning, and I was pissed that he had almost killed us by not clearing the Arc-glide area enough. I let a little of my anger enter my voice as I finally said, "Hey, Chief, I think we're wasting time. Why don't you finish my orientation ride before we run out of fuel?"

He turned north toward Dak To as he answered. "Okay, sir. We'll continue up to Dak To and the northern boundary of our area."

Dak To was located in the flatlands where the Play Trap and the center valley joined. Twenty-five miles west of Dak To was where the borders of Vietnam, Laos, and Cambodia came together. It was usually referred to as the triborder area. From Dak To, we continued north.

I could see the rising terrain ahead, and Benet applied power and started climbing. We followed Highway 14 along its route through the Play Trap. When Benet reached seven thousand feet, I could see the pass that Highway 14 ran through. The NVA antiaircraft positions were plainly visible as we neared the pass. Suddenly, we could see figures running for the positions. Benet banked around to the south and lowered the nose, and we descended back into the valley. He said, "That's about as close as I ever want to get to those guns."

I blurted out, "I agree with that," relieved that he didn't want to do some hot-dog act, such as fire one of our rockets at the positions. "Do you have any idea why the air force doesn't attack those guns?"

He answered, "We have never received an answer as to why they don't destroy the positions. We check them every day or so and update the information on them, but no one seems to be concerned about their existence."

He was flying toward Kontum now, and I was feeling better. I vowed to myself that I would never fly in the backseat with him again.

When we got back to the airfield, all the pilots were there, including Captain Bill Mark, the air force FAC. Captain Mark was based at Kontum and worked out of the platoon's area. The platoon provided him with ground support and occasionally unofficially lent him an aircraft when his was down. In turn, he was always ready to support us when we had a target suitable for attack by air force fighters or bombers. He was a nightly poker buddy and a hell of a pilot considering that before he went to FAC school and Bird Dog transition, he flew B-52s.

Captain Tom first introduced us and then said, "Captain Griffin is the new operations officer, and Lieutenant Darrel is the new maintenance officer. We will continue to conduct operations like always. Captain Griffin will schedule flights to ensure we cover the province each day. If you have any questions about the schedule, resolve them with Captain Griffin first. If you are still unhappy, come see me, and I will reaffirm Captain Griffin's decision." Everybody looked at him in silence. "Okay, Chief Donald is doing the evening perimeter flight. The rest of us can go have a beer and dinner."

As everybody turned to leave for the officers' club, I asked Captain Rater to stay with me and help me with the flight schedule for tomorrow. Chief Donald left to preflight. Because Kontum was isolated, one of us would fly a recon extending out ten miles around the city each night. The idea was to find any NVA units moving in for an attack on the city. The flight would last until dark. We had no way to tell whether it was effective or not. Until now, no one had seen any activity, and no one had attacked the city.

With Captain Rater providing recommendations, I planned the flights for the next day. Because of the treacherous mountains and valleys, many of the flights needed two aircraft. One would fly low while the second aircraft stayed high, watching the low aircraft. This was mainly for safety purposes since an aircraft lost radio contact when down in a valley. If you had an emergency in that situation, no one would ever hear your mayday call.

The Second Platoon had eight aircraft assigned to it. One was in maintenance, one was for Captain Thompson so he could oversee the missions in progress and provide command and control when needed, and the six left were for recon missions. I scheduled two recons with a high-aircraft requirement. I scheduled Darrel and me for the high aircraft. That gave us more time to learn the area. The remaining two aircraft I scheduled for single-aircraft areas. I reversed the schedule for the afternoon and scheduled myself for the evening perimeter flight.

After I posted the flights on the flight operations board, the maintenance sergeant entered the aircraft tail numbers. The maintenance sergeant assigned the aircraft for each mission, so he could rotate aircraft and schedule needed maintenance with minimum interruption of the mission. After posting the missions, I made two paper copies, one for Captain Thompson and one to post on my BOQ door, so pilots would not have to go to the airfield to check their assigned flights.

I took my job as operations officer seriously. I ensured I covered the entire province each day. I balanced flights so every pilot flew a different sector each day. I was demanding about recon reports. When a pilot came in bragging about an enemy position he'd attacked and how many KIAs he estimated, I asked him about his primary job of collecting information. I made sure he understood that I did not care how many KIAs he reported, as our job was to collect and report information on the enemy. That information, when analyzed and linked with other intelligence, provided a picture of enemy activity. That picture was far more important to the commander than the few NVA soldiers we might kill.

At first, the response was "We are the only ones in this area who can attack them most of the time."

My response was "Okay, attack them after you can describe their activity, weapons, uniforms, number, location, and direction of movement. I don't care as long as you get the recon report information." After a couple of weeks, my reports started to improve. The company reported that there were more platoon reports than they had seen in a long time.

Some of the pilots wanted to fly the hot areas all the time. They would try to convince me that because of their experience, they should fly these areas. In response, I told them that was exactly why they should the fly the quieter areas too: their experience would enable them to see activity that less-experienced pilots and observers might miss. Some went to Captain Thompson to complain and present their cases. They only went once, and when he finished with them, I had no more complaints.

Kontum Province was active compared to Binh Dinh Province. There were daily sightings of new bunker complexes and signs of NVA movement, especially in the Play Trap. By late December, activity was peaking. We did not know it at the time, but it was preparation for the Tet Offensive, which took place in January 1968.

One day after a recon in the Play Trap in support of the Fourth Division, Darrel reported that he believed the NVA was improving the dirt road running through the valley. It looked as if in some areas, they had bulldozed and filled bomb craters. When we reported this, we received instructions to continue recon of the Play Trap as a priority. We were to map the roadwork and find all positions. In no case were we to attack any troops caught in the open or to even suggest we were aware of what was going on. In response, I scheduled two recons a day at random times— early morning, midday afternoon, and early evening. Besides our flights, Mohawks flew infrared missions by night.

The information from our careful and thorough recons produced some alarming results. We were watching the NVA rebuild and repair the road running south through the Play Trap from the intersection with the road that ran out of Laos to Dak To. Each day, we mapped the progress as the work inched south. We found and identified map coordinates of camouflaged areas where they had stacked fifty-five-gallon drums of what we believed to be fuel. There was one of these areas about every fifteen miles. The NVA put a great deal of effort into camouflaging their work. Many times, we watched people scatter and hide as they heard us approaching. However, the fact that there had been no attacks must have lulled them into believing we were unaware of what was going on.

After about three weeks, the roadwork reached the Se San River, and work ended. Earlier, air force assets had detected armored trucks just across the border in Laos. Our guess was that the NVA had made the repairs in preparation for an all-out attack on Pleiku. The sign the attack was about to begin would be when they built a bridge across the Se San River. A week passed with no activity reported. Then an imagery interpreter, analyzing infrared imagery from a Mohawk, identified what looked like a truck in the middle of the Se San River.

The next morning, we received an urgent order to recon the river closely and confirm or deny the existence of a bridge or a fording site. I scheduled four flights that day for that purpose. I flew one of the missions. I directed the other three pilots to recon in such a manner that would not reveal we were purposely looking for a bridge. We were still under orders not to reveal our knowledge of the road.

I flew my recon and pretended interest in the mountains and small valley about two miles northeast of where the interpreter had seen the truck. I would make wide turns that took me over the river so I could check for any sign of a bridge or fording site. To the casual observer on the ground, I did not appear interested in the river. I saw nothing suspicious, and after about five flights over the site, I moved farther northeast and continued my recon.

Chief Walker, on the third flight that afternoon, solved the puzzle. The sun was at just the right angle, so as he flew over the river, he could see the bridge under about a foot of water. The NVA had built the bridge underwater to hide it. They could attack at any time.

The report of the bridge location attracted much attention. The Fourth Division CG asked for confirmation. I sent Chief Walker on another flight, and he confirmed the location. I sent the confirmation report to company operations. Orders came down to avoid flights in the Play Trap for the next couple days.

That afternoon, as I was rescheduling flights, Bill dropped by platoon operations and asked me for the coordinates of all the fuel storage areas that we had plotted in the Play Trap. I pulled out my copy of the reports and resolved the map locations with him. I could sense something was up and asked Bill if he was flying tonight.

He grinned and told me to watch the sky over the Play Trap around 2100 tonight and have pilots standing by for immediate recon missions in the morning. That was it. The air force was going to hit targets in the Play Trap. With that, he climbed into his Bird Dog and left.

That night around 2100, I walked outside and looked to the west toward the Play Trap. After about twenty minutes, the sky started flashing from the rolling explosions of thousand-pound bombs. It lasted for about fifteen minutes and covered the entire Play Trap. By then, Darrel had joined me, and all we could say was "Wow!"

We were about to go in, when Captain Tom walked up. "As you can see, the air force just attacked the Play Trap with a massive rolling thunder. The Fourth Infantry Division commander wants to know the extent of the damage from the attack, so, Neal, schedule two birds to take a look at first light. Make sure whoever you send coordinates with Bill Mark before entering the area. Bill will put in F-4s as soon as he can see and mark any targets not destroyed."

I didn't hesitate. "Darrel and I will go. No sense trying to find two sober pilots and brief them for the mission." He agreed, so Darrel and I took the mission.

We were airborne at first light. Darrel headed south to the bridge. He would start his recon there and fly north. I headed for Dak To so I could enter the Play Trap and recon south. Bill Mark was already airborne, and as we proceeded to our start points, I gave him a call.

He was putting F-4s in on an undamaged fuel depot. I told him Headhunter 25 and I would be doing damage assessment recon and would pass any targets to him. He said he had plenty of F-4s stacked up and waiting for targets. I told him, "Roger," and I said to keep us informed so we could stay out of his way. A midair with an F-4 was not favorable to longevity.

Darrel found the bridge still intact and told Bill. Bill told us he was heading to the bridge to attack it. I was happy to hear that because our flight path would be clear of any aircraft attacking the bridge.

At two hundred feet over the ground, I could see the destructive effects of thousand-pound bombs. Most of the destroyed depots were now huge fires with smoke plumes rising thousands of feet into the air. The attack had also cratered the road from start to end. Of course, the NVA could repair it, but it would take awhile. Occasionally, I could see bodies flung about. At one depot, several trucks were burning amid the fifty-five-gallon drums. As I approached an area where the road passed between two hills, I caught a glimpse of movement off the right side of the road.

Not sure what I had seen, I added power and climbed up to five hundred feet as I banked around. Crossing over the sight, I could see about twenty-five NVA troops crouching under some low trees. I went on guard and called, "Any gunships in vicinity of Play Trap, come up Headhunter frequency."

Almost immediately, I heard, "Headhunter, this is Headhunter Test One. I'm in vicinity. What do you need?"

Headhunter Test One was the call sign of an OH-6 Loach helicopter with a minigun mounted on it. The 219th was testing its use for flying recon missions with a Bird Dog. The idea was to provide both recon and attack means.

"Headhunter Test One, this is Headhunter 28. I've got troops in the open. Coordinates 672134. Are you looking for a target?"

"Roger that, Headhunter 28. I'm on the way. I'm on heading ten degrees at four hundred feet. ETA five minutes," the slightly excited voice answered.

I climbed to eight hundred feet to ensure good separation as I circled the NVA location. I was sure they would start moving after I detected them, but so far, they were sitting still. I suspected the bombing had disoriented them. Looking south, I saw Headhunter Test One approaching. "Headhunter Test One, this is Headhunter 28. Got you two miles approaching from the south. I'm in a left bank at eight hundred feet. Do you have your fixed-wing with you?"

"Negative, HH 28. I am working alone today. I've got you in sight. You can mark the target anytime."

"Roger, Test One. I'm rolling in hot." I lowered the nose and lined up on the spot where the NVA hunkered down. When the spot was close enough to see several of the NVA looking at me, I fired my rocket. It was a good shot. As I pulled up and banked, I could see the WP explode in the middle of the NVA position. "Okay, Test One, the WP was dead center."

"Roger, HH 28. I'm rolling in. I've got the NVA in sight."

I watched as Headhunter Test One descended to about ten feet above the ground and opened fire with his minigun. It amazed me how he just hovered and turned the nose of the OH-6 using pedal turns. Of course, where the nose pointed, the rounds from the minigun went. After about twenty seconds, which seemed like an eternity, he pulled pitch and climbed up and away from the target area as he contacted me. "Headhunter 28, take a look. I don't see any moving targets left."

"Roger, Test One," I answered as I descended toward the target area. I was hesitant to slow down and take a good look, but since Test One had hovered without drawing fire, I lowered full flaps and entered slow flight. As I passed over the target at thirty feet, I saw no movement. I could count twelve bodies scattered about. The minigun had shredded the vegetation at ground level and even knocked over several small trees. Climbing out, I called, "Good job, Test One. I confirm twelve KIA. Will you be in the area if I need you again?"

"Negative, HH 28. I'm heading back to Pleiku. I've used all my ammo and need to refuel."

"Roger, Test One. Take care." I watched him turn toward Pleiku as I continued my recon. I spent the rest of the flight recording the damage without seeing any more live targets. Bill contacted me, confirming that he had destroyed the bridge with F-4s. I called Darrel and told him to get a confirmation on the bridge. It wasn't that I did not trust Bill's report, but when I filed my reports, I could include that I had confirmed it. If the NVA rebuilt it the next night, there would be no questions about my reports.

The Play Trap would remain a hotbed of activity. We would continue to fly daily missions in it and find activity on every flight. It was obvious the NVA was moving many troops and supplies into Vietnam from the triborder area. Shortly after the rolling-thunder night, the Fourth Division began operations in the valley. We did not know that what we were seeing was the NVA preparing for the Tet Offensive, which would erupt throughout Vietnam on January 31, 1968.

One afternoon, Captain Rater returned from his recon looking excited. He bounced into the operations building and started describing what he had done. While returning to the airfield, he'd flown over an NVA platoon hiding on a small mound about twenty miles south of Kontum. He'd immediately called and gotten clearance to attack. He'd happened to have one fleschette rocket in his tubes, and he'd fired that one first. The fleschette rocket contained hundreds of small darts in its head. At a set distance, after being fired, the head busted open, spreading the darts in a large circular pattern. The dart pattern had covered the mound. He'd then fired his HE and WP rockets. When the smoke had cleared, he could count fifteen KIA, which he reported to sector and the Fourth Division. He finished his recon report and took off for the compound. After all the pilots had finished their reports, I reviewed them and noticed that Captain Rater had only described his attack of the NVA position and nothing else.

That night around 2130, Darrel and I were in our room, writing letters, when Captain Rater knocked on our door. I opened the door, and he handed me some forms. When I looked at the forms, I saw that they were a nomination for the Distinguished Flying Cross, and he had completed them on himself. "What's this?" I asked.

He looked at me and replied, "You're the awards officer for the platoon, and that's my nomination for the DFC. You need to sign off on it and forward it to company."

I turned and held the papers in the light so I could read them. His account described an action in which he had been under fire and had attacked a force that was preparing to attack a Fourth Division patrol. His actions had destroyed the enemy force and prevented a possible ambush of the patrol.

His account surprised and angered me with the deliberate lie he had developed to justify recommending himself for the DFC. With disgust, I challenged him. "Captain Rater, this is not what you told me this afternoon. Where in the hell do you get the nerve to lie and put yourself up for a Distinguished Flying Cross and think I will approve it? Your primary job is recon and to report information for use in developing intelligence. From my view, you failed to do your job, for which I should reprimand you."

Shocked at my rebuke, he said, "I did my job. I reported a suspected NVA platoon."

"Really?" I answered. "How were the NVA armed? What type of unit, infantry, and artillery? What direction were they traveling? Were they preparing a fighting position? Did they appear to be part of a larger unit? This information is far more important to the commander than your report of fifteen KIA. Now all we know is that you killed fifteen NVA. Get info first, and then attack if you can. That's what the army pays you to do."

He was still not satisfied. He started pleading. "Look, Captain Griffin, this is the only war we've got now, and we need to get medals when we can. Awards are important when the DA considers you for promotion. I need to get a DFC before I rotate in January."

Now I was really pissed. I had a captain who outranked me standing before me, demanding I approve an untrue nomination for the DFC that he'd written for himself. I wanted to kick his ass. I was confrontational now. "Captain Rater, if you don't like my decision, take your paperwork to Captain Tom, and get him to approve it."

He said, "It's your job, dammit. You need to sign it whether you agree or not and forward it."

That was when we heard the sound of an M16 being charged. Turning, we saw Darrel standing there holding his M16. I have never seen Darrel as angry as he was. "Captain Rater, I'm tired of this bullshit. Captain Griffin has been polite and professional and has told you what to do. You are totally out of line and insubordinate. Now get your ass out of my doorway, or I'm going to send you home with a medal—a Purple Heart." He said this as he was walking toward the door and Captain Rater.

Captain Rater's red face turned ashen, and he started to say something, but then he spun around and left.

Darrel cleared his weapon and looked at me, saying, "Neal, you are a nice guy and way too patient. You should have told him to leave after you saw what he was trying to do."

That Darrel might have put himself in a jam by pulling a weapon and threatening a superior officer now concerned me. "Darrel, you know the army can court-martial you for that stunt."

"Who's going to court-martial me?"

I said, "If he runs to Captain Tom and presses charges, Captain Tom will have to take some form of action. What you need to do is go to Captain Tom right now and tell him what happened before Captain Rater gets to him."

Darrel was thinking about the implications of what he had done. "I guess you're right, Neal." He put his shirt on and left to find Captain Tom.

I was in bed when he returned. "Did you find Captain Tom?"

"Yes, he said not to sweat it but never to do it again."

We never heard anything else about the incident. Captain Rater avoided Darrel and me as much as possible until he rotated back to the States three weeks later.

While he avoided me, I did not avoid him. The following week, I scheduled him to fly a mission for the SF team in Plateau GI. That afternoon on the return flight, he declared a mayday on Guard frequency. He reported losing power and going down halfway out of the valley. The tower told me on our platoon FM radio. I immediately diverted two of our planes to look for him.

When they reached the spot where he had put the aircraft down, a helicopter that had heard his call was picking him up. The aircraft and the tall grass were on fire. After the medics checked him for injuries and released him, I went to his BOQ to get his description of what had happened. As the operations officer, I had to file an incident report and launch an accident investigation of the accident or incident.

Before I talked to Captain Rater, I talked to the pilot of the helicopter that had recovered him. The helicopter crew reported that the plane was intact and undamaged when they first flew over it. Captain Rater caused the fire when he popped a smoke grenade so the helicopter could see him and get wind direction. The grenade started a brushfire, and the wind blew it to the aircraft, setting it on fire. The helicopter crew was in communication with him via the survival radio all pilots carried. In fact, they had him in sight and told him that it was not necessary to pop smoke. They had the wind direction by observation of the waving grass. But he popped smoke anyway.

When I talked to Captain Rater, I congratulated him on doing a fantastic job of landing the aircraft on the upslope of a small hill. I asked him to write a statement regarding what happened from the time he left Plateau GI until he was forced to land. I reminded him that this report was an official document and part of the accident investigation packet. He said, "Okay," and he started the account of what happened.

From there, I went back to the platoon operations building and called the depot maintenance unit to see if they could recover the remains of the Bird Dog. They flew their heavy-lift helicopter out to the sight and put a team on the ground to assess the possibility of recovering the aircraft. They found that the fire had not consumed the aircraft. It had burned the tires and scorched the remaining parts. They attached a harness to the aircraft and flew it back to depot maintenance for analysis.

That evening, Captain Rater brought his statement to my room. I told him I would read it and get back to him if I had any questions.

He described checking his oil at the airstrip at Plateau GI before starting the flight back to Kontum. This was SOP after flying for three hours and landing. On the flight back, he reported that everything was normal until he heard two pops that sounded like rounds hitting the aircraft. Almost immediately after that, oil began to hit his windshield.

The only clear area he could see was the grassy knoll of a hill a mile to his left. By then, oil covered his windshield. Knowing that his engine was going to seize at any moment, he began the mayday call. When he got to the hill, his engine seized, and he dropped full flaps and pushed the nose down toward the center of the hill. When he was at the roundout position, he pulled back on the stick as if to climb, and the Bird Dog settled into the grass in a relatively soft landing. Frightened, he grabbed his survival vest and weapon and fled from the aircraft. Almost immediately, the helicopter appeared, and he contacted it on the survival radio. Before they told him not to throw smoke, he'd already pulled the pin and was throwing it. He believed the two pops were rounds hitting his engine, resulting in the oil lost. He lost his .45 from the holster while running from the aircraft. That was the end of his statement.

Although we'd lost an aircraft, there was no loss of life, which satisfied us. I completed all of my incident reports while we waited for the results of the depot maintenance report on the aircraft.

The afternoon before Captain Rater left for the States, I received the final report on the results of the incident. I was furious. There were glaring discrepancies between what Captain Rater had reported in his statement and what the helicopter crew and depot maintenance reported.

The helicopter crew's statement said the crew heard the mayday before Captain Rater landed the aircraft. Because of their nearness and immediate response, they watched Captain Rater land the aircraft. They watched him exit the aircraft, run a short distance, and then turn around and run back to the aircraft. It looked as if he pointed something at the nose of the aircraft and then ran away from the aircraft. They circled over him, and he waved. They motioned for him to move to his right, which was a better landing site. Then they heard him on the survival radio and told him to move to his right. He responded that he was throwing a grenade to mark his position. Before the pilot could respond, he threw the green grenade, which set the brush on fire. After that, he moved to where the pilot told him to go for pickup.

The depot statement said there was no pin in the oil cap. Two rounds had struck the engine, doing some damage. However, the angle at which they struck the engine suggests the trajectory angle was parallel to the ground. This meant whoever fired the rounds was level with the aircraft. This was inconsistent with the altitude that Captain Rater reported when he heard the pops. His statement meant that whoever had fired the rounds had to be even with him—fifteen hundred feet above the terrain.

After reading the report, I decided that Captain Rater was lying. I called the SF team at Plateau GI and asked if Captain Rater had put oil in the aircraft before leaving for Kontum. The sergeant who'd driven Captain Rater to the airstrip confirmed that yes, he had added a quart of oil. Another rumor going around about Captain Rater was that supposedly, he wanted to buy a .45 pistol to take home with him.

What I heard and the maintenance reports confirmed my suspicions about what must have happened: Captain Rater had failed to pin his oil cap after adding oil to his engine. This was a classic failure that had caused many crashes over the years. Without the pin, the oil cap vibrates loose, and because the oil system is pressurized, the oil blows out. Oil hitting the windshield is the classic sign. Without oil, the engine seizes, and the propeller stops turning. The aircraft stops flying.

To his credit, Captain Rater did a remarkable job landing the plane on the hill. But knowing he caused the crash, he tried to cover it up by firing two rounds from his .45 pistol into the engine. In the obvious excitement, he failed to consider the possibility of the army recovering the intact aircraft. The entry angle of the rounds would be obvious. So being downwind from the aircraft, he threw a grenade, knowing it would start a fire and burn the aircraft. At the same time, he saw an opportunity to steal a .45 pistol by claiming he lost it while running through the grass.

I took my suspicions to Captain Tom. He listened and then said, "Let's go see Captain Rater."

We went to Captain Rater's room and knocked on the door. He opened the door, and Captain Tom walked in, so I followed. Captain Rater looked a little puzzled. He had everything packed for his return to the States. Captain Tom explained there was an inconsistency about what had happened in his forced landing. Captain Tom then advised him of his rights under Article 32 and asked him to unpack his duffel bag. I was praying that I was not wrong, because it would be embarrassing if I was.

Captain Rater was visibility upset as he started unpacking his duffel bag. Halfway through, out came the .45 pistol that he'd reported as lost. Captain Tom turned to me and said, "I'll take it from here, Neal. You can leave."

I left and returned to the flight line to fly my last mission of the day. I never saw Captain Rater again. Captain Tom never mentioned it again. I never brought it up again. It's difficult to accept that an officer would lie and steal. When the dishonesty is found out, it cancels out all the officer has ever done and is a discredit to the officer corps. I had no sympathy for him.

I became competent at flying recon in mountainous terrain. I loved the beauty of the mountains and was careful not to let it lure me into dangerous situations. Foremost in my mind was the most common mistake pilots make in mountainous terrain: they try to recon by flying up the mountain. I always obeyed the rule of gaining altitude first and then flying down the mountain on recon. Also, the high-density altitude and the operating weight of the Bird Dog made it impossible to climb uphill faster than the rising terrain.

Wind is an ever-present danger in mountainous terrain. The constant updrafts and downdrafts and the sudden and unexpected wind gusts can have you suddenly fighting for control. Both conditions can throw the small Bird Dog around like a kite in a hurricane.

One afternoon, I was flying high aircraft for Headhunter 27 in the mountains north of Dak To. Headhunter 27 entered a valley and flew along the foothills, heading for a ridge that separated two six-thousand-foot mountains. At the proper distance, he started climbing to clear the ridge by fifty feet. Everything looked good to me, when all of a sudden, he called, "Headhunter 28, I'm caught in a downdraft!"

Headhunter 27 had to clear the ridge because there was no room to turn around. "Headhunter 27, are you going to clear the ridge?"

Headhunter 27's voice was tense and strained as he answered. "I don't know, HH 28. I've got full power in, and I'm losing airspeed trying to climb over the ridge."

I felt my stomach turn into a knot. I wanted to help, but there was nothing I could do.

Then Headhunter 27 called again. "I'm not going to make it. I am going to put it between two trees. Have you got me in sight?" He seemed resigned to his fate.

There was a line of trees running along the top of the ridge, and I could see the two he was talking about. He was using the correct technique for landing or crashing into trees. The intent is for the trees to sheer off your wings and slow you down enough so that the fuselage can bear the impact without major damage. The less damage to the fuselage, the better one's chance of surviving.

I felt as if I were watching the event in slow motion. It looked as if Headhunter 27 would clear the trees if he could just gain five feet of altitude. He had already confirmed that he was just above stall speed and would not get any lower. That meant at full power, he could not raise the nose any higher. The nose of the aircraft would have to come up for it to climb. However, if Headhunter 27 raised the nose, he would lose airspeed and risk stalling out. If he stalled the aircraft, it would pitch nose down, and he would crash into the ridge. It is always better to crash with the aircraft in control than out. The graveyards are full of pilots who lost power on takeoff and, at low altitude and airspeed, tried a steep turn to get back to the airfield. They crashed out of control instead of lowering the nose and landing straight ahead under control. A steep turn at low altitude and slow airspeed will invariably stall the aircraft and send it nose down to the ground.

Suddenly, I thought of something I had seen before. I'd watched a Caribou take off from a short field with a berm off the end of the runway. I'd noticed that the pilot did not lower flaps until he got to the end of the runway. The Caribou had responded by seemingly jumping into the air momentarily, clearing the berm before it settled. I started broadcasting to Headhunter 27. "Flaps, HH 27. Drop flaps, 27. Drop flaps, 27!"

I watched, amazed, as Headhunter 27 lifted ten feet as if the plane had jumped. It was not much, but by lowering the flaps, Headhunter 27 gained just enough lift to avoid slamming into the trees. He merely brushed the treetops going over the ridge. When Headhunter 27 cleared the ridge and started to settle, he was over terrain that dropped abruptly for more than two thousand feet, giving him the altitude to regain control of the aircraft. Headhunter 27 lowered the nose and was flying again. I was holding my breath, not believing he had made it, when Headhunter 27 called, his voice still a little shaky. "Thanks, Headhunter 28. That was damn close. I didn't think there was any way I was going to miss those trees. It never occurred to me to drop flaps. I kissed the trees going over, but I don't think I did any damage to the aircraft."

By then, I'd entered the strong downdraft that had shoved Headhunter 27 downward, but I was a thousand feet over the terrain and had no trouble flying through it. I said, "Headhunter 27, let's swap positions and continue the mission." So Headhunter 27 and I switched positions and continued the recon.

That night at the officers' club, drinking beer and basking in the emotional relief of what had not happened, we retold the story at least six times. I went to sleep that night thinking about all the unforeseen dangers of our mission. I had expected hostile fire to be the daily threat, not the weather and terrain.

By the middle of December, we were sighting more and more evidence of the enemy's presence. NVA movement in the SF team's area at Plateau GI was so heavy that they asked for a daily recon. The weather was much cooler at night now. Clouds socked in most of the valleys until around noon, when the sun's heat lifted the clouds. Each flight going to support Plateau GI had to creep up the valley under the clouds and scoot through the narrow pass into Plateau GI.

In this weather pattern, few supply aircraft could get into Plateau GI. The SF team there depended on air resupply because there was no way they could get trucks into Plateau GI. Before a Headhunter went in to support them, I would call the team on radio to find out what they needed that we could bring. Most of the time, they needed ammo and rations, and we would pack as much as we could carry into the rear of the aircraft. Needless to say, the SF team did not care much for the air force. The air force, after taking over the Caribou, refused to fly supplies in during bad weather, as the army did.

The Caribou was a rugged twin-turbo jet cargo aircraft developed by the army to land on short, unimproved strips. The army employed it so successfully that the air force began to complain that the army was doing their missions. The issue became political, and eventually, the army lost the Caribou and turned it over to the air force. Unfortunately, the air force applied their rules for flying it. The result was that they would not fly into areas or under conditions for which the army had designed the Caribou.

Luckily, the Australians had bought Caribous to support their ground troops and had no qualms about flying them to their maximum capability. The Australians provided the main support to the SF team on Plateau GI when the air force would not fly.

One cloudy and rainy morning, I was en route to Plateau GI with four cases of C rations in the backseat, when Wallaby 11 called. "Any Headhunter aircraft, this is Wallaby 11. Over." Wallaby was the call sign for the Australian Caribou unit.

"Wallaby 11, this is Headhunter 28. How I can I help you?"

"Roger, Headhunter 28. I am trying to get into Plateau GI with supplies. I need you to lead me up the valley to the pass. This weather has socked Plateau GI in, and this is the only way we can get supplies to them."

"Roger, Wallaby 11. What's your location?"

"Headhunter 28, I'm just entering the valley."

"Roger, Wallaby 11. I'm about five miles ahead of you at seven hundred feet. Slow down to my airspeed of one hundred ten knots, and I will circle back and pick you up. I'll stay at seven hundred feet, and you stay at eight hundred."

"Roger, Headhunter 28. Slowing down to one hundred ten and at eight hundred."

"Roger, Wallaby 11. I'm turning around."

Halfway through my turn, I saw Wallaby 11 about two miles back. "Wallaby 11, this is Headhunter 28. Tallyho."

"Roger, Headhunter 28. We'll follow at this distance."

They would stay two miles behind me as we continued into the valley. As we flew into the valley, I watched for decreasing visibility. If the weather worsened so that Wallaby 11 could not safely turn around and go back, I would warn him. Being two miles back gave him the time to turn safely and fly out of the valley. Since I had the shortest turning distance, I could go farther into the valley in bad weather. When I could see the pass and could safely enter it, I would tell Wallaby 11, and he would continue to Plateau GI. Using this technique, Headhunter and Wallaby pilots consistently provided critical support to the SF team that they would not have received otherwise. I will always remember and admire the dedicated and skillful Australian pilots with the call sign Wallaby.

Unlike the often-boring recon flights in Dinh Binh Province, recon in Kontum was always full of action. Sightings were plentiful. We spotted new bunker complexes every other day. Troop sightings were not as common. Most of the time, we saw evidence of troops as they infiltrated into South Vietnam from Laos and Cambodia. The NVA and the Vietcong rarely fired at us. Their commanders told them that if they fired on a Bird Dog and did not destroy it, they would reveal their location. The Bird Dog then would bring in artillery, gunships, and bombs. Therefore, the only time we drew fire was when the enemy realized that we had detected them.

To get enemy troops to reveal their positions, we would use a technique known as recon by fire. As soon as we spotted a freshly prepared bunker void of activity, we would clear with sector control to ensure no friendly troops were in the area. Once sector control verified that no friendly troops were in the area, they would give us clearance to fire. We would then attack the target with an HE rocket in hopes of fooling any enemy present into thinking we had seen them. If they were present and hiding, they would think they had been seen and start firing at us. That would reveal their position, and we could hand the target off to Bill Mark for attack by the air force.

Sometimes recon by fire had its surprises. One afternoon, I was in the Play Trap, when I spotted a newly built and large bunker. After getting clearance, I lined up on the bunker and fired an HE rocket. As usual, with our grease-pencil-mark-on-the-windshield sighting system, I was close to the bunker when I fired the rocket. At an altitude of thirty feet and a hundred yards from the target, I followed the rocket toward the bunker.

I saw the rocket slam into the bunker opening, and to my surprise, the whole area exploded in front of me. In a split second, the sky was full of dirt and debris that billowed up three hundred feet into the air. Startled, I tried to bank and pull away from the exploding cloud but could not. I was too close and was in it before I could do anything.

The debris and concussion pounded and buffeted me, tossing me in every direction. The dirt plume was so thick that for about two seconds, I was in total darkness until I punched out the other side of the cloud of dirt and debris. As I fought to control the aircraft, I could hear debris ping and bang it. *Crap*, I thought. *I just shot myself down.* But the Bird Dog came of the debris cloud, climbing and banking under my control. The whole incident, from the time I fired my rocket until I was safely out of the debris, lasted no more than ten seconds.

Shaken by what had happened, I kept climbing and leveled off at a thousand feet to regain my composure. My mind was racing, trying to figure out what the hell had happened. Then it hit me that my rocket had exploded in an enemy ammo storage bunker, causing the massive secondary explosion that I had flown through. *Damn*, I thought, *I am lucky to still be alive.* Turning back to look, I could see the cloud of smoke and debris that had risen to seven or eight hundred feet. I heard my radio squawk. "Headhunter aircraft, this is Eagle Control 12. Do you have that explosion at your eight o'clock?"

It was Bill Mark. "Eagle 12, this is Headhunter 28. Roger that. I just flew through it. I fired a rocket at a bunker and got a secondary from it. Don't know if there are any bad guys around. I'm going in to take a close look, so stand by." Hearing Bill's voice calmed me down, and I went back to work.

"Roger, Headhunter 28. Got you in sight."

I lowered the nose and pulled off power to make a rapid descent. I leveled off at fifty feet and headed for the huge crater where the bunker had been. The explosion had flattened small trees and brush out to about a hundred yards around the crater. Fresh dirt, various debris, and the remains of ammunition boxes covered the area like dust. As I approached, I could see what looked like two bodies lying about fifty feet from the crater. There was no other sign of life or movement. I circled the crater out to about a mile but did not see anything else. I called Bill. "Eagle 12,

I don't see anything. There are a couple bodies about fifty feet from the crater, but other than that, nothing."

"Roger, Headhunter 28. I'll be in the area for another hour. Give me a call if you find anything."

"Roger, Eagle 12. I am going to continue my recon toward the south."

My crew chief, Specialist Four Wheeler, guided me in after landing. I could see him looking at the aircraft in disbelief. After I shut the engine down, he walked up to the door and asked, "Sir, what the hell happened to you?"

I smiled, mostly in relief that I was safely on the ground, and answered, "I did a recon by fire and had a huge secondary explosion that I couldn't avoid."

By then, the maintenance sergeant was walking around the aircraft, inspecting it. I completed the log entry and took the book with me to inspect the aircraft for damage. There were several minor dents in the fuselage and wings. Two quarter-sized holes were in the tail section of the fuselage, and one was in the right wing. Clumps of dirt still stuck to the aircraft. I entered the damage into the logbook and, looking at the maintenance sergeant, asked, "Can you fix it?"

"Yes, sir, we'll pop the dents out and put some hundred-mile-an-hour tape over the holes until it goes back to the company for its hundred-hour maintenance."

I felt relieved that the damage was minor and would not put the aircraft into a nonfly status. It was the first time I had damaged an aircraft, and it upset me little. The danger of a secondary explosion had never occurred to me. I changed my recon-by-fire technique after that experience. From then on, when I fired a rocket into a bunker complex, I fired from a couple hundred yards out. That gave me enough room to avoid a secondary explosion, should one occur.

That night at the officers' club, I took plenty of kidding. Bill Mark said, "With Headhunter 28 in the air, we don't need F-4s. I could have him attack the target." Darrel thought it was funny that I'd almost shot myself down. He mimicked me explaining to Captain Tom how that had happened. After three Black Labels from rusty cans, I relaxed and laughed with the chiding.

That night, I thanked God for his hand in getting me through each day. As with my attack on the bunker in Binh Dinh Province, I'd had no fear during the event, but as I lay in bed, my nearness to death caused me to tremble. I asked God to please let me survive until I at least saw Claudia once more. It was only ten weeks until we were to meet in Bangkok, and I was aching at the thought of holding her.

I was getting a pleasant letter every three or four days from Claudia. She too was excited about meeting in Bangkok. She had made a down payment on reservations with the option to cancel three weeks in advance without a penalty. The commander had approved my R&R leave, so we were prepared. I just needed to stay alive. Of course, I had no doubt I would survive—no one believes death will happen to him. If he did, he probably would not keep doing his job.

The war had become a routine for me: get up in the morning, shave and brush my teeth, go to the mess hall to eat breakfast, get to the flight line and make sure the early flights got off, consolidate and file the previous day's reconnaissance reports, review the hotspot report and schedule a recon of the hotspots in our area, update the weekly reconnaissance schedule, review any recommendations for awards, fly my assigned morning recon, eat lunch, fly my afternoon recon, recheck the following day's schedule for any adjustments necessary, eat supper, take a shower, hit the officers' club and join the continuing poker game, and, after the two or three cans of Black Label or Schlitz took effect, go to my room and hit the sack. I had no complaints. Compared to an infantryman's daily routine, my routine was a piece of cake.

The food was mundane in our mess hall. I believed it was because we were at the end of the supply line. Most of the meals in the mess hall consisted of veal, which came in various forms. We had veal stew, veal chops, and veal steaks. In some places, people consider veal a delicacy, but when you eat it every day, it becomes a hated menu item. Maybe it was the way the cooks prepared it. I am sure that in army cook school, they did not teach the fine art of cooking veal. Our cooks only knew how to boil it, stew it, or fry it. One thing we could count on was a full mess hall on pork chop day.

In Vietnam, certain food items were valuable in the barter system. A case of steaks, not veal, would fetch an AK-47 for some rear-area stud, whereas a case of veal steaks was worthless. To understand the importance of food is to understand how far a crafty person will go to fool another person in the barter system.

Aviation units had an advantage in bartering. We had transport and could go places to get the treasured items. One day Captain Tom was talking to a supply sergeant in Qui Nhon who said he had a case of rib eye steaks that he would trade for an AK-47. Well, we had three AK-47s hanging in the platoon locker in the operations building, so Captain Tom took him up on his offer. Captain Tom told me to set up a barbecue after the day's mission. That afternoon, he flew over to Qui Nhon and traded an AK-47 for the steaks. I invited the cooks to our barbecue in exchange for some salad, potatoes, and cake. They, like us, were weary of veal steaks, and they readily accepted. It was the first time in months the platoon had come together for some fun. The thought of sinking our teeth into those rib eye steaks was titillating.

The grill was going, and the beer from rusty cans was flowing, when Captain Tom called on the platoon net to say he was inbound with steaks. There was applause as he taxied into the revetment area and shut down the aircraft. Someone handed him a beer as he climbed down from the Bird Dog. The maintenance sergeant slid the pilot's seat forward and hauled out the case of steaks from the backseat. Sure enough, stamped on the box in big letters was the label "Rib Eye Steaks, 64 Count." Condensation covered the box, testifying to its freshness. The maintenance sergeant ripped the box open on the way to the grill and set it on the field table by the grill. As we gathered around, he pulled out two steaks to put on the grill—and stopped in disbelief. We gasped when we recognized the pale color of veal steaks.

The supply sergeant had ripped us off. He had taken a box of real steaks, replaced them with veal steaks, and swindled us out of our AK-47. Captain Tom was rabid. He ran to the platoon landline and called the supply depot in Qui Nhon. After talking to the duty officer, he slowly hung up the phone. The sergeant who had traded us the steaks had left for the States that afternoon. That left us with veal steaks. However, after we grilled them with lots of Tabasco sauce and salt and pepper, they did not taste half bad. So amid the war, realizing that as smart as we were, we were still gullible, our steak dinner turned out okay. Even Bill Mark, who heard about the steaks and came by to scrounge one, agreed the veal steaks were okay if grilled properly.

The movie *The Blue Max*, starring George Peppard, was the story of a German aviator during World War I. I was in flight school when Claudia and I saw it. The movie contrasted the good but dangerous life the German aviators lived as they fought their part of the war with that of the infantry struggling in the trenches. Now I was at war and could make the same comparison. By day, we flew over the enemy and did our part, but at night, we returned to a clean room, a shower, and beer at the officers' club. The infantry stayed on firebases and slept in the rain and the mud. In recognition of that, I always went out of my way to help the infantry in any way I could.

One day I looked at the calendar, and lo and behold, it was December 20. Christmas was less than a week away. The volume of mail had already announced the approach of Christmas. The number of packages and Christmas cards arriving in the mail alerted everyone to what time of year it was. Other than that, nothing else changed. The mess hall posted a Christmas dinner menu on the door. Thank God the menu listed turkey as the Christmas meal and not the usual veal. Claudia sent me a small package full of candy. I am not sure why or how she got the idea for candy, since I didn't eat hard candy, but it is the thought that counts.

We had our monthly fly-in on December 23. The highlight of the fly-in was the company Christmas party, which reminded us that we were far from home and lonely for the families we held dear. The company mess sergeant fixed a grand Christmas dinner for December 24. We had real turkey and mashed potatoes, not the ones that come from cans. I think I ate enough at that meal to last me for the rest of my tour. After the meal, we climbed back into our aircraft and returned to the war. There were no specific intelligence reports to support whether the NVA would or would not attack over Christmas. Because of that, we had to beef up our recon effort to find an answer to the question.

Occasionally, I had noticed a Catholic nun on the compound gathering leftover food from the mess hall. I asked around and found out that she ran an orphanage for children with leprosy about fifteen miles out of Kontum. One day as I flew over the orphanage, the children ran out and waved at me. The thought occurred to me that I could in some way provide a little joy to these children.

Two days after Christmas, I went around the compound and asked for all the hard candy the soldiers did not want or would give to the orphanage, and I got several pounds of hard candy. I packed it in three shell canisters, taped them shut, and wrapped them in some padding material. My plan was to fly over the orphanage and drop the canisters full of candy for the children. The canisters were sturdy, so I figured they would survive the drop.

On my afternoon recon, I loaded my canisters into the backseat. After my mission, I headed for the orphanage. Flying over the orphanage, I could see children out in the yard, playing. When they heard and saw me, they waved. I waved back as I looked for a place to drop the canisters. There was a large clearing in front of the main gate to the orphanage. I decided that was where I would drop the candy. It was in plain view of the children, but it would take them several minutes to get there. I knew they would run to get whatever I dropped, and I didn't want the falling canisters to hit one of them. Having picked my drop spot, I banked the aircraft around, dropped down to about fifty feet, and lowered full flaps. The aircraft slowed down as I entered slow flight. Approaching the drop spot, I popped the window open and pulled the canisters from the backseat. Over my drop spot, I threw the canisters out the window.

Adding full power as I raised my flaps, I banked over and could see the canisters hit the ground. They kicked up some dust as they bounced along several yards. They seemed intact as they stopped. I could see the nun approaching the gate with a mob of kids behind her. I banked around again, flew over the drop spot, and waved at them as they picked up the canisters. It wasn't much, but to those kids, it would seem like a gift from God, which it was.

About a week later, a thank-you note addressed to the platoon came. It said, "Thanks to Headhunter pilot who dropped the candy on December 27. It was a blessing for children who know few blessings in their life. God bless you, and merry Christmas." After that, soldiers started writing home and asking their families to send hard candy and any small toys suitable for kids. Dropping packages to the orphanage became a weekly event for someone after his mission was over.

Compound security became a hot item over Christmas. We had areas of responsibility and duties to protect the compound in case of an attack. I was responsible for the defense of the west fence, which ran from the front gate about a hundred yards to the northwest corner of the compound. A trench topped with sandbags ran along the base of the fence to provide cover and fighting positions. Three bunkers about thirty yards apart provided automatic-weapons positions. From the bunkers, machine guns could provide interlocking fire along the fence line. Fifty yards forward of the fence, three lines of barbed wire topped by razor wire ran parallel to the fence. My security force consisted of mechanics, crew chiefs, clerks, and cooks. It was a small force of noninfantry soldiers to defend such a large area. After the intelligence warning over Christmas, I became concerned about the condition of the bunkers and defense wall and the readiness of the soldiers assigned to me.

One day, acting on my concerns, I inspected the trench and bunkers and found them in poor condition from complacency over the years. I could see that I needed some cement and bags to repair the areas that had collapsed. I checked with the supply people and found that no cement was available anywhere in the area. I called the depot at Qui Nhon. The sergeant I talked to said they had bags of cement available, and all I needed was a request form signed by the commanding officer to pick it up.

That afternoon, with a request form signed by Captain Tom, I took off for Qui Nhon to pick up five bags of cement. I needed more, but I figured five was all I could get in the small Bird Dog. After I landed, the airfield duty driver took me to the depot. I had no trouble getting the five ninety-pound bags of cement. I could see by the many pallets of cement stored at the depot that I could get all I wanted. Back at the airfield, the driver helped me load the five bags into the Bird Dog. It was a hassle to load ninety-pound bags with the rear seat still in the aircraft. I made a note to remove the seat for my next trip.

Everything seemed normal as I taxied out to the runway for takeoff. The tower cleared me for takeoff, and I taxied onto the runway, applied full power, and started down the runway. As I approached takeoff speed, I put forward pressure on the stick to raise the tail. However, my tail did not come up, and in an instant, I was in danger. I started to pull off power and stop the takeoff, when the aircraft, having passed takeoff speed, lifted off the ground, flying in a tail-low configuration. I calmed down after I got airborne and turned toward Kontum while I climbed to four thousand feet. When I reached four thousand feet, I lowered the nose for level flight. That was when I realized I might have a serious problem.

The tail would not come up to level flight. It stayed slightly low, keeping me in a slow climb of about ten feet per minute. Stupidly, I had not considered the effect that 450 pounds of cement would have on the aircraft. That much weight exceeded the gross weight limits and had shifted the center of gravity to the point where I could not lower the nose. That meant I would be in a continuous climb until I reached the maximum altitude for the Bird Dog. A little wave of fear moved up my spine.

I had to think of some way to overcome the nose-high attitude of the aircraft. There was no way I could dump the heavy bags resting behind me, so I had to figure a way to fly out of this fix. Because of the nose-high attitude, my airspeed at maximum power stayed at ninety knots, which was safe but not the 110-knot cruising speed. Thank God my habit of practicing emergencies after a mission had prepared me for the fix in which I found myself.

Talking to myself, I started checking the courses I could take. The first decision I made was to make a turn and see how the aircraft handled. I made a shallow turn to the right, and the aircraft responded, except the airspeed bled off to about eighty-five knots. When you turn, you put in back pressure to maintain altitude in the turn. Without the back pressure on the stick, the aircraft will lose altitude because of a loss of lift during the turn. Since I already had the back pressure from the cement, the aircraft tried to climb. I leveled the wings, satisfied that I could safely turn.

Now I needed to figure out how to lose altitude. Then I thought of my rear horizontal stabilizer. I had not checked the trim tab on it, and I was praying there was enough adjustment to raise the tail, which would lower my nose. Cautiously, I started turning the tab control to down trim, which would act to raise the rear of the aircraft. God was with me. The nose slowly came to level flight. That was okay, but I still could not lower the nose to descend, so my problem was finding a way to lose altitude.

I had several choices to lose altitude. I could stall the aircraft, go into a spin, and pull out when I had lost enough altitude. However, that was a scary solution, and I had no idea how the aircraft would act with its shifted center of gravity. Besides that, I had not done a spin since flight school, and even then, I'd not been comfortable doing one. Even if the spin worked, I still could not land without losing altitude under control.

My other choice was to slow the aircraft down to slow flight and see if I could lose altitude that way. Reluctantly, I lowered full flaps and watched the airspeed drop. I already had full power, so I eased the nose up in slow-flight attitude. When my airspeed stabilized to just above stall speed, I could see that I was slowly losing altitude, which was how it should work. The only problem was that I would have to hold this attitude all the way to the ground to land. I slowly raised flaps and adjusted my course to Kontum, happy that I could safely lose altitude.

The last problem I had to face was my approach to the runway. It had to be perfect. I had to start a final approach in the slow-flight attitude from an altitude higher than normal. My descent angle had to result in my running out of altitude at the approach end of the runway as if I were making a normal landing. I wanted to avoid making a go-around and trying a second landing approach. That would require me to give a reason for the go-around, which I did not want to do. It's hard to tell your boss that you did something stupid, but to announce it to the world is even more embarrassing.

At last, I saw the Kontum airfield and asked for a straight-in approach. When the tower cleared me for the straight-in, I lowered the flaps halfway and reduced some power. The aircraft began to settle and lose airspeed. When my descent angle looked perfect, I lowered the rest of the flaps. I was already in a nose-high attitude, and my descent started. By adding and reducing power, I kept a perfect angle of descent and airspeed just above stall airspeed. With unbelievable relief (and a heavy thump), I planted the Bird Dog on the end of the runway. I had just executed the perfect short-field landing. Soaked in sweat and elated, I told tower that I was doing a 180 to taxi back to the platoon revetment area.

I wanted not to report the incident, but my integrity required me to do so. After getting the cement unloaded, I briefed Captain Tom on what had happened. He looked at me as if I were missing some of my marbles and then grinned and said, "Well, you're one hell of a pilot or just damn lucky—or both. Make sure you relate the incident at the next safety class. It is a good example of not overloading these small Bird Dogs."

I liked Captain Tom. He could see how upset I was for my stupidity, and he let that be enough reprimand. I think the fact that I reported the incident, when I did not have to, raised his esteem of me. The situation could have turned out differently, but at least I had the cement I needed to fix my bunkers.

Christmas and New Year's passed without incident. We had a New Year's party at our little officers' club. I woke up the next morning with one hell of a hangover.

The day before New Year's, I did not put myself on the flight schedule. I told Captain Tom that I was going to stand down and work on the bunkers. I got most of my security team excused from their duties so we could do all the work in one day, which was what it took to fill bags with mixed sand and cement and repair all three bunkers. The good thing was that we did not have to mix water with the cement. The bags would absorb enough water from the humidity to set the cement in a couple weeks. After the bunkers, we worked on the trench line, fixing areas that had caved in. By day's end, I was satisfied with the bunkers and the trench line. I checked the barbed wire with binoculars because no one knew where the mines were along the wire. I sure as hell was not going to walk it and find out. We went to the enlisted club after we finished, and I bought a case of beer for the men. I felt that if, for some reason, we had to defend the compound, I had done the best I could to ensure we had a sound defensible position.

There was one task left to do. I needed to sight in the machine guns in each bunker. A couple days after New Year's, I had the two men assigned to each machine gun sign it out and report to the bunkers. These were cooks and mechanics, and they had probably forgotten most of the techniques for using the machine gun. One by one, we mounted a machine gun in its position and zeroed the gun. When we were through, each team had a firing scheme for their gun. Each gun had settings for interlocking fire and grazing fire. The gunner could turn the traversing knob to the proper setting, and the gun would transverse to the proper position. The gunners now had more confidence in their abilities, and I think they gained confidence in my ability to lead them.

The Vietnamese New Year (Tet) was a month away, and most intelligence reports suggested that any attack would occur during that period. There had been no attacks on the compound since the French had occupied it, but I wanted to be ready for an attack. My men were ready, and I intended to keep them ready with a practice drill once a month. Some of my peers have described me occasionally as being highly perceptive. I think that sensitivity was working at maximum when I decided to repair the trench and bunkers.

The thought on my mind each day was how soon I would see Claudia. I could not help but look at the calendar each day and count the days left until I met her in Bangkok. It was hard not to let my dream of holding her again preoccupy my thoughts and interfere with my flying. That would cause an unsafe condition. Pilots preoccupied in thought had caused numerous accidents.

The second week in January, we received intelligence that the NVA had taken a German nurse prisoner. The nurse had been working with the Vietnamese in a small village when the NVA took her. The intel people believed the NVA would move her north. They asked us to look for any signs that would point to that movement.

Two days later, I was flying in the mountains northwest of Kontum. As I crossed a ridgeline, I saw twelve men in NVA dress and four civilians in black pajamas moving along the valley trail. The group froze as I flew overhead. That was their best chance of remaining unnoticed since they were out in the open and more than fifty meters from any cover. I continued my flight path as if I had not seen them. All the time, I was recording as much information as I could. The NVA were armed with AK-47s, wore backpacks, and carried an assortment of combat gear. The civilians formed two teams, each carrying a pole on their shoulders, from which hung equipment bags. They stood still, tensely watching me as I flew over the next peak as if I hadn't spotted them. Once out of sight, I called control and reported the party's location and description. Because one of the individuals in black pajamas might be the German nurse, I decided I would not attack the group. I had collected all the information I could about them, so I decided I would at least give them a fright.

Out of sight behind a higher peak, I climbed a thousand feet higher. Then I turned back toward the group and slowly pulled the power back so it would sound to them as if I were flying away. I lowered the nose and glided as quietly as an idling engine would let me toward them. When I crossed the peak hiding them, I pushed the stick forward and dove toward the group.

They had resumed their movement along the trail, believing that I had not seen them. When they finally heard my idling engine, I was about three hundred meters behind and above them in a simulated rocket attack. They froze momentarily as they all stared at me with open mouths. In a panic, they finally reacted and rushed for cover to both sides of the trail. The civilians dropped their poles before running, and I could see that two of them were female. Although I had barely a glimpse, I believed that one had blonde hair. Once past their location, I did a 360-degree turn and flew slowly over the spot. I could see several NVA soldiers crouching beneath brush, but I didn't see the women. They were lucky for the possibility of the German nurse being among them. I could have destroyed many with my rockets. To this day, I believe I saw the missing German nurse. I do not know what became of her.

While January signals the middle of winter to most Americans, the only signs there were the cool nights and the thin fog layer each morning along the river basin. By 0900, it was hot again, and the fog had burned off. Intelligence reports were insistent that a big attack would probably occur during the Tet holiday. In response, we intensified our recon efforts, looking for any sign of new NVA activity, but despite our intense efforts, nothing significant surfaced. It was as if the intelligence reports were saying they were there, and we were saying we could not see them.

On January 26, in reaction to the intelligence reports, we heightened our security level, and the sector commander issued orders for a 100 percent alert status each night. So each night, after the evening meal, we moved into our defensive areas. I was happy I had taken the time to repair and reinforce my positions. We spent all night sitting in the dark and waiting for a possible attack. I let half of the men sleep four hours beginning at 2000 hours, and then the other half would sleep until 0400 hours. That allowed 100 percent to be at the ready until two hours after darkness and two hours before daybreak, the times most likely for an attack.

Being 100 percent on alert each night had an effect on pilots. We were flying most missions a little exhausted from the lack of sleep, but luckily, no incidents resulted from inadequate rest. Despite our complete coverage of Kontum Provence, we saw no signs of an NVA buildup. On January 29, the third day of our 100 percent alert status, word came down to go to 50 percent. January 30 was Tet, and obviously, General Westmoreland did not believe the NVA and Vietcong would attack on their New Year's Eve. That night, I flew the evening patrol around the city. As I was walking to the aircraft, Captain Tom stopped me and said, "Do a good recon, Neal. The NVA could catch us by surprise if they slip into town after dark."

So I did one of the most detailed recons of the area around Kontum. I saw nothing moving other than civilians going about their daily routines. It was after dark when I landed and closed down the platoon. The maintenance sergeant was waiting for me. I completed my reports, and we left the airfield in our jeep for the compound. As we turned left from the airfield onto the MSR (main supply route), our lights swept the rice paddy, and I clearly saw four soldiers in the dark green uniforms of the NVA standing by the road. The soldiers had AK-47s slung over their shoulders. The sight surprised us both. I grabbed for my M16 as I yelled for the maintenance sergeant to get the hell out of there. I watched them nervously as we sped away, and I swear I saw one of the soldiers salute me as if the group were a friendly patrol.

When we pulled into the compound, I called Major Dan, the intel officer, and asked if he had any reports of NVA infiltrating Kontum. He said some unverified reports had come in. I told him about the four soldiers I had seen. He said he would pass the report on and let me know if he got any reports that would confirm or deny NVA infiltrating Kontum. I told Captain Tom about the incident, and he laughed and asked if I'd returned the salute. He said it was probably an SVA guard at the intersection, and their green fatigues looked different in the jeep headlights.

After chow, I moved into the trenches and checked on my defense team. The first shift of seven was in place. I felt a little apprehensive because of what I had seen, so I checked each position carefully. The machine guns were in place and ready. Each soldier was in the right position, and they understood that if we were attacked, they had to hold until the rest of the team joined us. I spent the next two hours moving back and forth along our part of the perimeter. I would stop occasionally to scan out to the outer wire to reassure myself that no one was trying to penetrate our defensive wire.

At about 2200, the field phone rang. It was Major Gates, the compound commander. After each command post answered, he said, "Okay, everybody can stand down. The threat level is down, and the commander expects no attacks tonight. No need to spend the night in the trenches. Keep your equipment ready to go if something comes up. We will post the usual guard detail for security the rest of the night."

I released my people, and they returned to their billets, happy for a good night's sleep. I returned to my room and found Darrel writing a letter. He would have relieved me at 2400 hours. I told him we were standing down. No one expected an attack on the Tet holiday.

I took a shower and got into bed by 2300 hours. Drifting off to sleep, I thought of Claudia. I had gotten a letter that day, and she was ready to meet me in Bangkok but needed me to confirm that I would be there before she paid for the tour. I had mailed a letter the day before, telling her to go ahead. I had my leave in my hands, and I would be there.

I was sound asleep when the sound of rifle and automatic-weapons fire woke me. Jumping out of bed, I grabbed my rifle and flak jacket, and I headed for the door. Everybody was running for the trenches, when a sergeant came by, saying it was a false alarm. The Vietnamese were celebrating Tet by firing their rifles into the air. Cautiously, we returned to bed. The false alarm had pumped me full of adrenaline, and now, although I was exhausted, it was difficult to go back to sleep. Eventually, I drifted off.

This time, a .50-caliber machine gun firing woke me. The gun was in the corner bunker fifty yards to the west of the communications tower and thirty meters from my room. The bunker was one of the perimeter guard posts and provided a clear view of the line of barbed wire and mines protecting the north and west approaches to the compound. Some past commander had made the bunker a strong point by mounting a .50-caliber machine gun in it. The army taught most of the young soldiers in the compound to fire the .30-caliber machine gun in basic training. Most had never seen a .50-caliber machine gun, much less fired one. Because of this, the sergeant of the guard had to give each new soldier stationed in the bunker a quick class on the .50.

As the *thump-thump* of the .50 firing slowly awakened my sleepy brain, I realized I heard explosions with small-arms fire. I jumped up, donned my pants and flak jacket, and grabbed my rifle. Darrel was still sound asleep.

I shook him and said, "Wake up, Darrel! We are under attack!" I headed for the door.

I have never seen Darrel move so fast. Before I could get out the door, he had all his equipment and was following me out the door. The compound was buzzing with movement as soldiers darted toward their fighting positions. When I got to my position in the battle trench, most of my fifteen guys were there. Everybody was asking what was going on.

I finally got a hold of the compound command post on the field phone and found out what was happening. The sector headquarters building, located about a mile from the compound, was under attack. We could visually confirm that because we could see the exchange of tracers. So far, our compound was not under attack. It appeared that a sapper team had tried to infiltrate the wire in front of the .50-caliber bunker. The guard had spotted them and asked for instructions just as the attack on sector headquarters began. He was ordered to fire on the team, which he did. That was the firing that woke me up.

I walked up and down the trench line, telling each soldier what I knew and checking to make sure they all had their equipment and were ready to fight. Captain Tom joined me after about fifteen minutes. He was the second-in-command of the compound and was checking the perimeter. We talked for a few minutes, and he left to continue his checks.

The fighting at the sector headquarters continued all night. The rest of Kontum seemed quiet. Around 0500, dawn started its slow creep. Captain Tom called me on the field phone and told me to get all the pilots together behind the barracks by the tennis court. We were going to start recons at first light, and Major Dan would brief us there.

It took me about ten minutes to find all my guys and get them to the barracks location. By now, the firing at the sector headquarters was slacking off. Captain Tom arrived and told everybody to go eat and be back there ready to fly at 0600. Major Dan would brief us then. We headed for the mess hall and had some hot coffee. The mess hall personnel had heated C rations for breakfast, but the coffee was fresh. I drank two cups and ate a can of sausage and crackers.

By 0600, we were all back at the end of the barracks. It was eerily quiet considering how noisy the night had been. We watched Major Dan run from the compound CP toward us. When he got to us, he paused to catch his breath and started his briefing. "Okay, here's the situation. Kontum is under attack by an estimated NVA brigade. Right now, the MACV headquarters is the primary target, as we have witnessed all night. NVA units have surrounded the airfield and are probing its perimeter. No attack against this compound other than the sapper team has occurred. That could change. The intelligence reports suggest an NVA heavy-weapons company is moving into position northwest of the airfield. We need to verify that and find that unit. An NVA heavy-weapons company has 4.3 mortars and antiaircraft weapons. If they get into position, they can damn well destroy the compound with mortar fire. We need to find them and destroy them before they can destroy us. A helicopter will be in to pick you guys up in about fifteen minutes. Any questions about your mission?"

Everybody shook his head, and Captain Tom said, "Okay. Neal, lay out recon areas for each pilot."

I quickly drew a circle on the ground and divided it into north, south, west, and east quadrants, using the runway as the centerline. I drew a larger circle around the first to depict the area I wanted to recon. I assigned each pilot a quadrant out to fifteen miles. Then I assigned two pilots the areas past the fifteen-mile line. I took the northeast quadrant. I asked for questions as we heard the helicopter inbound.

The Huey came in hot as if under fire and barely sat down. Captain Tom said, "Let's go," and with us following, he ran from the cover of the building toward the Huey.

As I ran past Major Dan, he hit me on the butt and shouted, "Find that heavy-weapons company!"

I was halfway to the Huey, when the first eighty-two-millimeter mortar round landed about sixty meters away. The NVA were adjusting in on the Huey. It was the first sign of an attack against the compound. I dove into the Huey just as the second round landed approximately thirty meters from us. By then, the pilot had the Huey light on the skids and was moving away from the burst of mortars while trying to gain translational lift. I looked at the mob of soldiers on the helicopter and realized there were too many—we'd overloaded the Huey. Two more mortar rounds exploded in front of the Huey. The pilot did a quick pedal turn back in the direction of the mortars. The Huey bounced along as it slowly entered translational lift and started to fly. I was holding my breath, thinking I did not want to die in an overloaded helicopter crash. Two more mortars exploded behind, as if they were chasing the Huey. At last, the Huey was flying and gaining altitude as it headed for the airfield runway.

The crew chief started yelling for everyone to hang on. Because of the overload, the pilot was going to make a running landing on the skids. Landing an overloaded helicopter is difficult and dangerous. It is safer to make a running landing on the skids if possible. Five minutes after takeoff, the pilot was on final approach. The Huey was still flying when it touched down, and we slid about fifty feet before halting. The crew chief started yelling for us to get out as we jumped off, running for the revetment area. In less than ten seconds, the pilot was pulling pitch, and the Huey started climbing almost vertically before the pilot pushed the nose over and started flying away.

Once in the revetments, each pilot found the Bird Dog I had assigned and began a preflight. That was when small-arms fire started hitting the fifty-gallon drums. Darrel got to his plane and found it was in maintenance and not flyable. The rest of us started the aircraft in the revetments and reported to the tower that we had incoming small arms. We asked for takeoff clearance for all six Bird Dogs. Waiting my turn, I saw Sergeant White, the intel sergeant, run up to my plane. I opened the door, and he said he wanted to fly as my observer. I slid my seat forward, and he jumped in. While he fastened his seat belt, I pulled out behind the next plane speeding out of the revetment area for the runway. It was Captain Tom. As soon as he reached the centerline, he did an immediate turn and started his takeoff roll. I waited about five seconds for spacing and then sped toward the runway. Turning down the centerline as fast as possible, I applied full power for takeoff. We were under small-arms fire the whole time. As I gained speed, I heard the metallic whack of a round hitting my fuselage. As I lifted off, I hoped it had not damaged any control cables.

I climbed out on the runway heading and entered the usual wintertime fog. I kept climbing and was through at 250 feet AGL. I leveled out. I planned on staying just on top of the fog until it burned off. I made a right turn over the end of the runway and started the outbound leg on the right side of my recon quadrant. I planned to fly out fifteen miles, fly an arc to the line extending from the runway, and then fly inbound on that line to the end of the runway. This flight path outlined my quadrant. On the next

outbound leg, I would fly ten degrees to the left of my first leg and start
the arc at fourteen miles, and so on, until I covered the entire quadrant. I
could see straight down through the fog with no difficulty, but the fog was
just thick enough to prevent slant vision. This meant if we saw anything,
we would only have a few seconds to identify it as we flew overhead.

I followed my plan. I flew the fifteen-mile arc until I came to the line
extending from the runway and turned inbound. The inbound leg took us
over the rifle range located about half a mile off the end of the runway. As
I passed over the rifle range, I thought I saw movement, but with no slant
vision, I could not tell exactly what I'd seen. I asked Sergeant White if he'd
seen anything. He said yes, but it had been just a glimpse of movement,
and he wasn't sure what he'd seen either. I said, "Okay, I am going to fly
the same track again. Maybe we will be able to identify what we saw."

I banked around, flew out fifteen miles, and turned inbound on the
course I had previously flown. I could see the rifle range firing positions
passing below but no movement. I turned to ask Sergeant White if he
had seen anything, when all hell broke loose. The sky filled with tracers
crisscrossing around us. Then the aircraft shook violently as bright flashes
walked across the wings and fuselage. Then we were out of it.

I sat frozen, startled and dazed by the flashes that had exploded across
my aircraft. At first, I did not grasp what had happened. Then my mind
woke up, and I realized that antiaircraft fire had just hit me hard. "Are
you okay?" I asked Sergeant White. I heard him say yes, but I was already
checking my oil pressure to make sure I still had a working engine. The
oil was in the green, and the engine was running smoothly. I looked at my
body to make sure I had not been hit. I was happy to see that I was okay.

Then I noticed that I was putting in moderate left stick with some
right rudder to keep the aircraft flying in a straight line. Looking out the
right window, I could see a big hole just past the rocket pods. When I saw
my right strut, a little knot of fear formed in my stomach. A large-caliber
round had cut it almost in half. A piece of aluminum no larger than two
fingers held my right wing in position. If that round had been an inch
more to the right, I would have been dead in the mangled wreckage of
my aircraft by now. I had visions of that thin piece of aluminum failing.
I could see my right wing folding up and over me as I spiraled into the
ground. The same results would happen if I put any negative Gs on the

aircraft. I could tell by the sound of rushing air that I had a hole in my fuselage somewhere. Then I saw that the end of my left wing was gone. That was the source of my control problem.

My heart was pounding as I fought to calm down. I told myself at least I was still flying, and other than the strut, I saw nothing else seriously wrong. Over the initial shock of being shot up, I switched the radio control and broadcasted on Guard channel. "Attention, all aircraft in Kontum vicinity: this is Headhunter 28 reporting heavy antiaircraft fire from positions half a mile off the west end of the runway. Estimate at least three or four antiaircraft guns. Advise all aircraft to avoid the area." As I broadcasted the warning, I realized how lucky we had been while taking off. The fog layer had deprived the enemy gunners of slant vision as well and had hidden us as we climbed out from the runway. There is no telling how many pilots were still alive because of that fog. I had been stupid to refly my track. The movement Sergeant White and I had seen must have been the gunners running to their guns. They had missed sighting me the first time. Then all they'd had to do was listen and, from the sound of my engine, know that I was turning around. The next time, they'd been waiting for us. Their initial rounds had struck me before I was out of their sight and hidden by the fog. Without the fog, it could have been much worse.

While I transmitted on Guard radio, I turned toward the airfield to land. I had found the heavy-weapons company. Although I was still flying, I felt the extent of my damage warranted landing as soon as possible.

In the middle of my turn, I heard, "Headhunter 28, this is Cobra Lead. Flight of two gunships two miles south of airfield. We have you in sight. Please mark target."

His request surprised me. Gunships did not attack antiaircraft positions. "Cobra Lead, this is Headhunter 28. Recommend not attacking antiaircraft positions. The fire is extremely heavy."

"Roger, Headhunter 28. Understand but request you mark target."

I could not believe he wanted to attack a heavy antiaircraft position. On top of that, he wanted me to mark the position. I did not want to fly into that antiaircraft fire again. All I wanted to do was land as soon as possible, but it was my job to mark targets, and there was no way I could refuse, so I answered, "Roger, Cobra Lead. I will mark on an azimuth two hundred seventy."

I wanted the sun at my back. I hoped that position, combined with the fog, which was starting to burn off, would help blind the gunners and give me a chance.

"Roger, Headhunter 28. We have you in sight."

Trying not to stress my hurt airplane, I carefully banked around, setting up for my rocket run. I saw the gunships orbiting about a mile north of the rifle range where the antiaircraft positions were located. I told Sergeant White to hang on tight. I did not have my heart in doing this. I was not sure if my airspeed in the rocket run, or any other evasive maneuver, would rip the wing off.

When I was in position at 1,500 feet and about two miles east of the rifle range, I could barely see the area where the guns were located. The fog had burned off enough for some slant vision. If I had it, so did the enemy gunners. *This is going to sting,* I kept telling myself, and I turned to 270 and pointed my nose at the center of the rifle range.

"Cobra Lead, this is Headhunter 28. Going in to mark target."

"Roger, Headhunter 28. Got you in sight."

As my speed increased, the aircraft began to shudder. I had to slip to try to fool the gunners as to my flight path. It was not going to be like the time I attacked the bunker. These were trained antiaircraft gunners, and I could not fool them for long. I did not know which way would put the most stress on the right wing. With a deep breath, I pushed the stick to the right and applied left rudder. The nose moved to the right about forty-five degrees from my direction of flight as I slipped almost sideways toward the rifle range. Then, as if by magic, green lights flew at me and past me, until it seemed as if the air were full of tracers crisscrossing in all directions. It reminded me of the World War II films of aircraft flying through a sky of tracers while attacking naval ships. However, this was not a film. They were shooting at me, and I was scared shitless. I could see the smoke of firing guns, which marked five antiaircraft positions. I armed the number-one WP rocket on my left wing. I sure as hell didn't want to fire a rocket from the wing with the damaged strut. At three hundred feet, I took out the cross controls, and the nose of the Bird Dog moved to the left and lined up on about the center of two gun positions. With slight rudder input, I centered the ball and fired the rocket. I followed the rocket until it exploded about forty meters to the left of one antiaircraft gun position. I thought I could see figures running as I pulled the nose up, banked hard left, and applied full power.

Simultaneously, I pushed the radio button. "Cobra Lead, two gun positions fifty meters right of rocket. Total of five positions. Recommend you not attack. The antiaircraft fire is too heavy."

"Roger, Headhunter 28. We saw it. We're rolling in for attack on northwest heading."

I watched tracers follow me as I pulled up to a hundred feet and leveled, and the tracers stopped. I turned to the north and gently climbed to a thousand feet while watching Cobra Lead begin his attack. I was trembling from fear and relief that I had made it safely through all the antiaircraft fire.

I held my breath as I watched the two gunships fly toward the antiaircraft positions. Then, as if in slow motion, tracers lit the sky up, reaching from the ground and encompassing the two gunships. Almost immediately, smoke began trailing from the gunships, and I heard the cry on Guard. "Mayday! Mayday! Cobra Lead going down half a mile east of Kontum runway. Mayday! Mayday! Cobra Lead going down half a mile east of Kontum runway."

This was followed by "Mayday! Mayday! Cobra 2 damaged and autorotating to airfield."

I followed Cobra Lead's spiraling flight to the ground as the pilots fought to control their damaged aircraft. He hit hard, kicking up a cloud of dust that hid him. I looked for Cobra 2 and saw a helicopter sitting to the side of the runway with smoke pouring from it. I presumed that was Cobra 2.

I was turning toward the airfield to land, when I heard, "Headhunter 28, this is Croc Lead about two miles north of area. Have you in sight. Please mark antiaircraft positions."

I could not believe he was serious at first. "Croc Lead, this is Headhunter 28. Recommend no attack of antiaircraft positions. Cobra Lead and wing just got shot down trying to attack."

"Headhunter 28, this is Croc Lead. Understand but request you mark target."

Damn, I thought. *These crazy gunship pilots are going to get me killed!* There was no way in hell I wanted to mark the target again. I felt a little nausea touch me in the stomach. "Croc Lead, this is Headhunter 28. Recommend holding attack until we get some tactical air on the position. Antiaircraft fire is too heavy."

"Headhunter 28, this is Croc Lead. I understand, but we don't have fuel to linger. Need to attack and return for fuel. Not sure exactly where target is. Request you mark target."

I banked back to the east. "Roger, Croc Lead. I'll advise when I get into position." I was really scared now. I had to fly back into that wall of fire to mark the target. I did not want to get myself or my observer killed. I did not want to do it, but I could not refuse to do my job. I was an officer and charged with doing my job regardless of the consequences. As I maneuvered the Bird Dog into a position east of the rifle range, I tried to come up with a plan that would provide me the most protection and still let me mark the target.

While I was out of range of the antiaircraft guns, I was in plain sight of the gunners. They had watched me do this once before and knew what I was planning. It was still early in the morning, and the sun was low. I felt my best plan would be to go in lower than I had before and try to keep the sun at my back all the way. I did a 360-degree turn to lose altitude and line up on the target. As I flew around, I looked at the city and airfield. There were several areas of smoke where current battles raged. I leveled out at five hundred feet and looked at the sun. It seemed right, and I figured if I made my run from this position on an angle straight to the rifle range, I would be in the sun all the way.

I looked at my damaged strut and then turned and looked at the observer. Sergeant White gave me a little smile and held up two grenades he was holding. I knew by the look on his face he intended to drop them as we pulled up after marking the target. *Why not?* I thought, half smiling back. If we made it that, far those grenades would only help. I pointed the nose at the rifle range and added power to increase speed. There were three results facing me: the strut would fail, and I would spiral in nose first; the tracers would find me and rip us apart; or I would mark the target, pull up, and get safely away from the target.

"Croc Lead, this is Headhunter 28. Marking the target on heading of two hundred seventy. Do you have me in sight?"

"Headhunter 28, this is Croc Lead. Got you in sight."

I could feel my heart pounding in my chest. My breathing was short and rapid as I waited for the tracers to start reaching for me. As a kid, when I would stub my toe on something, I would hop around crying, "Oh we, oh we, oh we!" I caught myself saying it now as if I were hit already. I was halfway to my release point, closing fast, and still saw no tracers. Maybe the sun was blinding the gunners, and for a moment, I thought I might get away with my ploy. The sudden bright flashes of the tracers going past my canopy startled me into reality. I realized that I was flying straight in and quickly applied right aileron and left rudder. The nose moved left, and the tracers followed it. The dance they made as they zipped around me had a hypnotic effect.

The rifle range rushing up at me broke my trance on the tracers. I could see three antiaircraft positions and the smoke from the barrels of the guns that were firing at me. I was close enough. I let up on the left rudder, and the nose of the aircraft swung around and pointed at the center of the gun positions. I could see the gunners' movements as I checked to make sure the ball was centered and fired the second WP rocket on the left wing. I watched the rocket hit the center of the guns before I began pulling up.

I banked hard right and pulled up on the stick right on top of the guns. I do not know if that maneuver fooled the gunners or they were ducking from the white phosphorescence. All I know is my wing did not fall off, and for a few seconds, the tracers stopped searching for me. Then a burst of tracers passed behind me, and I was clear of the area as I called, "Croc Lead, this is Headhunter 28. Three guns located around my WP round. Two more about one hundred meters north of burst." I looked back at Sergeant White, who was bent over trying to see where his grenades had landed.

"Headhunter 28, this is Croc Lead. Roger location. We are rolling in on a heading of two hundred seventy."

I thought, *At least he is attacking with the sun at his back,* as I scanned to the east, trying to pick up the two gunships. Then, as if to help me, the tracers reached up and marked the gunships. Before I could recommend they break off their attack, I heard, "Mayday! Mayday! Croc Lead going down east of town." I watched, shaking my head as the smoking helicopter spiraled toward the ground.

Then I heard, "Croc Lead, this is Croc 2. Breaking off attack. Antiaircraft too heavy. I am hit but still flyable."

I watched Croc 2 follow Croc Lead down to cover and rescue the crew. *Thank God*, I thought, *for one pilot recognizing the stupidity of attacking the antiaircraft position.*

Then I heard Captain Tom call, "Headhunter 28, this is Headhunter 26. Over."

"Headhunter 26, this is Headhunter 28. Over."

"Roger, Headhunter 28. I've got Bill Mark on the way. He's got F-4s stacked. Can you put artillery on the position until he gets here?"

"Negative, Headhunter 26. My FM went out when I got hit. I can adjust if you relay."

Before Headhunter 26 could answer, I heard, "Headhunter 28, this is Eagle 12. I'm over Kontum at two thousand feet. I've got a stack of four F-4s. I saw the antiaircraft gun positions as they attacked Croc Lead. Unfortunately, I have no rockets left. Need for you to mark the position for the F-4s."

"Roger, Eagle 12. Wait!"

I told Bill to wait because I needed time to come up with a reason I could not mark the target other than that going near those guns again terrified me. The only rockets I had were on the wing with the damaged strut. The stress of firing the rockets could possibly cause the strut to fail. Could I use that as a reason? I looked at Sergeant White, as if he could help me with an excuse. He looked at me as if resigned to what he had no control over. I turned to the only strength I had left. *Dear God, I am asking much of you, but I need the courage to do this one more time.*

"Eagle 12, this is Headhunter 28. I am setting up east of the rifle range. It will take about two minutes for me to get close enough to fire a rocket accurately. Let me know when the F-4s are ready to watch the target area."

I had committed myself. I banked the Bird Dog around and headed east to my start position. The sun was higher now, so I decided to start my run from eight hundred feet. I thought of Claudia. I was so close to seeing her again. "Eagle 12, I'm in position. Let me know when the F-4s are ready."

I circled, waiting for the F-4s to get in an orbit from which they could see the rockets when they impacted. Eagle 12 would direct them from the impact point.

"Headhunter 28, this is Eagle 12. Got you in sight. Go for it."

I lowered the nose as I said, "Roger, Eagle 12. I'm inbound." The rifle range was about two miles away when I started my dive. I could see the two-hundred-yard and three-hundred-yard firing positions. As I picked up speed, I pulled some power off so as not to red-line airspeed. The two times before, I had slipped to the left to protect my right wing. This time, I was going to slip right so I might fool the gunners for a few seconds. I felt numb, as if I were functioning like a robot. As before, the suddenness of the tracers reaching up for me was startling and caused me to jerk. With a quick breath, I pushed the stick to the left and applied enough right rudder to maintain my first path toward the target. Tracers flew by left, right, and in front of me. The target was looming, and again, I could see the gun positions pumping smoke as they fired at me. I armed my first rocket and then a thought hit me: *Fire both rockets, and you will not have any left. With no rockets, you cannot mark a target.* So I armed both rockets, giving in to fear and the need to end this madness.

About four hundred meters away, I could no longer contain my fear, and I fired the first rocket before I centered the ball. The rocket flew to the right of the center of the targets. I quickly took out the cross controls and centered the ball. I called out, "Eagle 12, ignore first rocket."

Then I fired the second rocket and watched it explode in a white cascade of WP. "Eagle 12, gun positions are all around the second rocket."

Before he could answer, I banked hard left, pulled the nose up, and added full power. The Bird Dog shook, and I thought at first the wing was coming off. Tracers were still flying all around me. A large flash came from under the aircraft, and the engine started running roughly. I heard Eagle 12 say, "Roger, Headhunter 28. Got the guns in sight. Clear the area. The F-4s are rolling in east to west."

"Roger, Eagle 12. I am clearing to the north." I turned north and made it to around six hundred feet with the engine running roughly. I watched my rpm drop to 1,800. As the rpm fell, my airspeed started to bleed off. I was talking to myself by now, telling myself, "I've got to land now before I crash." I flipped my radio selector button to Guard and called, "Mayday.

Mayday. Headhunter 28 unable to maintain airspeed. I'm headed for runway twenty-eight."

I heard the tower answer, "Roger, Headhunter 28. Got you in sight. You are cleared for landing. Be advised the airfield is under attack from sporadic automatic-weapons and small-arms fire."

The engine was running so roughly that I couldn't maintain my airspeed and altitude, so I had to lower the nose to keep flying. I headed for a spot on the runway about two-thirds from the end. I was losing altitude fast, but it looked as if I could make the runway. In my peripheral vision, I saw the rifle range erupt in fire. The first two F-4s had covered it with napalm. I could see the second flight release four more napalm drops. I said in relief, "So much for the antiaircraft guns."

The airfield was coming up fast, and with a hundred feet of altitude left, I dropped flaps, turned a sharp final, and rounded out. I did not have to reduce power. The damage to the plane was enough to slow me down with the little power the engine still provided.

I touched down with a bump that was not my usual smooth landing. I braked and slowed down enough to do a 180-degree turn on the runway. I taxied as fast as possible for the platoon area and the safety of the revetments. I was shaking so much that I had trouble staying on the centerline. I heard a ping from a round hitting the fuselage. We were still under fire, and I was going as fast as I could to get in a revetment, where it would be safe. I turned into the line of revetments and pulled into the first open one, hoping I did not hit the sides with my wings. Normally, a crew chief would guide the aircraft into the revetment for safety. But with small-arms fire crisscrossing the area, I wanted the revetment's protection. I had had enough of people shooting at me.

When I shut the engine off, the fear that had gripped me for the last fifteen minutes eased and left me trembling and feeling weak. I bowed my head and thanked God for his grace. I had found the NVA heavy-weapons company—rather, it had found me—but it had come at the price of four gunships. Sergeant White snapped me out of my daze, asking me if I was okay. Darrel was opening the door to the Bird Dog, asking, "Damn, Neal, are you okay?"

"Yes," I answered as I unsnapped my seat harness. I climbed out of the aircraft, followed by Sergeant White, as Darrel and the maintenance sergeant checked the damage to the aircraft. "Something is causing the engine to lose power. I could only get eighteen hundred rpm at max power, and the engine was running roughly," I said as I joined them.

"It's a wonder that it would still fly with all the damage," the maintenance sergeant said as he popped the engine cowling open. "There's the cause of the engine trouble." He pulled four P-leads out of the engine compartment. "A round or shrapnel cut four of your P-leads," he said, looking for more damage.

Darrel turned to me and said, "Damn, Neal, I am sure glad to see you! We've been under attack from NVA elements across the airfield. There's a tank about a mile from the airfield firing. It looks like he is firing at us."

Just as he finished speaking, small-arms rounds began slamming into the revetments with loud clinks as they hit the fifty-five-gallon drums. We ducked down below the top of the revetment and peered around the edges to make sure no NVA were charging our position. Darrel said, "They've been doing this all morning."

While we were waiting, a Bird Dog made a low pass down the runway, did a 180, and landed midway down the runway. The pilot kept taxi speed just below takeoff speed as he raced for the revetments. We could see it was Captain Tom as he roared into an empty parking spot. The small-arms fire picked up for a minute or so and then stopped. Captain Tom dashed across the revetment taxi area to the revetment we were in.

He grinned as he quipped, "Damn, those guys seem pissed off at us." He looked at me and said, "Great job, Neal. The F-4s destroyed the heavy-weapons company. With it gone, the commander believes we can hold the compound against NVA attacks. Let me take a look at your aircraft."

The maintenance sergeant had finished inspecting it and discussed the damage as Captain Tom walked around the aircraft. He looked at it and asked, "Neal, did it fly okay before the P-leads were cut?"

"Yes, sir," I answered. "I had to use some rudder to compensate for the damage to the left wing tip. But other than that, it was okay."

He looked at the maintenance sergeant. "Replace the damaged P-leads. How about the right strut? Do you think it will hold up for a flight back to Pleiku?"

The maintenance sergeant answered, "Yes, sir, as long as there's no unusual stress put on it and no negative Gs."

Captain Tom turned to me. "Neal, I'm leaving you in charge of the platoon members left in the compound. All the other aircraft are recovering at Pleiku. A helicopter will pick you, Sergeant White, and the crew chief up and take you back to the compound." He looked at Darrel. "Darrel, as soon as the maintenance sergeant replaces the P-leads, I want you and Sergeant Lane to fly back to Camp Holloway."

Darrel looked shocked. "With due respect, sir," he answered, "I don't want to fly it back. Despite what Sergeant Lane says, that strut might fail. Let Captain Griffin fly it back."

Captain Thompson looked at Darrel and asked, "Are you the maintenance officer?"

Darrel nodded.

Captain Tom spoke in a no-discussion manner. "It's your job, Lieutenant. Do it. I will follow you back in case something happens."

Darrel looked at me. "Thanks a lot, Neal."

It took Sergeant Lane about fifteen minutes to replace the P-leads, while Darrel checked out the rest of the aircraft. I tried to comfort him while secretly glad I did not have to fly it again. "I think it will be okay, Darrel. I fired both rockets without any trouble. It should be okay in straight and level flight."

When Sergeant Lane finished and shut the engine cowling, Darrel opened the door and let Sergeant Lane climb in. He started the engine and did a magneto check. The engine ran smoothly. He taxied out to the runway, applied power, and was gone under a hail of small-arms fire. Captain Tom waited for a couple of minutes before he made a hasty takeoff. I watched them disappear, and a thought hit me: *Maybe it would have been better if I had flown it back to Camp Holloway.*

The clang of rounds slamming into fifty-five-gallon drums snapped my attention back to the situation on the ground. I saw Sergeant White wave at me and point across the runway. I looked in the direction he was pointing and was surprised to see what looked like a platoon of NVA moving toward us. They were about three hundred meters west of us. I brought my rifle up, aimed at the center of the platoon, and started firing. Sergeant White and Specialist Jones, the remaining crew chief, also began firing at the NVA. By then, the NVA had taken cover. A machine gun was firing at us, and the rounds hit the drums with an unbelievable racket.

"Hold your fire unless you have a clear target!" I shouted to the other two. I did not know how much ammo we had among us and did not want to waste what we had. We lay in position, watching the NVA platoon's location, when suddenly, a gunship roared by with guns blazing. It fired two rockets at the NVA position, and after the rockets exploded, I could see the NVA soldiers running back toward some houses. The gunship was chasing them with its door gunners blazing away. The gunship made two passes, and we had no more problems from that NVA platoon.

However, I knew that when night came, so would the NVA. Safe from the gunships under the cloak of darkness, they would come for us. For now, all we could do was wait for the helicopter that Captain Tom had said would come for us. Suddenly, Sergeant White firing his weapon to the east interrupted my thoughts. I ran to his position to see what he was firing at. "What's up?" I asked, crouching beside him.

He pointed toward the perimeter road and said, "Four NVAs were moving down the road. I think I got all four."

I looked at the area of road he was pointing at. I could see two bodies lying on the road. They had on the fatigues of ARVNs. "They've got ARVN uniforms on," I said as if to question his actions.

"I know, sir," he answered, "but I guarantee you they were NVA."

Shit! I thought. *I'm in charge here, and I hope he's correct. But I don't know how he could tell they were NVA.*

"Okay," I said, looking at him. "Don't engage any more troops unless they are firing at us. We do not know what the situation is, and until I do, I do not want to chance firing at friendly troops."

"Okay, sir," he answered. "But I assure you they were NVA."

During our discussion, the roar of small-arms fire and explosions became increasingly louder from the vicinity of sector headquarters. Sector headquarters was located about half a mile northeast of our position. We could see smoke rising from the area around the building. During Major Dan's briefing, before we'd left for the airfield, he had mentioned that the sector commander and about twenty of his staff were holed up on the second floor of the headquarters building. Obviously, that was the battle we were witnessing now.

The battle raged on all day. It was hard to judge by the sound who was winning, but based on the sound of the firing, the commander and his staff were holding on. Around 1300, we noticed four figures wearing ARVN uniforms climb the ladder to the Kontum water tank. The tank sat about three hundred meters west of sector headquarters and about four hundred meters north of our location. They began firing from both sides of the water tank. We watched them moving around and firing all afternoon. My thought was that they were helping the force trapped on the second floor of the headquarters building, but Sergeant White kept saying he thought they were NVA. We did not know for sure, so we watched, unable to act, blinded by the fog of war. After the battle for Kontum was over, I found out that they were NVA dressed in ARVN uniforms, as were the four whom Sergeant White had killed.

The NVA's tactics for the attack of Kontum included infiltrating the city the night before the attack and stealing American and ARVN uniforms from the laundries that catered to army personnel. They were successful at this, and NVA soldiers dressed in ARVN and American fatigues wreaked havoc before we found this out. This guise attributed to many of their early victories

Around 1400, I was starting to get hungry. We had not thought to bring rations with us, so I entered the platoon operations building, looking for something to eat. The only food I could find was a big wheel of cheddar cheese that Captain Tom kept in the refrigerator. I cut off a big chunk of it and went back outside. The crew chief and Sergeant White went in and helped themselves as well. That was my lunch on the first day of Tet 1968. Now, each time I eat cheese, I take a few seconds to remember that day, and I enjoy my cheese even more.

The crack of a large-caliber weapon firing interrupted my cheese meal and made all three of us duck for cover. About a kilometer north of us, I saw an ARVN tank firing toward sector headquarters. I also could see the figures on the water tank firing away, and I mentally cheered them on with a *Give them hell!* The tank fired again, and I could see the round impact in a building about three hundred yards east of us. "Okay, guys, be sure you don't aim this way," I said to myself. Tank rounds would do some damage to our revetments—and us if we were still here.

The tank fired several more rounds and then moved to another position, which hid it from my observation. Periodically, a small-arms round pinged off a revetment, reminding us that an enemy force still had us in their sights. There were several helicopters flying around the area, but none of them approached the runway. I needed to contact the tower to find out what was happening. I wanted to know specifically if they had any helicopters scheduled to pick us up. We had no communications with anyone. Something or someone had cut the landline, and for some reason, we could not set up radio contact with the tower.

I looked at my watch. It was 1600, and in about two hours, it would be dark. The NVA knew we were here and would come for us, so I started thinking about a defensive plan that would give us a chance. I motioned for Sergeant White and the crew chief to come over to my position. Crouched against the revetment wall, they looked at me with "What the hell are we going to do?" looks on their faces. I expressed my concern that if the helicopter did not come for us, we needed a nighttime defensive position that the NVA hopefully could not breach.

My plan was simple. In one corner of the wall, in the middle revetment, we would stand with three drums together to form a small triangle, leaving enough of a crack between them for a firing port. Between an end drum and the revetment wall, we would leave enough room for us to squeeze into the little cave we were building. We would form a top out of old timbers lying by the operations building and pile sandbags three layers deep on top. The result would be a small fighting position in which we could spend the night and hopefully survive any attacks. So we started working on our position and completed it in about an hour. Looking at it, I had my doubts that it would work. I kept them to myself. It was the best we could do if we had to spend the night.

About thirty minutes before nightfall, I noticed a helicopter north of us, flying low. It was on a flight path for the end of the runway. As it got closer, I intuitively knew it was coming for us. I yelled at the other two to get ready to dash for the helicopter. Sure enough, like an angel, the helicopter came in hot, sliding down the runway as it touched down. I could see a figure in the doorway, waving for us to get aboard. "Go! Go!" I shouted at Sergeant White and the crew chief. They piled into the helicopter with me behind them as the pilot pulled pitch, hardly slowing down from the running landing. I looked up and into the grinning face of Captain Tom. He shouted, "I bet you thought I had forgotten about you!"

With my best relieved grin, I shouted back, "The thought crossed my mind!"

The helicopter never climbed higher than three hundred feet as the pilot headed straight for the tennis court at the compound. Three minutes later, the pilot made a fast approach into the tennis court, and before the skids settled, we piled out and ran for cover. When we made it to the interior side of the row of billets and huddled, Captain Tom looked at us and said, "Go get some chow, and meet back at my room in thirty minutes. I'm going to the compound command group to find out the situation. Be careful moving around. There's been some sniper fire off and on."

We moved quickly to the chow hall and had all we could eat of warmed-up C rations. I had no trouble with that, because I always enjoyed C rations. I drank several glasses of iced tea. I had not realized how thirsty I was until I started drinking it. It dawned on me that we had stood out in the sun all day with just a little horrible-tasting water to go with the hunks of cheese we'd eaten for lunch.

When I got back to Captain Tom's room, members of the platoon who had not evacuated to Camp Holloway were there. "Listen up." Captain Tom started his briefing on the situation. "Around 0100 this morning, the VC, supported by NVA units, attacked major cities all across Vietnam. Here in Kontum, they have been attacking sector headquarters all day. The MACV commander and his staff are behind barricades on the second floor. So far, the NVA has been unable to breach his position. NVA soldiers have surrounded the airfield operations building. Operations personnel have set up a tight defensive perimeter around it. So far, there have been no major attacks there. The NVA troops have not attacked the compound yet, but Major Dan believes it will happen soon. So everybody get your weapons and combat gear, and move to your assigned positions. Neal, you've got the south side, and I will go with you. Thanks to Captain Griffin, we won't have to worry about heavy mortars destroying the compound tonight. But there are still some eighty-two-millimeter mortars that will be used against us. If there are no questions, grab your gear, and report to your security force OIC."

Captain Tom and I walked to my trench line. I took a count of my guys and checked the bunkers to make sure the machine guns were set and ready for action. I called everybody together and briefed them on the situation. I had them check equipment to make sure they had what they needed. During our preparations, we could hear the battle raging at MACV headquarters—a warning of what could be next for us. When I felt we were as prepared as we could be, I sat down with Captain Tom. We made small talk for a while, and then I asked him why he'd come back.

He looked at me and said, "The same reason you would have come back. To make sure you guys were okay. But tomorrow afternoon, I am taking a helicopter back to Camp Holloway. I'm going to leave you in charge here. You've got everything well organized, and I can do better flying recon than sitting on the ground here. That okay with you?"

I grinned and said, "Fine with me, sir." We both knew he did not need my concurrence, but that was his kind of leadership. I am sure if I had said I did not want to stay there, he would have gotten me out. But we both knew I would not object. He trusted me with the care of his men. It honored me. Besides, I considered myself a warrior, and while I made my presence felt as a pilot, I wanted to fight in ground combat. My first dream when entering the army had been to be an infantryman. Now I would have a chance to experience what it was like.

We spent the night in the trenches, listening to the constant sound of combat and watching tracers light up the sky. There was no direct attack against the compound, so we sat and waited for whatever was coming our way. I rotated my soldiers to the mess hall for breakfast. Captain Tom remained in the trench while I ate.

Around 1000, three shots rang out from the east side of the compound. Somebody yelled, "Sniper!" and everybody ducked for cover. Captain Tom and I moved to the east end of the trench to try to find the sniper. We had to find him because eventually, someone would get careless, and I did not want to lose one of my men to a sniper. The presence of a sniper interferes with performing your job. It would be like trying to work in an office with a rattlesnake crawling around.

An open field the size of two football fields separated the east side of the compound from a neighborhood of Vietnamese houses. We studied the row of houses for several minutes. Packed closely together, the houses' windows appeared tightly shuttered. Neither Captain Tom nor I could detect any possible sniper position. Snipers need a hidden position from which they have a clear view of their target area. After studying the housing area for a while, we took a look at the open field. It was possible the sniper had dug a hole and hidden himself in it.

There was no sign of any fresh dirt anywhere in the field. The only possible position in the field was around a small shrub growing about in the middle. The shrub was about three feet high and about two feet wide and was the only logical place left for the sniper position.

Captain Tom studied the shrub with his binoculars. Finally, shaking his head slightly, he said, "I don't see anything. I think I might see some fresh dirt in the shade of the shrub, but I'm not sure."

He handed the glasses to me to take a look. I also did not see any of the signs I would expect if there were a sniper hiding there. We studied the field and line of houses for another thirty minutes without seeing any sign of a sniper. Finally, I said, "Hey, sir, maybe it was a VC moving through the neighborhood who decided to take a potshot at us."

"Yes, that's a possibility," he answered.

One way or another, we had to confirm if a sniper existed and was targeting us. If he did exist, we had to locate and neutralize him, because the threat of a sniper targeting us restricted our movement. When one of us left the trench to go to the toilet or to the mess hall, we had to do it on the run. Captain Tom was convinced he could get the sniper with his M49 grenade launcher if he could find him. I believed him because I had seen him shoot the M49. He could hit targets at a hundred yards with it. Of course, all he had to do was come close, because the bursting radius of each M49 was twenty meters.

I was working my way back from the mess hall, when I heard the thump of the M49 firing. I started running for the trench. By the time I reached it, Captain Tom had fired four times. When I got to his position, I could see a grin on his face as he pointed toward the shrub. I looked at the shrub and could see where the M49 rounds had exploded. I could see part of a body at the base of the shrub. Several of my men walked up to see the sniper.

Captain Tom looked at me and asked, "Did he hit you?"

I looked at myself to make sure and answered, "No, why? I didn't even hear a shot."

Captain Tom was shaking his head. "He fired at someone. I thought it was you."

"Maybe we shouldn't have killed him," I said. "If he was firing at me, he missed me from fifty meters. He had to be a lousy shot. Now they might replace him with an expert."

Captain Tom replied, "You might be right. Cover me while I check him." With that, he darted across the field to the sniper position. We watched him as he lay in a prone position, searching the body and looking into what had to be a hole. He pushed the body back into the hole. After that, he jumped up and ran back to the trench.

Catching his breath in the trench, he said, "I pushed him back into the hole. He had plenty of supplies and was prepared to stay there for a while. If nobody saw what happened, they might think he is still active and not send a replacement." That must have been the case, because we had no further problems with snipers on my portion of the fence.

We spent the rest of the day hunkered down in the trenches and bunkers, listening to the battle going on at sector headquarters. Major Dan came by several times to update us on the situation and make sure we were ready for any attack. Based on his intelligence, two brigades of NVA and VC units had attacked Kontum. Aerial recon of the rifle range confirmed the F-4s had destroyed the antiaircraft guns and the 4.3 mortars. As soon as we regained control, he would send a team out to confirm the aerial photos. Gunships attacking positions near sector headquarters interrupted his briefing several times. They flew over the compound on their firing runs and cheered us up as we cheered them on. Other than the sniper incident, my sector remained quiet all afternoon.

Around 1600, Captain Tom decided he was going back to Camp Holloway. "Neal, you're in charge. As soon as friendlies regain control of Kontum, I'll bring the rest of the platoon back. Get word to me if you need anything." I walked him to the tennis court helipad, and he jumped aboard the courier helicopter.

On the second night of the Tet Offensive, the battle shifted to the MACV compound. It started with a steady eighty-two-millimeter mortar barrage, followed by an attack. The point of the attack was against Special Forces team B24's perimeter, located on the north side of the compound. Fortunately, during the day, the B team had brought in a company of Montagnards to reinforce their perimeter. The NVA assaulted their position on the nights of January 31 through February 2. At one time, the

NVA took two bunkers on B24's perimeter. The fearless gunship crews and several other attack helicopter teams from Pleiku again saved the day. Two gunships remained in the air throughout each night as the Gladiator flare ships circled overhead, dropping flares that provided eerie daylight brightness over all of Kontum City. On February 4, ARVN troops finally cleared the city, pushing the NVA out. Throughout the six-day period of January 30 to February 4, the body count in the Kontum area reached 785 NVA troops dead.

For two nights during that period, the NVA hammered the B team's defensive position. We hunkered in our position, ready for an assault as we listened to the battle taking place three hundred yards to our rear. The battle had a rhythm. When the gunships were overhead, the roar ebbed into a shot or two. When the gunships returned to Pleiku to rearm, the roar soared into a deafening crescendo. We nervously watched the hundreds of tracers arching through the sky. Then, miraculously, the gunships would appear, and the battle sounds ebbed. Each time, I prayed the Montagnards would hold until the gunships returned. The cycle played out seven or eight times each night.

Each morning brought us relief. The NVA stopped attacking during daylight. They were too vulnerable to air attacks. You could almost hear a loud sigh of relief when morning light arrived and we still held the compound. During the day, we slept and prepared for the night.

At 1000 on the third night, Major Dan came up to me and said, "Captain Griffin, I want you to take six of your men and reposition them along the crumbled wall separating us and the B-team area. The NVA are hammering the SF perimeter, and it's likely they might overrun the defenses. If they do start coming this way, I want you to hold them until I can redirect our forces to your position. The NVA have already temporarily occupied two bunkers. Each time they attack, it's more violent than the previous attack. Any questions?"

"Got it, sir," I answered, and I started down the trench line. I picked every other man until I had six and told them to follow me. When I reached the end of the trench, I briefed them on our mission. "Does everybody understand what we are going to do?" I asked. I checked each one to make sure he had plenty of ammo. Then I asked, "Who knows the exact location of the broken fence?" I was not sure, because it was in an area I had never been to. One of the soldiers raised a hand, and I said, "Okay, lead the way,"

We moved in single file, and I took up a position in the center of the file. It took about five minutes to get to the wall in the dark. When we reached the wall, we took up prone positions behind it. After taking a look at the several buildings between us and the SF perimeter, I shifted the group about fifteen yards to our left. Then I moved the soldiers to positions about ten meters apart, with me in the center. I stressed to each man not to fire until I gave the command. I made the specialist who had led us to the fence second-in-command in case anything happened to me.

After one last look around, I was comfortable that I had set up the position in the best manner possible. As we set up our position, the crescendo of the current attack rose to its highest level as a steady stream of tracers went back and forth. Occasionally, several would create a *twang* as they passed over us. Just when it seemed impossible the SF would hold their positions, the gunships arrived.

The noise of their exploding rockets increased the crescendo. They flew directly over us at a height of about sixty feet. As they peppered the NVA with their rockets, their door gunners were raking the attacking NVA with machine gun fire. The spent casings fell on us as they flew overhead. In the light of exploding mortars and tracers, I could clearly see both door gunners stretched out as far as they could lean and blazing away with their machine guns. The image of the attacking gunship is etched forever in my brain.

Within five minutes of the gunships' arrival, the pandemonium faded into occasional potshots. Once more, SF held. As soon as they used up their ammo, the gunships headed to Pleiku to rearm. Slowly, the crescendo started its climb in intensity, and we repeated the scenario again. I lay peeping over the broken wall, praying that they would get back to save us again. By 0300, I was thinking the next attack would surely breach the perimeter. The NVA would wreak mayhem if they got inside the compound. We would do our best to hold, but in the dark, it would be difficult. These were clerks and mechanics lying here, not infantrymen. I was an artilleryman and aviator. Of course, I had SF training to help me.

I thought of Claudia. We were to meet in three weeks. I remembered that I had bought her two rings, a princess-cut diamond and a blue star-cut sapphire dinner ring. The rings were in my BOQ room, and if the NVA took the compound, they would surely find them. I decided then that we would hold as long as possible. If it was certain that they were going to overrun us, I would fight my way back to my room and destroy the rings. There was no way the NVA would get Claudia's rings.

A figure appeared, moving between the buildings and coming our way. This surprised me and caused a little tremble to rack my body. "Hold your fire!" I commanded as I studied the figure. The man was tall and dressed in army fatigues. When he was about twenty meters from the wall, I yelled, "Halt! Who goes there?"

The figure froze, surprised by the challenge. "SFC Benet, Special Forces."

I got up and, keeping my rifle trained on him, walked over. It was Benet. We'd been on the same A team back in 1963 and 1964. "What do you need?" I asked. He did not recognize me, and now was not a time to rehash old times.

"Sir, my major sent me over to pick up the fifty-caliber machine gun you have on your perimeter. Major Dan said we could have it to increase our firepower against the NVA positions."

"Okay, Sergeant Benet, head toward the barracks on your right." I pointed toward the .50-caliber and continued. "It's located in the corner bunker." I did not question his claim. SF was in a fight for the compound, and if they needed more firepower, I was not going to question their need.

Sergeant Benet said, "Thanks, Captain," and he headed toward the .50-caliber position. The crescendo was starting to rise now, and I hoped he would hurry back with the .50. Ten long minutes passed before I saw him returning with the gun.

He was carrying the gun over his shoulder with a box of ammo in his other hand. Following him was one of our soldiers with two cans of ammo. As they passed by one of my men, the soldier hauling the ammo told him he would be back as soon as he dropped off the ammo. "So please do not shoot me."

He returned within minutes, and soon after, I heard the .50-caliber start firing. Soon its loud pops were lost in the noise of firing weapons. The intense fighting was only a hundred meters from our position. I thought that at any minute, the NVA would breach the perimeter. I kept straining my ears for the sound of the gunships, but there was no sound of them. "Okay, men!" I shouted over the crescendo. "Be alert, and remember, no firing until I give you the okay!" Then, as if by magic, the gunships were overhead, changing the course of the battle. We cringed through two more attacks before dawn eased in and quieted the battlefield.

We withstood three nights of attacks, and then it was over. The ARVN Twenty-Fifth Division counterattacked and drove the NVA out of Kontum. We had, by someone's count, 462 dead NVA around our perimeter, which were beginning to rot, making the air almost unbreathable. When MACV reestablished communications with the command in Saigon, they reported the number of dead NVA. The command in Saigon told us to stop all actions until their representatives counted the bodies. Around three o'clock that afternoon, a helicopter landed at our little landing pad. Four colonels in neatly pressed uniforms got out and walked around the battlefield, counting the bodies. When they finished, they told us to go ahead and bury them. Nobody ever explained why we had to wait until higher headquarters counted the bodies. This remained a puzzle to me until many years later, when I watched a special on TV about General Westmoreland. I put it together then: he had been underreporting enemy strength.

The Tet Offensive of 1968 caught everybody by surprise. Based on combat ratios, 462 dead would suggest another 1,200 wounded. When you added survivors, the NVA force was much larger than what General Westmoreland and his staff had officially reported in the Kontum area. They sent the colonels to ensure that we were not inflating the enemy KIA. That made the battle for Kontum the third-largest battle of the Tet Offensive. The NVA and Vietcong had captured Kontum on the first night and had gone on public radio, announcing that Kontum Province was now under the control of the People's Republic of Vietnam. Since we lost all communications during the fighting, our higher command did not know for sure if we were still alive.

With the battle over, the Second Platoon returned to Kontum, and we started tracking the retreating NVA. Friendly fire had demolished the platoon area. The ARVN tank that we had witnessed firing while pinned on the airfield had obviously missed the target a couple times, and the rounds had hit our operations hut. The revetments had come through okay, although we had to repair them. I used my BOQ room as the operations room until we repaired the damaged hut. The routine quickly returned to normal, and my mind turned to Claudia.

The Tet Offensive caused considerable damage throughout Vietnam. Reconstituting combat capacity was the priority for aircraft. Most personal amenities, such as mail delivery, were delayed by other priorities. No mail was coming through, at least not to us. By February 10, with no mail, my plans to meet Claudia became my primary concern. I was supposed to meet her in two weeks, and in the last letter I'd had from her, she was waiting for me to confirm I would be there before she paid for the tour. When my patience ran out, I called the depot at Qui Nhon and tracked down the postal officer. "Where the hell is the mail for Kontum?" I blurted out after I identified myself.

"Well, Captain Griffin," he replied, "the short answer is it's sitting in mailbags at the airfield. Right now, mail service does not have the priority to move it; I think it will start moving in a couple days."

"Okay," I said. "I have an airplane. If I fly to Qui Nhon, can I pick up the mail for Kontum?"

"You can if you are on orders as the postal officer," he replied.

"Okay, sir, I will be there in a couple hours."

I hung up the phone and went to Captain Tom. "Sir, cut some orders making me the postal officer, and I can get our mail at Qui Nhon."

Captain Tom was also waiting for mail. When I explained that it was sitting at Qui Nhon, he called the MACV commander and explained the problem. The MACV commander told him to send me to the MACV admin office, and the orders would be waiting for me. As I got in the jeep to leave, Captain Tom looked at me and said, "Neal, no more cement flights!"

"Roger, sir," I answered. He did not have to remind me of that. My desperation with the cement was still fresh in my memory.

Surprisingly, when I got to the MACV admin office, the orders making me a postal officer were waiting for me. It seemed everybody was eager to get mail.

Two hours later, I borrowed a jeep from the operations sergeant at the Qui Nhon airfield and drove to the mail section at the depot. The captain I had spoken to earlier was expecting me. After checking my orders, he took me to ten bags of mail that were waiting for delivery to Kontum. I loaded the bags into the jeep and headed back to my Bird Dog parked on the transient ramp.

Fortunately, the mail bags were not as heavy as the cement had been, but they were bulky and filled up the entire rear of the Bird Dog. I was still a little concerned about the bags shifting the center of gravity, but I figured I had the experience now to handle the situation if it affected the aircraft.

After returning the jeep, I did a quick preflight, started the Bird Dog, and contacted the tower for taxi clearance. When I completed my run-up check, the tower cleared me for takeoff. The aircraft seemed okay while taxiing to the takeoff position, which gave me a little more confidence. I would know on takeoff roll if mailbags were going to be a problem. If I could not get the tail up for normal takeoff, then I would know I had a repeat of the cement flight and would stop. But when I applied forward stick, the tail slowly came up as designed.

About thirty minutes from landing at Kontum, I called MACV and told them I was inbound with ten bags of mail. I asked for the mail clerks to meet me at the airfield so we could speed up the mail distribution. They agreed, and when I landed and taxied into the platoon revetments, a clerk from each unit was waiting. Within twenty minutes, we had broken down the mail, and it was on the way to the soldiers waiting for it.

Receiving my five letters from Claudia was like finding a treasure. I sat down and arranged them in the order in which she'd written them. The first two were just chitchat about the kids and missing me. The third expressed some worry about not hearing from me in time to take advantage of the cheap tour to Bangkok. The fourth letter expressed concern for me because the news had just reported the massive attacks across Vietnam, and Kontum Province had fallen to the Vietcong. In the last one, she prayed I was okay and said she had decided to pay for the tour despite not hearing from me. I felt bad that she did not know my status, but if mail could not get in, it could not go out. I could not do anything about getting the mail out of Vietnam. *Don't worry, darling. I will be there,* I told her mentally.

The mop-up of NVA and Vietcong forces continued throughout the province. We doubled our flying time supporting the infantry troops on the ground. When we were not flying, we worked on rebuilding our operations hut. I counted the days left before meeting Claudia.

The day after the siege of Kontum ended, Major Dan came to my BOQ. I stopped working on my flight schedule and asked, "Sir, what can I do for you?"

He smiled and said, "Nothing for me. I just wanted to let you know that I got the report from the intel people who looked at the site of the antiaircraft position. They found a hundred and fifty-two bodies. The napalm the F-4s dropped killed most of them. The heavy mortar position was next to the antiaircraft positions and destroyed with everything else. Just wanted you to know your actions that morning probably changed the course of the battle for Kontum. If you had not found the guns and if they had brought them into action against us, we would be history now. I just wanted to thank you for doing a good job." With that, he turned and left.

He left me with a good feeling. But in reality, I had not found the guns. They'd found me. The problem was the residual twinge of fear I felt each time I thought of flying again and of the possibility of being shot at. I feared I was pushing my good luck. Eventually, I would run out of it. I was flying Bird Dog 713, denoted by the tail number on the airplane, the morning of the Tet attack. When we started flying recon missions, I found myself afraid and too cautious on each flight, to the point that it was interfering with my ability to perform. I needed to clear my mind and reassure myself of my ability. I wanted to come to grips with my fear and, at the same time, find some humor in what had happened. I wrote the following description of what I was going through with the idea of rewriting it one day as a ballad.

The airfield at Kontum was under heavy attack, so we took off at daylight under heavy enemy fire. The other seven planes in my platoon recovered at Pleiku, about seventy miles away, which was well protected and not under attack. I, on the other hand, lost a confrontation with some heavy antiaircraft fire and was fortunate to make a forced landing on the Kontum airfield. After the battle for Kontum was over, the maintenance folks started repairing 713. It took about three weeks to replace the engine and one wing, which had two feet missing from it. Then there were the many holes in the fuselage and the other wing, not to mention the need to replace the pilot's seat, which had been rendered useless because of brown stains and a foul odor.

Finally, 713 was repaired and all nice and shiny. It sat on the flight line, ready for action. But each time I drew 713 for a mission, when I approached the aircraft to preflight, it seemed as if 713 would shrink away from me. When I did the engine run-up, something was always not quite right. The fuel pump wouldn't go to maximum flow, or the magnetos seemed to fail, and the engine would run roughly. So I would get the maintenance folks and take the standby aircraft for my mission. None of the other pilots seemed to have any problem with 713, and some of them were starting to look at me as if I might have been the reason the pilot's seat was replaced.

The fourth time this happened, I decided that enough was enough. I was going to fly 713 regardless of what problems it pretended to have. I must admit that on the takeoff roll, I was a little nervous and started to question the wisdom of what I was doing. 713 seemed to question the wisdom of what we were doing by responding sluggishly to my control input and running roughly occasionally. After we were safely airborne and headed for our mission area, I said, "Look, 713, I know you blame me for getting you all shot up and damaged. It's true that I did put you in harm's way, and as a result, you got hit pretty badly. I know you were hurting and wanted to land right away, but I kept flying you back into harm's way, and you kept taking more hits and more damage. But you know we had to do our job. People were counting on us. On that last run on the target, I think it was wrong of you to stop your engine and try to dump us right on top of the bad guys who were shooting at us. Look what you made me do to the seat. Just remember, it was my superb skill as a pilot that got us back safely on the ground with no further damage to you, not to mention my butt." After that conversation, 713 regained confidence in me, and we had no further problems.

A week before my R&R leave started, Captain Tom told me that his tour would be up at the end of February. He had decided not to extend. He had been in Vietnam for two years and felt that it was time for him to move on. He was going to Pleiku the next day to start clearing and to complete all his OERs and award recommendations. I would be in charge until the new company commander assigned the new platoon leader. I was sad to see him go, but on the other hand, it gave me the opportunity to be platoon leader. I thought I would be the natural choice.

To my surprise, three days later, Captain Tom returned with the supply officer to inventory platoon equipment. When I had a chance to see him, he said, "Neal, the new CO, Major Baker, is looking for a sharp officer to be his operations officer. I put in a good word for you. He wants to interview you tomorrow afternoon."

My heart sank. There was no way in hell I wanted to be the company operations officer. "Oh, sir, I wish you had not done that. I want the platoon. I want to rebuild it."

Captain Tom looked at me as if I were not thinking correctly. "Neal, the operations position is the third-ranking position in the company. It will be a feather in your hat. It will look good on your OER that the commander picked you, a junior captain, over more-senior officers for that position. I thought I was doing you a favor."

I liked and respected Captain Tom, and though I didn't like the position he had put me in, I didn't want to push the point with him. "Okay, sir, I will talk with Major Baker tomorrow." I intended to convince Major Baker that making me platoon leader was a better use of my skills than having me sit behind a desk, pushing paper. The next day, I flew a Bird Dog back to Camp Holloway for maintenance while I interviewed with Major Baker.

I knocked on the door to Major Baker's office, and when I heard him say to come in, I entered, stood before his desk, and saluted. "Sir, Captain Griffin reporting, as directed."

He returned my salute and stood, reaching across the desk to shake my hand. "Good to meet you, Captain Griffin. I've heard a lot about you. Captain Tom thinks you are the best-qualified captain in the company for the operations officer position. After reviewing your records and OERs, I am inclined to agree with him. That's why I want you for the job."

While he was speaking, I studied him. He was about five foot six inches and a little overweight. He was bald and freckled. Somewhere from the depths of my mind, the memory of another officer of his stature and complexion surfaced. I remembered how hostile that officer had been. Intuitively, I sensed that Major Baker had the same personality.

When he finished and it was time for me to speak, I said, "I appreciate the good word Captain Tom put in for me. But, sir, I have no wish to be operations officer. The Second Platoon is reconstituting from the aftermath of Tet. I would much like to command the platoon as it rebuilds. As the oldest member of the platoon, I am the best qualified to get it back up. I believe sitting behind a desk would waste my expertise and drive. I respectfully ask that you leave me as platoon commander. There are two captains who outrank me. They should be considered for the third-ranking position in the company."

As I spoke, I could see his freckled face turning a little red. "Captain Griffin, I'm not concerned with what you want. I'm concerned with running this company, and to do that, I want the best officers in key positions. I've made up my mind, and you are my new operations officer."

As he spoke, his voice rose in pitch, and I knew he was on the edge of anger, but I couldn't give in. "Sir, I wish you would reconsider. I'm not your best choice for operations officer."

He was angry now. "Captain Griffin, you are my new operations officer. Do I have to stand on that box and tell you before you understand?"

As he spoke, he pointed to a two-foot-high wooden box sitting by the left of his desk. I looked at the box, astounded. My instinct had been right. For the second time in my military career, I was working for a tyrant. "No, sir," I muttered.

"Good. Then after you return from midtour, I expect you to go to work as the operations officer. Any questions?"

"No, sir," I answered.

"Then you are dismissed."

I saluted, and he half-ass returned my salute.

I walked out of his office feeling bad. This was not going to be good. I could do the job, but I did not want the job. Major Will, the XO, was standing outside the door as I exited. He looked at me apologetically. "Welcome aboard, Captain Griffin." He smiled as he shook my hand. I immediately liked Major Will. He gave me the feeling that he sensed the problem with Major Baker and would try to mediate it.

"Thanks, sir," I responded. "I guess I will move my stuff up here and get a feel for the job before I go on midtour."

"That's a good idea, Captain Griffin. We are going to need every opportunity to stay ahead of the power curve for the next six months." The tone in his voice as he approved my plan gave me the sense that he also had some misgivings about Major Baker. However, we were officers and were loyal to the code of conduct required of officers. We would perform to the best of our ability despite personal preferences or how much we disliked it.

I flew back to Kontum to pick up my gear and say good-bye to the men and officers I had served with during the last three months. Darrel flew me back to Camp Holloway.

After we were airborne, I switched the radio to Guard frequency. "Hello, Vietnam. This is Headhunter 28, saying good-bye and good luck to all the warriors I have had the privilege of supporting over the last three months."

Within seconds, I heard, "Headhunter 28, this is Cobra Lead. Hey, man, good luck. I hate to see you go. You were the calmest pilot I have ever worked with. So many times, your calm voice in the middle of action reassured me and enabled me to do my job. I hate to see you go. Take care." There were several more "Ditto, Headhunter 28" calls.

Then I answered, "Thanks, Cobra Lead, and take care, all. Don't crash and burn." Cobra Lead's comments lifted my spirit a little. It was good to know other pilots thought well of me. I knew them only by their voices and call signs, but together we had destroyed enemy emplacements and personnel, resupplied friendly forces, and plucked wounded men out of hotspots. Many times, our presence overhead had turned the battlefield around and changed what could have been defeat into victory. What memories they were! But my days as Headhunter 28 had ended. Now I was Headhunter 3, a desk jockey. I felt like shit, but I told myself that I was still in the army and in combat, so I had to shape up my mental attitude and apply myself as operations officer. But first, I would see Claudia.

When I got back to Camp Holloway, I carried my bags to the BOQ that Major Will had assigned me. The BOQ was a large GP tent placed over a wooden frame. Sandbags were stacked around the sides to a height of three feet to provide protection from small-arms fire and shrapnel. The interior was divided into rooms by metal lockers and plywood panels. The floor was plywood on two-by-four trusses. The door was a heavy curtain. Each cubicle was large enough for a field table, two metal folding chairs, two metal wall lockers, and a bunk. My room was not as good as my quarters at Kontum but adequate.

Another large GP tent over a wood frame housed the toilets and showers. The toilets were on one side of the tent. They were fifty-five-gallon drums cut in half, sitting under a frame that ran down the side of the tent. Over each drum, to add some class to what was otherwise just a shit can, the engineers had bolted a toilet seat and lid over the hole. A plywood panel divided the toilets from the showers. The stench that hung around on days with no wind came from details pulling the half cans out and burning the contents.

The showers were a work of art. The engineers had mounted six fifty-five-gallon drums on a wooden frame. Protruding from the bottom was a showerhead. Between the showerhead and the drum was an off-and-on valve. A lever attached to the valve activated the shower. The user pulled on the rope attached to the lever and held it down. This turned the shower on, and it remained on as long as the user held the rope down.

It was simple to take a shower. You'd stand under the drum, pull the rope, and wet yourself. Then you'd lather down and pull the rope to rinse yourself. The secret, of course, was a fifty-five-gallon drum full of water. The Vietnamese women who cleaned the toilet and shower room and the BOQs, commonly called hooch maids, also were responsible for filling the fifty-five-gallon drums. They did this by once a day hauling buckets of water until each drum was full. If you were lucky, you could take a cold shower at least once or twice a week. That wasn't so bad. What was bad was getting in the shower and lathering up and then having the drum run out of water before you could get the soap off. As Murphy's law would predict, one could run quickly to another shower only to find it empty.

Wiping soap off with your towel was not enjoyable and always left you chafed in your crotch.

The other problem affecting the showers was water. Unbelievably, the Camp Holloway well would go dry about once a week. Without water, we had no shower. Fortunately, since the toilets didn't flush, there was no problem in that area. The irony of the situation was that we could look across a rice paddy and watch airmen at the air force base about a quarter mile away diving into their Olympic-size swimming pool. The army had no water, but the air force swam in it. Go figure.

After I unpacked my bags and set up occupancy in my new room, I walked up to the operations Quonset hut. There were six desks in the hut, three on each side of the building. The two at the end opposite the entry door were empty. Three enlisted men and an SSG occupied the other four. When I walked in, the SSG said, "Sir, may I help you?"

I looked at his name tape. "Yes, Staff Sergeant Flynn, you can. I'm Captain Griffin, the new operations officer. Which desk is mine?"

SSG Flynn jumped to attention and saluted. He pointed to the end desk and said, "That one, sir." By then, the three enlisted men were standing at attention.

"At ease. Sit down. Don't ever jump to attention when I come in. Do that when the CO comes in, because I think he will expect it. I'm just checking in right now because in the morning, I am going on midtour. When I get back, I want each of you to brief me on your job. Whose desk is that?" I asked, pointing at the desk across from mine and on the right of SSG Flynn's desk.

"That's the assistant operations officer's desk—Lieutenant Kubrick, sir," SSG Flynn replied.

"Where is Lieutenant Kubrick?" I asked.

"Sir, he's new and is getting his orientation training now. He will be at work on Monday," SSG Flynn replied.

I walked to my desk and sat down. I opened the drawers and took a brief look at the papers. One drawer contained files on flying hours, awards, safety meetings, and miscellaneous administrative actions. Another drawer contained a record file for each pilot assigned to the company. The last drawer contained a file with record copies of intelligence reports and reconnaissance reports. The files provided me a brief idea of what I would be doing for the next four months. On the wall to the left of my desk was a big board covered with acetate.

The board listed all the pilots assigned to the company and their flight statuses. It provided a quick view of their qualifications, check rides, and flight hours. It was a good management tool. The only data missing from the board were the daily flight assignments. The flight platoons made those assignments, as I had done in the Second Platoon. That meant I was not really an operations officer. I was the flight records officer with many extra duties.

I had communication with the platoons and in-flight aircraft via a VFH and an FM mounted in the building. I did not know what use they were, because the pilots, when on recon, were busy and communicated with their platoons. They certainly would not be interested in chatting with me. The possibility existed, of course, that I might get some hot intelligence and redirect an ongoing flight. Maybe that was one use for the radios.

I left the operations building and wandered over to the company headquarters building to pick up my leave papers. The first sergeant gave them to me, and I went ahead and signed out while I was there. CW-3 Akins was flying me to Saigon in the morning in the company Beaver, or the U-6, officially. The U-6 was a four-passenger aircraft assigned to the company for administrative support. It was manufactured by De Havilland Corp. My first flight in it had been back in Germany in 1958, when mortar battery jumped from one. Later, in Special Forces, I had jumped from one. It was the same aircraft in which I had given up my seat to the photographer, which had cost him his life.

I heard someone call my name, and turning, I saw that the door to Major Baker's office was open. He was motioning for me to come in. I walked in and said, "Good afternoon, sir."

He looked at me and asked, "Are you ready to go on leave?"

"Yes, sir," I answered. "CW-3 Akins is flying me to Saigon with the Beaver in the morning. I'm all moved into my BOQ, and I started orienting myself on the operations officer's duties this afternoon."

"Good." He seemed pleased and asked, "Are you rated in the Beaver?"

"No, sir," I answered.

"Okay. When you get back, I will check you out in the Beaver. You can use it to fly administrative runs to Qui Nhon."

"Great, sir," I answered enthusiastically. "I would love to fly the Beaver."

With that, he turned his attention back to his work, and I left his office, feeling a little better. I might get something out of the operations job after all. On the way back to my BOQ, I went by the mail room and told the mail clerk of my change of address. I did not expect any mail, since Claudia did not yet know I had changed jobs. I planned on giving her my new address in Bangkok. After that, I went by the mess hall and ate dinner.

CW-3 Akins was there, so I sat with him and confirmed our takeoff time for the morning. He was flying the Beaver to Cam Ranh Bay to pick up three new pilots and would drop me off at Tan Son Nhut on the way. I would fly out of Tan Son Nhut on the R&R flight to Bangkok at 1300 that afternoon. At the time, he and Major Baker were the only ones in the company rated in the Beaver. That was why the CO wanted me checked out so I could fly the administrative missions.

Back in my BOQ room, I packed my few civilian clothes and a suit I'd borrowed from one of the officers who shared the BOQ with me. In the last letter from Claudia, she had written that she had booked the tour and would be in the Hotel RS, a Thai hotel used by many European tour companies.

That night, I listened to the sound of artillery in distance. I tried to sleep but kept waking up to check my watch. Finally, morning came, and I was up and dressed in my khakis. I met CW-3 Akins at the mess hall for breakfast. I convinced him to leave as soon as we finished eating. I wanted to get going before anything happened to prevent my departure.

After a slow flight over the interior of Vietnam, CW-3 Akins dropped me off at the Tan Son Nhut base operations. In the passenger area, a sign over a window directed soldiers going on R&R to report there. I got in line behind several soldiers and waited my turn. I presented my leave form and passport to the sergeant staffing the window. He checked the information against a list and told me to get on bus 15 in front of the operations building at 1100.

By 1110, the bus was full of GIs headed for Bangkok, and we left for the commercial jet passenger area. There, we boarded a leased 707 for the short flight to Bangkok. Two hours later, I was in the R&R reception center in Bangkok with a hundred other soldiers, receiving our briefing on R&R in Bangkok.

The army specialist briefed us on the dos and don'ts and areas of Bangkok to avoid. He gave us emergency numbers to contact if we had a problem. He gave me my departure day and time since I was not staying at one of the several hotels the army leased. Because the hotel Claudia was at was not an army-leased one, I had to leave the name and the room in which I would be staying. I arranged to call back with the room number since I did not yet know it. Finally, the specialist said, "That's it. If there are no questions, enjoy your leave. Stay safe, and report in on time."

Just like that, I was out of combat and walking out the door of the R&R center into the hot, humid air of a Bangkok street. The rest of the GIs were boarding army buses that would take them to their assigned hotels. I had changed into civilian clothes in the center, and as I hailed one of the many cabs lined up in front of the center, I thought about how fast life can change.

In the cab, I showed the driver the name of the hotel in which Claudia was staying, and he looked a little puzzled. He did not know where it was. He got out and walked back to ask some other drivers how to get to it. After several minutes, he returned, and we were on our way.

I could understand why the driver did not know the hotel's exact location. Bangkok was a big, sprawling city, and the Hotel RS was way across the city in a more upscale area. My heart raced as he pulled up in front of the entrance. I paid the driver and walked into a huge lobby with marble floors.

Walking up to the desk, I wondered if the clerk spoke English. When I told him that I was Neal Griffin and was there to meet my wife, he replied, "One minute, please." He thumbed through some cards and then looked at me and smiled. "Oh yes, she is waiting for you. She said you would be in from Vietnam. She is in room 521. The elevators are down the hall on your left."

"Thank you," I replied, and I headed for the elevators. I knocked gently on the door to 521. There was no answer. I knocked a little louder. A couple of minutes went by, and no one answered. *She's not here*, I said to myself, and I returned to the lobby desk.

The clerk seemed surprised to see me. I said, "Mrs. Griffin was not in her room. Did she leave a message for me?"

"I'll check," he answered, and he checked a bank of small boxes against the wall. "No, there's no message. She has her keys, so I think she's in the area. Check the pool. I believe I saw her earlier in her bathing suit. The pool is at the end of the hallway," he said, pointing to a hallway.

"Thank you," I replied, and I started down the hall. I could see a sign over a door: Pool Entrance. *I hope she is here*, I said to myself as I opened the door.

I stepped out into the hot, muggy air, onto the deck of a huge pool area with a bar at one end. Looking around, my eyes came to rest on several women sitting in lounge chairs. In one sat the most beautiful woman in the world. She was wearing her white bikini. She saw me at the same time I saw her, and she stood up and started walking toward me. We stood there holding each other until the rush of joy eased and we could begin our brief time together.

At first, I felt awkward and was unsure what to say. It had been six months since I had seen her. All I could think of was "I love you. It's so good to hold you again." Then I explained how I had gone to her room first.

She said she had told the clerk that she was expecting me and to tell me I was in the pool area. That broke the ice, and our conversation started flowing as we took the elevator to our room.

The week flew by. We saw all the famous sights. We dined, shopped, and made love. When I gave her the two rings I had bought for our anniversary, she was ecstatic. She loved both, and she wore the blue sapphire ring with diamonds for many years.

The morning I had to leave, she cried. Getting into the cab that would take me back to war and my despised desk job was one of the hardest things I'd ever had to do, especially since her tour group did not leave Bangkok for another two weeks.

Then, just like that, I was back in the dirty, mildewed atmosphere of Camp Holloway. It took a day to get reaccustomed to the constant drone of helicopters and other aircraft. There was something new now: while the Tet battle had mostly ended in the rest of Vietnam, the VC periodically attacked Camp Holloway with mortars and rockets.

I signed in on the afternoon of my return, and Major Baker called me into his office. "Good to have you back. I hope you had an enjoyable time and are ready to get back to work."

"Yes, sir," I responded. "It was great."

"Good," he said. "You need to hit the ground running. The new battalion commander will visit the company on Friday, three days from now. He wants a briefing by each key staff officer and all platoon leaders. My plan is to give him a review of the company and then take him on a tour to each office to receive individual briefings. He will arrive at 1300 on Friday. I will greet him and escort him to my office for my briefing. After I finish briefing him, I will take him to your office for your briefing. I have assigned thirty minutes for your briefing. After you finish, I will escort him down to the flight line for the platoon briefings. Any questions?"

"No, sir," I answered. Hell, I did not know enough about my job to ask a question! But from the little bit I had seen before going on midtour, it would be difficult to develop a thirty-minute briefing.

I spent the afternoon studying my responsibilities as company operations officer. Since I did not schedule daily flights—a major operations responsibility—I did not have much in the way of tasks to perform daily. That centered my briefing on flight records and flying hours, awards, safety programs, recon reports, and intelligence summaries. At best, I had a ten-minute briefing. If I tried to make it longer, it would be clear to anyone that I was throwing in trivia just to kill time. So I got on the phone with Major Baker.

I had to wait a couple minutes to speak to him, and when he finally answered, he did not seem to be in a good mood. When I explained the best I could do on the briefing, he became enraged. "Captain Griffin, you have thirty minutes in which to brief the battalion commander, and I expect you to use it. Do I have to stand on my box to get you to hear what I am saying?"

His outburst stunned me. "I'll do the best I can, sir." I think he hung up before I finished my reply. Well, at least I'd warned him.

It took me a couple hours to prepare a draft of my briefing. I spent most of the next two hours familiarizing myself with each subject area as I drafted it. I spent the next two days refining it, and as I had expected, it was about ten minutes long. I could see what concerned the CO. A major part of his command was theoretically company operations, but because the platoons did all the scheduling work, his empire was not as complex as it looked on paper. The battalion commander might question why it took a captain and a lieutenant to do the operations job. That was my question also.

At staff call Friday morning, Major Baker reminded us of the battalion commander's visit in the afternoon and wanted assurances that we were ready. I answered, "Operations is ready to go." After he dismissed us, I caught Major Will before left. "Sir, I need to talk to you about my briefing."

I needed to confide to someone that my briefing was not going to be thirty minutes long. I knew it was useless to talk to Major Baker. The XO was reasonable and could advise me. "What's up?" he asked.

"Sir, Major Baker is insisting that I give a thirty-minute briefing on operations. I have developed a comprehensive overview briefing that covers everything in operations, but it's only, at best, ten to twelve minutes long. Because we do not schedule flights, it removes the major portion of any briefing on flight operations. That leaves administrative functions, which do not take thirty minutes to cover."

He looked at me as if to say, "I understand your predicament," and he said, "Do the best that you can. The CO is new, and so is the battalion CO. Major Baker is just eager that we do a good job of briefing our new battalion commander. I don't know what else to tell you."

That did not help my predicament, but I felt better after telling the XO. I would just do my best and hope all would go well. Maybe the battalion commander would ask many questions and help take up the thirty minutes.

At 1230, the orderly room called to tell everyone the battalion commander was on the way, and his ETA was fifteen minutes. I heard an inbound helicopter and felt a tenseness start. I was prepared and would give a good briefing. The only problem was that I didn't have much to brief him on. I checked the operations room's appearance once more and made sure my staff knew what to do.

Sergeant Flynn would call attention as soon as the battalion commander entered the room. I would greet him and lead him to my desk, which served as my briefing area. During the briefing, my men would continue working. Usually, I felt good about briefing someone on my job and responsibilities, but this was not one of those times.

Sergeant Flynn called attention as Major Baker led the battalion commander into the room. I saluted and introduced myself as we shook hands. As I led him to my desk, I introduced each of my men and Lieutenant Kubrick. The battalion commander and Major Baker took the seats I pointed to, and I began my briefing.

I briefed the five major functions performed by the operations section. I covered flight records and aviator qualifications, flying hours, awards, safety programs, and intelligence reporting. In each, I pointed out successes and challenges. It was a good, concise briefing fitting for a battalion-level commander. I think because the battalion commander had, during his career, been an operations officer several times, he had few questions about the responsibilities I talked about. When I said, "Sir, that ends my briefing. Do you have any questions?" he had none. It had taken fifteen minutes, and he appeared surprised that the briefing was over or that there was so little responsibility for a captain, lieutenant, sergeant, and two enlisted clerks. Major Baker gave me a look that would kill. The battalion commander stood and said, "Thank you, Captain Griffin. Good briefing." With that, they left.

I sat at my desk and waited for the call I knew was coming. Two hours later, I heard an outbound helicopter, and ten minutes later, the phone rang. It was Major Baker. "Get your ass in my office."

I stood at attention in front of Major Baker. His face was red with anger as he chewed me out. "You had the opportunity to impress the new battalion commander, but you failed miserably. I don't think you take me seriously. From now on, when I tell you to do something, I will stand on my box. Maybe then you will take me seriously. Your OER will certainly reflect your actions. Any questions?"

"No, sir," I answered.

"Get back to work," he said.

That was my start in my new job. Despite my shock at Major Baker's stand-on-the-box comments, I vowed I would do a good job and see if I could redeem myself. I did not think that giving a good briefing to impress someone equaled doing a good job and showing someone what you could do. I had given a good briefing. However, the way the company was organized relegated the operations job to a recordkeeping role with little substance to brief.

The first duties I focused on were the flying hour program and aviator qualifications. During the following week, I checked each assigned aviator's records to ensure he was current and properly documented to fly the Bird Dog. At the same time, I looked at the awards program. All nominations for the Air Medal required my signature as the awards officer. My signature meant the nominee had met the combat flying hours to justify the Air Medal.

A recipient needed twenty-five hours of combat or combat support time to qualify for the Air Medal. At the end of a mission, the pilot completed the logbook by entering the number of hours flown and the nature of the flight. Combat entries did not apply to recon pilots unless they were required to attack a specific target with their rockets as part of their mission. Most of the recon missions fell under the category of combat support missions.

An observer earned the Air Medal by flying the same number and category of hours. Before someone other than a pilot could log time as an observer, he required flight orders placing him on flight status. The company had no assigned observers, so if we flew with one, it was often another pilot from the company. Sometimes the unit we were supporting would train an individual and put him on orders to fly a mission, as in the artillery missions I had flown in Qui Nhon. The award of the Air Medal was readily subject to misuse if the awards officer did not oversee the process closely.

One of my first actions as the awards officer for Air Medals was to review all flight records on file for observer flight hours. I found several records belonging to cooks and maintenance personnel. They had orders issued by the maintenance platoon, placing them on flying status as observers. Unfortunately, the maintenance platoon did not have the authority to issue this order. It was obvious that it was an under-the-table effort to award Air Medals to individuals not qualified to receive them. There were files showing that previous awards officers had approved the requests for Air Medals going to these individuals.

My view on awards was different. I believed those officers abused the awards program each time an award was given for a performance that did not deserve it. I believed that practice reduced the award's significance. In World War II, the army awarded the Air Medal to the airmen who flew the bombing raid over Japan with Jimmy Doolittle. That was my standard for the Air Medal, and I was not going to let individuals get it for just flying twenty-five hours in the backseat of a Bird Dog.

I called the maintenance platoon leader and explained my position to him. As I expected, he was upset. He tried to convince me to allow it because it served as a morale booster for his maintenance soldiers. I was sympathetic but adamant that if they wanted Air Medals, they would earn them by the rules. He said he would take it up with Major Baker and hung up. I felt bad about creating a problem between me and the maintenance platoon leader, but if I gave in on this issue, I would be more prone to give in on the next issue. I was being a hard-ass about it, but in doing so, I fixed the standards I expected. That would make my job easier down the line.

I did not hear from Major Baker until that afternoon. His call was not about awards. His tone was pleasant as he said, "Captain Griffin, meet me down at the flight line at 0900 in the morning. We are going to start your checkout in the Beaver."

"Okay, sir, I'll be there," I answered with a little excitement in my voice. It would be a thrill to fly the Beaver. I had checked Major Baker's records and learned that he had more than a thousand hours in the Beaver, and most of that time had been as an instructor. I checked our publications and found a manual on the Beaver, so I spent the rest of the afternoon studying the operating procedures for it. I wanted to be as prepared as I could when I met Major Baker in the morning.

The next morning, Major Baker was friendly and professional as he began my transition into the Beaver. First, he walked me around the aircraft, explaining each part and function. My taking the initiative to learn something about the aircraft pleased him. The Beaver was designed for use in the rugged Canadian wilderness, which made it a perfect aircraft for military use.

It was a tail dragger like the Bird Dog and had high overwings with tremendous lift. Its better stability made flying it easier than the Bird Dog. One major difference was in the flaps. The pilot lowered or raised the flaps by pumping a handle up or down. This was different from the electric flaps on the Bird Dog, but the aircraft had a variable-pitch prop similar to the Bird Dog's. All in all, it was like flying a big Bird Dog, except it was more fun.

I completed my transition in ten flying hours. Major Baker signed me off, and I entered my qualification into my flight records, which he signed. At the time, I did not recognize how important my qualification in the Beaver would be to my career. I had not yet developed my belief that each event in life occurs for a specific reason. A simple example is that had I not volunteered for airborne training, I would not have met Claudia. When Captain Tom did me a favor by convincing Major Baker that I was his new operations officer, he put into effect a long line of events. These events would significantly affect my life. I only saw each event's significance in hindsight.

While flying the Beaver boosted my morale and eased the pain of not flying recon missions, I still had the boring job of operations officer. One problem I had was keeping Lieutenant Kubrick busy. There was not even enough work for me. When I wrote his OER, I needed something on which to rate him. He also was disappointed with his assignment as assistant operations officer.

The second week, we were sitting around the office, acting as if we were busy, when I looked at him and asked, "Lieutenant Kubrick, what the hell is a cubit?" The pronunciation of his name was the same as the word *cubit*.

He looked at me, surprised, and replied, "What do you mean, sir? It's my name."

I laughed at his confusion. "Didn't you ever hear Bill Cosby do his skit on Noah talking to God? When God told him to build an ark three hundred cubits by forty cubits, Noah said, 'Okay,' and then he said to God, 'What's a cubit?' Now I am asking you. What's a cubit?"

Not knowing for sure if I was joking or serious, he answered, "Sir, I don't know."

I stood and said, "Look it up, Lieutenant Kubrick. I want to know what a cubit is." I turned and walked out the door, saying, "I'm going down to the flight line. I'll be back in a little bit."

I walked into the First Platoon operations and knocked on the platoon leader's door. Captain Smith yelled, "Come in!"

Walking in, I said, "Stan, I need to talk to you for a couple minutes. You got time?"

"Sure, what do you need?"

"I've got a new lieutenant just sitting around my office, doing nothing. I need to put him to work on something that contributes to the war effort. Can you work him into missions for half a day each day?"

"Hell yes, I can! You're talking about Lieutenant Kubrick, aren't you? I told Major Baker I needed him, but he said you needed him more."

"Stan, that's a bunch of crap. The operations officer's job is, at best, a part-time job. But for some reason, Major Baker thinks it's more and needs two officers to run it. Now, if I was scheduling all the missions the company flies each day, maybe it would be a real job. But it's unfair to Lieutenant Kubrick to sit around each day doing nothing and flying for just currency."

"Send him down. I can use him right now."

"Thanks, Stan. We need to keep this low key. I don't want Major Baker to find out. I can cover for him if he's gone a half day. I will take any flak if Major Baker finds out and is upset over it. Just tell him I'm the one who set it up." I got up and, leaving, said, "Thanks again, Stan. I'll have him down here in about fifteen minutes."

I walked back into the office and looked at Lieutenant Kubrick. "Okay, Lieutenant Kubrick, what the hell is a cubit?"

He looked at me, a little shocked. "Sir, I haven't found the definition of a cubit yet."

"All right, keep looking. But for now, I want you to get your flight gear and go down to the First Platoon and report to Captain Smith. I've arranged a deal where you will fly recon missions half a day and work in here the rest of the time. You keep this to yourself. You understand?"

I saw sincere gratitude in his eyes as he jumped up and said, "Thank you, sir! You will never regret this."

"Be careful," I told him as he left. Looking at my sergeant and two E-4s, I said, "You guys keep this quiet also. If anybody asks about Lieutenant Kubrick flying recon missions, tell them they have to talk to me."

The nemesis I struggled with the most as an officer was my lack of education. My high school English was not strong, so in jobs where I had to write reports, my stress levels went out of sight. To ensure well-written reports, I always had to get help from individuals with college degrees. Lieutenant Kubrick had a college degree and was an excellent writer, so I made him responsible for the weekly intelligence summary. I, of course, reviewed it for relevance, accuracy, and quality before I sent it to Major Baker for signature. By arranging for Lieutenant Kubrick to fly recon missions, I got his full and motivated cooperation in doing the summaries. Between us, we produced, according to the battalion S2, some of the best he had ever seen. This pleased Major Baker and kept him happy and out of my business.

Company safety officer was one of my extra duties. Like my predecessors, I scheduled and prepared the agenda for the monthly safety fly-in. I liked safety and had been involved in safety either as the safety NCO or safety officer since my tour in mortar battery. I enjoyed giving the monthly safety briefing, which I always put a lot of effort into, and I always received praise for its content and relevance. I had attended so many safety briefings that amounted to the presenter fulfilling a need with boring and disjointed information that I swore I would never be guilty of that. Again, Major Baker was happy with my performance as safety officer and even invited the battalion commander to attend two of my briefings.

I could sense that the major still felt I had let him down in that first briefing. In turn, I had to accept that my OER was not going to be a good one. A bad OER in combat could destroy an officer's career. I was not the only officer who had a problem with Major Baker.

It seemed that he had a chip on his shoulder associated with his short stature. I heard other officers remark about how he had threatened to stand on his box so they would listen. Though I know Major Will had a problem (he was six feet two inches tall and laid back), he never mentioned any friction.

Flying the Beaver three times a week to Qui Nhon to deliver and pick up distribution provided my only pleasant distraction from my office duties. Before leaving for Qui Nhon, I always contacted Pleiku's airfield to see if they had any passengers looking for a ride to Qui Nhon. When they did, I would stop by Pleiku Air Base en route to Qui Nhon and pick up any passengers waiting there. I did the same on the way back. I felt like an airline pilot.

One day in Qui Nhon, I picked up three soldiers. As I helped them aboard the Beaver, I looked into the eyes of Corporal Jones. The last time I had seen him, he was Major Jones, the same Major Jones who had questioned me when I appeared before the OCS board in 1964. I recognized him immediately. His arrogant manner and the tone of his questions had fixed his image in my brain forever, and although he did not recognize me outright, I must have seemed familiar to him.

As he was fastening his seat belt, he looked at me and asked, "Sir, have we met before? You seem familiar. Were you ever in Tenth Special Forces?"

I fought the urge to say, "Yes, we have met. You were the arrogant major sitting on the OCS board who told me I did not have the qualifications to be an officer. Now I'm a captain, and you are a corporal." But I did not. Whatever had happened to cause him to lose his commission was more than enough payback, so I answered, "No. I don't think we have met that I can remember." There was no need to rub it in. I dropped them off at Pleiku Air Base and watched Corporal Jones walk toward the base operations building. I never saw him again. Running into him was a good lesson on how time and events can change the course of one's life.

The main problem with having a do-nothing desk job is the slow passage of time. My days dragged by. No matter how I applied myself, I still had too much free time, and free time creates an idle mind. When it's far from home, a busy mind does not know how lonely it is. I found myself thinking too often of Claudia, Michele, and Ron. The problem with that was remembering the tension between Claudia and me. Our time together in Bangkok was wonderful. We were like two young lovers who had just met. However, in my heart, I knew that time was not characteristic of our marriage.

The tension was obvious in her quick anger over simple statements or gestures on my part. My often immature response always fueled the situation. Thinking about it without being able to take some action to resolve it was painful. When we were together and tried to address the problem, the resulting discussion always turned into a fight. We would never get past that point. Adding to the trouble was her association with Marcy Smith in Georgia. It worried me sometimes that she might be drifting toward the possibility of being unfaithful. Staying busy was my way of avoiding these thoughts.

There were some interruptions to the boredom of my do-nothing job. Every third or fourth night, the VC would entertain us with a mortar attack. The attack usually consisted of about thirty or forty rounds of eighty-two-millimeter mortars. They were trying to hit the fuel storage area but could not get close enough to Camp Holloway to get in range. As a result, the rounds fell all over the camp. The attacks were not too effective but did occasionally hit a barrack and do some damage.

One attack caused several injuries and one death when a mortar round fell through the door to a bunker and exploded. The bunker contained more than twenty aviators who had just entered it for protection from the attack. The round killed one mechanic and wounded six others. We seldom suffered casualties, because we usually knew when the attacks were going to occur.

The warnings about the attacks came from the hooch maids who did our laundry and cleaned the barracks, BOQs, and latrines. On the night the VC planned an attack, a hooch maid would say to me, "Captain Griffin, you go bunker tonight." Every time she warned us to go to the bunker, an attack occurred around 0015, so everybody would take blankets with him and head to the bunkers around 2300.

One night, I was writing to Claudia and wanted to finish the letter before I went to the bunker. Major Will headed for the bunker at 2300 and asked, "Neal, you going to the bunker?"

"Yes, sir," I answered, "but I want to finish this letter first."

"Okay," he replied, leaving. "Don't wait too long."

I finished the letter and left for the bunker at 2330. I was in an open field, about one hundred meters from safety, when I heard in the distance the *thump-thump* of mortars firing. *Oh shit*, I said to myself. *I'm too far to make it to the bunker.* So I hit the ground in prone position, holding my helmet on my head. I was lying along a four-inch-deep depression that draining water had cut. I squeezed myself into those four inches as far as I could, and almost immediately, I heard in the still night a swishing sound of something flying through the air. Then I heard a crump and saw the flash of an exploding mortar round, followed by four more all around me. At the same time, I could hear the thumps of the mortars firing again. The crump of exploding mortars moved away from me toward the bunkers and then back over me toward the airfield. I lay there trembling with my eyes shut tight as a volley of forty mortars hit the base. Even with my eyes shut, I saw the flash of each exploding mortar round. The closest one landed ten meters from my position. The explosion lifted me and covered me with dirt, while the concussion stung my ears. Then it was over. After I heard no more thumps, I waited another fifteen minutes, jumped up, and ran the rest of the way to the bunker.

I explained what had happened and listened to everyone agree I was lucky. While waiting for the all clear, I thought about the times when I'd taught forward observer procedures to Expert Infantryman Badge candidates. In discussing the use of mortars versus artillery, I would point out that mortars were effective in surprising enemy troops because you could not hear them coming, whereas you could hear inbound artillery rounds. Now I knew how wrong that was! I promised myself that I would correct the manuals describing mortars as being undetectable when I got out of Vietnam. As usual, about thirty minutes after the attack had ended, the camp commander gave the all clear, and we returned to our BOQ.

About two weeks after the mortar attack that caught me in the open, one of our hooch maids told me to sleep in the bunker that night. About five minutes to eleven, Major Will declared that it was time to go to the bunker. He had just finished saying that, when we heard a distant but loud whooshing sound, followed by several more. I looked at him and asked, "What the hell was that?"

Before he could answer, a massive explosion shook the ground. The concussion from the explosion shook a cloud of dust loose in the BOQ. I froze as Major Will yelled, "They're one-hundred-twenty-two-millimeter rockets! Let's get to the bunker!" and he headed for the door.

By then, I was remembering that artillery and rockets are most effective against personnel in the open. I yelled to Major Will as he exited the door, "I'm staying here, sir!" Two more rockets exploded; they were farther away but still shook the BOQ. There was no way I was going to run three hundred meters through this barrage. I put on my flak jacket and helmet and crawled under my bunk. It seemed as if every minute, I could hear the whoosh of another series of rockets launching, followed by earthshaking explosions. The intensity and power of the exploding rockets made the mortar attacks seem like child's play. Toward the end of the attack, I heard a whoosh and braced for an explosion, but nothing happened except a thud, which also caused the ground to shake. The whole time, I cringed in fear under my bunk. It was the most helpless feeling I have ever had in my life. Then there was one final whoosh, and it was over. Still, I lay under my bunk, waiting for Major Will to return and reassure me that the attack was over. The rocket attack killed three soldiers, wounded fourteen, destroyed two billets, and damaged the runway.

The rockets hit the runway three times. Each rocket destroyed twenty meters of PSP (pierced steel plank) and created a crater twenty feet deep and thirty feet wide. It was one of the most damaging attacks on Camp Holloway while I was there. Despite the damage, all units were operational by noon the following day. Thank God that was the only rocket attack, but mortar attacks continued.

At the April fly-in and safety meeting, Major Baker awarded me my first Air Medal and then, to my surprise, the Distinguished Flying Cross for my actions on October 20, 1967. I expected the Air Medal, but the DFC was a complete surprise. When Major Baker pinned it on during the awards ceremony, he congratulated me, but the expression on his face was one of disappointment. Although I was doing an outstanding job as operations officer and even received kudos from the battalion, Major Baker still did not appreciate me. I guess my resistance to taking the job and my later battalion commander briefing still galled him.

Besides my job, I was having another problem. I started suffering from persistent diarrhea. I lost my appetite for anything but toast at breakfast. This went on until I started having ten to fifteen bowel movements a day, which interfered with my flying. I finally went to see the flight surgeon, and he was upset that I'd waited so long. He gave me some pills to take and promised that they would "dry me up like a cork."

After taking them for a week, I saw no improvement, and I started losing weight. I went back to the flight surgeon. The pills' ineffectiveness perplexed the flight surgeon, and he became a little concerned. "Okay, Captain, I'm putting you in the hospital until this clears up."

His suggestion troubled me, and I responded, "Dr. Griff, I don't think I need to go to the hospital just because of a little diarrhea. Besides, I feel good, except that I don't have an appetite. I'm losing a little weight because of that."

"I want you in the hospital until we can find out what's causing the diarrhea. You don't want to ignore this and have a liver problem develop," he said.

The possibility of a liver problem convinced me, and that afternoon, I checked into the army field and evacuation hospital located on the

Pleiku AFB. When I told Major Baker, the issue of who would do the operations job concerned him more than my problem. I told him there was no problem with that, because Lieutenant Kubrick could handle it for a few days. I wanted to add that Lieutenant Kubrick was more than capable of doing the job, period, but I decided not to rock the boat. Major Baker had his jeep driver take me to the hospital.

Captain Griff had called the hospital and told them I was coming. When I got there, they gave me a gown and a bed in a ward that housed wounded soldiers. The OIC nurse was a major, and she explained the rules to me. I had to get up each morning and make my bed. After that, I could get back into it. She hung a medical chart at the end of my bed and told me the doctor would be around to look at me later. Although the doctor never showed, an enlisted medic came by and took my blood pressure and gave me some pills. By then, I had to go to the latrine.

Back from the latrine, I lay on my bed and looked at the wounded soldiers around me. Some had serious wounds and were awaiting evacuation to the States. Others had less-serious injuries and would return to their units. All I had was diarrhea. The contrast had me feeling as if I were a gold brick, but my raw ass reminded me that I could be sick.

Evening chow was at 1700, and the major told me that I could walk to the mess hall to eat. Mess personnel served the rest of the patients. I walked down to the mess hall to make an effort to eat. I took a little food on my tray and some Jell-O. After trying the food, I could only stomach the Jell-O. My first night passed with several trips to the latrine and more pills.

I got out of bed at 0600 and made it for the major's ward inspection. After that, I headed for the mess hall for breakfast. I managed to eat some toast and bacon and down some coffee. When I got back to the ward, I took a hot shower in a real shower room with clean, hot water, and that activity made me feel a hell of a lot better. Back in the ward, I got back in bed and waited for the doctor. I dozed off and on, visited the latrine, took some more pills, and waited.

When the doctor didn't show by noon, I walked to the mess hall for lunch. I was able to eat a little of the meat loaf and some chocolate cake. That was the first solid food other than toast and bacon that I had been able to eat in about a week. On the way back to the ward, I picked up a book from the library. I spent the afternoon waiting for the doctor, taking pills, reading my book, and visiting the latrine. When the major made her last walkthrough of the ward, I asked when the doctor would see me. She told me an emergency had delayed him, and he would see me tomorrow.

That was my routine for the next three days. I made my bed, ate breakfast, took pills, and visited the latrine. Then I lay in bed and read my book while waiting for the doctor. I ate a little lunch, and then I visited the latrine and read my book while waiting for the doctor. I ate a little supper, realized the doctor probably would not come today, took some pills, and visited the latrine.

On the fourth day, I still had not seen the doctor. But the good news was that my latrine visits were down to about five a day, which was manageable. My appetite had returned, and I could eat a normal meal. I believe the clean environment the hospital provided allowed my body to defeat the bug that was trying to devour me. That morning, I asked the major if the doctor was going to see me today. She acted surprised when I told her that he had not seen me yet. She told me she would check on when he would see me.

When she left, I went to the nurses' station and asked an orderly to use the phone. I dialed the company headquarters, and when the first sergeant answered, I told him, "Hey, Top, this is Captain Griffin. They've released me from the hospital. Send the CO's driver to get me. I'll meet him out front."

"Okay, Captain Griffin, he'll be there in about fifteen minutes."

"Thanks, Top," I answered, and I returned to my bed. I got my fatigues out of my bag, dressed, and left the hospital. To this day, I have no idea what I had. No one ever questioned what happened to me. I think, and rightly so, with the numbers of seriously wounded, a case of diarrhea was not that important.

By the middle of May, I had fully recovered and was again entrenched in the boredom of my do-nothing job. At about 1000, the phone rang. It was the Second Platoon leader, Captain Damon. He said, "Captain Griffin, we've got a plane down. It's HH 23 with an observer aboard. They went down about ten miles south of Firebase Charlie. HH 21 is over the crash site. I can't contact him, because he keeps breaking up because of range from my location. Please tell Major Baker. We are arranging for a security force to get to the crash site. I'll keep you posted as events change."

"Roger, Captain Damon. I'll start recovery efforts from this location. Any word on the fate of the crew?" I asked, because that would be the first question the CO would ask.

"The only facts I know now are that the observer is out of the plane, but the pilot is still in it. The plane is still intact," he responded.

"Okay, keep us informed."

I called the orderly room and asked for Major Baker. The first sergeant told me that he and Major Will were at a meeting with the camp commander. I told him what had happened and asked him to get that information to Major Baker as soon as possible.

I pulled out the procedures on downed aircraft and started down the checklist. The first step was notification of the chain of command. I called the battalion S3 and told him of the situation. He said he would get back to me shortly. The SOP required an accident investigation team to look into all aircraft accidents. I did not know if it was an accident or if enemy fire had brought the aircraft down. I needed to find out, because we did not investigate an aircraft downed by enemy fire.

I tuned the operations FM radio to the Second Platoon frequency and called, "Headhunter 21, this is Headhunter 3 on FM. Over."

There was a short silence, and then I heard, "Headhunter 3, this is Headhunter 21. Over."

"Roger, HH 21. I need to know if Headhunter 23 was shot down or crashed accidentally."

"Roger, HH 3. As far as I know, there was no enemy fire involved. The observer reports that they were flying over the trees; the pilot made a steep turn; and all of sudden, the plane went into the trees. Headhunter 3, I've got three radios going, trying to coordinate rescue efforts. I'll call you back when I get time."

"This is Headhunter 3. Roger that. Let me know if I can help." I understood his problem. Flying the aircraft and working three radios was tough. He did not need staff officers interrupting him just for information.

Just as I finished talking to him, my field phone rang. It was the battalion S3. He asked if the crash was an accident or enemy fire. I told him that at this point, information from the crash site suggested that it was accidental. He said he was organizing an accident investigation team to investigate it. Three of the members would be the maintenance officer and the flight surgeon from Camp Holloway and me. He asked me to let the others know and have them ready to go at 1500. The other member would be Major Hill from the Mohawk company at Tuy Hoa. The S3 would have him meet us at Camp Holloway by 1500. He asked me to check with the air assault battalion at Camp Holloway and arrange for a helicopter to fly us to the accident site.

After we finished talking, I contacted CW-4 Berry, our maintenance officer, and Captain Griff and told them of the situation and asked them to be at my location at 1430. Then I called the S3 of the assault battalion to arrange for a helicopter.

Captain Smith, the battalion S3, wanted to help, but he had all his flyable copters committed to an air assault mission. They would not return until around 1700. He told me he did have the CO's B model if I wanted it. I would have to provide a pilot because all his pilots were flying. I thanked him and told him I would check with my pilots to see if anyone was currant in a B model and get back to him.

I was checking flight records, trying to find a pilot to fly the B model, when Major Baker burst into the operations building. "What's the status of the downed aircraft?"

I stood, greeted him, and briefed him on the situation. He seemed surprised that I had everything under control. He grabbed the FM radio handset and called Headhunter 21.

Headhunter 21 responded, "Roger, Headhunter 6. Wait one, please."

I interjected. "Sir, Headhunter 21 has asked we stay of the net until he gets rescue efforts under way."

Major Baker looked at me with a pissed look and called, "Headhunter 21, this is Headhunter 6. I want an update on the situation now!" He stressed the number six to ensure Headhunter 21 understood that it was the company commander talking.

Headhunter 21 answered with irritation in his voice and gave Major Baker the same information I had. I was amazed at how arrogantly Major Baker had acted. When Headhunter 21 finished, Major Baker told him to keep us updated every ten minutes.

Then he turned to me. "Get a hold of the assault battalion S3 and tell him we will take the B model and get it ready to go. I will fly it. As soon as Major Hill arrives, we will leave, so get everybody down to the flight line." For the second time, Major Baker put me in a position to really piss him off.

I picked up his flight records and told him, "Sir, you are not current in helicopters. I just checked your records, and the last time you flew a Huey was six months ago. You need a check ride every ninety days to be current in an aircraft." Even as I spoke, I knew my words were going to anger him. However, I was the operations officer and the safety officer. It was my duty to tell the emperor he had no pants.

Major Baker was red in the face from rage as he looked at me and spewed out, "Captain Griffin, I don't give a shit about those regulations. If I say I can fly the B model, then that's what I will do. Now, get everybody down to the flight line so we can get to the accident site!"

I was on thin ice now. As I answered, "Yes, sir," I was debating whether I had enough courage to refuse to fly with him. I knew for sure if we survived, he would court-martial me. I was still too much of a soldier to refuse. Perhaps he was good enough to fly the B model safely, but I had warned him at my expense. I got everybody down to the flight line. We walked over to the revetment holding the B model.

The crew chief met us there. He had the copter ready to go. Major Baker directed us to get aboard, and then he would move the aircraft down to the runway to wait for Major Hill. He told me to get in the copilot seat. Major Baker started the B model and let it warm up. Then he pulled pitch and lifted it up to a shaky hover. Right away, I realized that he was not proficient in the aircraft. He wobbled around and almost hit the sides of the revetment several times. Finally, he got it out of the revetment, hovered to the runway apron, and set it down. I turned and looked at the passengers and the crew chief. The crew chief looked at me with an expression on his face that asked, "Can he fly this thing?" I gave him a half-assed reassuring grin.

As we sat there waiting for Major Hill, I was having a problem controlling my fear. This flight frightened me and gave me a bad feeling. After about five minutes, a Mohawk landed and parked on the apron. Major Hill got out, and Major Baker waved at him. As he walked to the Huey and started to climb aboard, that strange sensation struck me again. It was like the time in Bad Tölz, when it had urged me to give my seat to the photographer. It was compelling me once again to give up my seat. To this day, I'm not sure whether it was fear or some other force, but I looked at Major Hill and asked, "Sir, would you like to take this seat? I'm not rated in the helicopter, and it does not matter to me."

Major Hill nodded and said, "Yes, I would like to sit copilot. It's been a long time since I've logged helicopter time." So I got out of the copilot seat, and Major Hill climbed into it. I took a seat beside the flight surgeon. Major Baker pulled pitch, and we slowly gained altitude and headed for the firebase.

The firebase was about fifty miles north of Pleiku. I was still wearing my helmet, so I plugged my cord into the service bar so I could monitor the radio traffic. Headhunter 6 contacted Headhunter 21 to let him know we were on the way. Headhunter 21 asked Headhunter 6 to pick up the infantry security at the firebase and insert them before inserting the accident investigation team. He had arranged for the security team but so far had been unable to find transport. A medevac had dropped a harness and pulled the observer out, but the pilot was still in the aircraft. The observer had confirmed the pilot was dead. Headhunter 6 gave Headhunter 21 a wilco and continued to the firebase.

It took us about thirty minutes to reach the firebase. A 105-millimeter artillery battery and an infantry company occupied the firebase. It had a medical station and several CH-47s using it as a forward base. The CH-47s were all committed and could not support the rescue effort; Headhunter 6 would have to put in the security team.

As we approached the helipad on the firebase, I could see six infantrymen with combat gear sitting on the edge of the pad. I looked at them and the seven of us in the helicopter and shuddered. There was no way this B model could lift that load. Then Major Baker told me and Captain Griff to get out and wait. He would come back for us as soon as he inserted the security team.

I felt an instant surge of relief as I exited the copter, but I looked at the infantry climbing aboard and shook my head. The copter was still overloaded. B models are so underpowered that they are only used as command ships. Plus, I knew that Major Baker was not proficient, although his control of the copter had smoothed out a little on the way to the firebase.

When the security team was aboard, Captain Griff and I watched Major Baker struggle to get airborne in the high-density altitude. He got it light on the skids and slid across the ground until he reached translational lift speed and slowly climbed out and toward the accident site. I looked at Captain Griff and expressed my concern. "The copter is overloaded. It's going to be tough for Major Baker to insert those troops."

We took a seat alongside the helipad and watched Major Baker as he flew toward the crash site, which was about ten miles away. By watching Headhunter 21, which was circling over the site, we could see the general location. When Major Baker reached the area, we could see him make several circles over the site, and then he started a descent and disappeared against the dark background of trees.

It was hot sitting on the helipad, and after about an hour, sweat soaked us, and dust covered the sweat, making us muddy. Still, Major Baker had not returned for us. We could see Headhunter 21 still circling. When another twenty minutes went by, I turned to Captain Griff. "Something is wrong. He should have returned by now."

I kept asking myself what could be taking so long; even if Major Baker had decided not to return for us, he should have recovered the pilot and been back by now. But he would not do that, because Captain Griff would have to check the pilot first. Deep in thought about what was going on, I noticed a CH-47 approaching the crash site. We watched it descend below the tree line. Ten minutes later, it rose above the trees and turned toward the firebase. As it approached, medical personnel with stretchers started running toward the helipad. Captain Griff got up, saying, "There must be injured coming in. I'm going to see if I can help."

The CH-47 landed in whirl of dust and lowered the rear ramp. The medics with stretchers rushed up the ramp and disappeared inside. Within seconds, they reappeared with soldiers lying on the stretchers. The soldier on the second stretcher rose and looked at me.

It was Major Baker. Blood covered his face. His legs were wrapped and bloody. He looked at me as if he were trying to say something, and then he lay back and disappeared as the medics carrying his stretcher rushed toward the aid station. The medics took eleven stretchers off the CH-47 before it powered up and left in a cloud of dust. I was sitting alone on the side of the flight line, thinking about the expression on Major Baker's face.

I found out later that he had tried to insert the security force, but the B model had run out of lift and settled into the trees. The crash, fortunately, killed no one. Broken bones were most of the injuries.

The crash lacerated Major Baker's face and broke both his legs. The army evacuated him back to the States, and I never saw him again. I often thought of the look he gave me. It was as if he rose up to find me. I tried to believe the expression on his face was one of pain and contrition, but knowing him, it might have been one of anger at me for being right about his currency. I am sure he was thinking about the accident investigation board, knowing I would have to testify about his qualifications and currency. In the end, the board would hold him responsible for what had taken place. Captain Griff and I caught a ride back to Camp Holloway that afternoon on the last medevac helicopter evacuating the last injured soldier to the evacuation hospital at Pleiku.

Battalion headquarters organized another accident investigation team to investigate both accidents. They did not include anyone from the company, since with the pilot of the Bird Dog, we had lost three members to the accident. A month later, we found out the crash did not kill Headhunter 23. The impact smashed his nose and knocked him out, and with his head slumped forward, he drowned in his blood. There was some bitterness toward the observer because he had jumped out of the aircraft and run away from the aircraft. He said he had run away to avoid detection by any NVA or VC coming to check the downed aircraft; however, he admitted that he did not check the condition of the pilot. He was so frightened that he panicked. Only after he calmed down and realized there were no enemy forces around did he return to the aircraft. That was when he checked on the pilot and used the radio to call on Guard frequency and report being down. By then, the pilot had choked to death on his blood. However, it is hard to blame the observer, because no one really knows how he will act in those circumstances until it happens.

Major Will became CO, and my life as operations officer improved. I was fortunate that such an unfortunate event had occurred. It probably saved my army career, because under Major Baker, I would have received a bad OER. I had to prepare a statement about my actions leading up to the crash. I never heard the official findings of the investigation, which took several weeks to complete. Other than my statement, I had no more involvement in it and turned my attention to finishing my tour in Vietnam.

Looking for more work to do, I inspected the company's portion of the perimeter that we were responsible for defending. As in Kontum, it was in disrepair, so I organized a work detail and began repair work. It took two long weeks to complete, and the whole time, I was thinking, *The last time I undertook a task such as this, we were soon under a major attack.* However, this time, nothing occurred except the occasional mortar attack.

Letters from Claudia were coming once a week. She wanted me to ask for an assignment in Germany after Vietnam, so I put in a request for an intertheater transfer, and the DA approved it. I received orders in May assigning me to the Thirty-Fourth Signal Battalion, near Ludwigsburg, Germany. Claudia was happy. Since Claudia and the kids were already there, it was much easier for us to move to Germany than to move back to the States.

Around the second week in May, Major Will asked me if I wanted to take another R&R leave. The company had plenty of quotas but no takers, so I called Darrel and asked him if he wanted to go to Hong Kong. He jumped at the chance, so I told Major Will I would take one for Hong Kong if Darrel could also go. He approved it, so Darrel and I spent six days in Hong Kong, doing nothing but eating, drinking, and seeing the sights. At night, I sat around the bar in the hotel and talked with several other married aviators. Darrel, on the other hand, was Darrel and spent his time chasing women.

My tour was almost over. I had orders to leave Vietnam on June 30 for a PCS (permanent change of station) to Germany with a report date of August 1, which gave me a thirty-day leave. I decided to take government transport to Fort Dix. From there, I planned on flying commercially to Jacksonville Beach and spending some time with my family before continuing to Germany. I felt the war had been over for me since I took the operations officer job. Other than the mortar and rocket attacks and the occasional distant sound of artillery and small-arms fire at night, my job could have been any boring army job at any location in the States.

I found flying the Beaver the only enjoyable and thrilling thing I had left. On June 28, the Second Platoon called me and asked if I could get up to Kontum. They had a package for me from the Special Forces team at Plateau GI. June 28 was my last currier flight, so I swung by Kontum and stopped by the Second Platoon operations.

The platoon had repaired the Tet Offensive damages, so it looked newer than the last time I had seen it. Captain Daniels, the platoon leader, was there when I entered the operations building. We greeted each other, and I complimented him on the work he had done in repairing the damage. We talked for a while, and he gave me the package the Special Forces team had left for me.

To my surprise, it was an M1 Garand rifle in its original wax paper wrapping. The data printed on the wrapping had the date November 1944. The note attached to the wrapping said, "Thank you, Captain Griffin, for all the support you provided us. You often spoke of wanting an M1. When we found a VC cache containing several new M1s, we thought of you. Good luck on your next assignment, and don't crash and burn somewhere." Emotion overwhelmed me. To me, this was the crowning recognition of their appreciation. No medal could equal the significance of this gift.

As I was about to leave, Darrel landed. For some reason, the army had scheduled him to leave two days later than I. He was working on changing it because we wanted to return together. "Neal, when are you leaving for Bien Hoa?" Darrel asked.

"Darrel, this Beaver is leaving at ten hundred hours tomorrow morning. If you want to go with me, be at the apron then. I'm not waiting one minute for anyone. I want to get out of this place!"

"Okay, I'll be there," he promised.

That night, they had a small farewell party for me at the officers' club. I picked out the Headhunter statue that I wanted. When I'd signed in, I'd given twenty dollars to the souvenir fund to pay for it. The company presented the statue to you when you departed. Periodically during the year, an officer would take an R&R leave to the Philippines and order the statues. The business that carved the statues would ship them to the company. The one I picked had a small nick in it from a piece of shrapnel that hit it during a mortar attack.

That night, I packed my duffel bag and wrote Claudia my last letter from Vietnam. I was ready to leave. There was a formation scheduled for 0800 in the morning. After that, I had to turn in my equipment, sign my OER, and get on the Beaver. That night, I lay in bed and replayed my year in Vietnam in my mind. I had survived a couple of tight spots thanks to God. I had done some duties well, but most importantly, I had satisfied my need to get into combat. Looking back, I found that I really did not like it. War was not the fun it had been when Bobby, Butch, and our friends played it along the big ditch. I was a soldier, and combat was what I existed for, but for now, I hoped that when I got out of it, I would never have to return to it. Compared to others, I had had an easy tour.

The next morning at the 0800 formation, Major Will surprised me when he called me to report front and center. I marched out and came to attention in front of Major Will. He presented me with the Distinguished Flying Cross First Oak Leaf Cluster. The citation read, "For heroism while participating in aerial flight during the battle for Kontum in the Tet Offensive." I was stunned—two DFCs within a year! Did I deserve them? There was no way the fear I'd felt could be described as heroism. No matter how I looked at it, I could not accept that I was heroic.

After the formation, everyone congratulated me and said good-bye. I hauled my equipment to the supply room and turned it in. I had cleaned my M16 the night before, and now, as I turned it over to the armory, I held it for a minute. It had been my constant companion for a year. I was attached to it. Of all the pilots I had talked to, I was the only one who had taken the time to zero mine.

At 1000 hours, I threw my bag into the rear of the Beaver. Darrel was nowhere in sight. CW-3 Taylor was flying with me to Bien Hoa and would fly the Beaver back to Camp Holloway. At 1005, I walked into the maintenance office and called the Second Platoon. I asked the crew chief who answered the phone if he had any idea where Darrel was. He told me he was back at the BOQ, so I called the BOQ office. They sent a runner down the Darrel's room to get him.

"Neal, you have to leave without me, my friend. They wouldn't change my orders, so I don't leave until the day after tomorrow. Take care, don't crash and burn, and I will see you somewhere sometime."

"Okay, Darrel. The same to you, buddy." I hung up the phone and returned to the Beaver. "Let's go, Chief," I said, and I climbed into the pilot's seat and flew my last flight in Vietnam.

It took about three hours to fly to Bien Hoa. Upon arrival, I reported to the replacement company, and CW-3 Taylor returned to Camp Holloway.

After signing in, I attended a debriefing session centered on the dos and don'ts of returning to the States. It was over with by 1600, and they assigned me a bunk in the officer billeting area. My plane would leave at 0730 the next day.

After dinner, I packed my bag again. This time, I left the M1 out. I wanted it desperately, but in the debriefing session, they'd warned about taking weapons back to the States. The penalty, if someone was caught, was more than I wanted to pay. The next morning, I left the M1 lying on my bunk.

At 0800 the next morning, the packed 707 lifted off the Bien Hoa runway, headed for McGuire AFB. I was on my way home. My Vietnam tour was over. Now it was time to focus on reuniting myself with my family. After my little prayer asking God for a safe trip home, I said good-bye to Vietnam.

CHAPTER 2

Back to Germany

A time for joy, a time to grieve.

Ater refueling in Anchorage, the 707 continued to McGuire AFB and landed at 0430 in the morning. After entering the terminal, I got in the line for customs. Signs posted everywhere warned against bringing unauthorized weapons and material through customs. The irony was that I could have brought back an AK-47. But the American-produced Garand M1 was banned.

Officers and enlisted men separated into different lines for customs checks. There were only about fifteen officers on the flight, so I cleared customs quickly. As I dragged my duffel bag to the counter and handed the customs officer my declaration statement, he glanced at it and waved me through. That was it. Now I was upset that I'd left my M1 on the bunk at Bien Hoa. But the risk had been too great. I would have to buy an M1 one day.

When I got to the main terminal, I headed for the snack bar. There, I ordered eggs, bacon, and grits. As I moved along the line to pay, I saw some large tomatoes. They looked delicious, so I had the server cut me three slices and add them to my plate. It had been so long since I had tasted a good tomato. That was my best breakfast in more than a year. It felt good to be back in the United States despite the warning that protesters often scorned soldiers returning from Vietnam. The army warned against wearing uniforms in public. I wore mine because I was not going to let a bunch of protesters deter me from my pride in being an American soldier.

I caught a military bus in front of the terminal, which took me across the AFB to the BOQ. After I took a shower and shaved, I called American Airlines and booked a flight to Jacksonville. The flight left at 2400, so thoroughly exhausted, I went to bed and slept until 2000. After dressing, I caught a cab to the civilian airfield. My flight left on time, and I arrived

149

in Jacksonville around 0400. I had to wait for a bus going to Jacksonville Beach. I finally got to the bus station in Jacksonville Beach at 0730.

Jacksonville Beach had not changed much since I'd last visited. It still had the feel of the place I grew up in but not the feel of home. My home was where Claudia and the kids were. The Beach was just a place where my family and friends lived. I decided I would call Mom to see if there was someone there who could pick me up. My call surprised everyone, and ten minutes later, my brother arrived and drove me to Mom's house.

It was good to see my family again. I was the son who had been to war and had come home. Though they were happy to see me, it disappointed them that I was only going to stay one night. Mom got upset when I told her I was going back to Germany for another tour. I think she thought that one day I would be there permanently to care for her. She still had not accepted that I had a family and had dedicated my life to them and not her. She did not understand how eager I was to get to Claudia and the kids.

Mom fixed me a big breakfast of sausage, grits, and eggs. While I ate, we caught up on each other's lives. After an hour, Bill left to go to work. Mary and Buddy stopped by later in the morning. Laura was teaching in Jacksonville and was coming by after school. Grace was in school in Jacksonville, and I did not get to see her.

Dad, to my surprise, was sober. He was still trying to work, but his lifestyle had destroyed his health. He worked enough for Mom and him to get by; they were trying to hold on until he could start drawing social security. That afternoon, we sat in the kitchen and talked. He asked me about what it was like to be in combat, but I did not have a good answer for him. My only taste of ground combat had been at Kontum during the Tet attack.

He wanted to know if I had been afraid. I thought for a while and said, "Yes, Dad, I was afraid, but performing your duty distracts you from your fear. So you function the way the army trained you and hold the fear down in the pit of your stomach so it does not harm you."

He nodded as if agreeing with me. Then he put his hand on my shoulder and said, "Son, you have done and experienced everything I ever dreamed of doing. I'm proud of you."

For a moment, I saw sadness in his eyes. They lost focus on the present, as if his mind were back in time. Then they cleared and became a bit shiny and moist. I knew that my father had tried to join the army in World War II, but the army had rejected him because he worked in the Jacksonville shipyard, and they considered his job essential to the war effort. When I joined the army, I remember how serious he was when he told me to serve half the time as an enlisted man and then become an officer. Had circumstances deprived him of his dream of serving in the military and going to war? Could that somehow have led to his descent into alcoholism? I would never know the answer to that question; I only know that that moment was the closest I had ever been with my father. From that day on, his drinking did not bother me.

I also realized that I knew little about my father. That realization made me decide that one day I would write the story of my life. I would leave a journal of my life in the military for members of my family who were interested in knowing who I was and what I did. More importantly, I wanted them to know what my thoughts were and what I believed. I wanted them to know how I got to be the person they knew.

Saying good-bye is always difficult. When the taxi arrived to take me to the bus station, I could see the hurt in their eyes and feel it in their voices over my leaving so soon. But I was eager to press on and get to Germany. I promised that when I returned from Germany, Claudia and I would spend a week visiting everybody.

I spent the rest of the day and all night traveling. By noon the next day, I was back in the terminal at McGuire AFB. There, I showed the operations NCO my orders, and he booked me on a military flight leaving that night to Germany.

I was in the Frankfurt terminal, booking a Lufthansa flight to Munich, at 1330 the next day. I caught the flight leaving at 1430 and was in Munich by 1530. I gave the taxi driver the address of Claudia's apartment and sat back to enjoy the ride and the joy of knowing I was just minutes away from seeing my family again.

Claudia first had stayed with her mother in Munich after she left Fort Benning and returned to Germany, but her mother's one-bedroom apartment in downtown Munich quickly had become too small for two kids and two adults, so Claudia had found a little one-room apartment a block from the Isar River and close to McGraw Casern. It also was close to the army school that Michele attended. An army bus picked her up each morning and brought her home after school.

I had written to Claudia that I would be there today but did not know exactly what time, though I was sure it would be in the afternoon. It turned out to be a thirty-five-minute drive from the airport. When the taxi pulled up in front of the apartment building, I could see Michele and Ron standing on a little second-story balcony overlooking the street. When I got out of the cab, I could hear them yelling, "Mama, Daddy is here!"

As I paid the cab driver, the door to the apartment building flew open, and Michele and Ron came running out to hug me. By now, Claudia was standing on the balcony, waving. She was stunning. We were together again as a family.

The apartment was a large room with a kitchen area and a sleeping area that also served as a living room. It was okay for Claudia, Michele, and Ron but did not afford privacy for intimate relations.

Mom was there with Claudia's cousin Traudl to greet me. We had coffee and some good German cake while we got reacquainted. Then Mom and Traudl took Michele and Ron to a movie to allow Claudia and me some time together. Our love was wild and passionate. It made me eager to get into quarters and regain our privacy.

I knew I loved Claudia beyond all else. I would never be capable of loving another woman as long as Claudia lived. This frightened me because I was at her mercy. If she did not feel the same about me, I was in for a lot of hurt.

For the first couple of days, I took it easy and caught up on the interests and problems of Michele and Ron. After Michele left for school, I would take Ron down to the Isar to feed the ducks. Then we would play games until Michele joined us when she got home. While I did this, Claudia would clean the apartment and then visit her mom or Traudl.

Claudia and Traudl were close, and they spent a great deal of time together. Traudl's husband was a fireman for the city of Munich and spent considerable time at work, which left Traudl alone a lot with their young son, who was about the age of Ron.

As the days passed, I noticed a slight change in Claudia. The bliss we'd felt in Bangkok was gone. She would get angry with me for the smallest reason. It was as if I were intruding into her life. I had known it would take some time to readjust to each other, but I had not expected this new attitude. She wanted to continue the lifestyle she'd lived while I was gone, wherein she and Traudl would go out occasionally in the evenings for drinks. Though I was okay with that, I felt that she should be going out with me now. She disagreed, and of course, that would cause an argument.

Sometimes I got the feeling she wished she were single. It looked to me as though she were trying to live the lifestyle that marrying so young had deprived her of. I did not think she was being unfaithful to me, but I could tell that during all the separations we had experienced since I'd left for OCS in December 1964, she had grown apart from me. During the last three years and eight months, duty had separated us for two years and ten months. Obviously out of loneliness, she had started going out and having fun, as young and beautiful single women would want to do. I hoped she was careful not to cross the line. Now that I was back, although I believed she loved me, she did not want to end the lifestyle she had been enjoying while we were apart.

This attitude had a terrible effect on me. I loved her dearly and could not understand why, if she loved me, she wanted to continue this practice. If she did not love me, why did she want to stay married? It was not the homecoming for which I had yearned. There was no denying the rift between us. However, we were husband and wife, and I had the responsibility of supporting my family. I hoped that in time, she would turn back to the wife I once knew and trusted. Thus was our frame of mind as we resumed life together. I did not know that it was only the beginning.

With some excitement and anger, we started preparations for our move to my assignment as the aviation officer for Thirty-Fourth Signal Battalion in Ludwigsburg. To get quarters, I had to sign in so that I was officially in Germany for duty. A week after my return, Claudia and I drove to Ludwigsburg so I could do this. When we arrived at the casern, I went to the battalion S1 office and signed in, and then he put me back on leave for the rest of my thirty days.

While I waited for the clerk to type my leave, LTC Kirk, the battalion commander, came out and welcomed me to the battalion. He told me I would be replacing Captain Brede, who was leaving in two months. My office was in Carly Barracks, also the home of Fifth Corps headquarters. The Thirty-Fourth Signal Battalion provided communications support to

Fifth Corps. The aviation section provided aviation support for the corps' administrative needs.

I found out the aviation section's aircraft and equipment were located at Stuttgart Airfield, about forty kilometers from Ludwigsburg. LTC Kirk recommended I get quarters at the Echterdingen housing area, which was five kilometers from the airfield and six kilometers from Carly Barracks. I thanked him, and he left, wishing me good luck. From there, Claudia and I drove to the Echterdingen housing area and found the housing office. We were in luck: there was a three-bedroom apartment available.

The apartment, located on the second floor, was in the center stairwell of a large apartment building. There were three stairwells and eighteen apartments. We entered the apartment and liked it immediately. The apartment was large and came well appointed. We drove back to the housing office and told the clerk we would take it. We returned with the housing clerk, inventoried all the furniture in the apartment, and signed for it. When we'd completed that process, the apartment belonged to us. We had a late lunch at the officers' club in the housing area and began the three-hour drive back to Munich.

During the drive back, our conversation centered on the tasks we needed to do to move. Claudia seemed happy and enthusiastic over moving into our new home, and that raised my spirits enormously. We kept this mood during the move with only a minor spat or two.

By the time my leave was up, we were in our new apartment and comfortable. Michele was happy because she had a bedroom of her own. She still had to catch a bus to school, but the bus stop was at the end of the building, which was convenient. We had our personal belongings, which we'd put in storage while I was in Vietnam, sent to our new address. The transportation office said they would arrive in about two weeks. Now it was time for me to go back to work.

The aviation section was part of headquarters and the headquarters company, so I signed in at the headquarters company's orderly room. I met the company commander and first sergeant and then went over to battalion headquarters and met the staff. Captain Brede met me there, and I followed him to Carly Barracks and our office. There, he briefed me on the aviation section, corps support roles, and my duties. After about two hours, we drove to Stuttgart Airfield to meet the men in the aviation section.

The aviation section occupied a large hangar and apron area across the runway from the civilian side of the airfield. The section had three CH-34s, two OH-13s, and one Beaver assigned to it. Personnel assigned to fly and maintain the aircraft and section equipment consisted of four warrant officers, two captains (me and Captain Brown), a section sergeant, and thirty-two enlisted men. The section equipment included two fuel tankers and three two-and-a-half-ton trucks to haul our maintenance equipment, supplies, and personnel. The enlisted men lived in barracks at Carly Barracks. Officers' quarters were in Echterdingen.

Captain Brede introduced me to everyone and showed me around the hangar. As I met and talked with everyone, I wondered why Captain Brede had located himself across town in Carly Barracks. I saved that question for later, when we were alone, but I decided then that when I took over the section, I was moving to the hangar unless there was some compelling reason not to. In my book, the leader had to be where his men were in order to lead.

Back at the Carly Barracks office, I asked Captain Brede why the office was there and not at the airfield. He explained that he felt our presence there improved our status because the corps staff had easy access to the section leader. I dropped the subject then because I wanted to learn more about our relations with the corps staff.

Captain Brede left midafternoon with instructions for me to read all the corps regulations and the aviation section SOP. Sitting alone in that big office, I started reading the stack of regulations. After an hour, I was praying the phone would ring and assure me that I was not alone in the world. It did ring about thirty minutes later, and it was Captain Brede on the other end, telling me he would not be returning today and would see me in the morning. I read regulations until 1700, locked the door, and went home. It was an understatement to say that my first day at work had not excited me about my assignment. So far, it was too much like my last job in Vietnam.

At home, Claudia had dinner ready. During dinner, everybody had something to tell about his or her day. Our family routine had begun. I came home from work, we ate, Michele did her homework, and I played with Ron. When Michele finished her homework, we might play a game until it was time for them to go to bed. I would read a story to them and say good night and then join Claudia to watch German TV.

On the first weekend, we drove around Stuttgart and the surrounding area, sightseeing and learning the area. We shopped at the commissary and PX. Claudia wanted Mom to see the apartment, so on Sunday, she drove to Munich to pick Mom up, while I watched Michele and Ron. The two of them returned around 2200. It was good having Mom around, because she loved the kids and always wanted to babysit.

I was eager to start flying again, but first, I would have to get current in the Beaver since it was the only aircraft in the section I could fly. I also had to renew my instruments ticket. It had expired while I was in Vietnam. I'd had no need for one there, since we flew all recon flights under VFR. The weather in Germany demanded a current instrument ticket, and the Beaver was the only plane in which I could renew my instrument rating.

Fortunately, USAREUR ran an aviator standardization school in Augsburg. The army sent new aviators there to get current in their assigned aircraft and renew their instrument tickets. Captain Brede had already scheduled me to go the following week to the course for the Beaver. It was a one-week course and a perfect opportunity for Claudia and me to spend time together and get to know each other again. Claudia was all for going with me, and Mom was happy to take care of the kids.

We drove to Augsburg and checked into a guest BOQ. Claudia waited at the BOQ while I found the aviation transition office. I signed in and picked up my class material and flying schedule for the next four days. We spent the rest of the day touring Augsburg. That evening, we had dinner at the officers' club and went to a movie. Back in the BOQ, we made love, and I felt the happiest I had in a long time.

My first class was at 0800, so we got up early and had breakfast at the officers' club. When we returned to the BOQ, I got ready to go to class and asked, "What are you going to do until this evening?"

She looked at me and answered, "I'm going to Munich, Neal. I'm going to stay with Traudl until Friday. I'll be back here Friday afternoon to get you."

I am not sure how she expected me to take that. I had expected to be spending time together. Angrily, I replied, "Claudia, we just spent a year apart. Now you are going to leave me here for four days so you can see Traudl, whom you have spent the last nine months seeing?"

She was also angry now and came back at me. "What do you expect me to do all day while you are training? Sit in this room?"

"No. Why don't you drive to Munich, spend the day with Traudl, and come back in the evenings? It's only an hour drive."

We were arguing now. I did not want to argue, and I had no time to. She said, "You know Traudl works during the day."

I was mad and hurt. I did not understand why Claudia did not want to spend time with me as much as I wanted to be with her. I thought, *Damn, I'm losing her—or I have already lost her.* I was in a lose-lose situation. I could insist she stay, and she probably would, but she would be angry and bitter, which would spoil our being together. "Look," I said angrily, "I don't know why you did not stay home to begin with if you had no plans of staying with me. Dammit, go to Munich. Stay there. I don't care. Just be back to get me on Friday." I turned and stormed out the door.

There was a pain in my stomach as I walked across the casern to my classroom. I had to rid my mind of this hurt and frustration; it would be hard enough to deal with the stress the transition course would cause me, and on top of it, I would have to deal with marriage problems. I felt the same despair I had felt when I was sixteen and my drunken father fought with my mother. All I could do was shake my head in disbelief and pray for the strength and wisdom to make a better life someday.

Then, as always, when it came to Claudia, I would start making excuses for her actions. It was a little unrealistic to expect her to sit in the BOQ and wait for me, but we could have settled that before she came. Did she only come this far to go out with Traudl? I once asked her where they went, and she told me they went to a bar in a hotel for drinks. I could understand that while I was away but not with me there.

The day was long and difficult. I had to fight back thoughts of Claudia and what she might be doing that night while I concentrated on the training. In the first two hours of class, the instructor covered USAREUR flight regulations and flying in the DMZ. After that, an instructor gave a class on instrument flying in Germany and reviewed flying under instrument conditions. Then we broke for lunch.

There were eight of us in the class. Six were there for helicopters, and another captain and I were there for fixed-wing. We went to the officers' club for lunch, and though the food was great, I was careful not to eat too much, as I always suffered from sleepiness after eating a large lunch. While I engaged in conversation, my mind kept slipping back to Claudia.

A bus picked us up at the officers' club and transported us to the flight line. We entered one of the hangars and went to a briefing room that would serve as our flight line classroom. There, my classmate and I met CW-4 Turner, our SIP (standardization instructor pilot) in the Beaver. After introductions and a short briefing on what we would do during the next four days, he led us to the Beaver sitting on the apron. He spent an hour discussing the operating systems and details of the aircraft. When he finished, we conducted a preflight, and he told me to climb into the pilot's seat. I would fly for the first two hours. The other captain would fly the next two, and we would rotate after that.

I was a little rusty as I moved through the start-up checklist, but when the big radial engine roared to life, I started feeling a little more confident. I always had a problem with nervousness when flying with an instructor pilot. I hated the idea of making a stupid mistake that would embarrass me and cause the instructor to question my piloting skills. But I also had a habit of working hard to perfect newly learned skills. That had been the case in Vietnam, and now my effort was paying off, as my competence in the Beaver quickly returned.

The first two flying hours were designed to regain competence in takeoffs and landings. Within the first hour, I was doing perfect takeoffs and landings despite any emergency the instructor put me in. Satisfied that I could fly the aircraft, he pulled out the hood and started my instrument training.

I had no experience flying the Beaver under the hood to stimulate instrument conditions. I was all over the sky as I adjusted to controlling the Beaver strictly by what my instruments were telling me. CW-4 Turner would give me a heading and altitude to maintain using only the instruments. As I turned to the new heading and climbed or descended to the assigned altitude, I realized how much instrument flying skill I had lost during my year in Vietnam. While the Beaver was a stable aircraft, it was not as stable as the two-engine Beechcraft Baron in which I had learned instrument flying.

The first hour under the hood was a struggle. I had difficulty focusing on what the instruments were telling me and ignoring the sensations my body was giving me. The key to instrument flight is trusting in your instruments and not your body. The more the Beaver bounced in the turbulent air, the more the sensations that I felt differed from what my instruments were telling me. The hour under the hood exhausted me. I was wet with sweat when the hour was over, but toward the end of the session, I started to control the aircraft satisfactorily.

After we landed and taxied back to the apron, CW-4 Turner critiqued me on my flight while the maintenance crew refueled the Beaver for the other captain's flight. He pointed out some rough areas I had to work on, but my progress satisfied him overall. He released me for the rest of the day and told me to be back at 1000 in the morning. I would fly second then. He also directed me to study ADF approaches and tracking procedures before tomorrow's flight.

I grabbed my flight bag and caught the bus back to the BOQ. On the way back, I kept hoping Claudia had changed her mind and would be at the BOQ, waiting for me, but she wasn't there. I felt a new surge of anger. As I took a hot shower to wash away the stress I was feeling, I thought about how I would have acted if she had been there.

I realized her presence would not have made things better. I was too angry and hurt at her for not wanting to stay with me, and I would have ignored her just to show her that I did not care. We would have sat there not speaking to each other, because she would have been angry and blamed me for making her come back. My anger and hurt would last for days, and I would not speak to her until it faded. This was the usual course of our fights: we'd ignore each other until we slowly came back from the mental isolation in which we took refuge. She would not apologize for her actions, nor I for mine. We would just pretend they had not happened until the next fight.

The next three days were grueling. I dealt with the worry and hurt of what Claudia was doing while I struggled to master instrument flight in the Beaver. The biggest problem was the ADF system. It was an old navigational system and much harder to fly than VOR. The ADF approach, although simple in theory, was hard to fly. The instrument landing system (ILS), VHF omnidirectional range radio (VOR), and ground-controlled approach (GCA), which I'd learned in flight school, were much easier. But by Friday afternoon, I took my check ride and instrument certification ride in the Beaver and passed without problems. My performance pleased me; I could achieve success in the face of personal obstacles. However, it saddened me that I was the only one who cared. There was no one to make me feel appreciated for my accomplishments; there was no one other than me to say simply, "Good job, Neal."

Each day, I would rush back to the BOQ, hoping Claudia would be there waiting for me. When she was not, despair and bitterness would swell up in me. I tormented myself over why she would treat me this way when I loved her so deeply. I did not want to accept the idea that she was being unfaithful to me. However, something was affecting her. I just could not recognize what.

Between our fights, we had great days and nights together. We had fun, and the sex was wonderful. We never had arguments over money or any of the typical issues that cause major problems between married couples. Claudia's falling asleep while watching TV was the issue that triggered most of our fights. This would anger me because I saw it as her attempt to avoid sex. I would respond in a childish manner, which would anger her, and we would start another period of being mad at each other. However, I could not believe this would cause her to become unfaithful.

Friday afternoon, after everybody had completed his check ride, the OIC of the transition course had a final meeting. He congratulated us and wished us well. After that, we headed to the officers' club to celebrate our completion of the course. Now we were qualified in our assigned aircraft and cleared to fly in German airspace. After a couple of beers, I said good-bye and headed for the BOQ. I was eager to see if Claudia was there and, at the same time, dreaded the meeting if she were.

As I neared the BOQ, I spotted our VW sitting in the parking area. She was there! Walking up the stairs to my room, I tried to think of the right words to say. I was glad she was back but still angry that she had left me. It was not purely anger I felt; it was more the heartbreaking sensation of finding that the person you love the most does not feel the same about you.

When I entered the room, she was sitting in the lounge chair, reading a magazine. She looked at me and, in a terse voice, said, "Hi!"

I did not look at her as I set my flight bag down by the closet door and said in a disgusted tone, "Thanks for coming back to get me."

Defensively and in a firm voice, she replied, "I told you I would be back today. You don't have to act as if I were going to leave you here."

My heart was breaking. She was so beautiful. All I wanted to do was take her in my arms and hold her, but the anger that I had held all week wanted out. In a slurred voice of resolve, I said, "I'm surprised you did come back. I guess in the future, I know what to expect. If there's a choice of running around with Traudl or being with me, Traudl wins. So I guess I shouldn't put myself in such a position ever again."

She was fighting to hold her anger. "Neal, let's not fight. I'm hungry. Can we go get something to eat?"

She was pulling the teeth out of my anger. I sensed that she knew my devotion to her, and that was her strength. If she did not get mad, my need for her would eventually defuse my anger, and I would fall back under her spell. It always worked. My attraction to her was so strong that I allowed her abuse for the little bit of love that she would give me. Years later, I would understand that my behavior was characteristic of the children of alcoholics.

With a deep sigh, I exhaled the rest of my venom and answered, "I'm hungry too. Let me take a quick shower, and we'll go." That was it. I suppressed the pent-up anger and frustration and put on a friendly face. This was to become a major problem in the future. The pressure of keeping so much contained anger and frustration built up in me would eventually change me into a man I did not want to be.

We had dinner at the officers' club and sat at the bar for a while. When we returned to the BOQ, it was as if nothing unpleasant between us had happened. In bed, she was in my arms, and I felt good again.

I was happy to be back at work. Captain Brede was leaving and stayed gone from the office most of the time. Officially, he was clearing and finishing OERs. Unfortunately, before I officially took charge of the flight section, he had been my boss for ninety days and had to write an OER on my work.

It was my worst officer efficiency report. He felt that I was not aggressive enough in seeking out flight missions from corps headquarters, yet he stressed to me each day not to bother corps headquarters. They had complained about too many non-corps-level calls tying up the communications system. So my job for the ninety days he rated me on amounted to sitting in the office, waiting for the phone to ring, and flying the courier mission once a week—not much meat for captain-level work. Each time I wanted to take the initiative, he stifled it. He was leaving and did not want to make any changes.

The day after I officially became the aviation section chief, I let Major Davy, the battalion S3, know that I was moving my office into the hangar at the airfield. He agreed and commented that he did not understand why Captain Brede had not done so. While I was packing up the office records, Captain Brede stopped by to show me my OER.

It was clearly just an average OER. I looked at him as I signed it and said, "You know, I couldn't do more because you restrained me from any actions other than sitting at this desk and answering the phone. I should have been at the airfield, supervising the work there. Now you give me a poor OER for doing what you told me to do, so obviously, I will never think highly of you as a leader since my OER is also a rating of you."

Captain Brede looked shocked at what I'd said. He looked lost for words and finally said, "Well, it's just for a ninety-day period. I'm sure if it had been a longer period, it would have been better." He took the signed copy and left. By evening, I had completed my move into my office in the rear of our hangar. My soldiers seemed happy that I moved my office. I became someone who did not come to the hangar only to address a problem or to fly.

Now, not tethered to a phone, I had more time to manage the section. One of my first actions was to rewrite the section SOP. Captain Brede never spent time inspecting the aircraft or vehicles or reviewing the logbook and maintenance records. I changed the SOP to make a compulsory weekly inspection of one vehicle and one aircraft and associated records. At the end of a cycle, the crew chief and driver with the best aircraft or truck and records received a three-day pass. In addition, I would inspect the barracks each Saturday morning, which required a GI party on Friday night to prepare for it. There was some grumbling about the Saturday morning inspections, but that soon ended.

I managed to instill my philosophy of completing all maintenance immediately and keeping maintenance records always current. I explained that if we did that, we would have the best aircraft in USAREUR and would be ready for any command inspection on a moment's notice. By doing our work every day, we would never have to work day and night before a command maintenance inspection (CMI) to prepare for it. My being at the hangar ensured that happened.

One of our standing missions was the courier flight each Tuesday and Thursday. We picked up correspondence and other freight from the V Corps distribution office and delivered it to major commands at Heilbronn, Fulda, Nurnberg, Regensburg, and Grafenwoehr. We brought back correspondence and materiel from those commands to V Corps. The flight, depending on the weather, took around four to five hours in the CH-34 and about four hours in the Beaver. I always flew one of the days to get my flight time in.

During training exercises in which the Thirty-Fourth Signal Battalion was in the field, we flew supplies and personnel from site to site for battalion elements. We used the OH-13s to provide general transport and fly commanders and staff on reconnaissance missions.

The month after I took command of the aviation section, three of my pilots left. That left CW-2 Opie, Captain Jones, and me to fly our missions. Fortunately, two weeks later, I received two new warrants to replace the ones I'd lost. CW-1s Roy and Quito were right out of flight school and disappointed that they had not gone to Vietnam.

I managed to get them into the USAREUR CH-34 transition course within a week of their arrival. The course was six weeks and necessary for them to fly the CH-34. It also provided them with instrument training in the CH-34 and awarded them an instrument ticket if they passed the instrument check ride.

CW-1 Quito was a handsome young man and a coordinated and skilled pilot. After he'd been gone for six weeks, the phone rang. It was CW-1 Quito. He was excited as he spoke to me. "Captain Griffin, I completed the transition course today and got my instrument ticket."

I told him, "Congratulations, Mr. Quito. Did Mr. Roy complete it successfully?"

"Yes, sir, but the reason I'm calling is my flying impressed the CO of the transition team. He told me he would put me through the instructor pilot course if you approved it."

I thought for a while before I answered. "No, Mr. Quito. I don't think you have enough experience to become an instructor pilot. You have never flown a mission other than in a training environment. There's more to being an instructor pilot than flying the aircraft. When you get a couple hundred hours of flying missions under your belt, I will send you to the instructor pilot course."

That did not sit well with him. He said, "Well, I don't understand. The instructor pilots here think I am well qualified to be an instructor pilot."

I was firm. "Mr. Quito, I am not going to argue about this. My answer is no. Have one of the instructors give me a call."

I hung up and waited for a call. About five minutes later, the phone rang. It was a CW-4 Johnson on the line. "Captain Griffin, this is CW-4 Johnson. Mr. Quito asked me to call you about attending instructor pilot training in the CH-34. He is one of the best pilots I've seen in a while. We have an opening in the instructor pilot course starting Monday. It would be convenient for him to attend it. But of course, we need your permission to cut the orders."

"Chief, like I told him, I don't think he's ready to be an instructor pilot. I don't believe he is mature enough. He has never flown a mission in any aircraft other than training in a school environment. You know an instructor pilot has to be more than just an expert on the aircraft. Imagine him giving an experienced captain a check ride. What conditions would he be able to judge the captain against? How would the captain feel knowing a junior pilot with no operational experience was rating his ability to fly the aircraft? I told Mr. Quito that when he got a couple hundred hours of operational time, I would send him to instructor pilot training."

"I understand your point, Captain Griffin. We didn't know that his only flying experience was training. Most helicopter pilots go directly to Vietnam from flight school. We didn't realize that he had come to USAREUR for his first assignment."

Needless to say, Mr. Quito's attitude was not the best after that. He had the idea that his only job was flying, and I had killed a great opportunity to do that job. When I assigned him the extra duty of supply officer, he was resentful. He'd thought flying would be his only duty, so he took the supply officer duties lightly. I explained to him that keeping six aircraft and eight trucks with trailers in running condition demanded an efficient supply system. It was his responsibility to make it work, and half of his OER would reflect how well he'd performed as supply officer. It took me several inspections and counseling sessions to convince him to take the supply officer duty seriously.

His first courier mission as the aircraft commander justified my concern about his lack of operational experience. It happened about a month after he and Mr. Roy returned from the transition course. I had them fly as copilot with CW-3 Opie for six missions to learn the route and procedures. I asked Mr. Opie if he thought they were ready to handle the mission as the aircraft commander. He said he thought so.

For the next mission, I assigned Mr. Quito as aircraft commander and Mr. Roy as copilot. Mr. Quito was excited about being aircraft commander. Before they left, I had them brief me on their plan. It sounded good, so I released them.

All day, the crew chief, Jim, and I waited for their return. When 1600 came and passed, I began to worry a little. Their ETA was 1600. At 1630, the phone rang. It was Mr. Quito. My heart almost stopped beating.

"Where the hell are you?" I asked.

Mr. Quito hesitantly answered, "Sir, we're lost."

Relieved that they were okay and pissed at them for getting lost on a simple flight, I asked, "Okay, what airfield are you at?" I automatically assumed they were at an airfield.

I could tell Mr. Quito did not want to have this conversation. "Sir, we are not at an airfield. We were running low on fuel, so I landed at a road intersection near a gasthaus. I'm calling from the gasthaus."

I wanted badly to chew his ass out, but I could tell he was upset, so I remained calm. "Okay, Mr. Quito, ask the people at the gasthaus the name of their town."

I waited while he found out what town they were near. I motioned for Mr. Opie to get our map and bring it to the desk. Outside, it was starting to get dark.

"Sir, we are in Eswanger."

"Okay, wait until I find you on the map." Mr. Opie and I scanned the map until we finally found the little town of Eswanger. I asked Mr. Opie to get me an azimuth from Eswanger to Stuttgart.

He set the compass on the map and reported, "Sir, it's two hundred ninety degrees, and they are about sixty-five kilometers from Stuttgart."

I thanked him. I had to get them airborne as soon as possible. It would be dark in a few minutes. I was not sure about Mr. Quito's night flying ability since we normally did not fly night missions. "Okay, Mr. Quito, what's the weather at your location?"

"Sir, it's partially cloudy with about ten miles' visibility."

"How much fuel do you have left?"

"Sir, we are down to a quarter tank."

"Okay, Mr. Quito, this is what I want you to do. Climb out of there on a heading of two hundred sixty. Climb to four thousand feet, and maintain the heading of two hundred sixty degrees and four thousand feet. You need the four thousand feet to clear the Stuttgart mountains safely. You won't be able to see Stuttgart until you are over the mountains. If you can't maintain four thousand feet, you are going to have to contact Stuttgart approach and asked for a GCA into the airfield. It's about a twenty-five-minute flight from your location. You should have enough fuel but not enough to get lost again. Call me on the FM radio when you have Stuttgart in sight. Once you get Stuttgart in sight, it's just standard procedures. You got any questions?"

"No, sir," he answered in a dejected tone.

"Then get going!"

Now it was a waiting game. My decision to deny Mr. Quito the instructor pilot training had been correct. Maybe after this, he would understand my concern about him being an instructor pilot. Forty minutes after I hung up, the FM radio blurted out, "Flight section operations, this is CH-34 Flight 41. We are over the Stuttgart mountains and have airfield in sight. We should be landing in about six minutes. Over."

Mr. Opie picked up the mike. "Roger, Flight 41. It's about time." We both looked at each in relief. Our young birds were home. Of course, we had some choice words for them or at least for Mr. Quito. He was the aircraft commander and responsible for the flight.

They landed and taxied the CH-34 into its position on the apron. As Mr. Opie and the crew chief left to guide them in, I told Mr. Opie to tell Mr. Roy to come see me while Mr. Quito completed the logbook.

I watched Mr. Roy walk across the apron toward my office. He looked a little upset and unsure as to how much trouble he was in. He knocked on the door, and when I told him to enter, he saluted and reported. I left him standing at attention to emphasize how serious I was about this incident. "Okay, what the hell happened? How on earth did you two manage to get lost in daylight?"

He responded with the neutral "Sir, there was no excuse."

His expression made it clear that he did not want to explain what had happened. He was a good soldier and was willing to share the blame for what had happened. "Mr. Roy, no excuse is not an answer. Who was flying the aircraft?"

He answered, "I was, sir."

I'd suspected that. "Who was doing the navigation?"

"It was Mr. Quito, sir."

"How did both of you miss the en route checkpoint?"

Mr. Roy was obviously uncomfortable. "Sir, we had a difference of opinion about our location."

"Okay, Mr. Roy, you are dismissed. I'm glad you guys made it back safely. Make sure you take away a lesson from this experience."

I could hear the sigh of relief in his voice as he saluted with a "Yes, sir" and left. I had the answer to what had happened, and I did not have to put Mr. Roy in a bad position. If there is a difference of opinion about location, the AC decides.

Mr. Quito knocked on the door, and when I told him to enter, he saluted and reported.

I returned his salute and asked, "What happened, Mr. Quito?"

He looked a little shaken as he answered. "Sir, I made a mistake and got us lost. It was not Mr. Roy's fault. Had I listened to him, we would have been right on schedule."

His absolving Mr. Roy raised my respect for him. His admission was as I'd expected. "Mr. Quito, I hope you learned a couple of lessons from today. One, had I approved your instructor pilot training, you would have lost all creditability by this screwup. This is what I meant by your not having enough experience to be an instructor pilot. Once you realized that you were lost, you had no idea what action to take other than to land. No one expects an instructor pilot to get lost. They expect him to handle any problem, not just one with the aircraft. You had all the instruments in the aircraft to locate yourself. Why didn't you use them?"

"Well, sir, we turned on the VOR but could not receive the Stuttgart VOR."

I interrupted him. "What was you altitude?"

"Fifteen hundred feet AGL," he answered.

"How high are the Stuttgart mountains?" I asked.

His face reddened as he answered. "Three thousand feet, sir."

"You told me the weather at your position was partly cloudy with a visibility of ten miles. Why didn't you climb until you could pick up the Stuttgart VOR? Fifteen hundred feet was too low. These are actions you learn by gaining experience, Mr. Quito. Both you and Mr. Roy are inexperienced, but I had you fly several missions with Mr. Opie to gain enough experience to fly the courier mission. In Vietnam, that's about the exposure you get before they make you AC and you fly combat missions. You still have a lot to learn, and I expect you to start learning it. Any questions?"

He looked relieved that I was just talking to him and not chewing him out. "No, sir," he answered.

"Okay. I don't expect you to get lost again. But if you do, I expect you to take the proper actions to find yourself. Landing is not a proper action unless you have an emergency or circumstances are beyond your ability to handle. If you have no questions, that's all I have."

Mr. Quito's attitude and performance improved after that incident. He became part of the team effort, and I began to trust him more with each mission.

That was my tour in the Thirty-Fourth Signal Battalion as the aviation officer. One day could be indistinguishable from the next day. Mostly, it was just another day at the hangar. My insistence on high standards of work each day resulted in fewer supply and maintenance problems. I settled into a weekly routine at work. At home, I had a different problem.

Claudia and I had settled into what I would call a loving but tense relationship. We attended numerous parties and events because of the social duties that came with being an officer. At these functions, Claudia met other German wives and made several friends. We had fun and enjoyed ourselves during these events. I think we were like most of the other couples there. We dealt with the pressures of military life during a time of war.

If there were no parties or coffees to attend, Claudia and I would go to one of the several nightclubs in Stuttgart. We often met other couples at a club and spent the evening dancing and having fun, but always, just below the surface, I could see that Claudia was changing. I loved being with her and paid no attention to any other person while I was out with her.

She had a different attitude. She was a beauty and invariably drew the attention of other men in the club. They would ask her to dance, which she did. That never bothered me. What did bother me was when they flirted with her, and she flirted back. Many times, I could see them watching her and smiling at her. She would look at them and smile back. Finally, one night, I asked her why she wanted to flirt with other men.

Her answer hurt. She looked at me defiantly and said, "It makes me feel good when other men look at me and find me attractive. I feel young again."

A little shocked, I said, "Do you care that it hurts me when you do that? Don't you believe that since you are married, you shouldn't be doing that?"

I could see the anger in her eyes, and just like that, peace would turn into a fight with her retort. "Neal, you are just jealous. Why don't you flirt with other women if you are so concerned about me?"

That response always hurt me more than anything else. She did not understand that I did not want to flirt with other women. I loved her, and she was all I wanted. In her dismissal, I was the one with the problem. I am sure I was not smothering her in any way. I was not trying to control her. On the contrary, I encouraged her involvement in clubs and social activities.

I had an idea about how married couples related to each other. Unfortunately, I based it on the only example I had of a happy family. My mother and father were no example. I honestly believed the shows *Leave It to Beaver* and *The Nelson Family* portrayed the true example of how married couples should act within a family. I expected and worked for that example of a marriage, but Claudia was on a different wavelength and expected something different. Slowly, I was becoming even more convinced that Claudia had changed. It was hard to tell if she loved me or felt she was stuck in our marriage.

Many times during our frequent arguments, I accused her of not loving me. I would cite examples of what I believed were proof of that fact. Then I would ask, "If you don't love me and don't want to remain married, why don't we get a divorce?"

Her answer was always "You know I am Catholic and can't get a divorce."

That never answered my question, and it left me frustrated. I did not want a divorce, but neither did I want to have all these arguments. I did not want her hurting me the way she did. I was concerned that one day, she would cross the line. I did not want a wife I could not trust.

What did not make sense was how well we got along about half the time. During each good period, I would start to believe that everything was going to be okay, and then Claudia would decide that she wanted to spend the weekend in Munich without me. I believed she wanted it that way, because she always planned the trip when she knew I couldn't get away because of duty. This action would start the angry cycle again.

Fortunately, I was better at being an officer and aviator than I was at being a husband. Friday morning the week before Thanksgiving, Major Davy called and wanted to know if I could fly three new captains to Bremerhaven so they could pick up their cars. If I flew them there on Saturday morning, they would be back Sunday evening and would not have to take leave. I eagerly agreed and told him to have them at the airfield at 0800 Saturday morning.

As usual, when I told Claudia about flying to Bremerhaven in the morning, she said, "Good. I'll take the kids and spend the weekend in Munich with Traudl."

The argument started by my replying, "You don't have to run off to Munich. I'll be back Saturday afternoon." However, she got up early on Saturday and left with the kids at the same time I left for the airfield with Mr. Roy.

I had talked Mr. Roy into going as my copilot. Although not fixed-wing rated, he had a current instrument ticket, which satisfied the copilot definition. Since it would be an instrument flight, he could log the time too. It also would be good training for him.

The weather Saturday morning was terrible. A solid deck of clouds from four hundred feet to eight thousand feet socked the airfield in and reduced visibility to two miles. That meant I would have to fly on instruments to Bremerhaven. The good news was that the weather there was broken clouds and ten miles of visibility.

The weather at Bremerhaven was critical because if it was not VFR conditions when we got there, we could not land. The army runway at Bremerhaven was on the army golf course. Army engineers had placed runway markers at each end of a long fairway to create the runway. There were no instruments for landing. Bremen control, located in Bremen, a town about twenty miles from Bremerhaven, provided radar control for the area. The flight procedures for an approach to the golf course strip consisted of contacting Bremen control for current weather and traffic and a radar vector to the golf course. Once over the golf course, you had to locate the strip and make a low pass to warn golfers that you were about to land.

While I went to the army flight operations building to file the flight plan, Mr. Roy checked on the Beaver to make sure it was ready to go. The flight to Bremen was simple, except it would be under instrument conditions for at least an hour of the flight. My route going would be from Stuttgart, Frankfurt, Hannover, and Bremen to Bremerhaven. I filed for a flight altitude of eight thousand feet en route except for Frankfurt.

The airspace around the Frankfurt area is designated a high-density area. Because of the high-density status, aircraft flying through Frankfurt airspace must do so at ten thousand feet or higher. That was no problem going. The weather forecast for ten thousand then was clear with a temperature of negative twenty degrees. Once past the high-density area, I could drop back down to eight thousand feet. I filed for the same flight path for my return trip, except in reverse order. I filed my plan and walked back to the hangar to preflight the aircraft.

By 0730, the captains had arrived, and I briefed them on emergency procedures for takeoff and landing. We loaded into the Beaver, and I started the engine and contacted flight departure for my clearance. The controller told me to wait. I had filed for a 0800 takeoff, so I still had plenty of time.

As I sat there with the engine idling, I realized that I was a little nervous. Maybe it was fear. I had never flown an instrument flight other than in training. Now, in a few minutes, I was going to taxi out on the runway and, at three hundred feet, go into the clouds on instruments to fly and control the aircraft. I could feel the apprehension in the pit of my stomach. The voice on the radio interrupted my thoughts. "Army 62378, you are cleared to the Bremen Beacon via Frankfurt and Hannover. Barometer is 30.04. Execute a picture-two departure. Squawk 1125. Cleared to taxi to departure runway. Contact departure control on 169.45 when ready for takeoff."

"Roger, control." I repeated his instructions to him and applied power and headed for the departure end of the runway. I completed a pretakeoff check and power check on the engine. "Departure control, this is Army 62378, ready for takeoff."

"Roger, Army 62378. Cleared for takeoff."

I taxied out onto the runway, looked back to make sure everybody was secure, and applied full power. The Beaver sprang forward, gaining speed to lift off. As we sped down the runway, I started my instrument scans and focused on calming the fear that was knotting in my stomach. I pushed forward on the yoke and felt the tail come up. I eased the yoke backward softly, and the Beaver left the runway, climbing slowly toward the dark gray clouds waiting to engulf us.

What was good about bad weather this time of the year was its stable air. That made flying on instruments much easier than bouncing around in unstable air. With my attention fully on the flight instruments, the Beaver entered the gray clouds. At first, I felt a slight sense of vertigo, but I quickly overcame it by focusing on my instrument scan. The Beaver climbed smoothly in the gray darkness while the rotating beacon reflection gave the cockpit an eerie glow.

I was calm now and starting to feel a sense of exhilaration. I was flying my first instrument flight, and I was confident now that I could do it without any problems. I looked back to check on the passengers. They looked calm. Mr. Roy was checking instruments with me and ready for copilot duties. We were passing through four thousand feet, when Stuttgart control directed us to contact Frankfurt control.

I concentrated on flying while Mr. Roy switched frequencies and contacted Frankfurt control. "Frankfurt control, this is Army 62378, climbing through four thousand to eight thousand. Over."

"Roger, Army 62378. Radar contact thirty miles west of Frankfurt. Continue climb to ten thousand feet. Barometer 30.04. Report ten thousand. Over."

"Roger, Frankfurt control. Report ten thousand. Over."

I expected the change from eight thousand to ten thousand, so it didn't bother me. The moisture and surrounding air temperature were above icing conditions, and ten thousand feet wouldn't be a problem now. However, the forecast for return weather was different. I would have to contend with it on the way back.

When we reached ten thousand feet, Mr. Roy reported to Frankfurt control. As we climbed through 8,500 feet, we came out of the thick deck of gray clouds and entered a thin layer of light clouds. Visibility was still zero but much lighter. With the aircraft trimmed, it needed little control input in the still air to maintain altitude and flight course. That gave me the chance to sit back and relax my tense muscles.

I looked at Mr. Roy and said, "This is your first instrument flight. What do you think?"

He looked at me with a grin. "I'm impressed. I don't think I want to do this in a helicopter. But so far, it's just like they told us in training. I was a little nervous when we first entered the clouds, but I'm okay now."

We crossed the Frankfurt VOR, and I turned to the outbound radial that took us to Hannover. The air was incredibly calm but cold. The heating in the aircraft hardly worked, so we started to feel the chill. Fortunately, everybody had worn field jackets with liners.

Fifteen minutes later, Frankfurt told us to contact Hannover control. Since I was out of the Frankfurt area, I asked Hannover for a lower altitude. Ten thousand feet is the limit for flying without oxygen, so I figured we would feel better at a lower altitude. Hannover cleared us to descend to eight thousand feet. I pulled back on the power and eased down to eight thousand feet. I do not know if anyone noticed the difference. Mentally, I felt better.

As I've said before, flying is hours of boredom interrupted by minutes of sheer terror. The flight now was one of boredom. Sitting in a cold aircraft while watching instruments can slowly get old. I kept thinking about how proud I was of myself while sitting in that seat. I was flying instruments and doing a good job so far. As far as Mr. Roy and the passengers knew, I did this all the time and was an old hand at flying in weather. I halfway smiled at myself, thinking it would probably scare the hell out of them if they knew it was my first time.

I watched the VOR needle rotate as we flew over the Hannover VOR. Mr. Roy confirmed passing the VOR, and I turned to the outbound heading for Bremen. A few minutes later, Hannover control handed us off to Bremen control. We were getting close now, and I started running the procedures for landing at Bremerhaven through my mind. We were beginning to experience light turbulence. I could tell by the way the clouds darkened and then lightened that we were flying through cumulus formations.

"Army 62378, this is Bremen control. Over."

"Bremen control, this is Army 62378. Over."

"Roger, Army 62378. You are ten miles southwest of Bremen VOR. Turn to heading one hundred sixty and descend to three thousand for a direct vector to the Bremerhaven airstrip. Barometer is 29.42. Report three thousand feet. Over."

Mr. Roy answered with an "At last" tone in his voice, "Roger, Bremen control. Heading one hundred sixty, descending to three thousand feet."

I turned the aircraft to 160, pulled the power back, and started our descent to three thousand feet. We were bouncing around now in the unstable air. At four thousand feet, the cloud cover became broken, and we could see patches of ground. We leveled off at three thousand feet in scattered clouds with about ten miles of visibility. Over us lay a deck of dark clouds. It felt good to be out of clouds and in clear air. Mr. Roy reported us at three thousand feet.

"Roger, Army 62378. You are five miles south of golf course. Report golf course in sight."

Mr. Roy repeated their instructions, and we both leaned forward, searching for the golf course. It was winter, and the grass on the golf course was greenish brown, making it hard to identify. The first sign we were over the golf course was when I saw sand traps around a green. Then we both recognized fairways by the sand traps. Mr. Roy reported that the golf course was in sight as I pulled off power and banked to get beneath the scattered clouds.

"Roger, Army 62378. Cleared to land at golf course. On leaving golf course, fly heading two hundred forty, and climb to and maintain three thousand feet. Contact Bremen control on takeoff. Over."

While Mr. Roy repeated the departure instructions, I descended to a thousand feet. I found the clubhouse, dropped down to three hundred feet, and made a low pass down the fairway in front of the clubhouse. As I passed the clubhouse, I could see a wind sock showing that the wind was blowing from my rear. At the end of the fairway, I could make out two white cones marking the end of the landing area. There were no golfers present, so I did a teardrop turn, climbing to five hundred feet. I rolled out of the turn on final approach about half a mile from the markers. I lowered the landing flaps, set the landing rpm, and landed just past the markers.

I continued to roll out until I had to add power to taxi to the clubhouse. At the clubhouse, I pulled off the runway and shut the engine down. A sergeant walked out to the Beaver as we got out. He was there to pick up the captains. They thanked me for taking them and made comments like "A good flight, but I am glad I don't have to fly back with you in this weather." I thanked God for guiding me safely there.

Mr. Roy and I took a fifteen-minute break in the clubhouse to use the restroom and stretch our legs. Walking back to the aircraft, I could see the clouds were starting to thicken. I think we were lucky to land when we did, because in another thirty minutes, weather would have socked us in.

I taxied the aircraft back down the fairway to the markers. I turned it around and did an engine run-up. All instruments were good, and we still had more than half a tank of gas, which was enough to make Stuttgart with a thirty-minute reserve. I lowered the takeoff flaps, set the rpm to take off, and applied full power. We bounced down the fairway and lifted off.

I continued climbing on the runway heading until I reached six hundred feet and then turned to a heading of 240.

Mr. Roy tried to contact Bremen control but could not until we reached two thousand feet. "Bremen control, this is Army 62378. We are airborne, climbing out of golf course on heading of two hundred forty, passing through twenty-five hundred feet."

"Roger, Army 62378. Cleared to the Bremen VOR on the three-hundred-fifty-degree radial. Climb to and maintain eight thousand feet. Barometer 29.03. Report reaching eight thousand feet."

I was in the clouds now and on instruments. I turned right to a heading of 295 to intercept the 350-degree radial. I watched the VOR needle swing to 350, and I turned with it to stay on the 350-degree radial. When we leveled off at eight thousand feet, we were flying through heavy snow. Mr. Roy reported our flight level of eight thousand feet. I was thinking to myself, *Man, what else am I going to have to deal with before we get to Stuttgart?*

"Army 62378, cleared to Stuttgart via Hannover, Frankfurt. Maintain eight thousand feet."

Mr. Roy had barely answered the transmission, when Bremen said, "Army 62378, you are headed directly toward a large cell. Would you like a vector around it?"

I motioned to Mr. Roy that I would take the radio. "Roger, Bremen control. Request a vector around the cell."

"Army 62378, wait one."

I could see ice building up on the leading edges of my struts and wings. That, to say the least, was alarming. The weather forecast had not predicted icing at eight thousand feet. I was starting to get a little concerned, when Bremen directed me to turn to heading 210 for a vector to intercept the 330-degree radial to the Hannover VOR."

I repeated the Bremen controller's instructions and turned to 210. I noticed Mr. Roy looking out the side windshield at the ice building on the strut. He turned to me with a questioning look on his face. Before he could say something, I told him, "I see it. I think it will be okay. We are obviously in a large snow cell. But we should be through it soon. They built these planes for use in Canada, and they are very capable in snowy conditions. What we have to prevent is an icing buildup on the prop. That's why I am going to cycle the prop periodically." With that, I pulled the rpm control knob back and forth a couple times.

Mr. Roy nodded as if reassured. He did not know that I meant for my words to have a calming effect for both of us, especially me, since I needed some reassurance just now. I knew we were in a shaky position. I scanned the engine and flight instruments, continually looking for the slightest sign of something going wrong. As hard as I tried not to, I could not help looking at the ice buildup on the struts. I estimated the ice was sticking out almost half a foot, and now I could see it protruding from the leading edges of the wings. The way the plane was bouncing around, I could not believe the ice remained on the struts and wings and continued to grow.

Suddenly, the cockpit got dark. We could not see outside the aircraft. The snow was so thick that we could not see the struts any longer. I had the sensation that we had flown into a winter thunderstorm. That alarmed me, and I pushed my transmit button and called Bremen control.

I could not understand their reply. It was too broken up. I tried to keep the panic out of my voice as I called again and told them that they were breaking up. Still, we could not hear them well enough to understand their transmission. As I recycled the prop, I noticed that Mr. Roy's face was ashen. As calmly as I could, I said, "Well, it's good that we got the instructions to intercept the three-hundred-thirty-degree radial to Hannover before we lost communication with them. Tune it in, and let's see where we are."

With something to take his mind off the problem, Mr. Roy snapped back to being copilot. "Good idea, sir," he said as he turned the radio dial. We watched the VOR needle swing slowly to the Hannover VOR. We were crossing the 355-degree radial.

"Good," I said. "We may not be able to talk to control right now, but we have a clearance to the Hannover VOR. Bremen control knows where we are, so all we have to do is continue as directed. Keep trying to contact Bremen control." I wanted him busy to keep his mind focused on our flight and not the terrible weather we were in.

For what seemed like an eternity but was only ten minutes, we bounced through the icy, snow-filled sky. We were both starting to feel the effects of the cold. A thick coat of frost covered the inside of the windshield, and occasionally, a piece of it would fall off the top console and hit me.

At first, I thought I had a hole in the canopy, but I finally realized it was just condensation freezing. The fear in my stomach was like nothing I had experienced in Vietnam. It was taking all of my skill to hold our heading and altitude while praying for an end to the weather hammering us. Then, slowly at first, it started to get lighter, and just like that, we popped out of the massive snow cloud and escaped the demon trying to tear us apart.

A minute later, we heard Bremen control loud and clear. "Army 62378, this is Bremen control. Over."

"Bremen control, this is Army 62378. Over."

"Roger, Army 62378. We have been trying to contact you. How do you hear this station?"

"Bremen control, this is Army 62378. We hear you loud and clear now. We must have lost communication in the snowstorm we flew through."

"Roger, Army 62378. What's your heading and altitude?"

"Roger, Bremen control. Our heading is two hundred ten, and altitude is eight thousand feet."

"Roger, Army 62378. Radar contact ten miles northwest of Hannover. Continue heading two hundred ten, and intercept the sixty-degree radial of the Frankfurt VOR. Maintain eight thousand feet. Report intercepting sixty-degree radial. Over."

I repeated Bremen's instructions as Mr. Roy tuned in the Frankfurt VOR. The air was almost calm, with little pockets of minor turbulence.

Six or seven inches of ice protruded from the leading edges of the struts and wings. Most of the ice had cleared off the windshield. It looked as if we were in a thin layer of clouds. The outside temperature had to be below freezing, because the ice was sticking to the struts and wings. It was not increasing, but it was not going away.

I took a deep breath and looked at Mr. Roy with a half grin. "That was something we can tell our grandchildren about."

He spoke in a strained voice as he folded our en route chart. "Well, I've got to make it back so I can have children who can have grandchildren if I want to tell anyone."

"We're going to be okay," I assured him. I could tell he was regretting volunteering for this flight. I could understand the fear he felt. He could not fly the aircraft, even though he was the copilot. All he could do was sit there and help me with the radios. I'd had that feeling when I was in the backseat of the Bird Dog and Darrel lost eyesight temporarily from a sinus block. It was a shitty feeling.

Time passed slowly as we watched the sixty-degree radial slowly swing to the nose of the aircraft. In the ten minutes it took to intercept the sixty-degree radial, our nerves calmed down, and we felt much better. We began chatting about the sensations the snowstorm had had on us and even talked about what we'd have done if the plane had iced up so badly that it would not fly. I told Mr. Roy that the reported weather was no freezing temperatures at four thousand feet and lower. I would have declared an emergency and headed for four thousand feet to clear the ice off. He nodded as if he agreed with that alternative.

When the course indicator needle showed us about three degrees from crossing the sixty-degree radial, I turned to sixty to intercept it. Mr. Roy reported intercepting the sixty-degree radial to Bremen control. Bremen control directed us to contact Frankfurt control and said good-bye.

Mr. Roy tuned in Frankfurt on the VRC radio while I fixed us on the sixty-degree radial. "Frankfurt control, this is Army 62378, eight thousand feet, sixty-degree radial, Frankfurt VOR. Over."

Frankfurt control came in loud and clear. "Roger, Army 62378. Radar contact sixty miles north of Frankfurt VOR. Barometer 29.03."

"Roger, Frankfurt control. Barometer 29.03."

I dialed in the new setting on my altimeter. The new setting changed our altimeter altitude to 8,140 feet, so I slowly descended back down to eight thousand. I estimated that we would be back in Stuttgart in about forty minutes. Since Frankfurt had not mentioned anything about altitude, I hoped we would slip through the Frankfurt airspace at eight thousand feet. The first weather forecast had projected clouds and freezing conditions above eight thousand feet. I did not want to contend with icing conditions ever again!

We flew in silence, watching the instruments and checking the ice protruding from the struts and wings. Each time I looked at the ice, I mentally measured it, trying to detect any change. I kept replaying in my mind the flight through the snow cloud that had deposited the ice and snow. I racked my brain, trying to remember the instructions for flying in icing conditions, but all I could come up with was "Don't fly in those conditions, and cycle the prop to prevent ice from building up on it."

Strangely, the longer we flew with no problems from the ice, the more comfortable I became with it.

I guess Mr. Roy was also in deep thought, because when Frankfurt called on the radio, it startled us. "Army 62378, this is Frankfurt control. Fifteen miles north of the Frankfurt VOR. Climb to ten thousand feet. Barometer 29.03. Report at ten thousand feet. Over."

I answered before Mr. Roy could repeat the instructions. "Frankfurt control, this is Army 62378. Roger. Climb to ten thousand feet. Request a lower altitude if possible."

"Roger, Army 62378. Because of heavy traffic in Frankfurt area now, a lower altitude not available. Report ten thousand feet."

"This is Army 62378. Roger. Report ten thousand feet."

With a trembling hand, I eased the prop control forward to climb rpm and moved the throttle forward to maximum power. I simultaneously applied back pressure on the yoke, and we began climbing toward ten thousand feet. I mumbled over the intercom, "Man, it's sure cold up here," to explain my trembling hand. Mr. Roy agreed with me as he stared at the dark layer of clouds we were climbing toward.

The plane entered the dark clouds at 8,600 feet. We experienced a slight increase in turbulence and an instant increase in the ice forming on our struts and wings. When Mr. Roy reported ten thousand feet, there was at least a foot of ice protruding from the struts and wings. To add to our troubled state, ice had started forming on the outside of the cockpit. When I returned the power and prop settings to cruise, the airspeed slowly increased to 106 knots. That was four knots below the normal cruise speed of 110 knots.

Okay, I told myself. *Ice covers the aircraft, and it would be normal for it to slow down. One hundred and six knots is still a good airspeed.* I kept watching the ice buildup on the struts and wings as the cockpit slowly iced over. When I could no longer see the struts, I pulled the prop rpm control handle to the rear and pushed it back to cruise rpm. The aircraft slowed slightly and then returned to 106 knots. Five minutes after we reached ten thousand feet, ice encased us, making it impossible to see outside the cockpit.

With a pounding heart, I watched my airspeed slowly fall to a hundred knots, and the little knot of fear in my stomach got bigger. I calmed myself by telling Mr. Roy. He had not noticed the lower airspeed. He looked at me, and I could see the question in the expression on his face: "What the hell are we going to do?"

Most of the time, I had the ability to stay calm under stress and override fear, so I could focus on finding a solution to whatever problem was before me. Now I faced the most stressful situation ever. I had to do something. I had to reassure Mr. Roy, who was just as stressed as I. I pushed the intercom button. "Mr. Roy, our only recourse is to cycle the prop and try to descend to a lower altitude. I sure as hell don't want ice on the prop, so I'm going to cycle it every thirty seconds or so. I will hold altitude as long as our airspeed does not get below eighty knots. If I can't maintain ten thousand feet and eighty knots, then I will start descending to maintain eighty knots. That's a safe airspeed for this aircraft. But first, I am going to see if I can get a lower altitude."

He nodded, agreeing, as I pushed the transmit button. "Frankfurt control, this is Army 62378. I am experiencing heavy icing and request a lower altitude."

"Negative, Army 62378. Maintain ten thousand."

I answered his transmission. By now, the airspeed was down to eighty knots, and the controls were starting to feel sluggish. I had to force myself to stay calm as I thought, *Neal, you are in real trouble. You don't know if eighty knots is a safe airspeed for a flying hunk of ice. There's a good possibility that ice could jam the controls and cause you to lose control of the aircraft.*

Alarmed by that thought, I lowered the nose to descend. *Just keep the wings level, and maintain eighty knots. Don't worry about altitude,* I told myself.

Dear God, I need your help now, I prayed as I pushed the transmit button. "Frankfurt control, this is Army 62378. I am iced up and unable to maintain ten thousand. Request a lower altitude immediately."

"Roger, Army 62378. Are you declaring an emergency?"

"Negative, Frankfurt control. I just need a lower altitude."

"Roger, Army 62378. Maintain ten thousand feet."

"Frankfurt control, unable to maintain ten thousand feet and safe airspeed. Descending through ninety-eight hundred feet."

"Army 62378, are you declaring an emergency?"

"Negative, Frankfurt control. I cannot hold altitude in these conditions. I am descending about two hundred feet a minute to maintain airspeed and control of aircraft."

"Army 62378, your assigned altitude is ten thousand feet."

I decided then that I was going to continue descending and just give Frankfurt my altitude. It was obvious that they were not going to clear me to descend lower unless I declared an emergency. If I did that, there would be all kinds of paperwork and investigations. Besides, in my mind, I did not technically have an emergency. I was flying the aircraft, but I was in a condition where a wrong action on my part could lead to a disastrous end. I had visions of stalling and spinning out of control with nothing but instruments to go by. I knew that might be beyond my ability to handle.

Mr. Roy was fidgeting in his seat, trying to remain calm. I was still working the radio. "Frankfurt, this is Army 62378. Descending through ninety-two hundred feet."

"Roger, Army 62378. Maintain ten thousand feet."

To this day, I believe the reason he was insisting on my maintaining ten thousand feet (even though I could not) was to avoid filing a violation against me for violating Frankfurt airspace. At the time, it did not matter. I just wanted to get out of this frozen mess without declaring an emergency or killing myself and Mr. Roy.

Each time I cycled the prop, I would try to hold the altitude without losing airspeed, but each time I leveled the Beaver, the airspeed started to bleed off. So I would quickly lower the nose to regain eighty knots and call Frankfurt to report altitude. I wanted to hold altitude if possible because Frankfurt had denied me a lower altitude because of heavy traffic. I could be descending through another airplane's airspace.

Along with the spinning-out-of-control image, another image of disaster kept entering my mind: I could imagine blindly slamming into another aircraft and the resulting destruction. "Frankfurt control, this is Army 62378. I am descending through eighty-eight hundred feet." I hoped that since Frankfurt knew I was descending and had me on radar, they could keep me separated from other traffic. I had no choice other than to descend until I could get enough ice off the control surfaces to let me maintain altitude and a safe airspeed.

"Army 62378, this is Frankfurt control. Ten miles south of Frankfurt VOR. Cleared to Stuttgart VOR. One-hundred-seventy-degree radial. Contact Stuttgart control. Good day."

My heart leaped with joy. Stuttgart had no flight limits approaching their terminal. I immediately regained some confidence that this was going to turn out okay. "Stuttgart control, this is Army 62378. Descending through eighty-four hundred feet. Request lower altitude as soon as possible."

"Roger, Army 62378. Radar contact thirty-five miles north of Stuttgart. Barometer 29.04. What altitude do you want?"

"Roger, Stuttgart. Barometer 29.04. Request four thousand feet."

"Roger, Army 62378. Descend to four thousand feet. Report four thousand feet."

I motioned for Mr. Roy to take the radio, and he answered, "Stuttgart control, out of eighty-two hundred for four thousand feet." There was relief in the tone of his voice, and I know I was feeling much better than I had three minutes ago.

I hoped the temperature at four thousand feet was above freezing. I had to at least get some ice off the windshield so I could see well enough to land. The Beaver did not have side windows that I could pop open to see enough to land the aircraft, as the Bird Dog did. Boy, was I relieved to see ice start sliding off the front of the windshield as we passed through five thousand feet! Mr. Roy, relieved, looked at me and grinned.

When Mr. Roy reported that we were level at four thousand feet, the windshield was free of ice. We could see that about six inches of ice remained on the leading edges of the wings and struts. As I pulled the yoke back to level at four thousand, the airspeed started climbing toward 110 knots. I could see Stuttgart ahead. Everything was okay. I thanked God for getting us safely down and enjoyed the strongest feeling of euphoria that I have ever had.

When I could clearly see the airfield, I asked Stuttgart control to cancel my IFR flight plan. They cleared me to contact the Stuttgart tower for landing. I made a visual approach to Stuttgart, and when I touched down on the runway, Mr. Roy and I heard a strange sound. As we rolled down the runway, the tower called. "Army 62378, something fell off your aircraft when you touched down."

I answered, "Roger, Stuttgart. Request permission to do a one eighty and check."

"Roger, Army 62378. Cleared for a one eighty on active. Hurry, please."

I did a 180 and taxied toward a pile of debris lying on the runway at the spot where I'd touched down. As I got to within fifty meters of it, we could see a pile of ice scattered along the runway. "Stuttgart Tower, this is Army 62378. The debris on the runway is ice. We were iced up when we landed. The touchdown shock must have shaken it loose from the aircraft."

"Roger, Army 62378. Cleared to taxi to army apron. Good day."

I taxied to the Beaver's parking spot in front of my hangar. The crew chief guided us into the chocks, and I shut the big engine down. We got out and checked the aircraft for any damage the icing might have caused. It felt good to be on the ground. The crew chief pulled the fuel truck up and started refueling the Beaver. "How did it go, sir?"

"It was a good flight," I answered, looking at Mr. Roy. "We got some good instrument time. We ran into a little icing. But I don't see any damage to the aircraft." Mr. Roy smiled and nodded, agreeing.

I completed the logbook entries and gave the book to Mr. Roy to enter his data. Looking at the crew chief, I said, "Chief, it has been a long day, so we are going to cut and let you finish here."

"Okay, sir. See you Monday."

Mr. Roy and I dropped our flight bags off in the hangar and walked to his car. He humorously said, "Sir, you are going to have to order me to go on another flight like that. There's no way in hell I'm volunteering for that ever again."

As we got in the car, I answered, "It wasn't all that bad. Where else could you spend Saturday morning getting paid to have the shit scared out of you?"

When Mr. Roy let me out at my building, I looked at him and said, "Thanks, man. You did well, and I'll fly with you anytime. Tell your wife hello for me, and I'll see you Monday." He smiled and drove off.

I walked into my empty apartment, hoping Claudia would be there. But I knew she would not. It was three thirty in the afternoon, and the tension and stress I had gone through were starting to affect me. I felt exhausted and mentally drained. I stripped and took a hot shower to relax my tense muscles and unwind.

As I stood under the hot water, my mind kept replaying the flight and the fear I had felt. It was different from the fear I'd suffered while flying into the antiaircraft fire in Vietnam. That fear had lasted only for the two minutes it took to dive in and fire my rockets. Today the fear had lasted for more than thirty minutes, from the time we entered the snowstorm near Bremen until Frankfurt cleared us to the Stuttgart VOR. The ice could have caused me to lose control of the aircraft, and I could have been dead now. The army would be trying to find Claudia to tell her that her husband had crashed and not survived. Boy, would that have surprised the hell out of her. I was not even sure she would have been that upset over it.

After I showered and dressed, I fixed myself a rum and Coke and sat down to watch TV. I was over the flight now. My mind occupied itself with trying to understand the German-language TV program I was watching. The house was quiet, and sitting there on the couch, I felt lonely. I had never felt this lonely in Vietnam. There, I'd accepted the separation from my family. Here, I could neither accept nor fathom why I was here and she was in Munich. Why were the people in Munich so much more important to her than I? After a while, the rum and Coke on my empty stomach, coupled with the restful sense of being safe, dazed my mind. I stretched out on the couch and drifted off to sleep.

It was 1800 when I woke from my nap. I felt rested and hungry. I went into the kitchen to find something to eat. While I stood there trying to decide what I wanted, it occurred to me that what I wanted was not to have to eat by myself. If she could go out and party, so could I. I decided I would catch a cab to the restaurant that Claudia and I occasionally ate at and have dinner.

The restaurant was in downtown Stuttgart, near several nightclubs. The taxi dropped me off in front of the restaurant. It was early, and I found a free table. I wanted company but not the strangers who would be sitting with me soon. I could not get over the way Germans did not consider an occupied table as private. If there were free seats, others would politely ask if they were free and then sit down as if it were their table. Of course, one met many people that way, but for me, it was difficult because of my poor ability to speak German. By the time I finished my roasted chicken, diners occupied all the seats at my table. I paid the server, said good-bye to everyone, and walked out into the cold night.

I was not ready to return to my lonely apartment, so I decided to have a drink at one of the nightclubs. I crossed the street and entered the first one I came to. The club was about half full. The three-member band was in the middle of a song, and several couples were on the dance floor. I found a seat at the side of the bar, from which I could watch the dance floor. The pretty, sexily dressed bartender asked me in English what I wanted to drink. After I ordered a rum and Coke, I took a slow look around the club. There were many tables with couples sitting at them, and unescorted women sat at several other tables. Most of the unescorted men were at the bar, as I was.

I started to loosen up after my second rum and Coke. The band was not bad. I thought, *If Claudia can go out dancing, why can't I?* I was looking around the room for a woman who looked as if she might like to dance, when I spied an attractive brown-haired woman staring at me. When our eyes met, she looked away quickly, as if I had caught her doing something she should not. *She's the one*, I thought as I got up and walked toward her table.

She was sitting with three other women and one man. I did not know her relationship to the man sitting at the table, so I asked him if it was okay to ask her if she wanted to dance. He answered, "*Bitter*," which was "Please" in German, so I turned to the woman, who was looking at me, and asked her to dance. She nodded and, with a half smile, stood. I took her hand and led her to the dance floor.

The band was playing a slow song, so I held her loosely, looking her in the face. "My name is Neal," I said.

"My name is Heidi," she answered, looking me in the eyes.

"Nice to meet you, Heidi," I replied with a smile.

Then she pulled my left hand down, looked at my wedding band, and asked in German, "What is your wife's name?"

"Her name is Claudia," I answered in English.

"Why is she not here with you?" she asked in a mix of German and English.

"She would rather be in Munich with her friends than here with me," I answered in English.

"That's too bad," she said with a warm smile, and she moved closer to me.

As I felt her body swaying against mine with the music, I was in awe. Eight hours ago, I'd been in a crisis, frightened. Now this woman attracted me, and the way she was responding, as if she were attracted to me, frightened me. Just as I was going to ask her what she did, the song ended.

We stood and applauded the band with the rest of the dancers. The band began playing a rock-and-roll song, and again, we started dancing. That gave me the chance to check her body out. She had a nice body and moved with the music with a seductive rhythm. We moved together well and had a good time dancing. This time, when the song ended, the band announced that they were taking a break. I walked her back to her seat and thanked her for the dance. She squeezed my hand as she sat down, and I returned to the bar and my seat.

During the band's break, she kept glancing at me and smiling. When the band started playing again, everybody at her table got up to dance, leaving her sitting alone, so I walked over and sat down. I started the conversation by asking her how she'd learned to speak such good English. She revealed that she had married a GI and had lived in Louisiana for two years. When she got pregnant, she realized how unhappy she was. She and her husband started fighting all the time, so a month after the birth of her baby, she filed for divorce and returned to Germany. Her divorce was finalized last month, and she now had a healthy six-month-old baby girl.

Then she said teasingly, "So you go out on the town when your wife leaves you alone?"

I did not want to tell her my problems, but her smile and friendliness were pulling answers from me. Responding playfully and trying to move away from the subject, I said, "No, I don't take off when my wife leaves me alone. I just had a bad day and decided to eat something and have a couple drinks to relax. I saw you and was smitten by your beauty."

My diversion might have worked, because she asked me, "What is your rank in the army?"

I answered, "I am a captain."

She tilted her head in an "I am impressed" nod and said, "My ex-husband was a corporal. He was only in the army for three years. I think we might have stayed together if he had stayed in the military. But back in Louisiana, he started running around with his friends and spending little time with me. He felt that as long as his family visited me, I should be happy."

The band announced another break, and her friends returned to the table. I got up so they could have their chairs and told Heidi, "I'll ask you for the next dance." I returned to the bar.

The next move was up to me. I took a sip of my rum and Coke and debated what I should do. Did I want to start an affair with this desirable woman? It would be a good way to get even with Claudia for the way she treated me. It would be easy to lie to Claudia and make excuses for being gone. But the reality was that unless Claudia knew what I was doing, it would not be getting even. I would just be proving to myself that I could get even and taking the chance of ending my marriage. I had never slipped around and cheated on Claudia, nor had I condoned other men doing it to their wives.

I realized that was not what I wanted to do. I just wanted Claudia to make me feel as Heidi had during the seven or eight minutes we'd danced and talked. I did not want Heidi. I wanted Claudia. Despite the hurt she caused me, I loved her and only her. I finished my rum and Coke, got up, and walked to the door. At the door, I turned and looked at Heidi. She was looking at me with a questioning expression. I raised my left hand, pointed at my ring, waved, and left.

I spent Sunday moping around the apartment, waiting for Claudia to get home. With no transport except taxis, I did not feel like going anywhere. Finally, she returned around 1800. Despite still being angry, I was happy to see her and the kids. However, being happy did not prevent me from showing my anger, which in turn angered Claudia.

Later, while lying in bed and trying to sleep, I wondered why she had not asked me how my flight went. I had asked about her weekend in Munich because I cared about her. If I had to pin down the exact time the major problems between us began, it would have to be the fall and winter of 1968. We could not come together fully, as we had after previous separations.

We had a white Christmas that year. We picked up a small but nice-looking tree and decorated it. On Christmas night, the kids opened one of their gifts. As was customary, they had to wait for morning to open the rest. As a family, we had a great Christmas. The weekend before Christmas,

Claudia drove to Munich to get her mom and brought her back to spend Christmas with us.

Over the Christmas holidays, the battalion sponsored several social events. On Christmas Day, I put on my dress blue uniform and, with Claudia, her mom, and the kids, ate Christmas dinner in the battalion mess hall. It was a scrumptious Christmas dinner that brought the officers, enlisted, and their families together to dine and enjoy the spirit of Christmas.

After dinner, the battalion commander invited all the officers to his quarters for an impromptu party. Mom did not want to go, so we took her and the kids back to the apartment. Claudia and I had an enjoyable time together at the commander's party, and that told me that it was possible for us to be happy if we wanted to be. That was followed by New Year's celebrations and waking up in 1969.

The weather stayed cold, with snow on the ground. Sometimes during each day, we would go outside and have a snowball fight or go sledding. The weather cleared up after New Year's Day, as if to say, "Enough of that."

The Bremerhaven flight had given me a healthy respect for German weather when it came to flying. It seemed it was bad most of the time. You could start your flight in perfect conditions only to have the weather turn bad at a moment's notice. At some point in time, on most flights, you would have to contend with rain, snow, low clouds, or poor visibility. The constant threat of these conditions made me strive to keep a high degree of competence at flying in instrument conditions.

In early January, the Thirty-Fourth Battalion was in the field on a training exercise. Major Davis remained behind for a couple of days, tied up with a court-martial. When the court-martial was over, I flew him to the field to join the battalion. I filed an instrument flight plan from Stuttgart to Nuremberg and back. The weather was not bad, but it was a good opportunity to practice instrument flying.

We left Stuttgart Airfield at 1000, and I followed Stuttgart control's instructions to turn to a heading of 260 degrees and climb to and maintain four thousand feet. That put me on the airway to Nuremberg, which would take an hour and fifteen minutes. It was clear over Stuttgart, but I could see clouds about twenty miles away in our flight path. They were dark—a sure sign of moisture. The weather forecast was for intermittent clouds from three thousand to ten thousand feet. That did not worry me, because we were flying instruments, and a base of three thousand feet was way above landing minimums at Nuremberg.

What did worry me was the air temperature at four thousand feet: it was twenty-five degrees Fahrenheit. That was cold enough for icing conditions, although the forecaster had not mentioned any in-flight reports of icing.

When I was on course and altitude, I trimmed the Beaver to hold those settings. Major Davis was also an aviator and my rater, and I wanted to impress him with my piloting skills. He was rotary-wing rated and on a ground assignment. We engaged in small talk as we approached the dark clouds. While I sounded calm and collected, I was a little jittery inside, remembering my last battle with icing.

We experienced the usual bumpy turbulence as we flew into the clouds. I was looking at the struts, waiting for the ice to start building, and sure enough, it appeared. Major Davis noticed it when it was jutting out about two inches. He turned to me, alarmed, and said, "You know we are picking up ice?"

"Yes, sir," I answered. "That little bit is nothing to worry about." About the time I said that, we popped out of the clouds, but up ahead were more clouds. It looked as if we would be in and out of clouds all the way.

I was hoping the ice would clear off each time we were free of the clouds, but it did not. After we'd been flying through clouds for about fifteen minutes, the ice was about six inches on the struts. The good part was that the windshield stayed free of buildup.

I could tell Major Davis was getting a little concerned, so I said, "Sir, I am going to cancel our instrument plan and go VFR so we can get a lower altitude and out of these icing conditions."

"That's a great idea, Neal. I've never experienced this before, and it makes me a little nervous, especially when we don't have to fly in it."

I called Stuttgart control and changed my instrument flight plan to a VFR plan. When they gave me approval, I descended to three thousand feet. That kept us clear of the clouds, and in about five minutes, the ice had disappeared from the struts. I did not mention the Bremerhaven flight to him, but I had gained much confidence in my flying ability from that flight. It was an experience that few pilots would ever know. Although the little icing had disturbed Major Davis, I had been calm. I knew I could easily handle this little icing.

Snow and ice had a positive effect on me that winter. One January morning, after a night of snow, I was just about to leave for the hangar, when Mr. Roy knocked on my door. He needed my help in getting his car moving on the snow-packed road. His quarters sat below a slight rise in the road, and without snow chains, he could not get the car to the top of the rise. I walked with him back to his quarters and his car, and while he drove, I pushed. That gave him just enough energy above his spinning tires to get enough traction to get up the rise. From there, the road was clear.

I pushed him for about twenty yards before he pulled away, but the exertion left me gasping for breath. That shocked me because I considered myself to be in good shape. I reached into my pocket, took out my pack of Pall Malls, and threw them into a roadside garbage can. I knew that smoking was the problem.

I had stopped smoking after OCS, but when I got home from Vietnam, I started again. I blamed it on the stress Claudia was causing me and on stress from my job. Since Claudia smoked, I joined her. However, that morning, I stopped, and I never smoked again.

In March, our personnel office told me I needed to file an officer preference form for my next assignment. I thought about it for a while before deciding where I wanted to go next. I knew that Claudia wanted me to request another assignment in Germany, but because of the conditions between us, I believed it was better if we got out of Germany. I asked for Mohawk and rotary-wing transition. I figured if I got it, we would be in Fort Rucker in a school environment, and that might help us resolve some of our problems. Of course, when Claudia found out that I did not request Germany, she was upset and bitter for a while.

I loved flying the Beaver and looked forward to the weekly courier missions. I pushed for the battalion commander to use the aviation section assets more. Slowly, he started scheduling flights to field sites instead of driving. We started getting more flight time, and it helped keep my people busy.

One time, I flew him to Grafenwoehr for a training meeting. It was my first time flying into Grafenwoehr, and the mission excited me. Because Grafenwoehr sat next to the border with Czechoslovakia, pilots had to be careful when flying into Grafenwoehr to avoid crossing the DMZ, commonly called the Iron Curtain. There were special procedures for entering the area near the DMZ to reduce the chance of straying across it and causing an international incident.

The procedures for flying into Grafenwoehr included command approval of the flight and an ADF approach for all flights. There was a fixed corridor for entry into Grafenwoehr's airspace. One had to enter that corridor within five minutes of the estimated flight plan time. Once in it, one had to contact Grafenwoehr approach for landing clearance and any special instructions needed to avoid interfering with the units training there. The entry flight direction was 180 degrees to intercept the eighty-degree radial into the airfield. The danger was failing to intercept the eighty-degree radial. If one missed it for some reason and was not familiar with the area, one could continue 180 degrees, which would take the plane into Czechoslovakia.

To trick a pilot into doing that, the Czechs had set up a more powerful ADF radio on their side of the border. They used the same frequency as the Grafenwoehr ADF and would jam the Grafenwoehr beacon in an attempt to deceive a pilot into using their beacon. To prevent pilots from accidentally using the Czechoslovakian beacon, the army required all pilots to tune in to the Fürth civilian radio station on a second ADF. Fürth was located east of the corridor. The safety rule was to never fly past the Fürth 270-degree beacon. If a pilot had not intercepted the Grafenwoehr eighty-degree beacon by then, the Czechoslovakians were trying to deceive him, and he needed to do a 180 and try again.

I flew several missions into Grafenwoehr but only had a problem on one mission. It was one of those bad weather days, and the Czechs knew I would have trouble using terrain features to make my approach. Knowing I would be mostly depending on instruments, the Czechoslovakians turned their ADF on and tried to deceive me into crossing the border, but thanks to the Fürth radio, they failed.

Everything was going smoothly on my approach, when my DF needle flickered, spun, and then locked back onto the Grafenwoehr radio. At the same time, there was a burst of static. I did not think too much of it, until my estimated time to intersect the inbound course passed, and I had not intersected it yet. Then, in a bit of a shock, I watched the ADF needle turn to the Fürth radio past the radial that I should have turned on. I quickly turned to the inbound heading and told Grafenwoehr approach that I had lost the ADF radio transmission and was continuing inbound VFR. They confirmed the Czechs were jamming the ADF.

Then, realizing I had not fallen for their deception, the Czechs turned their radio off. I immediately picked up the Grafenwoehr ADF, intercepted it, and landed safely at Grafenwoehr. It was a strange feeling knowing that had I not been alert, I could have easily become an international incident by crossing the DMZ. Just like that, I could have ended up in a burning tangle of metal while the Czechs complained about the American army plane they'd had to shoot down after it had illegally entered their airspace.

Despite the dangers of weather and the threats arising from the cold war we were in, I loved flying the Beaver. It was a controllable and forgiving aircraft. I wish now that I had learned the reason the one crashed while I was in Special Forces.

One afternoon, I was returning from flying the courier mission. Stuttgart's tower had cleared me for landing, and I was turning to final, when the tower called and asked me if I could speed up my landing and take the first turnoff possible. There were two civilian Lufthansa 737s waiting for takeoff as soon as I cleared the active. I could see them sitting on the departure end. I called the tower. "Stuttgart Tower, this is Army 62378. If you clear me to land on the overrun, I will turn off on the departure end of the runway."

"Roger, Army 62378. Cleared to land at your discretion."

I pumped down sixty degrees of flaps and set a short-field landing approach. I added power to compensate for the barn-door effect the sixty degrees of flap had. My speed bled off quickly to fifty knots, and my rate of descent increased to three hundred feet per minute. Using power and rudders, I maintained my nose-high attitude and rate of descent all the way to the ground. I was on show because I knew the tower and the pilots of the two Lufthansa aircraft were watching me. I was back in Vietnam now, under pressure and applying all the flying skills I had. I could not screw this up, because by asking to land on the overrun, I was clearly showing off my skill. The overrun came up to meet me, and at the right moment, I rounded out, adding a little power to cushion my descent.

The Beaver planted itself in a perfect three-point landing. My rollout was all of about a hundred feet, and I had to add power to taxi to the end of the runway and turn off into the run-up area. The tower came on the radio with a "Thanks, Army 62378."

One of the Lufthansa pilots said, "Great landing, army pilot," as he added power to take the runway. The other Lufthansa pilot pushed his transmit button twice for ditto.

The compliment made my day. Had I made a normal landing, it would have taken three or four minutes to roll out and turn off the runway. The two Lufthansa aircraft would have burned costly fuel while sitting there waiting for me to clear the active so that they could takeoff. It was my first flying compliment since leaving Vietnam.

My job as aviation officer had become routine. I just focused on doing my job satisfactorily. I did not look for ways to excel and impress the battalion commander. I wanted to succeed at my job and, at the same time, work on relations with Claudia. Improving my relations with Claudia was actually harder than doing my job.

With the coming of spring, the weather turned warmer, and Claudia and I began to get along a little better. We were having fewer arguments and spending time together as a family. All the time, I had an image of a woman, an ideal wife, in the back of my mind. I wanted Claudia to be that woman, but of course, she was not. She had many of the qualities of the woman in my image but not all of them.

She was capable of deep passion yet seemed uninterested in sex at times. I did not understand how we could have such good sex, yet our anger toward each other was often because of sex. I was mostly the one to blame for that. I could not handle rejection, and when I wanted sex and Claudia did not, I felt she was rejecting me. Of course, her flirting and always wanting to go to Munich for the weekend fueled some of the anger.

The army had gotten away from working a half day on Saturday, so for the first time in our marriage, we had most weekends free. I, of course, wanted to spend time together, but she saw it as a chance to spend more time in Munich. To keep her happy, I would drive to Munich for the weekend. This cut down on the arguments, and most of the time, I would find some way to enjoy myself.

As far as duty went, I had begun to enjoy the five-day workweek. There was still a need for inspections, and Saturday morning had been the ideal period to conduct them, so I began a one-Saturday-a-month inspection of the billets and my soldiers. I still required them to have a GI party each Friday night. They appreciated that unlike the rest of the company commanders, I did not inspect every Saturday. As far as my aircraft and equipment went, I inspected them daily.

On a Friday morning around the middle of May, USAREUR told the battalion that they would conduct an inspector general and command maintenance inspection (IG and CMI) the following Monday. The inspection was a big event. Inspectors would descend on the unit and inspect all equipment, vehicles, logistics, records, training, and personnel to ensure the unit was fit and ready for combat and was following prescribed army directives. Commanders who failed to pass it often found their careers ended, so understandably, when a higher command told a unit of a coming IG and CMI, it was jump-through-your-ass time. Personnel worked twenty-four hours a day preparing for the inspection.

Major Davis called me Friday morning and told me of the inspection and a meeting at 0900 to go over the inspection schedule. I called for my people to gather and relayed the information. My instructions were to begin rechecking aircraft and their logbooks and vehicles and their logbooks; they were to check all logbook entries to ensure maintenance and logistic requisitions supported any uncompleted maintenance problem. When each logbook was ready, one of the warrants would sign off on it, make sure all priority requisitions were current and had follow-up action for those overdue, and check the hangar for cleanness and safety requirements. I had SFC Rhodes send two men to the barracks to draw all weapons and CBR equipment and clean them. They began working, and I left to attend the IG and CMI planning meeting.

The meeting was short and to the point. LTC Kirk expected each company to work all weekend if necessary. He expected at least a satisfactory rating for each unit. The mood during the meeting was somber. Everybody knew that if the mass of communications equipment, trucks, and trailers in the battalion were not ready for inspection now, there was no way they could get everything ready in three days.

Unlike me, the rest of the commanders did not focus on maintaining their equipment daily. Honestly, they probably had too much equipment to have it inspection ready each day. I could pass any unannounced inspection any time because of my procedures. Unfortunately, the inspectors would combine my inspection results with the higher headquarters company's results. That meant my aviation section could pass but still fail if the other part of the higher headquarters company scored too low.

When I returned to the hangar, the work in progress pleased me. Captain Brede was always critical of personnel in the section. It was obvious to me his leadership skills were the only problem, not the soldiers. By 1700, we had completed all work and checked it. I released all personnel and told them to be back Monday morning at 0700. I reminded them of the GI party for Sunday night. After leaving the hangar, I drove over to Kelley Barracks and inspected the weapons and gas masks. They were spotless. Satisfied, I went home to Claudia and the kids.

Saturday afternoon, the phone rang. It was Major Davis. "Captain Griffin, I'm at the hangar, and there's no one here. The battalion commander wanted everybody working this weekend to prepare for the IG and CMI."

"I know, Major Davis," I replied. "I'm ready for the inspection. My folks will GI the barracks Sunday night, and I will inspect it Monday morning at 0600. I don't think it's necessary to have my people working, when I require them to have my equipment and aircraft ready for inspection on a moment's notice."

He was silent for a couple of seconds before speaking. "Well, I hope you are right, Captain Griffin, because this could reflect on your OER."

"I understand, sir," I replied. "But I don't perform every day because of the threat of an OER. I conduct myself professionally and efficiently because of who I am and the high standards I set for myself. I hope my OER reflects that."

"Well, just be warned," he said, and he hung up.

About thirty minutes later, the phone rang. It was LTC Kirk. He asked, "Are you ready for the IG and CMI?"

"Sir, I am ready for an IG and CMI any day on a moment's notice. I demand that of myself and my people. I don't believe that you win by letting work slide and trying to catch up at the last minute."

"Okay," he said, "that's all I wanted to know. See you Monday."

Because of my verbal swagger, I was a little apprehensive over the weekend. I was confident in my ability and trusted my soldiers. I had spot-checked everything and found no errors. Still, if I did badly on this inspection, it would kill my army career.

Monday morning, I was up at 0400 and at the Carly Barracks at 0600 to inspect my soldiers' living area and personal equipment. SFC Callahan met me there, and we toured the barrack room. It was perfect. We could not find one thing wrong. I was happy.

I arrived at the hangar around 0700 and picked up an egg sandwich and some coffee at the little cafeteria on the military side. Now, according to the schedule, we would stand by until the inspection team arrived. My soldiers looked good. While we waited, they started rechecking equipment and aircraft. At 0830, the inspection team leader, a major, called and asked me to send one of the OH-13s to pick him up and bring him to the airfield. The rest of the team was on the way in trucks.

I sent Mr. Quito to pick up the major. He had gained the needed experience, and there was never a question of his flying skills. Rumor was that the major, although not an aviator, could fly the OH-13. In the past, he had asked to fly it back to the airfield. I directed Mr. Quito to let him if he asked but to watch him as if he were a student and Mr. Quito were an instructor pilot.

The inspection team arrived in two trucks at 0900. They gave a quick briefing on how and what they would inspect. After the briefing, they scattered to each of their areas of expertise to conduct the inspection. At 0915, Mr. Quito called on the section radio and reported that he was inbound to the hangar. I watched them do an approach and hover up the landing spot in front of the hangar.

They shut the helicopter down, and while the rotor was winding down, they talked. Then the major got out, and I walked up to him and reported. That he had his own flight helmet impressed me. We talked for a while, and he left to confer with his inspection team members. I walked around to watch the inspection. My guys were busy with the inspectors, but all gave me a thumbs-up.

By noon, the inspectors had gathered into a group and were briefing the major on their findings. They excluded us from the briefings since the findings were preliminary and had to be consolidated with the HHQ company's findings. The inspection team members climbed back into their vehicles and left while I walked the major to the OH-13 for his flight back to the battalion location. His only comment about the inspection was that everything looked good. He thanked me for letting him get some stick time in the OH-13. After they left, I called the battalion and reported what he'd said to Major Davis.

The IG and CMI team scheduled their exit briefing for 0800 the following morning at the battalion headquarters in Ludwigsburg Casern. All the company commanders, officers, and key NCOs assembled in the briefing room for the results. The corps signal officer and aviation officer were also there. The team commander, a colonel, gave the opening remarks and turned the meeting over to each team leader to brief the individual findings.

The results were not good. One by one, each letter company heard the list of major discrepancies found during the inspection. Each company had scored below the 70 percent mark. The only company to pass with a score just barely above 70 was the HHQ company. The team leader pointed out that the only reason the company had a satisfactory score was because of the aviation section inspection score. The aviation section had received a mostly unheard-of high score of 98.6, which, when combined with the HHQ score of 50, resulted in a passing score for the HHQ company. The major closed his briefing by stating, "I commend Captain Griffin, the aviation section leader, for his section's excellence. It is the best aviation section I have seen during my three years on the IG and CMI team."

The IG and CMI team commander then told LTC Kirk that they would be back to reinspect the battalion minus the aviation section the following Monday. I breathed a sigh of relief when I heard his comments. I looked at LTC Kirk as he thanked the commander. He looked at me and smiled and nodded as if to say thanks. The IG and CMI team left, and the rest of the meeting was about the plan of action to correct all the problems before next Monday. I sat through it because I was part of the unit and wanted to be of help if I could. After they decided on the plan, LTC Kirk stood up and spoke. "Gentlemen, take a lesson from Captain Griffin. The way he achieved excellence was by doing work every day and not letting it pile up. He does not have as much equipment as you do, but he also does not have the personnel you do. It's a matter of taking care of business every day. I expect that from you now. There will be no excuse for failing the reinspection."

I was exuberant as I left the meeting and headed back to the hangar. I had been on thin ice. The section's results could have been bad, and LTC Kirk would have held me responsible because I hadn't worked my soldiers over the weekend. Back at the hangar, my guys were eagerly waiting to find out how we did. They were happy and proud when I told them the results of the inspection. When they quieted down, I said, "Okay, the inspection is over with. I will see if LTC Kirk will give us a training holiday next Friday as an incentive to keep up the good work, but for the rest of the day, we have work to do. We've set the bar high, and we will have to work to keep it high. Let's get back to work."

I was still walking on air when I went home that evening. When Claudia asked how the inspection went, I told her how I had saved the HHQ company. I think she felt a little pride in that fact. When she showed me affection, I was in a special world. She had an astounding power over me. I worked hard to please her and make her proud of me, which was why when she treated me badly, I would be so devastated. But what was unique was the commitment between us. So far, we accepted living with our problems with the hope of better times ahead.

One of the mistakes I made was not going to church with her. To this day, I regret not doing so. I had various excuses. I was not Catholic, or I had work to catch up on; those were my usual reasons. I believed in and called on God but had an idea that you did not have to go to church to be in good standing with him. I felt all one had to do was have faith in him. Each Sunday, she dressed the children and went to Mass without me. This confused me because I could not reconcile her actions with her devotion to the church. The children were grown and gone before I started going to church with her every Sunday. Our relations became much stronger and closer after that. It was as if God said, "I've been waiting on you to make a difference."

Michele and Ron no longer attend church, and I blame myself for that. They claim a belief in God, and I remind them that Satan believes in God. However, they saw me not go to church as they grew into adulthood, and now they have other interests more important than attending church. One cannot say, "I believe in God," and leave it at that. You have to try to live the way God wants you to. You find out how by being in his presence at a church to hear his Word. I believe that only when you accept God into your heart, mind, and actions are you able to sense his presence and reap the love and peace he offers.

Despite my good showing on the IG and CMI, Major Davis clearly held a grudge over my telling him that I did not base my performance on the fear of getting a bad OER. I began to come up on extra duty details more often than normal for a section chief. In addition, the aviation section started getting assigned more details than they had in the past. My men noticed the increase and grumbled about how the S3 was punishing them for doing a good job. I took a positive outlook and explained that the battalion needed good results, so they picked the best to do it. After a while, feelings smoothed over and got back to normal.

The detail I came up on most often was as a member of a court-martial board. The army was on a downhill slide in 1969. The war in Vietnam was unpopular and was the priority for equipment, personnel, and funding. Drugs were a problem, and discipline in units like the Thirty-Fourth Signal Battalion was difficult to uphold. Thus, there were, at times, a high number of Article 32 investigations and court-martials.

In May, during a surprise billet inspection, the Company A commander found a bag of hashish and weighing scales in a specialist four's wall locker. The company arrested the specialist, charged him with seven counts of drug dealing, and referred him to a court-martial board. The board consisted of five officers. Major Worth was the senior officer and president of the board. Another captain, three lieutenants, and I made up the rest of the board.

The board convened at 0800 on a Friday morning. The specialist had hired a civilian lawyer to represent him. The trial counselor was a first lieutenant. The board continued normally until it was time for the defendant to exercise his challenges for cause. The defense challenged Major Worth, and he had to excuse himself. By seniority, I became the president of the board.

While as a lieutenant, I had served many times as the defense counsel or trial counsel, but I had never served as the president of the board. The responsibility and duties equaled those of a judge in a civilian trial. Honestly, when they challenged Major Worth, it shocked me because that usually did not happen. While I had the utmost confidence in myself when it came to performing soldiers' duties, I was apprehensive about these types of duties. Plus, I did not feel that with just my high school education, I was smart enough to be the board president. Nervously, I took the president's chair and resumed the proceedings.

After the challenges, the script called for presentation of charges and pleas. The trial counselor read the seven counts and specifications. I asked the accused specialist, "How do you plead?"

The lawyer for the specialist stood and replied, "If the court drops the first five counts, then my client will plead guilty to the last two counts. Otherwise, not guilty."

The two counts the specialist wanted to plead guilty to were minor counts, such as having unauthorized equipment in the wall locker. If I accepted the plea, then he would get off lightly. I called a five-minute recess and asked the trial counselor to approach the board. I asked him how strong his proof on the first five counts was. He assured me the proof was ironclad. He had witnesses who'd seen the specialist selling drugs, he had one witness who would admit to buying drugs from the specialist on several occasions, and the CID reports showed that his fingerprints were all over the scales and the bags containing the hashish. They had arrested his supplier, who'd given a statement that he'd sold drugs to the defendant.

I called court back to order. Looking at the defendant's lawyer, I thought to myself, *How on earth am I going to survive being president of the board?* I was facing a well-educated lawyer and deciding on points of law with no more than my simple high school education. However, I knew I was smart, or I would not have made it this far in the army. The problem was that I did not feel smart because I knew I lacked a formal education. The lawyer and trial counselor were standing, waiting on my decision about the defendant's plea.

I looked at the trial counselor and asked, "Lieutenant Brown, what's your recommendation on the proposed plea deal?"

He answered, "Sir, I recommend the court not accept the plea deal."

I looked at the lawyer and said, "The court does not accept the plea. Trial counselor, you may go with your opening argument."

The trial counselor continued to lay out the case against the defendant and enter the evidence into the record. It took him until around 1600 to complete his opening argument. When he rested, I directed the lawyer for the defense to begin his argument. He began by making a motion that the court throw out the charges against the defendant because of a lack of due process. His justification for the motion was an undue delay in bringing the case to court. The military court-martial manual required the army to try a defendant within six months of being charged. It was now seven months past the date when the army had charged the defendant.

Shit! I thought. *What do I do now?* I said, "The court will take a thirty-minute recess while I consider the motion. Lieutenant Brown, I want you to brief me on why the army exceeded the time limit."

He looked at me and said, "Sir, I will have to review the records first because I am not sure what caused the delay."

"Okay," I said. "Get everybody back in here."

As soon as everyone was back in the courtroom, I announced, "The court will adjourn until 0800 in the morning. Lieutenant Brown, you research the records and report the reason for the delay to the court in the morning."

That evening, I told Claudia about the proceedings and said I would have to work Saturday. She said if that was the case, she would go to Munich for the weekend. Again, it felt as if she were always looking for an opportunity to spend the weekend in Munich without me. As expected, on Saturday morning, she fixed breakfast, and while she packed to go to Munich, I left for the casern.

When everyone had assembled in the courtroom, I called the court to order. "Lieutenant Brown, are you ready to explain the delay?" I asked.

"Yes, sir," he answered. "The late receipt of lab results caused the delay. The commander sent the container of hashish to the army lab for analysis two weeks after he filed charges. Because of a backlog, the lab could not complete the analysis within the six-month window. The commander received the results from the lab six days ago and convened this court as quickly as possible. Since there was no dereliction by the convening authority, I recommend the court throw out the defense's motion to dismiss all charges."

I sat there for a while, thinking about the implications of what he had said. While the convening authority was not in dereliction of duty, there were grounds to dismiss because of a lack of a speedy trial. The lab's failure to complete a timely analysis was the fault of the government and not the accused. It would be within my purview to dismiss the case. But would that stand in the judge advocate's review of the court proceedings? If it did not stand, I would be at fault for making a bad decision. On the other hand, if I did not throw out the charges and a review board found that I should have, then I would have wasted a lot of the government's time and money.

The members of the court sat looking at me, waiting for my ruling. I thought, *Okay, exactly how many days are we talking about?* I opened the copy of the charge sheet and looked for when the army had charged the defendant. Then I calculated the time when the court-martial had started, which was sixteen days past the six-month period. That did not appear an undue delay, especially since the convening authority had acted immediately upon receiving the lab results.

In a court-martial, the president of the court could call on the judge advocate to provide an opinion on a point of law. The army recognized that not all of their appointed presidents of a court-martial board were brilliant lawyers. They would be like me and need help. Therefore, when a court-martial was in progress, the judge advocate stood by to provide help if needed. I needed it! "All right, here's what I am going to do," I said. "Lieutenant Brown, I want you to contact the judge advocate office. Speak to a lawyer, and explain the circumstances of the case and delay. Then ask if a sixteen-day delay with no dereliction by the convening authority is an undue delay. My opinion is that it is not an undue delay. Therefore, the court will be in recess until I have an answer from the judge advocate. Stay in the area, so we can reconvene as quickly as possible."

It was Saturday, and as expected, all the lawyers had left for the weekend. Lieutenant Brown spent almost two hours trying to track someone down to answer my question. Frustrated, he came back to tell me that he could not reach anyone. I asked him if he had tried to reach the judge advocate himself, a full bird colonel. He said no, so I sent him out again to try to get hold of the colonel. It was noon by then, so I told everybody that we would reconvene at 1500. It made no sense to have them sit around waiting.

I went to the officers' club and had lunch. Some signal officers I knew were there, so we talked for a while. At 1500, I called the court to order. I looked at Lieutenant Brown and asked, "Well?"

He shook his head and replied, "Sorry, sir. I tried every number I could but could not find him."

"Okay, Lieutenant Brown, you keep trying, and I do not care if you have to wake him up at midnight. I want that opinion. The court is in recess until 0800 in the morning."

The defense counselor looked at me and said, "Captain Griffin, tomorrow is Sunday. I would prefer we continue Monday instead of Sunday."

I looked at the defense counselor and replied, "I would prefer we continue Monday too. But you have made a motion about undue delay in bringing your client to trial. It is that motion that is delaying us now. I do not intend to let the day of the week influence continuing this court-martial. In my mind, that would subject us to an undue-delay claim. Court will convene at 0800 in the morning." The defense counselor shrugged, accepting my decision without further argument.

It was lonely back in my quarters. I could still smell Claudia's perfume. Some toys and books left by the kids were lying on the couch. I missed Claudia and the little encouragement she might give me after I told her about the court-martial. I do not know if my wish to spend all my free time with Claudia comes across as being controlling. It was not that I wanted to control her; I just wanted her company. I wanted her to love me with the same fervor and passion with which I loved her.

I convened the court-martial at 0800. "All right, Lieutenant Brown, what's the story?"

All eyes were on Lieutenant Brown as he stood and spoke. "Sir, I finally got a hold of the colonel at his quarters at 2230. He was a little upset at first, but when I explained the problem, he cooled down. He is going to call you at 0815 to give you his opinion personally."

"Thank you, Lieutenant Brown. Everybody take a break in place until I talk to the colonel."

At 0815, the CQ stuck his head into the courtroom and, looking at me, said, "Sir, the judge advocate wants to speak to you. He's on the phone in the orderly room."

I walked past several doors to the orderly room and picked up the phone. "Captain Griffin speaking, sir."

The voice on the phone answered, "Captain Griffin, this is the judge advocate. I am calling about your question about whether sixteen days is an undue delay. The answer is no. There's no way to consider sixteen days, without a blatant neglect of duty, an undue delay. Two, three, or four months without some plausible reason would be an undue delay. You can dismiss the defense's motion and continue with the court-martial."

"Thank you, sir," I answered.

I returned to the court-martial room and ruled on the defense's motion. "The motion to dismiss the charges is denied. Defense counselor, you can begin presentation of your arguments."

We sat in session until 1600, through the defense's arguments and then through rebuttal from each side. At the end of the defense's rebuttal, the court-martial board began deliberation of the evidence and testimony. It took us two hours to work through all the facts and witnesses' statements. I thought it was interesting that we found the defendant guilty of all charges and specifications except for the two he'd wanted to plead guilty to.

After hearing the extenuating and mitigating arguments, using the legal guide, I reduced him to the grade of private and sentenced him to six months in the stockade and a dishonorable discharge. I am proud to say that my conduct of the court-martial and following sentence, although challenged two times, was upheld by the judge advocate at the headquarters of the Department of the Army.

When I got in Sunday night, Claudia had already returned from Munich. Surprised that I was in my class A uniform, she asked, "Where have you been?" That I had been in a court-martial all weekend long astonished her.

By the end of May, I had accrued almost eighty-five days of leave. The army only allows you to carry over sixty days into the next year. That meant that by the end of September, I would have to burn up thirty-five days of leave or lose them, so Claudia and I started planning a vacation for the summer. I wanted to go somewhere and stay for two weeks. I wanted to go to an interesting place where we could spend time together but not have events rush us. Claudia came up with a good idea.

She suggested we book a two-week stay at Tenerife in the Canary Islands. That was a popular site for German tourists, and most travel agencies had cheap vacation packages. We booked a two-week stay at the Icarus Hotel for the last two weeks in July 1969. Mom was going to stay in our quarters and take care of the kids.

I was excited about spending two weeks with Claudia. Nothing was going to spoil my time. I intended to be a perfect husband and dazzle her. At least that was the way I fantasized about it.

Our tour left from Frankfurt Airport, so we drove up early on the departure date. The flight route was from Frankfurt to Lisbon for refueling and then on to Tenerife. Tourists filled all the seats on the 737. A mixture of Germans, a few Italians, and one other English couple were all headed for a holiday in Tenerife.

The flight was fairly smooth to Lisbon. I was a little nervous because of the steep circling approach the pilot used going into Lisbon Airport. I had never seen an approach like that in a commercial jet. Claudia was a nervous wreck. She was always afraid of flying. The least little noise, rattle, or turbulence intensified her fear. However, she withstood it, mainly by grasping my arm with bruising force.

A couple of hours after leaving Lisbon, we started our approach into the Tenerife airport. The airport's altitude was 4,500 feet with intermittent clouds. The pilot had to do a missed approach on the first try, as he could not see the runway. Circling, he announced he would try another approach, and if that failed, he would have to return to Lisbon.

Now I was a little nervous. I knew the pressure he was feeling. That pressure would cause him to try a little harder and take a little more risk than he usually would. To return to Lisbon would cost the airline a lot of money. There was light to moderate turbulence as we descended through the clouds toward the runway. I kept staring out the window, looking for signs of the runway. I listened to the roar of the engines change from power-up and to power-down mode as he worked to stay on the glide slope. Then, surprisingly, I could see terminal buildings through the window, and simultaneously, the 737 bounced onto the runway. I am sure the pilot made an almost zero-zero landing, because fog covered the airport. We taxied to the terminal amid the "Welcome to Tenerife" announcement over the intercom. This was the first time I'd felt uncomfortable flying commercially. I knew what it took to make an instrument landing, and my gut told me the pilot had exceeded minimums to land. He had put us at risk. I was glad to get off the aircraft. Even Claudia sensed that it was an unusual landing, because she had never landed in such dense fog.

When the courtesy bus arrived at the Icarus Hotel, the fog had burned off, and the sun was shining. Our vacation coincided with another major event that had the world's people on the edge of their seats. Apollo 11 was orbiting the moon in preparation of landing American astronauts. During our ride to the hotel, the bus driver had the radio on so all could follow the Eagle's descent to the moon. When those immortal words "Eagle has landed" came over the radio, everybody on the bus started cheering and clapping for America. Then they all started congratulating Claudia and me. I felt enormous pride in being an American.

We had a wonderful time in Tenerife. By day, we lay by the pool and sunned. Our tour package included two meals a day, so we mainly ate breakfast and dinner. When we toured the sites, we would eat lunch and eat dinner out. About thirty of us took a one-day side trip to North Africa. We flew across in an old C-47 and landed at a crude airport. After processing through customs, we boarded an air-conditioned bus and left to visit an oasis for lunch. The temperature was around 130 degrees as we motored across a flat, barren expanse of land. Somewhere, we turned off the main road and descended into a small canyon.

At the bottom of the canyon, a collection of tents surrounded a spring. There, we sat with bedouins and drank hot tea flavored with rock sugar. Lunch was snacks of shish kebabs. The bedouins offered camel rides, and Claudia climbed aboard one and rode for about five minutes. I took pictures and laughed at her bouncing around. From there, we continued to a large town located along the coast.

There, the tour guide took us to a bazaar for shopping, and afterward, we retired to a restaurant for dinner. We sat on cushions to eat, as there were no chairs or tables. This was real Arab dining. After a tasty meal of spicy foods, we returned to the airfield for the return trip to Tenerife. It felt good to get back to a cold beer after spending a day in blazing heat with nothing to drink but hot tea or warm soda, since they did not allow alcohol in Muslim countries.

All good times end. Other than when we'd met in Bangkok, this was the first time Claudia and I had gone on vacation and spent the whole time at one location. It was the most enjoyable time I had during the year and a half I spent in Germany on that tour of duty. As we boarded the 737 for the flight back to Frankfort, Claudia saw some fluid venting from a vent tube on one of the wings. She sat terrified the whole flight back, believing that it was fuel leaking from the wing. Nothing I could say convinced her that the fluid was only excess moisture venting from the aircraft.

The kids and Mom were happy to see us. I know they could feel the tension between Claudia and me, and for us to come back happy and peaceful made them feel better. I still had fifteen days of leave to use, so I took another two-week leave in September. This time, we spent my leave in Germany, some of it in Munich and the rest in Stuttgart. It was relaxing to be away from the grind of army duty.

My job was starting to bore me, so I returned to work in a "Wish I didn't have to" mood. I loved flying and commanding my people, but the details, inspections, meetings, and endless make-work orders from the battalion were getting me down. The army was suffering from poor-quality soldiers brought about by the war raging in Vietnam and the demand it placed on recruitment.

Poor-quality junior-grade soldiers overloaded the battalion. Despite the best effort of the NCOs and officers, it floated from one performance deficiency to the next. That was not the case with my soldiers, but as part of the battalion, we suffered with the rest and endured the training exercises and inspections designed to correct nonperforming elements.

In October, Mr. Quito got orders for Vietnam. He was happy to go. I called him in to counsel him and show him his OER. Because I was responsible for the professional development of my officers, I had held up his promotion to W-2 for three months. The three months got his attention and convinced him that flying was not the only job for which he was responsible. He improved rapidly, and I was now able to give him a good OER.

During our session, he asked me how I thought he would do in Vietnam. He wanted to fly gunships and not lift helicopters. I told him I thought he would return from Vietnam either as a hero or dead. I based my opinion on the way he always pushed the envelope when flying, whether it was necessary or not. That would get him killed or make him a hero. He was a tremendously skilled pilot with superb coordination. That ability gave him, I think, a false confidence in his ability to handle any situation. I believed that it would lead him to take risks not because the mission demanded it but because he believed he could do it and get away with it. I hoped that I was wrong and that he would get experience with a wiser aircraft commander before he became a combat aircraft commander.

CW-3 Opie left a week after Mr. Quito. His departure left me in a bind for a good maintenance officer. He had been training Mr. Roy on those duties in preparation for his departure. Mr. Roy was both good and competent, but I did not know if he would have the drive and passion for being a maintenance officer that Opie had. His absence also left me with two assigned officers with which to provide the battalion aviation support. I worked out a deal with Major Davis to let one of the rated captains assigned to the S3 staff fly until I got some more pilots.

I started flying all the courier missions and used Mr. Roy and the captain to do the tactical support missions. We got in many flying hours and managed to support the missions asked of us satisfactorily. However, my boredom evolved into dissatisfaction with my job.

I began to look around at other units to which I might seek a transfer. It turned out our battalion was the only unit in Germany with a Beaver. All the other aviation units had either helicopters or U-21s. I was not rated in either one, so I was stuck in the battalion.

My dissatisfaction began to surface in my family life. Claudia and I began to argue more. This time, I could see that it was not necessarily what she was doing that angered me. I was unhappy.

My OER was due in November. Major Davis, as my rater, called me in to discuss his rating. It was not a bad OER narrative wise. The problem with it was that he put me in the average category of officers. Normally, this would have been okay, but because of the inflation, an average category was now below average, and the above-average category was the average. For an officer to have a chance for promotion or stay in the army, he had to have all above-average ratings. My face was blank as I listened to him, but my mind was saying, *This is payback for the comments I made to him about OERs.* Finally, he asked if I had any questions. I told him no and signed my OER. It went to the senior rater next, LTC Kirk. My fate now rested with how he rated me and what narrative he put in his block.

A week later, LTC Kirk called me in to discuss the OER. I reported to him and took the seat by his desk. He said, "Captain Griffin, I have talked to Major Davis about his rating. He feels strongly that it is correct. I'm sure you are aware that it's a killer for promotion boards. But I believe that you are much better than Major Davis has rated you. I cannot change his rating, but in my narrative, I have described how your leadership and performance were responsible for the higher headquarters company passing the IG and CMI inspection. I have also noted several other accomplishments that I believe distinguish you. Often, the senior rater's comments carry more weight than the rater's. I am hoping that will be the case for your OER. I certainly believe you are a much finer officer than Major Davis describes. Do you have any questions?"

I was thankful as I answered, "No, sir. Thank you for having confidence and faith in my ability and future value to the army." I signed my OER and left in a much happier mood.

At the same time my OER was due, an officer preference sheet was due. I dropped by the personnel office and filled one out. In it, I asked for Mohawk and rotary-wing transition as my next professional development training. I signed it, and the personnel officer said he would include it in my OER packet.

The two OERs I received in the Thirty-Fourth Signal Battalion were the worst in my record. I do not believe I could have performed any better than I did. The daily evaluations of my unit and my performance were all outstanding. I was thirty-one years old and had thirteen years of service. I also was, for the first time in my career, unhappy with my job and hoping it would change soon.

I was happiest when flying. My mind focused on flying the aircraft and took a break from handling the unhappiness. While flying dampened the pain I was feeling over Claudia and my relations, it did not erase it. Sometimes, with the Beaver trimmed and the weather clear, I would think through my choices to make our relationship better. I had a sense that somehow, the way I acted was part of the problem. Was my poor self-esteem causing me to feel insecure and untrusting? Did my reaction come across to Claudia as controlling? I wanted a bond that I could depend on.

I wanted one that was good continuously. Even a continuously bad one would be better than the up-and-down one we endured. We could walk away from a totally bad relationship.

One day Major Davis called to say he was in Kitzingen and needed me to pick him up at 2000. It was mid-December, the season for winter weather. It was about an hour's flight to Kitzingen, and the weather forecast called for snow and icing above three thousand feet. I did not want to file a night IFR plan in snow and icing, so I filed VFR at three thousand feet. I figured this would keep me out of the bad weather and at a safe enough altitude to clear any terrain features en route.

It was dark when I took off and climbed to three thousand feet. It was clear, and the many lights from the array of small towns sparkled like diamonds. Occasionally, I would fly though a heavy snow shower, but most of the time, it was clear. After a while, I began to think about Claudia and our relations. I did not know what to do. In my mind, I provided her with a good life. She had been an inspiration for me to be the best I could be and achieve all my goals. In turn, I felt let down by the way she treated me.

In the smooth night air, I lost track of time. Fortunately, I had tuned my ADF receiver to the Kitzingen ADF transmitter. I was flying through a snow shower, when the ADF needle surprised me by rotating 180 degrees. That meant I was flying over the Kitzingen AAF. While I had little forward vision, I could see clearly when looking down. Sure enough, I could see the airfield lights below me. I had become so engrossed in my thoughts that I had failed to see the landmarks alerting me that I was approaching Kitzingen AAF. Hastily, I banked right and called the Kitzingen tower for landing instructions. I did not want to lose sight of the airfield in the snowstorm.

The tower called back, asking for my location. It is routine on a VFR flight plan to report your location when calling the tower for landing. I had failed to mention that I was over the airfield, because a pilot does not overfly an airfield without permission. Now I had to report my error. "Roger, Kitzingen Tower. I unintentionally overflew the runway in the snowstorm. I'm in a right bank at three thousand feet."

"Roger, Army 62378. Enter a right downwind for runway sixteen. Report downwind."

I repeated the tower's instructions and felt fortunate that they did not press the issue. Overflying a runway can be dangerous, especially if there are other aircraft in the traffic pattern. Of course, at three thousand feet, I was over the altitude for airfield operations, except for instrument traffic, and maybe that was why it did not concern them. I counted myself lucky and took it as a warning not to work on my personal problems while flying. There is no way of knowing what would have happened if I had not turned my ADF on.

We had another white Christmas. We had battalion parties to attend, and overall, it was a fun Christmas season. We had a small tree, and Michele and Ron helped decorate it. There was peace between Claudia and me. I like to think the spirit of peace and goodwill reached our hearts for a while.

Time dragged on for me. January 1970 came and passed, and the restrictions of winter intensified my frustration and unhappiness. All I hoped for each day was a new assignment. By February, I was desperate and was considering calling my branch assignment's office at the DA and begging them to send me back to Vietnam. The war was raging there, and the army was struggling to keep up the flow of replacements. The army gladly accepted and quickly honored all requests to go to Vietnam.

On February 15, I was sitting in my office at the hangar, when the phone rang. I answered and found myself talking to Major Beck, the artillery assignment officer. "Captain Griffin, I'm looking at your latest assignment preference form, and I see that you want rotary-wing transition and Mohawk transition. Is that correct?"

It was as if Major Beck, sitting in the Pentagon, had read my mind. "Yes, sir, that is correct," I answered.

"Okay, if you can be at Fort Rucker by April 1, I can get you into a rotary-wing transition course, followed by Mohawk transition. Can you be there?"

Excited, I replied forcefully, "Yes, sir! If you send the request to cut orders to my battalion personnel office today, it would help."

"Okay, Captain Griffin, as we speak, I am sending a message to your personnel office. The message asks them to cut orders sending you TDY to Fort Rucker for rotary-wing and Mohawk transition en route to Vietnam. You have a good day."

He hung up before I could say, "Wait a minute." I had just volunteered to return to Vietnam without even knowing it. At first, I was tempted to call him back, but then I rationalized that I had been fixing to call branch anyway and ask for a transfer to Vietnam to get out of Germany. Now I had the schools I wanted and the trip back to Vietnam. I was better off than before.

I called Claudia to give her the news. She was not as excited about it as I was. I told her we would talk about it when I got home. Then I called the personnel officer and alerted him that a message requesting orders reassigning me was on the way. I asked him for any help he could give me because of my short report date. Then I called the S1 and told him, so he could alert the commander. Then I called all my people together and told them.

That evening, when I explained exactly what I was doing, Claudia was not happy about the short notice. I told her I was not either, but if I wanted the rotary-wing transition and Mohawk transition, I had to accept it. At first, she wanted to remain in Germany while I was at Fort Rucker, and that angered me. I told her bluntly that if I had to spend six months alone at Fort Rucker and then a year in Vietnam, it would result in a divorce. The anger and frustration in my tone must have gotten her attention. She angrily said, "Okay, I will go with you. When you finish your training, then what?"

She had a point. Where would she stay? It would be unfair of me to ask her to stay in the United States, when her family was in Munich. Softening my tone, I said, "Look, after my training, I will fly you and the kids back to Munich. I probably can get quarters for you in Perlacher. The army has a program that lets families of soldiers deployed to Vietnam stay in government quarters if they are available. There's hardly any military left in Munich, so there should be plenty of quarters available in Perlacher."

She immediately lost her confrontational mood and responded excitedly, "That would be great. Do you think you will have time to move us to Germany before you go to Vietnam?"

"I'll have plenty of time. We'll fly back with Davis Agency, and it shouldn't take more than a couple of days to sign for quarters if they are available. In fact, once you're in quarters, why don't you fly back with me, and we'll spend the rest of my leave driving to Fort Lewis and vacationing along the way?"

She was happy now. Although she would have to spend six or seven months in the States, she knew she was coming back to her Munich. I felt a twinge of apprehension, wondering what was waiting for her in Munich. Whatever it was, it had a strong hold on her, and she wanted it more than she wanted me. At least she would be with me for the next six or seven months, and I vowed to do my best to make her forget about Munich. Once that discussion was over, we seemed closer to each other as we began planning our move to Fort Rucker.

The most troubling problem was what to do about transport. We had bought a new 1969 Cougar XR7 through the PX. It would take two weeks from the time we shipped it for it to arrive in the States. If we shipped it two weeks before we left, we would not have a car just when we needed it the most.

Fortunately, we had become friends with a WO-4 and his wife who lived in the apartment above us. He was retiring and had sent his wife on to the States while he cleared quarters and cleared the army. His home was in a town in New Jersey about five miles from where the cars arrived. He indicated he had an extra car that we could use. He told us to catch a cab to his house when we got to McGuire AFB, and we could use his car to go on to Fort Rucker. When our car arrived, I could drive his car back and pick up my car. He was a godsend, and that solved our car problem.

I was happier than I had been in a while. Storing household goods, clearing quarters, and getting a flight back to the States in time to be at Fort Rucker went smoothly. The battalion threw a going-away party for Claudia and me. At night, lying in bed, I could not believe I was really going to helicopter and Mohawk transition. It was a little scary to think about. I hoped I could live up to the challenge.

We waited until the day before we left to take Michele out of school. That was one of the unfortunate things about the military: the frequent moves bounced kids around from place to place. Michele and Ron would tell me later, when I retired, that they did not want to move, because where we lived then was the only hometown they had known.

We left Frankfurt AFB on March 25 on an air force–chartered 707. The flight was nice, and we landed at McGuire AFB on schedule. It was midday when we cleared customs and found a cab to take us to the chief's house.

He was not home when we got there. He had found a job in a town about a hundred miles from New Jersey, but his wife was waiting for us and had the car ready. She wanted us to spend the night, but I wanted to get on the way, so we thanked her and left with the promise to return the car as soon as ours was ready for pickup.

We stopped at a small town in Virginia to spend the night. It felt good to be back on US soil. The kids loved the number of TV programs they could watch (in Germany, there were only a couple of channels, and only a few had shows designed for kids). After dinner, we were all so exhausted that we went straight to bed.

We were on the way by 0900 after a big breakfast. I had eggs, grits, sausage, and biscuits for the first time in two years. Claudia did not like grits, so she had potatoes, and the kids ate cereal. They were picky eaters anyway. I was eager to get to Fort Rucker as early as possible because with all the students going to the various army aviation schools at Fort Rucker, housing was hard to find, and I wanted to live as close to Fort Rucker as possible.

CHAPTER 3

Transition to Rotary Wing and Mohawk

W e got to Daleville, the little town at the front gate of Fort Rucker, around 1500. I remembered my previous experience with finding a place to live, so it was the first item on my agenda. The first place I tried was the Daleville Inn, a large inn with kitchenettes. We were in luck. A party had just checked out, so we took a look at the kitchenette. It had a large bedroom, large kitchen and dining area, and small bedroom with two single beds. It was perfect, so we moved in.

After moving in, we drove around Fort Rucker to familiarize ourselves with the fort. After finding the commissary and PX, we bought groceries at the commissary. Next, we drove around Daleville and then to Enterprise, a larger town about six miles from Fort Rucker. Enterprise had a giant statue of a boll weevil on the highway entering the town as a tribute to the farmers' win over the pest. Enterprise was the second-largest town close to Fort Rucker. Ozark, a little larger than Enterprise, was on the west side of Fort Rucker.

It felt good to be in my country again and in the wonderful, warm Alabama weather. I was looking forward to the peace of a school environment, where I did not have to worry about missions, inspections, and personnel problems. I just had to worry about flying. I could make it a six-month vacation for Claudia and the kids.

That night after dinner, as we sat around watching TV, I felt maybe Claudia and I could strengthen our relations. I had no Munich or Traudl with which to compete. The school environment would allow us to live like a normal couple. My flight training would be from eight to five each day, giving us plenty of time to have fun together. Even better, Claudia had a

German girlfriend whose husband was midway through Mohawk training. They could keep each other company during the day while Michele was in school. This was my chance to ease the tensions between us.

We spent the weekend exploring the area. We drove to Dothan, the largest nearby city that had a shopping mall. We found the school Michele would attend, and Claudia called Karen, her friend, to let her know she was there. Karen invited us over for coffee on Sunday afternoon. She and her husband, Don, had two young boys Michele and Ron's age.

Don was an artillery major. He had attended OCS four years ahead of me. We had a good time talking aviation, and he filled me in on Mohawk transition. Of course, he would finish long before I started, since I was doing rotary-wing transition first.

Monday morning, we enrolled Michele in school. Because of the large number of military families living in the Daleville Inn, a school bus stopped at the office each morning and afternoon to pick up and return students. In addition to families, a number of young warrant officer candidates attending flight school stayed at the inn.

After enrolling Michele, I dropped Claudia and Ron off at the inn and drove to the base to sign in. I found the student officer company in the same location as when I'd attended flight school. I signed in, completed all the personnel paperwork, and filed for travel pay. The personnel sergeant gave me a student packet with my class schedules and locations. Once I finished there, I drove to the quartermaster issue point and picked up a flight helmet, after which I went to student issue to pick up twenty-eight field manuals detailing helicopter flight and aerodynamics, plus maintenance manuals on the OH-13.

The OH-13 was the helicopter I would be transitioning into. I was one of four active-duty officers going through the army reserve rotary-wing transition course. Though I had hoped for UH-1 transition, they were overcommitted with training warrant officers. The war in Vietnam was still raging, and it was an air war, so the demand for UH-1 pilots never ended and far exceeded the supply. Therefore, there were no extra UH-1s for transition training.

That night, I reviewed my training schedule and checked the read-ahead requirements. The transition consisted of classroom instruction with a focus on hands-on learning in the observation helicopter 13 (OH-13).

I read several chapters on the OH-13 and its systems. It was a simple helicopter that had been around since the Korean War. It had a reliable rear-mounted air-cooled flat-head eight-cylinder engine that resembled a Volkswagen engine and was the same as the one I'd had in my aviation section in Germany. Now I wished I had learned more about the OH-13 when I'd had the chance.

Our first morning of rotary-wing transition began in a classroom and flight room. The room was at a field training site away from the main base. The location allowed us to fly without interfering with traffic arriving and leaving Cairns AAF. The class consisted of about forty officers and WOs divided into two flights. We met our instructor pilots that morning.

My instructor pilot, W-3 James, was a skilled pilot with two tours in Vietnam. The other student on my team was a National Guard lieutenant. Chief James spent the first hour discussing the training plan and what he expected of us. Then he took us to the flight line to explain a preflight on the OH-13. He pointed out what to check and how to check it using the checklist. He was moving through the checks faster than I wanted him to, but because we were pilots, he expected us to grasp the concepts faster. After completing the preflight check, he said, "Okay, Captain Griffin, get your helmet, and let's start."

I strapped myself into the pilot's seat of the OH-13 and looked at the instruments. They were mostly the same as the instruments in the Beaver and Bird Dog. The differences were the gauges, such as rotor rpm versus prop rpm. Prop rpm equated to engine rpm on the Beaver. However, in the OH-13, there was a separate engine rpm gauge. Chief James explained the use of each gauge and then went over the controls.

Flying a helicopter requires the use of three control inputs. The cyclic is similar to the stick on a fixed-wing aircraft. On a helicopter, it is used to control the rotor. When you push the cyclic forward, left, right, or rearward, the rotor tilts in that direction, causing the helicopter to move in that direction. The next main control is the collective.

The pilot uses the collective to move the helicopter up or down by changing the pitch on the rotor blades. The power control for the engine is on the collective control handle. It works like a motorcycle handle: when you roll the handle to the right, you increase power to the engine; when you roll it to the left, you reduce power. The pilot must coordinate the use of the collective and power controls. As you pull the collective up, you increase the pitch on the blades, and the helicopter wants to rise. At the same time, that loads the blades and requires an increase in power to preserve the proper rotor rpm, so while pulling the collective, you roll on more power. When you lower the collective, you roll off power. If you do not, there is no load on the engine, and it will quickly overspeed, damaging the engine.

The next control input is for the pedals. When you pull the collective and roll on power, the increased pitch on the blades will make the fuselage turn with the blades. To control this, you apply right or left pedal, which controls the tail rotor. Pedal changes increase or decrease pitch to the tail rotor. This counters the sideward spin of the helicopter and keeps the fuselage aligned with flight direction.

I had to learn to pull the collective as I rolled on the correct amount of power. Simultaneously, I had to move the cyclic forward so the helicopter would start moving forward, and I had to apply the right amount of pedal to maintain straight flight. To stop forward motion, I had to pull back on the cyclic, lower the collective, and reduce power just enough to stop moving forward and, at the same time, reverse input to the pedals, which would bring me to a hover.

Ideally, you hover three feet above the ground. The pilot uses the hover to move the helicopter around the airfield just as you would taxi a fixed-wing aircraft. The hover is the first phase of a normal takeoff.

To take off in a helicopter, you bring it to a hover, and if on a helipad, you turn into the wind, apply forward cyclic, and pull the collective to move the helicopter forward. As the helicopter moves forward, gaining speed, the rotary blades will begin to act like wings, and the helicopter will enter translational lift and begin to fly. Landing a helicopter is the opposite.

Landing the helicopter was more difficult for me; I had to concentrate to avoid the tendency to round out, as you do in fixed-wing aircraft. The procedure is similar. You pick your landing spot and reduce power and collective to begin a descent. You set up a descent line to your landing spot and maintain it until you have to add collective and power to stop your descent. At the same time, you move the cyclic to the rear to halt forward motion. Ideally, you come to a three-foot hover over your landing spot. If you are over your landing spot, then you lower the collective and reduce power to ease the helicopter onto the spot. If not, then you taxi at a three-foot hover to your spot.

I spent the next two weeks training four hours a day—two in the morning and two in the afternoon—learning to coordinate movement of my hands and feet together to fly the OH-13. Like all the other students, I bounced around the field on my first try, but after an hour or so, I could hover anywhere between two feet and ten feet. Finally, I began to get the grasp of it and started to improve. It would take another two weeks of hovering to the active, taking off, flying the traffic pattern, and landing before I began to feel comfortable with my ability to fly the OH-13 safely. On Friday afternoon of the second week, I had my first check ride.

Chief James had me hover over to a spot near the briefing room and land. He got out of the aircraft, and another instructor got in. It was my check ride to show that I could hover, take off, and land the OH-13. I did okay on the check ride, but because of checkrideitis, I did not perform the maneuvers as smoothly as I normally did. However, I passed, and that was what counted.

Now the more serious training began. Chief James got back into the aircraft, and I hovered out to the runway for takeoff. He took control of the aircraft and demonstrated an autorotation. He made it look easy.

A pilot uses the autorotation to land if he loses the use of his engine and has no power to make a normal landing. The key to an autorotation is getting your collective down the instant the engine loses power. The object is to keep the rotor rpm in the green. If it starts getting too high and out of the green, you apply rearward cyclic to flatten your approach. This loads the rotor blades and reduces rpm into the green. If your rpm starts bleeding off, you put forward pressure on the cyclic to steepen your descent and increase the flow of air over your blades. This increases rpm.

As you descend, you prepare to land just as you would with power. When you reach your touchdown spot, you pull the collective just as you would in a typical landing. The inertia in the rotor rpm is enough to bring the aircraft to a hover and allow you to set it down before the rpm bleeds off completely. Of course, you have to make a good approach because you only get one application of collective to land the aircraft.

A strong feature of army aviation is being prepared for an emergency. After you learn the basic techniques of takeoffs and landings, 90 percent of the remaining instruction and training are on handling an emergency. As in fixed-wing training, you always have an area in your mind to which you will autorotate in case of an emergency. You must constantly note wind direction and mentally keep the nearest site located. This allows you to turn toward it immediately if an emergency, such as an engine failure, occurs. In a helicopter, you cannot waste any altitude deciding where you are going. When you fly out of range of one site, you must pick another.

The instructor stresses emergency procedures until they become automatic reflexes. You can expect him to ask you where you plan to go in case of an engine failure. At any moment in the middle of any training maneuver, you can expect to hear the instructor say, "Engine failure," or name some other emergency. He expects you to react correctly and immediately to the emergency. I believe lack of emergency training is the cause of the high number of civilian deaths in small-aircraft crashes. I think private pilots fail to make successful emergency landings because of the lack of discipline in being prepared for the emergency.

After I showed my ability to safely fly the OH-13, Chief James started autorotation training. First, he demonstrated one as we were making a normal approach to the airfield. Speaking as he simulated an engine failure, he lowered the collective while rolling off power and maintained direction using pedals. He used pedals to maintain direction and forward cyclic to keep rotor rpm. He declared an emergency and headed for the landing spot. Of course, he made a perfect autorotation to the end of the runway. After he asked me if I had any questions, he said, "Okay, show me what you can do."

I waited until it was clear for takeoff and then pulled collective and took off, staying on runway direction until I reached the traffic pattern altitude of 1,200 feet. I made a right bank and entered a right downwind. I turned base and to final just as I would for a regular landing. As I rolled out on final, Chief James said, "Engine failure," and he notified the field tower of a simulated autorotation. As soon as he said, "Engine failure," I lowered the collective and rolled off power. I'd never done this in the air, and the OH-13 yawed to the left before I could get right pedal in. Concentrating on getting the aircraft turned in the right direction, I forgot about the cyclic until Chief James asked, "What are you going to do about your rotor rpm?"

"Shit," I said as I looked at my rotor rpm, which was below the green. I had forgotten to put in forward cyclic to start down, and the helicopter continued in level flight, bleeding off valuable rotor rpm. I immediately pushed the cyclic forward, and the rpm started back up, but I was way past my touchdown point. I had to go for a spot farther down the runway. While I focused on that, I heard Chief James say, "Watch rpm"—it was now in the red.

"Shit," I said again as I pulled the collective to get the rpm under control. Pulling the collective without pushing the cyclic forward caused the aircraft to climb. Of course, climbing without adding power caused the aircraft to yaw to the right and bleed off forward airspeed. Chief James was laughing now at my plight while muttering singsong-like, "We're going to crash, and we're going to crash." As I fought to regain some likeness of coordination, I told myself to calm down and think.

Chief James was about to take the aircraft, when I got it under control. I aligned the aircraft with the runway and had the rpm under control when we got to three feet. I pulled the collective and the cyclic back too far, and we touched down halfway down the runway, sliding about twenty feet before stopping. I sat there shaking my head in disgust and waiting for Chief James's comments.

He finally looked at me after he composed himself, and he said, "Hover over to the hover area, and let's talk about your autorotation."

I set the aircraft down in the hover area, and Chief James gave me his critique. "What was good about your autorotation is we survived it. You took an area two thousand feet long to set it down. Let's say you were operating at three hundred feet over triple-canopy jungle, and the only spot you had was a clearing thirty feet square. In that scenario, we would have crashed into the trees. An autorotation is only good if you can hit your spot. I know this was your first one, but an autorotation is just a landing without power. Don't let the idea that you have no power distract you. At the end, you brought everything together to land the aircraft. I want you to concentrate on doing that immediately, and when you pick your spot, I want you to do whatever is necessary to land on that spot. Any questions?"

I wanted to defend myself because it was my first autorotation, but he was right. If I'd gotten everything together at touchdown, then I could get it together at the beginning. I responded, "You're right, Chief. I have to admit that I was a little apprehensive about an autorotation, and I let that cause me problems. I've handled several flying emergencies, and there was no excuse for that so-called autorotation."

Thus, my autorotation training began. As usual, after a while, I became skilled at doing an autorotation. At the same time we practiced autorotation, we learned how to make a no-hydraulics landing.

Most helicopter controls move with the help of hydraulics. Without hydraulics, the pilot needs a tremendous amount of cyclic pressure to move the rotor head. This makes the cyclic stiff. It is difficult to fly the helicopter, especially when landing, and almost impossible to hover. The slower the speed, the harder it is to make cyclic and collective changes. Because of that, there is a special technique for landing with a hydraulic failure.

The technique for a no-hydraulics landing is the same as a normal landing, except you maintain a higher airspeed. The object is to take it all the way to the ground with no hover. As you reach hover altitude, you put back pressure on the cyclic to slow your forward speed and, at the same time, lower the collective to touch down and slide to a halt. It's almost like landing a winged aircraft on skids.

Once I mastered all of these techniques, I began to have fun flying the OH-13. At the end of the sixth week, I took another check ride to show my ability to autorotate and do a no-hydraulic landing. As usual, while I passed the check ride, checkrideitis ensured it was not one of my best flights. After I hovered back to the pad, we went into the debriefing room, where the captain who'd given me the check ride asked me questions about the OH-13 and all aspects of each maneuver. Afterward, he completed my check ride form and said, "Okay, you are cleared to solo."

The clearance to solo boosted my morale but also left a twinge of apprehension. I could have fun over the weekend, knowing I was doing okay in my transition program and had reached a milestone a week early. The National Guard lieutenant was still struggling with autorotation. I was bubbly with satisfaction when I got back to the apartment. Claudia congratulated me, and we had a nice dinner. We made plans to go to Dothan Mall on Saturday.

I had spent the last weekend on the road. The transportation office had notified me on Tuesday of that week that my car was ready for pickup at the Brooklyn Navy Yard. I had asked for a one-day leave so I could leave that Friday, but the regulations would not allow it. The army only approved emergency leaves during a formal transition course, so immediately after training that Friday, I left for the Brooklyn Navy Yard.

I drove all night and got to the chief's house in New Jersey around nine o'clock on Saturday morning. Claudia had called to let them know I was coming to return their car. When I got there, the chief was still out of town, so I dropped the car off and thanked his wife for their kindness. Fortunately, I could catch a bus in front of their house that would take me by the navy yard. I waved good-bye and invited her and the chief down to visit us. She said she would love to, but sadly, we heard a year later that they had divorced.

I picked up my Mercury XR7 and was on my way back to Fort Rucker by 1300. I got back to the apartment around 2200 on Sunday night, dead tired and sleepy. I'd chanced driving all weekend to get the car. If I had broken down, had an accident, or for some reason not made it back in time to be at class on Monday, the army could have charged me with being AWOL.

Monday morning, Chief James rode around the pattern with me one time to make sure I was still safe. He then got out and told me to practice landings and takeoffs on my own. He shut the door, and I was alone at the controls. *Well, here goes,* I said to myself, and I called the field tower for clearance to hover for takeoff. The tower approved my request. I slowly brought the helicopter to a hover and moved toward the line of OH-13s waiting to take the active for takeoff. There were several other solo students waiting to take off. The turbulence from the rotor wash was causing all of us to work hard to keep the aircraft under control at a three-foot hover and a ten-yard separation.

The tower cleared me for takeoff, and I hovered onto the active. I took a deep breath, pushed the cyclic forward, and made my first solo flight in a helicopter. I smiled as I climbed to traffic pattern altitude behind the aircraft in front of me. I followed him around the traffic pattern, and then the tower cleared me to land and hover for another takeoff.

I turned final, and selecting my touchdown at the end of the runway, I lowered the collective and power and started my approach. I kept telling myself not to round out but to take it to the ground. After all the time flying fixed-wing aircraft, it was difficult for me to control the tendency to round out. As I neared the hover altitude, I became a little wobbly as I worked the controls to bring the OH-13 to a three-foot hover over my landing spot. When I finally set the aircraft down, I was about fifteen feet forward of my landing spot, but I was happy. At least I had soloed.

I called the tower for clearance to hover around for another touch-and-go. I spent the next hour and a half taking off and landing. It was boring as hell, but it was necessary to develop my skills and coordination. By my last touch-and-go, I could land within a foot or two of my intended spot. I was exhausted but happy when I returned to the apartment.

We spent the rest of the week practicing turns, climbs, recon, and approaches into confined areas. There were many small landing sites around our training area. Some were among tall trees; others had one or two obstacles that we had to avoid on landing. Chief James had me fly to one, recon the site, and then make a landing approach. He would critique my performance and have me fly to the next one and repeat the landing approach. Of course, along the way, I could expect a simulated autorotation anytime, so I was careful to pick emergency landing spots along the way. The good feature about the helicopter was that almost any small, cleared area could serve as a landing site. In fixed-wing aircraft, you needed a runway-sized landing site.

While I trained and looked forward to the weekend with my family, Michele went to school and looked forward to the weekend so she could watch cartoons on TV. It was the first time Ron and Michele had seen the array of Saturday and Sunday morning cartoons on TV. In Germany, cartoons were not shown often, and now all they wanted to do on the weekends was watch cartoons. It was hard to drag them away from the TV to go shopping with Claudia and me.

One Saturday morning about four weeks after we moved into the apartment, Claudia and I were going to Dothan. Michele and Ron did not want to go, and Michele pleaded with us to let them stay and watch TV. Michele was nine years old at the time and an unusually mature young lady for her age. I walked up to the office and explained to the women there that I wanted to leave my nine-year-old daughter and five-year-old son in the apartment while we went to Dothan. The women were nice and assured me they would act as babysitters if Michele needed help with anything.

They told me not to worry; several of the military families staying at the apartment left their children alone under the same agreement.

So I relented and agreed to let Michele and Ron stay while we went to Dothan. Claudia fixed some sandwiches and snacks for their lunch. I had Michele repeat what she was to do in case of an emergency and made sure she understood that they would not leave the apartment for any reason other than an emergency. Michele was smart and capable of caring for Ron. Some people might criticize Claudia and me for leaving our young children alone, but I trusted Michele, so we prepared them and let them stay.

Claudia and I had a wonderful time in Dothan. Claudia loved to shop, and I just hung around because I loved her. We returned around 1600 so we could fix dinner for everyone. As we approached the apartment door, I could see a note on it, telling us to please come to the desk. The apartment was dark, and the note scared the hell out of Claudia. We hurried to the office.

The clerk on duty saw the looks on our faces, and before we could speak, she said, "Don't worry; nothing bad has happened." That was a relief to hear. It seemed one of the students in the warrant officer course who lived over us had been celebrating the night before. He placed some beer in the bathroom sink and put some ice in to keep it cool. After the ice melted, he turned the cold water on to keep it cool. He left the next morning, forgetting about the running water, and one of the bottles shifted and stopped up the sink. The sink overflowed, and after a couple hours, it started filling the apartment with water.

Meanwhile, in our apartment below, Michele and Ron were watching TV. Michele noticed that water started dripping from the ceiling, so she put a pot on the floor to catch the water. The one leak did not bother her since she figured she had it under control. Within an hour, there were six more leaks, and Michele ran out of pots. She told Ron that something was wrong and that they had to shut off all the power and go to the office. I knew then that she was going to be a take-charge woman.

When Michele told the lady in the office what was going on, she rushed to the apartment to check it out. She called the maintenance man and had him start moving our clothes to another apartment. She opened the apartment above us and found the problem. Both apartments suffered major damage from the leak.

Claudia and I were proud of Michele, and we had her tell us the story several times so we could compliment her on her actions. She was nonchalant about the leak but upset about it interrupting them while they were watching cartoons. After we settled down, I told Claudia we needed to move; we needed a place where only we lived and where we did not have to worry about people living in the apartments around us. She agreed.

Because of the large number of transient soldiers and families at Fort Rucker, housing was at a premium. I got lucky and found a three-bedroom mobile home that would be vacant in two weeks in the same trailer park I'd stayed in when attending flight school. The trailer park, located about a half mile from the front gate, did not have the run-down look associated with most. I signed an agreement, and when it became empty, we moved in.

The mobile home was comfortable. It was clean, the furniture looked new, and it provided more privacy than the apartment did. Michele and Ron had their own room, which they enjoyed. We also had a little yard, which I was happy to see, because I had the urge to plant a garden. Within the grounds was a small playground with swings and climbing bars, and the school bus stopped at the entrance to the park, which was convenient for Michele.

The downside was that we had to buy sheets, towels, pots and pans, and dishes, but since we were going to be there for another four months, it was worth it. Also living at the trailer park was one of the National Guard students attending rotary-wing transition. This enabled me to catch a ride with him on days when Claudia wanted to keep the car instead of driving me to work and picking me up.

A week after we moved into the mobile home, I decided I would get a vasectomy. Claudia's fear of getting pregnant was often a problem in our sex life, so I decided a vasectomy would solve the problem, and she agreed. The only problem was that I could not do anything to interrupt my training, so I had to plan around that. I found a doctor in Enterprise who performed vasectomies and scheduled the procedure for a Friday afternoon. I did not have to fly until the following Tuesday, so that gave me three days to recover. As advertised, I was well enough Tuesday to fly. Again, I had taken a chance and pulled it off.

Chief James was preparing us for our cross-country flights. We had to do one day solo and one night solo cross-country flight to complete the course. By then, I could handle the OH-13 well, and a cross-country flight was no challenge because of my previous flying experience. However, I was not looking forward to it, because the OH-13's speed was about eighty knots in level flight. That would make it a boring flight from point A to point B to point C and back. I liked flying from field site to field site and practicing landing or autorotation. Flying straight and level was easy and boring but necessary to demonstrate navigational ability.

On the first day cross-country flight, Chief James flew with me to explain the technique. I, of course, knew as much about cross-country flying as he did, except all my experience was in fixed-wing aircraft. The flight was routine, so we talked most of the way about our families and past experience. About halfway through, he gave me a simulated engine failure. I smoothly entered autorotation and turned toward my emergency landing spot. He was checking to see if I was picking emergency landing spots. By then, I was picking landing spots without thinking about it. I always had in mind where I would go if the engine failed. He gave me an "Attaboy" on my response and my composure.

The next day, we were going into field sites, when he commanded an engine failure. I immediately pushed the collective down and turned toward the site from which we had just taken off. Unfortunately, as I shoved the collective down, I rolled on power instead of rolling it off. The engine sounded like a car engine does when you are sitting in neutral and rev the engine to full power. Of course, as soon as I did it, I realized my mistake and rolled it off. However, it was too late. The engine rpm needle had sped past the green and into the red, showing an overspeed. Chief James came unglued and grabbed for the controls, but I had the power off before he took them. "Shit!" I muttered. "Sorry, Chief. Do you want to break off the autorotation?"

"Hell no," he said. "We've got an emergency. You oversped the engine. We might as well land and have maintenance check it out."

"Are you going to take it?" I asked. Although we practiced autorotation at the field sites, they didn't allow students to take them all the way to the ground.

Chief James had a grin on his face now as he said, "Hell no. You created the emergency. You'd better make a damn good autorotation, because we don't know if that engine is going to work if we have to apply power. It could break up and blow us out of the sky." Then he crossed his arms as if to signal he wanted nothing to do with the autorotation.

I was sweating now. My stomach felt as if there were a dozen or more hundred-pound butterflies trying to get out. I figured I was in trouble, and the only way out was to make a perfect autorotation. I was headed for a site about forty yards wide and sixty yards long with trees surrounding it. I had picked my touchdown spot for the center of the clearing. I could see I was too high and would overshoot my spot, so I turned thirty degrees to the left to lose some altitude. I turned back toward the site, but I was still too high. I turned thirty degrees to the right and put more forward cyclic to increase my descent speed. Of course, as my descent speed increased, my airspeed increased. As my airspeed approached the top level, I pulled in a little collective and brought my cyclic to neutral. At the same time, I turned back to the landing site.

My turns had worked. I was on a perfect descent angle to the site, and all my instruments were in the green. I was breathing rapidly because this, in my mind, was a real emergency. I knew that if my handling of the situation got dangerous, Chief James would take over, but he was sitting there pretending to be dead, and I did not know how fast he could react if my autorotation got out of hand. I saw the treetops go by and knew I was nearing touchdown. Just as I had been trained to do, I pulled a little collective and put back pressure on the cyclic to stop my forward movement.

The OH-13 started to settle as I kept it straight with pedals. As I reached my landing attitude, I pulled the collective all the way up, moving the cyclic to keep the aircraft level. With a slight bump and about a two-foot slide, the OH-13 stopped. As we sat there with the blade turning and the engine idling, I looked at Chief James, and he was looking at me, shaking his head as if he could not believe what had happened. I was saying to myself, *Say something, Chief.*

Then he spoke. "Why did you do some stupid-ass move like roll on power? For six weeks, you have not even come close to doing something dumb. Fortunately, your autorotation was as good as any I could have done. Therefore, I am not failing you for this flight. I don't know what maintenance is going to say about the engine." With that, he switched to the FM radio and called the maintenance support at the training field.

I was pissed at myself for doing such a stupid act, but I was happy about the way I had handled the emergency. I had done a perfect autorotation to the ground. Never mind that the engine was still running, because I had not used it. In my mind, I'd been without an engine, and I'd made a perfect landing. I had to force myself not to smile, because I was so elated. However, the idea that I had let Chief James down in a moment of stupidity bothered me. I replayed the incident over and over in my head and still could not understand why I had done it. I credit the mistake to complacency. Complacency is a big cause of aviation accidents, and I never believed it would happen to me.

Chief James interrupted my self-admonishment. "Okay, let's fly it back to the airfield. Let's do a run-up. If the engine checks out, maintenance thinks we should be able to fly it back."

I sat there waiting for him to take the controls. After a minute or two, he looked at me and said, "What are you waiting for?"

I answered, "I thought you were going to take it."

"No," he answered. "You screwed us up. You are going to fly it out."

"Sorry," I replied as I started the engine run-up. The engine came up to full power, and all instruments stayed in the green. I called out the checks for him to hear as I completed the checklist. Slowly, I lifted the OH-13 to a hover and did a pedal turn and hover out to the end of the field. I did another pedal turn to face into the wind. I was nervous because I knew he was giving me a check ride, and if I screwed anything up, I would get a pink slip.

I completed the pretakeoff check and asked the chief if he was ready. When he replied that he was ready, I nudged the cyclic forward and pulled in the collective. The OH-13 moved forward into translational lift, and we soared up past the tree line. So far, I was doing well. I banked around as we climbed out to a thousand feet and headed directly to the training field. My eyes constantly raced back and forth over the instruments, looking for any sign of an engine failure. At the same time, I was checking off emergency landing sites so I would be ready for an immediate landing.

I had felt this way before in Vietnam. However, this time, I was in a helicopter that I had barely learned to fly. I was a little concerned about what the flight leader would say about the damage I might have caused to the engine, but I was still proud of how I was handling the mishap. I would have thought nothing of it had I been in a fixed-wing aircraft. The training field came into sight, and the tower cleared me for a direct approach and landing at the maintenance pad. I made the approach and anticipated that my only problem would be when I pulled the collective to land. I would increase power and strain the engine, so I was mentally ready for any possible emergency.

I made a perfect approach to hover and landing. I had to keep Chief James from giving me a pink slip. I shut the engine down, and as the blades were spinning down, he looked at me and said, "Other than damaging the engine, your performance today was flawless. Keep that up. I'll see you in the morning."

I exited the aircraft, and a maintenance warrant got in and sat down. He and Chief James were talking as I left. Chief James was explaining exactly what had happened so they could make a determination about the engine. I found out the next day that they pulled the engine that night and installed a new engine. That was the only time I was responsible for damage to an aircraft.

When I got home, I was eager to tell Claudia about my experience. She listened patiently, and when I finished, she said, "Wow, you're lucky!" I'm not sure she understood exactly what I was telling her or why I was so exuberant, but that was okay. I felt good about myself. That was what I wanted more than anything from Claudia: I wanted her to make me feel that she was proud of me. I wanted somehow for that to translate into her love and desire for me.

While I concentrated on flying, Michele became a force with which poor Ron had to deal. The primary issue was that Michele was angry about having to go to school every day, while Ron could watch cartoons. She told Ron that on Saturday mornings, she was going to teach him reading, writing, and math for two hours until the cartoons she wanted to watch came on TV. She prepared a little lesson plan laying out her subjects, and on Saturday morning at 0800, she began.

Ron came to me and said, "Dad, I don't have to do this, do I?" I told him I thought it would be a good idea. It would be like going to kindergarten. He was not happy with my answer, so he went to Claudia, but Claudia also agreed it was a good idea. I softened the pain for him by telling him just to go along with Michele, and she would probably grow tired of teaching a two-hour class each Saturday morning. Reluctantly, he agreed, and classes began.

It amazed me how well Michele prepared the subjects she was going to teach. She started in math with addition and subtraction. After an hour, she gave Ron a list of problems to solve and told him to go into the bedroom to work on them and, when he was finished, bring them to her so she could grade them. With much complaining, Ron went to the bedroom, and Michele turned on the TV and watched cartoons.

After about twenty minutes, Ron came and got me to help him with a problem. He had done nine of the ten problems correctly. The tenth problem was a word problem, and he could not read well enough to understand it. I helped him and expressed my pride that he had done so well. He took his paper to Michele, and she graded it and gave him an A in math. He could then watch cartoons with Michele.

This went on for six weeks. Michele's tenaciousness impressed and amazed me. Ron was not happy, but when he realized how impressed Claudia and I were with his work, he kept at it without too much complaining. When his classes were over, which coincided with the end of school, Michele gave him a final test and a report card. We made a big affair out of it by taking them both out to eat whatever they wanted, which was pizza. With school out for the summer, they both watched cartoons every morning.

The Monday after my engine overspeed incident, I flew my cross-country solo. The flight was uneventful. I had flown cross-country hundreds of times, so other than the fact that I was flying a helicopter this time, it was boring. The flight took about an hour and forty-five minutes. Chief James knew I considered it a waste of time to fly a cross-country instead of doing tactical work, but a cross-country flight was part of the training syllabus.

What I wanted to work on was my landing technique. I still had a tendency to round out. Every time I did that, I would overfly my touchdown spot. The only way I would break the habit was to make touch-and-gos until I broke myself of the tendency. However, the curriculum did not have the flight time within it to do that, so I had to work on it in the course of doing other training. Chief James recommended I wait until I graduated and then sign out an OH-13 and practice on my own. However, to be truthful, I never overcame this tendency, even when I later flew the OH-58 Bell Ranger and the Huey.

The day after my cross-country solo, I took my check ride covering all the training I had received so far. As usual, I suffered from checkrideitis but managed to pass all the flight checks. The next day, we started night training.

This part of the curriculum was a repeat of day flight techniques, except we did them at night. One night, I would fly with Chief James first, and the next night, I'd fly second. Each flight lasted about an hour and a half to two hours, depending on how well we did. All classes were scheduled for the afternoon, after which we would eat and start flying. On the nights when I flew second, I would get home around 2300, but if we did not have classes, I would not have to be at the flight line until 1900. Again, I had plenty of night flying experience, so that part did not bother me.

Learning to land the helicopter and doing an autorotation using landing lights did tax my skills, but I managed to perform the skills and pass a check ride. The night after my night check ride, Chief James flew a night cross-country with me.

The night ride was the same as the day flight, except it was dark. The most taxing problem of flying at night is identifying your emergency landing spots. You can identify a clear area fairly well but not any power lines or other obstacles that would interfere with an emergency landing. The best approach is to pray that you do not have an emergency, such as an engine failure.

Night flights are more scenic than day flights. The lights of the towns and homes fill the countryside and provide what I always thought was a wonderland setting. The automobiles moving along the roads and highways add motion to the scene and provide paths of light to follow from point to point. During the day, it is more difficult to look ahead and identify your next checkpoint. At night, towns and intersections stand out because of the lights.

Chief James and I were between two towns on my cross-country route. I could see the traffic on the highway below us. The cruising speed of the OH-13 is only eighty knots, and we had a fifteen-knot headwind, so many of the cars on the highway were moving faster than we were. I muttered to myself that I could have driven the route faster than we could fly it. Chief James must have heard me, because he asked, "What did you say?"

At first, I thought maybe he was upset at my remark. It could have sounded as if I felt this were a waste of time. I said, "I was looking at the cars passing us on the highway and said how it would be faster to drive than fly in this slow aircraft."

"I agree," he said. "This is the slowest helicopter in the inventory. The army is phasing it out of the inventory. It's just more economical to use it for transition than a Huey."

About halfway through the ride, he gave me a simulated engine failure. I made sure I did not roll the power on as I put the collective down and turned toward a pasture alongside the road. I had just selected the pasture, and although I could not tell if there were any obstacles, I felt the pasture was large enough to change my landing spot the closer I got to touchdown. Of course, Chief James did not let me go to touchdown. About halfway, he told me to recover and resume our cross-country.

Back in the debriefing room, he told me it was a good flight, and he cleared me for my solo night cross-country. After that, I would have to take one more check ride, and if I passed it, then I would be finished with the course and rotary-wing qualified.

When I got back to the trailer, Claudia and the kids were in bed asleep, so I undressed and quietly slipped under the sheets. I wanted to sleep, but my mind refused. It was wide awake. Fueled by the idea that I would soon be rotary-wing qualified, it was randomly drifting from one event and thought to another. It wanted to rehash all my problems, as if it were asking me to resolve those problems still troubling me. I lay awake for almost an hour, dealing with the hurts and pains I had suffered. I do not remember drifting off to sleep, but when I did, it was a deep and restful sleep.

The next morning, Claudia asked me if I was flying that night. I told her about my solo night flight and said I would finish the course next week. We made small talk and talked about when I would start Mohawk transition. I thought I would have a week off between courses. My instrument ticket had expired, so I would have to renew it before I started Mohawk transition.

I went in early the next day to prepare for my night solo. I wanted to talk to the Mohawk transition committee about getting my instrument ticket renewed. The operations major told me to contact the Fort Rucker standardization board, and they would schedule a check ride for me.

I called the standardization board number and got a hold of a captain. He listened to my request and asked me what instrument-capable aircraft I was current in. I told him the only one would be the Beaver. He told me to call him once I finished rotary-wing transition, and he would schedule me an instrument check ride in the Beaver.

My night solo flight was without incident, though I have to admit I was a little nervous during the flight, mostly because of my lack of comfortableness when I flew helicopters. I never gained the experience in helicopters that allowed me to relax the way I did in fixed-wing aircraft. Maybe I would have felt differently if I had learned to fly helicopters first. I asked Chief James once which was easier: teaching a helicopter pilot to fly fixed-wing aircraft or a fixed-wing pilot to fly helicopters. He was quick to answer: teaching a helicopter pilot how to fly fixed-wing aircraft. I guess I was not the only pilot who felt the way I did.

I took my final check ride the last week in May and graduated from the rotary-wing qualification course. The OV-1 aviator qualification course began on June 13, which gave me more than two weeks to renew my instrument ticket. As soon as I was officially through with rotary-wing transition, I called the captain at the standardization board to schedule my check ride. He told me to wait a few minutes while he checked some schedules, and after a couple of minutes, he said, "All right, you're scheduled for the second of June at 1000 hours. Meet your examiner, Mr. Broker, in the base operations at 0900 to do your flight planning. Any questions?"

"Yes," I answered as I wrote down the information. "Would it be possible for me to get a ride in the Beaver before the second? I haven't flown the Beaver in five months or done any instrument training. The last two months, I've been flying the OH-13, and I would feel better with a training ride."

The captain answered, "There's no way I can schedule you a training ride before the second. As a matter of fact, it was difficult to find an instrument examiner qualified in the Beaver."

"Okay, I'll be there at 0900. Thanks, Captain."

The combination of finishing rotary-wing training and taking my check ride left me with a week with nothing to do, so I went to the training company and signed out on a four-day pass. Normally, if I were staying around the local area, I would not have to sign out on pass, but I was planning on driving up to Gainesville, Georgia, to see my grandmother on my father's side.

Grandmother Crisp was in her late nineties and had told my mother that she would like to see Claudia, her great-grandkids, and me before she died. We had not seen her since she took Claudia and me to dinner after I got out of the army in 1959, so I wanted to drive up to Gainesville to spend the day with her.

That Sunday, we packed the kids in the car and took off for Gainesville. I found her little house on the outskirts around 1500. After we greeted one another, she asked me to go get a Kentucky Fried Chicken meal for dinner. She was spry and in good health for her age but could not cook a big meal. She insisted on paying for the chicken. I left to get the chicken while she and Claudia chatted.

We had a nice chicken dinner with my grandmother. I had only seen her two times in my life that I could remember. I am glad I took the time to visit her and wish I had spent more time with her. I realize now there were many subjects I would have loved to discuss with her, and that is one reason I am writing this memoir. Someday people might say, "I wish I knew more about Neal Griffin." They will have my memoir to answer some of their questions.

We left around 1900 for the drive back. Grandmother Crisp hugged us all, and I could tell that we knew we would never see one another again. Michele and Ron interrupted the drive back. They had eaten too much of the chicken and pie that Grandmother had given them. About halfway back, they threw up all over the backseat. I had to stop and clean it up. They were upset, and Claudia did not handle it well either. We finally got back to the trailer around 2400.

I met Mr. Broker, the DA civilian instrument examiner who was giving me my check ride, at 0900. He was an old, heavyset pilot who gave me the impression that I had imposed on his time. As I did the flight planning for the flight, he questioned me about instrument flight procedures. He did not like the way I answered some of the questions, although I had answered them correctly. After he checked my flight plan for accuracy, we filed a VFR flight plan and walked out to the aircraft.

Mr. Broker watched me like a hawk while I did the preflight. Satisfied, we climbed in and started the engine. I checked the gauges and flight instruments, and we called for clearance to taxi. The Beaver controls felt both familiar and strange as I taxied to the run-up area. I guess that was what hovering everywhere for two months had done to my senses.

After I'd run up the engine, the tower cleared us for takeoff. I rolled out onto the active and made a good takeoff, considering I had not been at the controls in five months. As soon as we were airborne and at our altitude, Mr. Broker told me to put the hood on. He flew the aircraft while I attached the hood to my helmet. Then he gave the flight controls back, told me to tune in an ADF frequency, and gave me a flight clearance to the station. He was acting as flight control to check my reporting ability. I banked the aircraft and followed the needle until it pointed to the ADF station. As I did that, I said, "Flight control, this is Army 70991. Cleared to the ADF beacon on radial one hundred sixty. Altitude three thousand feet. Report over beacon."

It was summertime, and as usual, the air was humid, hot, and turbulent, which gave me some problems holding altitude. However, I was starting to regain some of my control touch and managed to hold the altitude and heading within ten to fifteen feet.

After a few minutes of straight and level flight, he directed me to enter a holding pattern west of radial 160. I responded as if I were talking to traffic control and did a thirty-degree bank to the left. I maintained my bank until I rolled out on heading 160 and noted the time on my clock. I flew heading 160 for two minutes and did another thirty-degree bank to the left. I rolled out on heading 340 and noted my time. When I rolled out, I saw that I was east of the heading, so I calculated that I had a west crosswind. Two minutes later, I banked thirty degrees left, and this time, instead of rolling out on 160, I rolled out on 155 to compensate for the crosswind.

A holding pattern looks like a racetrack. The thirty-degree bank is the end, and two minute legs are the sides. While I was flying the pattern, looking only at my instruments, Mr. Broker was checking my flight path on the ground to verify my accuracy. Satisfied that I could do a holding pattern, he directed me to continue to the ADF beacon. He had me change altitudes several times and then told me to put my head between my knees.

He took control of the aircraft and made several steep turns left and right, climbing and diving. With my head between my knees and the hood on, I could not tell what flight condition the aircraft was in. Then, to test my ability to recover from unusual attitudes on instruments, he told me to recover.

I raised my head quickly and looked at the flight director to determine my attitude. I was in a climbing left bank. I banked the aircraft to the right to bring the wings level while I added power and lowered the nose. I knew that in a steep climbing left turn, my airspeed was bleeding off, and to correct, I needed to lower the nose and add power. When you fly a lot under instrument conditions, it only takes a glance at the instruments to decide recovery procedures. Had I been in a dive, I would have known without looking that my airspeed was increasing, so as I rolled the wings level, I would have pulled off power and raised the nose to recover the aircraft. I was good at recovering an aircraft from unusual positions.

Satisfied with my recovery, he cleared me for an ADF approach to field landing strip X-ray. That was when I started to worry a little. I had not done an ADF approach since the transition course in Germany. I had used ADFs for checking my VOR approaches but not for landing. My mind rushed to remember the procedures: I had to fly on the runway heading until the needle reversed, fly another minute on the reversed needle, and then turn fifteen degrees to the left and fly that heading for forty-five seconds. At the end of forty-five seconds, I'd make a standard rate turn to the right, rolling out on the inbound heading to the runway, and start my descent. I'd have to do all of this while under the hood and bouncing around in turbulent air.

I screwed my first approach up and missed the runway by a couple hundred yards. My next approach was worse. I could not get the timing and the turns coordinated. He gave me one more chance, which I also failed. Then he said, "Okay, take off the hood, and let's go back to Fort Rucker."

I was devastated. It was the first time I had ever failed a check ride. I could not believe that after flying instruments in the rigors of German weather, I had failed an instrument check ride. I wanted to blame something or someone other than myself, but no matter how I looked at it, I was the one to blame. What hurt the most was the importance of this ride. I needed the current instrument ticket to enter Mohawk training.

Mr. Broker was not kind in his debrief. He insinuated that I'd wasted his time by not being ready for a check ride. I asked him why we had not done a VOR approach, which I was confident I could do. His reply was that I should be able to do any instrument approach. I saw that I was not going to win any concessions from him. He ended by telling me he was going to recommend that I have some instrument training before retesting.

I had one week to practice and take a retest in order to start my transition class on June 13. When Mr. Broker finished, I immediately called the captain in standardization branch and told him I had not passed my check ride. I told him I needed a couple of hours of instrument training so I could take a retest and pass it. I asked him if there was any way I could do it in the next couple of days. He said no because he did not have any aircraft or pilots available until the end of the month, when the current officer fixed-wing aviator course would end their instrument qualification phase. That would free up some aircraft and instrument examiners.

I was crushed. That meant I could not attend Mohawk transition. "Okay," I said. "What's my recourse since I will miss my Mohawk transition class start date?"

He said, "Let me call the Mohawk committee and explain the situation, and I will get back to you. Give me the number of the phone you are calling from, and stay by it until I call."

I sat in the debriefing room for about fifteen minutes, waiting for my fate to be decided. I beat myself up for missing my opportunity. I had asked them to send me to Mohawk transition first because my instrument ticket would have been current. It had expired in April while I was in rotary-wing transition. That fifteen-minute period was one of the low points in my professional life. Failing the check ride did not look good on my record as an aviator or as an officer. I said a little prayer because I needed help.

Finally, the phone rang. I took a deep breath, grabbed it, and answered. "Captain Griffin speaking, sir."

It was the captain, ready to tell me my fate. "Okay, Captain Griffin, here's what we are going to do. We are going to reschedule you into the Mohawk transition course starting on the first of August. Meanwhile, I am going to put you on blackbird status and attach you to the OFWAC tactical phase committee. They need someone to fly the Beaver to the field training site each day and support their needs. I will schedule you for instrument training and a check ride as soon as the aircraft and examiner are available."

Thank you, dear God, I said to myself before thanking the captain profusely. I felt I'd been rescued from disgrace and given another chance. The captain gave me the number of the OFWAC tactics committee and directed me to call Major White for instructions. My spirit rose from the gloom of the last two hours as I called Major White.

The term *blackbird* identifies aviators awaiting entry into a specific class. They report to the various committees and provide administrative help and any ash-and-trash support needed. It can be fun work, and I anticipated my assignment would be. Furthermore, I would get to fly the Beaver each day.

I dialed Major White's number. He was pleasant and happy to get a Beaver-qualified blackbird. He gave me his building number and told me to report there at 0800 on Wednesday morning. That was great—it gave me a week of free time. After talking to him, I called the captain back and told him that they did not need me until next Wednesday. He said, "Okay, leave me your home phone number so I can reach you." I gave him my number, and I was free for a week. However, I was not really free. The need to renew my instrument ticket hung over me, and I knew that until I did that, I would not be able to relax.

I felt bad telling Claudia about my failing the check ride. It was the first time I'd had to tell Claudia that my performance was anything less than outstanding. Surprisingly, she said it was unfair of them to fail you. That small show of love touched me, and I said, "Look at the upside: I get an extra two months before I have to go back to Vietnam." However, she seemed a little disappointed that because my time was extended, the day when she could go back to Germany was delayed.

With my extra free time, I planted a little garden behind the trailer. It was not much of a garden, just some cucumber plants. Claudia loved cucumbers in salads and had several good recipes. Boy, did those cucumbers grow! We provided neighbors and all our friends with cucumbers the whole time we were there. I took pride in the cucumber garden and got the yearning to garden more. It was the first time I became aware of this interest.

I had fun being in blackbird status. Each morning, I would load up the training site cadre on the Beaver and fly them to the tactical airstrip where OFWAC students were undergoing tactical training in the Bird Dog. During the day, I might have to fly back to the Fort Rucker airfield to pick up supplies, students, or instructors and fly them back to the training field. I got in a couple hours of flying each day. While I was not flying, I helped the cadre with administrative tasks. I recalled when I'd gone through the tactical training phase and seen other pilots pulling blackbird duties. I wondered then how they'd gotten roped into blackbird status, and now I knew.

I used some of my free time to practice instrument flying at the link training facility. Sitting inside a link trainer was close to flying on instruments. Each trainer had a set of aircraft controls and flight instruments mirroring an aircraft. The instructor could set up any flight for you to practice. I wanted en route and instrument landings, so in each session, I would practice en route procedures, such as reporting, intercepting airways, and holding patterns. Then I would do a VOR or an ILS approach and landing. I did several ADF approaches, but the instructor thought I was wasting my time. The ADF was old and phased out of most airports. After several two-hour sessions in the link trainer, I was satisfied that I could pass my instrument check ride.

I started calling the captain at the standardizations branch to remind him that I was waiting for a check ride. Finally, about the middle of July, he told me that my check ride was scheduled for Friday morning. He directed me to be at the flight planning room in base operations at 0900 to meet with Captain Killen, my flight examiner. My spirits lifted. I was ready. My link training had refreshed my instrument flying skills. I had my confidence back and was eager to get my instrument ticket renewed.

That Friday, I met Captain Killen on schedule. He wore master aviator wings showing that he was both rotary- and fixed-wing rated and had hours of instrument flying time. As before, we went through flight planning procedures, but Captain Killen was more personable and made it seem as if we were planning a flight. He asked me about what had gone wrong on my first check ride and who the examiner had been. When I told him it was a Mr. Broker, he said, "Oh yeah," as if that were part of my problem on the ride. He went on to say that Mr. Broker was noted for being harsh on officers. He had been a warrant officer and must have had a problem with officers before he retired.

When we walked out of flight operations, I expected to go to one of the five Beavers tied down on the ramp. Instead, we walked to a T-42 Beechcraft Baron. The Beechcraft Baron was a two-engine four-passenger aircraft and was the one the army used for instrument flight training. I had flown it more than fifty hours during my instrument flight training phase. Suddenly, my confidence evaporated in the hot July air. Captain Killen looked at me as we did the preflight and asked, "When is the last time you flew the T-42?"

Shaking my head, I answered, "In flight school in 1967."

"Don't worry about it," he replied. "I'll give you a fifteen-minute check ride in it before we start on instruments. With your flying experience, you shouldn't have any problems."

Easy for you to say, I thought. Inside, my stomach was churning. My mind was racing to bring back all I could remember about the T-42. *Calm down*, I told myself, *or you will blow the ride even before you take it*. My mind was already wondering what they would do to me if I failed the ride again.

In the cockpit, he talked me through the engine start-up procedures. Once both engines were running, we turned on the radios and called for taxi instructions. I taxied to the active run-up area and stopped. Captain Killen said, "Go ahead and study the flight and engine instrument arrangement for a few minutes so you will be familiar with them."

That was a godsend. Knowing each instrument location on the instrument panel increases your ability. Good technique calls for an instrument scan every thirty seconds, and knowing the instruments' locations makes that possible. During the time it would take to search the panel for an instrument to check your altitude, you could be drifting off course. By the time you got to your course indicator and recognized that you needed to correct, you could get behind the aircraft quickly.

After about ten minutes of study, I could shut my eyes, open them, and immediately find any instrument I wanted to. "Okay," I said to Captain Killen, "I'm as ready as I can get right now."

"Okay," he said, and he started reading the pretakeoff checklist. When we were ready for takeoff, he called the tower for clearance.

The tower cleared us for takeoff, and I taxied out on the departure end of the runway. I stopped and applied full power and released the brakes. The T-42 started down the runway. When we reached about eighty knots, Captain Killen said, "Pull the nose up."

I pulled back on the yoke, and the T-42 slowly lifted off the runway. We climbed out on runway heading, and when we were about three hundred feet above ground, Captain Killen pushed the gear handle to the up position. He said I could retract flaps. I pushed the flap handle to the up position. Our speed increased to 130 knots, and when we reached three thousand feet, Captain Killen told me to turn to a heading of 270. "Okay," he said, "I am going to let you fly the aircraft for a while so you can get comfortable with it. I am not checking you on your ability to fly the aircraft, but you need to fly it well enough to do instrument procedures. I am going to give you some turns, climbs, and descents so you can get the feel of the controls, and then we will start the instrument portion. Okay with you?"

Of course it was okay with me, so he told me to make a thirty-degree turn to the right. That started me on a series of turns, including descending and climbing turns. After about ten minutes of that, he told me to put the hood on, and we would start. Just as Mr. Broker had, Captain Killen acted as traffic control and gave me a flight clearance for a VOR approach into Dothan International. I changed VOR to the Dothan frequency, and he cleared me to intercept the 270 radial to Dothan.

I completed a VOR approach into Dothan and did a go-around before landing. He cleared me for an ILS approach into Fort Rucker and gave me a radial to intercept to Fort Rucker. En route to Fort Rucker, he had me enter a holding pattern for five minutes.

I left the holding and did an ILS approach into Fort Rucker. On this approach, I landed, and my ride was over. Wet with sweat, I felt I had done well. I'd not performed as smoothly as I would have with practice in the T-42, but I'd made successful instrument approaches that would have allowed me to land safely in weather.

Back in the debriefing room, Captain Killen discussed each approach with me and pointed out my strong and weak areas. He completed the form renewing my instrument ticket. He talked about Mohawk training and told me I would have an instrument training phase in which I would have to take another instrument check ride to pass the course. He wished me luck and went to file my paperwork.

I was walking on air. My career was back on track; I could start Mohawk training in August. My morale was back at its usual high. I checked in with the tactical training office and found out that they wanted me to take the Beaver to the field site as soon as I finished my check ride, so I grabbed a sandwich at the PX snack bar and then returned to base operations, filed a VFR local flight plan, and took the Beaver to the field site. That night, I felt good telling Claudia that I had passed my check ride.

Mohawk Transition

Finally, the first of August arrived, and I started OV-1 aviator qualification class 71-2. There were only eight of us in the class. Two, like me, had done tours as aviators and had flying experience. The other five were right out of the last officer fixed-wing aviator course (OFWAC). There was one instructor assigned for every two students. My teammate was Captain Jonas, who was right out of OFWAC. Our instructor was a Captain Mack.

On the first day, we met in the student debriefing room. Captain Mack introduced himself and discussed what he expected of us during our training. He was tall and lankly and seemed like a no-nonsense guy. He had done two tours in Vietnam flying Mohawks and was an expert in the Mohawk. At the end of his briefing, he gave us a Mohawk checklist and directed us to memorize it. Next, he told us to read the maintenance manual on the Mohawk because he would ask us questions on the various systems and expected us to know the answers. After that, he took us out to the flight line, where eight Mohawks sat.

The OV-1 Mohawk was an awesome airplane. The large cockpit bubble at the nose and its curve length gave it the distinctive shape of a dragonfly or mosquito hawk. It stood twelve feet high and was forty-one feet long, with a wingspan of forty-eight feet. Another distinctive feature of the Mohawk was the fact that it had three vertical stabilizers. The army had designed the Mohawk to be an armed military observation aircraft, hence the large bubble cockpit nose for visibility. As the Mohawk was used chiefly for battlefield surveillance, the army armed some of the early models for light strike abilities. The aircraft had twin turboprop engines and carried two crew members with side-by-side seating. The Mohawk was designed to work off short, unimproved runways in support of army maneuver forces.

The armed models became a point of dispute for the air force. They accused the army of taking on the role of the air force with light strike capability, so the army phased out the A (armed) models and replaced them with B models.

While using the A model to attack targets in Vietnam, the army lost several pilots and aircraft. As a result, the Mohawk became known as the Widow Maker.

The B models carried side-looking airborne radar (SLAR) and vertical-looking cameras. They had two L-7 Lycoming turbine jet engines that were much more powerful than the L-3s on the A models. The SLAR could beam out to a hundred miles from the side of the aircraft and detect moving and fixed targets on the ground. SLAR film displayed these targets on split imagery as blips on one side and terrain features on the other side. It gave commanders a clear picture of what was moving in the area forward of his lines.

The need for an infrared detection system led to development of the D-model Mohawk. Besides the SLAR, the army installed an infrared detection system in the bottom bay of the Mohawk with the vertical camera and a forward-looking camera. The infrared system could detect heat differences of one degree. The results displayed on imagery gave commanders a picture of what the aircraft flew over. It was especially useful for detecting targets at night. To handle the additional weight of these systems, Grumman mounted more-powerful L-15 Lycoming engines on the OV-1D. Speed boards were another feature of the OV-1D.

The speed boards were mounted on the fuselage just forward of the rear stabilizer. Just as the name suggests, the pilot could activate the speed boards and quickly slow the aircraft down. This feature gave the Mohawk better tactical maneuverability.

The OV-1D had an advanced navigational capability. The newest system was a flight director coupled with autopilot and an inertial navigation system. The rest were standard ILS, VOR, and TACAN (tactical air navigation). Because of its sophistication, the OV-1D was the only single-pilot aircraft approved to enter high-density flight areas around major airports.

The Mohawk could perform in all weather conditions. An oxygen system gave it the ability to operate above ten thousand feet. The propeller nose cones had heating to prevent prop icing. The wings had deicing boots to remove wing icing. It was approved for aerobatics. It had Martin-Baker ejection seats for pilot safety. Like I said, it was an awesome aircraft, and as I walked with Captain Mack out to the waiting Mohawks, I could feel my familiar butterflies in my stomach.

As always, the first task was a preflight of the aircraft. Captain Mack explained the 120 items that a pilot checks on preflight. You cannot do it correctly without using the checklist. After the preflight tour, he had us climb into the cockpit. We spent the next hour sitting in the cockpit and finding and memorizing all the instruments.

A few of the instruments in the Mohawk were similar to those I was used to. The flight director and artificial horizon were new and more complex than those on the Beaver or the T-42. Engine instruments were new, with an array for each engine. Instead of manifold pressure, the Mohawk had pounds of torque. A new instrument was the exhaust gas temperature gauge (EGT). Instead of oil pressure, the Mohawk measured oil temperature. Propeller rpm gauges were tape gauges instead of dials. The switch and circuit breaker panel covered the back space between the pilot and the technical operator. I sat in the seat in the hot Alabama sun and applied myself to memorizing each instrument's location. After an hour, Captain Mack returned and told us to shut it down; it was time for ejection-seat training.

It was a relief to get out of the hot canopy of the Mohawk. We shut the hatches and followed Captain Mack to the ejection-seat training area for classes on the ejection seat. The whole class was there. The first hour focused on how the seat functioned. The next hour focused on the proper technique for ejecting from an aircraft and recovery. From the classroom, we went to the ejection-seat trainer.

The trainer was an ejection seat mounted on two vertical rails. The rails slanted about fifteen degrees and were about thirty feet high. A forty-millimeter round drove the seat up the rails. It simulated well the G forces one experiences when ejecting. To use the seat, the student, with flight helmet on, straps into the seat the way he would in the aircraft.

There are two handles available to use the seat. One is at the top of the seat. This is the preferred handle to use. The first step in the proper ejection sequence is to blow the canopy by pulling the handle for that function. Then, with both hands, you grasp the handle above the seat and pull strongly down in front of your face. As the handle comes down, it pulls a canvas curtain over the face and fires the shell. You feel a jarring blast, and then, instantly, you are sitting about twenty feet up the two rails. The next step is stimulating seat separation, and the seat slides slowly down the rails into position for the next student to ride.

The second handle is found below your knees, at the bottom of the seat. In case of an emergency in which you cannot use the overhead handle, you can easily reach the one between your legs. You should always try to blow the canopy when possible, but it's not necessary to eject successfully. The top of the seat extends out over your head. If you eject without blowing the canopy, the top of the seat will knock a hole in the top of the canopy. The purpose of the face curtain is to protect your head from pieces of canopy. Of course, there is no face curtain with the bottom handle. Therefore, you only use it in an emergency in which you cannot use the top handle.

When it was my turn to ride the ejection seat—or, as it's fondly called, ride the rails—I was a little tense as I climbed in. I strapped myself in tightly and waited as the instructor checked me. Then he reminded me to keep my chin down and back straight. If you are not straight in the seat, the G forces can injure your back. Then the instructor commanded, "Eject!"

I pulled the top handles down forcefully and felt the jar, and before I could open my eyes, I was twenty feet in the air. It happens so fast that you cannot feel the ride. It's over with before the sensation of the jar leaves your mind. No matter how straight I sat, I always felt sore the day after ejection-seat training.

Mohawk pilots must ride the rails once a year for refresher training. Studies have shown that this training instills confidence in the pilot. It makes it less likely that he will hesitate in an emergency when he only has a split second to decide to eject. During the six years I flew Mohawks, I rode the rails each year.

That night, I studied the Mohawk manual. To be honest, the complexity of the Mohawk intimidated me, but I kept telling myself that I would forget these feelings in a few weeks. The Mohawk was like all new challenges. At first, new challenges seem overpowering, but when they are no longer strange, you wonder what you were worried about. I had felt that way about flying the Beaver, but after a few hours in it, I'd had no qualms about my ability to master it.

The next morning, our training started in full. Captain Mack told my teammate to go to the link training building to study the cockpit layout using the Mohawk mock-up and to be back at 1000. Then he told me, "Get your helmet and harness, and let's start."

We walked out to a Mohawk that was sitting on the apron. Several crew chiefs were standing around waiting for engine starts. Captain Mack suggested popping the hatches so the cockpit could cool off while we did the preflight. Normally, the crew chief or the technical observer (TO) reads the checklist. The pilot checks each item and responds, "Check." Captain Mack read the checklist and watched me while I did the check. He expected me to know each item I was checking and what I was checking for. After several pauses in which he had to help me, we completed the check. We put our harnesses on and climbed into the cockpit.

The harness is similar to the harness on a regular parachute and serves the same purpose. After the pilot gets in the cockpit, he first snaps his harness to the parachute risers that are part of the seat harness. As before a parachute jump, it is important that you fit your harness for comfort. On a long flight, a poorly adjusted harness can cause agony.

The Mohawk's cockpit is small and compact. There is only enough room for two men. To enter the cockpit, you have to put your left foot in the recess and swing your right leg into the cockpit. You cannot get in any other way unless you crawl in headfirst. Once seated, you hook your harness up to the ejection-seat risers and adjust your seat belt. The only adjustment to the seat is an up-and-down switch. This allows you to raise or lower the seat to have proper leg reach to the rudder pedals. At best, the Martin-Baker ejection seat is hard and uncomfortable, but over time, you get used to it.

Captain Mack talked me through the prestart check and then demonstrated starting the engines. By then, the crew chief was standing in front of the aircraft. When Captain Mack looked at him and nodded, the crew chief pointed to the number-one engine, which is the left engine, and made a circular motion with his hand. Captain Mack pushed the engine start toggle switch, and the engine started whining to life. The crew chief watched for exhaust as the engine started. With all engine starts, the pilot watches the gauges to ensure oil pressure and prop rpm come up to the green mark. On the Mohawk, the critical gauge during start-up is the exhaust gas temperature (EGT) gauge.

Correct EGT temperature is 650 degrees. During an engine start, the EGT surges to above 700 degrees and then drops back down to 650 degrees. The pilot must watch the gauge to ensure the temperature does not stay above 650 for more than three or four seconds. When the number-one engine was running and all the gauges were in the green, Captain Mack looked at the crew chief. The crew chief pointed to number two, the right engine, and made circular motions with his hand.

Captain Mack pushed the start toggle switch to the on position, and we repeated the sequence. Once the number-two engine instruments were in the green, Captain Mack looked at the crew chief. The crew chief gave him a thumbs-up, which signaled that all was okay. Had there been a problem, the crew chief would have pulled his finger across his throat, signaling a problem and telling the pilot to shut the engine down. Once the engines were running and all instruments were in the green, we turned on the radios, and Captain Mack called for taxi instructions. "Cairns tower, Mohawk 61500, VFR local area, ready for taxi."

When the tower cleared us to taxi, he said, "I've got the controls. I am going to demonstrate taxi, engine run-up, and takeoff procedures. Then we will go to our auxiliary field and do some touch-and-gos." He looked at the crew chief, and the crew chief pointed to the left, clearing us to taxi.

As we taxied, we kept the hatches open for cooling. The odor of JP-4 exhaust permeated the cockpit, and closing the hatches would make it worse. Captain Mack taxied to the run-up and turned the aircraft around, with the engine exhaust facing away from the runway. "Okay," he said, "let's start through the checklist."

There were about ten items on the list. I called them out, and he checked them and responded with the proper responses. The last item was the engine run-up. He locked the brakes and pushed the throttle handles forward, and the two L-15 engines roared to life. He took the power to max while checking to make sure all instruments came up to the proper level and then pulled the power back down. During run-up, the Mohawk shook as if it were trying to get away.

He next explained the takeoff checks as he performed them: the pilot would lower the flaps to the takeoff position, advance the engine rpm handles to 1,600 rpm, turn autofeather on, ensure the hatches were shut and locked, and arm his ejection seat.

When he finished, he called the tower. "Cairns tower, Mohawk 61500 is ready for takeoff."

"Roger, Mohawk 61500. You are cleared for takeoff."

Captain Mack narrated the takeoff. "Taxi onto the runway, and line up on the centerline. Make sure the runway is clear. Apply brakes, and synchronize your flight director to runway heading." He punched the synchronization button on the flight director and held it until it was set to runway heading. He continued, "Advance power, keeping the power handles together to fifteen pounds of thrust. When the engines spool up, release the brakes and apply full power."

The Mohawk jumped forward on takeoff roll and quickly gained speed. Captain Mack continued his narrative: "Watch airspeed, and when it reaches one hundred knots, apply back pressure on the stick, and the aircraft will start flying at one hundred twenty knots. Once on a positive climb, about one hundred forty knots, raise your landing gear and check the gauges visually to ensure they are up." He pointed to the landing gear gauges and then to the mirror outside the hatch.

I looked at the mirror, which allowed me to verify that the left gear was up I reported, "Gear up."

He looked at the right mirror and reported, "Gear up and locked. Now raise flaps, and turn autofeather off." He moved the flap handle to the up position and turned off the autofeather. The Mohawk surged upward.

When we reached an altitude of three thousand feet, he said, "Set your prop rpm to fourteen hundred fifty," and he pulled the prop handles back. "Set the thrust on sixty pounds," he said as he pulled the power handles back. "Fourteen fifty rpm, fifty-four pounds of thrust, and airspeed of one eighty to one ninety is the desired cruising setting. Any questions?"

It was impressive. The whole takeoff process had taken roughly two minutes, and Captain Mack had made it look smooth and simple. "No questions right now," I answered.

"Okay, you've got the controls. Turn to two hundred ten, which will take us to the auxiliary field. Remember, you don't need to apply rudder when you bank. The rudder controls are synchronized with your aileron controls."

I gingerly took the controls and responded, "I've got the controls."

All aircraft fly the same. Once you learn how to fly, learning to fly a new aircraft is a matter of getting used to the controls and how they respond to your touch. I flew the T-41, T-42, and Beaver with my left hand on a yoke, and I flew the Bird Dog with my right hand on the stick. I flew the OH-13 with my left hand on the cyclic stick. Now I was flying the Mohawk with my left hand on the stick. The Mohawk's hydraulics made the controls sensitive, or at least more sensitive than those on the Beaver, so when I first took the controls, I had a tendency to apply too much pressure and overcorrect. Correcting this tendency was a matter of practice. I could hold the aircraft within two or three degrees of my heading and a hundred feet of altitude. That is not that good, but for me, it was success.

As we approached the training field, Captain Mack told me to descend to 1,200 feet and enter a right downwind. I pulled off power and lowered the nose, which was instinctive from my flying experience. However, I did not know how much power to reduce to get the wanted results. I was not sure until Captain Mack said, "All right, pull back your power to thirty pounds, or you're never going to get down to twelve hundred feet in time to enter a downwind." Then I knew.

I pulled the power handles to thirty pounds and lowered the nose a little more. I reached 1,200 feet, and Captain Mack said, "I've got the aircraft," and he took the controls.

I responded, "You've got the aircraft." Pilots do this exchange each time they switch control of the aircraft, to ensure someone is piloting the aircraft. There have been many crashes simply because one pilot thought the other pilot was flying the aircraft.

"Okay," Captain Mack said, "I am going to demonstrate entering the traffic pattern and landing." He turned downwind and said, "This is about the right distance from the runway to fly downwind."

I fixed a picture of how far we were from the runway in my mind, noting that the distance was about twice as far from the runway as I would fly in the Beaver.

Captain Mack continued. "Leave your power around thirty pounds. The approach speed for landing is one hundred forty knots, and somewhere around thirty pounds will maintain that speed."

There were two other Mohawks in the pattern, so we entered behind the one on downwind. The other one was on a short final. Captain Mack said, "Here, we do the prelanding check—props at sixteen hundred rpm, speed boards in, gear down." He smoothly pushed the prop handles forward until the tapes showed 1,600 rpm. Then he pulled the gear handle to the down position and pulled the speed board toggle switch to the in position, even though we had not used the speed boards.

I could feel the gear coming down. Captain Mack said, "Check gear down and locked."

I looked in my mirror and confirmed that my gear was down and appeared locked. I responded, "Left gear down and locked."

The Mohawk ahead of us was turning to base. Captain Mack said, "We'll have to extend the downwind a little to keep proper clearance. When you lower the gear, you have to increase power to maintain one hundred forty." He added power to compensate for the gear being down. "You see where he turned base? That's about where we would turn if we were not extending our downwind."

Captain Mack was talking to me on intercom while he was talking to the other instructors and coordinating our approach to keep a safe distance between aircraft. He had switched my radio to intercom, so I could not hear the other traffic. This allowed me to concentrate only on what he was telling me. I made a mental note of where the proper distance to turn base was.

Captain Mack turned base and lowered the nose to allow the Mohawk to start descending. He performed a smooth turn to final, rolling out exactly on runway heading. The aircraft was doing the usual bouncing around in the hot, humid, unstable air, but he compensated with a smooth control touch that canceled the turbulent effect on the aircraft. He continued, "As with all the landings you have made before, get your descent glide path, and add or reduce power to maintain it. Because we extended our downwind, we have to add power to get us into the proper descent angle." As he spoke, he added power. "Don't forget the engine lag and wait too long."

Turbine engines have a two- or three-second lag from the time you apply power until they respond, so a pilot has to be ahead of the aircraft and apply power two or three seconds before he wants the aircraft to respond to the power change. Captain Mack added enough power to drag us to where we would have been had we turned a normal base. "Okay, I've got my angle to the runway. I am going to lower the nose and reduce power to maintain that angle all the way to the end of the runway. My speed should bleed off to one hundred twenty knots but not lower than one twenty."

My eyes flickered from the flight and engine instruments to the runway. Captain Mack was good. The Mohawk descended in the turbulent air as if it were sliding down a cable to the end of the runway. I could do that in a Beaver. I knew that in time, I would do it in a Mohawk.

As we crossed the end of the runway, Captain Mack spoke again. "Once you're over the runway, pull the power handles back to the detent, which gives you about fifteen pounds of thrust, and looking down the runway, round out." He rounded out as he said, "Round out," and the Mohawk planted the two main gears on the runway. He held back pressure on the stick to hold the nose up to bleed off speed. When the nose started to come down on its own, he lowered the nose and pulled the power levers into reverse thrust, which quickly slowed the Mohawk to taxi speed.

As soon as we reached taxi speed, we popped the hatches to let some cool air into the hot cockpit. The warm, humid Alabama air mixed with JP-4 exhaust fumes rushed into the cockpit. Captain Mack said, "Flaps up, landing light off, ejection seat deactivated. All right, you've got the aircraft. Taxi back to the departure end; we're going to practice touch-and-gos for the rest of the morning."

I responded, "I've got the aircraft." I was hot and starting to get my flight suit wet with sweat. The open hatches did not offer much in the way of cooling. In fact, the odor of JP-4 exhaust was irritating and causing me some queasiness. It did not bother Captain Mack. I decided to try to ignore it. While it never made me sick, I had to contend with a queasy stomach whenever we popped the hatches.

As I taxied toward the departure end, Captain Mack, reading the pretakeoff checklist, said, "Flaps."

I responded, "Takeoff position," as I moved my hand, looking for the flap switch. Everything was new, and I knew I would fumble a little. Captain Mack would expect that the first couple of times, but I needed to learn control positions as soon as possible.

"Props," he called out.

"Sixteen hundred rpm," I responded as I pushed the prop handles forward. That was easy.

"Fire handles," he said.

"Fire handles in," I responded as I pointed to the two engine fire handles above the prop and power control panel.

By then, I was trying to turn right into the run-up area. I had applied brakes to turn the Mohawk, and now it was hardly moving. I added power to the number-one engine to pull the wing around and face us outward. The Mohawk ahead of us was taking off, and there were two behind us, so Captain Mack began to speed up the commands. "Brakes locked, area clear, power to full, engine instruments power up in the green, power to low, pretakeoff, props, speed boards, flaps, circuit breakers, hatches closed and locked, autofeather on, ejection seats armed. All right, take the runway, and let's go."

I tried to keep up with him, but a couple of times, he had to help me. I lined the aircraft up on the centerline, and he said, "Sync flight director."

It was my first takeoff, and I could not find the flight director sync button! Not five minutes ago, I had watched him do it. Captain Mack reached across, pointed to it, and said, "Make sure you spend time learning the instrument positions."

"I will, sir," I answered.

"All right, let's go. We're ready for takeoff. Apply the power slowly until you start rolling, and then take it full forward."

I followed his instructions, and the power the two L-15s produced surprised me. We jumped forward, and from my experience, I knew to keep it on the centerline of the runway, but the power steering was extremely sensitive. I kept weaving back and forth across the centerline. I let that distract me as the Mohawk sped down the runway until I heard Captain Mack say, "Are you going to take off or drive around the airfield?"

I looked down at my airspeed; it was approaching 110 knots. I was supposed to rotate at one hundred knots. I reacted like a novice and quickly pulled back on the stick. The Mohawk jumped off the runway. Captain Mack expected my reaction and had his hand on his stick to prevent me from pulling it back too far. That could have put us in too steep of a climb. *Calm down, Neal,* I told myself. I heard Captain Mack say, "Gear up."

I was sitting in the pilot's seat like a dummy. *Calm down,* I told myself again. I reached for the gear handle and raised it to the up position. I felt the gear coming and checked my mirror. My gear was up and locked. I pointed to Captain Mack's mirror, and he reported that the right gear was up and locked. I checked altitude and airspeed. I was climbing through a thousand feet at 140 knots, and I was behind the aircraft.

Captain Mack jarred my thinking by saying, "Clean up the aircraft."

That put my mind in gear. I reached for the prop handles, pulled them back to 1,600 rpm, and reported it to Captain Mack. Then I called, "Flaps up," and raised the flaps. The aircraft shot forward when I raised the flaps, and my airspeed hit 150 before I remembered to pull power off to thirty pounds and turn off the autofeather. I was already at 1,400 feet. I was two hundred feet too high and far left of the centerline of the runway.

I was going to turn right and lower my nose to get back to 1,200, when I heard Captain Mack say, "I've got the aircraft."

"You've got the aircraft," I responded. My performance upset me. I had more than a thousand hours of flying time, and I had done so badly that Captain Mack had to take the aircraft.

Then he said, "Relax now. Life happens real fast in this aircraft, and it can get away from you. But that was not too bad for your first takeoff. I have seen much worse. We've got to lose some altitude and airspeed, so I want to explain the use of the speed boards." He pushed the speed board toggle switch to the open position, and I could hear and feel the effects.

The aircraft vibrated slightly and slowed so quickly that it moved me forward against my harness. Captain Mack lowered the nose and added a little power, simultaneously popping the speed boards. In just three or four seconds, we were at 140 knots and 1,200 feet. "Okay, you've got the aircraft," he said.

"I've got the aircraft," I answered as I took the controls. I noticed that the airspeed was going down, so I added power. Pretty soon I had applied fifty pounds of thrust, trying to hold the 1,200 feet of altitude. I knew something was wrong. Captain Mack let me go until we were getting close to the point to turn base. Then he said calmly, "You know, if you pull in your speed boards, you won't need so much power to control the aircraft."

I reacted with "Shit!" as I woke up and retracted the speed boards. The boards slammed shut, and the airspeed jumped to 160 knots. I grabbed the power handles and reduced power to thirty knots. I was behind the aircraft in thought and actions. As soon as I retracted the speed boards, I should have reduced power all in one smooth motion. Now I was at the point where I should turn to base, I had done no prelanding check, and my airspeed was too fast to lower the landing gear. Captain Mack was looking at the runway as if to say, "I wonder if this fool is going to fly away or land."

It was then that I took the first action to show that I might be capable of flying the Mohawk. I popped the speed boards and watched my airspeed start down, and when it hit 140, I retracted the speed boards and called for the prelanding check. Captain Mack started reading: "Flaps, rpm, gear down, landing light on."

I stayed with him, and in the middle of the check, I turned base and lowered the nose. I finished the prelanding check halfway through base. I was piloting the aircraft again. I had done this many times in the Beaver;

I had to get over this big, powerful Mohawk intimidating me and fly it. I noticed Captain Mack nodding in silent approval.

I turned final and looked for my descent angle. I was too far out, so I added power to hold my altitude until I had the descent angle. When it looked right, I pulled power back to fifteen pounds and lowered the nose on my descent angle. The aircraft bounced in turbulent air even with my working the controls to keep it on course to the end of the runway.

The touchdown end of the runway came up fast, and I honestly was not sure when to round out. When I thought I had the right picture, I pulled the power all the way off and started to round out. Captain Mack put his hand on top of mine and pushed power back in, and his hand on the stick stopped me from rounding out. "Too high—you're twenty feet in the air." He held his hand over mine until I thought we were going to slam into the runway. Then he said, "Okay, land."

I pulled the power off and rounded out, trying desperately to keep the wings level in the choppy air. Two seconds after I rounded out, the Mohawk plopped down with tires squealing and bounced a couple feet before settling firmly on the runway. I forgot to hold the nose up, and it came down with a bounce. I had to work the pedals to keep us on the runway. Sweat was pouring off me. Captain Mack calmly said, "Reverse your engines. Make sure you reverse both at the same time. I don't want us cartwheeling down the runway."

I reversed the engines, and the aircraft slowed to a controllable speed. Captain Mack started the after-landing checklist as I struggled to follow and taxi the aircraft. The thought ran through my mind that this was more difficult than flying helicopters. Halfway down the runway, Captain Mack said, "I've got the aircraft," and I surrendered control to him. "I'm just going to speed up taxi. There's another bird behind us on final." He applied power and smoothly raced to the end of the runway and exited onto the taxiway.

I did eight more touch-and-gos before Captain Mack said, "That's enough for today. Let's head back to Cairns."

By then, the Mohawk had physically exhausted and mentally drained me. Sweat soaked my flight suit. The many mistakes I had made over and over had wrecked my ego. In my opinion, I had performed like a student pilot with no flying experience. Captain Mack had shown some frustration at my handling of the aircraft. I am sure he expected more of me.

Finally back in the debriefing room, he asked me if I wanted a Coke. I said yes, and he walked over to the Coke machine and brought back two Cokes. I told him thanks and said I had to go to the bathroom first. He waited, and when I returned, he had a training sheet out and was marking it. I sat down and took a long swig of the cold soda.

Captain Mack finished making marks on the student training sheet and took a swig of Coke. He looked at me and started his critique. "Overall, it wasn't that bad for your first flight. It wasn't as good as I expected but was passable. Your biggest weaknesses are instrument location and procedures. You take too much time trying to find an instrument, and that lets something else go, like altitude. Then you start correcting altitude, and something else goes. You have to be a minute ahead of this aircraft, or you can get into trouble fast. I want you in the Mohawk mock-up trainer this afternoon, practicing takeoff and landing checks and memorizing instrument locations and settings so there's no hesitation finding an instrument. Do you have any questions of me?"

"No, Captain Mack. I'll do better next time." That was all I could think to say.

"Okay, I'll see you here at 1030 for your next flight."

Walking out to my car, I was thankful. He had filled out a white training form and not a pink one, so I had passed my first flight. It was 1015, so I decided I would go home to eat something and relax before going to the link trainer. My struggles had overwhelmed my brain. I would not be able to concentrate any more without a break. I tried not to let my morale go down. I kept telling myself that in two weeks, I would laugh at how badly I had performed.

After a sandwich and a hot shower, I felt new again. I told Claudia how I had struggled with flying this aircraft. She did not understand why I would have any problems, since I was already a pilot. She compared flying an aircraft to driving a car. I do not know if she was trying to cheer me up or believed that flying different planes was like driving different cars. When I was ready to go, Claudia wanted to use the car, so she agreed to drop me off at the link trainer and get me at 1500.

Sitting in the link trainer, I looked at the array of instruments. I told myself that before I left, I would find and memorize the location of every instrument. Then I would memorize the checklist. I had to do better on my next flight for the sake of my ego. No one could chastise me worse than I could. I could not stand another self-flagellation.

I spent the first two hours closing my eyes, mentally picking an instrument, and putting my finger on it. Then I would open my eyes to see if I was correct. I was slow at first, but as I began to fix each instrument's location in my mind, I started getting faster and making fewer mistakes. By the end of two hours, I could name every instrument and immediately touch it without hesitation. Satisfied that I at least had a good idea of instrument locations, I started on the checklist.

I began with the engine start procedures. I read each one and simulated doing it and reciting the correct response. I continued this until I worked my way through all the checks. When I finished, I knew each function, setting, and response. Well, I did for now. I knew that when I got back in the Mohawk, it was not going to be as smooth as it was in the mock-up trainer. My need to excel caused me to view any minor mistake as a major failure on my part. Learning to fly is unlike any other learning experience. You have to display with hands-on application in real-life time what you have learned. Once you learn the technique, you must do it over and over until you develop just the right control touch. Unfortunately, my personality would punish me for any failings while developing those skills. I held myself to such high standards that I suffered when I fell short of my expectations.

I was exhausted when Claudia picked me up. I hoped the effort I had put into the trainer would pay off, except I knew myself, and that meant that tomorrow I would somehow screw up again. I had to accept that I was not the perfect pilot. I had to learn as everybody else had to learn. I did not want Captain Mack thinking, *How in the hell did this hot dog get into Mohawk transition?*

That night, I lay sleepless in the darkness for an hour or so. Claudia and I had made passionate love, and she had fallen asleep before I could share my emotions with her. I would have thought that helicopter transition would have affected me more than Mohawk qualification, but the size and complexity of the Mohawk had me questioning whether I could complete the course. The way I'd gotten lost at times during the morning training flight worried me. I have said that flight training was the most difficult and, at the same time, most fulfilling experience I had been through. Now learning to fly the Mohawk appeared it was going to be more taxing than flight school. I knew I needed God's help to do complete the training, and I asked him for it that night.

The next morning, I went to the flight room first to check in with Captain Mack. My teammate was already there. I asked how he had done on his first flight. "Man," he said, "that is a tough bird. I don't think I did anything right. I hope I can do better this morning. How did you do?"

"I think the same as you did. I have more than twelve hundred hours of flight time, but it was if I had never before flown. You'll be okay. But I think Captain Mack expects more of me. I basically flew the aircraft okay, but the checks and procedures killed me."

Captain Mack walked in and, looking at us, said, "I am glad to see you two are ready to give me a good flight today. I'll be right back as soon as I get a cup of coffee."

He returned with his coffee and sat down. "All right, do you have any questions about yesterday? Both of you need to learn the cockpit layout and procedures like the back of your hand. Shit happens fast in the Mohawk, and you must be at least sixty seconds ahead of the aircraft. The way you get there is to learn the instruments and procedures so you do them without pause. That allows you to fly the aircraft and stay ahead of it. All right, Captain Jonas, you start the preflight on 821. Captain Griffin, you get some more mock-up training and be back here at 1030."

I spent the next two hours in the trainer. It became boring after a while, but I forced myself to stay focused on the array of instruments. I repeated the procedures from my session yesterday. I shut my eyes, called out an instrument, and pointed to it. Then I opened my eyes to see if I was pointing at the right instrument. My work yesterday paid off. I would occasionally misplace an instrument, but I could zip through the whole array quickly. I spent the next hour going through each checklist procedure and response.

I was waiting at the briefing table when Captain Mack and Captain Jonas returned. Captain Jonas's flight suit was soaked with sweat, and he looked beat. The expression on his face caused my stomach to flutter.

Captain Mack said, "Captain Griffin, you can start the preflight on 821, and I will be with you after I debrief Captain Jonas."

I was almost finished with the preflight when Captain Mack walked up to the aircraft. He asked me where I was at, and I told him I was about to check the infrared and camera bays. He told me to go ahead. I opened the bay doors and performed the prescribed checks. Then we climbed into the cockpit.

As soon as we buckled our harnesses to the ejection seat, he began the engine start-up checks. This time, I did better. He called out the check, and I touched the instrument or switch and called out the proper setting or response. When we'd finished, I sat there, expecting him to do the start. He looked at me and said, "What are you waiting for? Start the engines."

I looked at the crew chief. He was pointing at the number-one engine with his right arm and was rotating his left hand in the start-engine signal. I turned the engine start switch to the start position, and the left engine prop started turning as the engine whined to life. I let go of the start switch as I heard the engine start, and I looked at the EGT gauge to make sure it was not a hot start. I quickly checked the engine gauges, calling out the readings as I waited for the EGT to stabilize.

When all the instruments were in the green and the EGT had stabilized at 650 degrees, I looked at the crew chief. He gave me the signal to start number two, and I repeated the procedure. While I was starting the engines, Captain Mack called for taxi instructions. When both engines were running in the green, he told me to taxi to runway twenty-eight.

I taxied to the departure end of runway twenty-eight, and my second flight training period began. It was a repeat of the first flight, except I was quicker and smoother in the cockpit. I was not good, but I was better than I'd been the first time. The sheer size and power of the Mohawk still awed and intimidated me. My work in the mock-up trainer had improved my knowledge of the instruments and controls, but I was still timid about making control changes.

After ten touch-and-gos at the auxiliary runway, I could see improvement in my performance. I had begun to picture the correct angle for descent to landing and had a feeling for the height at which to round out. I was still sloppy at holding the exact altitude in the hot and turbulent air, but I knew that with time, that would become an automatic control touch, and I would be able to hold it without thinking about it.

Back in the debriefing room, I waited for Captain Mack's critique of my flight. Again, I was oily from sweat and mentally exhausted. Captain Mack, to my joy, filled out a white critique sheet. When he'd finished, he looked at me and said, "Much better today than your last flight. You are still hesitant and slow on power and control changes, but in time, I think you will overcome that. Keep working in the mock-up trainer, and in the morning, get in one of the Mohawks on the flight line and practice all the procedures. I'll see you tomorrow afternoon at 1300. Any questions?"

"No, sir," I answered. "I can't think of any right now."

I went home again to shower and eat lunch before going back to the trainer. I had a total of three hours and forty-five minutes of flying time in the Mohawk. The entire qualification course was twenty-five hours of contact training to learn to fly the aircraft, followed by twenty-five hours of instrument training and qualification. I still had much learning to do before I could pass any check ride, and I had only twenty-one hours left in which to do it. That thought worried me. I knew I had to get better—and fast—if I were going to get through this course. The only positive sign I had so far was that Captain Mack did not seem concerned with my progression.

The next morning, I went to one of the Mohawks not scheduled to fly and climbed into the cockpit. I found that sitting in the aircraft and running through the flight procedures and checks was much better than using the mock-up trainer. I could better imagine the aircraft in flight, and that helped me run through the checks as if I were flying it.

We flew in the afternoon for the rest of the week. I'd thought the mornings were bumpy, but after the moist air heated up, there was real bouncing around. Fortunately, the weather had still been cool during helicopter transition, and there had been little turbulence. The flights followed the same pattern: I'd fly to the auxiliary runway and do touch-and-gos. By the end of the week, I was beginning to believe I would make it through the course. I had improved, and I knew it. My main problem was that occasionally, unexpectedly, I would do something dumb, such as forgetting to orient my flight director or rounding out prematurely, but I could take off and land well enough, which was a big boost to my morale.

After my flight on Friday, Captain Mack said he was happy with my progress. He told me to study emergency procedures over the weekend, because Monday morning, we would start working on those. That meant that as in helicopter transition, from now on, I would have to contend with an emergency on every flight. My first reaction was *Oh no, just when I was starting to have confidence in flying the Mohawk!* I did not feel ready to handle emergencies on top of still being stressed from just flying the aircraft. I knew the emphasis the army placed on safety and handling emergencies. I also knew I had shown my ability to successfully handle every emergency that had come my way, but the idea of an emergency in the Mohawk was intimidating.

Over the weekend, between going shopping with Claudia and washing and waxing the car, I managed to study all the emergency procedures on the checklist. Occasionally, I stopped to counsel myself. Mentally, I was making the training more difficult than it was. This course was important to me, and for some reason, whenever I faced a challenge like this, I would seesaw emotionally. One minute, I would feel confident, and the next minute, I'd feel overcome by a challenge that seemed beyond my ability. From jump school to OCS to OFWAC, I had gone through similar mental doubts. I kept asking why I did this to myself. Finally, I would shut my mind down and focus on the task. I could do that successfully but still feel that I was in over my head.

Monday morning, I was ready to test myself but dreaded the ordeal I faced. After we took off, Captain Mack told me, "Turn to a heading of sixty, and climb to ten thousand feet." We were going to an area set aside for aerobatics and unusual maneuver training, where normal en route traffic was barred. After I reached ten thousand feet, I flew on a heading of sixty for about five minutes. At ten thousand feet, we were in broken cumulus clouds. Cumulus clouds harbor stronger turbulence than moist air, and I had not yet gained the control touch to let the aircraft bounce around and still keep it on course and altitude. I still tried to correct every little bounce, which kept me working all the time. I was glad when Captain Mack said, "I've got the aircraft."

I gave up the controls, saying, "You've got the aircraft."

Captain Mack flew the aircraft for a minute or two and said, "Okay, I am going to explain an engine-out procedure. First, let's make some turns to ensure we are clear of any other aircraft."

After we made turns to the right and left, he said, "Okay, I'm going to set up an engine failure by turning off the fuel to the number-one engine."

A few seconds after he turned the fuel switch off, I could hear the left engine spooling down. I glanced at the engine gauges to verify it was not running. I could feel the Mohawk yaw to the left as the right engine tried to turn the aircraft into the dead engine. Captain Mack smoothly applied right aileron and right rudder to hold the aircraft on course. He demonstrated each procedure as he called off the check. "Quickly verify which engine is dead. Left foot dead, left engine dead. Confirm by checking the left engine gauges. " His left foot was dead because his right foot was holding rudder to keep the aircraft on course. He pointed to the left engine gauges, which confirmed that the engine was not running.

"Next, feather the number-one propeller." He pulled the number-one engine rpm handle to the rear into the feather position. "Verify the blade feathers by watching it."

I watched the three big blades, which had been flat and turning, align themselves so that the edges faced the direction the aircraft was flying. That immediately reduced the drag on the aircraft and allowed Captain Mack to reduce the aileron and rudder needed to hold the aircraft on course. Before he feathered the props, he had to add power to maintain a safe single-engine airspeed of 140 knots. With the blades feathered, the airspeed increased, and Captain Mack reduced power to hold 140 knots.

Captain Mack pointed to the autofeather switches and said, "I feathered the props manually. I also could have used the autofeather switch. Whichever method you use is your choice. What is most important is to get the aircraft under control; identify the dead engine; get the blades feathered; and, after that, clean up the aircraft. It's absolutely critical that you correctly identify the dead engine. Too many times, pilots, in the shock of having an engine quit running, feathered the wrong prop. Several could not figure out what they did wrong and had to eject and lose the aircraft. Others figured out what was happening and unfeathered the props." He continued, "Had the engine failed in downwind and had I already lowered my gear, I would have feathered the props first and then raised my gear. I would continue the approach and lower them when I was sure I could make the runway. The Mohawk will fly safely on one engine, but you don't want to push your luck, because what caused the one engine to fail could cause the other engine to fail. Obviously, it doesn't fly well with both engines dead. We engage the autofeather system on takeoff because you won't have the time to worry about feathering the engine. You are already low and slow, and keeping control of the aircraft will demand your attention, but you have to check to make sure the autofeather is working. After you get some time in the bird, you can tell by the aileron and rudder you're using if you feathered the prop.

"All right, let's do an engine start in the air. When you have an engine failure, always try to restart after you have everything under control. The restart procedures are the same as on the ground—props to sixteen hundred rpm, full power, fuel pumps on, and switch to start."

The number-one engine started turning, and the engine gauges came up to the green. When Captain Mack advanced the rpm handles, he took the prop out of feather. As the left engine began to run, he eased off the aileron and rudders, adjusted the power, and synchronized the props. We were again flying normally. "Any questions?" he asked.

"No, sir, not at the moment," I answered.

"Okay, you've got the aircraft."

"I've got the aircraft," I replied. It was my turn now, and I could feel little butterflies in my stomach.

Captain Mack said, "Okay, make some clearing turns, and make sure we are clear of any other traffic."

I banked the bouncing Mohawk to the left, checked the airspace, and then banked right to clear us. While doing the turns, I did not notice Captain Mack turn off the fuel to the number-two engine. When I leveled the aircraft, I felt it yaw sharply to the right. Instinctively, I applied left rudder and aileron to right the aircraft, but the yaw caught me by surprise. It was as if I were in a daze until Captain Mack said, "All right, you've got an engine failure. What are you going to do?"

"Shit," I muttered to myself. I was already behind the aircraft. Fortunately, I respond well under pressure. I started the checklist, calling each check as I performed it. "Right foot dead, right engine dead. Confirm with engine gauges, feather right engine, check that aircraft is clean, and add power to maintain airspeed." I got power in, but by then, the airspeed had bled off to 120 knots, which was too slow, but when the right prop feathered, the airspeed quickly increased to 140 knots. I pulled off power to preserve that speed and eased off the aileron and rudder. The power of those big engines amazed me. If I had applied full power without left rudder and aileron, the left engine could have put the aircraft into an inverted condition—not something you want to happen, especially when you are in downwind for landing.

Captain Mack said, "Good job. But you were too slow in recognizing your engine was out. Remember, you are not going to expect an engine failure, so you've got to be ready always. All right, let's do a restart."

After I completed four more engine-out recoveries, Captain Mack said, "Let's head for the aux field." By then, I knew the way, so I banked and headed for it.

Captain Mack said, "Descend to six thousand feet, and I'll show you a high-speed tactical approach." When we could see the aux field, he said, "I've got the aircraft."

"You've got the aircraft," I responded, releasing the controls.

"A high-speed approach keeps you over the airfield and away from any antiaircraft fire. Start the approach by flying about halfway down the runway. Then, when cleared to land, you pop the speed boards and begin a left or right thirty-degree descending turn. The object is to make a three-hundred-sixty-degree descending circle and roll out on final. Halfway through your circle, you perform prelanding check. Also, by this point, you should have lost half of you altitude."

He continued talking as he lowered the flaps and moved the props to full rpm. "Lower gear when you roll onto final." I felt the gear come down, and the aircraft slowed to 140; we were on a perfect final. We did landing check, and he said, "Once you are on final and on the right glide path, retract your speed boards."

He touched down right on the end of the runway. It was a perfect landing, and the whole process had taken us about three minutes. He smiled at me and said, "Don't worry; it takes practice to do an approach that good. You only have to perform one later. I won't expect it to be perfect. I just want you to know the technique. Okay, you've got the aircraft."

I spent another hour doing four touch-and-gos. On each one, he gave me an engine out to contend with. I did not know it, but there was another way to cut the fuel to the engine, so my first engine out came as a surprise. Captain Mack had reached behind us and pulled the fuel pump circuit breaker. However, this time, I recognized the yaw. Other than losing a hundred feet of altitude before I got it feathered and got the gear up, I did a good job. Finally, he said, "Let's head back to Cairns."

Those were sweet words. It's difficult to understand that learning to fly a big, complex aircraft, such as the Mohawk, is hard work. The tension and stress of responding to each situation and the knowledge that the instructor is grading you on how well you do take a toll mentally and physically. I was wet, and I could tell I had no mental stamina left. I could not gain anything from continuing past this point.

As he completed my student critique sheet, Captain Mack said he was happy with my progress. He asked me how I thought I was doing. I told him I was gaining more confidence in my ability with each flight but had a long way to go. I was giving it my best, and barring any major problems, I had no doubt I would complete the transition. He seemed satisfied with my response and parted with a "See you tomorrow."

The rest of the week was a repeat of Monday. I did touch-and-gos with engine outs and at least one high-altitude approach. By the end of the week, I was still in awe of the monster the Mohawk was, but I had to admit I could fly it satisfactorily—or at least I was happy with my progress. I no longer felt apprehensive each time I walked up to the aircraft.

Friday afternoon, at the end of my second touch-and-go, Captain Mack told me to taxi over to the field tower apron. When we got there, he told me to shut down the number-two engine. After it spooled down, he said, "Okay, time for you to take it solo. Make four touch-and-gos. I'll be in the tower, so if you have problems, call me." With that, he got out of the Mohawk and walked away.

My heart was beating two hundred beats a minute. The casual way he'd told me to go solo had surprised me. The small cockpit seemed big without him sitting there beside me. I could see other Mohawks taxiing toward the tower to let their instructors out. *I'd better get moving,* I thought, so I secured his hatch, laid the checklist on his seat, and called the tower for taxi.

As I taxied to the run-up area, I said, "Dear God, let there be no problems until I have enough time in the aircraft to handle them." I taxied into the run-up area and turned the aircraft around. The pressure of having an instructor sitting next to me and evaluating each move eased, but the pressure of realizing that I was about to solo in the most sophisticated aircraft the army had in its inventory replaced it. After completing the run-up check and takeoff check, I glanced at the side mirror and looked at my reflection in it. I thought, *Neal, you have come a long way from the unsure and immature boy who joined the army back in 1956.*

"Tower, this is Mohawk 671, ready for takeoff." I sounded a hell of a lot more confident than I felt.

"Mohawk 671 cleared for takeoff."

I taxied out onto the runway and oriented my flight director. Everything looked good, so I held the brakes as I firmly applied power, and then I released the brakes as the engines spooled up. The aircraft jumped forward, and I shot down the runway, as I had many times before, except I was by myself. There was no one sitting beside me to keep me from screwing up.

A hundred knots came up fast. I rotated, and the Mohawk lifted off smoothly. I ignored the elation I felt and focused on flying the aircraft. I cleaned up the aircraft and quickly checked the checklist to make sure I had not missed anything. The procedures were coming automatically now as I climbed out and banked right to enter a downwind. I was flying solo in total command of a big aircraft, and I was starting to feel comfortable. I wanted a feeling of sure control, of mastery, when piloting the Mohawk. I wanted to feel the way I felt when I flew the Beaver or the Bird Dog. I was not there yet, but I knew I was well on the way to gaining that confidence and skill.

I made three more touch-and-gos before Captain Mack called and told me to pick him up. I felt great while taxiing to the tower apron. I popped the hatch, and for the first time, the odor of JP-4 did not bother me. Even the hot, wet Alabama air seemed tolerable. I glanced at the side mirror. I looked great and professional with my sunscreen visor pulled down. Captain Mack climbed into the cockpit and said, "Take me back to Cairns."

At the pilot debriefing table, Captain Mack asked me if I had any questions. I said no as he added up my flight hours. "You've got nineteen hours. We need to fly six more hours before you start instrument training. Next Tuesday, we will start aerobatics. Monday will be a no-flight day because of compression chamber orientation, so I will see you Tuesday morning at 0730. Have a great weekend."

I stopped by the student company on the way home to check my message box. There, I found an amendment to my orders. After finishing the transition course, I was to report to the US Army Combat Surveillance and Electronic Warfare School (USACSEWS), Fort Huachuca, Arizona. I had not known that Mohawk pilots had to attend three weeks of training on the SLAR (side-looking airborne radar), infrared, and camera systems. Hell, I had not even known there was a Fort Huachuca or its location.

That evening at dinner, I told Claudia about my solo flight. She was happy for me, but I could tell it did not mean all that much to her. She seemed as if she were in some form of transition. Everything had been going well for us over the last four months. We had little fights but nothing serious. Many times, she seemed bored, and I could understand that; she spent her days cleaning house and taking care of the kids. I was the one who came home telling her of something exciting that had happened. When I was not flying, I tried my best to shower her with love and attention.

We both knew a year of separation lay ahead of us. I was not looking forward to returning to Vietnam. I feared I would have to fly helicopters, and I had an ominous feeling about that. The war in Vietnam was a stalemate, and US casualties were high.

While I dreaded going back to Vietnam, Claudia was looking forward to returning to Germany, especially Munich. I loved her deeply, but we had spent much time apart, and now we were fixing to spend another year apart. To me, that was as ominous as going to Vietnam. It was the middle of August, and I did not have to report to Vietnam until November 26. I had almost three months to make her fall back in love with me.

That night, lying in bed, I thought of my solo flight. I found it hard to believe I had come so far from the floundering kid I had been when I'd joined the army. I had made some good choices and an occasionally bad choice that had ultimately turned out to be good. I had proven I could succeed in anything I wanted if I applied myself. The only case in which that was not true was my relationship with Claudia. No matter how hard

I applied myself, I did not seem to get a response that made me feel secure about our marriage. At the time, I did not realize I probably lacked the ability to even recognize that response. I was in the dark because I had no real role model for the man and husband I wanted to be. The best I had were my father and the army.

We went to a party at Claudia's friend Karen's house. There were several couples there; all were aviators and, like me, in a transient state. Karen's husband, a major, had completed his course and was on the way to Vietnam. Karen was staying with her mother in Munich while he was gone, and she and Claudia were happy that they had someone to hang out with while both of their husbands were in Vietnam. I celebrated my solo in the Mohawk by drinking enough rum and Coke to get me falling-down drunk. Karen's husband did too, and they blamed me. But it was a good party.

Monday morning, sixteen students reported for high-altitude compression chamber orientation. Because the Mohawk can fly at a ceiling of twenty-five thousand feet, they have an orientation on the effects of high altitude. Army regulations require any pilot operating an aircraft above ten thousand feet to be on oxygen either with a mask or in a pressurized cabin. The lack of oxygen at altitudes above ten thousand feet can cause a pilot not on an outside oxygen source to black out and lose control of the aircraft.

The eight students in my class and eight from the class following attended the orientation. Inside the chamber were eight stations, as they were called. Each station was a small table extending from the wall, with a stool on each side. There were four stations on each side of the chamber. Two students sat facing each other at each of the small tables. Each student wore his flight helmet with oxygen mask attached.

Once we were all seated, the NCO in charge of the chamber briefed us on what we were going to do during the orientation. He had us plug in our headsets and hook up our oxygen masks to the receptacles at each station. After each student checked his mask to ensure it was working, we were ready to start our ascent to an altitude of forty-five thousand feet.

The instructor explained that since humans had unpressurized bodies, the gases in us would expand as we went up. That would cause many of us to pass gas, so we were told not to hold back. It also meant we would have to constantly clear our sinuses and ears. To show the degree of expansion, he hung an empty balloon in the center of the chamber. He stressed that each of us was responsible for watching his partner for any sign that his partner was having a problem.

When his assistants checked us and determined we were ready, he started the simulated ascent to forty-five thousand feet. The sensation was normal other than the sound the oxygen regulator made as I breathed. The instructor stopped us at ten thousand feet. He had us take off our oxygen masks to get a sense of how we reacted to breathing the oxygen-low air at ten thousand feet. I, like some of the others, had flown at ten thousand feet many times and felt no unusual symptoms. However, several of the newer pilots had not been at ten thousand feet without oxygen. One obvious result was the chamber's odor. As the instructor had warned, we passed a lot of gas. Thank God we were wearing oxygen masks.

The instructor pointed at the balloon, which had started to expand. Our bodies, especially those parts containing gas, such as our intestines, were also expanding. We had to pass the gas or suffer pain and possible damage to our bodies. Of course, we were familiar with clearing our ears and sinuses.

We donned our masks and started the ascent to twenty-five thousand feet. When we reached that altitude, we removed our masks to experience the effects. The air was dry and smelled of human flatus as I breathed it. Other than that, I noticed nothing else.

The instructor kept us at twenty-five thousand feet until we could feel ourselves starting to take deep breaths to intake enough oxygen. Then we began to feel light-headed. After we verified feeling these effects, the instructor had us remask. It was a relief to have oxygen flowing into the lungs and not to struggle to breathe. Again, the instructor pointed to the balloon. It was stretching the rubber. The purpose of removing our masks was to teach each of us the symptoms of oxygen deprivation. It is critical for a pilot to recognize oxygen deprivation and take the proper actions while he still can.

Once everyone affirmed that he was okay, the instructor started climbing again. This time, we went all the way to forty-five thousand feet. The balloon expanded to the bursting point. During the last twenty thousand feet, everybody had been squirming as he passed gas. At forty-five thousand feet, the instructor again had us remove our masks.

This time, we saw the fast and insidious effects of oxygen deprivation. He had us play patty-cake with our partners and chant as we played. He asked us to watch each other for slurring of words, loss of coordination, and lips turning blue. The three assistant instructors stood with him between each station, watching us. I decided I would try to last longer than my partner, but it was only about four minutes before the instructor at our station hit us on the head and told us to put our masks on. By then, most of the students had put their masks on or were putting them on. The instructor had to put one student's mask on. Oxygen deprivation is so insidious that I had not even recognized that I was slurring, and my partner and I were missing each other's hands. As I put my mask on, I could see that his lips were turning blue. That was an unforgettable lesson. I vowed never to let it happen to me.

After we recovered from the demonstration, the instructor took us down to sea level, and the orientation was over. We left the chamber because of the odor and debriefed outside. The instructor discussed what we had done and the exercise's purpose. He reviewed the signs we needed to be aware of when flying over ten thousand feet and the actions to take if we got into an oxygen-deprivation situation. Before he dismissed us, he told us we might have headaches from the exercise, but that was normal; we should just take a couple of aspirin.

Several of us decided to have lunch at the officers' club, and after lunch, we continued to party. By 1600, I figured I'd had enough to drink, so I headed home. Claudia was unhappy that I'd spent the afternoon at the officers' club, which led to an argument.

The disturbing problem with Claudia was that when she got angry and we started arguing, she flew into a rage. She would bring up every mistake or fault with me, no matter how long ago it had occurred. I learned early on that I would never redeem myself, because she never accepted that I regretted my faults and constantly tried to do better and correct them. She never noticed that I rarely made the same mistake twice; she harbored the missteps just under her skin. My recourse was to keep silent, and that fueled her anger. We ended up glaring at each other and not speaking for several days until the anger had passed. However, with her, it passed but was never forgotten.

The flight schedule had me flying first on Tuesday morning. I was sure that eating a big breakfast before flying aerobatics would be bad, and I told myself, *No food before flying aerobatics.* After we took off, Captain Mack told me to climb to ten thousand feet and gave me a heading that would take us to the area cleared for aerobatics above eight thousand feet.

After about five minutes, he took the controls. "Okay, I am going to explain each maneuver and then let you perform it. In some of the maneuvers, we will pull about four Gs, so remember to tighten down your neck to prevent passing out. Air force fighter pilots wear G suits when they fly. These suits automatically inflate and apply pressure to the abdomen and chest area to prevent the blood from leaving the head, which causes unconsciousness. G suits are required to fly maneuvers in which you will experience anything greater than four Gs.

"Even flying without a G suit, you can experience tunnel vision around three Gs. Unconsciousness follows tunnel vision, though most of the time, it is a momentary condition. But occurring at the wrong time, it could cause a disastrous chain of events. The remedy is to tighten your neck and squish your chin down into your chest. This stems the flow of blood from your brain long enough for you to complete the aerobatic maneuver and be out of a G-pulling configuration."

Captain Mack did some turns to make sure the area was clear of other aircraft and said, "The first maneuver is going to be a simple roll. To do a roll, you lower the nose to pick up airspeed to three hundred knots." I watched the airspeed gauge as he spoke. "When you reach three hundred knots, you pull the nose up to level flight and move the stick to full left or right aileron, depending on which direction you want to roll."

He pulled the stick all the way to the right, and the Mohawk started rolling to the right. "As you move the stick, put in a little back pressure to hold the nose up."

When we were inverted, he continued. "When you reach the inverted position, you have to take out the back pressure and put in forward pressure to hold the nose in the level position."

The Mohawk was now rolling through 270 degrees toward the upright position. "As you come out of the roll, ease the stick to the neutral position, and return to straight and level flight. Your airspeed will bleed off during the roll. That is why we start at three hundred knots, and when we roll level, we should be at one hundred eighty or so. If you complete a perfect roll, you should come straight and level at the altitude you started at."

I checked the altitude: it was 8,980 feet. We were at nine thousand feet when we reached three hundred knots and started the roll. He had lost twenty feet in the roll. Looking at the gauge, he said, "Not bad. Anything within a hundred feet above or below is good."

During the maneuver, I felt no Gs. The only noticeable effect was that while inverted, I could feel my harness and seat belt holding me in position, and I felt a slight sensation of motion sickness. Then Captain Mack said, "You've got the aircraft. Climb back up to ten thousand feet, and do a clearing turn."

After I made my clearing turn, he said, "Okay, I'm going to talk you through the first one. Lower your nose, keeping this heading, to increase airspeed to three hundred knots."

I followed his instructions and watched my airspeed increase to three hundred. We were at 9,200 feet when he said, "Okay, pull your nose up level, and move your stick all the way to the right. Apply a little back pressure to maintain altitude."

I moved the stick all the way to the right, and the Mohawk rolled abruptly to the right. "Okay," he said, "as you reach the ninety-degree angle, start letting out back pressure so that when you reach the one-hundred-eighty-degree inverted position, your stick is neutral."

I did my best to follow his instructions precisely, but it was hard to do so in the bouncing aircraft. Moving the stick to the right was easy, but holding it all the way to the right and applying the right amount of back and forward pressure was difficult. I heard him say as we reached the inverted position, "More forward pressure—your nose is falling off."

I added more forward pressure, but in doing so, I let the stick move a little to the left, which slowed the rate of roll. As I rolled past the 270-degree angle, I was wobbling all over the sky. Finally, I reached the level position with my nose up and airspeed at 160, climbing past 9,400 feet. I was thirty degrees off my heading. It was not a good roll.

After I got the aircraft under control, Captain Mack said, "All right, do it again."

I did three more rolls. Each one got a little better, but it was obvious to me that I would never be a stunt pilot. By the third roll, the little sensation of nausea was much stronger.

After my third roll, Captain Mack said, "I've got the aircraft." He took the controls and said, "This time, I am going to talk you through a loop. The entry is the same as for the roll. Climb to ten thousand feet, do your clearing turns, and lower the nose to increase airspeed to three hundred knots. At three hundred, holding your heading, move the stick firmly to the rear, up against your stomach. Keep the wings level."

As he spoke, the Mohawk started up in an arc, went inverted, and started back down. He still had the stick all the way to the rear, and I felt some slight Gs as we climbed and entered the inverted position. Captain Mack kept speaking. "Squish your neck muscles as we fly through the inverted position to level flight. That is where we will pull up to four Gs. When your nose points straight down at the ground, release a little back pressure to lessen the Gs and keep them under four."

He was not kidding. As we began to loop through the vertical position, I could feel the Gs pressing down on me. Even though I squished my neck muscles as hard as I could, I still experienced slight tunnel vision. I heard Captain Mack continue. "As you pull out, ease your stick to neutral so you roll out on your starting altitude." As he said that, we rolled out on 9,200 feet, the altitude we'd started at.

His skill impressed me. Also, my stomach was queasy. He said, "Okay, you take the controls, and I will talk you through a loop."

With a queasy stomach, I took the controls, climbed to ten thousand feet, and did my clearing turns. As he talked me through each step, I did a sloppy loop, rolling level five hundred feet below my starting altitude. My main fault was not holding enough back pressure on the stick when we reached the vertical position. I was concerned about pulling too many Gs, which caused me to miss my altitude. I did pull some Gs but not enough to give me tunnel vision, as the last loop had.

Before he called it quits, Captain Mack had me do two more loops. When he detected that I was not going to pull the stick back enough, he pulled it, saying, "Like that." By then, I was starting to get over my fear of pulling too many Gs, and my last loop was my best one. I missed my starting altitude by a hundred feet, but that satisfied me. I was unhappy at the way my stomach felt. I was not sick, but I was uncomfortable while trying not to get motion sickness. After my third loop, I was relieved when he said, "Let's head back to Cairns."

Movement of fluids in the inner ears causes motion sickness. I think the constant odor of JP-4 exhaust, the heat, and just sitting there as Captain Mack ran through each maneuver were the primary culprits in my case. I never felt the sensation of motion sickness when I was at the controls, but once I started feeling the effects, they hung with me even for a while after I got out of the aircraft. Later, while flying missions, I would witness TOs get airsick and upchuck in bags they carried with them. It did not faze them; they kept on working the cameras and sensor systems.

In the debriefing room, Captain Mack discussed my mistakes. He said my main problem was being too timid with my controls when performing the roll or loop, but he had no doubt I would improve with a little practice. He said, "Tomorrow plan on doing split S's and stalls, plus a couple rolls and loops to reinforce what you learned today."

I finally got rid of the queasy stomach on the way home. I knew there was no way I was going to do aerobatics just for fun! I honestly did not get any thrill from doing those maneuvers. Some pilots loved to do all maneuvers, but I was not one of them. I loved using the aircraft to perform a mission. That was fun for me. From classes, I knew the split S was the only defense the Mohawk had against the surface-to-air (SAM) missile. I would concentrate on doing that maneuver, because it was necessary for the safe accomplishment of the mission, not to mention my butt.

Claudia was still mad at me, but at least she fixed dinner. I played games with the kids until it was time for them to go to bed. Claudia and I sat in silence, watching TV until I tired and went to bed.

Lying in bed, I reran the techniques for loops and rolls in my mind and tried to imagine myself doing them. I could do them flawlessly in my mind—but of course, I had no bouncing aircraft and Gs with which to contend. I also knew I could take a Mohawk and practice each maneuver until I could do it flawlessly—but I had no intention of ever doing that.

Taking off from Cairns the following afternoon, I headed for the aerobatics area while climbing to ten thousand feet. The air was cooler at ten thousand, and the vent air allowed it to flow into the aircraft, which provided some relief from the heat. Unfortunately, the air bore the odor of JP-4 exhaust.

When we got into the aerobatics area, Captain Mack took control of the aircraft. "Okay, I'm going to demonstrate a split S. The split S is a combination of the roll and loop. First, we do our clearing turns. We don't dive to gain airspeed in a split S. Most of the time, a pilot enters an evasive maneuver from a straight and level attitude, so that's the attitude in which we'll enter it. We're clear, so we roll inverted. Once inverted, pull back on the stick, and when you reach the nose-down position, let up some of the pressure on the stick so you lose altitude quickly. Watch your airspeed, and keep enough backward pressure on the stick to fly out of the split S a thousand feet or so below your start altitude and on a heading one hundred eighty degrees opposite your original heading."

As he spoke, he smoothly did a split S. "Any questions?" he asked. I shook my head, and he said, "You've got the aircraft. I'll talk you through a split S. Go ahead and climb to ten thousand feet, and make your clearing turns."

I was making a clearing turn to the right, when I saw a Mohawk about two miles away in the middle of a roll. Captain Mack said, "I've got him. He's plenty clear."

I turned the aircraft on a heading away from the other Mohawk. Captain Mack said, "Anytime you are ready."

I took a deep breath, moved the stick all the way to the right, and held in a little back pressure. In less than a second, we were hanging inverted from our seat belts. I was moving the stick to the center to stop the roll, when Captain Mack said, "Center the stick to stop the roll. Back pressure to start the aircraft down; let it fall to nose-facing-the-ground position. Keep the wings level."

I was looking straight down at the ground in a vertical position. I started putting backward pressure on the stick to pull out of the dive we were in. I could hear Captain Mack saying, "Not too much back pressure. You want to lose some altitude, and you don't want to pull too many Gs."

I had my neck muscles tightened and my head pulled in, but I could still feel the Gs building. I eased up on the back pressure, the Gs lessened, and we slowly pulled out of the dive to level flight. I was at 8,800 feet, and my airspeed was160 knots.

"Not bad," Captain Mack said. "Let's set back up and do another one. This time, bring the stick back slowly but firmly until you feel the onset of G pressure, and hold it there. Let the aircraft fly itself out of the dive."

I did three more split S's before Captain Mack was okay with my performance. By then, my stomach was again queasy but not as bad as it had been the day before. Captain Mack said, "I've got the aircraft. Let's get back up to ten thousand feet and do some stall recovery procedures. I'll do the first one."

After clearing turns, Captain Mack put the Mohawk in a stall. "Power back to the detent, and rpm to 1,600. Let the speed bleed off while you hold altitude."

As the airspeed started to decrease, Captain Mack slowly brought the stick back, holding the nose up to preserve ten thousand feet and using rudder and aileron to keep the wings level. The nose rose higher and higher as the speed bled off. Captain Mack said, "We should stall somewhere around seventy to eighty knots. When it stalls, it will try to roll off to one side, but don't let that happen. We don't want to get into a flat spin."

Finally, at seventy knots, the Mohawk shuddered, and the nose dropped, pointing to the ground and putting us into a vertical dive. Captain Mack continued to speak. "Once you get a positive stall, release pressure, and apply full power. As the airspeed increases and the aircraft starts to fly again, apply back pressure to fly out of the dive and recover."

Captain Mack gave me control of aircraft and had me do four stalls and recoveries. Recovering from a stall was not new to me. All during my flight training and transitioning into each model of aircraft that I flew, I'd had to do a successful stall recovery. However, the Mohawk was huge, and its two big engines intimidated me at first. On my first stall, I was hesitant in putting enough back pressure to get a clear stall. Only after Captain Mack pulled the stick back with me did the aircraft finally stall. After that, I was okay.

After the fourth stall, Captain Mack told me to head for the aux training field. We still had thirty minutes left of training time. After one touch-and-go, he took control of the aircraft. "Okay, I'm going to explain a no-hydraulics landing."

Loss of hydraulic pressure in the Mohawk can be a serious problem. Without hydraulic pressure, you cannot lower the landing gear or flaps.

The hydraulically operated controls become stiff and need a strong force to control the aircraft. To lower the landing gear without hydraulics, you have to use a backup emergency system of air pressure. The Mohawk has a tank filled with compressed air. By activating a switch, you release that air and blow down the landing gear.

Once the landing gear is down and locked, you land without using flaps. To do this, you set up a long final to compensate for the stiff controls. You should maintain a high airspeed and fly the aircraft to the runway. Captain Mack simulated blowing the gear down, turned off the hydraulics, and explained the approach and landing.

His landing was almost perfect. When I tried it, I was all over the sky. The stick was really stiff, and I had to use heavy pressure to make the control inputs I wanted. This resulted in my overcontrolling and constantly correcting for the overcontrol, but in the end, I landed the aircraft safely. I knew that once I had a couple hundred hours of flying time in the Mohawk, I would be much smoother on the controls.

The next morning, Captain Jonas and I were in the flight room, waiting for Captain Mack, when he stormed in, obviously angry. He walked to the table and told me to go preflight, and he would be there shortly. I grabbed my helmet and harness and headed for the flight line. As I walked to the aircraft, I wondered what had happened to upset Captain Mack.

I found our aircraft and started preflight. As usual, I wore my field cap as I did the preflight. I reached the last item on the checklist, which was to check the camera and infrared system's bay. To this day, for some reason I cannot explain, I knelt to open the bay door. As I described previously, the bay door weighs more than a hundred pounds and swings downward when it opens. I pushed the release locks, and the door swung downward, catching me by surprise. Because I was kneeling, the edge of the door hit me in the bridge of my nose, pushing the bridge of my sunglasses into my nose and knocking me on my ass.

I jumped up, hoping no one had witnessed my act of stupidity. Blood was streaming down my face into my mouth from the cut on my nose. I pulled out my handkerchief and got the bleeding to stop. I noticed blood spots on my uniform as I inspected the equipment bay and shut the door.

My nose hurt, and I was cussing myself out when Captain Mack walked up. He looked at me and asked, "What the hell happened to you?"

Without waiting for me to answer, he said, "Get in the aircraft, and let's go." He guessed that since I was standing by the equipment bay, I had completed the preflight.

I put on my helmet and climbed into the hot cockpit. I could still taste blood as I shut the hatch and put my field cap in the nook. Captain Mack was already in and hooking up his harness. "Let's go. Start the prestart check."

I quickly hooked my harness to the ejection seat and tightened my seat belt. It was obvious that something was bothering Captain Mack. Halfway through the start-up check, he said, "I've got the aircraft."

I stopped what I was doing, sat back, and said, "You've got the aircraft." I watched him fly through checks and quickly start the engines. I knew I was not as fast as he was at this stage of my training, but it still angered me that he took the aircraft from me. He called for taxi, and three minutes later, we were airborne.

Captain Mack turned the aircraft toward the aerobatics training area and climbed to ten thousand feet. When we arrived at the area, without saying a word to me, he made a clearing turn, lowered the nose to pick up speed, and did a loop. When we came out of the loop, he did a double roll. He did a split S next and then another loop. As he did the maneuvers, I fought blacking out from the Gs.

After about thirty minutes and two times in tunnel vision, I was fighting nausea.

I was thinking, *What the hell is he doing? This cannot be part of the training.* I was a little worried about what he was doing. Finally, I said, "Captain Mack, you have tumbled my gyro. If you don't let me fly or stop the aerobatics, I am going to be sick."

My comment snapped him out of whatever was driving him to release his anger through aerobatics. He looked at me and said, "I am sorry. You've got the aircraft. Let's head for the aux field and do some touch-and-gos."

I took the aircraft and turned to the aux field. I did several touch-and-gos, but the knot in my stomach was becoming a force too strong to control. The hot, humid air and the odor of JP-4 fumes as I taxied with the hatches open worked with the knot to overpower me. The taste of blood from my nose did not help. After the third landing, I said, "Captain Mack,

I've had enough of this. You tumbled my gyro with the aerobatics, and I can't overcome nausea. I think I need to return to Cairns."

Surprisingly, he answered, "Yeah, I think we've had enough. Fly it back to Cairns."

I flew back in silence, struggling with the overpowering urge to vomit. About halfway back, I realized I was not going to make it. I had to puke and get the pressure off my stomach. In anger at what Captain Mack had caused, I acted as a captain and not as a student. "Captain Mack, you have tumbled my gyro, and I can't erect it. You are going to have to fly while I throw up, or I'll put it on autopilot and throw up."

Captain Mack replied, "I've got the aircraft."

I let him have the controls. I was seconds away from emptying my stomach, but I had nowhere to puke but my lap. Then I saw my field cap in the canopy. I grabbed it just in time and filled it half full of yellow vomit. I was pissed. Getting the bile off my stomach made me feel a little better, so I said, "Captain Mack, if you will hold my cap, I will take the aircraft back and finish my flight to Cairns."

Captain Mack turned and looked at me. He could see the anger in my eyes. He answered, "No, I will take it in. You sit and relax."

I sat there holding my cap filled with stinking fluid, thinking, *My Mohawk transition is over.* I wanted to blame Captain Mack for my nausea. I knew that if I had been doing the aerobatics, I would have not gotten as nauseated, as the flying would have taken my mind off it. But sitting there for more than thirty minutes while fighting Gs and enduring rapid movements from right side up to inverted was more than I could handle. However, I was a pilot, and I should have been able to avoid throwing up.

After Captain Mack landed and shut the aircraft down, I climbed out carefully so as not to spill my cap. With one hand, I took off my helmet, and in rage at my predicament, I quickly turned my field cap over and put it tightly on my head, puke and all. We walked into the flight briefing room together, me with yellow puke oozing down the sides of my head. At the table, Captain Mack said, "Go clean up. I'll wait for you here."

I stood in front of the mirror in the latrine, looking at myself. I looked like shit. Dried blood mixed with sweat crusted the sides of my nose. Blood crusted the cut across the bridge of my nose. Added to that image was the puke dried to the sides of my head. I looked the way I felt inside.

I walked over to the commode, lifted my field cap off, and dumped the thick substance into the bowl. Back at the sink, I washed my field cap out and dried it as much as I could with paper towels. I stuck my head under the faucet and let the cold water run over it. Fortunately, I wore my hair in a crew cut. Though it took awhile, I finally cleaned the puke from my hair. As I cleaned the blood from my face, I could see the beginning of two black eyes.

I dried my face, put my cap on, and looked at myself. I did not look too bad, considering. My cap was wet, but it would dry. The only thing I could not wash off was the odor of the vomit. I would have to take a shower with soap to do that. Shaking my head in frustration, I turned and left the latrine.

I walked to the table, where Captain Mack was sitting, filling out the training sheet. My spirits lifted. It was a white sheet and not the pink sheet I expected. I considered my flight a failure and expected the pink form. I did not say anything as I sat down.

Captain Mack looked at me and spoke. "You look a hell of a lot better. I can still smell you, though." He paused and then continued. "I owe you an apology. What I did was inexcusable. My wife and I have been having problems in our marriage. This morning, we had a terrible argument, and she told me she wanted a divorce. I responded by storming out of the house and sought some refuge in flying a series of aerobatics to still my anger. I should have been alone when I did that. I cannot fail you for the flight. I can fail myself for losing control of my emotions. If you want, I will ask the flight commander to replace me."

I looked at Captain Mack with a blank expression. I could see that his eyes were teary, although he was not crying. I was unsure how to respond to his admission of marital problems. I empathized with him. Many times, I had endured the pain and frustration with which he was trying to cope. Finally, I said, "Captain Mack, I'm sorry to hear about your marital problems. I too have marital problems. I hope you can work them out. I don't want another instructor pilot. I think you are one of the best. If you want to work out your anger, just don't take me with you—especially after I do some dumbass stunt like knocking myself silly by dropping the bay door on my nose."

He looked at me and smiled. "Okay, we will chalk up today as a practice ride for your check ride. I think you're ready, so I am putting you up for a contact check ride tomorrow afternoon. I am going to take tomorrow off to work on my problem. You feel up to a check ride?"

"I think I'm ready," I answered. "I don't think I can do the aerobatics perfectly, but I can do them satisfactorily."

He shook his head and replied, "Don't worry about the aerobatics. All you have to do is show you can enter and recover safely. The key requirements are landings, takeoffs, and emergency procedures. You do those well. Report in at 1300 tomorrow. I don't know who will give you the ride right now. I'll set it up so that the instructor will meet you here. Any questions?"

I had no questions, so Captain Mack dismissed me, saying, "Today will never happen again."

Driving home, I could still smell puke and taste blood. I thought of what Captain Mack had said about himself and his wife. It occurred to me that it was possible that Claudia and I were headed down that road. I wished him well because he was really a nice guy. He was professional, skillful, and compassionate. I vowed that I would never let the problems and hurt in my personal life affect my professional life, especially my flying.

When I got home, Claudia and the kids were in the pool. She was standing in her bathing suit and telling the kids something. She loved lying in the sun. She was a beauty, and I loved her deeply. I just could not get her to return love with the same intensity that I felt. I waved to them as I got out of the car. Inside the trailer, I stripped and entered the shower.

I stood in the hot shower and let the stream of water pelt me. I was looking for some form of relief in the hot water. If only the hot water pelting my body could wash away my fears and the smell of my vomit. I knew the odor would go, but the fears and mental stress I felt would not. My struggle against feeling inadequate never seemed to end, no matter how much I achieved. I lathered myself and wished that my relations with Claudia were such that she would slip into the shower with me and wash away my worries. How good would that be?

The shower revived me. I did not smell like puke. I put on my bathing suit, grabbed a beer, and joined my family in the pool. I played with the kids while Claudia lay on a lounge chair. She wanted a deep tan for when she returned to Germany.

The weather clouded, and rain drove us inside. When we entered the trailer, we could still smell the odor of vomit. I had put my flight suit in the washing machine but left my cap out. The odor was coming from my cap.

Claudia asked, "What is that odor?"

The kids only said, "Oh, it stinks," and headed for the TV.

"It's coming from my flight suit and cap," I answered.

Claudia looked at me with concern. "What happened?" She noticed my nose and eyes and added, "What happened to your nose?"

"Well, to start, I dropped a hundred-and-fifty-pound hatch on my nose. Then we did some aerobatics, and I got a little woozy and threw up," I answered. "But the good news is, I take my check ride tomorrow. If I pass it, I will start instrument training."

"Are you going to pass it?" Claudia asked, as if I could guarantee passing. She started the washing machine and put my cap in some soapy water to soak. She was warm and passionate for the rest of the day.

I spent the next morning in the link trainer, practicing each event involved in flying the Mohawk. I ate a light lunch and was sitting at the briefing table, waiting for my check ride, at 1300. At about 1305, a captain entered the room and walked over to the table. "Captain Griffin, I'm Captain Jenkins. I will be the one giving you your check ride."

He sat down and took out my training folder. "Let's go over what I expect from you. First, I expect you to know all the items on the checklist for each phase. After takeoff, we will go to the aerobatics area, and I want you to do each aerobatic maneuver. After that, we'll go to the aux field and do two or three landings and takeoffs. I will test you on your ability to handle the aircraft under emergency conditions during the flight. That's about all there is to the check ride. Do you have any questions?"

I told him I had no questions, and we headed for the aircraft. The flight lasted an hour and fifteen minutes. I performed well, considering my usual struggle with checkrideitis. I was funny that way. Even after I had more than five hundred hours in the Mohawk and was skilled at flying it, each time I took a standardization ride, I still suffered from checkrideitis. During a check ride, I could never match the skill and competence I had when flying alone. It had been that way in all the aircraft in which I flew.

I do not think average people like to display their abilities for someone to judge and criticize unless they are in some form of competition.

That is what happens in a check ride. You fly, and the instructor pilot (IP) watches and notes the problems you have or mistakes you might make. Despite the tension IPs can cause, they are effective in finding and correcting bad or dangerous habits some pilots might develop. I have seen active pilots grounded for poor techniques. As an operations officer, I had some pilots train with an IP until they could pass a check ride. It had never happened to me until my instrument check ride in the Beaver.

At the debriefing table, Captain Jenkins completed my check ride form and told me, "Good ride. No problems. Captain Mack will start your instrument training next week." He completed my form and signed it. He stood up, shook my hand, and left. I was now partially qualified to fly the Mohawk. My next check ride would be an instrument check ride.

Monday would be August 30, 1970. I had three weeks left at Fort Rucker to complete my instrument training. Then I had three weeks at Fort Huachuca, wherever the hell that was, to attend electronic surveillance and warfare school. My time with Claudia and the kids was running out. My time to return to Vietnam was drawing near. Each time I thought of it, a sense of dread shook me. I did not feel good about going back a second time.

That weekend, I partied and gave Michele and Ron all my attention. Both of them would start school the following week, and I would have less time to be with them. I did my best to be especially sweet to Claudia. When we next parted, I wanted her to have good memories of our time together.

I flew the first instrument training flight Monday morning. Captain Jonas had failed his check ride and was retaking it. When Captain Mack walked in, he appeared to be in a good mood, unlike the last time I'd seen him. I presumed he had resolved the problems in his family life. He had a hood with him. He sat down at the table, handed me the hood, and said, "That's yours for the next three weeks."

He opened my training folder and studied it for a couple of minutes. "Okay, from what I see, you should not have any problems flying instruments in the Mohawk. You have plenty of logged instrument time, so all you need is to learn the flight instruments in the Mohawk. Have you worked on instrument procedures in the link trainer?"

I affirmed that I had.

He said, "Let's go then. You preflight, and I will meet you in a few minutes."

I was sitting in the aircraft, waiting for him, when he climbed in. "All right, start the engines," he said as he hooked his harness to the ejection seat. "From now on, let's not waste time. When you finish preflight, start the number-one engine, and as soon as I get in, start the number two."

When I had both engines running and all instruments were a go, he asked, "Do you have any questions about the flight director and attitude indicator?"

"No questions right now," I answered.

"All right, as soon as you get airborne, climb out on a heading of eighty, and I will take the aircraft while you put your hood on."

Captain Mack took control of the aircraft while I put on my hood. As in my early instrument training, the hood obscured all vision except the engine and flight instruments. Except for landings and takeoffs, that would be the extent of my view for the next twenty-five hours.

At first, I felt a sensation of vertigo as Captain Mack told me to level off at nine thousand feet. I told myself to calm down; I had plenty of experience flying on instruments. I leveled off at nine thousand feet, and Captain Mack allowed me to maintain that altitude and the eighty heading for a few minutes to get the feel of flying the Mohawk under the hood.

After five minutes passed and I had settled down and was holding altitude and heading, he directed me to make a thirty-degree standard rate turn to the left. For the next hour, I made level turns, descending turns, and climbing turns. Then Captain Mack said, "I've got the aircraft."

When he had control of the aircraft, he explained how to engage the autopilot. I took control of the aircraft and engaged the autopilot. He had me fly the aircraft using the autopilot control knob found on the panel between us. I did the same turns I had done manually. Then I returned to nine thousand feet, and he had me make turns using the arrowhead on the flight director attitude indicator. That was neat. All I had to do was turn the arrowhead to the heading I wanted, and the autopilot turned the aircraft to that heading while holding perfect altitude.

After ten minutes, he had me release the autopilot. Jokingly, he said, "Don't get excited about the autopilot. We won't use it anymore during your training."

In a way, that made me happy; it would have been too easy to fly instruments using the autopilot. I wanted to struggle with flying the aircraft manually. I had a philosophy of not wanting to depend on automation until I had assured myself that I could fly the aircraft under any conditions without it.

Two hours had passed, and I could feel fatigue setting in from the intense concentration of flying on instruments. Finally, Captain Mack told me to turn to a heading that took us back to Cairns. "Okay, descend to four thousand feet, and make a thirty-degree turn to the left and right."

I was rolling back on course from my right turn, when the aircraft suddenly yawed to the left. This surprised the hell out of me. Automatically, I applied right stick and rudder to maintain my heading, while my mind raced to understand what was happening. Then it dawned on me that I had an engine out. I started calling out checks: "Engine out. Left foot dead, left engine out. Engine gauges confirm left engine. I am going to feather prop on left engine."

As soon as I feathered the number-one prop, the yaw lessened, and I got the aircraft back on course and continued my descent. I could not believe it. He'd shut the number-one engine down without my knowing it or expecting it. I'd thought we had an actual engine out. During the time I was calling the engine-out procedures, Captain Mack was saying, "Check," at each step. Only when he said, "Okay, let's restart number one," did I realize he had shut it down.

After I had the engine restarted, he said, "Take your hood off. That was an excellent handling of the engine out. It took you a few seconds to realize what was happening, but when you did, your responses were perfect."

I could see Cairns in the distance and called for landing. I was exhausted but exuberant at his remarks about my handling the engine out. Back in the debriefing room, he told me that today was my instrument orientation flight. From now on, we would file instrument flight plans to different airfields and make actual approaches at each runway. He recommended I go to the link trainer that afternoon to practice ILS, VOR, and GCA approaches.

I spent the afternoon shooting approaches in the link trainer. There was no trainer that mirrored the Mohawk. The only Mohawk trainer was the mock-up of the Mohawk cockpit, in which I had spent so much time. However, since the instrument approach procedures are the same for any aircraft, I could fly any trainer and benefit from it. I wore out after two hours. The intense concentration from the morning flight and the repeated approaches in the link trainer drained me, so after two hours, I felt I had improved considerably and called it quits.

The next morning, Captain Mack had me file an instrument departure from Cairns to the Mobile airport and from there to the Dothan airport and back to Cairns. He had me put the hood on when we took the active, and he did the takeoff. After we were airborne, he gave the aircraft to me to perform the instrument departure. At Mobile, I did an ILS approach and a missed approach. I circled the airport and did another ILS approach and a missed approach. As I climbed out on the missed approach, control cleared me to Dothan.

En route to Dothan, he had me do a holding pattern. When we reached Dothan, I did a VOR approach and a missed approach. I did another VOR into Dothan, and on the missed approach, I went to Cairns. At Cairns, I did two GCA approaches, and on the second approach, Captain Mack told me to remove my hood at two hundred feet AGL and land.

Fatigued, I was happy to hear that. I was wet with sweat, and my deodorant had failed. On a normal instrument flight, you might have to do one instrument approach and landing. Most of the time, when you arrive at your destination, the weather has cleared enough for a VFR landing. In the two hours we had been flying, I had done six different approaches and five missed approaches, which are in themselves difficult. The average person cannot understand the mental strain a pilot goes through, especially in training, when the instructor is evaluating his every move.

At the debriefing table, Captain Mack spoke as he filled out a white training sheet. "That was okay for a first time. You need to get some more link time and work on reporting. Remember, on a mission in the Mohawk, you are the only pilot. You have to do everything: fly the aircraft, copy flight plan instructions, and do the reports. It's a matter of practice. So get all the link training you can."

That pretty much defined my schedule for the next two weeks: instrument flights to surrounding airfields, instrument approaches and missed approaches, and link training. The only new subject added to the training was recovery from unusual attitudes. Captain Mack would have me put my head between my legs, and he would put the aircraft in some unusual attitude. Then he would tell me to recover. Since the Mohawk could fly inverted or vertical, when he told me to recover the aircraft, I would have no idea what attitude we were in.

I did this exercise so many times that it etched into my mind the technique for recovering from an unusual attitude. I can still do it automatically to this day. When told to recover, you should check the attitude indicator and flight director to decide where the wings and nose are in relation to the ground. As you level the wings, you should check the airspeed to add or decrease power to bring the nose up or down to level flight. If you are in a dive and at high airspeed, you should pull off power as you raise the nose; if your nose is high and you are at low airspeed, you should add power as you lower the nose to fly out of a possible stall. All of this takes no more than four or five seconds.

The instrument training block passed quickly, and I improved with each flight. As I improved, my confidence and comfort level in flying the Mohawk increased. I began to see the Mohawk as an extension of myself. This big, complex machine simply responded to whatever control input I made. Of course, I could say that about any aircraft, but the pride I felt in my ability to pilot the Mohawk successfully made it special. After twenty-three hours of flying under the hood, Captain Mack said, "Tomorrow I am putting you up for your instrument check ride. Are you ready?"

Of course I said yes, but despite my newly gained confidence, I felt a tinge of checkrideitis. That evening, I told Claudia about my coming check ride and how important it was. She assured me that she had full confidence that I would do well on it. Claudia was always there to encourage me when I faced a specific test.

As she'd predicted, I did well on the ride. I was now a Mohawk pilot with a renewed instrument ticket. The flight qualification course was over. I now had to go to Fort Huachuca for training on the camera, SLAR, and infrared systems. I had to wait around two more days until the rest of the class completed their check rides before I could officially graduate and get my diploma.

I used that time to clear post and clean the trailer so we could check out and get our security deposit. The day they handed out our diplomas, I thanked Captain Mack for all his help in training me. I also asked him how to get to Fort Huachuca. He laughed and said, "Get on Interstate 10, and stay on it until you get to Benson, Arizona. Go about half a mile past Benson, exit, and follow Highway 90 to the main gate. You can't miss it."

The army combat surveillance and electronic warfare course started on Wednesday, September 23. I figured it would take me two or three days to drive to Fort Huachuca. Michele had started school, so Claudia and I planned on leaving Fort Rucker on September 19 so Michele wouldn't miss more than a couple days of school. I signed out on the eighteenth, and early in the morning on the nineteenth, we headed west.

It took me three days to drive to Fort Huachuca. We spent the first night in San Antonio and the second night in Van Horn, Texas. If you have never driven from San Antonio to Van Horn, Texas, you have missed a beautiful transition from populated areas of green pastures and forests to an arid, sparsely populated high Sonoran Desert. From Van Horn to El Paso and on to Tucson is one big no-man's-land except for the farms and small towns along the Rio Grande.

The unlimited visibility of the desert impressed me the most. With no forest and clouds, I could see for miles. The Maker sprinkled the mountains randomly across the landscape. Most are treeless, except for the catclaw brush and occasional mesquite tree. All the bridges cross dry washes and dry stream beds. I only crossed two bridges that had water flowing beneath them: one was the Rio Grande at El Paso, and the other was the San Pedro at Benson, Arizona, a distance of about three hundred miles.

I reached Benson and the Highway 90 exit around 1400 on the third day. The personnel officer at Fort Rucker warned us about the lack of housing in Sierra Vista, the little town outside Fort Huachuca. Also, there was no housing available at Fort Huachuca. Since Tucson was only forty-five minutes from the turnoff at Highway 90, I decided we would drive on to Tucson and spend the night. We could get a good night's rest and drive to Fort Huachuca the next morning.

The decision to spend the night in Tucson worked out well. We were all tired from driving for three days. It was early when we checked into a motel on the outskirts. It was still hot, so the kids and I went swimming in the pool. Afterward, we had a nice dinner and went to bed early for some needed sleep.

I was surprised the next morning to find that it only took an hour and a half to drive to Sierra Vista. Sierra Vista and Fort Huachuca sit at the base of the Huachuca Mountains, which are the tallest southernmost mountains in the United States. Two of the mountains, Miller Peak and Carr Peak, are nearly ten thousand feet tall. I could see them as soon as I turned onto Highway 90, even though they were thirty miles away. Highway 90 runs almost due south along the east side of the Whetstone Mountains. The Whetstones run south twenty miles from the interstate, where they meet the foothills of the Huachuca Mountains. There, they form a pass known as Apache Pass, named after Apaches who used it in the pre-Columbian times.

As I drove south on Highway 90, the panorama spread out before me was fascinating. The terrain fell away to the east until it met the San Pedro River flowing north. Then it rose slowly to the mountains on the east side, forming the San Pedro Valley. This was a land like none I had ever seen. The vastness had an enchanting effect. I mentioned to Claudia how beautiful everything was, but she did not appear too enamored with it.

About ten miles out of Fort Huachuca, Highway 90 intersects Highway 81. Highway 81 starts in Nogales, Arizona, and runs north through the tiny old western town of Patagonia. Then it turns east through Sonata Junction and continues east through Apache Pass, intersecting Highway 90 and continuing east to Highway 80, which runs out of Tombstone.

Highway 80 loops south from Interstate 10 about twenty miles east of Willcox, Arizona. It runs south on the east side of the Chihuahua Mountains to the border town of Douglas and then west through the Mule Mountains and the town of Bisbee. It continues west out of the mountains and turns north to the famous outlaw town of Tombstone. From Tombstone, it turns north and returns to Interstate 10 in Benson.

At the intersection of Highways 90 and 81, I could look east and see the old courthouse in Tombstone some eighteen miles away. Although September normally signals the end of the monsoon season, which brings thunderstorms and rain to southeast Arizona, the monsoon rains in 1970 continued until the middle of October. The results were rolling hills and green mountains with views that by this time had usually turned brown. The mesquite trees, catclaws, and ocotillos spotted the landscape, thick in some areas but never interfering with the view.

We arrived in Sierra Vista around 1000 and immediately started looking for a place to stay for the three weeks I would be there. After trying two of the three motels in Sierra Vista, I finally stopped at the last one. They had nothing available either. This was a shock. I was in the same predicament I had been in at Fort Rucker. Luckily, the clerk said there was a scheduled checkout of a kitchenette at 1300. I told her to put my name down for it and said I would be back at 1300.

When I told Claudia, she was upset and said angrily, "Where in the hell are we going to stay? You dragged us off to this hellhole. Now find us a place to stay! You could have sent me back to Germany."

I could not get a word in edgewise, so I waited for her to calm down. When she was ready for me to speak, I said, "Look, let's drive on post and find where I have to sign in, and then we'll see if there are any temporary billets available. We can eat lunch and check back at the motel to see if the kitchenette is available."

Fort Huachuca looked old and abandoned as we drove on post. The army had constructed most of the wooden buildings during World War II. However, Captain Whiteside had built the ten or so three-story buildings surrounding the parade field and created a frontier post in the 1878. He'd built the post to protect the settlers from marauding Apaches. The US Army Communications Command and the US Army Combat Surveillance and Electronic Warfare School were the only units based at Fort Huachuca. The lack of activity and empty buildings gave me the impression I was driving through a deserted city.

I followed signs directing me the USACSEWS location and found the school's S1 building. I signed in and picked up a student welcome packet. The packet had class schedules, course instructions, and a post map. Using the map, I found the snack bar, and we had lunch.

After lunch, I found the billeting officer and inquired about temporary or transient quarters only to find out there were none available. By now, the kids and Claudia were getting restless and irritable. I drove back to the motel and said a small prayer as I entered the office. The clerk said I was in luck; the party had checked out, and I could check in as soon as the maid finished cleaning. I could look at the place in an hour and decide if I wanted it. I told her I did not have to look at it; I wanted it and was ready to register.

I knew accepting the kitchenette sight unseen was chancy, but I did not want to take a chance of losing the only housing available within fifty miles. After completing the registration, I asked the clerk where I could find the nearest elementary school. We were lucky again. The school was only four blocks away. Michele could easily walk to and from school each day.

Back at the car, I told Claudia the good news. It improved her mood, but it disturbed her that I had taken the kitchenette without looking at it. My response was that we had no alternative unless we wanted to live in Tucson. She agreed somewhat and tried to look on the bright side. I pointed out there was a pool, and it was close to Michele's school. Also, there were stores nearby, all within walking distance. We finished the discussion about the kitchenette with her saying she hoped it was clean and not full of roaches.

While we waited for the maids to finish cleaning, we found the school and registered Michele. We managed to meet her teacher, who gave us the books she needed and a list of school supplies. She also gave us her assignment for Monday. We drove down the main street of Sierra Vista until we found a Kmart, where we bought her supplies. By then, I figured our room should be ready, so we headed to the motel.

It was ready, and my luck held. It was a clean little kitchenette with two small bedrooms surrounded by a large living, dining, and kitchen room. It had all furnishings, so Claudia agreed that it would do for three weeks. I could relax then. We had a suitable place to live, and I could concentrate on my course.

It turned out that we were fortunate not to delay coming to Fort Huachuca. Four of my married classmates who had gotten there over the weekend could not find lodging and had to live in Tucson. That meant they had an hour-and-a-half drive each way. The commute would have created extra stress for us.

After moving in our few clothes, Claudia and I went shopping for food and cleaning supplies. Michele and Ron pleaded to stay and watch TV. On the way back, we picked up some Kentucky Fried Chicken for dinner. After dinner, Claudia went through the kitchenette, washing all the surfaces and recleaning the bathroom. While she did that, I started reviewing my training schedule for Monday.

As usual, the first hour Monday morning was an orientation class. Following that was a three-hour class on the side-looking airborne radar (SLAR). In the afternoon, we reported to Libby Army Airfield for orientation flights. That evening, I read some of the literature on the SLAR, and by then, exhaustion had set in, and I went to bed. Claudia was already sleeping in front of the TV.

We spent the weekend exploring the area. Michele wanted her horse that I had promised her when I left for Vietnam. I finally convinced her that we could not get a horse for only three weeks. I told her there was a riding stable on post and promised we would go riding after church on Sunday. That appeased her, and she cheered up. Ron was quick to point out that he was not going to ride a horse.

We drove to Tombstone on Saturday afternoon. I was awed by the pristine condition of the town too tough to die. Allen Street was the main street where all the gunfights took place. The bars, other than repairs to keep them in business, were just as they had been when the cowboys and outlaws drank whiskey and played cards in them. I immediately fell in love with the town. To this day, it is still my favorite town. I have a pact that anytime I am within five miles of Tombstone, I will stop in and have a beer in the Crystal Palace Saloon. I have kept that pact to this day.

When I was growing up, my heroes were cowboys, and Tombstone let me stand in the same places where some of my heroes had walked. I could stand at the same bar and drink a beer while looking in the exact mirror that had reflected their faces. Tombstone, on the other hand, did not thrill Claudia. Cowboys were not her heroes. Michele loved it because she loved horses, and horses were everywhere. Ron liked it because I did.

The USACSEWS commandant was the first one to greet us Monday morning at 0800. A briefing on Fort Huachuca and the local area followed his introduction. Personnel clerks were there to aid us in putting in our requests for travel pay and ensuring our personal records were up to date.

After processing in, we moved to the classroom lab to begin our classes on the SLAR. Like all radars, the SLAR sends out a signal that is reflected by objects in the target area. The SLAR receives the reflected signals and converts them to an image of moving targets and fixed targets. These targets are recorded on film as split images. One side of the film displays moving targets (MTs) as black dots. The film displays fixed targets (FTs) and terrain features, such as roads, mountains, and buildings, as images on the other side. By overlaying the moving target imagery on the fixed target imagery, the analyst can see where movers are in the target area. Analyzing the dots, the analyst can pick out targets of military interest.

We spent three hours in the lab, studying the features and capabilities of the SLAR and how to use it. The last class focused on how to read and interpret the imagery. The main emphasis for us was how to plan and employ the SLAR in combat. Technical observers (TOs) were assigned to all Mohawk units and operated the SLAR during missions. Imagery analysts assigned to the company interpreted the collected imagery. Our job was to plan and fly the aircraft so that the SLAR covered the mission area and recorded MTs and FTs.

After lunch, I drove to the airfield and found the Mohawk hangar. The rest of my classmates were arriving, so I waited, and together we walked to the operations office. Sitting on the ramp in front of the hangar were six Mohawks and three UH-1D helicopters. CW-3 Wellers was waiting for us at the hangar door.

Chief Wellers was a Mohawk SIP and the chief instructor for our flying part of the course. He introduced himself and led us upstairs to the operations office. In the pilot briefing area, he introduced us to three other IPs. After the introductions, he discussed the procedures and importance of our orientation flights scheduled for that afternoon and night.

Because of Fort Huachuca's nearness to the Mexican border, the army required all new pilots to have a border orientation flight. The border was only twenty miles south of Fort Huachuca, and many of our training flights were along it. International law forbid us from crossing into Mexico. At the time, only a barbed-wire fence marked it, except at the official crossing points staffed by customs and immigration officers. The orientation flights were essential to ensure new pilots could identify the border while flying above the featureless eighty miles of desert along the southern boundaries of our training area.

The orientation flights consisted of a one-hour day flight and a one-hour night flight. The instructors would give us our orientation flights. I was one of the first to fly with Chief Wellers.

As Chief Wellers taxied to the active for takeoff, I was aware of how relaxed I felt. I was not at the controls, and even if I had been, Chief Wellers would not have judged my handling of the aircraft unless I'd shown some dangerous trends. I was there to note the terrain, identify landmarks that would keep me from unintentionally crossing the border, and orient myself on our training area. As we climbed out and turned southwest to fly around the west side of the Huachucas, the raw beauty of the desert, mountains, arroyos, and dry river beds unfolding below me was enchanting.

I listened closely as Chief Wellers pointed out the key terrain points to use as guides to stay north of the border. He climbed to ten thousand feet and flew southwest forty miles until the Nogales airport came into view. The airport was a small one with a tower manned only during the day. However, at night, its rotating beacon was easily seen for many miles. The airport was nine miles north of the border and at the west end of our flight training area. It became the first landmark used to identify the border.

Chief Wellers crossed the airfield and made a wide turn to the east, rolling out on a ninety-degree heading. As we turned, he pointed out the Nogales border crossing complex and the large fence that ran east five or six miles from the complex. It divided Nogales into the US and Mexican sides and was easy to identify until it became just a barbed-wire fence in the desert. It was a good landmark in daylight, but at night, it was difficult to see because of the size of Nogales. At night, the airport rotating beacon was the safest landmark to use as a guide.

As we flew east, I could see clearly the south end of the Huachuca Mountains. Chief Wellers pointed out a road that ran around the south end of the mountains and cut through a monument known as Montezuma's Pass. There was a small building there. Looking closely, I could just make out a barbed-wire fence about three miles south of the building, which was the border.

Then identifying the border became easier. From there, I could look about fifteen miles to the east and see the small border town of Naco. A highway ran around the south end of the Mule Mountains north into Highway 80, which ran between Bisbee and Douglas. Looking past Naco, I could see Douglas about fifty miles to the east. I would be safe flying on a line between these landmarks.

Chief Wellers continued flying past Douglas for about ten miles and pointed out the only building I could see. It was a ranch that once had belonged to the marshal of Tombstone. This was the eastern boundary of the training area. Nearby was an infrared target, which I would learn more about during training.

We then turned north and flew eighty miles until we crossed Interstate 10. Chief Wellers pointed out the various mountain ranges. The vista was beautiful. There were no barriers to visibility, and I could twist in my seat and, from ten thousand feet high, see miles in all directions. One could not do that in the Southeast. The clouds and haze never let you see more than ten miles at the most.

It took about five minutes for me to orientate myself on the whole area. Ahead of us were the Willcox Playa and Willcox. To my west were Tombstone and the San Pedro River running into Benson. I could see the Whetstone Mountains and the Huachuca Mountains. It was incredible to have this much visibility. I did not know it at the time, but that flight was making a lasting impression on me. When we returned to the ramp, Chief Wellers shut down the number-two engine so I could get out and the next student could get in.

I had to be back at 2100 for my night flight, so I drove back to the apartment to check on Claudia and the kids. Michele was home from school and was playing in the pool with Ron. Claudia was lying on a lounge chair, working on her suntan. I greeted them and went up to the apartment. Part of the student issue was a 1:50,000 scale map of the area. I wanted to study it and fix in my brain the locations and landmarks I had seen during the orientation flight.

I studied the map for an hour until Claudia and the kids came in. The map helped me fix all the towns, roads, and mountain ranges clearly in my mind. I could shut my eyes, see the entire area, and picture each main feature's location. There was still a lot I had to learn, but I felt confident in my knowledge of the area.

I stood on the ramp while the Mohawk taxied in. The left engine shut down, the student pilot climbed out, and I climbed in. As soon as I plugged my helmet cord into the intercom box, Chief Wellers greeted me with "Evening, sir. As soon as you are ready, I'm ready. I want you to fly the route we flew this afternoon. Any questions?"

I responded, "Evening, Chief. No questions."

The wind had changed and was now out of the east. I took off and banked left as I climbed to ten thousand feet. I rolled out of my turn on a heading of two hundred. The view before me was striking. I could see the lights of Sonoita and Patagonia on my right. The Nogales airfield and its rotating beacon, with Nogales in the background, were easy to spot. Off to the northwest was the glow of Tucson sixty miles away. It was so clear that from ten thousand feet, I could see lights of towns that would have been impossible to see in the Southeast. The mountain ranges formed dark areas and were easy to distinguish, although I could not tell how high they were. Terrain like this made it essential for a pilot to know the height of all the mountains in his flight path, especially at night. I had no trouble flying the afternoon course.

After all had completed their orientation flights, we were ready for training flights. The curriculum called for classes during the day and night flights to operate the sensor. One student would fly the aircraft while the other student ran the sensor. Then they would rotate.

Conducting the training flights at night reduced weather delays. Because the monsoon was still active, almost every day, beginning around noon, thunderstorms would roll across the San Pedro Valley. The storms would usually end in the late afternoon. Since we obviously could not fly during thunderstorms, night flights provided the perfect solution. I loved doing a night flight, because it enchanted me each time. The down side was that we seldom finished flying before midnight.

On the weekends, Claudia, the kids, and I visited all the surrounding towns. In Nogales, we crossed the border and toured the Mexican side of Nogales. There were great bargains on many items in the stores, and Claudia found perfume that in the United States would have cost three times what she paid for it in Mexico. It was the same with booze, though of course, the law only allowed you to bring a certain amount back duty free. We visited Tucson to shop in the mall and have dinner. We went to Tombstone twice. It had the most historic attractions and, of course, the Crystal Palace.

The old mining town of Bisbee, high in the Mule Mountains, was the quaintest. The houses along the main street had a European look. The town had become a mecca for artists and the hippie crowd. That town and one of deepest open pit mines in the world attracted many tourists. Some of the best turquoise in the world came from that mine. Known as Bisbee blue, it was gem quality and expensive.

During the three weeks we were at Fort Huachuca, the relations between Claudia and I improved. We had fewer fights once she got over the first shock of how isolated we were. I do not know if the peace was because of our coming separation or just better behavior on my part. I know I counted the days and nights as they became fewer and fewer. It was there that we discovered that our sexual drive was strongest in the mornings. That came about because of the lack of privacy in the apartment. Early morning, before the kids woke up, gave us enough privacy. Making love in the morning reduced the stress between us if she fell asleep watching TV. Over the following years, it became the usual routine for us.

During the last week of training, we were flying photo and IR missions. These were fun to fly. We had a series of targets to image. After we flew the mission, the imagery analyst would develop the film, and we had a chance to view it the following morning to see how well we'd carried out the mission.

My last mission was an IR search of the main road running south out of Tucson to Nogales. Captain Jonas was acting as my student TO. I completed the run about ten miles north of Nogales and turned toward Libby AAF. As I climbed up to five thousand feet, I could see a wall of lightning covering the Huachuca Mountains and Fort Huachuca. Then I heard the Libby tower announce, "Attention, all Mohawks: request you recover at Davis-Monthan AF Base in Tucson. There are severe thunderstorms over Libby Army Airfield and throughout the area. Repeat: recommend you recover at Davis-Monthan AF Base until storms are out of the area."

I answered, "Libby tower, this is Mohawk 882. Roger." I told Captain Jonas to look up the approach control frequency for Davis-Monthan.

While he did that, I turned north. I could see the lights of Tucson about forty miles north of our location. Captain Jonas found the frequency on the list of frequencies that we had for emergencies. He put it into the VHF radio, and I called, "Davis-Monthan approach control, this is Mohawk 882 on a local training flight out of Libby AAF. Request a GCA approach to Davis-Monthan."

"Roger, Mohawk 882. Squawk 1160, and report altitude and location. Altimeter is 30.79."

"Roger, approach. Squawking 1160. Altitude five thousand. Estimate position about thirty miles south of Tucson."

"Roger, Mohawk. Radar contact thirty-six miles south of Davis-Monthan. What is your status and purpose for landing at Davis-Monthan?"

"Roger, approach. We are on a local training flight plan out of Libby AAF. Libby advises us there are heavy thunderstorms over Libby and surrounding area and advises us to land at Davis-Monthan until weather improves."

"Roger, Mohawk 882. Turn to heading three hundred forty, climb to and maintain six thousand feet, and report six thousand."

"Roger, approach. Turn to heading three forty and climb to six thousand."

I turned to a heading of 340 and climbed to six thousand. "Approach, this is Mohawk 882 at six thousand."

"Roger, Mohawk. Twenty-two miles southwest of Davis-Monthan. This will be a GCA to runway eighty. Contact GCA on 286.55. Good day."

Captain Jonas put the radio on 286.55, and I called, "GCA approach, this is Mohawk 882, heading three forty, at six thousand."

"Roger, Mohawk 882. This is GCA controller. Altimeter 30.80 inches. Turn to heading three hundred sixty, base for eighty. Descend and maintain three thousand."

"Roger, GCA control. Turning to three sixty and descending to three thousand." I put the Mohawk on 360, pulled the power back, and lowered the nose. In the clear night, I was flying half on instruments and half visual. It was neat to see how the approach would look if I were in the clouds and on instruments.

"GCA control, this is Mohawk 882 at three thousand," I reported as I added power to maintain three thousand feet.

The lights of Tucson appeared like a sparkling diamond mounted in the desert. We watched the Tucson airport passing to our right. "Mohawk 882, turn to heading thirty-five and descend to two thousand."

"Roger, GCA approach. Turning to thirty-five and descending to two thousand,"

I answered.

That heading put us on a forty-five degree intercept to eighty. I looked off to the right and could see the Davis-Monthan runway about eight miles away. I had the runway heading set on the flight director and could watch us approaching the eighty inbound course. I called for a prelanding check, and Captain Jonas read the checks to me.

"Mohawk 882, turn right to eighty. Eight miles west of runway, begin descent."

"Roger, GCA. Turning to eighty and beginning descent."

I rolled out my turn on eighty and pushed the prop controls to 1,600 while pulling back on the power to maintain 140 knots.

"Mohawk 882, on course two hundred feet above glide slope."

"Roger, GCA."

I pulled off more power and lowered the nose. My airspeed increased slightly, but I lost two hundred feet of altitude, and when I pulled the nose up to the right angle, the extra airspeed bled, and I added power to maintain 140.

"Mohawk 882, come right two degrees on glide slope." Losing the two hundred feet had distracted me enough to drift left of course.

I called for landing check. Captain Jonas read the checks as I lowered the flaps to the landing setting and lowered the gear. When I lowered the flaps, the Mohawk wanted to climb. I put pressure on the stick, and when the gear came down, it wanted to settle, so I added power to maintain my 140 knots and rate of descent. We checked that the gear was down, and I was ready to land.

"Mohawk 882, you are on course on glide slope and two miles from touchdown. Report gear down and locked."

"Roger, GCA approach. Gear down and locked."

"Mohawk 882, you are half a mile from touchdown on course, on glide slope. Report runway in sight."

"Roger, GCA. Runway in sight," I reported.

"Roger, Mohawk 882. Clear to land runway eighty. Wind southeast one hundred at ten knots. Contact tower on 377.7. Good day."

"Roger, GCA. Thank you for the help."

Captain Jonas tuned the VHF to 377.7, and I called the tower. "Davis-Monthan tower, this is Mohawk 882, short final for eighty."

"Roger, Mohawk 882. Cleared to land. Contact ground control on 378.9 for taxi."

"Roger. Clear to land. Contact ground control on 378.9."

I greased the Mohawk onto the runway and reversed props to slow us down as Captain Jonas tuned ground control. As we were rolling out, he turned to me and said, "So that's what it's all about."

I did not understand his meaning. I'd forgotten that he was just out of flight school and had no flying experience outside of flight school. "What do you mean?" I asked.

"Well, I've never done a GCA, except in flight school with an instructor aboard. I see now how you use approach control to get vectors to a GCA and landing. It was not that clear to me until now."

I assured him that after he had some flying time, he would be familiar with all types of approaches.

Ground control had us taxi to an apron located in front of the base operations building. Air force ground crews directed us into a parking spot, and we shut down the engines. After we climbed out of the aircraft, a ground crewman came up and told me there were two more Mohawks landing to wait for clear weather at Fort Huachuca. Ground control wanted us to move the Mohawk back two rows. I climbed back into the aircraft and started the number-one engine. I gave the crewman a thumbs-up, signaling I was ready for him to guide me into the new spot.

He pointed to my number-two engine and gave me a start-up signal. I shook my head, and he looked puzzled for a moment. Then he gave me the signal to start taxiing and guided me to a spot two rows to my rear. The Mohawk, as far as I know, is the only two-engine aircraft that can taxi on one engine. If a two-engine aircraft tries to taxi with only one engine operating, it will just turn in a circle. However, due to the unique engine alignment, the Mohawk can taxi straight ahead or turn left or right on one engine. During my time flying Mohawks, I impressed many ground personnel by taxiing on one engine.

We stood on the apron and watched the other two Mohawks land. After they parked, we walked into the operations building to check if or when the storms at Libby and Fort Huachuca would end. The forecaster on duty checked his data and told us that they should be clearing up now. The last report was light rain. He recommended we wait another thirty minutes or so.

An hour and a half later, we landed at Libby. My training was over. I was a Mohawk pilot and could perform every mission for which the aircraft was designed. We received our certificates of completion on October 15, 1970. It was time to move Claudia and the kids back to Germany. I was proud that I had completed the training and now flew the most-complex aircraft in the army. However, no matter how hard I tried to ignore it, a feeling of dread stayed with me.

I had a sense that this separation was going to be bad. At first, the separation was because I was going back to Vietnam, but to my surprise, when I was clearing the personnel office, they told me that the DA had changed my orders, and I was now going to Korea. That was a big relief, but for some reason, the sense of dread did not go away. I chalked it up to the ordeal of our separation for another year and turned my attention to the move back to Germany.

Our plan was to drive to Fort Dix, leave our car parked in a long-term parking lot at McGuire AFB, and take a Davis Agency charter flight to Frankfurt. In Frankfurt, we planned on renting a car and driving to Munich. Claudia had arranged for us to stay with her mom while I applied for quarters in the USA Perlacher Forst housing area. The army had a program under which military members assigned to Vietnam or Korea could use government quarters on a space-available program. The army had moved most of the units in the Munich area to other posts, which left many empty quarters available in the Perlacher Forst housing complex. After I got Claudia and the kids moved into quarters and Michele in school, Mom would stay with the kids while Claudia and I returned to the States. We would pick up our car at McGuire and spend the rest of my leave driving across the States and spending time with each other.

With that plan in mind, we left Fort Huachuca on October 16, 1970, bound for Fort Dix, New Jersey. According to my amended orders, I had to report to Fort Lewis-McChord AFB in Washington on November 20. That gave us thirty-five days to carry out our plan. Since Interstate 40 was the most direct route to Fort Dix, we had to go north to get to I-40. The shortest route to I-40 was through Silver City, New Mexico.

The highway through Silver City might have been the shortest route, but it wasn't the fastest. Silver City lies in the mountains, and travel there is on mountain roads. Although it was only the middle of October, snow covered the mountains above the four-thousand-foot level. The snow and winding roads slowed our progress but treated us to a beautiful winter scene. Silver City was enchanting as we drove through it. We talked about one day coming back to visit it and spending some time there, but we never did. The drive through Silver City was the eventful part of the trip.

Once we reached I-40, it was just a long drive as I tried not to waste any of the time I had left. I made it to Fort Dix in two days, though I had allowed three travel days. Since we had bought our airplane tickets before we left Fort Huachuca, we had to spend one day in the guesthouse at Fort Dix. That was not bad, because we were tired and needed the rest.

After leaving Fort Dix, we reached Munich on the afternoon of October 20. Mom had gathered friends to welcome us back, so I had to spend some time socializing. I had wanted to go immediately to the Perlacher Forst housing office to complete the application for quarters, but the little party lasted well into the night, so I accepted that I would have to do it the next day. I was not trying to be unfriendly; it was just that I had a lot to do, and the faster I got it done, the more time I had for me and Claudia. Plus, I did not know how long it would take to get quarters.

Our priority the next morning was to take Michele to school and get her registered. Next, we went to the housing office, where I completed the forms in about an hour and returned them to the clerk. I asked how long it would take to get my request approved. The response was that they had to send the paperwork across town to the housing officer for his review and approval, and that would probably take a couple of days.

I said, "That's unacceptable. What if I personally carry the paperwork to the housing officer, get it approved, and bring it back to you?"

The clerk replied, "Sure, you could do that. It would speed up getting it approved."

It took me two hours to take the paperwork to the housing officer, get it signed, and return it to the clerk. At first, the housing officer's secretary wanted me to leave the paperwork and come back for it. I explained my hurry, so she took it in to see if he would sign it. I waited with a nervous stomach for what seemed like an eternity. Then she came out, handed the packet to me, and said, "It's approved."

The housing office clerk checked the paperwork to ensure the housing officer had signed it and asked, "When do you want to inspect the quarters? We have several three-bedroom units available."

I answered enthusiastically, "What about right now?"

The clerk said, "I know you are in a hurry, but it will take an hour or so to do the paperwork and schedule an inspector. Come back at 1300, and it should be ready."

My first inclination was to question what would take so long, but I decided I had already pushed the limits, and there was no sense in pushing too far. "Okay," I answered. "We will go eat lunch and be back at 1300."

Claudia and I ate lunch at the snack bar near the housing office. She was nervous that the quarters would not be ready at 1300 or would be old and dirty, among other things she could think of that could go wrong. I tried to assure her that we had done our best so far and had to trust in everything working out. Finally, it was 1300, and we entered the housing office once more.

There was a couple in line ahead of us, so we had to wait another fifteen minutes. When I stepped up to the window, the clerk said, "Okay, Captain Griffin, the inspector will be here at 1330 to inspect a set of quarters with you. You can take a seat to wait for him."

I responded, "Sir, thank you very much. You have been a big help."

We had waited probably five minutes, when a man stuck his head in the door, looked at me, and asked, "Are you Captain Griffin?"

I answered, "Yes."

He replied, "I'm Mr. Deter. If you will follow me, we'll look at some quarters."

We followed him outside, got into our car, and followed his sedan to a row of standard army quarters. They were copies of the ones we'd occupied in Stuttgart. He led us into the corner building and up the stairs to the second-floor apartment and opened the door. Claudia and I walked in and found it to be a large three-bedroom apartment. It was the same design and size as the one in Stuttgart.

The apartment was clean and furnished. I looked at Claudia and asked, "Okay?"

She nodded and said, "But I need some items. There are no end tables, and I'm sure I'll find something else."

Mr. Deter told her in German not to worry; all she had to do was ask for any furniture she needed, and the supply office would deliver it. They had a warehouse full of furniture. That soothed her, and I said, "Okay, let's inventory and sign for it."

It took us an hour to do the inventory and complete the forms. I signed them, and Mr. Deter handed me a set of keys and bid us good day. We started moving in that afternoon.

It took all the next day and several trips to the post exchange and commissary before Claudia felt she was ready to live there. We compiled a list of furniture that she wanted, and I arranged with the supply people to have it delivered on December 1. That gave Claudia time to return to Munich and get a handle on events.

Three days after arriving in Munich, Claudia felt safe in leaving the kids with Mom while she returned to the United States with me. I went by the Davis Agency office and bought tickets for our flight to McGuire AFB and a ticket for Claudia's return on November 24.

The next morning, I kissed the kids good-bye. Michele was still intent on getting a horse. Her last words to me were "Daddy, when you get back, can I have my horse?"

I said, "Yes, if we live in a place where we can have a horse." I could not believe she was still so insistent about owning a horse. I hoped that over the next year, she would grow out of that notion. Ten days after leaving Fort Huachuca, Claudia and I were back in Fort Dix.

We picked up our car and, in a relaxed mood, headed west toward San Antonio, Texas. Our plan was to meander along and visit places that struck our interest. The Alamo was a place we wanted to see. We made a habit of stopping at every historic marker along our route. It surprised me how interested Claudia was in what had happened to shape US history.

We found a closeness that had not existed before. To my joy, there was more sex and less bickering. For the first time, I felt content with our relations. I do not know if it was our approaching separation or the lack of stress that helped us enjoy each other, but it was one of the happiest times I had had in a while.

In San Antonio, we saw the Alamo and walked the River Walk. The number of Germans among the Alamo defenders surprised us. That was where we found out that Germans had settled much of Texas.

The next place I wanted to visit was Pueblo, Colorado. My sister Laura was attending college there, and I wanted to see her while we were in the area. The shortest route to Pueblo was a highway running northwest from San Antonio to Pueblo. It ran through the backcountry of Texas and, according to the map, passed through many small German towns. After two days in San Antonio, we headed for Pueblo on a backcountry road. We would pass through a small German town and then drive for miles without seeing another car or house. All the street and store signs in the little towns were in German. It was like being in a Germany that we had never seen.

It was about five hundred miles from San Antonio to Pueblo, and we were about halfway, when we saw a historic marker. We pulled off the road to read it. To our surprise, it marked the spot where the Chisholm Trail passed through the area. While we were standing there, a pickup truck pulled out of a dirt road about a mile away and headed our way. It pulled off the highway and parked by our car.

An old cowboy climbed out of the truck and walked over to us. He was thin and leathery and wore old blue jeans and a faded flannel shirt that looked to be a hundred years old. When he got to us, he extended his hand and said, "Hi. My name's Tom."

I extended my hand to shake hands. His hand was thin and callused but gripped mine like a vise. "I'm Neal Griffin, and this is my wife, Claudia," I said.

He looked at Claudia, tipped his beat-up cowboy hat, and said, "Pleased to meet you folks. What do you think of this marker?"

Claudia and I answered that it was interesting and said we had seen many movies depicting cattle drives along the Chisholm Trail. It was neat to see the place where they'd occurred.

He turned, pointed to some small hills, and said, "The trail came up around those hills, passed along here, and then turned north."

As I looked at the landscape, it was hard to image driving a large cattle herd through the thick scrub oaks and mesquites.

Then he spoke again. "The movies make it easier than it was. I was on the last two drives to come through here. We fought harsh weather, Indians, cattle rustlers, wild animals, poisonous snakes, and illness. Most punchers wouldn't do it again if they survived the first time. I don't know why I did it the second time. I think it was because I had just gotten married and needed the money. We would get bonuses if we didn't lose many cattle along the way. I am now a member of the Texas Historical Society. I finally got them to erect the markers. When I see folks reading them, I always like to know what they think. Well, I've got to get going. I've got some shopping to do, and it's a long drive to town. You folks take care, and thanks for your interest."

Claudia and I stood in awe as he told his story. We watched him walk away with a limp that came with old age and the pain of arthritis. He got into his truck and drove off. We stood in the lonely silence of that remote area, and I tried to imagine the sound of the herds moving through. We drove away, fascinated by the old man. We wondered how old he was and why we had not thought of asking him. We shared the story of our meeting with everyone we knew.

We got into Pueblo around 1800 and checked into a motel. After we had dinner, I called the university registrar and found Laura's phone number. I called, and after some delay, she came to the phone. My being there was a surprise to her. When I told her I wanted to see her, she put me off. She said her schedule was so full that she would only be able to see me that night for half an hour. We met at a student hangout and talked for a while. Then she said she had to leave, wished me good luck, and left. Claudia had stayed in the motel, and when I told her what had happened, she thought it was kind of strange.

The next morning, we drove around Pueblo, read some more historic markers, and headed west again. We saw the Grand Canyon, stayed a night in Las Vegas, drove to Los Angeles and Hollywood, and finally headed north toward Fort Stewart.

The drive through Northern California, Oregon, and Washington impressed us the most. The landscape of mountains, forests, and green valleys was absolutely beautiful. We reached Fort Stewart on the afternoon of November 19. I drove around post until I found the replacement company and signed in. They gave me a training schedule for POR qualification before leaving for Korea. I had to take some cultural classes, attend DMZ briefings, update my personnel and finance records, and get several shots for an assignment in Korea. They scheduled me to do all of that on Monday, November 21. My flight left McChord at 1400 on November 23.

After signing in, I drove to the billeting office and rented a room in the military guesthouse. The guesthouse had a coin-operated laundry room, and Claudia wanted to wash dirty clothes that had piled up. I helped her wash and fold the clothes. We packed her suitcase for the trip back to Germany and then went to find something to eat.

That night, lying in bed, I looked at her beautiful face as she slept. In three more nights, she would be gone. It would be six months before I would see her again. I was so in love with her. We had had fun-filled days over the last three weeks. Now, for the first time, I was leaving her without feeling the excitement I usually felt about going to a place I had never been. I was happy I was not going to Vietnam but was not enjoying the prospect of going to Korea. I did not want to admit it, but I knew the fear eating at me was that another separation might destroy the gains we had made in the last six months. I drifted off into a restless sleep.

We woke up Sunday morning and came together passionately. I have never lost that first-time feeling when making love to her. I think that was part of my fascination with her. After we had breakfast at the PX cafeteria, we went to church.

We spent the rest of the day exploring Seattle. We drove to the Tacoma-Seattle International Airport. I wanted to know where it was, so I could get there with no delays. It was late when we returned to our room. We watched a little TV and went to bed. I counted off another day.

Monday morning, we had breakfast before I dropped her off at the room, where she stayed while I went to POR training and processing. It was noon before I returned to the room. Claudia was glad to see me. After all, it was boring just sitting there waiting. My arms were sore from the shots, and I had one class left for the afternoon. I talked her into going to the PX to go shopping while I attended the one-hour class. Then I would pick her up, and we would do whatever she wanted.

That afternoon, we went to a movie and had dinner. The weather turned colder and became windy and rainy. We did not have the proper clothes on, and the weather drove us back to our room. We watched TV until we fell asleep.

The next morning, we made love again. Claudia's libido was always equal to mine when we were not fighting. After breakfast, we drove over to the American Airlines office on post to buy Claudia's ticket to Fort Dix. To our surprise and dismay, the ticket agent would not accept my check. Claudia and I had no credit cards, since we always paid in cash or with a check. The problem was that when we were in Munich, I had opened an account with the American Express bank and transferred all our money into it. The check I was going to write was an out-of-country check, and the agent could not accept it. Claudia and I did not have enough cash between us to pay for the ticket. Claudia, of course, panicked.

I calmed her down by convincing her I could go to finance and get an advance on my pay. Everything would be okay. We drove to the finance office, and after an hour, I walked out with an advanced pay of $600, which was more than enough to pay for her ticket. We made a vow then that we would get credit cards as soon as possible to prevent something like this from happening again.

I bought her a ticket for a flight scheduled to leave Tacoma-Seattle at 0700 on November 23. That would put her in Fort Dix the night before her flight left for Germany the next morning. After that, we had one more item to take care of: what to do with the car. I had hoped a dealer would buy it from us, but none would. One said they would sell it on consignment if I left it with them. To do that, I had to go to JAG (Judge Advocate General's Corps) to get a power of attorney giving my consent for the dealer to sell it. After that, we were all set. In the morning, I would drop Claudia off at the airport and, on the way back, drop the car off at the dealer, who would have his courtesy car drive me on post.

When we finished running around, it was afternoon, and Claudia wanted to go shopping at a mall. She loved to shop. Mostly, she just looked at clothes and shoes but seldom bought anything. We found a big mall near base and spent the afternoon there. We had dinner at a nice restaurant in the mall.

After dinner, we were trying to decide what to do. We discussed going to a movie, when Claudia took my hand and, looking at me, asked, "What do you want to do?"

I studied her beautiful face for a few seconds. I knew what I wanted, but I did not want to anger her on our last night. Finally, I said, "I want to go back to the room and make love and just hold each other."

Then, totally out of character since we had made love that morning, she said, "Let's go."

To say that surprised me would be an understatement. She had never been receptive to sex two times in one day. Maybe there had been a change in her that I had not noticed. I know sex is not everything in a marriage, but I believed the amount and quality of sex were signs of the strength of a marriage.

We made love and spent the night holding each other until we drifted off to sleep. Morning came too early. We had breakfast at the airport, and I kissed her good-bye. I watched her walk through the gate to the airplane, and she was gone. I waited to make sure her plane left, and then I left. The dealer took our car, and his courtesy car dropped me off at flight operations. I checked my duffel bag and boarded the charter 707 for Seoul, Korea. Emptiness and dread pounded at my senses. As always, I ignored the feeling.

CHAPTER 4

Korea

To all things there is a season:
A time for trust, a time for betrayal.

T he 707 left McChord and headed west toward Japan. It was full of men headed for Vietnam, Korea, and other assignments in the Far East. The plane was noisy with the roar of the engines competing with the sound of a hundred conversations. I sat quietly nursing my thoughts of Claudia and my kids.

Claudia was changing, but so was I. She had become beautiful and desirable and seemed aware of it. I had changed from a confident and trusting husband who loved his wife dearly into someone unsure of how his life was going to turn out. We had just spent more than two years together amid pleasant and unpleasant times. In retrospect, our union was not much different from most marriages. Maybe it just seemed different. All I knew was that I was devoted to her and had no desire for any other woman. I guess that's why I spent so much time troubled over her love for me.

My feelings caused me to think there was some flaw in my character and personality. My lack of higher education and the conditions under which I grew up almost guaranteed that. However, I didn't know how to change it and make it better. Somehow, those influences hadn't affected my conduct and performance of duty as a soldier. I was a good, competent officer. So far, there had been nothing in the army that I didn't excel at. I anguished over why I couldn't meld my military traits into the person I was as a husband. After a while, with my thoughts rambling and no solutions, I drifted off to sleep.

The 707 crossed the international date line and landed at Yokota AFB in Japan. It was early Thanksgiving morning 1970. Soldiers bound for Vietnam and other destinations got off, and those en route to Korea remained aboard. The 707 refueled, and an hour later, it took off for Seoul, Korea. We landed at Kimpo Airport in Seoul, Korea, at 0800.

I walked into the military portion of the airport to wait for the baggage handlers to unload my duffel bag. I was one of few officers and the only aviator on the flight. As I walked into the lobby, I saw a full bird colonel standing by the flight operations desk. When he saw me, he approached and, seeing my name tag, extended his hand. "Captain Griffin, I'm Colonel Goody, the Eighth Army aviation officer. I want to welcome you to Korea. How was your flight over?"

I was a little stunned. I had never heard of a colonel meeting a captain. As I shook his hand, I said, "Good to meet you, sir. My flight was great."

He could see that I was a little uncomfortable and unsure about what to do now. He spoke again. "As the Eighth Army aviation officer, I make it my duty to greet all new aviators arriving in Korea. My driver will grab your bag, and we'll go to my office. I have a briefing I give all aviators. Since you are taking command of the Sixth Aviation Platoon, I wanted to impress upon you from the start that you are taking on an important and urgent mission."

As we drove through the bustling streets of Seoul, he asked, "Is this your first tour in Korea?"

I answered, "Yes, sir."

He replied with a smile, "You won't understand it now, but Korea is the best-kept secret in the army. You'll enjoy your tour here, and when you leave, you will understand what I just told you."

After about twenty minutes, we entered a heavily guarded compound and continued to a large building and parked. An Eighth Army Headquarters sign painted in large letters hung over the entrance. Inside, we walked up a flight of stairs to an office with the words *Aviation Office* on the door. Colonel Goody ushered me into a room with several desks.

Three captains and two SMs occupied the desks. A secretary sat to the left of the entrance door. He led me into his office and motioned for me to take a seat. I was a little amazed that a full bird colonel was personally briefing a captain. I had never heard of this happening before. He took a packet off his desk and handed it to me. "This is your copy of the Eighth Army aviation SOP. You need to read it and become familiar with its contents."

He took a seat and, pointing at a chart on the wall, said, "You are taking over one of the most important missions in Korea. The intelligence picture developed from the imagery collected during Mohawk flights plays a key role in establishing the daily alert posture for the military in South Korea. The importance of that imagery places those collecting it under intense pressure. General McCall uses the information the Mohawks collect to decide the daily readiness status for the military. His staff briefs him twice a day—once in the morning and once in the evening—on the data you will collect. From that, you can see the importance of the Mohawk mission. Problem is, you only have four aircraft. Vietnam has the priority for repair parts and film. You will find that it's a constant battle to keep the aircraft flying and conduct four missions a day, but failure is not an option. So far, the captain you are replacing has been up to the task."

As he spoke, I looked at the chart he was pointing at. It showed four Mohawks and their status. The date on the chart was that day's date. That meant somebody updated it each day. I was becoming a little impressed now. I also could see that I was taking a job that could well end my career if I failed.

Colonel Goody continued, "The Mohawk missions are part of the Peacetime Army Reconnaissance Program, or ARPRO, effort. There are seven different classified flight plans available for each mission. There is a different route and classified time for each fight plan.

"The G-2 of Eighth Army Air is responsible for planning imagery acquisition and delivery. Major Whams, the assistant G-2, is specifically responsible for that effort. He develops missions and recommends them to the Joint Chiefs of Staff for approval. They send the approved missions for each month to the G-2 a month ahead of the execution month. The G-2 will identify which flight plan to use for each mission.

"The air force provides in-flight control of each mission. During each mission, F-4s will be on standby for tactical support while search-and-rescue aircraft fly holding patterns on each coast. The North Koreans would like nothing better than to shoot down one of our Mohawks, so the threat is always there, thus the need for protection on each flight."

He opened another chart depicting a platoon organization. "The Sixth Aviation Platoon is a small aviation company with all maintenance personnel, TOs, and sensor technicians assigned to it. Also, attached to the Sixth Aviation Platoon is a second echelon maintenance platoon. This platoon ensures rapid response to any maintenance problem with the Mohawks. The Sixth Aviation Platoon is attached to the Fifty-Fifth Aviation Company for administrative, supply, and court-martial support. The Fifty-Fifth Aviation Company provides aviation support for Eighth Army headquarters, high-ranking Korean officers and politicians, and visiting dignitaries.

"The Fifty-Fifth has no tasking control of the Mohawks. Tasking will come to you from the G-2. When you get to the platoon, Captain Olson will check you out and mission qualify you. Then he will train you and sign you off as an SIP in the Mohawk. There is no other Mohawk SIP in Korea, so you will perform those duties. Instrument examiners assigned to the Fifty-Fifth will perform instrument renewal flights. In a nutshell, that's it. If you don't have any questions, let's go meet the G-2 and his staff. After that, we'll have Thanksgiving dinner. The Eighth Army officers' club is putting on quite a spread."

He rose, led us out, and told his secretary that he was going to see the G-2 and go on to lunch at the officers' club. I followed. I have to admit I was a little uneasy about having dinner with a colonel I hardly knew. I had always found it difficult to engage in small talk with a superior officer. I had listened closely to his briefing, and I wished I could get on over to the Fifty-Fifth Aviation Company.

We entered an office with *G-2* on the door. It was a small office with a secretary and a captain. The captain greeted Colonel Goody with "Hi, sir, and happy Thanksgiving."

Colonel Goody returned his greeting and introduced me to the captain. The G-2 was Major General Timer, and the captain was his aide. "Is the general in?" Colonel Goody asked.

The captain responded, "Yes, sir. He is. He is going to the Thanksgiving dinner in a few minutes."

Colonel Goody said, "Captain Griffin is the new Sixth Aviation Platoon commander, and I wanted to introduce him to the general if he has a couple of minutes."

The captain said, "I'll check," and he knocked on the general's door and opened it.

I was hoping this would not turn into my having dinner with a general. It was bad enough to eat with a colonel. The general stepped out.

Colonel Goody said, "Good morning, sir. Happy Thanksgiving. The new Mohawk commander got in this morning. I've finished briefing him and just wanted to introduce him to you and your G-2."

"Great," the general replied, extending his hand. "Glad to meet you, Captain Griffin. We had to put in a special requisition to get you. I'm sure you have taken away from Colonel Goody's briefing that you've got a tough job ahead of you. You can count on me and my folks to provide any support you need."

Shaking his hand, I replied, "Glad to meet you, sir, and to be here." That was true because I didn't want to be in Vietnam. "I will give a hundred percent of myself to get the job done. I will call if I need help."

With that, he turned and went back into his office. Generals seldom spend time talking to captains. Colonel Goody said, "Let's walk down the hall. I'll introduce you to the G-2."

We entered a large office with several desks. Sitting at one was a major. Colonel Goody led me over to his desk and introduced me to Major Whams, the assistant G-2. Major Whams welcomed me to Korea, and as we exchanged greetings, the phone rang, and he answered it. Colonel Goody raised his hand and said we were going to Thanksgiving dinner, and we left. On the way to his sedan, he said, "You will see more of Major Whams." He was right. I would come to find him a competent and dedicated officer who did not accept mission failure, regardless of the reason.

The Eighth Army officers' club was one of the plushest clubs I had ever seen. I could understand why, considering its primary clientele were generals, senior officers, and civilians. They did serve a splendid Thanksgivings menu. I was hungry and ate a big meal. It didn't seem like Thanksgiving. It was more like just another day, except for the menu. The colonel and I talked a little, and at last, dinner was over. We walked back to his office, and he directed his driver to take me to K-16. We shook hands, and he wished me good luck.

The driver left the headquarters compound and headed for Yeouido Island and K-16. K-16 was the name of the Fifty-Fifth Aviation Company's compound. Yeouido Island sat in the middle of Seoul in the Han River. The

Han River ran north and south through Seoul, dividing it into two parts. Several bridges crossed the Han. One small bridge connected Yeouido to the east side of Seoul.

As the sedan went through heavy traffic surrounded by sidewalks full of people, I took in the sights and odors. Garlic was the predominant odor. The city reeked of it. Mixed with it was the odor of burning charcoal. I would learn that charcoal was the primary heating and cooking fuel.

Korea had a 2400 to 0600 curfew each night, so millions had to take care of their business, travel, and shopping before 2400. The punishment was jail or possibility death for people caught moving after curfew. To detect and prevent attack from North Korean infiltrators, the Korean army set up checkpoints at every intersection during curfew. The Korean people were conscious of the curfew and did not violate it. If they could not get home before 2400, they stayed where they were until it was safe to travel after 0600.

I was mentally replaying my morning and Colonel Goody's orientation, when the driver turned off the main road onto a road in need or resurfacing. Up ahead, I could see a bridge and a security post with a guardhouse and gate. Soldiers from the Korean army manned the security post. The driver stopped at the gate, and one Korean guard looked into the vehicle, snapped to attention, and saluted me as the other Korean soldier opened the gate. The sharp military manner of the Korean guards was impressive.

We drove past the ROK guard barracks about two hundred yards and stopped at the entrance to a collection of Quonset huts that appeared old and dirty. Across the street to my left was a hangar facing south. A huge hangar, obviously a maintenance hangar, sat to the east of the smaller hangar. The hangar sat on a large aircraft apron built of PSP. Several UH-1s, OH-58s, and U-21s and two B-model Mohawks sat on the apron. Beyond the hangars, to the east, I could see the taxiway and runway.

The road entered the compound, but there was a No Traffic sign at the open gates. The driver grabbed my duffel bag and said, "Come on, sir. I'll take you to the orderly room."

I let him carry my bag because I had greens on, and the strap on the bag would easily knock off my captain bars. As we walked toward a modified Quonset hut that had the words *Fifty-Fifth Aviation Co.* painted over the door, we passed a large building just inside the gate. It had a sign hanging on a post: Fifty-Fifth Aviation Company Officers' Club. When we stepped into the orderly room, the CQ stood and greeted me. I responded, "I'm Captain Griffin. I'm reporting in."

The driver said, "Sir, if you don't need me any longer, I'll return to headquarters."

"No, I'm fine," I said. "Thank you for your help."

I heard the CQ on the phone, telling someone to tell Major Franks that Captain Griffin was in the orderly room.

He hung up the phone and turned to me. "Sir, have a seat. Major Franks, the CO, will be here shortly. Everybody is off for Thanksgiving except us poor souls who have to work."

I asked him where the latrine was. He pointed to a door in the rear of the hut. I walked in and straightened my uniform as best as I could. It was a little wrinkled after almost two days of travel. I straightened my tie and shirt and combed my hair. I needed a shower. I walked back into the orderly room just as the front door opened, and Major Franks walked in. Behind him was Captain Benson.

I saluted Major Franks and said, "Sir, Captain Griffin reporting for duty."

He gave me a waving half-ass salute and walked up with his hand extended. "Captain Griffin, I'm glad to have you aboard. You have a wealth of experience and a good reputation, according to your officer assignment sheet."

Turning to the captain, he said, "Meet Captain Benson. He's happy to see you, because you are his replacement, and I've told him he can't leave until you are ready to take command of the Sixth Aviation Platoon."

Captain Benson extended his hand with a smile and said, "Jake Benson. Glad to meet you, and glad you are here."

I extended my hand. "Neal Griffin. Jake, glad to be here, and glad to meet you."

With that, we retired to Major Franks's office. Major Franks wanted to know a little about me, so I spent a few minutes describing myself, my experiences, and my family. After that, he talked a little about the Fifty-Fifth Aviation Company. There was a lull, and he said, "Okay, Jake, you get Neal a place to bunk, and help him settle in. I'm going back to the officers' club, if you need me. Make sure you get Neal up to the club so you can introduce him to the rest of the officers."

Jake stood and said, "Come on, Neal. I'll get you checked into K-16."

I grabbed my bag and followed Jake to a Quonset hut with an Officer BOQ sign. We entered it, and Jake led me to a small cubicle with a GI cot and a mattress folded on it. On top of the mattress were a pillow, blankets, and linens. The cubicle was about six feet by twelve. A wall locker stood at one end. Plywood on two-by-four frames formed the cubicle and the other eleven cubicles in the Quonset hut. A four-toilet and four-shower latrine sat at one end. It was dark inside, making it necessary to keep on the table lamps in each cubicle to see. The interior had a musty odor blended with cigarette smoke. It was the odor of an old room where men live and do not thoroughly clean and air it out. The good part was that once you were inside, the odor vanished.

Jake said, "That's your room. Let's make up your bunk and get down to the club. There's still Thanksgiving food left, and the movie starts in about twenty minutes."

Jake helped me make my bunk. I put my duffel bag in the locker. I figured I would straighten the rest later.

As we walked toward the club, Jake explained the club. The Fifty-Fifth was the only unit to have a private officers' club. All the rest in Korea were annexes of the Eighth Army club. When the Eighth Army club had annexed all the other clubs, Major Franks had convinced the commander our club was different. He used it as an officers' mess and a place of duty for officers not flying or working on administrative duties. He held officers' call there each morning at 0800 and conducted officers' classes and meetings there. Since it was used as a classroom and work area, it was not an officers' club by definition. He won the argument, and we retained it as a private club. One of the assigned officers managed the club as an extra duty. The officers' club part opened after 1700 on duty days and on the weekends and holidays. The bartender was named George, and he had been working as a bartender for the US Army since the Korean War.

I followed Jake into the club. Like the BOQ, it had a well-worn look, and an old whiskey, beer, and vomit odor blended with cigarette smoke. The engineers must have built it by putting two Quonset huts together and cutting out the inside walls. A big horseshoe-shaped bar divided it.

Tables lined the walls and surrounded the bar. About twenty-five officers and Korean and American girls were sitting at the tables and bar. The dress varied from flight suits to civilian clothes. Some were playing the five slot machines on one wall. The jukebox was playing a country and western song. A few of the officers, at their own expense, had brought their families over and were living on the Korean economy. The Korean women belonged to the single officers.

When we walked into the bar, a few of the officers looked our way. The expressions on their faces indicated that they knew I was a new officer. I was still in my dress greens, so they could tell my rank and guess my experience by the ribbons on my uniform. I thought Jake would start introducing me, but instead, he walked to a bell hanging on the wall in the middle of the building. He grabbed the rope attached to the clapper and rang the bell two times. Everybody stopped talking and looked at Jake.

Jake immediately said, "I'm not buying; I only rang the bell twice, so don't let it excite you." Everybody booed. He later explained that if you ring the bell three times, you have to buy a round for the house.

Jake continued, "I want to introduce my replacement, Captain Neal Griffin." Everybody cheered.

Jake said, "He just reported in. So you know him now. Make sure you introduce yourself to him, especially you officers in the Sixth Platoon, since he is your new boss."

The major talking to Major Franks was the first one to come my way. He extended his hand and said, "Good to meet you, Captain Griffin. I'm Bill Eliot, the XO. What are you drinking?"

"Good to meet you, sir," I answered. "I'll have a beer."

Over the next twenty minutes, just about everybody in the club introduced himself to me. I knew there was no way in hell I was going to remember everybody's name, but at least the formalities were over. I met the two WOs assigned to the Sixth Platoon. Their names I remembered. The other pilot, Lieutenant Fatty, was flying. He would be back in about an hour.

There was a commercial popcorn popper beside the bar. One of the officers was popping popcorn. The club officer had set up a movie projector, and everybody was grabbing drinks and a bowl of popcorn. Jake and I were sitting at a table about four feet from the bell. The movie started, and we watched and ate popcorn.

I heard someone moving behind me. I heard the bell ring two times, and something hit me in the top of the head, knocking me forward out of my chair and to my hands and knees. Stunned, I could feel blood running down the sides of my head. I heard Jake yell, "What the shit? Turn the lights on!" He had me by the arm and asked, "Neal, are you okay?"

Someone stopped the movie and turned the lights on. Everybody was looking at me. Still stunned, I rose and turned around to see what had struck me. Standing there was Lieutenant Fatty, looking shocked with his mouth open and the detached clapper rope in his hand. "The rope broke," he said in disbelief.

Lieutenant Fatty, who stood six foot three inches, had returned from his mission and read a letter from his girlfriend. She had said yes to his marriage proposal. He had come to the club to buy the house a round. He had been ringing the bell vigorously, when the rope broke. The iron clapper had swung forward and clobbered me a glancing blow on the top of the head. The force of the blow had knocked me to my knees.

By now, Major Franks was looking at my head. He said, "You've got a deep cut, Neal. I think you are going to need stitches. Come on with me, and I'll have the duty driver take you to the hospital emergency room."

As we walked out, I heard Jake telling Lieutenant Fatty, "Dammit, Art, I hope you realize what you have done. That was your new boss. You haven't even met him yet, and you have already put him in the hospital."

The army doctor looked at my head and asked, "How did that happen?"

I explained what had happened, and he shook his head and said, "I've heard about everything you can think of but never someone getting hit in the head by a bell clapper. You are going to need some stitches."

He put six stitches in my scalp and gave me some pills for pain. He told me, "Come back in ten days to get the stitches out. Don't wear your flight helmet until I take the stitches out."

On the way back to K-16, I was thinking, *What a hell of a welcome to Korea. I get royal treatment from a colonel, and a lieutenant splits my scalp with a bell clapper.* It was a Thanksgiving I would always remember.

When we got back to K-16, I got out at the club. The movie had ended, and about half of the people had left. When I walked in, those remaining let out a cheer, and I waved. Jake was still there, so I walked to his table and sat down. He looked at me and smiled, shaking his head as if in disbelief. He asked, "You okay?"

"Yes, I'm okay," I answered. "The doctor put six stitches in. He also said I couldn't wear my helmet until the stitches came out. That's going to delay my transition ten days—and your departure date."

Jake looked shocked. He hadn't thought of that. "Damn that lieutenant," he muttered.

"I'm going to the BOQ, Jake," I told him. "My head is starting to hurt, and it has been a long day. I'm tired, so I'm going to hit the sack before anything else happens to me."

I found my cubicle in the dimly lit BOQ. Several of the officers were already asleep. I could hear them snoring. CWO-4 Bob Night, the instrument examiner for the company, was still up and reading by the lamp at the side of his bed. He rose, pointed at my head, and gave a thumbs-up sign. I gave him a thumbs-up sign in return, signaling that it was fine. I pulled my shaving kit out of my duffel bag, brushed my teeth, and took a shower. It felt good to lie down. I was sore from the force of the blow and lucky that it had not knocked me unconscious.

Had it knocked me unconscious, a medical flight board would have had to evaluate me. The board could have ended my flying career. As I previously related, the army booted one of my classmates from flight school in the last month of training. He had failed to note on his application an incident in which he'd been unconscious. A medical board reviewing his records had discovered the incident and ordered his relief from flight training for evaluation.

I took one of the pain pills before I got in bed. It eased the pain, and I drifted off to sleep, thinking of Claudia. She was back in Germany by now. I hoped everything went well on her trip back.

I slept soundly until around 0500. Then I heard a ritual that I would hear every morning in the BOQ. Around 0500, the time most soldiers were accustomed to waking up, I would hear someone fumbling in the dark. Then I would hear the rustle of paper, followed by the snap of a Zippo lighter. The smoker would take a deep drag and say, "Ah," in satisfaction as he breathed out. Then the coughing would start. Five or six smokers repeated this ritual almost in unison each morning for the four months

I slept in the BOQ. It was strange that I'd never noticed this ritual in Vietnam.

I got up then, not concerned about disturbing anybody. I grabbed my shaving kit and headed for the latrine. I shaved and brushed my teeth. I was leaving when Jake came in. "How do you feel this morning?" he asked.

"I'm a little sore," I replied. "But other than that, I feel great."

"Give me a few minutes, and I'll go to breakfast with you," he replied.

I returned to my cubicle and put on my flight suit. I started to make my bunk, when Bob said to leave it. The housekeeper would make it up and take all dirty laundry to the cleaners. So I left the bed and unpacked my duffel bag. I put all my belongings into the locker and little dresser at the end of the bunk. By then, it was 0600, and Jake came by and asked, "You ready?"

The club served breakfast between 0600 and 0700. Two of the company cooks brought cooked staples, such as bacon and potatoes, from the mess hall each morning. They prepared eggs to order on the club grill. Jake and I had breakfast, and he started filling me in on the platoon. By 0700, most of the forty-two officers and WOs were in the club. Officers' call was at 0730, and by then, most of the officers had finished breakfast and were drinking coffee, waiting for officers' call to begin.

Major Franks conducted officers' call, which was like a staff meeting, each morning. The difference was that a commander held a staff meeting once a week usually, and only principal staff officers attended. Officers' call was every day and included all the officers. The good point about the officers' call was that it informed all the officers about what was going on in the company. Work started immediately after officers' call.

I spent the rest of the morning meeting the men of the Sixth Platoon and reading SOPs. Lieutenant Fatty apologized profusely for hitting me with the bell clapper. I told him to forget it. It was an accident. Of course, he became the butt of many jokes and comments about officers trying to kill their new commander. He took it in good sport.

In the afternoon, I went to Young Sun, the name for the Eighth Army compound. I had to apply for travel pay and update my personnel records. I had to have a dental check. After that, I took care of some personal business. I had lunch at the Eighth Army officers' club and ate chicken fried rice for the first time. It was delicious.

The stitches in my head kept me grounded and relegated me to studying platoon operations. I spent time in each of my sections, learning their roles in detail. It became boring reading regulation after regulation, but I got smart about my new job. Jake was chomping at the bit to start my in country orientation flight training. He had twenty days left to get me up to speed, or he would miss his scheduled departure date.

Finally, I became eager to start flying. Reading regulations and watching operations each day got old. On the fourth day, with Jake's help, I used some gauze to make a pad to go over my stitches. I wrapped some gauze over the pad and under my chin to hold it in place. Gently, I slid my helmet on, and it felt good. I looked at Jake and said, "Let's go fly."

Jake spent the first two hours of my orientation doing touch-and-gos in the traffic pattern. He spent the next two hours orienting me on Korea. We flew to all the air force bases and landed at each one.

The rest of my orientation was at night. Jake loved flying at night, so we spent two hours in the traffic pattern at Osan AFB, doing touch-and-gos. There was a thirty-knot crosswind the whole time. It provided a challenge on each landing and took some of the boredom out of the training. During the flight, Jake gave me every emergency he could think of and some twice. I think that was the most intensive night training flight I have experienced.

The next part of my training consisted of two real-life missions with Jake as the TO. The takeoff time for my first training mission was 1900 the following night. The preparation for a mission began two hours before takeoff. That was when we sent the first classified message to the Joint Chiefs of Staff, stating the intent to fly the prescribed mission from their monthly schedule. After that, we called Kimpo departure control on a landline to give them our takeoff and landing portions of the flight. The controllers at Kimpo knew the nature of the Mohawk flights and had an SOP for their control.

We did the preflight in the hangar to uphold secrecy that we were about to fly a mission. Ground technicians checked the SLAR to ensure it was ready. One hour before takeoff, we sent another message, confirming the flight was still a go. We prepared another message identifying the crew, aircraft, and flight plan ID. We held this message until the aircraft actually took off. The platoon sergeant sent it. Eight minutes before takeoff, Jake and I climbed into the Mohawk, and the ground crew pulled the aircraft out of the hangar.

Once out of the hangar, I started the engines and called the tower for takeoff. I taxied to the run-up area, did the takeoff checks, and ran up the engines. I called the tower for takeoff. When the tower cleared me, I taxied onto the runway and oriented my flight director with the runway heading. Jake entered Kimpo's departures frequency into the VHF, I applied full power, and we headed down the runway.

As soon as I lifted off, I called Kimpo departure control and reported that we were airborne. There was a standing agreement with departure control for Mohawk mission flights. Control would confirm radar contact and give me a heading and altitude that would keep us clear of traffic. Then they would turn me over to Pine Tree control.

Pine Tree was the call sign of the air force ground control radar group that coordinated and controlled all flights into the DMZ. Kimpo departure and Kimpo approach controlled us during takeoffs and landings. Pine Tree took us from a civilian-controlled environment into a military-controlled tactical environment. When Kimpo told me to contact Pine Tree, Jake switched to Pine Tree frequency, and I called, "Pine Tree control, this is Mohawk 631. Heading two hundred ninety. Climbing to five thousand feet."

"Mohawk 631, this is Pine Tree control. Radar contact four miles northwest of K-16. Continue climbing to five thousand feet. Squawk 1311." We were now under radar control of Pine Tree.

Pine Tree would spend the next few minutes turning us to different headings to line us up on an entry heading for the DMZ. Once we turned to the entry heading, Pine Tree would clear us to the classified mission altitude. The monthly mission sheet listed the altitude, which was normally above eight thousand feet. Pine Tree had a copy of the mission sheet and knew what mission and track we were flying. As we flew toward the DMZ, Pine Tree confirmed that our support was standing by.

That meant two F-4 fighters were sitting on a runway at Osan, and a Jolly Green Giant (CH-54) was holding off the east coast of Korea. This was our search and rescue and tactical support for the flight. Pine Tree would launch the F-4s to counter any threat to us from North Korean fighters. The Jolly Green Giant was there to rescue us if a threat forced us to eject.

I reported mission altitude, and Pine Tree responded that I was two minutes from the first leg. I told Jake to engage the SLAR gyro, and I put the aircraft on autopilot. Autopilot controls the aircraft on an SLAR mission. The pilot cannot hold the aircraft straight and level enough to ensure pinpoint accuracy of the radar returns.

Once I was on autopilot and the SLAR was working, there was little to do except monitor the instruments and turn when Pine Tree told me to turn. I had the headings for each leg of our flight on my kneepad. When Pine Tree told me I had thirty seconds before the first turn, I checked the heading and waited. Pine Tree came back on the radio with "Turn to ninety. First leg."

I confirmed the instructions and moved the arrowhead on the flight director to ninety. The Mohawk banked to the right as the autopilot responded to my command. When the arrowhead reached ninety, the aircraft rolled level right on course. This leg would take thirty-two minutes to fly, so I marked that time. I would continue the mission as planned if I lost radio communication with Pine Tree.

Jake and I sat in silence, watching the aircraft instruments and the SLAR's oscilloscope. Mohawk 631 was a B model and outfitted with a first-generation SLAR system, so the only cockpit sign that the radar was working was the oscilloscope. The density of the rising and falling electrical waves on the green oscilloscope was an indication of the moving targets we were recording. The fluctuating electrical waves—or grass, as we called them—appeared normal, with no signal of unusual traffic.

Thirty-one minutes later, Pine Tree announced, "Mohawk 631, one minute from next leg."

I confirmed and checked my kneepad for the next heading. It was a dogleg to the southwest on a heading of 240 with a flying time of five minutes. I was waiting, when Pine Tree announced, "Turn to heading two hundred forty."

I confirmed while Jake set the SLAR in the standby for the turn. It was possible to tumble the gyro during a turn. That would cause us to lose data while bringing it back up, so we put it in standby during turns and back to run when we rolled out on course.

Barring no problems, most missions were essentially the same other than containing different legs and durations. They were all designed for best collection of moving and fixed targets in North Korea. The problems arose when the North Koreans would try to shoot us down or simply harass us.

Other problems most faced were maintenance and equipment problems. The aviation platoon only had four OV-1B Mohawks. The G-2 expected the platoon to fly without fail four missions a day seven days a week. Statistically, that was almost impossible with just four aircraft. Being the platoon commander meant I would have to contend with and solve a nightmare of logistic and maintenance problems to perform that task. The age of the OV-1Bs and our competition for repair parts with the units in Vietnam further complicated these problems. The OV-1 units in Vietnam had priority on all maintenance and logistical support for Mohawks. For me, as the platoon commander, I faced the added stress that too many mission failures could equate to career failure. Sitting at the controls while flying a tactical mission over the DMZ was the least difficult of anything I would do as the platoon commander.

After an hour and a half and six more legs, the mission was over. As we approached the end of the last leg, Pine Tree directed me to turn to a heading of 185 and descend and maintain five thousand feet. I confirmed and turned off the autopilot. As I turned to 185 and started my descent, Jake put the SLAR in standby to allow it to cool down before turning it off. I reported five thousand feet, and Pine Tree released me and told me to contact Kimpo approach for landing.

Jake switched the channel to Kimpo approach. We were back in civilian control now. I called Kimpo approach for a GCA to Kimpo. A GCA was the agreed-upon approach to get us down on returning from a mission. The pilot would begin a GCA into Kimpo Airfield as if he were going to land there. After breaking out of the clouds, or at minimums if he had visual flight conditions, he would end the approach and turn to a heading of 165 and fly at an altitude of five hundred feet. That heading would take him to Yeouido Island, ten miles from the Kimpo runway. Once Yeouido was in sight, he would call for a VFR landing. Yeouido had no instrument approach means.

Imagery interpreters assigned to the G-2 would be waiting at the airfield for the SLAR imagery. They would take it from the aircraft and rush it to the G-2's shop. There, they would develop it, analyze it, and prepare a report for the Eighth Army commander. If weather was so bad that the pilot could not land at Yeouido, he would tell the G-2 on the FM radio that he was going to Osan AFB, which was thirty-five miles southwest of Yeouido. He could get an instrument approach into Osan and land. The imagery interpreters would drive to Osan to pick up the film. The pilot and TO would wait at Osan for the weather to clear, and then they would return to Yeouido.

That night, the weather was clear. When I reached five hundred feet on the GCA approach, I reported that the runway was in sight and asked for clearance to Yeouido. The GCA controller closed my GCA and cleared me to Yeouido. I turned to a heading of 165 and maintained five hundred feet. Once I cleared the airfield boundaries, I climbed to 1,200 feet. I glanced around and could see by the array of city lights that Seoul was a large city.

My attention turned back to landing. The runway lights on Yeouido were indiscernible among the mass of light surrounding them. The trick was to look for the dark area running through Seoul. That was the Han River. Then it was easy to spot the dark ribbon formed by the river as it split and ran around Yeouido. Once you focused on the dark ribbon, the lights of the two bridges crossing the Han north and south of Yeouido stood out. The parallel row of faint lights between the bridges was then easy to identify as the runway lights.

I called the tower for landing, and three minutes later, I put the Mohawk on the runway. I had just flown my first Peacetime Aerial Reconnaissance Program (PARPRO) mission. After I reversed engines to slow us, Jake told me to shut down the number-one engine and taxi in on the right engine. That was to allow the imagery interpreters to enter the camera bay on the left side and remove the SLAR imagery immediately after the aircraft stopped on the ramp. They would have their imagery and be on the way to the G-2's shop before the number-two engine whined to a stop. The speedy delivery of the imagery was just another example of the importance placed on the intelligence provided by the SLAR.

Back in the office, I completed the postmission report to the Joint Chiefs of Staff. The purpose of this message was to confirm we had flown the mission and to identify any problems, unusual sightings, or hostile threats from the North Koreans. That night, the only information to report was that we had flown the mission successfully with no incidents. While Jake and I prepared the report, the platoon personnel working the night flights pulled the aircraft into the hangar and began checking it out for the next flight.

The esprit de corps of the men amazed me. They were proud that they were part of a unit with a tactical mission and not one that flew passengers. I was to see this pride many times while I commanded the platoon. No matter when—in the middle of the night or on a holiday—if a Mohawk was having a maintenance problem that was delaying the flight, the word got out somehow. Within an hour, every member of the platoon, even if he was off or on pass or whatever, would start drifting back into the hangar. They all knew the importance of the Mohawk mission, and they came voluntarily to do their part in getting the problem fixed and the bird flying again. Without a doubt, the men of the Sixth Platoon were a caliber higher than the rest of the men in the company.

When we'd completed the postflight message and Jake had debriefed me on my performance, it was 2130. It surprised me to find I felt tired from the flight. Jake wanted to stop by the club for a drink before going to bed. Despite my fatigue, I went with him and drank a beer. I was going to write to Claudia when I got back to the BOQ, but the beer was enough to end my day. I didn't even bother to take a shower. I just brushed my teeth and fell into bed.

I would fly my next training flight at 0100 the following night. I spent the day in the office, following Jake and reviewing each action he took. It was a form of overlap, because when he left in twelve days, I would take charge. By my nature, I was already doing some of the actions. Jake was happy to see me start taking charge, even though he was still officially in charge.

I left the office at 1700. Jake was working on the OERs he had to write. I stopped at the club and had dinner. I headed for the BOQ when I'd finished eating. I would have to be back in the office at 2230 to start preparing the first flight report. I wanted to write Claudia a letter before I left. I hadn't written yet, and I was sure she was waiting for a letter. I told her of my accident and a little about my training. I missed her and the kids and felt a little overwhelmed by our separation and the job I was taking on. I knew that after a week or so, the job wouldn't bother me. However, the loneliness came with a sense of apprehension I couldn't control. I knew that as soon as I felt comfortable in my position, I had to volunteer for some extra duties. I could suppress the loneliness by staying so busy that my mind had no time to mull on it. If I could get through the next six months successfully, I knew I could make the next six.

The flight that night was like the previous one, except it was thirty minutes longer. This time, Jake had me fly the aircraft and perform the mission as if he were not there. I stayed busy controlling the aircraft, leaning across the seat and operating the SLAR, and handling the radio. The flight challenged my skills and was a good way for Jake to judge my progress. I did okay. I didn't screw anything up. I got the imagery, and that was the measure of success.

It was 0345 before I got into bed. I thought the first flight had exhausted me. Boy, I was wrong. This flight was the king of exhaustion. I was sure the stress I put on myself was adding to the normal fatigue the mission would have caused. I convinced myself the fatigue would slowly go away as soon as I felt I was competent. It didn't matter if Jake felt I was competent. I had to feel it.

The next flight was a daytime flight. Jake scheduled it to show me the DMZ. So far, I had only seen it at night. Obviously, I hadn't seen much of it. The other reason for the day flight was the track. It was the longest mission, and it ran from coast to coast. The other missions, by design, mainly covered the three major avenues of approach that ran south to the DMZ. Any signs of the North Koreans massing equipment, men, and armor would by necessity occur along the corridors forming these avenues of approach. The mountainous terrain and lack of roads precluded any serious movement outside these corridors. Besides, historically, the attacks had happened along these routes. However, just to keep the North Koreans honest, we did fly a mission that covered the eastern half of North Korea.

Unfortunately, because of weather, I still didn't get to see the DMZ. We planned a 1300 takeoff, but by 1100, the clouds had rolled in, and it started raining. As a result, we had to do an instrument takeoff from Yeouido. The SOP with Kimpo called for us to file an instrument flight plan telephonically. They would give us the heading and altitude to leave out of Yeouido. On takeoff, we would leave Yeouido on that heading and start climbing to the assigned altitude before contacting Kimpo control. After that, we followed normal procedures. Instead of three hours of seeing the DMZ, I flew for three hours in the clouds on instruments.

It was my first instrument flight in the Mohawk. The ease of flying on instruments in the Mohawk compared to the Beaver was impressive. The GCA approach into Kimpo after the mission was on instruments. I broke out of the clouds at three thousand feet into a light rain. I canceled the GCA and got clearance to go to Yeouido. When I landed at Yeouido, my transition and orientation training were complete. Jake signed the form clearing me to conduct flights into the DMZ.

Jake's focus now was on completing the OERs and clearing the platoon. Before he left, we would have to inventory and account for all the equipment on the hand receipt that he had signed. Plus, he still had to certify me as a Mohawk SIP. I would have to be on orders as an SIP to give quarterly check rides to my pilots. During his last five days in Korea, he managed to squeeze in five hours to train me as an SIP.

For the entire five hours, I flew from the right seat of the Mohawk. He gave me every emergency possible. He showed me a check ride as required by army regulations and then had me give him several simulated check rides. Of course, he deliberately screwed procedures up to check my ability to correct them. It was some intense flying. When he was satisfied that I could perform the duties of SIP, he put in for orders appointing me as the Mohawk SIP. I gained a lot confidence in myself during those five hours of flying. I came away from the training feeling good about myself and with a marked increase in my self-confidence.

Finally, two days before he left, we did the inventory. It took half the day to go through the platoon's table of organization and equipment (TOE) and account for all the equipment organic to the platoon. It was necessary because I had to sign for it. Once I signed for it, I was responsible. If anything was missing, I would be the one holding the bag. There were some minor items missing, but after discussing them with the supply officer, we crossed them off the hand receipt. That afternoon, I signed for everything in the Sixth Aviation Platoon. I was now officially the commander of the platoon.

That night, lying in bed, I reviewed my life. I was a long way from the boy who'd enlisted in the army one Saturday morning. It was funny to me that no matter how much I accomplished, I still felt like that boy. The morning I'd enlisted, I'd had no idea, nor would I have dreamed, that I would go this far. It fascinated me that sometimes when you decide to do something, that decision changes the course of your life. My decision to join the paratroopers led to my assignment to the Eleventh Airborne Division. That took to me Germany and Warner Casern. Going out to eat one afternoon resulted in my meeting Claudia. My decision to apply to Special Forces led to my going to OCS. My decision to apply for flight school eventually brought me here. There was nothing in any of those decisions that foretold the result. As I drifted off to sleep, I wondered how future decisions could affect my life.

I spent the next day revising platoon SOPs to reflect my views and the way I wanted the platoon to run. I cleaned out several old files that were no longer needed. I met with the platoon and discussed my view of leadership, how I did business, and what I expected from everybody. I also pointed out how impressed I was with the esprit de corps I had seen in the platoon.

When I finished, Lieutenant Fatty, the platoon operations officer, asked me when I wanted to fly my first mission. I told him tomorrow night, preferably the one scheduled for 2300. He said, "You got it, sir."

I didn't want to fly that night, because we were having a party for Jake. All the officers not flying were at the club for his party. It was my first party in the Fifty-Fifth, or the Dragons. Dragons was the nickname of the company, and most everybody used it to refer to the unit. The partying ability of the Dragons officers was awesome. Everyone in the unit liked and respected Jake, and everyone bought him a drink that night.

I woke up as usual the next morning and felt good because I had restrained from drinking too much. When I saw Jake feel his way into the club for breakfast, he didn't look that good. He had one hell of a hangover and wasn't close to sobering up. It didn't matter, because he was catching an airplane to the States in a couple of hours, and that had him in a happy mood. He filled his tray, walked over to my table, and sat down.

I chatted with him for a few minutes before officers' call began. When it was time for the Sixth Platoon commander to speak, Jake stood and then laughed, pointed at me, and sat down. Everybody laughed, and I smiled, stood up, and gave my report on the status of the Mohawks and any potential maintenance problems. When I covered personnel, I pointed out that with Jake gone, I was now short three pilots. That left four of us to fly four missions a day. I had no sign of an inbound pilot. Major Franks told the administrative officer to check on the requisitions for Mohawk pilots.

When officers' call ended, I shook Jake's hand once more and wished him good luck. I had to go to work. I have to admit I wished it was me with the hangover. But it wasn't, and I had a year to go before I could get the hangover.

Because we flew missions night and day, the platoon worked in two shifts. This routine had been going on for several years, and it worked smoothly. I worked in the office during the day because it coincided with the time when the rest of the army commanders and staff worked. I was on call for the night crew in case they needed me. Of course I was available at night when it was my turn to fly a night mission. I spent most of my day dealing with maintenance problems, repair parts, and imagery for the SLAR system.

Many times, I would have to answer for the delay or failure of a mission because of equipment failure or a maintenance problem with an aircraft. When you have to answer to a general officer, you have to have your ducks in a row. That meant if a part on requisition delayed a mission or caused a no-fly, then I had to have the log of when I'd called to track the part through the supply chain. I had to have names and explanations that proved that my people and I had done everything possible to fix the problem. That was the only answer acceptable to the G-2 and the Eighth Army commander. It was the only way I covered my ass and saved my career.

On my first day in the office as the commander, I reviewed the status of every part on requisition. I reviewed maintenance schedules for the four Mohawks and write-ups that could potentially cause a delay or mission failure. Jake had left a list of contacts at the depot and GS maintenance company at the Eighth Army logistics office. I called them, introduced myself, and told them I wanted to work closely with them, as Jake had. I supervised the conduct of two day missions that went off on schedule.

By 1700, I was ready for a break. I had to fly my first tactical mission that night. I left the hangar and went to the club for dinner. Since takeoff was at 2300, I had to be back at 2030 to start mission planning and preparation. I went to the BOQ and took a nap. When I started back to the hangar, I noticed it had turned cold. If it was cold on the ground, it would be below freezing at mission altitude, so I returned to the BOQ and picked up my winter flight suit.

I was back in the office at 2000 and eager to start. A new pilot's first flight into the DMZ is kind of special. It's like your cherry jump as a paratrooper. There's much kidding, followed by a little celebration after it's completed. I noticed that most of the platoon was there. Some off-duty men were in civilian clothes. They had come to send their new commander off on his first mission. One thing I didn't notice then was how SFC Atchison, my platoon sergeant, kept supplying me with coffee. By the time I completed all the planning and reports, I think I must have drunk six cups of coffee.

Specialist Five Bent was my TO for the mission. He was an experienced TO and had served in Vietnam as a TO. He could keep me straight if I got into trouble.

I did the preflight, and ten minutes before takeoff, Specialist Five Bent and I climbed into the cockpit. The ground crew pulled the Mohawk out into the cold night. The weather was clear, with ten miles of visibility. It was good weather for my first flight. The weather forecaster at Kimpo had said the temperatures at mission altitude would be negative forty degrees Fahrenheit. That was cold, and the Mohawk's vent air system was not efficient at warming the cockpit. Both of us had donned our heavy winter flight suits.

At 2300, I applied full power and lifted off into the Korean night. I experienced no problems during the climb out and was soon under Pine Tree control. After about five minutes, Pine Tree told me I was two minutes from my start point. I put the aircraft on autopilot and checked the heading for my first leg. The flight so far had been picture perfect.

The mission was a two-hour-and-fifteen-minute one with seven legs. In the clear night, I could see lights extending almost the length of North Korea. The only exception was near the DMZ. The DMZ cut a ten-mile dark swath through Korea. The lights along the fence that ran in the center of the ten-mile swath were barely visible. After we turned onto our first leg, Specialist Five Bent asked if he could smoke. He lit up, and we sat in silence, watching the instruments and looking at the lights far to the north.

The flight was proceeding without incident. Judging by the small amount of grass fluctuating on the oscilloscope, it seemed most of the North Koreans had gone to bed to get out of the cold. About forty minutes into the flight, I was beginning to feel the urge to pee. For about ten minutes, I squirmed in my seat and tried to ignore the increasing pressure.

When we reached the one-hour point, I knew I had to pee. The Mohawk had a relief tube mounted to the stick. The tube had a little funnel on the end, and to use it, the pilot reached down and released it from its snap. He then pulled it up out of its recess and did his business. So far, as an aviator, I had never used a relief tube. I really didn't want to now, but the six cups of coffee had to go somewhere. They sure as hell wanted out of me.

I struggled with the pain for another ten minutes. I finally decided there was no way I could hold it until I landed. I wondered if Specialist Five Bent had ever used his relief tube or flown with a pilot who'd had to use his. Because I was in agony and concentrating on the mission, I didn't pay much attention to Specialist Five Bent. I failed to notice him turn my switch to the FM radio off so that I couldn't hear it.

That was our communication with the platoon. Unknown to me, he had watched my squirming and was describing it over the FM to the platoon. The way he was sitting with his arm resting on the radio control panel, I didn't notice him turn off his intercom button each time he transmitted, so I wouldn't hear him.

Finally, I was desperate. I pushed my intercom button and told him I was going to use the relief tube. He confirmed, and I reached down, pulled the tube out of the restraining snap, and pulled it up. Much to my surprise and chagrin, the tube only came up about a foot. There was still two feet between the end of the tube and where I needed it to be to pee and hit the cone. My reaction was *What the hell is going on?*

I grabbed the tube with both hands and pulled as hard as I could. It wouldn't budge.

Specialist Five Bent asked, "What's wrong, sir?"

Dumbfounded, I answered, "The damn tube won't extend. Have you ever heard of that happening?" I was jerking on the tube now.

"No, I haven't, sir," he answered. "Let me try mine." Although the TO doesn't have a stick, the tube is stored in the same position. I watched as he reached down, released his tube, and pulled it up to his crotch.

I couldn't believe it. Pine Tree interrupted my focus on peeing with instructions to turn to the next heading.

After I completed the turn, I looked at Specialist Five Bent's tube. I wondered if it was possible for me to switch positions with him. I was desperate and growing worse by the moment. I was going to pee in my pants if I didn't pee soon. To make the problem worse, when I had decided to use the tube, my mind and bladder had expected relief. Now the sensation was twice as bad as it should have been, because I had given in to peeing and not holding it. I mentally measured the space we had to swap positions and saw that idea was futile. I had to hold it or pee in my pants. I didn't even have my hat to pee in, as I'd had when I had to puke.

I was in misery and pain, but I couldn't concede to the notion that I was going to tell Specialist Five Bent that I had to pee so bad that, since I couldn't use the piss tube, I was going to have to pee in my pants. All I finally said was "Man, I have got to pee so bad. I don't know if I can make it back."

All right, I thought. *Settle down, and concentrate on something else. You can mentally focus and hold it until you get down. You are not going to pee in your pants.*

By then, we had only thirty minutes left in the mission. I flew those thirty minutes with sweat rolling down my face and in a state of ignored agony. I didn't know Specialist Five Bent had described my entire ordeal to the platoon, who had gathered around the FM radio, laughing their heads off. Finally, Pine Tree gave us confirmation that the mission was complete.

I wasted no time in doing an approach into Kimpo and breaking for Yeouido. I landed, shut down engine number one, and did a high-speed taxi on number two. I pulled into my parking spot and didn't bother with the checklist to shut down number two. I turned the fuel off, and while it was spooling down, I climbed out and, leaning against the aircraft, oblivious to anything around me, peed.

When I finished, I took a deep breath and relaxed the muscles I had strained in holding it back. I turned around as I zipped my flight suit, and the whole platoon was standing there. They all started cheering me and congratulating me. SFC Atchison walked up with a bottle of champagne, handed me a glass, and poured it full of champagne. "Congratulations. You're the second pilot who's made it back without peeing in his pants."

I raised my glass and toasted the platoon, and looking at the crew chief, I said, "That damn piss tube had better work the next time I fly."

SFC Atchison explained that the crew chief had tied the tube short so it wouldn't extend. The crew chief would release it when he did the postflight.

Although I was the official commander of the Sixth Platoon, I earned the respect of all the men and became a revered member of the platoon that night. Now they could brag about the size of their new commander's bladder and bet no other officer in the company could have done what I did. It doesn't seem like much, but when men are working grueling days and nights, small events become important to maintaining esprit de corps.

I quickly adjusted to the routine. My main job became one of solving problems and keeping the Mohawks flying. Major Whams became my nemesis when maintenance or a logistics problem prevented us from performing a mission. He expected me to fly four missions a day seven days a week without fail. In his mind, there was no conceivable excuse for a maintenance problem grounding an aircraft or causing one to cancel once airborne. It was my job to ensure none of that happened.

I tried once to explain that the main problem was the age of the aircraft and our competition for repair parts with the units in Vietnam. The OV-1 units in Vietnam had priority on all maintenance and logistical support for Mohawks. I had no control over when a part would fail and prevent us from flying or cause us to stop a mission. He listened, but I could see that he thought I was making an excuse. I only explained one time, and after that, I just sucked it up and took the ass chewing. I could understand his perspective. Shit rolls downhill, and when a mission didn't go and the general didn't get a current briefing, Major Whams caught hell. He just passed it on to me.

One day the mission aircraft developed an oil leak on run-up. We immediately switched to the backup aircraft. Unfortunately, the SLAR gyro would not erect despite all efforts to get it to work. The third mission aircraft was undergoing a hundred-hour maintenance inspection and was not flyable. Previous commanders had converted the fourth Mohawk to a training aircraft. It had an electrical problem that no one could isolate, and each time we tried to run an SLAR, it damaged it. That was why a previous commander had installed a stick in the TO side and made it the training aircraft.

After we were positive we could not fly the mission, I called Major Whams and told him. As expected, he was upset. The previous missions had detected increased North Korean movement toward the DMZ. The G-2 and the commanding general were waiting on the latest information, which was now not coming. The situation was tense. I called Major Franks and told him. He asked me if I had done everything possible to solve the problem. I assured him I had. He said, "Well, you will probably get the call to report to General McCall and explain to him why the aircraft are broken and what you have done to fix the problem. Just make sure you have your ducks in a row." His support made me feel better. He was my rater, and if he had confidence in me, then I was okay.

Just as Major Franks had predicted, the phone rang, and General McCall's aide told me the general wanted to see me in his office in one hour. I gathered my records on the aircraft and the log of actions my people and I had taken to keep the aircraft flying. I called Major Franks and told him I had to go see the general. He wanted to know if he needed to go with me. I said, "No, I need to handle this myself."

It's never pretty when a captain has to report to a four-star general to receive an ass chewing. Before you make it to the four-star level, you pass through a gauntlet of one- and two-star generals. They chew you a little just to let you know that shit has rolled down on them. I finally entered General McCall's office and reported to him.

He looked at me and said, "Captain Griffin, do you realize the North Koreans may be massing now for an attack on South Korea, and I won't know if that's the case, because your aircraft is not flying?"

I replied, "Yes, sir, I understand."

He looked stern and asked, "You're new, aren't you?"

I answered, "Yes, sir, I am."

He looked through me with expressionless eyes. "What are you doing to fix the problem, and how long will it be before I get my intelligence?"

I explained that we were pulling the good SLAR from the aircraft that had developed an oil leak and installing it in the flyable aircraft and should finish installing it within an hour. "If the gyro stabilizes, then we can fly. I have already sent a message requesting a special mission. The G-2 is working that end. If we get clearance to fly, the crew can start giving radio reports within the next two hours."

He turned and told his aide, "Get the PARPRO people in DC on the phone." He turned back to me and, looking at the records in my hand, asked, "What is all that paperwork?"

"It's my audit trail, sir," I answered.

The aide said, "I've got your number, sir."

The general walked over to the phone. "Brad, this is Doug. You know the situation in Korea. My people have a request for a special mission in your office. I need approval ASAP." He listened and then said, "Thanks, Brad," and he hung the phone up.

He sat down, looked at me, and said, "Captain, I don't have time to chew out captains. I don't want to see you in my office again. Your job is to fly airplanes and collect intelligence that I need. You go do that, and don't hesitate to call my aide if anyone or anything gets in your way of collecting my intelligence. If you can't do that, then I will get rid of your ass and get somebody who can. Do you understand?"

Before I could answer, he continued. "You may not believe I understand the problems with the maintenance and logistic nightmare we work under in Korea. I assure you that I do. But when you have done everything possible to solve a problem preventing the Mohawks from flying, then you start up the chain until you get to me. If it's not fixed when you reach me, I assure you I will fix the problem. Now, get back to work."

I saluted and said, "Yes, sir," and I did an about-face.

I left his office red faced from embarrassment. It's not pleasant when the highest-ranking general in Korea takes the time to chew you out. It hurt even more since I had done nothing wrong and everything I could humanly do to fix the problem. I prayed that my crew had the aircraft back up when I got back. I did not like having my name known by generals and associated with a mission failure.

When I got back to the hangar, Lieutenant Fatty was starting up 971. He saw me and gave me a thumbs-up. I felt relieved. My platoon had come through, as I'd hoped. In the office, SFC Atchison filled me in on what had taken place while I was gone. The maintenance crew was already pulling the engine with the oil leak. The new engine to replace it was sitting on a maintenance stand in the hangar. I called Major Franks and briefed him on what had occurred.

Lieutenant Fatty was back on the ground an hour and a half later. The imagery analyst was unloading the imagery. My guys had almost finished installing the new engine. The SLAR maintenance had repaired the faulty gyro. We were back in business but only barely. The maintenance people were going to work all night to finish the hundred-hour inspection on my third aircraft.

The mechanics finished installing the new engine that afternoon. WO Welsh took the aircraft up for a test flight with the fixed SLAR installed. Our test flight area was from K-16 northwest to Inchon and back. Other than actual missions, test flights were the only flights I allowed on the mission aircraft. We did all training flights in the dual-stick Mohawk. The engine checked out, but the SLAR people had to tweak the system, and WO Welsh took the aircraft on another test flight. This time, everything checked out.

I felt better now. I had two mission aircraft and one more coming online tomorrow. Of course, there were two more flights tonight and four more tomorrow. Because of the complexity and age of my equipment, the status could change within hours. I didn't know what else I could do.

I had first thought I would volunteer for some extra duties to help the time pass, but after my first full week, I changed my mind. Flying night missions and staying one step ahead of going back to General McCall's office kept me plenty busy. I spent sixteen to seventeen hours a day in the hangar, working with my people. By my first month, I knew everything about the maintenance problems, system problems, logistical problems, logbooks, and records of each aircraft. I was looking for trends that would enable me to forecast potential problems before they occurred.

One recurring problem was shortage of the film used in the SLAR and cameras. Because we were the only unit using the film, it came through the supply chain as a direct delivery. That meant the company in the States that produced it sent it directly to us. The film came in rolls of a hundred feet on a commercial jet, addressed to the military supply officer at Kimpo. The supply officer picked the film up and sent it via a supply vehicle to supply people at Eighth Army headquarters. For some reason, it occasionally disappeared during transport.

One week, we were critically low on film. The priority requisition had gone out a week ago, and we should have received the film by now. I got on the phone and called the company in the States. The people there verified that the shipment had left by air three days ago. I called the supply officer at Kimpo, and he verified signing for it and putting it on a supply jeep to go to the supply office. I called the supply office, and they reported that they had no record of it arriving. I called the G-4 office and explained the problem to a major. I told him I would give him an hour to get me an answer before I called his boss. I was doing what General McCall had told me to do: working my way up the chain.

The major called back in a half hour. It appeared the driver of the supply van had stolen the roll of film and sold it on the black market. He had been doing it for a while. It turned out that film was scarce and valuable. The buyers would sell it to a photo lab that converted the film into negatives for cameras. The army had turned the case over to the CID and Korean police for action. The major finished explaining and then asked, "Is there anything else I can do for you?" as if his explanation solved my problem.

"Hell yes, sir!" I exploded. "In two days, I will have no film for the SLAR. You need to get a hold of the company and have them send more film tonight. If you can't do that, let me know, because my next call is to General McCall. He told me a week ago to call him if there was a problem I couldn't fix that was preventing the Mohawks from collecting intelligence. Well, we are at that juncture."

I'm sure the major was not accustomed to a captain talking to him like that. There was a pause, and I'm positive I heard him thinking about what shape his ass would be in if I did call the general. Then, pissed and not sure how this was going to play out, he responded, "Okay, Captain Griffin, I'm going to get the G-4 involved in this. I'll get back to you."

"I'll be waiting, sir," I replied in a tone that let him know I wasn't going away. I was sure of one fact: if the general called me back to see him, there would be a few higher-ranking officers standing beside me.

After that, I called Major Franks and explained what was happening. He laughed and encouraged me. "Stay on it, Neal. If they blow you off, I will call the general and get it resolved."

I felt comfortable with my course of action. I know Major Franks laughed at the vision of the G-4 and the major jumping through their asses at the thought of becoming the ones responsible for the general not getting his intelligence. Most of the units in Korea considered the G-4 weak and unsupportive. They felt that instead of support, his office merely shifted the blame for logistical failures. Of course, I could suffer repercussions. I had put him on the spot with no way to avoid responsibility. His office was responsible for the delivery of supplies and the security of those supplies. The fact that there had been frequent loss of critical supplies in the supply chain would not play well with the general if he found out. I had surfaced that possibility.

About forty-five minutes later, the major called. "Okay, Captain Griffin, your film will be at Kimpo at 1630 tomorrow. Our supply people will pick it up and deliver it to you."

"That's not good enough, Major," I responded. "I want my people to pick it up. That way, I will have confidence that it will get to my location."

The major was angry now. My comments were a direct insinuation that the supply people could not ensure its delivery. His response was terse. "Your people do not have the authorization to sign for and accept supplies at depot."

"Well, here's the skinny, Major. Authorize them. Prepare an authorization for my two imagery technicians to sign for and accept the film at Kimpo. That saves the G-4 problems and ensures I get my film in a timely manner. I know we both want to accomplish our mission in the best way possible. Using a bureaucratic policy as an excuse for not performing our mission the best way possible is ridiculous, especially when granting an exception to the regulations will solve the problem." I knew it was clear to the major that I had contempt for using regulations as an excuse for not doing something. As officers and leaders, we were responsible for finding the best way to carry out a mission and doing it.

There was a pause, and I knew the major was considering what I had said and the tone in which I'd said it. I was a little concerned that I might be digging myself into a hole that would be difficult to get out of. However, my belief was that regulations were a guide. If a regulation prescribed one way of doing something, that didn't mean you couldn't do it another way if that way was legal and sped up completion of your mission. That was what Secretary of Defense McNamara had meant when he said officers should use regulations as a guide and perform the mission in the most efficient and effective way possible.

Finally, the major spoke. "Okay, give me the names you want on the authorization, and we will prepare it."

I gave him the names and serial numbers of my two imagery technicians.

He told me I should get the forms tomorrow. I said, "No, you call me when they are ready, and I will send my platoon sergeant over to pick them up."

He sounded frustrated but agreed. "Okay, we'll do it that way. From now on, we will tell you when the film is shipping from the States and when it will be available for pickup at Kimpo. Your guys will sign for receipt of it. Is that our understanding?"

"That's it, sir. I want to thank you for your help. I apologize if I was in any way disrespectful. But General McCall chewed my ass out the other day over failing to complete a mission. I never want that to happen again. I hope you understand."

He responded with a long "Yeah" that said, "I know what his ass chewing is like." He ended by saying, "Give us a call if you need our help again." However, I suspected he hoped he would never hear from Captain Griffin again.

It became a struggle daily for me to stay on top of the problems inherent to the complicated equipment I had to keep working, but I did it—while taking care of my men, flying missions, and keeping my pilots trained. I faced personal stress that came from knowing too many mission failures could equate to career failure.

My contact with Major Whams reminded me each day of the tough position I was in. After the mission failure, I made it SOP to call him each morning to advise him of my status. I was trying to elicit his understanding and support by confiding in him as if he were a member of my chain of command. Over time, we developed a relationship that was tense but not hostile. Still, I liked and appreciated his professionalism.

One day he suggested that he fly a mission with me. He said he would like to see the imagery collection mission from our end. He said he realized that he pushed us hard. Flying an actual mission would help him understand the difficult task we performed and help him gain an appreciation of our problems. As he put it, it would promote a "better understanding of one another's problems."

Finally, a perfect opportunity came on January 30. It was a Saturday and was quiet on the North Korean side of the DMZ. Major Whams called and said that day would be a perfect time for him to fly a mission if I could work it. I said absolutely. I was flying the first mission that night and would be glad to take him. I told him to be at the hangar at 1900. Before he could fly, I had to give him a class on running the SLAR and using the ejection seat.

He arrived right on time and was enthusiastic about flying. I introduced him to my night crew, and SGT Bent set him in the backup aircraft and gave him a one-hour class on running the SLAR. After SGT Bent was sure he could run the SLAR, I discussed the ejection seat and the procedures for using it. We completed his classes just as it was time to start mission planning.

Major Whams was familiar with mission planning but had never done it. We drank coffee while we waited for the report times. I warned him about drinking too much coffee, and he laughed when I told him about my initiation flight. Thirty minutes before takeoff, I did my preflight of the aircraft. Major Whams followed me throughout the steps. After the preflight, I had him put on an ejection-seat harness and helped him adjust it. Five minutes before takeoff time, we climbed into the aircraft and buckled ourselves into the ejection seats.

The ground crew pushed us out of the hangar into a cold winter night. I started the engines and had Major Whams turn on the SLAR so it could start warming up. The tower cleared me to taxi to the run-up area. I did the run-up and takeoff checks, and the tower cleared me for takeoff.

I taxied the OV-1 Mohawk onto the departure end of the runway. Patches of snow, barely visible in the cold overcast of the Korean night, spotted the runway as far as I could see. Braking gently, I advanced the throttles to thirty pounds of torque and carefully checked to make sure all systems were working and all instruments were in the green. I asked

Major Whams if he was ready. When he replied that he was, I released the brakes and smoothly advanced the throttles to takeoff power. Mohawk 631, with a whining roar from her two powerful turbine engines, leaped forward. The mission and our effort to gain an understanding of each other's challenges had begun.

Lifting off the runway into the dark night, I raised the gear and flaps. I contacted Kimpo departure as we entered the snow-filled clouds at an altitude of about three hundred feet. "Kimpo departure, this is Mohawk 631, heading three hundred sixty, climbing through three hundred feet."

"Roger, Mohawk 631. Turn left to heading three hundred twenty, and climb to and maintain six thousand. Report at six thousand."

I said, "Roger," and I turned to a heading of 320 and continued climbing to six thousand feet. My focus was now on flying the aircraft on instruments.

While I occupied myself with that, Major Whams readied the SLAR for operation. Since Major Whams was not a trained operator, each time he performed a function, I had to check it to ensure it was correct.

Reaching six thousand feet, I contacted departure. "Kimpo departure, this is Mohawk 631, heading three hundred twenty, maintaining six thousand."

"Roger, Mohawk 631. You're clear of Kimpo traffic. Contact Pine Tree control. Good night."

I switched to Pine Tree frequency. "Pine Tree control, this is Mohawk 631, heading three hundred twenty, at six thousand feet."

"Mohawk 631, this is Pine Tree control, radar contact. Turn right to three hundred sixty, and climb to and maintain nine thousand feet. Squawk 1233. Report ten thousand feet."

Soon we were at the tactical altitude assigned for the mission and still in the cloud cover we had entered at three hundred feet. Pine Tree had me fly several vectors before he announced that I was on course and approaching the release point. I engaged the autopilot and checked the SLAR's instruments to ensure it was ready and in standby.

Our flight plan that night had us flying six fifteen-minute legs: two out from the release point, a repeat of leg two, and two legs back to the release point. Pine Tree would tell us when to perform a standard rate turn to the next course.

When Pine Tree announced we were crossing the release point and on course, I put the aircraft in blackout conditions. Major Whams switched the SLAR to transmit and receive. We could relax now because the autopilot was flying the aircraft, and Pine Tree would tell us when to turn to our next leg. All we had to do was watch our instruments and hope that the North Koreans didn't feel like harassing us.

A couple of minutes into the first leg, the SLAR oscilloscope monitor lit up. The traffic appeared normal on the three major military corridors flowing south into South Korea. Thus, the first leg passed mostly in silence while Major Whams smoked a cigarette.

Pine Tree had just turned us on course for the second leg, when we popped into bright moonlight. Our spirits immediately soared as we marveled at the beauty that surrounded us. The clouds were below us now and looked like a carpet of cotton puffs in the bright moonlight. As we looked north and south, it seemed we could see the whole peninsula of Korea. Through the breaks in the clouds, the snow-covered mountains sparkled like thousands of diamonds. The beauty of the moonlight loosened us up, and we spent the rest of that leg reminiscing about other beautiful nights we had experienced.

When we completed leg two, Pine Tree directed me to do a 270-degree turn to the right to intercept my course for leg three. During the turn, I saw reflections of some bright red spark-like flashes in the right hatch canopy. At first, I assumed they were reflections from a firefight along the DMZ—a usual event. I was going to comment on this, when I noticed that Major Whams was staring at the number-two engine. From my seat, I could not see what was occupying his attention. Before I could ask him what he was staring at, he jerked his head around and excitedly yelled, "Fire and sparks are shooting from the number-two engine!"

I could feel the flow of adrenaline as I locked my eyes on the engine instruments and gauges. *Nothing.* I could feel the autopilot rolling us out of the turn. Try as I might, I found nothing out of the ordinary with the engine instruments and gauges. No firelight had appeared. The engine oil pressure, exhaust gas temperature, and rpm gauges never wavered. My scan of the gauges now included a look at the reflections on the canopy on his side, which verified what he continued to describe. Minutes passed, and the instruments and gauges remained steady. Not one needle made a scary move out of the green to suggest the sparks coming from the engine were causing a problem.

Pine Tree interrupted my attention to the spark problem with instructions to turn on course for leg three. I complied, and when we rolled out of the turn on course, the sparks and fire had subsided to an occasional spark or two. The engine instruments and gauges still signaled all was normal. I undid my ejection-seat harness and tried to stretch across Major Whams to see the number-two engine exhaust stack and sparks, but the cockpit layout and instruments made it impossible. I would have to rely on Major Whams's description of what was happening.

Still obviously shaken, Major Whams turned to me and asked, "What's going on?" Whatever was happening had me puzzled. Because of my experience and training, I was confident I could handle any emergency we might be having. Army flight training is thorough. It stresses carrying out emergency procedures and trusting in what your instruments are telling you. Despite the sparks, my engine instruments said everything was okay.

I answered, "I have no idea what happened to cause the fireworks." However, logic said that something was wrong. I just didn't know what.

I switched to my FM radio and called my maintenance sergeant. I explained what had happened and asked him for a possible explanation. Sergeant Atchison had fifteen years of experience with Mohawks, and if there was an explanation, he would find it. He said he was going to check the manual and get back to me. After about five minutes, he called back. He had been unable to find our problem in the maintenance manual, and he had never had a similar problem. Since all our instruments were still in the green, he offered the opinion that the sparks might have been carbon buildups breaking loose. I considered that a possibility but an unusual one.

"Okay, what's the worst-case scenario?" I asked.

Sergeant Atchison responded, "It could be turbine blades breaking loose, or maybe you ingested some debris or a bird on takeoff, and it's going through the engine."

There were no good results from what Sergeant Atchison was describing. Any one of the possibilities was going to damage the engine and, at worst case, cause it to break up. I thanked him and told him to let me know if he thought of anything else.

I turned to tell Major Whams that I had decided to end the mission at the end of this leg. Before I could speak, I heard Major Whams say that we had enough imagery and that it wasn't necessary to continue the mission. His statement surprised and angered me. I had stood before him too many times while trying to explain and justify why we'd had to end a particular mission. Too many times, I had heard his threatening emphasis of how important it was to complete each mission. Too many times, I had written reply by endorsements on the same subject. Now, because he was uncomfortable and feeling the stress that each of my pilots and I dealt with daily, he wanted to quit.

I heard myself firmly saying, "There's no need to end the mission right now. All instrument readings are still good. Besides, it would be a violation of your policy and my SOP if we ended the mission without a more definable reason." Without further discussion, I continued the mission.

Major Whams was not an aviator. While he outranked me as an officer, I was the aircraft commander. It was my decision, not his, whether we continued the mission. I could see that his anxiety was slowly rising. That was what I wanted. I wanted him to suffer the discomfort of being in circumstances that called for a decision to end or continue. I hoped that in the future, the experience might make him more tolerant and understanding of what could go wrong on a mission.

While I was professionally calm and mentally alert, I was agonizing over the fact that I had probably made what could be a bad decision. However, my confidence that I could handle any emergency, especially since I was expecting one, tempered my agony. Plus, I had my engine instruments' assurance that no problem existed.

Basing my actions on this rationalization, I turned outbound on leg four, and fifteen minutes later, I turned inbound on leg five. Thirty minutes later, I had my clearance for an instrument approach and landing at K-16 runway. The last forty-five minutes had passed in tense silence while we squirmed in our seats, staring at the instruments and watching the periodic emission of sparks from the engine. The tension eased a little as Pine Tree turned us over to the Kimpo GCA approach control for landing.

The GCA controller turned us on a course that took us back into the snow-filled clouds. As I intersected my inbound course, the controller directed me to begin my descent. When I reduced the power to begin my descent, the number-two engine responded with an eruption of sparks and fire the size of Mount Vesuvius. The clouds encasing us reflected the fire, worsening its effects. At first, I thought the engine had shattered. My eyes locked on the instruments, expecting the fire warning light to light up any second. I heard Major Whams mutter, "Damn!" But all instruments remained in the green. Again, the sparks settled down to a small, steady stream.

Major Whams turned to me and asked, "Are we going to make it?"

We were at 1,200 feet, and the controller had turned me on final approach to the runway and was saying, "You're on course and on glide slope."

"Roger," I replied, and I said to Major Whams, "I think so. We should be on the ground in a couple minutes if we break out of these clouds. Just in case we don't break out of the clouds when we hit two hundred sixty feet, I will have to make a missed approach and do another approach. That means I will have to add power, and I don't know what to expect from the number-two engine. So be ready to eject if I tell you to."

The GCA controller kept up his steady guidance. "Mohawk 631, you're on course, on glide slope. Report runway in sight. Cloud bases reported at three hundred feet. Report landing gear down and locked."

I heard myself calmly answer, "Roger, GCA control. Descending through six hundred feet." I should have already lowered my landing gear. I had delayed it as long as possible because I would have to add power to keep my rate of descent after I lowered the landing gear and fifteen degrees of flaps. So far, each time I'd changed the power setting, it had worsened the engine problem. However, I couldn't wait any longer. I moved the flaps handle to fifteen degrees and moved the gear handle to the down position. Holding my breath, I added power to preserve my rate of descent and compensate for the drag caused by the landing gear and flaps. Sure enough, an ominous burst of sparks and fire spurred from the exhaust stack on the number-two engine. Major Whams looked at the burst of fireworks and then at me, but I was too busy to speak to him.

"GCA control, this is Mohawk 631. Gear down and locked."

"Roger, Mohawk 631. You are left of course. Come right two degrees."

"Roger, GCA control. Coming right two degrees." The engine distraction had momentarily interrupted my scan, and I had drifted off course.

"Mohawk 631, you're on course, on glide slope, three quarters of a mile from runway. Report runway in sight."

"Roger, GCA control."

We were still in the clouds. My radar altimeter read 290 feet. I would be at 260 feet in three seconds, and if I couldn't see the runway, I would have to start a missed approached, climb back up to three thousand feet, and do another approach. I didn't want to do that with my sick engine.

Suddenly, the engine belched a large burst of sparks and fire. My rapid scan of the engine instruments caught the undeniable movement of needles. The exhaust gas temperature needle was moving rapidly into the red, as if the engine were on fire. The rpm and oil pressure needles were dropping. I had to shut the engine down before it caught on fire.

"Mohawk 631, you're over runway marker, on course, on glide slope. Do you have the runway in sight?"

Even under favorable conditions, there is an intense increase in pucker factor anytime an engine quits running. This was the worst possible time in the world to have an engine failure. I was in the critical phase of an instrument approach, almost at minimum altitude, and still in the clouds, and now I had the added stress of the engine. I pulled the fire handle and pulled the power off number two in one sweep. I turned the fuel pumps and engine switches off and turned the prop feather switch on. However, the plane lurched to the right before I could get the props feathered. I applied left rudder and got it back on the correct heading.

"Mohawk 631, you're right of course. Come left three degrees. Are you going to perform a missed approach?"

Simultaneous to GCA control's transmission, we popped out of the clouds at 265 feet. I breathed a sigh of relief, and Major Whams sank into his seat in relief.

"GCA control, negative. We have the runway in sight. Thank you." Mentally, I added, *Dear Lord, thank you.*

"Roger, Mohawk 631. You're cleared for direct flight to K-16 and landing. Altimeter is 29.28 inches, and wind is northeast at ten knots. Good night."

The approach to Kimpo got us out of the clouds. Now I had to stay under visual flight conditions and get to the runway at K-16. I raised the gear and flaps to ensure safe single-engine control and descended to 250 feet to make sure we did not reenter the clouds.

The rest of the flight was uneventful. I contacted my platoon sergeant on the platoon net. "Sergeant Atchison, get the direct support maintenance team and all our maintenance people to the hangar. The number-two engine is ruined. I want it pulled tonight and another engine installed tomorrow. I need it ready for me to do a maintenance test flight around 1500."

The single-engine landing went smoothly, and I taxied to the parking ramp and shut the number-one engine down. After it had whined slowly to a stop, we opened the hatches and let the tension and anxiety escape into the cold night air. We climbed down out of the cockpit and walked to the rear of the number-two engine. Most of my night crew had assembled there and were shining lights onto the exhaust stack. In the beams of light, I could clearly see the molten engine parts lying along the stack.

Sergeant Atchison had a puzzled look on his face. "Damn, Captain Griffin, I've never seen anything like that before. Most turbine engines disintegrate before they reach this stage. It looks like all your turbine blades have melted and are lying in the stack."

"I haven't either, Sergeant Atchison, and I hope I never see it again. Go ahead and get it in the hangar, and start pulling the engine. Crate it, and ship it to depot for examination and an explanation as to what went wrong."

While we were examining the engine, my imagery folks removed the SLAR imagery and handed it to Major Whams. He would take it with him to Eighth Army headquarters, where the imagery analyst would notate and interpret the moving target blips. I turned to him. "Hey, sir, sorry about the problems tonight, but we got the imagery."

He reached out to shake my hand. He looked at me with tired eyes and said, "Good flight." He got into his jeep and was gone. As I watched him drive away, I wondered if he had given any thought to the idea that I might have staged tonight's problem.

We had begun the flight at 0030 hours and landed at 0215. By 0500, I had finished all the required reports. I had to wake Major Franks to brief him on the incident. I crawled into my bunk, dead tired. Before I drifted off to sleep, I mentally replayed the flight. I was almost able to convince myself that continuing the mission had served a useful purpose. Maybe the pressures of mission accomplishment would slacken now that Major Whams understood the problems with which we dealt to collect the imagery. Perhaps, but the decision to continue the mission had been foolish and unwise. While the flight had ended without mishap, it could have ended disastrously. I recognized that fact, and it bothered me deeply. I considered myself too mature and intelligent to allow my emotions to dictate my decisions. I had gotten away with it this time, and I would have to ensure there would never be another time.

The pressure on mission completion didn't lesson, but Major Wham's attitude toward it changed. He was more sympathetic and more willing to delay or postpone a flight when I told him it was necessary. Fortunately, there was only one other canceled flight while I was platoon commander.

Two of my three technical operators rotated home in January. That was a critical loss for me. The next technical operator was due to report in April. The loss forced me to use pilots as technical operators. Because I was short two pilots, using the assigned pilots in that capacity put severe stress on the platoon. Despite priority requests for operators and several information papers sent to the commanding general, Vietnam had priority, and there was nothing I could do.

I had to do something. Sooner or later, fatigue from the flying schedule forced on my three pilots, one TO, and I was going to cause an incident. I thought of the analogy of two buzzards sitting in a tree. One, with a hungry look, says to other one, "Patience—hell. I am going to go kill something." If the army wasn't going to provide me with a TO, I would train one.

Over the next couple days, I reviewed all the personnel records of the men assigned to the platoon. I was looking for one with a GT score and the smarts to train as a TO. TO training is a highly technical four-month course at Fort Huachuca. I planned on training one in a week. Unfortunately, no one other than my maintenance technicians had scores high enough to consider. There was no way I could use a maintenance technician. I only had two of them, and they worked eighteen hours a day, keeping the SLAR and cameras working.

My lack of success was discouraging me, when on the way to lunch, I saw a soldier climb out of a jeep. I could tell by his uniform and his duffel bag that he was new. He saw me and saluted while greeting me. "Good morning, sir."

I returned the salute and asked, "Are you just reporting in?" He said yes. I could see that he was an E-4, and the name Mull was on the name tag he wore. "What's your MOS, Specialist Mull?" I asked.

He gave me an MOS for a camera repairman. Since I was the only one in the company with cameras, he was obviously coming to the Sixth Platoon. "What's your education level?" I asked.

"I have a master's degree," he answered, looking puzzled.

That got my attention. Anybody with a master's degree had the ability to learn the TO job. "What's your degree in?" I asked.

"It's in folklore, sir," he answered.

I started to say I had never heard of a degree in folklore but thought better of it. Instead, I said, "I'm Captain Griffin, your new platoon commander. Come on. I'll walk you to the orderly room." He followed me, probably wondering how I knew I was his new platoon commander. I led him into the orderly room and introduced him to the first sergeant. I told Specialist Mull I would talk to him after he processed in and Top sent him down to the platoon. I left for the club for lunch.

After lunch, I got SFC Atchison and Sergeant Bent together and explained what I wanted to do. I asked Sergeant Bent if he could train a camera repairman to perform the duties of a TO. I told him that Mull had the intelligence and the aptitude to learn the TO skills. He thought it was a good idea because we needed the help. He said it would be up to Mull. I said I could probably convince him because of the extra flight pay he would draw. I asked Sergeant Bent to come up with a training plan and let me see it. I wanted to start as soon as possible.

I called Major Franks and explained my plan to him. He knew my personnel status and the lengths to which I was going to keep flying missions. He supported the idea of training Mull but didn't think we would be able to award him the MOS. I agreed with that. It was a school-produced MOS, and a unit could not award it. However, units could cross-train soldiers to work in other positions if it was mission essential.

Specialist Mull reported into the platoon the next morning. SFC Atchison introduced him to platoon members and then brought him into my office. He sat down, and I started my spiel. "Specialist Mull, how would you like to cross-train as a TO?"

He looked puzzled and answered, "I don't know, sir. I've never thought about it."

"Here's my problem, Specialist Mull. I need a TO. I'm two short, and I'm forced to use pilots as TOs. I don't need another camera repairman. You have an MOS compatible with a TO MOS. You have the GT score and, I believe, the brains to cross-train as a TO. Also, you could earn another fifty-five dollars a month in flight pay as a TO. It's up to you. If you agree, I want to start training you today. Sergeant Bent will train you on the SLAR, and I will train you on the in-flight procedures. What do you say?"

Specialist Mull looked at me and said, "Sir, I can't answer you now. I need to think about it."

"Okay," I said. "Think about it, and let me know today. Talk with Sergeant Bent about it. He's a super TO and can answer any questions you may have."

He left with SFC Atchison, and I turned my attention back to the current platoon problem.

After lunch, Specialist Mull stopped me in the hangar and said he would do it. Sergeant Bent started cross-training him the next day.

A week later, Sergeant Bent and Specialist Mull came into my office. Sergeant Bent said, "I think Specialist Mull is ready for his first flight, sir. He knows the system, and there's not much more I can teach him on the ground."

I looked at Specialist Mull and asked, "You feel ready to try it in the air?"

He nodded. "Yes, sir, I think I'm ready."

"Great," I responded. "I fly tomorrow night at 2100. You will be my TO, and we will start your in-flight training. Any questions?"

He shook his head. "No, I'm ready to go."

The following night, when the ground crew pulled us out of the hangar, it was windy. The Kimpo weatherman's forecast was right. He'd said a front was moving in and would bring rain. While sitting in the closed hangar, we had no sense of what the weather was like outside. I glanced at Mull to see if the weather was causing him any apprehension. He didn't look bothered by it.

The tower cleared me to taxi to the run-up area. I ran the aircraft up and did the takeoff checks. The tower cleared me for takeoff, and I took the active. I looked at Mull and asked, "You ready?"

He answered, "Yes, sir," and I applied full power and took off. I contacted Kimpo, and they gave me my first vector and altitude and cleared me to contact Pine Tree. I turned to 290 and started climbing to six thousand feet. We entered the clouds at two thousand feet, and I was on instruments. I switched frequencies and tried to contact Pine Tree but got no response.

After several tries, I switched frequency back to Kimpo control. "Kimpo control, this is Mohawk 867, heading two hundred ninety, at six thousand feet. Unable to contact Pine Tree. Do you have another frequency for them?"

"Mohawk 867, this is Kimpo control. Negative on other frequency for Pine Tree. Turn to heading one hundred, and climb to eight thousand feet."

"Kimpo control, this is Mohawk 867. Roger heading one hundred, and climbing to eight thousand feet." I switched frequencies and tried again to contact Pine Tree. I barely heard Pine Tree, and what I heard was broken; I couldn't understand them.

I called again. "Pine Tree, this is Mohawk 867. You are coming in broken and weak. Say again."

Once again, I could hear the squelch break but could not understand Pine Tree. I started to call again, when I heard Kimpo on Guard frequency call and tell me to switch to Kimpo control.

I switched to Kimpo control. "Kimpo control, this is Mohawk 867. Over."

"Roger, Mohawk 867. Be advised that Kimpo has gone on red alert and will shut down all operations in five minutes."

All I could think was *What the shit?* I was flying in the clouds on instruments toward the DMZ. I couldn't contact Pine Tree, and now my only control was shutting down. If Kimpo shut down, I would be flying in the blind. My only recourse would be to turn south and try to contact somebody.

I had forgotten about Mull, who was hearing all of this. I looked at him. He was looking at me, and I could see fright in his eyes.

I only had seconds to decide. "Kimpo control, request immediate GCA to Kimpo. I'm ending mission."

"Roger, Mohawk 867. GCA to Kimpo. Turn right to two hundred seventy, and descend and maintain four thousand feet."

"Roger, Kimpo. This is Mohawk 867, turning right to two hundred seventy, out of eight thousand for four thousand."

As I descended through the clouds, I tried once more to contact Pine Tree. Unable to hear them, I made a blind transmission telling them I was canceling the mission. During the descent, I could see Mull was having vertigo problems. This was his first flight ever in the cockpit of an aircraft. It's scary when you are in the clouds under instruments conditions for the first time, even when you have the training for those conditions. Not having the instruments I had or the training to use them, he was having trouble with vertigo. This was adding to his fear.

We broke out of the clouds into the rain at two thousand feet. Seeing the runway and the blurred lights of Seoul allowed him to orient himself and calmed him. I turned on the windshield wipers, and—as a reminder that when you think problems can't get worse, they can—the wipers didn't work. The rain pounding on the windshield at 140 knots made it impossible see out of the windshield. Again, Mull was uncomfortable. I could see him shifting in his seat, praying for this ordeal to be over soon. What he didn't know was that I could fly the Mohawk with or without wipers. In Vietnam, Bird Dogs didn't have wipers. I'd landed in a driving rain many times by looking out the side window.

When we broke out of the clouds, I canceled my GCA and continued directly to Yeouido. Then the Kimpo control radio went silent. I dropped down to a thousand feet and flew to Yeouido.

When I turned final, Mull was looking out the front of the cockpit at the wall of water blurring forward vision. Flying the Mohawk felt like driving a car in a blinding rain with no windshield wipers. I was using my side window and touched the Mohawk down smoothly, much to his surprise. I heard later that he told some of his friends that he'd thought we were going to crash. Mull unvolunteered to be a TO, as I expected he would. The ordeal of his first flight had frightened him so much that he didn't want to ever fly again.

That mission was my second failed mission as commander. I had to write a reply by endorsement to the CG, explaining why I'd aborted. I sent the reply as directed and heard nothing further about the aborted mission. I was still short TOs, and my struggle to man each flight continued.

At last, I got some relief the first week in February. One of my new TOs reported in early. Three days later, Top called and said a new Mohawk pilot had just signed in, and Major Franks wanted me to pick him up. *Great,* I thought, and I grabbed my cap and headed for the orderly room.

When I walked into the orderly room, I noticed two officers and a couple of enlisted men standing across the room. One of the officers was using his hands to explain an aircraft doing aerobatics to the enlisted men. My first reaction was *I hope to God that's not my pilot.* I did not need a hot-dog pilot flying my hard-to-maintain Mohawks. That he was already verbally strutting the skills of a Mohawk pilot gave me an uneasy feeling.

My fear materialized when Top stood up and said, "Captain Griffin, meet your new pilot, Lieutenant Moray."

As I approached the two officers, the one who'd been explaining aerobatics turned, extended his hand, and said, "Glad to meet you, Captain Griffin."

"Glad to have you aboard," I responded. My friendliness belied my apprehension.

Just then, Major Franks stuck his head out of his office and said, "Neal, you and Lieutenant Moray come on in, and let's talk."

It was Major Franks's routine in-briefing. He and Lieutenant Moray did most of the talking. Major Franks liked to know his officers and their experiences and personal data, such as if they had a family. After a few minutes, he released Lieutenant Moray to me to get him processed into the company.

I led him to the BOQ and took him to his cubicle. On the way, he asked several questions about how much flying time he would get and when he would start flying. I gave him some brief answers and told him I would discuss all of that in detail in my office. I wanted him to settle in, see the administrative sergeant, and complete his in-processing. I pointed out the club to him and explained its use as a meeting place and officers' mess. I would see him there for lunch and take him to the platoon after lunch.

I returned to my office and got out the SOP and other references I wanted to discuss with him. My instincts kept telling me I was going to have problems with Lieutenant Moray.

I met him at the club and introduced him to the rest of the pilots in the club. During lunch, his comments focused on flying the Mohawk. He said he wanted to get as much flying time as possible. I found out that he was an only child and close to his mother. After lunch, we walked across the street to the Mohawk hangar.

I showed him around the hangar and introduced him to the soldiers on duty. Following that, I took him into my office to brief him on platoon operations. I covered the platoon SOP and gave him a copy to study. I spent time explaining the use of our Mohawks and stressed that they were used to only fly PARPRO missions and maintenance test flights as needed. There was to be no aerobatics—period. All training flights would be in the dual-stick bird, and I would conduct the training. He seemed disappointed when I told him no aerobatics, but he didn't say anything.

Then I took out a copy of the letter from the Eighth Army aviation officer on low-level flying on the Han River. The letter forbid low-level flying along the Han because of the number of cables spanning the river. Unmarked, they were impossible to see until you were right on them. They had already caused seven crashes over the years, killing fourteen pilots and crewmembers. After he read the letter, I asked him if he had any questions. He said no, and I had him sign a statement that he had read and understood Eighth Army policy on low-level flying. He signed it, and I put the form in his flight records folder.

The last item I discussed was his in-country orientation training. When I explained that he would need ten hours of orientation, he seemed puzzled. He asked why he needed ten hours, when he already knew how to fly the Mohawk and use the SLAR. When I explained the purpose of the orientation, I could tell he stilled questioned the need for it. I gave him a flight schedule with the time and objective of each session. I told him we would start in the morning.

Korea means "the land of the morning calm." That's pretty much how the weather ran. Unless a cold front was passing through, the mornings were dead calm and bitterly cold in the winter and hot and humid in the summer. It was still cold in the hangar the next morning when Lieutenant Moray started his preflight.

He started walking through the preflight, calling out checks from memory. I stopped him and had him use the checklist. That didn't go well with him, and he showed his dislike in the tone he used to call out the checks. The ground crew pulled us out of the hangar, and he called for taxi.

He taxied to the run-up area and completed the run-up and takeoff checks. His taxiing was okay, and as we taxied, I pointed out how narrow the runway was and how close the distance markers were to the runway. His takeoff was fine, and as he climbed out, I told him to level at a thousand feet. He said, "I thought the landing pattern altitude was twelve hundred feet."

I said, "Not here. Traffic patterns vary based on the terrain." He entered a right downwind, and his landing approach was good. When we were on short final, I pointed out that he was too far left of the centerline. I wanted him to land with the nose wheel on the centerline. I explained there was a chance of a wing clipping a distance marker on rollout if he got too close to one side.

When he touched down, he was still five feet left of the centerline. I told him again to put his nose wheel on the centerline. After five more landings, he still could not land with the nose wheel on the centerline. I guess my harping on that issue frustrated him, and he finally said, "The instructors at Rucker didn't seem concerned about the centerline. Sir, you'll have to demonstrate what you mean to me." His tone suggested he didn't think I could do it.

After he took off, I said, "I've got the aircraft." I entered downwind, lined up on final, and kissed the nose wheel on the centerline. I looked at him and let my agitation show. "Lieutenant Moray, I did that from the right seat. I get little flight time from this seat. If you can fly, you can do it from either seat," I said in a tone that let him know not to test me. "We are not going to get past touch-and-gos unless you can land the nose wheel on the centerline. Do you understand?"

He could sense that his attitude was ticking me off, and he answered, "Yes, sir." I had him make seven more touch-and-gos. He finally managed to put the nose wheel on the centerline on the last four landings. Satisfied, I ended the training flight.

Back in my office, I critiqued him on his flight. "First, Lieutenant Moray, you need to lose the attitude that you know everything there is to know about flying the Mohawk, because you don't. Next, this is a real-world mission we perform here. We only have three old B models with which to do it. Keeping them flying, under the best of conditions, is almost impossible. I'll be damned if I'm going to let some hotshot pilot damage one for any reason whatsoever. Do you understand what I'm saying?"

He was red in the face when he answered, "Yes, sir."

"If you want to fly my Mohawks, you'll have to satisfy me that you can do it the way I want you to. I'm the one who is going to sign you off to fly a PARPRO mission. You can bet your ass that whenever I do, you will be able to fly the mission as it's prescribed in the SOP," I said in a slow and deliberate tone. "Now, think about what I've said, and we will do your area orientation flight tomorrow afternoon and your night flights after it gets dark."

I took him on the area orientation flight at 1300 the following afternoon. There was improvement in his attitude. That night, I spent two hours with him, landing at Kimpo, Yeouido, and Osan. He did okay. I only had to remind him once to line up on the centerline. The following afternoon, I had him fly the day DMZ mission while I operated the SLAR. Again, he did okay.

Around 0900 the following morning, SFC Atchison stuck his head into my office and said, "Sir, we need a maintenance test flight on the SLAR in 609. Who do you want to fly it?"

I thought for a minute and asked, "Is Lieutenant Moray in the hangar?"

He said yes, so I left my desk and entered the hangar. Lieutenant Moray was talking with one of the TOs, and I called him over. "Okay, Lieutenant Moray, we need a maintenance test flight on 609. I want you to fly it. It's a simple flight, just like the SOP describes it. You take off and climb to eight thousand feet over Yeouido. Specialist Young will be the TO. He will be doing a maintenance check on the SLAR. You fly straight and level to Inchon and return directly to Yeouido. It's only a five-minute flight to Inchon, so you may have to make two trips or as many as it takes to complete the checks. The maintenance team will talk to Young on FM.

When he says he's finished checking the system, return to Yeouido and land. Any questions?"

Lieutenant Moray excitedly responded, "No, sir. I didn't think I was ready to fly yet."

"No," I answered, "you're not cleared to fly an SLAR over the DMZ. You're just flying a simple maintenance flight in the local area."

He was eager to fly, but he took the time to use the checklist during the preflight. That was because he knew I was watching him. They climbed into the cockpit, and the ground crew pulled them out of the hangar. I went back to my office and returned to work on the myriad of actions in my inbox. I heard Lieutenant Moray start the engines and the sound of him taxiing. A couple of minutes later, I heard him take off.

About thirty minutes passed, and then I heard a Mohawk taxi up to the hangar and shut down. Two minutes later, SFC Atchison stuck his head in the door. His face was ashen, as if he were in shock. He said, "Captain Griffin, I need you to come outside. There's something you've got to see."

The tone and urgency in his voice alarmed me. I couldn't imagine what he wanted me to see. When I stepped outside, I could see 609 sitting on the ramp with soldiers standing around it. Lieutenant Moray was standing in front of the aircraft, looking at me. Specialist Young was standing by his exit step, bent over as if in pain.

Suddenly, I realized something was wrong with Mohawk 609. The nose cone on the number-two engine was shattered. The leading edge of the left wing had a big rip in it. The canopy on the TO side was shattered. The nose section of the plane was bent inward. The right drop tank was gone. There was a large rip in the right engine cowling. The nose of the SLAR boom was shattered.

I stood looking at the damage with my mouth open in shock. I kept saying, "What the hell?" Then it dawned on me that this was damage from a wire strike. I looked at Lieutenant Moray. His face was as white as a ghost, and he said, "I'm sorry, sir. I screwed up."

I pointed at him and said harshly, "You! Go wait in my office."

I walked over to Specialist Young. He was standing up now. He had some blood on his face and hand. He was trembling as he wiped at the blood. "Are you okay?" I asked.

He looked at me, and I could tell he was shaken up. "Yes, sir, I'm okay, just a little woozy. I got some cuts from flying Plexiglas," he answered.

"What the hell happened?" I asked.

He looked at me as if he were reluctant to say. "Well, sir, when we finished the maintenance test, we were about ten miles south of Yeouido. I told Lieutenant Moray that we could return to Yeouido. He asked me if I had ever done a split S. I said no, and he said, 'Hold on.' Then he rolled inverted and dove to the Han River. He said, 'We'll low-level fly back to Yeouido, but don't tell Captain Griffin.' I told Lieutenant Moray that I didn't think we should be flying low level over the river because of cables. I had barely said that, when I saw the cable across the Han and yelled, 'Cable!' He yanked back on the stick just as the nose hit the cable. All I saw were sparks and Plexiglas flying. He got the aircraft back to five hundred feet and flew straight into Yeouido. The way it was vibrating and the noise scared me because I didn't think we would make it. Am I in any trouble, sir?"

I shook my head. "No, you didn't do anything wrong. I'm just glad you are okay. I want you to see the medics and then write me a statement about what you just told me." I told SFC Atchison to get the maintenance crew on the damage and prepare an estimate of the cost to repair the aircraft. Repairs cost control, whether the classification is an incident or an accident. I had to report the facts to higher headquarters and the USAVNASB at Fort Rucker within the next hour. The only good I could report was the fact that there were no injuries. I just hoped the drop tank had fallen into the river without causing any damage or injuries.

I walked into my office and shut the door. Usually, I left the door open. Lieutenant Moray was sitting, and I pointed at him and said, "I want you standing at attention in front of my desk—now!" He jumped up and stood at attention.

I sat down at my desk and called Major Franks. He couldn't believe me when I explained what had happened. He said he was on the way to the hangar.

I looked at Lieutenant Moray. To say I was angry was an understatement. I was raging. The acid in my stomach was boiling like a volcano fixing to erupt. This sorry sack of shit had destroyed one-third of my mission capability and damn near killed himself and one of my soldiers. I and the soldiers in the platoon struggled daily to meet mission commitments. Now we would have to struggle even harder with no guarantee of success.

I took a deep breath and let it out through my nose. Looking at him, I asked, "Do you know how close you came to killing yourself and Specialist Young?" I didn't give him time to answer. "I'll tell you. One inch—that's how close you came to having me write your mother and Specialist Young's family condolence letters. The cable struck the aircraft on the downward angle of the nose one inch below the upward angle. If it had caught the upward angle, it would have wiped out the cockpit—and you and Specialist Young with it."

He swallowed without saying anything. I opened my desk drawer and got out my court-marital manual. Deliberately and in a harsh tone, I read him his rights under Article 32. He stood red faced with pursed lips. When I'd finished, I said, "All right, Lieutenant Moray, it's your turn to speak. Do you want to tell me what happened?"

He knew that under Article 32, which I had just read him, what he said could be used against him in a court-martial. He spoke as if he were reluctant but accepted the consequences of speaking. "Sir, I conducted the test flight. When I completed it, I asked Specialist Young if he had ever done a split S and flown low level. He said no, so I did a split S and pulled out about a hundred feet above the river and started low-level flight back to Yeouido. Specialist Young saw the cable and yelled, and I pulled up but hit the cable. I flew directly back to Yeouido and landed."

He spoke while standing at attention, looking straight ahead and not at me. As I addressed him, the memory of him standing in the orderly room and using his hands to explain a split S came back. "Lieutenant Moray, didn't I make it clear to you there would be no aerobatics in our aircraft unless you were evading an SAM?"

He answered, "Yes, sir."

I continued, "Didn't I make it clear to you there would be no low-level flights, especially along the Han River? Didn't I have you read and sign the Eighth's policy letter on low-level flights?"

He answered, "Yes, sir."

I continued, "Lieutenant Moray, I praise you for getting the aircraft back on the ground in one piece after all the damage from the wire strike. However, that in no way excuses you from deliberately disobeying my orders and written orders while showing blatant disregard for the life of your TO and the mission of this unit. You have destroyed a third of my ability to conduct my mission. The Mohawk is a single-pilot aircraft, and the army places trust in the pilot to exercise the utmost professionalism and good judgment when at the controls. Specialist Young flew with you because you were the pilot. He put his faith and trust in your judgment and professionalism. Your conduct today displays a lack of the professionalism and trust granted a Mohawk pilot. Also, in my view, what you did today was counter to the conduct expected of an officer in the US Army. I intend to recommend that you never fly again and that you go before a board of officers to remove you from the army. Do you have anything to say on your behalf?"

Visibly shaken and trembling, he answered, "No, sir."

"Okay, I want you to return to your quarters and wait there for further instructions," I said. He saluted and left.

I pulled out a pad and wrote a draft letter, addressing it through Major Franks to the battalion commander, LTC Copper, describing Lieutenant Moray's actions and my recommendation that he be removed from the army. I gave it to my clerk, and he started typing it for my signature.

I walked back outside. Major Franks was standing there looking at the aircraft. He and SFC Atchison were going over the list of damages and the estimated repair costs. As I walked up, Major Franks asked, "Was it your new pilot?"

"Yes, sir," I answered angrily.

Then he said, "I've gone over the damage with SFC Atchison, and I think we can report this as an incident. That way, we won't need an investigation, and it won't look bad on our record."

I shook my head slightly and replied, "Sir, I don't think we can get by with that." I pointed to the damaged nose cone and said, "That nose cone costs twenty-six thousand dollars to replace. I'm positive that at the least, the right engine has foreign object damage from the cable. There's no way we can get the cost below fifty thousand dollars."

He answered, "I've got connections. Would you agree to let me take the list of damages and prepare the report to higher headquarters and USAVNASB?"

I looked him in the eyes. "Sir, you're my boss. If you say you can take care of this, then I believe you can. I have no problem with you preparing the report."

He smiled and said, "Good. What are you going to do with Lieutenant Moray?"

"Sir, my clerk is typing a reprimand and my recommendations now. As soon as I sign it, I will bring it to your office, if that's okay."

He said, "That's fine. You can start repairing your broken bird. I don't think there'll be anything else said about it."

I trusted Major Franks. He said he would fix the problem, and that was that. I knew that as the commander general's, pilot he was close with him and could ask for favors, so I turned my attention to getting my Mohawk repaired. I told SFC Atchison to start repairing everything we could at our level. I knew that the aircraft had to go to depot for repair of the skin damage to the wings and fuselage, but I would take care of that after we did our work.

I took the paperwork on Lieutenant Moray to Major Franks at 1400. He read it and looked at me. "Neal, this is a stiff recommendation. Let me study it for a while, and I will get back to you. Have Lieutenant Moray stand by. I will want to talk to him in a while."

I answered, "Okay, sir, but that's what I want done." He smiled, and I left.

Back at the hangar, I called SFC Atchison and my maintenance supervisors into my office. "Okay, guys, you know the fix we are in. We've got two aircraft to fly four missions over a twenty-hour period. I know we can do it. It's going to be tough, so tighten the maintenance schedules, and let me know the second it appears we are going to have a problem. At the same time, we have to concentrate on getting 609 flyable. I will work my ass off, and I'm counting on you guys doing the same until we get well." I thought about how having three operational aircraft meant being well. Just yesterday, I'd had three and thought I would be well only if I had four.

I gave some thought to trying to get the dual-stick aircraft up but dismissed it. I needed a bird to train pilots, and I couldn't chance the faulty electrical problem in the dual-stick Mohawk, which might fry an SLAR system. Besides, we would be too busy with 609.

By 1700, I was exhausted. The day's events had stressed me more than I realized. I had heard nothing else from Major Franks. Before going to chow, I went to the BOQ to find Lieutenant Moray. He was sitting on his bunk, writing a letter. My mind said, *I hope he is writing a resignation request.* I told him that Major Franks would see him sometime that night. "Go to the club, get some chow, and stand by here until told different." He looked so despondent that I wanted to feel sorry for him. However, I couldn't. He had willfully disobeyed my orders and had brought this on himself.

I went to the latrine and washed up. I looked at myself in the mirror. All I could see was an eighteen-year-old kid who'd joined the army fourteen years ago. How could that kid be me? I had done so much in those fourteen years—things that kid looking back at me had not dreamed of doing. How had I gotten to this stage of life on my own? I gently shook my head to say, *I don't know*, and left for the club.

When I got my tray of food and sat down at a table to eat, officers surrounded me, wanting to know what had happened that day. It amazed me how fast news traveled, especially bad news. I told everybody that because of the ongoing investigation, I couldn't talk about it. I didn't want to talk about it because of my bitterness toward Lieutenant Moray. I needed to get over that. I didn't see Major Franks at chow, so I returned to the BOQ.

The good about my life so far had been the letters from Claudia. They reminded me why I was working so hard. Once a week, and sometimes twice a week, I got a letter. The letters didn't say much other than "The kids are fine, and I love you," but that was enough to lift my spirits. There were two letters on my bunk when I got back to the BOQ. The mail clerk was sharp. He knew how important mail was. If an officer could not make mail call, the clerk would take any mail for him to the BOQ and put it on his bunk.

One letter was from Claudia, and the other was from the dealership in Seattle where I'd left the XR7. They had sold it, and included in the letter was a check for $1,600. The letter from Claudia was soothing. She had included some pictures of her that I had taken on our trip across the United States. On the back, she had written, "Taken by my favorite photographer." I answered her letter, but in the delightful mood her letter had put me, I could not talk of my problems. I endorsed the check from the dealer and enclosed it in my letter. I had just finished my letter, when the BOQ phone rang. Somebody answered it and yelled, "Captain Griffin, are you in here?"

I yelled, "Yeah, I am here!" and I went to the phone. Major Franks was on the other end.

"Neal, can you come to my office?"

"Sure, sir, I'll be there in a couple minutes," I replied.

It was 2000 when I knocked on Major Franks's door. He responded, "Come in."

I walked in, and seeing LTC Copper, the battalion commander, sitting there surprised me. "Good evening, sir," I said as I saluted Major Franks and LTC Copper. I extended my hand to LTC Copper and said, "Good to see you again, sir."

Major Franks pointed to chair at the table he and LTC Copper were sitting at and said, "Sit down, Neal, and let's talk."

I was a little leery at first. My thought was that LTC Copper's presence somehow involved action against me. However, Major Franks eased my concerns when he spoke. "Neal, LTC Copper and I have reviewed your reprimand and your request for a board of officers to remove Lieutenant Moray from the army." He smiled as he continued. "Now, hear me out before you unleash on us. I know you are still angry. LTC Copper and I agree that Lieutenant Moray deserves punishment for disobeying your orders and damaging a critical aircraft. But we both feel that he's a young officer who's made a serious mistake. We have made mistakes, and we are still here because the army gave us the chance to learn from our mistakes."

As he spoke, I could feel myself becoming upset at the direction Major Franks was going. I think LTC Copper could see me tensing up at what I was hearing. When Major Franks paused, he spoke. "Neal, on the way to LTC, I have seen several aviators make similar mistakes—some a lot worse because soldiers died. I've seen officers just as dedicated and professional as you are struggling to complete impossible missions. Hell, I've been one of them. I tell you this to make sure you know that I understand how you feel and to ask you to reconsider the board of officers demand. Lieutenant Moray screwed up, and there's no denying that. But as commanders, we have a duty to develop junior officers. The army has spent money and time training Lieutenant Moray. Now, it's strictly up to you, but Major Franks and I feel we need to recoup that investment. We do that by turning Lieutenant Moray into a productive officer. We need to give him a chance to redeem himself and, at the same time, learn from his mistake."

He paused for a few seconds to let me digest what he was saying. I liked that he'd said it was strictly up to me. That meant if I pushed it, they would support my request for the lieutenant's removal from the army. I was smart enough to know that Major Franks and LTC Copper could give any punitive action they believed necessary, with or without my consent. They were ensuring me that they would support me, while asking me to support them. "Okay, sir, I agree that we should try to develop Lieutenant Moray. But I believe, from my experience flying with him during his orientation, he lacks the maturity to serve independently as a pilot."

Major Franks spoke then. "Here's what I propose, Neal. I will give him an Article 15 for disobeying your orders and ground him for six months. During those six months, he will perform duties of motor officer. If he does that successfully, I will pull the Article 15 from his records. Of course, your reprimand will remain as a permanent entry in his records. What do you say to that?"

I could see both of them studying me as I considered what Major Franks had offered. That he had even discussed it with me was a sign of the respect they held for me. I looked at both of them and said, "Sir, I don't want Lieutenant Moray flying Mohawks ever again. I believe he will always need a copilot to ensure he doesn't do some hot-dog trick. He is a capable, pilot but the Mohawk is a single-pilot aircraft, and we must be able to trust the pilot at the controls. Based on my experience, Lieutenant Moray is not that pilot. I will agree to drop the demand for a board of officers if you will keep him out of Mohawks. There's not a man in my platoon who would ever fly with him again, and I think I owe them and any future TO who might have to fly with him that guarantee."

Major Franks looked at LTC Copper. LTC Copper said, "Transfer him to your fixed-wing platoon, and after his six-month probation period as motor officer, transition him to U-21s. He will always fly with a copilot who can keep him straight." He looked at me. "Neal, I will make a note in his records that I believe he does not have the aptitude and technical competence to fly the Mohawk, and therefore, the army should not assign him to those units. Will that do it for you?"

I nodded and replied, "Yes, sir." Then I looked at them and said, "I want to thank you for supporting my position. It means a lot to know I'm in a good outfit."

Major Franks stood and said, "Okay then, we agree." We nodded, and Major Franks continued. "Neal, please tell Lieutenant Moray to report to me. You can stay if you want to, but you don't have to be here."

I stood up and saluted. "I don't think so, sir. I'll send him to you, and then I'm going to have a drink at the club."

LTC Copper said, "Save some for us," as I walked out the door.

I entered the BOQ and walked over to Lieutenant Moray's cubicle. He was already in bed, reading a book. I told him, "Dress, and report to Major Franks now; he's waiting for you."

He muttered something as he jumped out of bed and started dressing. I turned and left for the club.

The club was empty except for five officers playing poker at one of the tables. I motioned to George for a beer and asked the players if they had room for one more. Two hours and three beers later, I'd had enough. I was about ten dollars ahead, so I decided it was a good time to quit and get some sleep.

The next day, I found out that Major Franks kept his promise. He gave Lieutenant Moray an Article 15, grounded him for six months, and fined him six months' flight pay. Then he assigned him to the service platoon as the company motor officer. After I heard that, I felt a little sorry for Lieutenant Moray. He was going to have a hard time redeeming himself.

I would like to say that life returned to normal after a few days, but after a major incident, such as the wire strike, I have never seen anything return to the same normalcy that existed before the incident. The adjustments and procedures needed to overcome the effects of any incident soon become the norm. The platoon faced tougher maintenance and repair parts challenges in keeping two aircraft flying. I had one less pilot. I couldn't complain about that, because I was responsible for that. It would be four months before I could get 609 into depot for repairs to its wings and fuselage. Fortunately, luck stayed with me for a while, and I stayed ahead of any potential problem that would interrupt a mission.

Apart from maintenance and system problems, there were two other serious threats to the crew and aircraft. First, there was the constant threat that the North Koreans would attack with a SAM. They had several SAM sites near the DMZ, well in range of the Mohawks' flight path. The other threat the Mohawks faced was an attack by a North Korean MiG (Mikoyan-Gurevich). Fortunately, during my time as platoon commander, there were no attacks by either threat. Most missions were routine. However, on two of my flights, the North Koreans decided to screw with me.

I was flying a mission in late February. It was a night flight, and everything was routine until about halfway through the mission. The TO and I were about half asleep, when the RC-25 (a radar detection system) squawked in a shrill tone. It was so loud that it caused both of us to jump in fright. I looked at the RC-25 mounted on the top left side of the cockpit. In astonishment, I saw that the acquisition radar light was on. A strobe light originating north of the DMZ was pulsating on the screen. I was wide awake now and shocked at what I was seeing. A North Korean SAM site had painted me on their acquisition radar.

The RC-25 is a passive radar detection system. Located at the bottom of its small screen is a row of four buttons. These buttons light up and show the radar painting the aircraft. The first button, the one that was squawking at us now, lets you know that acquisition radar has painted the aircraft. The strobe light shows the direction from the site to you and the range. It lets you see the SAM site compared to your position and read an azimuth from your position to the SAM site.

The next button is the targeting data radar, which is more accurate than the acquisition radar. When the acquisition radar detects a target and there is interest in attacking it, the operator turns on the targeting data radar. In response, the second button on the RC-25 lights up, and the squawking becomes more intense and louder. That tells the pilot the radar is loading targeting data into the SAM. The next light that comes on measures the intensity of the signals going from the targeting radar to the SAM. It signals that a launch is imminent. The fourth lights up to show a missile launch. The squawk becomes one continuous squeal. When that lights up, the pilot must take evasive actions to prevent destruction of the aircraft.

As soon as I recovered from the shock of the RC-25 coming on, I called Pine Tree to tell them a SAM site had set my RC-25 off. I gave Pine Tree the azimuth to the site. Pine Tree confirmed it and told me to continue my mission. With my eyes on the RC-25, I continued the mission.

Within seconds, the targeting button came on. That got my attention and caused me to tremble slightly. It scared the shit out of me. As I reported the increase to Pine Tree, I was mentally reviewing my choices. If they launched the missile at me, I only had one evasive maneuver. The instructions were to watch the missile until it looked as big as a telephone pole. That was when I must immediately do a split S.

In theory, I would dive faster than the missile guidance system could react. When it tried to reverse direction, it would tumble out of control. That was the good part. The bad part left me in a split S at night on instruments. That was enough to scare the shit out of me, not to mention that I might not evade the SAM on my ass. Pine Tree's response interrupted my mental agony: "Roger. Continue mission."

With my eyes focused on the buttons, I was as tense as a coiled spring. Then, just as suddenly as it had started, the targeting button light went off, followed by the acquisition light and the strobe light. The RC-25 went silent. Later, I understood the Pine Tree controller's calmness. He had been through many of these harassment tricks by the North Koreans. Of course, he was sitting on the ground at a safe site and not thousands of feet in the air as the obvious target of a SAM. I reported that the lights were off, and he responded, "Confirmed. Continue mission."

I think that was the first time I'd breathed since the acquisition button and strobe light had come on. I looked at the TO, and he smiled and said, "That's the second time that's happened to me. It was just as scary as the first time. If they fired, do you believe we could evade it by doing a split S?"

I shook my head. "I don't know. The split S is what they teach to evade a SAM. I don't even know if I can do a split S on instruments or at night. I've only done them in VFR conditions." I was sure my answer did not reassure the TO. It sure as hell did not reassure me.

Back on the ground, I filed a hostile-incident report. I thought about the F-4 pilots flying missions in Vietnam. They had my respect. The North Vietnamese fired SAMs at them daily. After the scare I'd had that night, I didn't think I could have handled that stress every day.

A month later, the North Koreans harassed me again. I was on an early night mission, when Pine Tree called, "Mohawk 867, bandits one hundred sixty nautical miles north on an intercept course. Continue mission. Will keep you informed."

That caused me to sit up in my seat. "Roger, Pine Tree." As if I expected to see something, I looked to the north. I asked my TO, "Have you experienced this before?"

He answered, "Yes, sir. They normally break off about fifty miles north of the DMZ."

"Mohawk 867, this is Pine Tree. Bandits one hundred miles north on high-speed intercept course."

Wow, I thought as I answered, "This is Mohawk 867. Roger." They were high speed. They moved fifty miles in a minute. As with the SAM threat a month ago, the Pine Tree controller seemed nonchalant about what was happening. Seconds later, he directed me to turn on my third leg.

My mind started asking me what I was going to do if they did not break off. They could cross the DMZ, attack me, do a 180, and be back across the DMZ before I crashed in flames. The instruction for foiling an attack like this was to turn south and dive for the ground. Before I could finish my thoughts, Pine Tree announced, "Mohawk 867, bandits now fifty miles north, high-speed intercept course. Prepare for evasive action on my command." This time, there was a little tone of urgency in his voice.

"Roger, Pine Tree," I answered. I turned to the TO. "Prepare to cage the gyro as soon as Pine Tree gives us the word to take evasive action."

I sat in my seat with my jaws tight, my left hand lightly holding the stick, and my right hand on the autopilot release switch. I was posed to disengage the autopilot, make a hard-right diving turn, and add full power to gain speed. The seconds passed as I kept saying to myself, *Come on, Pine Tree. Say something.*

Finally, after what seemed like a lifetime, Pine Tree announced, "Mohawk 867, bandits have broken off intercept and have turned to the north. Continue mission."

The rest of the night was uneventful. During the rest of my time as platoon commander, my flights over the DMZ were routine. For that, I was grateful. I was thirty-two years old, and to be honest, I had enjoyed all the excitement I could stand. I also believed the daily grind was wearing me down.

In the middle of February, Major Whams came into my office. He had a special photo mission for us. That was unusual because the platoon hadn't flown a photo mission in years. It was special because we could not reveal that we were flying a photo mission. Counterintelligence agents had discovered a unit of North Korean infiltrators hiding in a small village about ten miles south of the DMZ. They were planning a night raid to capture or kill the infiltrators. The problem was that they had no up-to-date maps of the village. They couldn't recon it, because the infiltrators would become suspicious and move.

They had asked for aerial photos of the village so they could study the layout of the houses and streets. With that knowledge, they could plan and conduct a night raid with confidence of success. The problem was that we had to do the photo mission without alerting the infiltrators that it was taking place. That meant no photo mission where the aircraft flew over the target several times. Major Whams wanted to know if there was any way we could do it under those guidelines.

I walked over to my large-scale map of South Korea. The village in question was just north of Seoul. The one imperative to take an aerial photo was to fly over the village. As I looked at the map, I saw that the village was about ten miles west of the route we routinely flew on our vector into the DMZ. If we could change that, we could overfly the village and take a photo. The challenge was how not to cause the infiltrators to become suspicious.

"All right, Major Whams," I said, "suppose we vary our flight path, lower our altitude a little bit each day, and move it closer to the village. The infiltrators are used to seeing us fly by, and if we change the path slowly, it may not cause them to be suspicious. After a couple of weeks, our track should be over the village, and we should be at five thousand feet, the maximum altitude at which we can get accurate imagery. Hopefully, the infiltrators won't become suspicious."

Major Whams liked my plan. He felt it was the best bet we had to get the imagery. He agreed to it. I told him I'd handle the flights, but he would have to contact Pine Tree and get them aboard, because they were the ones that vectored us into the DMZ. It would be their vector that would move us closer to the village. Major Whams assured me he would arrange it with Pine Tree and left happy.

I called all my pilots together and briefed them on the plan. I cautioned them to fly strictly the course Pine Tree gave them. We didn't want to do anything to cause the infiltrators to become suspicious of our flights. Of course, each pilot wanted to fly the mission that would take the pictures. I said, "Let's do it this way. The pilot who is flying the SLAR mission on the flight that overflies the village takes the photos." They all agreed that would be the best way to decide who would take the photos.

Two weeks later, Major Whams told me that Pine Tree had confirmed that the afternoon mission would overfly the village. Chief Dotson was to flying the mission. I called him in and made sure he understood the flight. I told him to run the camera en route to the DMZ and on the return flight. Hopefully, that would ensure we got some good imagery of the village.

Chief Dotson took off at 1330 and returned at 1540. The analyst took the film and sped away. Major Whams was going to let us know if we'd been successful as soon as his people analyzed the imagery. Two days later, he called and said congratulations. The imagery was perfect. It was so clear that the analyst could see an infiltrator who was using a large urn as a lookout post. The Koreans had conducted their raid the night before. They'd killed six and captured four of the infiltrators. Our imagery had made it possible for them to rehearse the raid and conduct it with precision. It had caught the infiltrators by surprise, and the South Koreans had suffered no causalities.

The success of the imagery mission and the raid boosted the morale of the men in the platoon. It had been a team effort, and they took pride in knowing the successful result of their work. I briefed Major Franks the next morning at officers' call. Because the project was secret, I had not mentioned it before. My news added some spice to the otherwise routine daily reports on maintenance problems and personnel shortages.

It was March, and the platoon status started to look up personnel-wise. In the first week of March, the platoon received two pilots and a TO. That brought me up to TOE strength. I immediately started their in-country orientation training. Everything seemed to be going well. Either I was becoming an expert at my job, or the daily grind was easing up. I still put in as much time as before, and the stress level remained high, but I was starting to feel relaxed, and the myriad of daily problems seemed easier to solve. I felt good about myself and my ability to resolve any problem that might arise. Something else was happening too. I didn't know it, but someone else was judging my performance.

Around the middle of March, Major Franks announced at officers' call that we were going to have to move off Yeouido. The Korean government wanted to use Yeouido as an international area to house the diplomatic community. Because of its location, Yeouido was easy to secure. It was therefore the logical place to build fancy hotels and government housing. That meant we had to move. To bring that transition about, the Korean government was building a new K-16 for us about fifteen miles south of Yeouido. It would be ready in April. The army ordered us to clear Yeouido by the end of April.

After Major Franks spoke, he looked at me and said, "Neal, I need to talk to you. Drop by my office after officers' call."

As usual, my first thought was *What the hell have I done now?*

However, after I took a seat in his office, Major Franks leaned back in his chair and said, "You know Major Baker leaves next week. That means I will need a new XO. I want you to be my new XO. What do you say?"

My reaction was just like the one I'd had in Vietnam when they'd made me operations officer. "Sir, I appreciate that you consider me qualified to be XO, but I really like commanding the Sixth Platoon. Besides, sir, there are six captains in the company who outrank me. Three of them are West Pointers. One of them needs to take the job."

He replied, "I have considered that, and it's true that six outrank you. But I'm looking for maturity, ability to thrive under stress, and some strong leadership skills. You have those and more. You have commanded the Sixth long enough to get credit for command time. If you accept, I would like you to take the position after we move to the new K-16. The Sixth Platoon is in good shape now with enough aviators and TOs to handle mission needs. Besides, you would still be able to aid the platoon anytime they needed you. An assignment as XO would look good on your record."

He paused and waited for my response. I looked at him for a couple of seconds and replied, "Sir, I don't think I'm the right man for XO. Sir, you know the army works on the policy of the ranking man in charge. What's going to happen when I have to overrule decisions made by those captains who outrank me? It's not going to sit well with them, and they will come to you for support. The results will create hostile relations that will hurt the company."

He nodded, agreeing, and said, "I don't think you have to worry about that, Neal. I have offered each one of them the job, and not one wants it. They want to stay as platoon leaders. I also pointed out that if they all refused to volunteer, I would have to pick one for the job. Still, no one volunteered. They all asked if I had offered you the job. They thought you would be the best officer for the job. I mentioned that they outranked you. Their response was that that wouldn't matter. They could work for you. I impressed on them that on any orders you issued as XO, I would back you one hundred percent. I asked if they were ready for that, and they all said yes. I think as ranking officers, they should have jumped at the job of XO. But they didn't, which cleared the way for me to offer it to you. You were my first choice anyway. What other concerns do you have about being XO?"

I had no reason now for not taking the job other than that I wanted to stay in the Sixth Platoon. I knew that was not an answer. Just like any of the other captains, Major Franks could make me XO if he wanted to, whether I wanted to be XO or not. Out of respect for me, he preferred to offer me the opportunity and have me freely accept it. That way, there would be no bitterness between us.

I smiled and, shaking my head in resignation, said, "Well, sir, I guess you have talked me into it. I'll take the job, but you know I don't put up with any bullshit about getting the mission accomplished, so I expect you to back me anytime I need it."

It was his turn to smile now. "Thanks, Neal. I knew I could count on you. I don't think there will be any problems. You handle issues in such a wise and mature manner that it leaves no dissent. I'll have personnel cut orders assigning you as XO effective the twenty-ninth of April. That gives you six months of command time and time to wrap up any loose ends and go to work as XO. What else?"

"There is one other point, sir," I replied. "I will need to check Captain Lobe out as SIP. I would still like to fly missions with the Sixth Platoon when possible."

He nodded and said, "You got it."

That was it. I stood up, Major Franks extended his hand, and we shook hands, sealing the deal. I left for the platoon to let them in on the news. I was the new XO. I would now be, in some way, responsible for 42 officers and 258 enlisted men. I hated to admit it, but I felt relieved knowing that I was leaving the stress and hectic pace of platoon commander. The XO job had to be a hell of a lot easier than the one I had been doing for the last four months.

The men and officers in the platoon were not happy about my leaving, except Captain Lobe. He would become commander, a job he wanted. He was a good officer and leader and always eager to take charge. I had two OERs to write, and I rearranged the mission schedule so I could start checking Captain Lobe out as an SIP.

Captain Lobe was an excellent pilot. Like me, he'd had plenty of flying experience before he transitioned into Mohawks. His in-country orientation training had been a breeze because of his attitude and skill. After four hours of flying with him for SIP qualification, I felt he was ready. I took him up for one more flight before I signed him off.

During the first hour we were up, I had him perform the role of SIP, and I acted as the student. He ran me through every maneuver necessary to show his skill and reaction as an SIP. During the second hour, I took over the SIP duty and gave him emergencies to react to.

My favorite way to give an engine out was to pretend we were going to do a roll. I would enter the maneuver by telling the pilot to make a right clearing turn, and I would look out the right hatch and call out, "Clear." Then I would have him turn to the left and clear. During the turn, I would lean forward and look too. At the same time, I would place my right hand on the console as if to brace myself. That let me lift the fire handle and turn the fuel off to the right engine without the pilot knowing it. When the pilot rolled level to begin the maneuver, the right engine would quit running, catching the pilot by surprise.

That was about as close to a real engine out as you could experience, and I could watch the pilot's reactions. Most of the time, there was a few seconds of confusion before the pilot realized the right engine was out. It was a good instructional technique.

The emergency didn't faze Captain Lobe at all. He quickly realized the engine was dead and took the proper action quickly and smoothly. Once he had the aircraft cleaned up and flying single engine, I told him to restart. I started reading the in-flight restart checklist. When I got to the engine start check, Captain Lobe turned the engine start toggle switch on and surprised both of us. The engine wouldn't start.

We looked at each other, and I said, "Okay, let's do it again." I read the checklist, and again, the engine wouldn't start. I turned to the air start check and said, "Okay, let's dive it and see if it will start with an increased airflow through the engine."

Captain Lobe nosed the aircraft over into a dive. We watched the airspeed increase to 250 knots and tried another restart. The engine did not start. I said, "I've got the aircraft," and I took the controls. I told Captain Lobe we were going to land and have maintenance check the engine.

This was going to be my second single-engine landing. I told Captain Lobe to act like the SIP and talk me through the procedures for a single-engine landing. I knew the procedures, but having him talk me through them was good training for him. On the approach, I called the platoon on FM and told maintenance of the problem. The maintenance crew was waiting for us when we taxied up to the hangar.

After Captain Lobe and I described what had happened and what we had done to try to restart, we walked to the club for lunch. Some of the officers called out to us as we walked in. One said, "Hey, didn't we see a Mohawk coming with the blade on one engine feathered? We thought it was against the regulations to practice single-engine landings."

Captain Lobe joked, "You guys wouldn't know a single-engine landing if it hit you."

Major Franks was eating lunch and motioned for us to sit down with him. He asked, "Neal, what happened?"

I answered, "I was giving Captain Lobe his SIP check ride, and we were doing single-engine failures and recovery. When we tried the restart, the engine wouldn't start. We tried three times, including a diving start. So I brought it back for maintenance to check."

When we returned to the hangar, the maintenance crew was shutting the right engine cowling. The maintenance sergeant walked over to us and said, "Sir, we couldn't see anything wrong with the engine. We're going to try starting it now."

As he spoke, we watched the crew chief point to the engine, and SFC Atchison flipped the start switch to start it. The blade started turning, and the engine started right up. Captain Lobe and I looked at each other, feeling a little sheepish. We were wondering if we had done something wrong or if some little genie had pissed on the engine while we were trying to restart it. We watched as the ground crew restarted the engine three times.

After the third time, SFC Atkinson climbed out of the cockpit and walked over to us. "Sir, we can't find anything wrong with it. You want to take it back up and finish the flight?"

Fifteen minutes later, Captain Lobe and I were at nine thousand feet over Yeouido. "Okay, Jim," I said, "shut number two down."

He reached up and, using the fire handle fuel-off switch, shut the right engine down. He cleaned up the aircraft, and we flew on one engine for about two minutes before I told him to do a restart. We looked at each other in disbelief when the engine wouldn't start. We ran through the restart procedures three times, and still, it would not start. Finally, I said, "Okay, Jim, let's take her back. You've got the aircraft." It was a good opportunity to check him out during an emergency.

I read the single-engine landing checks, and Jim made a perfect single-engine landing. When we taxied up to the hangar with the number-two engine prop feathered and the engine dead, it surprised my maintenance crew.

After we explained what we had done, SFC Atchison tried to start the engine. This time, it wouldn't start. I hated that we had a problem, but at the same time, Captain Lobe and I felt vindicated. I don't know what we could have said if the engine had started. The maintenance crew finally found the problem after taking apart the starter. A switch was sticking. We guessed that the temperature at nine thousand feet was cold enough to affect the switch, causing it to stick. After they replaced the switch, Captain Lobe and the maintenance sergeant took the aircraft up on a maintenance check flight, and when they shut the engine down, they had no problem restarting it.

I prepared the request for orders making Captain Lobe the Mohawk SIP. I completed the two OERs and discussed them with officers receiving them. That was it. I was ready to transfer command of the platoon to Captain Lobe, but first, I had to move the platoon to the new K-16.

The Koreans built the new K-16 on the north end of an old Korean airfield. They renovated the runway and three hangars to accommodate us. We would occupy the north end of the field, and the Koreans, with their couple of reconnaissance planes, would occupy the south end. On April 1, I scheduled one of our helicopters to fly Captain Lobe, SFC Atchison, a couple of my sergeants, and me to the new K-16 to recon the facilities. I wanted to look at our new hangar so we could plan how we would occupy it.

The recon provided valuable information that helped the NCOs, officers, and me decide how we would organize the move. I also wanted to look at the quarters for my men and the BOQ. The enlisted quarters, mess hall, and BOQ were the three new buildings the Koreans had to build for us. Our okay to move depended on their completion and acceptance by the US Army. Once the army accepted them, the Koreans expected us to move without delay. I wanted to be ready.

Once we decided how we would occupy our new hangar, I had SFC Atchison prepare a drawing of the hangar, depicting the layout and location of each section. We posted that on the bulletin board at the entrance to our Yeouido hangar. Every platoon member could see the layout of the new hangar. After that, I told them to begin packing non-mission-essential supplies and equipment. My plan was to start moving the second we received the word to move. At the time, I didn't realize how my actions stood out. I was just going about business the way I'd learned to in the airborne units I had served.

The next morning at officers' call, I reported the results of my recon and some of the problems I had seen, especially with the enlisted billets. I also let the service platoon leader know that I would need six two-and-a-half-ton trucks to move my equipment.

After the rest of the platoon leaders had provided their input to Major Franks, it was his time to speak. "How many of you other than Captain Griffin have conducted a recon of the new K-16?" There was silence, and Major Franks continued. "How many of you have scheduled a recon?"

Again, there was silence, and Major Franks continued more forcefully. "I suggest you start thinking about how you are going to move your platoons. It's not going to be simple. We have to continue to perform our mission during the move. I just heard Captain Griffin's plan. By the end of the week, I want to hear each of your plans. Any questions?" Major Franks dismissed us and walked out.

We rose, and as the other platoon leaders passed me, they jokily made comments, such as "Way to go, Neal, making us look bad."

I was ready and fired back, "I don't have to make you look bad. You do that better than I can." There was no hostility in the exchange. They were young officers in the sense of experience. Most had not had the combat arms experience that tempers you in the conduct of ground operations and teaches you to plan early and thoroughly. They had been pilots in aviation units, learning to be skilled in flight planning.

The next morning at officers' call, Major Franks suggested we have one last party on Yeouido. Everybody cheered. Then he asked for an officer to be in charge of the party. The immediate response from the other officers was "Captain Griffin! He's all ready to move, and we are still doing recon and planning our portions of the move!"

Major Franks was smiling when he looked at me. His smile said, "Neal, it's payback for putting them on the spot about moving."

I raised my hand and said, "Sir, I volunteer to do the party. Tell me what you want, and I'll get it done." I figured my volunteering would take away some of the pleasure of their payback. I could tell Major Franks I needed help, and he would let me pick officers to help.

As soon as I volunteered, all the officers started chanting, "Toga, toga, toga."

Major Franks said, "That's it; we'll have a toga party." He looked at me and said, "Toga party, Neal. Let's have it on the twenty-second."

"You got it, sir," I responded. Everybody cheered again. Major Franks dismissed us and told me to see him for a list of officers to invite to the party. My volunteering was premature because I had no idea what the hell a toga party was. I didn't even know what a toga was. I had never been to college or heard of anything like a toga party. They had not made the movie *Animal House* yet. I was totally lost. My first act when I got to the orderly room was to look up *toga* in the dictionary.

Once I saw that the definition was "a loosely fitting one-piece garment worn as an outer garment by Roman citizens," I inferred that a toga party was one where everybody wore a toga. That gave me enough information to act as if I were an expert on toga parties. When I went into Major Franks's office to get a list of officers outside the company whom he wanted to invite, I asked him how wild of a party he wanted. He replied, "As wild as it can be."

As I was leaving with the list of officers, he said, "By the way, Neal, there's an empty cubicle in the command BOQ. I want you to move into it. With Major Baker gone, I need you to take on some XO duties as soon as possible. With you in the command BOQ, we have better access to each other. Do you have any problems with that?"

I thought for a moment. I had no problem with starting some of the XO duties as long as I got the platoon moved. Besides, the command BOQ was plush and private compared to where I lived. I replied, "No, sir, that's a good idea. I'll move tomorrow."

When I got back to my office, I started planning the toga party. I remembered seeing some old pictures depicting Romans in togas lying around tables while drinking and eating. In my mind, those pictures represented a toga party in progress. I decided if it was a toga party, then everybody would have to be in a toga. I would somehow have to get togas. Sheets were the most obvious garments to use as togas, so I would have to get some sheets. I made my first rule: no entry unless you had on a toga. All the officers in the company could use their own sheets as togas. I estimated that I would need fifty extra sheets for folks who showed up in regular clothes thinking they would get in.

The next item I focused on was food. It wasn't reasonable to have us lying around tables, but I could have the food served the way I remembered it in the pictures. I decided I would have the food placed in large trays on each table. Attendees could stand around the tables and eat instead of lying down. I would have the club prepare and slice several different meats. I would serve bread, raw vegetables, and fruit, all of which could be eaten by hand. To go with that, I would have the bartenders serve all drinks in beer glasses. That was as close as I could come to the chalices used in Roman times.

Next was the cost. I estimated that I would have at least a hundred attendees. That included the forty-two officers in the company, plus six wives, maybe twenty Korean girlfriends, and the ten officers Major Franks wanted to invite. I called the Eighth Army club officer, explained what I was planning, and asked for a price on the food. The bar would be a pay-as-you-go setup. His price was $120 dollars for the food.

Before I ordered it, I decided to check with the company mess sergeant. I explained my menu to him and asked if he could do something like that. He said, "Sure, I already draw rations for forty-two. All I have to do is buy some more meat, vegetables, and fruit. I can bake the rolls." His estimate was seventy dollars. I liked that because it was cheaper, and I had control over the mess sergeant. I told him I would let him know tomorrow.

After I fixed the details in my mind, I sketched a draft invitation outlining my vision of the party. I would show that to Major Franks that night. I planned on charging each attendee ten dollars. I would use anything left over to buy the cooks a keg of beer in appreciation for their support. As an afterthought, I wondered about buying some wigs to wear. I decided I would mull over that.

I presented my plan to Major Franks, and he loved it. I had approval, so I put it into action. I told the mess sergeant to go for the food. I called the quartermaster support unit and talked to the laundry officer. He said I could sign for fifty extra sheets for the unit. I called the company supply sergeant and told him to pick the extra sheets up.

I took the invitation to Captain Rich, chief of the company admin section. As the administrative officer for the company, Rich was in his element. An English major with an ROTC commission, he loved writing. All anyone had to do was give him the main points he wanted addressed, and Rich would prepare a perfect letter, report, or OER that captured exactly what he wanted to say. He was one of the truly indispensable officers in the company. I gave the invitation to him and said, "Rich, this is my best shot. Can you make it better?"

I knew the answer to that question before I asked it. He would make it shine. He looked at it and said, "Yeah, let me make a few changes, and I'll make you a hundred copies." I thanked him and left.

The invitation made it clear that I would only admit people wearing togas. That meant I had to have togas available at the door. When I got back to my cubicle, I pulled a sheet off my bed and started experimenting with it to find out the best way to wear it as a toga. After a while, a couple officers joined me in the cubicle and helped with the experiment. Finally, I found the best way to use the sheets as togas, but I needed some big safety pins to make it work. I planned on buying a box of pins at the PX. I was set now. I had the plan for the party, and invitations would be ready tomorrow.

The next morning after officers' call, I returned to the BOQ and started moving my equipment to the command BOQ. It was great to get out of the dingy officers' BOQ and into a bright, clean BOQ. The company had recently painted command BOQ and put in new fixtures and furniture. There was a community room with a couch and chairs around a table. The latrine was clean and shiny. Command has its privileges and its headaches.

That night, I wrote to Claudia about my promotion to XO. I'm sure she didn't understand that becoming XO was a significant move for me, but she congratulated me in her next letter. It was April, and I would be eligible for my midtour leave in June. I couldn't wait to see her again and hold her. It's strange how being apart removes the memory of problems and replaces it with a need to be together again. Forgotten are the underlying causes of past anger—they have passed because of the time apart. Absence arouses a deep longing for the love that you imagine exists. Forgotten are past hurts, as if they never occurred. The belief that relations will be better now edges out the old doubts and despair. Such was my state of mind. I hoped that my joy was obvious to her in my letters and that she felt the same joy.

Captain Rich handed me my bundle of invitations at officers' call the next morning. When it was my turn to speak, I talked about the toga party and explained the details. I handed out the invitations and said I wanted the ten dollars per person by Friday. The response was positive. I explained how to best use a sheet as a toga and offered to show how to do it. Major Franks was happy with the arrangements. When he dismissed us, a toga chant started. The party mood was taking hold, and nobody can party harder than a bunch of aviators.

There is an inherent danger in arranging a party. People remember a good party and talk about it every time someone wants to do a party. People talk about a bad party and use it as an example of what not to do. The toga party was a huge success. Some of the guests were a little surprised when I greeted them at the door to ensure they wore togas. Those not wearing togas were a little unhappy about my not letting them in. However, the sounds of merriment coming from the club convinced them to wear the togas I provided. Some of the girls even stripped down to underwear and bras before they put on the togas. I had a prize for best dressed, and one of the women who went braless won it. The party lasted well into the night and produced some giant hangovers. I got many compliments about the party that night.

I flew five more missions during my final days as platoon commander. All but one was routine. On the third mission, I made a rookie's error. It was a dark, cloudy night with a light rain falling. When I took the active, I forgot to orient my flight director on the runway heading. I took off and entered instrument conditions almost immediately.

I contacted Kimpo, and they directed me to turn to 270 and climb to six thousand feet. That was when I noticed that my flight director read a heading of 290, when it should have been on 360. That was a shock. I quickly checked my magnetic compass, which showed a heading of 355, which was correct. I hurriedly pushed my reset button for the flight director while I confirmed Kimpo's instructions and started my turn to 270. When my flight director stopped spinning, it settled on a heading that did not agree with my compass.

Shit, I thought. *What should I do now?* I couldn't fly the mission on the magnetic compass, because the autopilot was synced with the flight director. I rolled out on the magnetic heading of 270, which was not exact because of the precession in the magnetic compass, which I had not computed. I was still waiting for my flight director to stabilize. I reached six thousand and reported to Kimpo, and Kimpo told me I was ten degrees right of course. That meant I was at a heading of 280, so I turned left to a heading of 260 on my compass. Kimpo then cleared me to contact Pine Tree.

I switched frequencies and called Pine Tree. I noticed my TO was looking at me with a "What's going on?" look. I pointed at the flight director, and he nodded that he understood. When Pine Tree answered, they were weak and broken, and I couldn't understand them. I called again and told them of the bad transmission. This time, I could barely hear the static breaking. I was in trouble now. I was flying west. *Shit, I need to check my clock. I can't fly west too long, because I'll be over the ocean.* I scolded myself as I punched my clock. *Come on, Neal. Start thinking.*

I couldn't hear Pine Tree, so I switched back to Kimpo frequency and called them. I heard only silence on the radio. Now I couldn't contact

Kimpo. I had been flying west for six minutes, and I had to do something soon. I tried once again to contact Pine Tree. I got nothing but static on the radio. I could see out of the side of my eyes that my TO was becoming nervous. He looked at me and shrugged as if asking, "What are we going to do?"

I knew what I wasn't going to do anymore: fly west. I made a blind call, telling Pine Tree that I was doing a 180-degree turn back to the east. I made the turn on my magnetic compass, and when I rolled out and the compass stabilized, so did my flight director on the same heading. At last, I could use my flight director. I punched my clock to keep track of the time I flew east and continued to make blind calls to Pine Tree. After about four minutes, I began to hear Pine Tree. Then they came in loud and clear: "Mohawk 671, how do you hear this station?"

"Pine Tree, this is Mohawk 671," I answered with a sigh of relief. "Got you loud and clear. Heading ninety. Eight thousand feet."

"Roger, Mohawk 671. Turn to heading three hundred sixty, vector to release point, and climb to ten thousand. We had you flying west and reversing direction to east. Are you experiencing any problems?"

"Pine Tree, this is Mohawk 671. Not now. Before, I could not raise you on the radio. I turned back to get closer to your position."

"Roger, Mohawk 671. We heard you loud and clear. We will check our radios."

The rest of the mission was routine. I can only say that flying lost in the clouds with no contact with anyone on the ground is, at best, terrifying. Even more painful was the knowledge that I had been the primary cause of the problem by failing to orient my flight director. It turned out there was a problem with the Pine Trees transmitter, which they quickly corrected. I still replay that flight in my mind and reason out what I would have done had I not contacted Pine Tree or Kimpo. I'm just glad I could make contact.

I flew my last tactical mission on the day before my thirty-third birthday. It was an early morning mission, and when I got back, I spoke with Captain Lobe and told him that Major Franks was pushing me to start the XO job early. If it was okay with Major Franks, I would turn over the platoon to him that afternoon.

Captain Lobe was eager to take charge and replied, "That would be great if we could do that."

I said, "Okay, let me call Major Franks and tell him that's what we would like to do. But I have one request. I want to fly the last Mohawk off Yeouido. Do you have any problems with that?"

He said, "Absolutely not."

I called Major Franks, and he agreed with turning the platoon over to Captain Lobe. He wanted me in the XO chair as soon as possible. I told Jim I would like to do it that afternoon. He was happy with that and said he would have the platoon assemble at 1400. That settled it. I told him I would be there at 1400.

When I returned at 1400, the platoon had set up a little party for me in the hangar. During the party, I shook hands with the men and thanked them for doing such a fine job. After the party, I shook hands with Jim and gave the platoon to him.

I felt a little sad as I walked up to the BOQ. I had put a ton of sweat and blood into commanding the platoon. I had the sensation that I was quitting a job because it was too tough, but I knew that wasn't true. I had mastered the job, and doing it successfully had become much easier and less stressful. I think it was the short time I'd commanded it that made me feel as if I were walking away from it. Flying a tactical mission over the DMZ was exciting, and I was going to miss that.

I walked into the orderly room and announced that I was ready to assume the duties of XO. As I expected, Major Franks immediately put me in charge of moving the company to the new K-16.

There were a myriad of details and issues to resolve to make a move of that nature. I would come to find that Major Franks didn't like to deal with details. He was a thoughtful leader who could quickly see the big picture and proper course of action, but when it came to the details necessary to make it happen, he would defer that work to me. His guiding principle was to continue the mission during the move.

I had made many moves during my time in the army, but a personnel move from one location to another is not like moving a unit as diverse and complex as an aviation company. My moving the artillery battalion to the Dominican Republic was simple in comparison. The first action I took was to get the platoon leaders together to create an advance party.

The advance party would be responsible for preparing the new K-16 for occupancy by the company. My plan was to move one platoon at a time. When the relocated platoon was up and performing, I would move the next platoon. That way, I would always preserve mission capability. At the end of my first day as XO, I had put together a movement plan for the company. I organized an advance party and put a captain in command of it. After I let the platoon leaders go, I briefed Major Franks. He made a couple of suggestions, but overall, he was happy with the plan.

My first day as XO also was my birthday. I was thirty-three years old. That night at mail call, I was a little disappointed that I didn't get a birthday card or at least a letter from Claudia. I knew that she had sent one and that it was in the mail somewhere. I would get it tomorrow or the next day with a couple of letters. After the evening meal, I stayed in the club and celebrated my birthday with four or five other officers. It wasn't a substitute for the letter I wanted, but it did the trick.

The Army Corps of Engineers inspected and accepted the new K-16 on April 24 and gave us the go-ahead to move. Major Franks told us to execute, and I launched the advance party. We were pressed for time now. The Koreans had already begun bulldozing the part of the island surrounding K-16.

On April 25, the captain in charge of the advance party told me that all the communications were in and working in the new orderly room. The next morning, I had a detail pack and move the orderly room and Major Franks. I would remain on Yeouido until the last piece of equipment had cleared the island.

Captain Lobe was leaving the training Mohawk for me to fly off the island, as I had asked. Major Franks wanted a company yearbook and had pulled Specialist Mull to do the photography and put it together. He wanted to fly out with me and take some aerial photos of the island as we left. I asked him if he was sure he wanted to fly with me, since our last flight had been less than successful. He laughed and said he trusted me for a photo flight.

The move went well with few interruptions. The main delays were getting the trucks unloaded and back to Yeouido to pick up another load. Although the new K-16 was only ten air miles from Yeouido, it was thirty miles by road. The operations platoon moved after the orderly room, and the maintenance platoon followed it. That put all the command, control, and support at the new K-16.

The rest of the platoons followed over the next three days, and by April 30, the company was clear of Yeouido.

On the morning of May 1, an OH-58 flew Major Franks and the first sergeant to Yeouido. They brought Specialist Mull with them. We did a walk-through inspection of all the buildings and the area to ensure no equipment remained. I threw my personal equipment onto the OH-58, and they left for the new K-16. Specialist Mull and I climbed into the training Mohawk, and I started it and taxied for takeoff. There was no tower, so I had to clear myself. I taxied onto the runway and sat for a moment while my mind flipped through all the other times I had sat there. I looked down the runway only to see bulldozers pushing dirt across the far end. That ended my reminiscing. I applied full power, and the Mohawk sprang forward. I kept thinking, *I hope those operators see me coming and stay off the runway.* Finally, I reached lift-off speed and rotated. No sooner had I lifted off the runway than bulldozers started ripping it up. I flew over the island several times so Specialist Mull could get all the pictures he wanted. When he said he had enough, I took one last look at where I had spent a significant part of my life, and then I turned toward the new K-16.

Slowly and surely, we turned the new K-16 into a functioning base. While most of the problems we faced were minor and easily fixed, some were not. The Koreans, in the rush to get us off Yeouido, had done some sloppy construction work. The enlisted barracks had cracks in walls up to an inch wide. This caused some to wonder if the buildings would stand. Major Franks turned the problem over to the engineers to solve, since they'd approved the buildings. They assured us the buildings wouldn't collapse.

The other major problems were the taxiway and apron. The Koreans had built them using steel planking over rubber sheeting. The problem was that when we taxied in a U-21 or Mohawk, the planking rolled in front of the aircraft. Air under the rubber blanket caused a bubble that pushed the planking up. This was no problem for the Mohawk because of its height, but the U-21 sat closer to the ground, and we feared the possibility that as the planking rolled, it would rise high enough to strike a prop. That would cause disastrous damage. The issue was turned over to the engineers to fix.

We instructed pilots to taxi slowly to avoid causing a high roll while the engineers worked on a solution.

The good part was moving into a newly constructed BOQ. The BOQ was a U-shaped building. Each wing was a two-story building consisting of twenty-four rooms. Connecting the wings was a one-story building that served as our officers' club and officer meeting room. Major Franks had the north downstairs room nearest the club. I had the one facing his on the other side. His room had a private bathroom.

My room was typical of all the rooms. It was larger than the rest, but I shared a bathroom with the next room. Still, it was 100 percent better than the quarters I had lived in on Yeouido.

From the first time Major Franks saw the BOQ, he wanted to build a swimming pool between the wings. As soon as we finished moving to the new K-16, he asked me to start rounding up the material needed to build forms and pour a pool. I added that task to the long list of my other XO duties.

A company XO is mostly responsible for maintenance and supply functions in a company. These are nitty-gritty chores. They would tie the commander down and take too much time from the command duties if he had to perform them. In the Fifty-Fifth Aviation Company, the commander was the commanding general's pilot and went wherever the commanding general went. Thus, the XO often acted as the commander and performed all the duties. Such was my case. Three or four days a week, Major Franks was gone, flying the commanding general out of country. That left me in charge.

At first, I was a little hesitant, but I immersed myself in the job, as was my habit. I was good at it. I understood maintenance and supply, and my tough but commonsense leadership earned me the respect I needed to perform well. Soon officers would come to me first with a problem, even when Major Franks was in his office. Only if I couldn't solve it did they go to Major Franks.

My one weakness at the job was my writing ability. I had learned all the other skills in the army, but I'd failed to master English and composition in high school, and it hurt me as an officer. It wasn't that I couldn't write. I could, but it took most of my time and many rewrites before I would get whatever correspondence I was writing correct. The time it took me was time I couldn't afford. I spent many late nights writing memos, OERs, fact sheets, requests, and other papers. However, now I had Captain Rich. All I had to do was scratch out the main points that I wanted to say and give them to him. Minutes later, it was back, well written and in perfect form for my approval. He made life easy for me, and what made it so nice was that he loved flying and doing correspondence. I learned from reading the way he structured my thoughts.

The XO job came with some extra duties. I was the Korean and American relations officer. I had to meet once a week with the mayor of the small Korean village that bordered the main gate to K-16.

As with all new army posts, bars and clubs sprang up overnight in the adjoining communities. They provided places for off-duty soldiers to hang out and socialize. They also become places for drunken soldiers to get into trouble.

My purpose in meeting with the mayor was to develop procedures to handle and resolve any problems arising from my soldiers. I didn't want my soldiers fighting and damaging Korean property, nor did I want them arrested each time they become rowdy. The mayor and I worked out a deal in which he would tell us if it appeared there was going to be trouble or a drunken soldier was becoming rowdy. Then I would post the sergeant of the guard to take care of the trouble. To simplify this, I installed a landline and put an army field phone in the mayor's office and at his home. Anytime his people called him about a problem, he could call directly to my office, night or day. This worked, and during the remaining seven months I was in Korea, we developed an excellent working relationship that allowed us to resolve all issues quickly before they developed into a major incident.

One day in the middle of May, Captain Davey walked into my office. Davey was the company SIP for the U-21. He looked at me and said, "I need to get you transitioned into the U-21 so you can start flying again. It's been a month since you have flown an aircraft. The Mohawks are too committed for you to use and stay current. When do you want to start?"

Davey was one of the super pilots that I imagined being one day. He had more than four thousand hours in the U-21 and had forgotten more about flying than most pilots will ever learn. He had a pleasant personality and was always smiling. I looked at him and thought, *He's right. I need to fly something other than this desk, which I have occupied for a month.* I had thrown myself at the job of XO. Now I was comfortable as XO, and it was time for me to start flying again. "Okay, Davey, let's start tomorrow morning."

He smiled and said, "Good. I am going to schedule twenty-five hours of training. Can I count on you to meet the schedule and not defer flying because of other priorities?"

I looked at him and said, "Davey, I will make every flight that's possible. The only postponements will be those that Major Franks causes. If he needs something, I will have to do it."

He agreed and handed me the training manual on the U-21. "Start reading this tonight, and I will see you in the morning at 0830. We'll get two hours in, and then you will have the rest of the day for XO duties."

The next morning at 0830, I walked out onto the flight line and found Davey standing by a U-21. He said, "Okay, let's start."

Once you learn to fly, transitioning from one aircraft to another is a matter of learning the characteristics of the new aircraft. It's similar to learning to drive a car with a stick shift and learning to drive one with an automatic transmission. The principles of driving, such as steering, braking, parking, backing up, and signaling, are all the same. It's the car that's different.

The first step in transitioning to a different aircraft is learning the procedures for preflight, takeoff, and landing, using the checklist. Learning those procedures is a repetitive process. Davey handed me the checklist, and we started around the U-21 with me calling out each check and Davey performing the check as he explained it to me. After that, we climbed into the aircraft and entered the cockpit.

The cockpit of the U-21 is similar to the Mohawk's except larger. The pilot and copilot fly it using a yoke instead of a stick. The yoke provides the same control inputs the stick does. The pilot turns it left or right to bank the aircraft. He pulls it back to climb and pushes it forward to descend.

In my case, the instruments were mostly the same, except the engine gauges in the U-21 were tape presentations instead of dials. Flight instruments were the same, except the U-21 had weather radar. The likeness in everything simplified the transitioning process.

Engine start procedures were the same as in the Mohawk. EGT readings and prop rpm were different, but the start procedures were the same. After we had the engines started, Davey called for taxi, and we taxied to the run-up apron.

Once we'd completed the engine run-up and set the U-21 for takeoff, Davey called for takeoff. The tower cleared us to the active for takeoff. I taxied the aircraft onto the active and halted. Davey explained the takeoff roll and at what speed to rotate. I applied power, and we rolled down the runway.

I flew eighteen hours in the U-21 over the following week. I spent most of the time doing touch-and-gos, emergency procedures, and instrument training. By the eighteenth hour, I was proficient in the U-21. We started flying night touch-and-gos and cross-county. Davey was ready to sign me off as qualified, but the regulation required twenty-five hours of transition, so we kept flying to get those hours.

One of the major differences between the Mohawk and the U-21 was single-engine performance. In a single-engine arrangement, the U-21 could not make a standard rate turn into the running engine with the gear down. So for example, if you were in a right downwind and the left engine quit running with the gear down, you had to raise the gear to turn a right base and then to final. If you didn't raise the gear, the best bank you got was about ten degrees. You need a thirty-degree bank to turn base and level out and then a thirty-degree bank or more to turn to final. You can see that a ten-degree bank would cause you to fly past final, still headed away from the runway.

Throughout the whole transition, I did not make a mistake until about my twentieth hour. Because I responded correctly each time Davey gave me an emergency, he was always trying to catch me in an error. We were doing touch-and-gos, and I was on a right downwind, when Davey killed the left engine. I immediately cleaned the aircraft up for single-engine flight, except for one item: my landing gear was down, and I forgot to raise it. Davey didn't say anything as I continued the approach.

I called the tower and reported we were turning base. As soon as I banked the aircraft to the right, I realized I had left the gear down and was not going to make final. Davey had finally caught me. I heard him say, "Aha. Did you forget something?"

I was always proud of my ability to remain calm and think of a solution when events were going wrong. I didn't want Davey to have the last laugh.

I knew I should raise my gear, break off the approach, make a go-around, and start over, but I had a solution. I called the tower and asked to fly past final and do a 270-degree left turn to final. That caught Davey by surprise. He sat up and asked, "What the hell are you doing, Neal?"

"Davey," I said, "I'm pretending my landing gear stuck down. I'm going to land the aircraft. I may not be able to turn right, but I can turn left. After all, the objective is to land the aircraft safely."

The tower cleared me to fly past final but wanted to know if I was having any problems. I told them no, we were just practicing a different approach.

Davey shook his head and said, "You're cheating, Neal; that is not the proper procedure."

I said, "No, I am not cheating, Davey. This is not the preferred procedure. But there's always more than one way to skin a cat. I am going to land this aircraft safely."

"Neal, suppose your right engines fails," he said.

"Davey," I replied, "if I raised the gear and did a go-around, my right engine could fail. This way, I will fly less time before I land, which means less time for the engine to fail."

By then, I was turning a 270-degree turn to the left. I rolled out on final and made a perfect single-engine landing. I looked at Davey and laughed. "Go ahead and pink-slip me, but I got us down safely without any damage to the aircraft."

He shook his head and laughed. "I'm not going to pink-slip you, but you owe me a beer for that landing." From then on, every time Davey saw me, he would shake his head and mutter, "I can't believe you did that."

Pilots sitting around the club held many discussions about my unorthodox landing. Some of the pilots jokingly insisted that since I was XO, I could land any damn way I wanted to. Others gave me credit for quick thinking and the idea that the landing gear could stick down. Davey said all I needed before he could sign me off was an international flight.

When we completed our move from Yeouido, I volunteered to be the club officer. However, after our move, the Eighth Army officers' club took away our independent club status and made us an annex of the Eighth Army's club. That forced us to keep complete records and file weekly reports. My first action was to inventory all the club property and account for it in a property book. After years of independence and doing whatever the commander at the time wanted, club officers had ignored several regulations governing clubs. Now it was time to pay the piper. Any impropriety could negatively affect Major Franks, even though he had inherited the club as it was. My job was to clean it up and protect him from any culpable responsibility.

I was going to need help with this task. I had become friends with Captain Jim Macy. He was one of the Mohawk pilots. Like me, he often volunteered for tasks on the premise that he had to do a job for it to be done right. I guess we both had the same seemingly arrogant nature, which made us friends from the time we met. I asked him to act unofficially as assistant club officer and help me clean up the club. His response was "Are you asking me or telling me? Because if you are telling me, then I'm not going to volunteer to help."

My response to his reaction was "I'm asking you, but it doesn't matter, because if you say no, then I'm going to order you to, and you will end up doing it anyway."

Anyone overhearing our conversation would have thought we were fixing to fight, but it was just the way we jousted with each other. His next response was "Well, okay, if you feel that way about it, I volunteer."

With George, the bartender, we went to work inventorying the club equipment and reviewing all the financial records. We found extra equipment that was not on the property books. That was easy to correct. We simply added it to the property books. The financial records were a little more difficult to correct.

Club officers had not kept a written account of most club funds. Army regulations direct strict accountability for any form of unit fund. The club had been a unit entity until the Eighth Army club made it an annex. Therefore, club officers should have kept exact records of all funds involved in its transactions. Sadly, previous club officers had been sloppy in keeping records. Since the commander was ultimately responsible, Jim and I had to figure out a way to correct the books and absolve Major Franks of any dereliction of duty.

It took Jim and me awhile, but we finally found a way to balance the books to the point where the Eighth Army club wouldn't question their accuracy. Regulations allowed contributions to other unit slush funds and some types of charitable activities. It also allowed the club to throw parties for its members. We used those activities to account for around $2,000 not reflected on the receipts and records. When the Eighth Army club officer audited our hand receipt and financial records, he looked at me with an expression that said, "Nice snow job." He accepted our club as an annex but made it clear that he expected strict accountability in the future.

When Jim and I inventoried the club's conex container, we found a new gas kitchen stove still in the box it came in. There was no record of it, and all the old-timers we asked knew nothing about it. We held that since we'd found it in the club's conex container, it belonged to club. In the seventies, most of the Korean people still used charcoal stoves for cooking. That was one of the prime causes of the heavy odor of charcoal that permeated the Seoul smog. Koreans considered people who owned a gas or electric stove fortunate and upper class. Jim suggested we give it to George as an anniversary present and a token of our appreciation for his long service to the army.

I thought that was a great idea. George had been working for the military as a bartender since the Korean War. He often spoke in admiration of the gas stove that was in the club. He used it to prepare short orders during lunch and dinner. He would say that one day he was going to get one for his wife. I told Major Franks about the mystery stove and what I wanted to do with it. He also thought it was a great idea. Fate intervened then, because much to our surprise, George invited Jim and me to his anniversary party. That was an honor because George had never invited an American to his home. Jim and I accepted and made plans to deliver the stove.

I scheduled a two-and-a-half-ton truck to take us to George's apartment. I asked the motor sergeant to use two of the company's KATUSAs (Korean soldiers attached to the US Army) to drive the truck. The company had more than thirty attached. They spoke English and Korean and could find George's apartment in downtown Seoul from the address he gave us.

The day of his party, we loaded the stove on the truck and left for George's apartment. It was a good idea to have the KATUSAs with us. Even though they spoke Korean, we still had trouble finding George's apartment and got there a little late. Loading the stove on the truck had been tough because of its weight. Unloading it and dragging it up three flights of stairs took all the strength that two KATUSAs, Jim, and I could muster. Finally, we had it outside George's door.

Jim knocked on the door, and George's wife answered it. She saw us, smiled, and immediately called George. We pushed the stove in front of the door, and when George appeared, we said, "Happy anniversary, George."

The greeting smile on George's face turned to one of surprise when he saw the stove. For a minute, he looked at the stove, and then he called his wife. She came to the door, and George spoke to her in Korean. She seemed confused at first but then extended her hand in respect, and although she spoke in Korean, it was clear she was saying thank you. Then, as if overcome with joy, she broke Korean tradition and hugged Jim and me. George said to come in and ushered us into his living room. Jim said, "George, let us help you move the stove in first."

He said, "No, no, my friends will move the stove. You sit and have a drink." He led us to some cushions surrounding a table with food and glasses sitting on it. There were several Koreans sitting on cushions around another table. George spoke to them and obviously was introducing us, because they got up and began to shake our hands. After we shook hands, George spoke again, and they all went to the door.

George's wife was still standing at the door. When the other men saw the stove, a big conversation started. The men would look at Jim and me, smile, and give us a thumbs-up. Then they started to move it. That was when George's wife took charge. I had no idea what she was saying, but from the tone, I knew she was telling them to be careful and not damage her stove. They were strong men, because the six of them picked the stove up and took it into another room. George said it was the kitchen. I could hear them tearing the box away from the stove, and then they returned to the pillows around their table.

"George," I asked, "do you have a gas hookup here?" He said no, but he would have one within a week.

Jake said, "George, let's all move so we sit together," gesturing with his hands to move the tables and pillows together. That pleased George and his friends. We moved together and had one hell of an anniversary party. At first, George's wife sat separately from us, but Jim told George that it was her anniversary too, and she should join us.

She was a little bashful at first, but after a while, with a couple of shots of Jack Daniels, she loosened up. I'm sure we broke all kinds of Korean rules and traditions, but soon we were talking to her with George translating. She was a delight. They had married forty years ago and were obviously very much in love. It wasn't long before she had us all laughing as she told stories about George. To his credit, he translated them as she spoke. We found out that before they married, George used to take her out on dates, but after they married, they had no more dates. We kidded George about that. Finally, we got him to say that he would take her out dancing.

Because of the curfew, the party broke up at 2330 so everybody could get home safely.

The next day, George again thanked Jim and me. He was so moved by what we had done that he had tears in his eyes. He said the gas company was going to hook him up on Friday. All of his wife's friends were coming by to see her new stove. He was going to take Friday off so he could show her how to use it. We cautioned him to be careful because gas was dangerous. He said not to worry; he had been using gas stoves in the club for years, and his wife had been reading a book on gas cooking. Besides, it wasn't half as dangerous as the charcoal cooking and heating used by most Koreans. He was right about that, because we would hear daily about families dying of carbon monoxide poisoning because of charcoal stoves malfunctioning.

Seeing George and his wife together made me eager to see Claudia and my kids. It was the middle of May, and the days passed slowly. The letters from Claudia were short and repetitive, mostly about Michele and Ron and how good it would be to see me again. I sensed from her words that she was not as impatient to see me as I was to see her. She once suggested that instead of coming to Germany, I should meet her for a week, as I'd done when I was in Vietnam. I didn't want to do that. I wouldn't see the kids, and besides, I wanted to spend more than a week with her. I guess in her defense, she had developed a routine, and I would interrupt that routine. However, it hurt me that a week was all the time she wanted to spend with me. As with all the times before, we would have to readjust to each other.

The orderly room shared the building with flight operations. The building was L shaped, with flight operations on the long leg and the orderly room on the short leg. My desk sat near the entryway that separated the two areas. Major Franks's office was at the other end. Between were Captain Rich's desk, the first sergeant's desk, the admin sergeant's desk, and the three clerk typists' desks. From my desk, I could oversee the activity in flight operations and the orderly room.

One evening around 2000, I was in my office, still working. I was there mainly because Major Franks was flying the commanding general and party on an inspection trip to the southern tip of Korea. Our policy was to have an officer in the command chain present whenever the commanding general was flying and would be returning to K-16. The operations officer was also working, because he was responsible for ensuring that the helicopter was ready to take the commanding general to the command helipad at Eighth Army headquarters when he returned.

I was conducting a review of the company TOE to identify equipment that we no longer needed. Suddenly, I heard Major Franks call flight operations on the FM radio. He told the operations officer that they were returning to K-16 and would land in about fifteen minutes. The commanding general had canceled the rest of his flight. Since it was 2000 and the general's schedule had him returning at 2130, his helicopter was not running and waiting for him. The operations officer had to find the pilots and crew chief and get it ready.

Before he had found the pilots and the crew chief, I could hear a U-21 in the landing pattern. The operations officer stuck his head into the orderly room and told me he was going to start the preflight on the helicopter. He wanted to know if I would greet the commanding general and party and have them wait in the flight operations area until the helicopter was ready. I, of course, said yes.

Major Franks taxied up to the hot spot and let the CG and party off. I greeted them and asked them to wait in the flight operations area until their helicopter was on the hot spot. The CG, to his credit, understood that canceling the flight had caught everybody by surprise and that it would take some time to react and reschedule events.

The CG and his party of five—two two-star generals and three one-star generals—followed me into flight operations. I asked if anybody wanted coffee. No one did, so I walked into the orderly room to my desk, and to my surprise, they followed me. Obviously, the CG was upset at something he'd found at an earlier stop. That was why he'd canceled the rest of the inspections. He also appeared angry with his staff of generals. I couldn't hear exactly what he was saying, but by the way he was pointing his finger at their chests, I got the feeling he was chewing ass. I assure you it's not a pretty scene when a four-star general is chewing out two- and one-star generals. It's even uglier when he chews out a captain.

He stopped talking for a moment and looked at me. "Captain Griffin, will you call the duty office and make sure the driver has the van at the helipad to pick us up?"

I stood and answered, "Yes, sir."

I dialed the Eighth Army duty officer, and when the phone rang, a specialist answered. I said, "Specialist, this is Captain Griffin at the Fifth Aviation Company. Is the duty officer there?"

He answered, "No, sir. He is performing security checks."

I said, "All right then, it's your responsibility. The CG will be at the helipad in roughly fifteen minutes. Send the duty driver and the van to pick him and his party up. Do you understand?"

He answered, "Yes, sir, I understand." I noticed the CG was watching me and listening to my conversation.

I could hear the helicopter hovering to the hot spot. I said, "All right, Specialist, I expect the van to be at the helipad in fifteen minutes."

He answered, "It will be there, sir."

I asked, "Once again, what is your name?"

When he answered that he was Specialist Brown, I repeated the name to him and wrote it down on my pad. When I did, the CG looked at the other generals and said, "See that? Dammit, that's what I mean. Captain Griffin knows how to fix responsibility for an action."

I think after that, he might have said that was something about responsibility they had forgotten, but I wasn't sure. The CG had heard the helicopter on the hot spot and turned and walked out of the orderly room. The generals followed him. One or two glared at me as if I had caused them problems. I never found out what the issue was about. I'm just glad the CG was happy with what I did.

It's amazing how slowly time will pass when you want it to speed by. I had ten days before my midtour leave started. I had finished my TOE review. I managed to identify some equipment that we no longer needed.

I wanted something else to do, when Captain Timmy, the OH-58 SIP, said, "Neal, you're rotary-wing rated. You want me to check you out in the OH-58? It'll only take ten hours."

I immediately said yes, and we started my transition into the OH-58. The OH-58 was a four-seat observation helicopter. The company used it to fly low-ranking officers and Korean generals to various sites. It was easy to fly, and the neat feature about it was the inertia the blade kept during an autorotation. It had so much inertia that in an autorotation, if you didn't like where you landed, you could pull pitch and move it to another spot. I spent my ten hours doing approaches, landings, and takeoffs. Of course, as always, Captain Timmy gave me an emergency on every flight. After ten hours, he signed me off as qualified in the OH-58.

May 31 finally arrived. My thirty-day midtour leave started tomorrow, and I was excited about seeing Claudia and the kids. It had been a long six months. I spent the morning working on correspondence and officer efficiency reports that would come due during my absence. While I was on leave, I didn't want unfinished work on my mind.

Around eleven o'clock, the motor sergeant called the orderly room. The first sergeant talked to him for a while and then came into my office.

"What's up, First Sergeant?"

"Hey, sir, sorry to bother you, but one of our soldiers in the motor pool is demanding that the motor sergeant dispatch him a truck. Something about his girlfriend drowning, and he needs to buy some ice to pack her body in before she rots. He seems highly upset."

The CO was down at the BOQ, working on the swimming pool with all the other officers not out flying missions. The CO had left me in charge to deal with official business. "Okay, First Sergeant, let's go down to the motor pool to see what the hell is wrong."

It took us about five minutes to get to the motor pool. A small crowd of off-duty soldiers had gathered around the motor sergeant and a specialist E-4, one of our aircraft mechanics. When we got there, the motor sergeant was telling the obviously upset soldier that he could not dispatch him a truck. It seemed the rest of the soldiers were taking sides with the specialist and asking why not.

The first sergeant yelled, "At ease!"

Everybody turned and saluted. Returning their salute, I said, "Everybody remain quiet until I ask you to speak. Okay, Specialist, why do you want a truck?"

In a frustrated and distraught tone, he said, "Captain Griffin, I had the day off, so I went swimming at the lake with my girlfriend. There were a few GIs and several Koreans there. I was lying on a towel, about half asleep, when people started yelling for help. I couldn't see my girlfriend, so I jumped up, and the Koreans were yelling that she drowned. They were pointing at a woman floating in the water. I ran to the lake and swam out to her, and it was my girlfriend. I brought her to shore and tried to revive her. No Korean would help. I was yelling for them to call an ambulance or the police, but no one would move. Finally, one of the GIs managed to get the Korean police to come.

"The Korean police said she would have to remain there until her family came for her body. It seems the reason no Korean would help was because of some law or custom that makes the person helping liable for the drowned woman until her family claimed her. If the family did not claim her, then they were responsible for her final disposition." I'm not sure that was the law, but it was what my soldier understood.

Tears edged out of the soldier's eyes as he continued. "Sir, the police contacted her family, but they won't be able to get here until tomorrow morning. I've got to get her out of the hot sun, but the police won't let me move her. I want a truck to pick up some ice to pack her body in so it won't rot in the heat. That's all I want, sir. We were going to marry in August."

"Okay, Specialist, let me see your military driver's license."

He handed me his license. I checked it and saw that it was current. "Okay, Motor Sergeant, why can't we dispatch a truck to him?" I asked.

The motor sergeant looked as if he were grasping for an answer. "Well, sir, it's not official business, and army regulations state that military trucks are used only for official business. Our SOP also states no trucks for private use."

"Do we have any trucks available right now?"

"Well, sir, we have some three-quarter-ton trucks available," the motor sergeant answered.

"Can they be dispatched?"

"Yes, sir, I don't see why not."

"If I put Specialist Nolan on detail to pick up ice for the mess hall, does that make it official business?"

"Well, yes, sir," the motor sergeant answered.

"Specialist Nolan, I want you to take a truck, go to Chumi Wah, and buy some ice for the mess hall. After you deliver ice to the mess hall, you can use the truck to take some ice to the lake for your use. I want the truck back in the motor pool by 2000 tonight. Understood?"

"Yes, sir," Specialist Nolan answered.

I turned to the first sergeant. "Get a hold of the mess sergeant, and tell him that he wants some ice and that Specialist Nolan will bring some to the mess hall in an hour or two. Also, tell the supply sergeant to issue Specialist Nolan some blankets to cover his fiancée."

Turning to Specialist Nolan, I said, "I'm going to put you on pass until tomorrow evening so you can take care of your fiancée. The first sergeant will take care of that. I want you back on duty by tomorrow evening. That understood?"

"Yes, sir. Thank you, Captain Griffin."

We saluted, and I headed back to the orderly room. I called the BOQ, got a hold of Major Franks, and filled him in on the situation with Specialist Nolan.

Around two o'clock, I finished all my work. On the way out, I stopped by Captain Rich's office. "Rich, is my leave ready?"

He handed me my leave papers. "Okay, Neal, here's what I did. I prepared courier orders and added them to your leave papers. Courier orders may help you get a hop faster than you normally would. Go ahead and sign out, and I will show on the personnel status report that you signed out in the morning. Get a ride to Kimpo tonight, and get a jump on catching a hop."

"Thanks, Rich. I'll see you in a month." See what I mean about his being indispensable?

I felt great walking back to the BOQ. The impending freedom of a month with my wife and kids had me walking on air. When I got to the BOQ, I paused and watched Major Franks and about twenty officers digging the hole that was to be our swimming pool. It was hot and humid, and they were dirty from their labor.

Captain Larson yelled at me, "Don't stand there watching! Grab a shovel, and start digging."

They knew I was going on my midtour leave in the morning. I expected to take some harassment about cutting out when the hard work started—which I did, but it didn't bother me at all. I was going on leave tomorrow. Besides, I had done all the preliminary work. Major Franks's method of giving orders had been simple: "Neal, I want to build a swimming pool in the space between the wings of the BOQ. Can you take care of that for me?"

Talk about a mission order. Major Franks was a master at it. I didn't feel bad about leaving now, because I'd done all the planning. I'd found and worked a deal for all material needed. My biggest problem had been finding lumber for forms, since we were going to pour the pool. I'd finally found the remains of a bowling alley in the depot at Inchon. The depot commander had said I could have the alleys if I picked them up. Major Franks thought the alleys would make excellent form material, so I'd arranged transport to haul them. Major Franks had picked the start day, which just happened to be the day before my leave, which he had already approved.

I yelled back at them, "I expect you guys to have this pool finished before I get back!"

I entered my BOQ, turned on my stereo, started my reel-to-reel tape of Charlie Pride's greatest hits, and got out my handbag. Since most of my clothes were in Germany with Claudia, I only planned on taking underwear, a shaving kit, and presents for Claudia and the kids. I would travel in my dress greens since it was necessary when traveling by military space available, commonly called space A.

By the time I finished packing, shining my brass and shoes, and putting my uniform together, it was 1630. The officers who'd been working on the pool were gathering in the officers' club. I was ready to go, so I decided to join them. I knew I would get all kinds of good-natured harassment. I walked in to the sound of someone shouting, "Hey, it's the XO! I hope you're not too tired from working on the pool. Your wife won't be happy with that."

I answered jokingly as I walked to the bar, "You can be damn glad I am leaving, because if I wasn't, your ass would still be out there working." That quieted them down. I had a reputation for not stopping until finishing a task. They knew that under my charge, we would work until it got so dark that you couldn't see. Major Franks laughed at my comments. Everyone knew that if I hadn't been going on leave, I would have been in charge.

I grabbed a stool at the bar and gave George my order for a beer and a bowl of vegetable soup. George brought my beer while the soup was warming. With a big smile on his face, he said, "You going to see Mama-San tomorrow. How long does it take to get to Germany?"

"I don't know exactly, George, since I am going space A. If I get lucky and don't have any big delays, it should take about two days," I answered.

Jim and Greg walked into the club. They had been flying all day. As they pulled up stools next to me, Jim yelled at George, who was bringing my soup, "Two martinis, George!" He looked at Greg and then at me with a half smile on his face. "I bet I know what you are going to be doing tomorrow night or the day after."

George set my soup down. Jim looked at George with the same smile and said, "I hope he gets enough pussy so when he gets back, he won't be such a hard-ass."

George laughed at Jim's comment as he mixed the martinis. Greg spoke up. "I don't think there's enough pussy for that."

George set a martini in front of Jim and one in front of Greg. Jim grabbed the one in front of Greg. "Order your own; these two are for me."

"Damn, Jim, I thought you ordered for me too. George, two martinis for me." Greg stressed the word *me*.

George shook his head at Jim and Greg's antics.

"Are you going to try to get to Germany on space A?" Greg asked.

"I hope to get a hop out of Kimpo to Yokota AFB in Japan. From there, I'll take the first available flight to the States. From wherever that takes me, I will try to get to McGuire AFB, Fort Dix, and check flights there. If it looks bad there, I'll go down to Dover AFB and try my luck there. If it starts to take too much time, then I will buy a ticket for a commercial flight," I answered.

George brought Greg's martinis and started talking to Jim. Turning to them, I asked, "You two have any last-minute questions about running the club while I am gone?" I had put Jim on orders as the assistant club officer so he could act on my behalf while I was on leave.

George shook his head, and Jim answered, "Don't worry. When you get back, George and I will have this club squared away, and we will be in Hawaii, enjoying life."

Major Franks walked up. "You set to go, Neal?"

"Yes, sir, as soon as I finish this soup. Izzy is going to fly me to Kimpo. He's returning from his mission in about thirty minutes and will drop me off before shutting down."

"Good. Have a great time, and I'll see you when you get back," he said as he headed out the door.

More officers were drifting into the club after finishing their flights. "Okay, guys, I've got to get going," I said. Walking out the door, I yelled over the din, "You'd better finish that pool before I get back!" I stepped out the door before anybody could reply.

I grabbed my bags and walked up to the flight line. I stuck my head into flight operations and asked the status of Izzy. "He's inbound and should be here in about five minutes."

"Thanks, guys," I said, and I headed for the hot spot. I could hear the inbound chopper as I walked to the hot spot. I braced myself against the rotor wash as Lieutenant Rogers put the chopper on the hot spot. The crew chief already had the door open, and I jumped in. As I fastened my seat belt, Lieutenant Rogers pulled pitch, and we were on our way to the military terminal at Kimpo, about a ten-minute flight. I put a headset on. "Thanks, guys. I owe you one for this."

Izzy turned and grinned. "It's going to cost you a case of beer, so save some money." He turned back and switched to VHF radio to contact Kimpo tower. As aircraft commander, Izzy handled communications while Lieutenant Rogers piloted.

Lieutenant Rogers set the Huey down on the hot spot by the military terminal. He turned as I was taking my headset off. "Hey, sir, have a good leave."

I entered the military passenger terminal, and it pleased me to see only three soldiers waiting for a hop to Yokota AFB. As I signed in at the operations desk, the sergeant on duty said, "You are in luck, sir; there's a flight headed for Yokota in an hour with seats available."

Taking a seat to wait on the flight, I thought, *This is a good sign.* After about thirty minutes, the operations sergeant announced that everybody waiting for a flight to Yokota should bring a copy of orders and ID to the desk. We were loading.

The aircraft was a C-130 Hercules loaded with cargo. It had six troop seats available. It would be uncomfortable, but beggars can't be choosers. We took off at 2215 and landed at Yokota two and a half hours later. I was elated. I was on my way, and everything was going well.

When I entered the passenger terminal at Yokota, my elation bubble popped. There were more than three hundred soldiers lounging around the huge terminal. As I checked in at the operations desk to add my name to the space-A list, my fears came true. I was number 354 on the list, and the operations sergeant said that tomorrow afternoon was the earliest he expected to have available seats. I sat down to think out a strategy. I hadn't expected this logjam at Yokota. If I could get past here, I would have more airfields and more flights to choose from. I asked the sergeant sitting next to me how long he had been waiting. He had been there for three days and was now number four on the list. He said that when he'd gotten there, there had been more than seven hundred people waiting for a hop. I decided I would wait one day, and if nothing became available, I would take a commercial flight to Fort Lewis, Washington.

The terminal had a large cafeteria, and I could smell bacon and eggs cooking. I dropped my bags off at a table and ordered a large breakfast and coffee. After breakfast, I found a cushioned seat and tried to sleep. Around 0700, I heard the loudspeaker announce, "Any officer with a top-secret clearance and courier orders, please come to the operations desk." I jumped up and hurried to the desk.

"I have a top-secret clearance and courier orders," I told the operations sergeant.

"Okay, Captain Griffin, may I see your orders and ID card?" the operations sergeant replied.

He looked at my orders and ID card and said, "We need an officer to deliver a classified briefcase to Hickam AFB in Hawaii. The C-141 is en route to March AFB in California but will stop long enough to transfer the briefcase to an officer at Hickam. I can put you on it if it suits your plans."

There was no hesitation on my part: "I'll take it." Two hours later, I was on my way to March AFB via Hawaii with a briefcase handcuffed to my left arm and a .45 automatic on my hip. If Rich had been there, I would have hugged him.

The C-141 was the military version of a 707 on a flight out of Vietnam. It was half loaded with cargo, mostly jeeps and eight military coffins. The seats were military canvas and uncomfortable. After we were airborne and could move about, I walked to each coffin and touched it. It was the only way I had to show respect for my fallen comrades.

We landed at Hickam around 1400. The pilots taxied to a remote part of the taxiway, where a jeep was waiting. After they stopped, they lowered the rear ramp, and a W-4 with Intelligence Corps brass came aboard and presented his orders and ID to me. I had him sign the transfer papers for the briefcase and the .45 automatic. With a "Thank you, sir," he took the briefcase and weapon and gave me a receipt, and then he was gone. I wanted ask him what was in the briefcase, but I didn't ask. I didn't have the need to know, and he wouldn't have told me anyhow.

Fifteen minutes later, we were at thirty-six thousand feet, headed to March AFB. I stretched out on the seats and fastened a seat belt around me so I would be secure if we hit turbulence. I had never forgotten the flight to Puerto Rico on a C-134 in 1961, when we had run into unexpected turbulence, and without warning, the aircraft had dropped a hundred feet, throwing everyone not wearing a seat belt to the ceiling of the aircraft. One soldier had been sleeping, and when he'd come down, he'd broken his back.

I drifted off to sleep, thinking about how to spend three weeks with my family. Seven hours later, a crew member shook me. "Sir, we are starting our approach to March AFB." Twenty minutes later, we were on the ground. I caught a ride with the crew to base operations.

March AFB didn't have a large personnel terminal. It was a tactical base and not the usual destination for flights that could also carry passengers. I checked in with the operations sergeant and found out there were no flights scheduled soon for McGuire AFB. The only flight with seats available was a scheduled medevac flight leaving for Elmendorf AFB, Alaska, in three hours. He recommended going to Elmendorf because more flights left there for the East Coast than from March AFB.

"Okay," I said, "I'll take the medevac flight to Elmendorf."

Seven hours later, I was in the Elmendorf terminal. I was in luck because the medevac flight I'd arrived on was continuing to McGuire after refueling. I grabbed some coffee and a sandwich while I awaited the boarding call. I calculated that I had been traveling for about thirty-one hours. I was beginning to feel the strain of napping instead of getting a good night's sleep, but I was on schedule, and if all went well at McGuire, I would be with Claudia and the kids within twenty-four hours.

The early morning descent into McGuire AFB presented an enchanting view of the East Coast. It was still dark enough for the lights of the cities to glitter like clusters of diamonds. Off in the east, the sun was pushing an orange sky out of the way as it eased up over the Atlantic Ocean.

Luck was staying with me. Although the flights to Germany for the next three days were booked, there was an admin flight to Dover AFB at 1000. The operations sergeant recommended going there because they had C-5As leaving for Germany several times a day. I had him put me on the manifest for the admin flight. With about two hours to kill, I went to the snack bar and ordered breakfast. I drank several cups of coffee while reading my first newspaper in three days.

The news was still bad. The war in Vietnam was dragging on, and casualties were high. The American people were demonstrating against the war, and the articles all blamed the United States. When I felt a touch of depression from what I was reading, I crumpled the paper up and threw it in the trash. I was going home to the woman I loved and my precious children, and I didn't want anything to depress me.

The flight to Dover took less than an hour. A bus picked us up at the airplane and took us to the flight operations and passenger terminal. I could get on a flight leaving for Frankfurt, Germany, at 0200. At last, I was nearing the end of my journey. I was tired, and I needed a shower badly. When I asked the operations sergeant if there were bachelor officer quarters nearby, he cordially answered, "No, but I'll have my duty driver take you to the BOQ and pick you up at 0130." I thanked him profusely.

It was a five-minute drive to the BOQ. Luckily, they had rooms available. The air force BOQs are much better than the army BOQs. They are large, with all the conveniences, and almost plush. They reflect the difference between a force that has a temporary-camp philosophy and one with a permanent-base policy.

I lingered in the shower for more than twenty minutes, letting the stream of hot water pound at my body until I felt my tense muscles relaxing. I washed my dirty underwear in the sink and hung it over the heater vent to dry. I was hungry, but the soft bed was too inviting, so I called the desk and asked for a 0100 wake-up call. I was asleep seconds after my head hit the pillow.

Ten hours later, I heard the phone ringing. Waking from a sound sleep left me confused and groggy at first. Then my mind finally realized that I wasn't in Korea, and I grabbed the phone. "One o'clock, sir," the voice on the other end of the phone said.

"Thanks," I answered.

Shaved, dressed, and feeling refreshed, I waited in the entrance for the duty driver to pick me up. I didn't want to miss this flight for any reason. The duty driver arrived at 0130, and five minutes later, I was in the terminal.

The rest of the passengers were arriving, mostly wives with children, going to Germany to join their husbands stationed there. The C-5A had a passenger deck that could hold up to thirty-five passengers, plus a full load of cargo in the bottom deck. The operations NCO announced that box lunches were available for $1.25. I picked up one. I knew that in a couple of hours, I would be hungry.

At ten minutes to 0200, we loaded onto two buses that took us to the flight line and parked beside the C-5A. An NCO started reading names off the manifest, and we started boarding the aircraft. We walked up the cargo ramp behind the aircraft and continued to stairs on the left side of the aircraft. The stairs led to the top deck and the passenger seats. After all the passengers were aboard and seated, there were still a few empty seats, so I guessed there were about thirty passengers in all.

The assistant crew chief seated everybody and gave the safety briefing. When he finished, most of the passengers were ready to sleep. The pilot had started the big engines, and soon we were taxiing for takeoff.

I always say a prayer while taxiing for takeoff; even today I say a prayer at the start of any trip. I ask God to guide us safely to our destination. In my case, he has always answered that prayer.

Turning onto the active runway, the pilot applied power. The big jet lunged forward, sped down the runway, and lifted smoothly into the calm night air. During the climb to altitude, air traffic control turned the pilot to his airway, and we headed east toward Europe and Germany. Once we reached altitude, the Fasten Seat Belt sign blinked off, and I settled into my seat for the six-hour flight to the Frankfurt's Rhein-Main Airport.

It had been almost ten hours since I had eaten, so I opened my box lunch. The ham-and-cheese sandwich, apple, and oatmeal cookies were delicious. The assistant crew chief provided sodas and coffee to go with the sandwiches. Although I had just slept for more than nine hours, I had no trouble drifting off to sleep after I finished my box lunch.

The sound of one of the big jet engines shutting down woke me from a deep sleep. Because I was a pilot, my mind stayed attuned to the sound of the engines even in sleep. The sound of one changing was enough to get my attention quickly, even in deep sleep. I sat up and looked around. All the other passengers were still sleeping.

I looked to the rear of the aircraft, and I could see the crew chief and assistant crew chief shining a light out the window of the side door. The Fasten Seat Belt sign was still off, so I got up and walked down the stairs to the side door. The crew chief was talking on the intercom, so I asked the assistant crew chief why the engine quit. He said the number-three engine's oil pressure light had signaled that the engine was losing pressure. They had visually checked it with the light and could see oil streaming out of the engine. The pilot had shut it down to prevent damage to the engine and a possible fire. My first thought was *Shit, I am not going to get to Germany.* I asked the assistant crew chief, "Are we going to turn around?"

"No," he answered, "C-5As fly just as well on three engines as they do on four. Besides that, we're past the halfway mark. It's shorter to keep going than to turn back."

"Thanks," I said, happy that we were still going to Germany despite the engine problem. Back in my seat, I was thinking of Claudia as I drifted off to sleep once more. Outside, the sky was showing the effects of a rising sun.

The flight was smooth in the morning air. The sound of passengers moving around woke me. Mothers were caring for their children, and a line for the plane's two toilets had formed. I unbuckled, got a cup of hot coffee from the big coffee urn, and took it back to my seat. Drinking it slowly, I pictured how it would be to see Claudia and the kids. I had many missed hours to make up. I loved Claudia so much. Of course, I loved Michele and

Ron. They were my blood, and my love for them was eternal and without reservation, but it was my beautiful wife who filled the holes in my soul and made me complete.

An hour and a half later, we were taxiing to the military area of the Frankfurt airport. As we left the aircraft, I could see a group of maintenance people and pilots looking at the bad engine. It reminded me of the night I'd landed with a broken engine, and we'd gathered around to look at it. I got through German customs and caught the subway to the German civilian side of the airport. For the rest of the way, I would have to pay for transport since there were no air force bases around Munich and, thus, no space-available flights.

At the Lufthansa window, I learned that the earliest flight going to Munich was at 1700, nine hours from now. That was a blow. I knew I would go crazy sitting around for nine hours when I was so close. Fortunately, the German train station was minutes away, so I decided to check the train schedules. I was in luck. There was a train leaving for Munich at 1000, an hour from now. It would arrive in Munich at 1545. Without hesitation, I bought a ticket.

In Germany, trains leave and arrive on schedule. I didn't want to miss this train, so I went to the departure track. The train was loading, so I boarded and found a seat in an empty compartment. I had forgotten how hard the wooden seats were, but I decided I could stand on my head for five hours as long as I was on the way to Claudia and the kids.

Right on schedule, we pulled into the crowded Munich main station at 1545. After grabbing my bag, I headed for the exit. The spring of 1959 was the last time I had been in the Munich main station. The Germans had still been repairing much of the damage from World War II. There had not been much in the station in those days except a little stand that sold ice cream, brötchen and wurst, and the best goulash soup you could buy. I always used to stop there for goulash soup before catching the streetcar to the casern. Passing through the main lobby, I could see that the stand was gone. A fancy-looking café replaced it.

Outside, the taxi stand was in the same location. The driver put my bag in the trunk, and I got in the cab. When I told him the address, he didn't know its location. I didn't speak enough German to explain where I thought it was, so in broken English, we discussed it. Finally, I mentioned

McGraw Casern, which was next to the housing area Claudia was in. He knew where that was, so off we drove.

As I watched the buildings and sights of Munich pass by, I was overcome with a strange feeling: the sense that my life was not in order. On the one hand, I felt thrilled and excited to see my wife and kids again, but on the other hand, I had a feeling of dread. Claudia's and my relationship was not the smoothest. Often, our treatment of each other made me sure that although we loved each other, we didn't like each other. I wanted more than anything to change that feeling.

As the cab pulled into the entrance to the US Army Perlacher housing area, the driver asked me for the building number, interrupting my thoughts. After I gave him the number, he turned down a street, and the building came into view.

"That's it," I said, pointing to the middle building in a row of six buildings. He pulled up, and I got out as he opened the trunk and got my small bag. As I paid him, I could hear the children yelling, "Daddy! Daddy!"

Looking up to the second story, I could see Claudia and Omi (Claudia's Mom) standing on the outside balcony, waving at me. The door opened, and Michele and Ron came running out toward me. I picked them up and hugged them tightly. They were hugging me and saying, "Daddy, we're so glad you're home." Holding my hand, Ron walked with me as Michele led.

Inside the foyer, Ron said, "We live upstairs, Dad."

I heard the apartment door open on the second floor as we climbed the stairs. When we reached the top of the stairs, Claudia was standing there. We hugged each other tightly and kissed. I stood back and looked at her. She was beautiful. *Dear God, how I love her. If only I could get her to like me.*

Then I was inside, saying hello to several friends who had gathered to welcome me home. Claudia's mom; Traudl, her cousin; and Paula, an old friend, and her son were there. It had been three years since I had last seen them. Michele and Ron were standing around my bag, waiting for me to open it. They knew I would have a gift for them. I opened the bag and took out a toy truck set for Ron and a Barbie doll for Michele. I gave Claudia a beautiful .9-carat princess-cut diamond ring.

After the greetings were over, I excused myself to take a shower and put on some clean clothes. Standing in shower with the hot water streaming over me, I thought about how fast life could change. Two days ago, I had been in the drudgery of a lonely life in Korea. Now I was standing in a shower a world away with my family in the next room.

The welcome-home party felt as if it went on forever. Claudia had the typical German fare: coffee, apple cake, wurst and brötchen, beer, and wine. Everybody smoked but me, and it took awhile to get used to that. I struggled to talk and understand everything in German, which, after a while, became easier as I remembered more. Of course, my southern accent would never let me speak German well. Through it all, my only thought was about that night after the kids were in bed, when Claudia and I would be alone. Then the beautiful woman sitting beside me, whom I loved so much, would at last be in my arms again.

Finally, the guests left, and the kids were asleep. Claudia and I brushed our teeth and got ready for bed. Then I was holding her. I made love to her with the tender passion of man who had been apart from the one he loved. However, I could not help but sense that her response was mechanical. I had expected the same passion and tenderness we'd felt on our last night in Fort Lewis before I'd left for Korea. It seemed she was merely taking part because she was my wife. I knew I was a good lover and had always satisfied her. Even that night, her orgasm was real and strong. I couldn't put my finger on the problem, but I drifted off to sleep with an empty feeling in my heart.

My sleep was heavy in the comfortable bed. When I awoke, Claudia was already up and fixing the kids breakfast. I shaved and joined them. The kids were happy to see me and eager to tell me everything that had happened since I'd left for Korea. I spent the morning playing and talking with them. Claudia had waited for me to get home to go shopping at the commissary, so around noon, Omi came to watch the kids while we shopped.

We made small talk as we drove to the commissary. I couldn't believe I was having a problem thinking of something to say other than commenting on how much Michele and Ron had changed. Whatever I said, Claudia would respond with a simple "That's nice" or "Everything's okay." She seemed satisfied with little conversation. With some anger and arguing thrown in, that was about the way it went during the three weeks I was there.

I spent most of my days playing with Michele and Ron or taking them to the zoo or a movie. I enjoyed that but wanted to do it with Claudia. Although she went once in a while, most of time, she would visit some of her friends. With me there to babysit the kids, she had the opportunity to see her friends more often. That seemed reasonable, except I thought that Omi would gladly come anytime to watch her grandchildren. Claudia had had the last six months to see her friends. It would have been nice if she'd just wanted to spend some time with me. We were together, but our relations were not what I had imagined in Korea. However, her seeing her friends reduced the tension between us, so I didn't strongly object.

No matter how hard I tried, I could not find the right word, emotion, or action to bring back the closeness that I envisioned in a loving relationship. I wanted her to want to spend time with me. In my view, she was finding ways to spend as little time as possible with me.

I always believed that physical contact was the basic form of affection. I could not ever picture sex with someone I didn't love. In my mind, a husband and wife touched, hugged, kissed, caressed, and had sex as the basic expression of their love for each other. However, since my first night back, she never appeared in the mood, or she created a problem whenever she could to avoid sex. I knew her libido usually equaled or exceeded mine, and normal sex for us was three or four times a week. Her efforts to avoid sex hurt me. I felt something was wrong, but if I asked, all I got was "Don't be silly; there's nothing wrong."

By the fourth day, my frustration level was at the breaking point. I tried to be pleasant always and hid any disappointment at the way I felt she was treating me. She had a slew of reasons to spend time away from me, and if I got upset, she became angry, and we ended up fighting. Then she left me with the kids anyway. She would always promise to be back by nine o'clock. I would give up at eleven and go to bed.

She always got up early, and a couple of mornings after I got back, I went into the bathroom while she was still there and caught her taking a pill. My entry surprised her, and she tried to hide the container of birth control pills. I said, "Why are you are taking birth control pills, when I had a vasectomy over a year ago?"

Her answer was "I don't trust the vasectomy."

I kept my temper and said, "The doctor tested me, and I have no sperm in my semen." She looked at me in anger, and the rift between us widened. She turned and walked from the bathroom as I stood there devastated by the birth control pill revelation.

I stood there for a while, and for the first time, I accepted the fact that she might be unfaithful. I didn't want to think or believe that, so I had no choice other than to accept her answer. The pain in my heart hurt. I looked at the reflection of my face in the mirror and asked, "What do I do?" Then, because I wanted to believe her, I began to rationalize that perhaps she was telling me the truth. After I'd had the vasectomy and the sperm-count test, she had expressed some doubt about whether it was safe to have sex without protection. I had convinced her it was safe. If I loved her, I had to accept her answer. Or what? I could not answer the "Or what?" so I took a deep breath, washed my face, and shaved

Because of the birth control situation, I became more desperate as each day passed, and I saw our time running out. That, of course, only aggravated the problem. One day a week later, we were shopping at the post exchange and stopped at the snack bar for lunch. Claudia had a hot dog, and I had a bowl of chili. We ate mostly in silence, and then, with a disgusted look, she said, "I don't see how you can eat that terrible stuff."

I responded, "It's good." But her comment had pushed the wrong button and angered me. She could have asked if it was good or why I liked chili. Looking her in the eyes, I said, "Claudia, we may love each other, but I'm sure we don't like each other."

Of course, that angered her. We didn't speak for the rest of the day. I cursed myself for losing my composure. Claudia seemed happy being angry and not having to speak. The loving was easy. It was the living that was hard.

One day she asked me if I remembered Dale and Marcy Smith. Of course I remembered them. "Well," she said, "Marcy lives in the quarters across the street in front of us, and Dale is here on leave from Vietnam. Next Friday, they want us to get with some other friends at a nightclub. Is that okay?"

I said, "Yes, that's fine."

That night, we made love again. When it was over and she drifted off to sleep, I lay there with the same feeling I'd had the first night. I felt as if

I were caught in a giant vise that I wanted to escape from, but the harder I tried, the tighter the vise became. The next morning, she turned into a monster.

I recognized the problem immediately. Her period was starting. It usually started with PMS, with which I was familiar. Fortunately, because of the birth control pill, her period only lasted for four days. I knew how to act during her period: leave her alone. We got along well when I left her alone.

That Friday, Claudia directed me to the club in downtown Munich. It was a typical nightclub of that era: a bar with a large dance floor and a room full of tables. When we got there, the club was about half full, with a steady stream of people entering the door. We found Dale and Marcy sitting at a table with another couple.

Dale and I shook hands, happy to see each other again. A lot had happened since we'd graduated from flight school. I said hello to Marcy, and Claudia introduced me to the other couple. The woman's name was Lilly, and her friend was Fred. It appeared she was a good friend of Claudia's. We ordered drinks and engaged in small talk as we got to know one another. By the second drink, the conversation was entertaining and funny, especially Dale's. Although he said they had gotten to the club just before us, he looked plastered.

Soon the club filled with partygoers. The loud music was good and included all the top songs of the time. I danced with Claudia a couple of times, and then, being polite, I danced with Marcy and Lilly. The seats at the bar were all taken. During lulls in the conversation, I noticed Claudia kept looking toward the bar.

Claudia had a habit of flirting. I once asked her why, and she said it made her feel good when men looked at her. She assured me that she never took it seriously. I could never convince her how bad it made me feel. Since she had never done more than that, I began to accept it as a little game she liked to play. After several dances, a man walked up to the table and asked me if it was okay to ask Claudia to dance. His request showed the proper respect, and I said yes. He spoke broken but good English. They danced to a couple of songs, and as I occasionally watched them, it seemed by their mannerisms and the way they talked that they knew each other. I let it go because more than anything, I didn't want to appear jealous and spoil a fun night.

We had fun that night, and Claudia and I seemed close, as we'd been before I went to Korea. The man asked Claudia to dance several times after asking me if it was okay. He had a seat at the bar, and though I didn't let on, I noticed Claudia smiling at him several times. As the evening wore on, I noticed that Dale seemed uninterested in Marcy, and he was beginning to slur his words. I knew he had consumed twice as much as the rest of us, so I figured he was not going to last much longer, and I began to worry about him. Finally, he said he was going to the car. I got up and went with him. I had to grab him a couple of times to keep him from falling down. When we got to the car, he crawled into the backseat and passed out.

When I got back to our table, Claudia was dancing with the guy from the bar, and Marcy was dancing with a guy I had never seen. Lilly asked, "Is he okay?"

"Yeah, he's okay. He got into the backseat and passed out," I answered.

When Marcy got back to the table, Claudia was still dancing. She didn't say a word about Dale. She grabbed my hand and said, "Let's dance."

We danced to several songs. I would start back to the table after each song, but she would pull me back as the next song started. During the slow songs, I could feel her body against me, and it seemed she was holding me a little tighter than necessary. Finally, the band took a break, and we returned to the table. I thought, *That's the attention I would love from Claudia.*

It was 0100 when the band announced the last song, so Claudia and I danced. On the dance floor, she held me a little tighter than before and smiled and said, "It looks like Marcy has a thing for you."

"How so?" I asked.

"Well, the way she was hanging on to you," she replied.

"I think we have had too much to drink, and that's why she was hanging on to me," I answered. I wondered, *Is she a little jealous?*

After the dance, we said good night and left. Claudia glanced at the guy at the bar as we walked out the door. We made love that night with a passion that felt normal again, and I forgot about the suspicions I had felt earlier. That was the magic Claudia used on me.

Dale had invited us to come over Saturday evening so we could talk and catch up. Later, at home, Claudia told me she didn't want to go to just sit there and listen to Dale and me talk about our experiences. Plus, she wasn't that close with Marcy anymore. That felt good to hear, considering my earlier assessment of Marcy. She said Lilly had invited her to a coffee, and she would rather go there. I understood. I knew Dale's and my reminiscing could be boring for her. I said, "No problem," and she said she would be home around nine o'clock. She picked up Omi to stay with the kids.

Around six o'clock, I walked across the street to Dale's apartment and rang the doorbell. Marcy answered and ushered me in. Dale was sitting on the couch and rose to greet me.

Shaking my hand firmly, he said, "Hey, man, good to see you again. Sorry about the other night. You want some rum and Coke?"

I could tell he had already had a drink or two. I said, "Yes, that would be fine." Marcy brought me a rum and Coke.

We sat there talking, drinking rum and Cokes, and eating snacks for about three hours. He was in a transport company in Vietnam. He flew Otters, mostly flying supplies to units in the field. He had extended for six months and was home on a six-week leave. He had been home for four weeks already and would go back two days after I left. He updated me on some of our classmates, including where they were and who was doing what. Sadly, three had been killed in Vietnam. I told him about what I was doing in Korea. Marcy sat there the whole time, smiling and getting us drinks.

After about three hours, I was starting to feel the alcohol. Dale was wasted. He drank three drinks to my one. He got his guitar out and started playing and singing. He loved country music, especially Merle Haggard. He was strumming the guitar and trying to sing the words "I want to settle down, but they won't let me." He seemed oblivious to Marcy and me.

Marcy finally said, "Dale, I think you have had enough."

He responded, "No! I've got to piss. Fix me another drink." Then he got up and staggered to the bathroom in the master bedroom. Marcy got up and helped him. He looked at me and said, "Don't go, Neal. I'll be right back."

A few minutes later, Marcy returned. She had put on a bathrobe. I had to go to the bathroom too, so I got up and told Marcy, "I've got to go too."

She pointed and said, "Right through there." I went through the master bedroom to the bathroom. Dale was lying on the bed, passed out. After using the bathroom, I tried to wake him, but he wouldn't budge. I decided it was time for me to leave.

When I got back to the living room, Marcy was sitting on the couch. I said, "Yeah, it looks like Dale is out for the night, so I think I will be going. Thank you for the drinks and treats. Tell Dale I enjoyed seeing him again."

She stood up, smiled, and said, "You don't have to go, Neal. Stay with me." With that, she let her bathrobe open to reveal her nude body.

Her brazen conduct surprised me. I had always believed she was capable of this type of conduct, but I'd never thought she would try it on me. I have to admit she was a beauty and tempting, but she was also my friend's wife. I looked at her and said, "Marcy, I'm sorry. I love Claudia, and I would not do anything to betray her or Dale." I turned and walked to the door.

As I left the apartment, I heard Marcy say angrily, "You are a fool, Neal. You don't deserve Claudia."

I still ponder what she meant by those remarks. Did she mean Claudia didn't deserve me, or I didn't deserve Claudia? To me, her words had two different meanings.

Staggering back to my apartment, I had a mental conversation with myself. The impression I'd formed of her in flight school was correct. I was right. She was a slut. I was a good judge of people. I had proved it over and over again in my assessments of the soldiers and officers with whom I worked. Captain Rich always said I was the most perceptive man he had ever seen. It was too bad I couldn't get Claudia to recognize how much I loved her. Any other man would probably have accepted Marcy's invitation.

When I let myself into the apartment, Omi had put the kids to bed and was asleep in Michele's room. *God bless her.* She loved those kids so much. Claudia wasn't home. *Hell, what did I expect?* I was there, but I could just as well have been in Korea for all Claudia cared. Being drunk and lost like that is difficult because it brings out the pain so intensely. There's no way to ease it except to sleep, which only shifts it to another day.

I woke up the next morning with a slight hangover. Claudia was dressing. She started telling me she was sorry for getting home so late, but so-and-so was at Lilly's, and nobody left until eleven o'clock. "You can call her if you don't believe me," she said. Then she asked, "How was the visit with Dale?"

Getting up, I answered, "Great! We had a good time. Marcy was a perfect host. I left at nine o'clock."

I think she sensed a twinge of anger in my voice. She responded, "You're mad because I wasn't sitting here waiting for you when you got home. You don't expect me to sit around and wait for you, do you? Well, you are wrong, mister."

We hardly spoke to each other for a couple days. Then I read in the paper that Neil Diamond was in Munich, so I asked her if she wanted to go to his concert. She said yes, and we were friendly again. The concert was great, and we had a wonderful time. Three days later, it was time for me to return to Korea.

I dreaded the thought of leaving. I loved her and Michele and Ron. However, I had begun to believe that Claudia had given up on loving me. I thought if that was the case, then I was to blame. It could be my fault since I'd had no role model for being a good husband. If I were to blame, then it would take time to fix. I wouldn't see her again for six months, and being apart for those six months might destroy us.

My heart was breaking the morning I left to go back to Korea. While Claudia and I had had a few good days, most had been tense, with us in an uneasy mood and arguing. It had not been the happy midtour leave I had expected. But we were cheerful while saying good-bye. We waited in the apartment for the taxi to come to take me to the airport. When it arrived, I hugged the kids, kissed Claudia, and left. They waved to me from the balcony as I walked out to the cab. As the driver put my bags in the trunk, I heard someone call my name. It was Dale. I waited as he walked up. "Neal, do you mind if I ride to the airport with you?" he asked.

"No," I answered. "Hop in."

It was obvious to me that Dale had a hangover. I had no idea why he would want to ride with me to the airport. After a couple minutes, he spoke. "Neal, you know I've been unhappy with my marriage for several years. That's probably why you see me drinking all the time. It helps me deal with the mess I am in. But I only drink like this when I'm around Marcy." He paused as if he were looking for more words or maybe wanted me to say something.

His admission surprised me, and I wondered why he was telling me this now. I didn't know how to respond, because I thought Marcy was a tramp. Perhaps he knew I felt that way and was trying to tell me why he stayed with her.

Finally, I broke the silence. "Dale, I'm sorry things are going bad with you and Marcy. I know all the separations we've been through with the war in Vietnam haven't helped you or me in our relations with our wives." Mentally, I was thinking, *Dale, why don't you see her for what she is and leave her?* I felt sorry for my friend, and the last three weeks with Claudia had planted the idea in my mind that I might be losing her. I could empathize with Dale. If I lost her, it would devastate me, and I would go through the same hell he was.

Dale took a deep breath, turned to me, and said, "Neal, Marcy is a slut and has been for years. I am surprised you haven't picked up on that. A part of what I wanted to tell you is that tomorrow I will serve divorce papers on her. I've spent these weeks here just to see my kids for the last time. Eight months ago, I met a nurse in Vietnam. We started hanging out together and fell in love. Now, for the first time in ten years, I have love, honesty, and caring that I never knew existed. She opened my eyes to what terrible compromises I was making in trying to keep my marriage intact. I have to admit that I thought one day Marcy would change, and I hung on for that. Carol—her name is Carol—has made me understand that even if Marcy did change, I would never be able to forgive the years of hurt she caused me. As soon as my divorce is final, Carol and I will marry. I extended my tour in Vietnam six months to stay with her and to get a six-week leave so I would have time to come here and begin divorce proceedings."

The driver pulled up to the departure gate as Dale finished speaking. I felt relieved at not having to say something right away. What would be fitting to say about what I had just heard? After we were out of the cab and I had my bag, I reached for money to pay the driver. Dale said, "I'll take care of that, Neal," and he told the driver to wait.

I looked him in the eyes and said the only positive words I could think of: "Man, I hope you are doing what's right. I wish you only the best, whatever course you take."

Nodding, he said, "Thanks, Neal, but there's something else I have to tell you. Now, you can knock my head off if you want to, but just hear me out. I never want one of my friends to go through what I've been through with Marcy. I am telling you this so you can make the right decisions."

I stood there calmly looking at him, but I felt as if my stomach had gotten on a free-falling elevator. He continued, "Neal, there's something going on between Claudia and the guy who kept asking her to dance that night we were in the nightclub. Marcy and I had been to that club a couple of times before you got here. Both times, Claudia was there and sitting with him, and she seemed nervous that I had seen them. She asked me not to say anything about it to you. He's not German, so they spoke English, and I could understand them. I may be wrong, but I've seen too much not to recognize that they are more than just friends. I didn't tell you when you first got here because I didn't want to spoil your time here, and I knew we were going to the club. I was sure he would be there and thought you could form your own opinion. It may be nothing at all, but I would hate to think I stood by and let you go through the hell I have been through."

The elevator with my stomach in it had just crashed into the cellar and knocked the breath out of me. His words stung, and all I could think to do was reach out, shake his hand, and say, "Thanks for the information, Dale. Be careful in Vietnam, man. Don't crash and burn."

We looked at each other for a second. His face was sad with knowledge of the hurt he had just caused. He turned and got into the cab. I watched it pull away and felt the nagging suspicion that I had harbored change into the pain that came with the realization that it was true. I felt tears flood my eyes as my mind sought some clue that would let me refute what was obvious and prove it was not true. I remembered reading a study on infidelity that found that when a woman engages in an affair with another man, she avoids sex with her husband. If this was true, Claudia was a textbook example. It would explain her constant anger with me, the birth control pills, her constant visits with friends, and the mechanical sex we had when we did have sex. It all made sense.

I was a little angry with Dale for not telling me earlier. I could have confronted Claudia. I turned and walked toward the terminal and then stopped. I felt like jumping in a cab and going back to the apartment to confront her. However, if I did, I would miss my flight and would not get back to Korea in time. What if I did confront her? She would deny it or confirm it. If she denied it, it would be a case of whom I believed: her or Dale. If she confirmed it, she might take it a step further and say she wanted a divorce. If she said that, what would I do then? I didn't want a divorce. Wrenching in the agony of discovering that the wife I loved and trusted was unfaithful, I turned and walked to the ticket counter.

I picked up my boarding pass and went to the departure gate to wait. I was numb. I thought about Dale and how he'd gone through this agony all those years. I tried to imagine how Claudia's betrayal had happened. What had occurred to make Claudia decide she was going to have sex with another man, and when? I sat there with my heart breaking. Finally, I decided the only choice I had was to try to win back her love. I wondered if this was the course Dale had taken all those years ago. How long would I try before I would give up? Would I be able to forgive her? My mind was racing through ideas, and each one only intensified my pain.

Finally, it was time to board, and I staggered through the gate to my seat. Fifteen minutes later, the Davis Agency charter 707 full of dependents and soldiers was climbing through the overcast sky on the way to Fort Dix. I smiled satirically to myself, thinking, *Boy, I came here with such high expectations, and now look how it turned out.* My hurt was turning to anger. *What the hell?* I thought. *Why don't I just get a divorce?* But each time I asked myself that question, the thought of life without Claudia, Michele, and Ron was unbearable. For the rest of the flight, my mind wrestled with what to do. When we reached Fort Dix, I had convinced myself that maybe Dale was wrong. Anyway, I would do the best I could through letters to show my love for her. Perhaps if I didn't blow it, I might have a chance to fix things when my tour was over in November. That was the best choice I had, so I convinced myself to focus on that and suck up the pain. After all, this had happened to many other men and women, and they had overcome it and lived happy lives. The separation that came with a career in the army took a terrible toll on families, especially all the turn-around rotations caused by the demand for manpower in Vietnam.

The flight to McGuire AFB took a little more than eight hours. The Davis Agency ran charters moving military members and families back and forth between Germany and the United States; thus, most flights left and landed at a military base. I spent the entire flight trying to compose mentally a letter to Claudia. I wanted somehow to allude that I knew what she was doing, just to get it off my chest. But I didn't want to come across as angry or accuse her. I was hurting too much to come up with the right words, so I gave up, deciding to wait until I got back to Korea. After landing and clearing customs, I headed to the operations desk to check on a hop to McChord AFB.

I was in luck. The operations sergeant put me on a C-141 leaving for McChord AFB in two hours. When the C-141 lifted off the runway at 2000, I was tired and sleepy. Slowly, I shifted my mind off Claudia and drifted off to sleep. The crew chief's announcement that it was time to prepare for landing at McChord brought me out of a deep sleep. When we landed at 0530, I noticed the hurt had faded a little bit. It was still there, but it didn't bring tears each time I thought of Claudia.

My luck turned bad at McChord. There were no available seats on any airplane headed to Korea. The operations sergeant didn't expect any seats available for a week or so, because the army had booked all planes for military headed to Vietnam. I said, *The hell with it. Why try to save the money?* My plan had been to use the money I saved on travel to buy a special present for Claudia. That didn't seem important at the moment, so I bought a ticket on a commercial flight back to Korea.

I was back in the Kimpo military terminal at 0930 on July 1. I was a day late, but I didn't care. Rich would take care of any problems with my being a day late. I called the orderly room, and First Sergeant Hodge answered. "Fifty-Fifth Aviation Company. First sergeant speaking, sir."

"Hey, First Sergeant, it's Captain Griffin. I am at Kimpo. I need a ride."

He responded happily, "Welcome back, sir. I'll see if operations has a chopper that can get you. If not, I'll send the CO's driver."

"Thanks, First Sergeant." I could tell by the sound of his voice he was glad I was back. With me gone, Major Franks had probably given him some of the work I should have been doing.

Just before I hung up, the first sergeant said, "Wait. Captain Rich wants to speak to you."

Rich's voice came over the line. "Neal, man, I am glad you're back. I carried you present on the personnel status report. If you hadn't shown up, we would both be in trouble."

"Thanks, Rich," I replied. "I owe you."

"I know you owe me," he replied. "The question is, when are you going to pay?"

I laughed and said, "See you in a bit."

About twenty minutes later, the loud speaker in the terminal announced, "Captain Griffin, your helicopter is waiting on hot spot for you."

Good going, First Sergeant, I thought. *You must really want me back.* I grabbed my bag, walked out to the pad, and got into the helicopter. Izzy and Lieutenant Rogers were inside.

I put my headset on and said, "Don't you guys ever fucking work? Don't you have more-important missions to do than fly captains around?"

Izzy replied, "Where the hell is my case of beer?"

I laughed. "Damn, Izzy, I'm not back yet. You're going to get your case of beer."

He laughed. "Welcome back, sir. How was your leave?"

That was the question I feared most of all. Lying, as people do in cases like that, I answered, "It was wonderful, Izzy. I recommend one like it for everyone." I'm sure he didn't detect the sarcasm in my voice.

Izzy called for clearance to land and then called operations. Captain Moore, the operations officer, answered the radio. "This is operations, 781."

Izzy replied, "Operations, this is 781. Please tell Major General Morgan's aide that we are going to be about thirty minutes late."

Captain Moore answered with disbelief in his voice. "Thirty minutes late? You left here forty minutes ago to get his party."

Izzy, in his most professional tone, replied, "Roger, sir, but we diverted on an emergency mission. I'll explain when we back."

I had to laugh. Captain Moore was going to shit when he saw Izzy land on the VIP pad and let me out of the helicopter. Captain Moore was responsible for scheduling flights and ensuring they picked up VIPs on time. Now the general was sure to complain and want to know what had delayed his flight. I was the XO, and he couldn't chew me out. He couldn't chew Izzy out, because Izzy would just say his leaders were more important than any Eighth Army general. If he came to me, I would tell him I was shocked but say, "Don't worry. I'll talk to Izzy and call the general to smooth it over with him."

I was back. It was good to have problems that commanded my attention. Work would be a welcome diversion from my personal problem. I would first have to get over the constant barrage of "Welcome back. How was your leave?" I debated just announcing, "It was terrible. My wife is cheating on me, and I had a miserable time." However, most men don't want to admit something like that. That would have been the truthful answer, but I couldn't bring myself to say that, because I didn't want to believe it. I knew how I'd felt for Dale when I knew about his wife, and I didn't want anyone feeling that way about me. So each time someone asked, I said my leave was great and changed the subject.

The officers had finished the pool, and it looked professional. All that remained was for me to build a barbecue pit. I had volunteered for that before I left. Now everybody was waiting for me to complete it before we could officially open the pool. My inbox was so full of paperwork that it almost overflowed onto my desk. I would usually reassign it to others to do, but because of the circumstances, I relished work that would keep my mind busy. The busier my mind, the less time I had to think about Claudia.

Major Franks briefed me on the hot topics and current actions. He also said he was leaving with the Eighth Army commander on a ten-day TDY to Alaska in two days. He told me to make sure that if I saw any potential problems while he was gone, I let him know. I said I would and retreated to my desk to plan and set priorities for my work.

Fortunately, most of the actions in my inbox were simple, routine matters. Preparing the responses was the most tedious and time-consuming task. Luckily, I could pen a solution or answer and give the draft to Captain Rich, and it would come out letter perfect.

The night before he left, Major Franks had a meeting for all officers, and he told them of his absence and said I would be in command. He said if any individuals had problems with that, they should let him know, and they could be in command. He did that each time because three of the platoon leaders were captains, all West Point graduates, and had date of rank on me. Any one of them, by date of rank, should have been the XO.

As usual, no one had any problems with my being in charge. Each time, I considered that the greatest show of respect I could ever receive. It meant that even though they outranked me, they trusted my decisions, respected my leadership abilities, and would follow my orders. With that, I immersed myself in long hours of work.

I dreaded the nights, so my goal was to exhaust myself each day so that each night when my head hit my pillow, sleep would be instantaneous. I told flight operations to schedule me for as many flights as possible. It didn't matter whether it was a day, night, or weekend flight. However, try as I might, keeping busy didn't work. As soon as there was nothing to focus my attention on, my thoughts turned to Claudia, and the hurt set in. By the third day, I was stopping by the officers' club and trying to ease the pain with alcohol. I think some of the other officers might have noticed that something was bothering me, but they never said anything to me.

One of the first chores I took care of was to contact my engineer friends and arrange to have a load of granite rocks and mortar mix dumped at our barbecue site. I built the barbecue pit with Jake's help on my first weekend back. Of course, I had much advice from all the officers who gathered around to watch. Since they had worked on the pool, they felt they had the right to provide advice, even though they knew nothing about building a barbecue pit. All in all, it was a good time. With the barbecue pit finished, the pool was ready to open officially. Major Franks would decide the date when he returned.

By midweek, I'd caught up on the paperwork and had the company running smoothly. I felt it was time to write to Claudia and at least let her know I was back safely in Korea. I wrestled for two nights, searching for the right words. Finally, I settled on the following:

Dear Claudia,

Well, I am back safely in the drudgery of Korea. Unfortunately, I had to pay for a ticket from Settle to Seoul. I couldn't get a hop that would get me back before my leave was over, so I didn't save as much money as I had expected.

It was painful to leave you and the kids. I enjoyed being together, even with our constant bickering. I know there was tension between us while I was home. I am sorry for any I caused. I only wanted our time together to be the happiest we've ever had. All these separations are taking a toll on us. Please tell me how I am failing you, so I can change whatever I do wrong and correct it. I love you so much. Without you and the kids, I don't know what future I would have.

All I have here is work and the thought of your beautiful smile. I have buried myself in work to make the days go by faster. The other officers were happy to see me return. You could translate that to mean they were happy to have another body to help with all the work that goes on here. But it did make me feel like they genuinely missed me. Knowing that in six months I will be able to hold you again is what comforts me now.

We have completed the swimming pool I told you about. Major Franks is TDY now, but when he returns, we will officially open it. I will take some pictures and send them to you. Well, I guess that's enough for now.

All my love,

Neal

I read it a couple of times, and each time, I thought it wasn't much of a letter, but I couldn't think of anything better to say, so I put it in an envelope and dropped it in the outgoing mailbox. My last thought before I drifted off to sleep was *Is it worth it? She's probably with him tonight.* The thought hit me again: *The loving is easy. It's the living that's hard.* He was getting the loving, and I was getting the living.

The night before Major Franks returned, I was in the club and about half plastered. Several of us were sitting around a table, drinking martinis.

Jim turned to me and said, "Neal, what the hell is wrong with you? You haven't been the same since you got back."

I looked at Jim and thought, *There it is—the recognition that something is bothering me and the direct question from my friend.* I answered, "Well, Jim, I just spent a month with my beautiful wife, and now I get to sit around with you bums for six more months. If that isn't depressing, then I don't know what the hell is. So my answer is that I hate this place. I don't hate you guys. Hell, I love you, especially you, Jim, because you've got such a cute grin."

Everybody was laughing at my response. Jim responded, "I think you are sweet too. Now buy us a drink."

Almost drunk, I crawled into bed. As usual, I turned the radio on to listen to Armed Forces Radio. The station played music all night long, and I would drift off to sleep while listening to the latest hits. After about fifteen minutes, the DJ said, "Here's one for all you lonely soldiers lying there, struggling to sleep. It's Sammi Smith with her new hit written by Kris Kristofferson, 'Help Me Make It through the Night.'" The words to the song were astounding—raw with the pain of not wanting to be alone. To this day, it remains my favorite song and one I believe captures the pure feelings of loneliness and emptiness. I cried myself to sleep that night.

The next morning, Major Franks was present at officers' call. "Welcome back, sir," I said happily. He just grinned at me.

He waited a few minutes for most of the officers to welcome him back and then said, "Let's start."

All the platoon leaders took turns updating him on their status and any problems with which they were dealing. Once they'd finished, Captain Rich briefed him on personnel status and OERs. After that, I briefed him on the company status and all actions completed and outstanding. When I'd finished, he asked, "Any issues with Eighth Army command?"

"No, sir," I answered. "Last night, they were happy with all we are doing."

He looked at me and said, "Thanks, Neal, for taking care of everything. Now, to open the pool officially, I think we should have a luau."

All the officers started sounding off: "Yeah, great idea!"

Major Franks turned to me and said, "Neal, set up a luau for the Saturday four weeks from now. Invite anybody you want, but make sure you invite Eighth Army staff."

Well, there it was—another one of his famous mission orders. Hell, I wasn't even sure what a luau was, and I was responsible for making one happen. "I'll take care of it, sir," I answered.

He turned back to the officers. "All right, let's get to work."

Before they could move, I yelled, "Wait a minute! Not you, Major Franks. I want four volunteers to help me with the luau. If I don't get four by close of business today, I'll pick four."

Major Franks spoke again. "No! Make that by noon. If Captain Griffin doesn't have four by noon, I'll pick four. Then I'll find something for the remaining thirty-eight of you to do."

I smiled. I could count on Major Franks's support. When he gave me something to do, he always supported me to the fullest.

The Luau

The luau would be my second major party and my priority for the next four weeks. I knew I would have much work to do to make it better than the toga party I'd set up on Yeouido Island. I first looked up *luau* in the dictionary. I had no idea what a luau was. After that, I called the Eighth Army officers' club officer and talked to him about it. He explained what support the Eighth Army officers' club could provide. He needed from me the date, time, and number of attendees.

I knew the date and time, so I made the number of attendees my priority. I called Captain Rich to my office. "Rich, I need your help. I need an invitation inviting folks to our luau with an RSVP, so I can find out how many people will attend." This was the work he liked.

"I'll have a draft for you to review in a couple hours," he answered.

Two hours later, he handed me a perfect draft. Other than correspondence, we seldom called on Rich to help with projects. Sometimes during planning meetings, I noticed that he seemed disappointed that he wasn't asked for ideas, so although I had my four volunteers, I thought I would see if he wanted part of the action.

431

"Beautiful, Rich," I said, looking at the draft. "Besides the command group Major Franks said to invite, who do you think we should invite?" I asked. He seemed pleased that I asked him for something more than perfect correspondence.

"Well," he said, "I would send invitations to all the USO clubs, inviting the women working there to attend, and I would invite some Korean dignitaries as a gesture of Korean and American goodwill."

"That's a great idea," I said excitedly. "Tell you what, Rich. Why don't you take care of invitations and accountability for who and how many folks are attending? Tell the USO women that we will send helicopters to get them and take them home the following morning. I will have rooms available for them here." I could see Rich was happy about taking care of the invitations. The task centered on what he loved to do but provided some added challenges.

"What's the latest you need the total number of attendees?" he asked.

"The Eighth Army officers' club requires five days to prepare the roasted pig and all the trimmings. The luau is set for the twenty-third of August," I answered, looking at my calendar, "so we need it by COB on the seventeenth, but keep me posted every other day or so."

"Can do. I'll keep you posted," he answered, and he left.

Sitting back in my chair, I mentally ran through my plan and then put it on paper as a checklist. I estimated the number of attendees to be around 150, based on the forty-two officers assigned to the company. Six were married and had their wives here. About ten more had Korean girlfriends, which made fifty-eight. I guessed that about ten to fifteen USO women would attend, especially since I was flying them here and putting them up for the night. The tough call was the Eighth Army command group. The Fifty-Fifth Aviation Company existed to fly them and any other VIP anywhere they wanted to go, so I guessed another thirty attendees from the command group. I had given Rich a list of sixteen officers from various commands whom I owed favors in return for help they had provided me. Then there were the Koreans. I could think of about twenty to thirty, such as the mayor of Seoul, the chief of police, and several Korean army generals we flew regularly.

So I planned the luau for 150 attendees. With that number in mind, I put my volunteers to work. Jim had volunteered immediately because he was my friend and liked a good party. He had a do-it-yourself attitude in terms of putting on a good party. I put him in charge of preparing the pool area for 150 people. I gave him my thoughts on table arrangements, decorations, and such. He listened to my guidance and then asked, "How many luaus have you been to?"

"None," I replied. "How many have you been to?"

"Three," he replied. "And one was in Hawaii on my honeymoon. Don't worry about the pool area, rookie," he said. He was right. As with the toga party, I had never been to one, and in fact, I didn't have the slightest idea what one looked like. But Jim was the only one who could get away with comments like that.

I prepped myself on luaus by reading, talking to officers who had attended one, and talking to the Eighth Army officers' club officer. All agreed that a mai tai was the proper drink for a luau. I got the idea to hollow out pineapples, fill them with mai tais, and hand one to each guest as he or she entered the party. The problem was getting enough pineapples. The Eighth Army club officer told me he got theirs from Taiwan. They had small, sweet pineapples that were perfect for mai tais. I asked Davey if he would schedule a training flight to Taiwan on August 21, pick up as many pineapples as he could get in the plane, and get them back on August 22. Davey loved to fly and was delighted to do that as long as I gave him the money to pay for the pineapples. He wanted me to go with him and get my international flight out of the way, but I said I would be too busy then.

I had invitations, tables and decorations, and mai tais checked on my list. My next volunteer was Lieutenant Moray. Since the wire-strike episode, he'd been doing his best to redeem himself. He knew I didn't like him and wanted him out of the army, but he volunteered anyway. He reported to me and stood at parade dress in front of my desk. I returned his salute and looked at him, nodding for a few seconds before I spoke. "Okay, Lieutenant Moray, I want you to get leis for all the women attending the party. I think about sixty should cover it. The afternoon of the luau, I will hand a mai tai to each guest as he or she arrives. Then I want you to put lei on each woman. Can you handle that?"

"Yes, sir!" he said.

"As soon as I get a good count on the number women attending, I'll let you know. Let me know if you have any problems getting the leis. Let me know how much they will cost, and I will provide the funds."

"Thank you, sir," he said as he saluted and left. I knew I would have no problems with the leis.

I was handling the food, so I checked that off my list. Two items remained: bar supplies and music. Many of the young officers had top-of-the-line stereos with tape-to-tape conversion, turntables, and big, loud speakers. I knew that because a couple of times, I'd had to tell them to turn the volume down so that the rest of the officers could get to sleep. I made a note to bring it up at officers' call in the morning and get one of them to provide the music. The bar drinks were no problem; George would take of that.

My plan was complete. It was time to brief Major Franks and see what he thought about it. He was in his office, so I walked over and knocked on the door. He looked up and said, "Come on in, Neal. What you got?"

I walked in, saying, "Sir, if you've got time, I can brief you on my plan for the luau."

"Sure," he said, and he motioned for me to take a seat. "I've got about thirty minutes before I have to go down to the flight line."

I sat down. "This won't take long, sir." Then I ran down my checklist, laying out each action.

He listened intently with his head slowly moving up and down as if approving each step. When I finished, he said, "Great plan! I love it. I've got two questions: What's the backup if you can't get pineapples, and how are you going to provide beds for the USO women?"

"Well, sir, if we don't get the pineapples, I'll have to use paper cups with canned pineapple slices. I am going to double up eight of the most junior officers for that night. That will free up four rooms, which will sleep eight of the women. I am hoping some of the officers will score with the women and solve most of the problem."

He laughed. "Good plan. Keep me posted, and let me see the invitation list as soon as you get a final draft. If you need my help, let me know."

"Will do, sir," I said as I got up and left. I felt good. He liked my plan. Now all I had to do was make it happen.

The next three weeks passed quickly. I was busy doing my XO duties, flying missions, working on the party, and waiting for Claudia to answer my letter. I had developed a nightly routine after work: I'd go by the club, have two or three martinis, go to bed, and try to blank my mind while waiting for sleep. Each night, Armed Forces Radio played "Help Me Make It through the Night." I would listen to the pure beauty of the words and drift off to sleep, thinking I needed something to help me make it through the long night of six months.

Two weeks later, I got a letter from Claudia. It was a simple, unemotional half-page letter that said, "We are all doing fine. The kids are well and miss you. Hope you are well. Looking forward to when you come back to Germany." They were the same words she had used in the last ten letters. I crumpled it up and threw it in the trash.

The weekends were my worst time. There were few flights, and most everybody was off work on Saturday and Sunday. There wasn't much to keep me busy except running the club. During those times, time stood still, and the pain and loneliness of my state hurt the most. I kept telling myself to get over it, but that didn't work. So I drank more, and each time I did that, I cautioned myself not to become Dale. Jim's girlfriend, Sjoni—or Johnny, as we called her—would come on Friday afternoon, spend Saturday and Sunday with Jim, and leave Monday morning. Many officers had Korean girlfriends who did the same. They lounged around the pool, having fun and making life seem normal. The remaining single officers would spend the weekend in Seoul. That left about ten married officers who spent the weekend alone with boredom for company. We did play poker and chess.

The weekend before the luau, Johnny asked me, "Captain Neal, why you drink so much? No good for you." No matter how many times I told her to call me Neal, she would say okay and still call me Captain Neal. Koreans are very respectful, and Jim said that since I was the number-two officer, she told him she must address me as Captain Neal out of respect. Since Jim and I were friends, she took it upon herself to watch out for my welfare. In a way, she provided a measure of comfort that I enjoyed. She was a nice woman, and her concern for me seemed sincere. She had a way of lifting my morale, and I looked forward to her visiting Jim each weekend.

"I don't drink that much," I answered.

She looked through me and said, "You were happy before you go on midtour leave. Now you not happy. I am sorry that you not happy."

I wondered how she'd picked up on that. I knew she would never say something to suggest a problem with my wife was making me unhappy, but the expression in her eyes said, "I know what you are going through." I kept a blank look as I thought, *How in the hell could she know?* Nobody knew. Then I did the only thing I could: I smiled and said, "Let me buy you and Jim a drink." I turned and walked into the club to end the conversation and get the drinks, and as I walked away, I barely heard her say, "Number ten," which expressed her unhappiness with me.

At last, it was luau day. I was happy with the way everything had come together just as I'd planned it. At officers' call that morning, Major Franks said a few words and thanked all who'd worked on the luau. After he finished, he turned the meeting over to me and left to attend a meeting at Eighth Army headquarters.

"Okay, everybody, listen up," I said to the group. "I want you to have a good time at the party today. What I don't want is behavior that will embarrass the CO and the company. We've got nine general officers attending the party, so let's watch our protocol. If you drink too much and start looking like trouble, I am going to tell you to go to bed. If I tell you to go to bed, I expect you to do so without discussion. Next, we've got twelve USO women coming in on a chopper around three o'clock. I want some of you young studs to meet them, escort them up here, and show them the rooms we've prepared. The mayor of Kumho is attending and is bringing twelve young ladies with him. Treat them with the utmost respect. By that, I mean they are not prostitutes, so don't offer them money to spend the night. But if you can woo them into spending the night with you, then that's your business. I don't want any damaged American and Korean relations.

"Captain Jim and his crew are going to start setting up the pool area after this meeting. Stay out of the area unless you want to help. Some of you still owe me ten dollars for your share of the cost for the party. I want that after this meeting. I want to thank Captain Rich for some of the best invitations I've ever seen. Next, Lieutenant Moray, the leis are beautiful. Good job. I want to thank Lieutenant Johnson, Izzy, and Captain Morgan for preparing the pineapples to hold the mai tais. I think they are going to be a big hit, and handing them out to the attendees as they enter will let them know that they are attending a first-class affair. I want to thank you lucky officers who get to spend tonight together so the USO women will have a place to sleep. If there's any change in sleeping arrangements or partners, I'll let you handle it.

"Okay, the luau starts officially at 1600, but I expect folks to start arriving around 1530, so let's make sure everything is ready by then. If there are no questions, the meeting is over. No questions? All right, let's have fun today. If you owe me money, stay until you pay me. The rest are dismissed."

By 1500, Jim had the tables and chairs set up around the pool area. As usual, he did an outstanding job. There were coconuts and flowers on each table. The area looked like a scene on a Hawaiian beach. Chief Warrant Officer Hawks had set up his stereo, and the speakers were belting out some of Charlie Pride's best songs. I loved it, but he knew he couldn't play it for the luau. He had equally good rock-and-roll and popular music for the luau.

Just as I expected, guests started arriving around 1500, when some of the married officers with wives arrived. Jim had set up two simulated palm trees to serve as the entryway into the pool area. I had coolers with the pineapple mai tais stacked. I had field tables set up so I could act as the host and greet each attendee, hand out a mai tai, and provide a name tag if he or she wanted one. Lieutenant Moray stood next to me with his leis so he could place them around the necks of those wishing to wear them. Major Franks also was standing there to greet and escort the general officers to their tables. You always had to lead generals. They expected it. By 1600, people were coming in a steady stream. Judging by their reactions, the mai tais and leis impressed them. The music was going. Couples were dancing or gathered in circles, talking and laughing. Drinks and trays of appetizers were plentiful. The Eighth Army officers' club cook and servers would arrive with the roasted pig at 1730 and serve dinner at 1800.

By 1630, there must have been 150 people, and a few more were approaching the entry. Officers, some of whom I didn't know, were coming up to me and congratulating me on a great party. I appreciated the thanks, especially so early in the party. First impressions will always last throughout the night and overcome any glitches that might arise. We ran out of mai tais and leis except for two of each. Jim told me to save one for Johnny and her friend she was bringing to the party. Jim went down to the main gate to sign them in.

I was standing there waiting for them and protecting the mai tais, when Major Franks walked up and put his hand on my shoulder. "Great job, Neal. I've had many compliments. The generals want the name of the officer who planned and organized it. They have your name now, so don't be surprised if they call you to plan a party for them."

I looked at him. "Damn, sir, I appreciate the good word, but I only do parties for you."

As he turned to leave, he grinned. "Don't worry about it. The way they're drinking, they won't remember." By then, I was feeling the few martinis I had put down. I decided I had better lay off for a while since I had to police the party.

Jim walked up escorting Johnny and the most beautiful woman I think I have ever seen. That wasn't the alcohol talking. She was five feet tall and in a shapely dress that was suitable for any nationality. She was Korean but had the delicate features of a Eurasian. She styled her long dark hair with a slightly modern flair. She was damn beautiful. *Wow,* I thought. *Wait till the rest of the young studs see her.*

Jim interrupted my thoughts. "Neal, I want to introduce you to Soon In."

She smiled and extended her right hand with her left hand lying across her wrist, a sign of respect in Korea. She said in broken English, "Nice to meet you, Captain Neal."

Her calling me Captain Neal made me smile because I knew Johnny had coached her in preparation of meeting me. I took her hand and smiled the smile of a half-drunk man who had just touched an angel. I bowed, kissed her hand in the fashion of the 1800s, and said, "Very nice to meet you, Soon In." Her left hand went to her mouth as it opened in surprise. In Korean society, what I had done didn't happen. Jim was laughing. Johnny said something in Korean, and Soon In's beautiful mouth stifled a smile.

Jim said, "Nice touch, Neal."

I turned, got the mai tais, and gave them to Johnny and Soon In. Soon In asked Johnny something in Korean and then said, "Thank you, Captain Neal."

I shook my head and said, "Please call me Neal."

She turned to Johnny, and Johnny rattled off something in Korean. Soon In looked at me and said, "Okay, Captain Neal."

I shook my head and motioned for Lieutenant Moray to put the leis around their necks. He was standing there staring at Soon In as if in a trance. When they passed into the pool area, Jim said, "Neal, I'll save you a seat at our table."

I answered, "Thanks, Jim. I'll try to drop by, but you know I've got to act as host and keep all our guests happy." As they walked away, Soon In gave me a parting smile.

I figured she didn't speak much English based on the way she'd obviously asked Johnny what I had said. Lieutenant Moray watched them walk away and turned to me, saying, "That was the prettiest Korean I have ever seen. Sir, if you don't need anything else from me, I'm going to join the party."

"No," I answered. "Thanks for a good job. Go ahead and join the party, and have fun."

I watched him walk away and smiled as he made a beeline for the table where Jim was pulling chairs out for Soon In and Johnny to sit. Then the thought hit me that Johnny had brought Soon In to meet me. I felt a surge of desire flow through my body. I looked at Soon In and realized that I was seriously tempted to take advantage of Johnny's effort. I had never had such a temptation placed before me, especially at a time when I was so vulnerable. Then I remembered that I was on duty that night.

I began my duty by checking on the food. The Eighth Army officers' club cook had finished setting the serving line and told me he was ready to serve. A few of the couples were starting to get in line, so I announced that dinner was being served. The cook had done a wonderful job. The centerpiece of the serving was a pig, roasted whole with an apple in its mouth.

As the food line started moving, I went to the bar inside the club to see how George was doing. The bar was empty at the moment because everybody was in the food line. "How's the booze holding up?" I asked George.

"We've got plenty, Captain Griffin. You want another martini?"

"No, I don't think so right now, George. Give me Budweiser," I answered. "I am getting a little tipsy, so I'd better slow down if I want to keep things in order tonight."

Specialist Porter, who had volunteered to help George tend bar, brought my beer and said, "Great party, sir. When are you going to throw one for us enlisted men?"

"That's a good idea, Specialist Porter. I'll get with the first sergeant and see what we can come up with. Do me a favor."

"Yes, sir, what do you need?" he answered.

"Three of the generals had their drivers drive them here tonight. They're all getting plastered and might not remember that their drivers need food. Go out to where the sedans are parked, and tell them to come in and get something to eat. And you get something too while everybody else is eating."

"Thanks, sir," he said, and he left to get the three drivers.

I walked over to the tables where the generals sat and told them I had asked their drivers to come get some food. I could see by their reactions that they had been having so much fun that the thought hadn't crossed their minds. One said, "Thanks, Captain Griffin. I don't need my driver being upset with me, and by the way, this is one fucking great party. I've told Major Franks that I expect an invitation to every party you throw."

I said, "Thank you, sir," and I turned and walked away. Under my breath, I said, "I hope you get so drunk tonight that you forget where you were and if you had a good time."

Leaving the generals, I looked for Jim, Johnny, and Soon In. I was going to grab a tray of food and sit with them to eat it, but when I found the table, at least twenty officers were squeezed around it, all trying to get Soon In's attention. Looking at her, I could tell she was accustomed to attention. I thought there was no need for me to join the crowd. As I turned, she looked up and saw me. She smiled, and it looked as if she moved her head in a motion that said, "Come get me out of this position." I smiled back and motioned that I was going to get something to eat.

I took my tray to the bar and talked to George while I ate. The food was great. George shared some of his kimchi with me. Everything was going well. The dance floor was full of dancers. A few couples were swimming in the pool, and everybody looked to be having a good time.

After I ate, I started circulating from table to table, making sure everybody felt satisfied. The USO women were in a party mood. They were impressed with my flying them in a helicopter for the party. It was the first time some had ever ridden in a helicopter. From what I could tell, several of them had hooked up with some of the officers. I sat with three of them for a while. We danced, and it was refreshing to talk to American women. I think I received a couple subtle invitations for something more, which I delicately ignored.

The Korean mayor sat with the generals and was having the time of his life. The young women he'd brought were all attractive and dressed in the different native dresses of Korea. Their presence added a special touch to the party. They were all dancing, and I couldn't help but think they would probably love to shed those traditional dresses for something more comfortable. I moved among them, and to my surprise, several spoke perfect English. That enabled me to learn a little about them. They were all graduates of Seoul University and worked in Seoul. The mayor was somehow related to each of them, so they had to mind their act. They told me this was the first time they had met American soldiers, and the young officers impressed them. Several of them started dating some of the officers after the party.

Occasionally, I looked at Soon In's table. I wanted to ask her to dance, but so many officers were sitting around her and competing for her attention that I gave up. Each time I looked in her direction, it seemed she was looking at me.

Sometime around 2300, the party started breaking up, and people began leaving. I had already put several of my too-drunk young officers to bed, but the night was ending with no major problems. Many of the couples had slipped off to BOQ rooms. I didn't hear of any problems caused by the sleeping arrangements set up for the UFO women.

As people left, they came by to shake my hand, tell me how great the party had been, and remind me to invite them to the next one. As they left, I helped George clean up the area. Around 2400, only George and

I were left. I had missed Jim, Johnny, and Soon In leaving. I figured she probably had given in to the advances of one of the officers. The pool area looked straight, so I told George to call it quits for the night. We turned off the lights, and George retired to the bed I had for him in the club. I made it to my room. I'd had way too much to drink, and lying in my bed, I could feel it. I turned the radio on, waiting for the DJ to play "Help Me Make It through the Night," when I drifted off to sleep.

It was 0600 when I awoke with a hangover and in desperate need of a cup of coffee. I took a shower and shaved. After that, I felt a little better and headed to the club for coffee, which I knew would perk me right up.

George was already up and had the big coffee urn full of fresh coffee. We greeted each other with a smile, as if to congratulate each other on surviving the night. I drank half the cup, refilled it, and walked out to the pool area to survey it for any damage. I picked up some trash George and I had missed the night before and put it in the garbage bag. I was looking for more, when I noticed someone leaning on the upstairs balcony. I looked up and right into the smile of Soon In. I smiled back and said, "Good morning!"

She answered in broken English, "Good morning, Captain Neal."

"Do you want a cup of coffee?" I asked.

She frowned as if she didn't understand what I had said, so I raised my cup and pointed to her and then to my cup. She smiled and said, "Yes."

I said, "Come on down," as I motioned for her to come down.

She raised her hand in a "Wait a minute" motion, said something in Korean, and went into Jim's room. I only understood the word *Johnny*, but it was obvious she was telling Johnny and Jim where she was going. She came out the door and walked down to me. I looked at her and asked, "Did you have a good time last night?"

She looked puzzled. It was clear she didn't understand. She said, "I sorry. I speak only little English," as she motioned with her fingers.

"It's okay," I said. "I speak only little Korean."

She looked at me and smiled with mirth in her eyes. She understood what I'd said and the humor behind it. I opened the door to the officers' club for her to enter. A couple of the other officers were there with cups of coffee. Captain Parker looked at me with admiration in his eyes and said, "Tell me you didn't."

"No, I didn't. Mind your manners."

He laughed, and they both said, "Good morning, Soon In."

She smiled and said, "Good morning."

I thought as I pulled out a chair for her to sit that everybody in the company must know her. I looked at her and said, "How do you like your coffee?"

She looked at me and raised her shoulders as if to say, "I didn't understand you."

Motioning with my hands, I said, "Wait!" I went to the coffee urn, poured her a cup of coffee, and brought sugar and cream back to the table. I pointed to the cream and said, "You like cream?"

She pointed to the cream and said, "Oh, cream. Yes, I like much cream."

I pointed to the sugar and said, "You like sugar?"

She beamed a smile back and said, "Yes, I love sugar." I handed her the spoon, and she piled the coffee full of sugar and cream. She took a sip and said, "Good coffee. Thank you."

As she cupped her hands around the coffee cup and sipped it, I thought, *Now what am I going to say?* The door opened, and Jim and Johnny walked in. Johnny sat down at the table with us while Jim got them cups coffee and then sat down. Johnny and Soon In were talking in Korean. Then Soon In pointed to the sugar and said the word *sugar* and then to the cream and said the word *cream*, as if she were telling Johnny that she had learned two new English words.

Johnny looked at me and said, "She learn English fast," nodding in approval. I smiled at Soon In, who smiled back at me.

Then Jim looked at me and said, "Neal, we are going downtown to have breakfast and then go to the zoo. Why don't you go with us?"

I thought for a minute and said, "You know, Jim, that sounds like fun. Other than flying, I haven't been off this base in almost two months. When you leaving?"

"Let's go now," he answered. "I am hungry."

I spent the day with Jim, Johnny, and Soon In. It was the most carefree fun I had had in what seemed like years. Soon In and I could communicate pretty well with sign language and a little help from Johnny. I had been through a similar experience since Claudia hadn't spoken English when

I'd first met her, so I was good at using sign language and arm and body motions to explain and communicate.

The day slipped by quickly, and by 1500, we began to tire. The imbibing and late hours from the night before were starting to remind us that you have to pay for what you sow. We went by the Eighth Army officers' club, had a fried rice dinner, and caught the bus back to K-16.

As usual, there was an impromptu party going on in the club, so we gathered there for a nightcap. Soon after we sat down, officers began to gather around and join our conversation, and it became a competition for Soon In's attention. It was turning out to be a contest, so I sat back to watch the antics of the young officers as they worked to attract her interest.

Then I started to feel a little jealously, which surprised me until I reminded myself that I was married and therefore had no romantic interest in her. However, it would have fixed my broken ego if she had selected me over the several handsome and socially smooth officers who had an obvious interest in her. At thirty-three, I probably seemed like an old man to her. Besides, I had no wish to involve myself with another woman. The one I'd married gave me enough heartbreak. Plus, casual sex had never appealed to me.

After about an hour, Soon In rubbed her neck as if it hurt her. She said something to Johnny in Korean, and Johnny said, "Okay, guys, party over. Time we go bed. Jim, you coming?"

Jim looked at everybody with a shit-eating grin on his face and, as he got up to go, replied, "Sorry, guys. It looks like I get the women."

After they left, one of the officers proclaimed, "That's the most beautiful woman I have ever seen."

Then one asked me, "Captain Griffin, are you going with her?"

"No," I replied. "I went with Jim and them to the zoo today just to get away from this place for a while."

"How long is she staying?" one asked.

"I think Jim said till Monday morning," I answered. "That's all I know. Well, guys, I am hitting the sack," I said, and I went to my room.

I was exhausted, and the two martinis I'd had at the club had made me sleepy. *Good,* I thought. *Perhaps I can sleep the night through without waking up.* I brushed my teeth and was about to undress, when someone knocked on my door.

"Come in!" I shouted.

The door opened, and Jim walked into the room. "Neal, I need a favor. The reason Soon In's neck is sore is because she's sleeping in a chair in my room." He saw the slight grin on my face and continued. "No, we are not all three sleeping together. Don't tell all those young studs. Let them think we are."

"Okay, Jim, but what's the favor?" I asked.

He pointed to the big couch in my room and said, "Let her sleep on that tonight. She can stretch out and get a good night's sleep if you leave her alone."

"She can sleep here if she wants to, Jim. But don't you think that might be a little awkward for her?" I asked.

"No. If you agree, Johnny is going to talk to her," he replied.

"Okay, get her down here, man, because I am dead tired and need to get some sleep."

"Great," he said, and he left.

I got out the extra sheet and blanket and made up the couch for sleeping. I was smiling as I worked, because when the word got out, no one was going to believe she'd slept on the couch.

About five minutes later, there was a light knock on the door. I opened it and let Johnny and Soon In in. Soon In looked a little embarrassed—or was it shyness?—but smiled at me and said, "Thank you, Captain Neal."

I was about to say, "If you call me Captain Neal again, you can't stay," when Johnny said, "Thanks, Captain Neal. She got bad neck hurt from sleeping on chair."

There was no way I was going to get her to call me Neal, so I said, "It's my pleasure, Johnny. I put out a clean towel for her. Tell her to make herself at home. Take a shower or whatever she wants. I am tired, and I'm going to bed. She can turn the lamp off when she gets in bed."

They talked for a few minutes, and Johnny left. We stood there looking at each other, and she said, "I take," followed by something in Korean while making the motion of a bath. I showed her the bathroom and the shower. She had a little overnight bag with her. Then I smiled and said, "Good night. I hope the couch is comfortable." The look on her face told me she didn't understand about the couch. I smiled and said, "Sleep well," and I shut the bathroom door and got into bed.

I must have been more exhausted than I'd thought, because almost as soon as I shut my eyes, I went to sleep. The last sound I heard was the shower running. I have never told anyone about that night, because I don't think many people would believe me anyway. Writing this journal is the first time I have mentioned it. Sometime in the middle of the night, I awoke briefly. Before I drifted back off to sleep, I heard her tossing and turning on the couch.

Sound sleep turned to restless sleep around 0530. I kept trying to return to sound sleep for about twenty minutes before I decided to get up. There was enough light through the closed curtains to see in the room. I was in my underwear and needed to pee. I wanted to get up, but I didn't want to wake Soon In or embarrass her or myself by being in my underwear. However, peeing became more important than embarrassment, so I quietly got up, went into the bathroom, and shut the door. I peed, showered, and shaved. Then it dawned on me that I should have brought my clothes with me, because I had to walk out in my underwear to get them. I was sure that by now, Soon In was awake. It finally occurred to me that I was acting like a high school teenager, so I opened the door, walked to my pants, and put them on.

I heard Soon In softly say, "Good morning, Captain Neal."

"Good morning," I answered, turning to look at her. *Man*, I thought, *she is so beautiful.* "Did you sleep well?"

Her expression told me she didn't understand the question, so I folded my hands against my head to symbolize sleep and asked, "Good sleep?" I knew she understood *good*, and the sleep symbol would make it clear.

It did help her understand. She made a so-so motion and replied, "Good." Then she pushed on the couch and said something in Korean while making a sign that I took to mean *hard*.

I pushed my hands together and showed my muscles to show the expression for hard and said, "Too hard?"

She answered in Korean, and I heard Johnny's name mentioned. I assumed Johnny would tell me. I told her, using sign language and words, that I was going to the club for coffee. She could shower or whatever and then come for coffee. She smiled and said, "Okay."

Jim was already in the club, drinking coffee, when I got there. He grinned at me and said, "You look much better this morning. Did you get good night's sleep?"

"Yes, I did," I answered, pouring myself a cup of coffee. I could see by the grin on his face that he wanted to know if I'd slept alone. I remained noncommittal and sat down at the table.

"Well, shit, Neal," he said, frustrated that I wasn't going to volunteer any information. "Did you get any last night?"

I looked at him with a playful grin on my face and answered, "No, Jim. I slept in my bed all night, and Soon In slept on the couch. I'm married, Jim, and you know I don't fool around."

He studied my face for a minute or two. I could see by his expression that he was having a hard time believing I'd spent the night in a room with a beautiful woman and done nothing other than sleep. Finally, he said in a disbelieving tone, "You're shitting me."

I was doing my best not to smile at my friend. He was having a hard time accepting my word that nothing had happened between Soon In and me. Hell, I would have had a hard time believing it too. "That's all we did, Jim. Wait until they come in here, and ask Johnny. Soon In was trying to tell me something this morning, but I couldn't understand her. I think she was trying to tell me that the couch was uncomfortable and that she didn't sleep well. She is going to tell Johnny, and Johnny will explain it to me."

"Well, if what you say is true, you are a better man than me," he said, shaking his head. "Johnny wants to go to the Seoul Museum today. You want to come along?" he asked.

My first thought was that it would be boring to spend a day in a Korean museum. I love to visit museums, and when I do, I read all the information posted for each display. However, all the information would be in Korean, and having to depend on Johnny for translations would kill the fun. Despite that, it would be fun to joke around with Soon In, using hand signs and broken English. It would beat sitting around there drinking martinis and swimming all day. "Yes, I'll go. What time do you plan to leave?"

Jim looked at his watch and said, "I don't know. Whenever the girls get ready. Johnny was still asleep when I came down."

I was hungry, so I said, "Let's go down to the mess hall and have breakfast. We can bring them something to eat."

When we got back, Johnny and Soon In were sitting at a table in the club, drinking coffee. Several of the officers had pulled chairs up to their table and were trying to talk to Soon In by using Johnny as a translator. When we walked in, Johnny looked up and asked, "Where you been?" Looking at me, she said, "You're number ten, Captain Neal."

Jim spoke up. "We went for breakfast." He set the scrambled eggs, fried potatoes, bacon, and toast—not a typical Korean breakfast—on the table.

That distracted Johnny since she loved to eat, but the officers hadn't missed the number-ten comment and were now chiding me.

"Whoa, Neal, what the hell did you do that brought that on?" Dan asked while the others laughed.

I raised my hands, shrugged, and, looking at Johnny, asked, "What did I do?"

Johnny looked at me and said, "You know."

Poor Soon In was blushing with her eyes on her food. The officers couldn't picture exactly what Johnny was talking about, which confused them. I honestly didn't know, unless she was upset because I had not slept with Soon In. Had Soon In expected me to make love to her, and because I hadn't, I'd hurt her pride? Johnny knew I was married and didn't mess around with the women. Maybe she'd thought Soon In's beauty would capture my desires.

Later, I would understand that my lack of attention had hurt Soon In. She was used to men falling over their feet for her and could have any man she wanted. She couldn't understand why I ignored her when she was giving herself to me. I didn't know that then. But she didn't know how fragile I was. What Claudia was doing broke my heart, and it was all I could do to resist the temptation she presented.

I figured I could gracefully end this by apologizing, so I said, "I am sorry for whatever I did. I won't do it again." Under my breath, I muttered, "Whatever it was."

That calmed Johnny, and she said, "You better not."

Jim had a shit-eating grin on his face and shook his head, saying, "I told you you were crazy."

We spent the day at the museum. Contrary to what I had originally thought, I enjoyed it. I learned much about Korean history and culture that day. Each display had English subtitles. To cap it off, Soon In was giving me her full attention, and it felt good to have such a beautiful woman so interested in me. We laughed a lot while trying to communicate with our broken English and hand and body motions. She was a fast learner and was quickly grasping English.

For dinner, they took Jim and me to a Korean restaurant. They ordered bulgogi, and it was delicious. The meat was cooked to perfection on a charcoal grill sitting on the table and mixed with rice and kimchi. It was the best I have ever had. Jim and I chased it with Korean beer, which was okay but not the best. It always gave me a headache. There was a rumor that the Koreans added formaldehyde to it.

After dinner, we caught the bus back to the base. On the bus, Soon In leaned against me to get comfortable. Her touch sent shivers through my body. I couldn't help but think how easy it would be to give in to the desire I felt. My mind kept saying I should get even. But I didn't want to become the many men I had disapproved of for cheating on their wives. It was good that Johnny and Soon In were leaving in the morning. Then the pressure would be off me.

We got back to the base at 1900. As we started walking back to the officers' barracks, I said to Jim, "You guys go on back. I'm going by the orderly room to check the charge of quarters log. I'll see you in a little while."

That was my routine on Sunday night. I would check the entries for the weekend so I would be ready for the company commander in the morning. He would review the log as soon as he got to his office. If there were any problems, he would call me in to discuss them and get my recommended solutions or actions. By reviewing them the night before, I could think about the problems and come up with a decent recommendation when the CO asked. That night, there were several personnel problems, such as fights, and the MPs had arrested some of our enlisted for disorderly conduct. When I finished my review and discussion with the duty NCO, it was 2100.

When I walked around the entry to the pool area to my room, I met Johnny sitting on the stairs. "Where's everybody?" I asked.

Johnny stood up and said, "Everybody go to bed."

I asked, "Where's Soon In?"

"She's in your room," Johnny answered. "You take it easy, Captain Neal. Korean girls not big like American girls."

The moment was cute and funny, and I stifled a smile. Johnny was giving me sexual instructions, and she was serious. I knew she cared a lot for Soon In, so I said the only thing that came into my mind: "Don't worry, Johnny. I'm not very big myself, and besides, I am married. Although Soon In is beautiful, I'm not interested in sleeping with her."

She looked at me for a few seconds and said, "You just be easy," and she turned and went up the stairs.

I stood there watching her disappear up the stairs. If anything was a turnoff, their calling me Captain Neal was. I entered the room, and Soon In was already in bed on the couch.

She looked at me and smiled. I looked at her, smiled, and said, "Okay, let's do sleep different tonight. Johnny says the couch is too hard and hurts your neck, so tonight I will sleep on the couch, and you sleep in the bed. Okay?" I pulled the covers back on the bed.

At first, she didn't understand, so I pointed at her and then at the bed and said, "You sleep here tonight."

She smiled and said, "Okay."

It dawned on me then that she had undressed and didn't want to get out from under the covers on the couch. I said, "I go to bathroom, and you get in bed." As I shut the bathroom door, I could hear her moving.

I smiled, took a shower, and brushed my teeth. I wrapped a towel around me and went to my dresser for clean underwear. I looked at her and asked, "Is that better?"

She replied, "Yes, much better."

I turned off the light, slipped into my underwear, and said, "Good night."

I heard her say good night. She was right; the couch was hard. However, I had slept on it before and could do it again. Surprisingly, I drifted off to sleep with no problem.

I had been asleep for about an hour, when the sound of her moaning woke me. I turned on the night lamp and looked at her. "Are you okay?"

She pointed to her neck and said, "No can sleep. Hurt." She motioned for me to massage her neck. She rolled over onto her stomach, and I got up and walked to the bed.

I firmly massaged her neck and shoulders the way barbers did mine when I got a haircut. Then, without warning, she rolled over, and I was looking into the eyes of the most beautiful woman on the planet. She reached up and pulled me down until our lips met. We came together in a passion I hadn't known existed, and I surrendered to it without even putting up a fight. Later, as we lay holding each other and waiting for sleep, the words from the song "Help Me Make It through the Night" kept running through my mind.

My sleep that night was restless. I kept waking up, aware of her presence beside me. I guess sleeping with a woman for the first time under those circumstances affected my ability to sleep soundly. The alarm clock sounded at 0500, stirring me from the deep sleep I had finally achieved around 0300. Soon In looked at me and smiled. "Wait," she said as she jumped out of bed and ran to the bathroom.

She was back in a couple of minutes. She got back in bed and pulled me to her. I said, "Wait," and I went to the bathroom to pee and wash my mouth with Listerine. Back in bed, we came together in a tender passion that was almost playful. She seemed interested in what we were doing and not the least bit shy. *Johnny was right,* I thought. *She isn't very big.* Some of the things we did seemed new to her, and I got the impression she wasn't too experienced in sex.

By 0530, I had to stop and get ready for work. We had officers' call every morning at 0630, and I still had to shower, dress, and eat breakfast. She would have to leave. After the weekend, guests had to be off the base by 0700. She waited in bed for me to finish. Watching me lace up my boots, she asked, "I come with Johnny next week?"

I could have ended it then by saying no, but looking at this beautiful woman, I could only say yes. I was dumbfounded by her interest in me. She could have had any of the young and handsome officers in company. Why would she want me?

I thought about that question for the rest of the week. I finally decided that Claudia's betrayal had caused me to question my desirability to other women. I was thirty-three years old, had been married for thirteen years, and felt old. Soon In was twenty-five and beautiful and didn't need to be wasting her time with me. I decided that after this weekend, if she came back, I would break it off. Besides, I felt a strange guilt for breaking my marriage vows and breaking God's commandments by committing adultery. I had gotten even with Claudia, but there was no comfort in getting even, because I still loved her and knew that cheating was no way to salvage our marriage.

It was a busy week. I flew several missions in the OH-58 and two Mohawk missions. After the weekend, I desperately wanted to hear from Claudia. It had been almost three weeks since she had written, and I needed something from her to help me readjust my direction. Finally, on Thursday, I got a half-page letter from her. It was the usual "How are you? We are fine. Nothing much to write about." At that time in my life, I needed more than that from her. Feeling let down, I crumpled the letter and threw it in the garbage. Now I understood and felt the line from "Help Me Make It through the Night" that said, "Yesterday is dead and gone, and tomorrow is out of sight. Come and lay down by my side, and help me make it through the night."

All week, I had halfheartedly wished Soon In wouldn't come on Friday. I didn't want to become a man who cheated on his wife. I always held myself to a higher standard. However, by noon on Friday, I was hoping she would come.

Friday afternoon passed slowly even though I buried myself in work. Around 1630, Jim dropped by my office. We sat and talked for a while, and then he asked, "Is Soon In coming tonight?"

"I don't know for sure, Jim," I answered. "She said she might. What time does Johnny usually come? She said she would come with Johnny."

"Johnny usually comes around 1900," he answered, and he got up to leave.

"Jim, wait. What do you know about Soon In?" I asked. "Did Johnny bring her to the luau to introduce her to me?"

"All I know about her is that she used to sing with a little band. She knew that Johnny was going with me and wanted to meet an American soldier. Johnny invited her to the luau so she would meet an American soldier. I think Johnny said she had a Korean boyfriend. Why she picked an old butt like you to hang with, I don't know," he said, smiling. "I'm going to the mess hall to get something to eat. I've been flying all day, and I'm starved."

"I've got one report to finish before I can leave," I said, "so I'll see you later at the club." I sat there thinking about what he had said about Soon In. At least I knew a little bit more about her. I finished the draft report on our August flying hours and took it to Major Franks for his review and approval.

He dropped the draft into his inbox and said, "That can wait until Monday." Looking at me, he grinned and said, "I would invite you to a party tonight, but the rumor is that you are going to be with that beautiful young woman again this weekend."

I looked at him and smiled. He knew that I knew there was no rumor and that he was just digging for information. "I hope I see her tonight," I volunteered as I turned and left his office.

I dropped by the mess hall and had dinner. I took some of the pork chops, rice, and cake with me to my room in case Soon In hadn't eaten before—if she came. I took a shower, dressed, and walked over to the club for a martini. I felt like a teenager on his first date.

The club was crowded. It was Friday and was happy hour. Jim was already there, and judging by the empty martini glasses on his table, he was getting into a party mood. I joined him, and George brought me a martini. Several of the officers had started a poker game, and a crowd of onlookers had gathered around the table. Several of the younger officers pulled up chairs around our table and started asking me about Soon In.

Jim laughed and said, "You guys wouldn't know how to handle a classy lady like her. You spent all night at the luau making an ass out of yourselves while trying to impress her. The XO played it cool and ended up in the sack with her. You guys only think you're studs." They all looked a little disappointed, because if I had slept with her, they didn't want to take the chance of pissing me off by chasing her.

George interrupted the discussion, announcing, "Captain Griffin, your party is at the main gate."

"Thanks, George," I said as Jim and I got up to go sign in Soon In and Johnny and escort them to the club. The main gate was about a quarter mile away, so on the way out, I asked Major Franks, "Hey, sir, can I use your jeep for a couple minutes?"

"Sure," he replied.

When we got to the main gate and I saw Soon In, my heart lost a beat. She was so beautiful, and she was there to spend the weekend with me. We spent that weekend together, as well as every weekend until the weekend before I left in December. In her arms and company, I received the affection, interest, and passion that had been missing from my life. It was hard at first to accept her wanting to please my every wish. In turn, she reveled in the way I treated her as an equal, which, at the time, was not the way Koreans treated females.

Time started to fly by. I wrote to Claudia once over the next three months. I didn't want to deal with that. In turn, I got three letters from her. I didn't bother to open them. I just threw them into my desk drawer.

By November, I knew it would be easy to fall in love with Soon In and forget everything else. Early on, I had cautioned her not to fall in love with me. She understood that I was leaving in December and that the bliss we shared would end. She never pressured me for anything other than to see me each weekend.

The second week in November, Davey and I flew a mission to Hong Kong for General McCall, the Eighth Army commander. Our mission was to take a U-21 to Hong Kong and bring back cargo that his wife was going to buy for a Christmas party. General McCall was hosting the party for a bunch of diplomats. The cargo would consist of gifts and items to support the party. His warrant officer aide and his wife flew commercial air to Hong Kong. The aide would escort the cargo back to Seoul with us. Davey took me along for training on international flights, which would complete my transition into the U-21.

The flight was an experience I never forgot. In 1971, Hong Kong was an enclave under British rule and surrounded on three sides by communist China. The only air route into Hong Kong International Airport was a narrow corridor from the southeast. Since inbound and outbound flights had to use the same corridor, all departures took place in the morning, and all landings took place in the afternoon.

We had to plan our flight to reach Hong Kong in the afternoon. Because of the range of the U-21, that meant we had to refuel in Taiwan. Taiwan—or Formosa, which was its name then—was still under military control. We landed there at about 1100 and refueled. From Taiwan to

Hong Kong was about a two-hour flight. Our international clearance to land at Hong Kong was for 1615, so we had a couple of hours to kill.

We took a taxi down to the market area to look for some LPs. This was the same market area where Davey had bought the pineapples for the luau. Taiwan was a bustling island of bicycles, cars, and crowded markets. Taiwan's population was made up of natives and Chinese who had fled communism. They were friendly, industrialist, and pro-American. Taiwan did not enforce copyright laws, so they would instantly copy every new record. At the stands in the marketplace, we could buy the copies for twenty-five cents a record. The copies wouldn't stand up to much use, but they were perfect for recording on tape. I bought several country and western LPs, and Davey bought several for other officers who had given him a list.

We returned to the airport and prepared for departure. The weather update showed no changes from planning weather, so our ETA to Hong Kong International Airport was still valid. That was important because the authorities only allowed a ten-minute deviation from the estimated touchdown time. If you didn't land within that time frame, they would revoke your landing clearance, and you would have to land somewhere else. That was not a desirable choice for an airplane with the limited range of the U-21.

Taxiing for takeoff was exciting. When we picked up our approved flight plan, the official handed us five five-by-eight cards with numbers on them and an instruction sheet directing us to show a specific card at each checkpoint. To reach the takeoff position, we would have to taxi past five checkpoints. Heavily armed soldiers stopped us at each checkpoint until we showed them the correct number. The idea behind this procedure was to prevent unlawful or hijacked aircraft from taking off. I hate to think what would have happened if a pilot did not show the correct numbered card.

Our flight to Hong Kong was smooth. Before entering the corridor, we contacted Hong Kong approach for a GCA to the runway. GCA directed us through the several doglegs that made up the corridor, and I landed the U-21 at 1612. Since this was a check ride for me, I did all the flying while Davey evaluated my performance. As I taxied to the parking ramp, Davey said, "Nice job, Neal."

While I refueled and secured the aircraft, Davey went into the terminal to find the aide who was to meet us there with further instructions. I finished refueling the aircraft and was completing the logbook entries, when a small Chinese truck pulled in beside the aircraft. Davey and the aide got out. "We've got some cargo to load," Davey said as he opened the U-21's cargo door and climbed into the cabin.

The aide greeted me. "Welcome to Hong Kong, Captain Griffin." He started unloading boxes off the truck and handing them to Davey.

"Good to be here, Chief," I replied, and I helped him unload seven boxes from the truck. Davey arranged them evenly in the cargo bay and secured them with cargo straps.

As soon as we had the cargo secured, the aide said, "Okay, I've got to get back to the general's wife." Looking at Davey, he continued. "As soon as you get to your hotel, call the number I gave you so we can coordinate our activity for tomorrow."

With that, he told the driver to go. Davey and I grabbed our bags, walked over to the flight operations building, and closed our flight plan. "What's the skinny?" I asked as we walked.

"Well, according to the aide, the general's wife has a lot more shopping to do. So we are going to wait until she's finished. We check with the aide each evening at 1800 for instructions. I guess we just have a good time meanwhile."

We caught a cab to our hotel. Davey had reserved rooms for us before we left. The hotel was in decent shape. It was one the army had contracted for military to stay on R&R leaves from Vietnam. The staff was pleasant, familiar with American soldiers, and tolerant of soldiers blowing off steam. It had a Chinese restaurant on the property, which was convenient.

Davey and I spent five days doing nothing until the general's wife decided she had done enough shopping. At first, it was a break, but after two days, it was boring. Each morning, we went to the airfield and checked the aircraft. After that, we would take a cab to downtown Hong Kong and explore the stores and shops. After our 1800 coordination call, we would go to the bar district and spend the evening drinking beer and joking with the working women. Most of the bars and nightclubs catered to the GIs on R&R leave from Vietnam. The atmosphere is always the same in those situations: several pretty women all work to get you to buy them a drink.

Of course, the drink is expensive and nonalcoholic, and they get a cut on each glass. The more you drink, the friendlier they are, and they give you the impression that you are going to end up in bed with them. This goes on as long as you keep buying drinks for you and them. The result is always the same: you get drunk and pass out, or you stop buying drinks, and the woman disappears. It was the same routine I fell for in 1957 in a bar on Gertigstrasse in Munich, Germany.

Whenever the women approached our table, started a conversation, and asked us to buy them a drink, Davey or I would respond, "Okay, we will buy what we are drinking, which is beer."

They would wrinkle their noses, saying, "We don't drink beer." We would stick to our offer, and after a while, they would head for another customer.

After we went a couple times to the same bar, the women knew us. They knew we would buy them only what we were drinking, so they would gather at our table and talk while waiting for customers. Occasionally, one would drink a beer with us. It surprised me to find that most of them were college graduates and highly intelligent. They could discuss most any subject and spoke perfect English. As they explained it, the problem was that when you graduated from college, there were no jobs available. Hong Kong had no way to grow and expand economically at the pace its population did. To find employment, most young people would have to move out of Hong Kong. Hustling drinks was a way for them to make some money until they found employment or married.

Finally, after the sixth day, the chief said, "The shopping is over. I will meet you at the airport at 0900 to load the aircraft and return to Korea."

Davey and I got to the airport at 0730 to preflight the aircraft and file a flight plan. On checking the weather, we found out that a frontal system was stalled midway between Taiwan and Korea. That put it right in our flight path. Davey and I decided to fly to Taiwan and recheck weather to see if there was any improvement. The chief arrived at 0900, and we loaded another eight boxes onto the aircraft.

We had to estimate the weight of each box to ensure we didn't exceed maximum gross weight on the aircraft. By our estimation, we were close to maximum gross weight, and the aircraft thought so too, as it seemed sluggish on takeoff. Once in the air, it flew normally.

The flight to Taiwan was uneventful. With the aircraft on autopilot, there was little to do except sit and enjoy the view, which was clouds and sea. At the weather office, the news was not much better. The front had not moved. In-flight reports from commercial airlines flying through the area described moderate to severe turbulence and estimated cloud tops at fifty thousand feet. Even though our aircraft was equipped with weather radar, there was no way we could penetrate weather that bad.

Neither one of us wanted to remain overnight in Taiwan, so we started looking at what our choices were to fly around the front. We had two choices: the Japanese mainland or Okinawa. The front extended far enough to the east to block our route to the mainland, which was our first choice. It looked as if we would have to take Okinawa.

The distance to Okinawa was just within the cruising range of the U-21. By our calculations, we would have about thirty minutes of our fuel remaining when we touched down on Okinawa. That would not be enough fuel to make it to an alternate airfield, so if we headed for Okinawa, that was where we would have to land or put it down in the ocean. However, there was a minor problem: a squall line about a hundred miles southwest of Okinawa. Pilot reports from the area didn't show any thunderstorms, just heavy rain. We asked the weather forecaster for a printout showing the squall lines so we could see firsthand what he was telling us. The squall line looked to be about twenty miles thick. The forecaster said he expected it to be mostly gone when we got there.

Davey and I looked at each other, and Davey, nodding, said, "That doesn't look that bad, Neal. With our weather radar, we should be able to get through the squall line without any problems. I say we go."

I heard myself say, "Okay, let's do it," as a little butterfly fluttered in my stomach. I had flown in bad weather before but never without an alternate airfield to go to if I couldn't make my destination. Thirty minutes later, we were on the way to Okinawa.

About an hour from Okinawa, we could see the squall line ahead of us. Small white cumulus clouds began to grow and thicken as we approached the squall line. Davey turned on the weather radar. The radar returns marked the areas of heavy rain on our screen. This was my first time flying on instruments and using weather radar to guide me. Davey, after changing the scale several times, selected the scale easiest for us to pick out the lighter rain areas between the thick cells. We wanted to fly through those areas. There would be less turbulence in those areas. Our biggest concern was flying into a thunderstorm, which could rip the plane apart.

Five minutes after entering the cumulus clouds, we met rain and light turbulence. The sky darkened as the rain intensified, and we turned on the red cockpit lights. I was flying on instruments while Davey watched the radarscope and directed me regarding how many degrees to come right or left to avoid the bad areas. I could tell by the darkness that we were in more than just light squalls. I was having trouble holding the aircraft level and keeping our altitude in the turbulence, which was bouncing us at least fifty to sixty feet in all directions. Finally, Davey took the controls and said, "Neal, I've got the aircraft. The blips are so close together I can't direct you fast enough. I can react faster flying the aircraft than you can following my instructions. Watch the scope with me, and try to guide me to light areas if you see any."

I let go of the controls, confirming that he had control of the aircraft by saying, "You've got the aircraft, Davey." I scanned the radarscope, and it looked solid to me. "So much for our weather forecast in Taiwan," I said, thinking out loud.

Davey had to use fifty- to sixty-degree banks to stay in the lighter areas the radarscope was marking. Downdrafts would drop us two hundred feet like a rock. Davey would pull back on the yoke to try to hold flight altitude. Then we would hit an updraft and bounce four hundred feet up. Davey was moving the yoke backward and forward and making steep turns, trying to stay out of the severe turbulence. Steep turns like that, coupled with the way the turbulence was tossing us about, would have given any passenger the idea that we were out of control. Our attention was so focused on controlling the aircraft that we forgot about Chief in the cabin. I turned to look at him and at the cargo to make sure it was not bouncing around in the cabin. Chief looked at me with terrified eyes. His face was ashen, and he looked as if he were about to vomit.

I motioned for him to turn on his intercom. He had his headset on but somehow had turned his intercom off. "Are you okay?" I asked.

"I am a little woozy, sir. Are we in trouble? Do I need to start throwing this cargo out?" he said.

459

"No, we are okay," I answered, trying to calm him. "We will be through this in a couple more minutes," I said. "At least I hope so," I added to myself.

I heard Davey say, "Neal, check fuel level."

Our attention had been so focused on controlling the aircraft that we'd neglected other checks. Under the conditions we were in, the aircraft was consuming more fuel than it normally would have, and when I looked at the fuel gauges, I got more than a little concerned. "Damn, Davey, the best I can tell, both gauges are borderline red," I reported.

Before Davey could tell me what to do, I started thinking again. I switched the VHF radio frequency to Okinawa approach control. "Okinawa approach, this is Army 613. Over."

"Army 613, this is Okinawa approach. Radar contact sixty miles southwest of runway and four miles north of course. Barometer 30.29. Airfield visibility twenty miles. Wind three hundred twenty at sixteen knots. Are you in squall line now?"

"Roger, approach. We are at nine thousand, flying weather radar. Once we get clear, request GCA."

"Roger, Army 631. You should clear squall line in a few minutes. Weather reports squall is located fifty miles from our location. Report clear."

"Roger, control," I answered, and I set the new barometer on the altimeter. By then, we were in light turbulence and flying through breaks in the clouds. Suddenly, as if we'd popped out of a dark room, we were in clear skies.

I looked at Davey and said, "Davey, that was fun, but I never want to do it again." Once again, the old saying that flying is hours of boredom interrupted by moments of sheer terror had come true.

He laughed and said, "You've got control of the aircraft."

"Roger. I've got control of the aircraft," I replied, and I took the controls with sweaty flight gloves. Sweat soaked my flight suit. I looked at Davey and noticed that his suit was also wet. I felt a little better. I figured if flying through the squall line had caused Davey to sweat, then it was okay that it had scared the shit out of me, being that it was my first time. I had thought that once I got over the icing incident in Germany, nothing would scare me again. So much for my macho image.

Davey contacted approach control and reported we were clear of clouds. Approach control switched us to the GCA controller, and fifteen minutes later, we were on the tarmac, refueling the aircraft.

The chief had his color back. He looked at us and said, "I don't know how you do it. I thought we were going to crash. I don't think I will fly in a small aircraft like this ever again."

After refueling the aircraft and checking it to ensure there was no damage from the turbulence, we grabbed sandwiches and ate them while filing our flight plan from Okinawa to Korea. The chief checked for but couldn't find a commercial flight back to Korea, so he had to continue with Davey and me.

The flight back to K-16 was uneventful, and we landed at K-16 around 1900. The route from Okinawa allowed us to skirt the squall line and avoid the area of severe weather that had forced us to divert to Okinawa first. General McCall's aide had a truck waiting for the cargo. The chief thanked us and left with the truck. Davey and I went into operations to close our flight plan and complete the logbook entries.

Major Franks wandered in. "Hey, I'm glad to see you two back. How did the flight go?"

Davey answered, "Great, sir. Captain Griffin is good to go in the U-21. We would have gotten back earlier today, but we had to divert around some severe weather."

I looked at Major Franks. "What's been happening in the company that I need to know about, sir?" I asked.

He shook his head and said, "Nothing. With you two gone, it's been quiet with just routine business. It's Friday night and time to party. I was on my way downtown, when I saw you two in operations, so I thought I would drop by and say hello. Neal, you're in charge this weekend. I'll be back Monday morning." With that, he turned and left.

Davey, watching him get in his jeep, said, "I bet he's going to the Green House to see that woman with those humongous tits."

Davey and I grabbed our bags and walked to the BOQ. The club was half full of officers taking advantage of happy hour. Davey threw his bag by the door of the club and said, "I need a drink. I'm buying, Neal."

"I'll take a rain check. I want to take a shower and put on something that doesn't stink from sweat," I answered, and I walked to my room.

Entering the room, I could smell Soon In's perfume. She was sitting on the couch, reading a magazine. When I walked in, she jumped up and ran to me. After a long, sweet kiss, she wrinkled her nose and said, "You need bathe."

I smiled and said, "Yes, I do. My deodorant failed near Okinawa." I started taking my clothes off. I'm not sure she understood the deodorant comment, but as I undressed, she undressed and led me into the shower. I stood in the steam of hot water as she bathed me. The sensation of her hands caressing and scrubbing me was pleasant and exciting. It aroused a feeling that was playfully teasing and sexual, one I had never before experienced. The most pleasing part was the half smile on her face that said she cared for me. Two hours later, we made it to the club for something to eat and drink.

The nights passed quickly now. I didn't think about Claudia at all on the weekends, but during the weekdays, I would think about the position I was in. I loved and missed Michele and Ron and, in a way, Claudia. It was the middle of November, and my tour would be up December 1. I already had orders to attend the artillery officer advanced course at Fort Sill, Oklahoma, beginning on January 6, 1972. My departure date from Korea was December 2, 1971, with a thirty-day leave before reporting in at Fort Sill. I knew I had a problem that had no easy solution. The decision I had to make in two weeks would cause somebody pain.

I tried to imagine starting a new life. Soon In's and my relations now were easy and not tested by the everyday challenges of living as a family. How would our relations change under the pressure of marriage? If I called it quits with Claudia, I would lose Michele and Ron and the thirteen years we'd spent together. Other than her infidelity, our marriage had been a happy one between the fights. In a way, I wished she would send me a Dear John. That would decide for me. But all I got was the same letter with the date changed.

I tried to war-game a course of action by asking myself, *If you go back to Claudia, can you forgive her and get past what both of you have done? If you forgive her, can you ever trust her again? Can you live with someone you can't trust? Suppose Claudia doesn't want to continue the marriage. What are you going to do? At thirty-three years old, do you want to start over with a new woman? Who do you love?* No matter how hard I tried, my mind refused to consider one course over the other.

The situation left me feeling bad because each week, I could tell that Soon In was falling more in love with me. She knew I was married. I tried to tell her that it was better if we just enjoyed each other's company and did not become attached. If I left without her, I knew it was going to hurt her, and the thought of that troubled me. I realized that was a sign that I was falling in love with her. Her response to that was "You can't tell me who not to love." I decided to let things go until I had to decide.

I lived in bliss with my problem until November 30, which was a Friday. The week before, I had gotten a letter from Claudia asking when I was leaving Korea and where I was going. I answered her letter the same day and told her I would be there on December 4. What I didn't know was whether I was going there to do what Dale had done six months prior or to try to reunite with her. I was torn between being with Soon In and trying to fix my marriage.

Major Franks was also leaving for a staff officer assignment at Eighth Army headquarters. A change-of-command ceremony was set for him and the new commander that Friday. Captain Peary, the operations officer, was responsible for setting up the ceremony. Around noon on Thursday, I walked to his office and said, "John, is everything ready for tomorrow?"

He answered, "Yes, it's all set up. The sergeant major and I are going to rehearse the events this afternoon with the platoon leaders and half of the men in each platoon."

"Great," I said. "Remember, this will be the new commander's first impression of the company, so it needs to be perfect. If you need any help, let me know." John was a young captain and had accepted a direct commission from the warrant officer corps. He lacked the experience that one got by being a second lieutenant and first lieutenant but was doing a satisfactory job as operations officer.

Satisfied that he was on top of the ceremony, I walked to the club. I had briefed my replacement, and since he was sitting at the XO's desk, my official duties as XO were finished. The new CO, Major Harris, had arrived and was sitting in the club with Major Franks, who was briefing him on the company. Major Franks saw me and waved me over. "Neal, I want you to meet the new company commander, Major Harris."

Major Harris stood up and extended his hand, and as we shook, he said, "Good to meet you, Captain Griffin. Major Franks has many good words to say about you."

"Well, I hope he puts them on my OER," I answered.

They laughed, and Major Franks said, "You're never satisfied. You packed and ready to go?"

"Yes, sir," I answered. "They picked up my hold baggage this morning. When are you leaving, sir?"

"I am leaving tomorrow after the change-of-command ceremony," he answered.

"Okay, sir, I'll let you get to briefing Major Harris, but I want to buy you a drink tonight. Nice meeting you, Major Harris."

I left them, got a beer, and took it back to my room. I looked toward the parade field and saw the troops practicing the change-of-command ceremony. I took a shower and dressed. I sat down and looked at my room. It had been my home for eight months, and within its walls, I had experienced a remarkable love. In two days, that love would be a memory if I let it become one. Soon In would be there in a couple of hours, and we would spend our last two nights together for a while. My heart was aching for the love I was about to leave and for the lost love I was going to. I felt tears flood my eyes. Sobbing, I thought, *If only Claudia could treat me the way Soon In does.* In my mind, I showed each woman the same love, tenderness, and respect, but the way they showed their love was different. I wondered if the man Claudia was having an affair with felt the same toward her as I felt toward Soon In. What irony that would be. The more I lingered in these thoughts, the more bitter I felt myself becoming. Shaking my head, I decided I needed another drink, so I got up and headed for the club.

On the way, I looked toward the parade field. The practice must have ended, because the troops were walking back toward the mess hall. I could see Captain Peary walking toward the BOQ. It was strange, I thought, that I hadn't heard the loudspeakers during the practice, because the field was so close. I stopped and waited for Captain Peary to get to the BOQ.

"John, how did the practice go?" I asked.

"Great. I think we are ready," he answered.

"I didn't hear the loudspeakers. You do plan to use the loudspeakers during the ceremony, right?" I asked.

"Oh yeah," he answered. "We are going to set the sound system up in the morning."

"But you checked it to see if it worked?" I said, pushing.

"No. The speakers should work. We checked them in the containers, and all the parts are there," he answered in a slightly agitated tone. I suspect he didn't appreciate my grilling him about the loudspeakers.

"Listen, Captain Peary, I've done many ceremonies in my fifteen years in the army. The one truth that has been consistent all those years is that the loudspeakers never worked correctly. You are putting yourself in an embarrassing position. In the morning, if it doesn't work, the first question Major Franks is going to ask is 'Did you check it out?' When you say no, he is going to ask you why. Standing beside him will be the new CO, Major Harris. His first impression of his operations officer will be your explanation of why you didn't think it was necessary to check the loudspeakers. Now, I don't know about you, but if it was me, I would take those speakers out of their containers, set them up on the parade, and make sure they work when you turn on the power. I've got my officer efficiency report, so whatever you want to do is up to you."

He looked at me as if weighing the effects of the speakers not working. Then he said, "Shit, I guess you're right," and he started walking back to the operations building.

When I picked Soon In up at seven, Captain Peary and four or five of his soldiers were still on the parade field, trying to get the speakers to work. In my room, Soon In, with tears in her eyes, said, "I only stay tonight, so tomorrow you have time to think what you do."

That night was both the saddest and most passionate I have ever experienced. We drifted off to sleep around 2300. I could still hear an occasional "Testing, one, two, three, four, five" coming from the parade field.

The next morning, we made love, and Soon In dressed. As she left, she smiled at me and left me in awe of her beauty and the knowledge that she was mine if I wanted her. Then, with a soft sob, she was gone. I felt terrible. My heart was hurting just as badly as hers. After getting dressed, I went to the club for coffee.

It was 0700, and a few officers dressed in class As were already in the club, drinking coffee and waiting for the change-of-command ceremony to begin at 0900. Since I was leaving tomorrow, I didn't have to take part, but I would attend as a spectator. I ordered an egg sandwich to go with my coffee and joined Jim and Johnny.

Johnny looked at me and said angrily, "You're number ten, Captain Neal."

I knew she was upset with me for letting Soon In leave without giving her some sign of what I was going to do. I couldn't do that, because I honestly didn't know what I was going to do. The only firm plan I had was to attend the artillery officer advanced course. I had no idea how I would feel about Claudia until I saw her again. I said the only words I could think to say: "I'm sorry, Johnny. I told you I was married before you brought Soon In to me. Before I can offer Soon In anything, I must first resolve my status with my wife. I hope you understand that."

She looked at me with intense dark eyes and, nodding, said, "Okay, Captain Neal, you not number ten."

Major Harris walked in, and the club went silent, as if we were all talking about him. Then everybody was saying, "Good morning, sir." I thought this would be a good opportunity to escape further conversation with Johnny, so I excused myself and walked over to Major Harris. "Good morning, sir," I said. "How was your first night in the Fifty-Fifth Aviation Co.?"

He smiled and replied, "It was pretty good except for that damn loudspeaker that kept blaring all night. Every time I drifted off to sleep, it woke me up. Is that a normal routine around here?"

I laughed. "Sorry, sir. That was my fault."

"How so?" he asked.

"Well, your operations officer, Captain Peary, was responsible for the setup and conduct of the change-of-command ceremony. He had the troops out practicing all afternoon. I noticed that he didn't check out the loudspeakers during the practice, so when he got to the BOQ, I asked him why. He said he didn't think it was necessary. I reminded him that this was your first look at the company. You would form a first impression of the officer in charge of the ceremony. If the loudspeaker didn't work and he hadn't at least checked it out, I didn't think you would have a good first impression of him. Besides, it was simply attention to detail to ensure he checked all facets of the ceremony and made sure they were ready. I guess that's why he spent most of the night trying to get the speakers to work."

"Well, Captain Griffin, I guess Major Franks wasn't bullshitting when he gave you credit for the successful daily operations of the company," he said with a smile.

"That's because he was gone most of the time, sir, and left me in charge. I had no choice in the matter," I quipped.

Major Franks walked in and joined us. That gave me the opportunity to excuse myself to join the rest of the officers who were leaving for the parade grounds.

The ceremony took about an hour. Major Franks spoke first, thanking all for the support they had provided and for the professionalism displayed in performing our mission. He then passed the company guide on to the sergeant major, who passed it to Major Harris. Major Harris spoke about how happy he was to assume command of such a fine company. He discussed some of his leadership values and expectations. Then the company did a march by, and the ceremony was over. When Major Harris dismissed the troops, he asked the officers to remain for a few minutes.

After the officers assembled around him, he told them there would be an officers' call in the club at 1500, after he returned from Eighth Army headquarters. With that, Major Franks shook hands with everybody and left with Major Harris. All the officers headed to the mess hall for lunch and then to the club.

I got a beer and went to my room to clean it out. The transport office had picked up my hold baggage Wednesday, so I had only my uniform and some underwear and toilet articles. However, I had several personal papers and books that I had to dispose of. Most went in the garbage. I left several books on the bookcase for the next occupant. By 1500, my room was clean and suitable for the next occupant. Of course, Tony, our houseboy, would clean it on Monday and put fresh linens on the bed.

At 1500, I walked back over to the club. The meeting was just about to start. Major Harris looked at me and said, "Neal, you don't have to attend if you don't want to."

It was my last afternoon there, and I knew those meetings could go on and on. I wasn't in the mood to sit through another policy session, so

I said, "Thank you, sir. I'll take you up on that." I grabbed another beer and walked back to my room. It was warm enough to sit by the pool, so I took my beer to a table and sat, looking at the pool and trying to work on my tangled emotions. Looking at the pool, I remembered when it had been just an emerging hole, and I had been happy because I was on the way home to see Claudia and the kids. Now I was on the way again, but I damn sure was not happy.

I sat for about thirty minutes, sipping my beer and feeling the pain of my life. My mind drifted over all I had been through there in Korea. I was sitting at the table Soon In had sat at on the night of the luau. I already missed her. I blanked my mind. *I need a martini,* I told myself, but the meeting was still in progress, and I didn't want to interrupt it. I had nothing to keep my mind busy, and the pain I was in kept edging through the blank wall I set up to halt it. Then the door to the club opened, and officers started exiting. The meeting was over, and I headed for the club for a martini. As I walked toward the club, I looked up at the balcony, and there was Johnny, watching me from in front of Jim's room.

I waved and entered the club. I was not in a good frame of mind. My heart was broken and full of pain. This was my last night in this place that had cost me a marriage but had given me a look at a different world. I was just a simple soldier from a humble past, and the weight of my predicament was overwhelming me, so I surrendered to the idea of just getting blown away and saying, "Screw tomorrow." I thought of the words in the song I loved so much: "Yesterday is dead and gone, and tomorrow is out of sight. Come and lay by my side, and help me make it through the night." No one was going to be by my side that night, so martinis would have to do.

The club was almost full. It was happy hour, and of course, everybody loves happy hour. Jim, Johnny, Dale, Richard, and Davey crowded around a table, so I got two martinis at the bar and joined them. They looked at me, and I said, "I'm too short to get into a long conversation, so let's just drink and pretend that tomorrow is going to be just like all the rest we have shared."

Jim grinned, picked up one of my martinis, and said, "I'll drink to that."

We drank and bullshitted for an hour or so. We had worked our way through several martinis, when Major Harris walked into the club. He looked around, saw me, and walked over to our table. We stood up and greeted him. "Evening, sir."

He motioned with his hands and said, "Sit down. You guys look like you're getting it on. I didn't mean to interrupt you. I just want to speak with Captain Griffin for a few minutes." He looked at me and asked, "Can we talk in private for a few minutes?"

"Sure, sir," I said. "Do you want to talk here or some other place?"

"Let's go to your room," he answered. We took our drinks to my room and sat down at my small conference table.

Looking at me, he opened the conversation by saying, "I want to make you a proposition, Neal. I want you to extend for six months and be my XO. I guarantee you a maximum OER that will strengthen your career. You can take another thirty-day leave and see your family. What do you say?"

I was stunned. He was offering me a solution to my predicament. But if I accepted his offer, I would lose my place at the advanced course; plus, I left tomorrow afternoon. I didn't see any way he could change courses this late in the game. "Sir, I've got orders to the advanced course, and I would hate to lose the opportunity to attend it."

He answered, "Don't worry about that. I'll get you another quota for six months from now. I really need you to stay and help me command the company until I get my feet on the ground. Major Franks credits you for the professional way the company has performed its mission and the esteem the Eighth Army command group has for it. I think we would make a good team."

He could see the interest mixed with reluctance in my eyes. He said, "Look, think about it tonight, and let me know in the morning. I will need to know by at least 0700 so I can change your orders if you accept."

"Okay, sir, that's a deal. I will let you know one way or the other by 0700 in the morning," I said, relieved that I didn't have to give him an answer right now. He left for somewhere downtown, and I went back to the club.

"What was that all about?" Jim asked when I returned to the table.

"He wants me to extend for six months and be his XO," I answered, smiling at everybody.

"Oh shit, I thought we were getting rid of you. Say you're not going to accept his offer," Jim said, feigning disappointment.

"Well, I haven't accepted his offer yet. He gave me tonight to think it over. I have to give him an answer by 0700 in the morning."

"Hell, Neal, why don't you stay?" Jim said seriously. "You get power for another six months, and you are good at the XO position. All the other officers will hate it because you're such a hard-ass, but you are a good leader. You set high standards and hold officers responsible for doing their job. Hell, I'll follow you anywhere, especially when you head for a party."

I didn't want to agonize over the decision now, so I said, "Speaking of parties, let's party." I motioned to George. "A round of martinis, George! I will deal with the decision drunk so I can think."

Drunk is what we got. Everybody was wishing me well and buying drinks to celebrate my departure. About 2100, the door opened, and several officers walked into the club. They had come to say farewell to me. Among them was my old friend Darrell. He surprised me, because I had not known he was in Korea. It turned out he had only been there for two weeks. When he'd heard I was there and leaving, he and several other officers I had worked with had driven out to say good-bye. We really had a party then. They had to leave in time to get to their compound before curfew, so Darrell and I said good-bye once again. An hour later, Jim and I closed the club and staggered to our beds.

Like all drunks, I fell asleep quickly and slept for three or four hours before waking. Then I felt like shit from all the martinis. I got up, brushed my teeth, and took a couple of aspirin. Back in bed, my mind turned to the decision I had to make.

I struggled for an approach to decide exactly what the hell I wanted. Did I want my life with my existing family, or did I want a new life? I thought about Michele and Ron. If I filed for divorce, Claudia would stay in Germany, and I would never be sure if I would see them again. I thought of Claudia. We'd had some good times together in the thirteen years of our marriage. I'd probably caused our problems by the way I acted. As a kid, I'd had no role model for a good husband, and my tours of duty had separated us often. I could see a reason for our problems. After one tour, we would hardly reacquaint before I was gone again. As a result, we'd developed separate lives and routines that conflicted when we reunited.

Something good had gotten lost along the way, and we just fought each other instead of compromising and working on being together. My tour in Korea must have been the straw that broke the camel's back, and Claudia had taken a course that forever changed life as I saw it.

What would life with another woman be like? What example was I setting for Michele and Ron? My lack of a role model had ill prepared me for being a father and a husband. Did I want to pass that on to Michele and Ron, or did I want to be there to ensure they had the proper role model?

The last six months had changed me. I had crossed a forbidden border. Did I have the strength not to go there again? I felt different, but I was still a decent human being. I still had compassion and empathy. I still had ethics and a conscience. I still wanted to do what was right. I still had my marriage vows, especially the one that mentioned "for better or worse." In my evaluation of myself, I didn't like the man I had become, because it worried me that I couldn't trust him. I honestly wanted the innocence I'd had before I'd come to Korea, but that was gone forever.

I guess the tough question I had to answer was if I could rebuild my trust and respect for Claudia. Was I strong enough to do that? Though it saddened me, I accepted that she needed someone to help her make it through the night, as I did. I was guilty of what she had done, and that had brought out a change in my attitude. Would I be able to remain faithful to her? I had strayed from my bond with God, and that hurt. I had relaxed my discipline and abandoned my principles and integrity. I had let her betrayal become an excuse for my behavior. If the man I prided myself on being had crumbled at the first serious threat to his image and marriage, how would I handle the next threat?

At last, I decided. In the end, the kids influenced my decision the most. I would go back to Claudia and do my best to regain what we had. However, I promised myself that I would not go through the hell that Dale had put himself through. If it was too late, then I could give life with Soon In a try. With that, my drunken and fatigued mind shut down, and I slept.

I was up at 0600, still a bit groggy and wishing I hadn't celebrated so hard last night. I showered, shaved, and put on my class As. I pulled the sheets and blanket off the bed and put them on the couch with the pillowcases. I took one long last look at this room filled with memories and then opened the door and headed for coffee at the club.

About halfway through my first cup of coffee, I saw Major Harris through the window. He walked up, knocked on my door, and then turned and headed for the club. I rose and greeted him. "Good morning, sir."

He smiled as he answered. "Good morning. You look a little hungover."

As we sat down at the table, I replied, "Yes, sir, I am definitely hungover." I knew he wanted my answer, so I continued. "Sir, I gave serious thought to your offer, and regretfully, I have to decline it. I know it would be great for my career, and I am honored that you wanted me for your XO. But if I stay another six months in Korea, I will lose my wife and children. I may have already lost them, so it's important that I go back and try to salvage what's left. I hope you understand."

He looked at me, nodding, and said, "I'm disappointed, but I understand." Standing, he shook my hand and said, "Best of luck, Neal. I hope all goes well with you. I've got to get on to a meeting at Eighth Army, so take care." With that, he turned and left.

George brought me some scrambled eggs and toast. In his accented but good English, he said, "I hate to see you go, Captain Griffin. You have been a good boss and a friend. I wish you a happy life."

"Thanks, George." I stood and shook his hand. "Good luck to you. I enjoyed working with you. I am sure with your help, Jim will make a good club officer."

He smiled. "I'll see to that." He returned to the bar to take care of the officers straggling in for breakfast.

Davey came in. Seeing me, he said, "Damn, I thought you were gone. Tell me you didn't extend."

"No, Davey." I laughed. "I am not leaving till 1100. Captain Lobe is flying me to the airport."

I sat around the club, chatting with everyone, until 1045, when Captain Lobe came in and asked, "You ready to go?"

"You bet," I answered, and standing up, I said, "Take care, everybody. Don't crash and burn." With that, I picked up my bag, and we walked to the Mohawk hangar.

The Mohawk platoon had old 631, the Mohawk used chiefly for training outside the hangar, ready for us. I put my bag in the camera bay and did a preflight while Captain Lobe filed a flight plan to Kimpo. As I got ready to climb into the plane, the guys I'd once commanded came up and shook my hand, wishing me the best. Captain Lobe returned, climbed in, and started the engines. Five minutes later, we were climbing up a thousand feet for the traditional farewell flyby of the club. We made a wide circle of the field and turned on a course straight for the club. We overflew the club at a hundred feet with an airspeed of 350 knots. All the officers were out by the pool and waved to me as Captain Lobe pulled back on the stick, and the 631 climbed like a lost angel to five thousand feet and turned toward Kimpo. I smiled and remembered what Colonel Tate had told me on my first day in Korea. I agreed with him. Korea was the best-kept secret in the army.

Ten minutes later, we landed at Kimpo. I climbed out and grabbed my bag. I shook hands with Captain Lobe and wished him luck.

In the passenger terminal, I was surprised to see Jim standing with Soon In and Johnny. He looked at me and said, "It's been fun, Neal. I hate to see you go. I hope your life turns out okay, and don't forget us."

I shook Jim's hand and said, "Thanks, my good friend. You stay out of trouble."

Soon In stepped up to me and kissed me softly. Then she shook her head, put a piece of paper with her name and address on it in my hand, and stepped back.

The loudspeaker directed us to start boarding the aircraft. With one last look at them, I started up the stairs with the rest of the soldiers to the boarding ramp. I turned back to wave at them. Soon In was waving good-bye to me. I could see that she was crying. My heart broke. Claudia had caused me pain. I had caused Soon In pain. I felt lousy. Tears came to my eyes. I didn't have the heart to play these games. I turned and entered the aircraft.

The 707 landed at the Fort Lewis, Washington, air force base. Right away, I caught a hop to McGuire AFB. There, I booked a Davis Agency charter flight that was leaving in a couple of hours. I had decided not to mess around on this trip. I wanted to get to Munich as soon as possible and start dealing with Claudia.

I had written Claudia a letter a week before I left Korea, saying I would probably be there on December 4, so when the cab pulled up to the building, the kids were waiting for me, as before. They came running out, yelling, "Daddy! Daddy!" I hugged them tightly. Their happiness in seeing me reassured me that I had made the right decision.

They led me upstairs to the apartment. Claudia met me at the door. She smiled and said, "Hi."

I returned her smile and said, "Hi." For an awkward moment, we looked at each other, and then we hugged each other and lightly kissed. There was no way to miss the tension between us. I knew the situation with her, but she did not know the situation with me. If she reads this memoir, she will know.

This time, there was no welcome party. Mom was there, so I hugged and greeted her. Michele and Ron were waiting for me to open my bag for their surprises. I opened it and gave them their small presents. For the first time, I didn't have a gift for Claudia. She seemed a little disappointed but didn't say anything. She was still beautiful. I felt a tug at my heart. I hated the betrayal that stood between us. We should have been happy to be together again. Instead, we engaged in polite talk as if we knew a storm was brewing.

Michele and Ron wanted to tell me everything that had happened since I'd left, so I spent an hour talking and playing new games with them. Claudia fixed some coffee to go with the apple cake she had baked. When I'd finished with Michele and Ron, I took a shower and put on some civilian clothes.

We sat at the table and had coffee and cake while making small talk. When I looked at Claudia, it was hard to not show my anger. She was friendly and acted as if everything were normal. That helped me control my feelings. I had decided I was not going to make any accusations. After all, I had no proof that she had been unfaithful. If I were going to trust her again, I had to start now. I relaxed, and we had a pleasant afternoon. I even felt a little guilty about being unfaithful to her.

Omi and Claudia fixed a schnitzel dinner that was delicious. I washed it down with two German beers that seemed much stronger than the martinis I was used to drinking. Claudia drank wine, and Omi drank beer. When dinner was over, I watched TV with the kids while Claudia and Omi washed the dishes.

As I watched TV, I thought about how different it was this time. The last time, I could hardly wait to get Claudia in bed. Now I seemed indifferent. I welcomed the delays before we would be together and I would have to make love. My hang-up about not having sex with someone I didn't love was troubling me. When we made love, would she be measuring my performance against her lover's? I had always satisfied her in every way, but it was different now. We both had felt different levels of passion, but the problem wasn't so much the sex. I was confident that I was an excellent lover. It was her decision to betray someone who loved her that hurt me so much. How exactly do you arrive at that decision? When do you let go of the controls and give in to temptation? I knew why I had surrendered. If Claudia had not betrayed me, no power on earth would have been strong enough to cause me to betray her. While I knew that to be the truth, I also knew that my character should have been stronger.

When we got into bed, we were like two strangers having sex for the first time. What we did was familiar. We were acting out our parts with no first-time feeling. It was a pretense that all was well. After it was over, I felt a terrible sadness. I drifted off to sleep with a feeling of utter despair.

I woke up with a feeling of enthusiasm. I felt that maybe I could make this work. We got up together, and I went to the kitchen to start breakfast. Claudia washed up while I set the table. When she'd finished, I washed and shaved, and she got the kids up to get ready for school.

We had a pleasant breakfast together. I was a little concerned that perhaps Dale had been wrong and had misled me into believing she had been unfaithful. Things seemed normal, the way we were going. After being gone for six months, I knew to expect a little awkwardness, but Claudia seemed glad to see me again.

When breakfast was over, I washed the dishes while Claudia drove Ron and Michele to school and took Omi home. When she returned, I had the kitchen clean and was reading an old *Stars and Stripes*. After she took off her coat, I said, "We need to start preparations for checking out of quarters and returning to the States."

She seemed hesitant at first, and then she said, "I've got an idea. Now, don't get mad. Why don't we stay here while you go to the advanced course? We don't have to interrupt the kids' school. You can ask for an assignment in Germany when you finish the advanced course."

I was a little stunned. Now her niceness made sense. I cautioned myself to be careful. With measured words, I answered, "No. I don't want to spend another ten months apart. Besides that, I want to spend my last years in the army in the States. I will have to retire in four years, and that will allow me the opportunity to prepare for a job after I retire. I can't do that from Germany."

I could see anger flash in her eyes. "I don't want to go to Fort Sill for ten months and then to God knows where like a bunch of gypsies. Staying here will give the kids time to finish this school year, and then we can join you."

She was mad, and I knew I was not going to give in to her demands. I had decided we would leave together, or I would ask for a divorce. Her lips curled in extreme anger. I cautioned myself to be calm. "Look, Claudia, we have spent so much time apart. I want to be together as a family for a while so we can reconnect with each other. The advanced course is a relaxed time and a chance for us to work on our problems. We really need some quality time together."

I could see by the expression on her face that she didn't care about us being together. She blurted out, "I'm not going, Neal. I want to stay here until you finish the advanced course. If you love me, you will let me stay."

She didn't understand that it was because I was trying to love her that I wanted her with me. I could see this wasn't going to work, so I tried another approach. "Claudia, you can't stay in government quarters while I'm in the advanced course. The rules only allow it for unaccompanied tours. The advanced course is not an unaccompanied tour."

"Then we'll rent an apartment on the economy," she snarled.

"Well, Claudia, I guess the only solution is for us to get a divorce," I calmly said. "I will not go back to the States by myself. You come with me, or let's file for divorce and end it."

She responded, "You know I am Catholic and can't get a divorce. You will have to file for a divorce."

I was slowly getting angry. "What's the biggest sin, Claudia—adultery or getting a divorce?"

She looked at me, a little shocked at the question. "What are you talking about? Adultery? I should ask you the same question."

I could see that we were going nowhere. "Okay, Claudia, you decide. Are you going with me, or are we getting a divorce? Let me know, because by December fifteenth, I am going to start checking out of quarters. We need to know before then where you are going. If you are not going with me, we need to get a place for you and the kids to stay."

I hated to force the issue like that. Again, I was looking for some sign that she wanted to be with me, but it wasn't there. Now I had become the villain by forcing her to either come with me or get a divorce.

She was livid. She got up. "You don't have to worry about me. I have a place to stay," she said, and she grabbed her purse and left.

I reminded myself that this was what I'd expected. I would have to do what I'd come for but remain calm and not show anger or bitterness. I honestly didn't know what else to do. I sat there for about an hour, going over in my mind what I needed to do to close out quarters and move to the States. After a while, I needed something else on which to focus my thoughts. I decided to walk to the housing office to tell them of when we would leave quarters, so they could schedule an inspection.

The morning was gray under an overcast sky, with a damp wind blowing. When I walked the mile to the housing office, I was on the edge of being cold. The office was warm, thank God. I signed the visitor sheet and didn't mind the fifteen-minute wait for my turn.

I completed all the documentation and scheduled an inspection for December 16. That meant we would have to clear the quarters by December 14 so I could clean them and have them ready for inspection on the sixteenth. I knew that what I was doing would anger Claudia even more, but I had to set a date because with us fighting, she would never agree to a date.

The transportation office was in the same building, so while I was there, I completed the paperwork to get our household goods picked up on December 13. I told the clerk that right now, I didn't know whether my wife was staying Germany or going to Fort Sill with me. She said that was okay for now, but she needed to know before December 12. I still had to arrange for shipment of our car, but that could wait. If I shipped it, we would turn it over to the transportation office at the military terminal in Frankfurt, where we would depart if Claudia went with me. I left the housing office building, feeling satisfied. I had started events, and I had a timetable to guide me.

It was getting late, and the kids would be out of school in a couple hours. I didn't know if Claudia would pick them up or if they would ride the bus home. I needed to be home if they rode the bus, because I didn't know if Claudia would be there. I felt like going to a bar and drinking myself silly, but I started walking back to the house. The weather had worsened, and it was raining lightly. On the way, I stopped by the quick shop and picked up a six-pack and the latest *Stars and Stripes*.

I was back in the house by 1400, wet and numb from the cold. It was too cold to drink a beer, so after changing into dry clothes, I looked in the cabinets and found some vodka. There was orange juice in the refrigerator, so I started drinking screwdrivers in the hopes of killing the misery I felt inside. Around 1530, I heard a key turn in the door, and Claudia and the kids entered.

Michele and Ron ran to me and greeted me with hugs. It felt good to be with them again. I asked them about school. They told me about their day as they took off their coats and shoes. I glanced at Claudia.

Anger was still on her face. In a terse voice, she said, "There are groceries in the car. Will you please bring them up?"

"Sure," I answered. "I'd be happy to." I brought up four bags of groceries and placed them on the kitchen table.

Claudia was telling the kids, "Okay, do your homework, and then you can watch some TV. Your daddy will help you."

I helped them with spelling lessons and arithmetic while Claudia fixed dinner. It felt good to be together as a family. It was familiar and relaxing, if only for a short while. Even so, I could feel the tension of being in an unaccustomed routine.

I thought Claudia must feel the same on top of her anger. She had a good life going. She had it organized to fit her schedule, and she was in charge. I sat in the living room. I was a disruption or maybe an intrusion into her life. My interruption was changing everything, and it was not going away. It took away her control of events, and that made her angry.

When the kids finished their homework and started watching TV, I got up and went into the kitchen to fix myself another screwdriver. Claudia gave me a cold look and said, "Save the kids some orange juice for breakfast."

I replied, "There's plenty left. Would you like me to fix you one?"

"No," she replied coldly. "I'll take a glass of wine."

We ate dinner mostly in silence except for talking with Michele and Ron. As usual, they didn't want to eat their vegetables, which always upset Claudia. I was mentally debating whether to bring up what I had done that day, but compared to that morning, the mood was too pleasant to start another fight. After dinner, I played a game with Michele and Ron while Claudia cleaned the kitchen. When she finished, she called someone and sat in the kitchen, talking. It must have been one of her girlfriends because she spoke in German.

At 1900, she hung up and said, "Okay, you two, after you finish this game, go take your baths and get ready for bed." When they were in bed, I read each a story of their choice.

While I was reading to Michele, Claudia stuck her head in the doorway and said, "I'm going to see Lilly. Good night, Michele." She went to Ron's room and said good night to him and then left.

When I finished reading to Michele and kissed her good night, she said, "Daddy, please don't fight with Mommy."

I looked at her and said, "I won't, honey."

After reading to Ron and kissing him good night, I sat in the living room, watching German TV. I switched to rum and Cokes to save the orange juice. I was watching TV to keep my mind occupied. I had forgotten so much German that most of the time, I had no idea what the actors were saying. I was starting to feel the effects of the rum and Cokes. It was just like being in Korea, except I was in Germany and should have been happy. At 2200, I shut the TV off and staggered to bed. I was back where I'd started, except there was no one to help me make it through the night.

I never heard Claudia come to bed. I was wide awake at 0600, and Claudia was sleeping by my side. I lay there and looked at her. She was beautiful. I felt a twinge of desire, and I wanted to wrap my arms around her and hold her tightly. It would have been wonderful to do that and start anew. However, I also felt the hurt of wondering if she had been with her lover. That spoiled the mood and made me mad. It was Saturday, so I got up quietly, went to the bathroom, and got back in bed. After a while, I drifted off to sleep.

When I woke up again, Claudia was out of bed and fixing breakfast. I took a shower and shaved. I wasn't feeling the best and dreaded the confrontation with Claudia. The kids were up and watching cartoons on

TV. I walked into the living room, feeling like a stranger. Michele and Ron saying, "Good morning, Daddy," and giving me kisses reassured me that I wasn't a stranger to them. A plate and cup were at the table for me, so I guessed Claudia was including me in breakfast. I walked into the kitchen and said, "Good morning," in my best indifferent tone.

Claudia's answer was barely audible: "Morning." She put rolls, butter, and jam on the table. She brought out milk, cereal, and juice for the kids. "Michele and Ron, come get your breakfast," she called as she put cereal in their bowls. I got the coffee, poured myself a cup, and, as a friendly gesture, poured her a cup. The kids got their cereal and took it back into the living room so they could eat and watch TV.

We ate in silence for a few minutes, not looking at each other. Finally, I said, "Claudia, we have to talk. We can't ignore the problem, because it won't go away. We have to talk without fighting so we can reach some sane conclusions. I'll do anything you want me to, except go back to the States alone without filing for a divorce."

She replied angrily, "What choice does that give me?"

"That's why we need to discuss what you want to do," I replied. "I've a timeline that I have to meet to get to Fort Sill by my report date. If you are not going with me, then please decide that now so I can help you resettle. I want to part on amiable terms if we have to."

"Wow, you are pushing for a divorce?" she spat.

"No, I am not," I said softly. "I want more than anything for you and the kids to come with me. I don't even know why we are sitting here at this table and discussing this. I can't understand why, if you love me, you want to remain apart for another ten months. You need to tell me why you're so angry that I want you with me. You need to tell me why, because the only reason I can think of is that you've lost interest in our marriage. If that's the case, you need to tell me."

She sat in silence, looking at her plate. Any second, I expected her to say she'd met someone and fallen in love with him, and that was why she didn't want to leave. But she didn't, and the kids interrupted our conversation by bringing in their cereal bowls. She got up and said to them, "Okay, clean up and dress if you want to see that movie you've been talking about all week. It starts in an hour."

She started cleaning up the kitchen, leaving me sitting at the table. I thought that the kids going to the movies would give us an opportunity to talk—and argue, I suspected. I picked up the old *Stars and Stripes* and started rereading it.

She said, "Please drive the kids to the movie while I clean the house," and she handed me the keys to the car. Michele and Ron were excited about the matinee. It was a Walt Disney kids' movie.

I walked them to the ticket window and bought their tickets. I said, "Okay, the movie is over in two hours. Either your mom or I will pick you up here."

I drove back to the apartment. The weather was lousy, with light rain and a cold wind blowing. It was a gloomy day, and it wasn't going to get better. Claudia was sitting at the table, talking on the phone, when I got back. After a while, she hung up and asked, "Do you think we could not fight this afternoon? I had planned a coffee, and I don't want fighting during it to embarrass me."

"No," I answered. "I will be a perfect gentleman. When does it start?"

"Three o'clock," she answered.

"Fine, but we need to talk right now while the kids are at the movie," I said. "I went to the housing office yesterday and scheduled the quarters inspection for the sixteenth. I scheduled pickup of our household goods on the thirteenth. That's next Friday. I will need to reserve seats on a Davis Agency flight by Wednesday. That's why you need to decide what you are going to do. I am flying out of Frankfurt on the seventeenth, either with you and the kids or alone."

She flew into a rage. "Why didn't you tell me this before?" she screamed. "You could have waited for me before making all these plans! I wish you had never come back."

I let the anger overcome me and raged back. "Well, if you would have stayed here yesterday, I would have consulted you. But you took off to be with someone else and ignored me, so don't complain." She was yelling back at me, and I was sure she wasn't in listening mode. I walked away because it was getting too loud, and I didn't want to disturb the neighbors.

I sat down in the living room, full of anger. I was trying my best to save our marriage, and in my mind, she was doing her best to destroy it. Why didn't she say yes or no, for Pete's sake? She came into the living room and looked at me. "What choice do I have? I either go with you, or you file for a divorce. Why can't you consider what I want for once?"

That statement fueled the anger in me. "Listen, Claudia, I am not sure you understand that we are married. Married people live together. I work hard and provide a good life for you. I want to live like some happily married people do. I'll be damned if I am going to support your free and wild lifestyle anymore. Either we are together, or you support yourself. I'll always provide for the kids. But the choice is yours. You're still young and beautiful, and I'm sure there are plenty of men willing to support you. You need to make your choice soon. I don't want to argue about it any longer. So hate me, curse me, leave, or stay with me—just decide!"

She looked at me with venom in her eyes and tersely spit back, "You asshole. I curse the day I ever met you. I feel dirty just knowing I sleep with you and let you screw me."

She continued as I mentally shut her out of my mind. I had long ago learned to let her go on until she got over her anger. Then we would give each other the silent treatment for a week or so until I would say I was sorry and make up. During these periods, I would start feeling juvenile and stupid at the way we were acting. Then I would apologize to make up. I was always the first one to say I was sorry, whether I was right or wrong. However, this time was different. I wasn't making up. I was just going to leave.

She finally stopped and went back into the kitchen. I waited, and right on cue, she started slamming objects around, venting her anger. I waited until the slamming stopped, and then I got up, saying, "I am going to pick up the kids."

As I left, I heard her yell, "Take them to lunch after you pick them up!"

It was still thirty minutes before the movie let out, so I went by the snack bar to drink a cup of coffee and read the *Stars and Stripes*. The weather was still miserable and only intensified the depression I was feeling. I wished Claudia and I could just talk and exchange our thoughts and views, but when we did, it seemed we always ended up fighting. If I suggested she had done something that made me feel bad, she took it as an accusation and would start throwing out what I had done wrong, and we could never go from there. I had read somewhere that feelings were neutral. Explaining how the actions of another person affected your feelings wasn't an attack on the other person. It was a statement of how you felt. But Claudia never saw it that way. We were never successful at resolving issues between us because of our inability to discuss them without getting mad at each other. I guess we were both rather immature.

I picked the kids up on time. They jumped into the car, and I said, "How was the movie? Before you tell me, where do you want to go for lunch? Your mom is having a coffee this afternoon and doesn't want to mess up the kitchen by fixing lunch."

"We want to go to the Wienerwald," they answered in unison. I'd hoped that would be their choice, because there was one just outside the housing area. On the way to the Wienerwald, they told me about the movie. It was cute the way they spoke back and forth, describing the movie in detail.

At the Wienerwald, we had a chicken dinner, for which the restaurant was famous. As we ate and talked, I could see that I didn't want to lose them. They were precious to me. I felt remorse over my failings. I prayed Claudia would not force me to file for divorce.

On the way back to the apartment, Michele asked, "Daddy, what are we doing this afternoon?"

"I don't know," I answered. "What do you want to do?"

"We want to go to a German movie," she answered.

"Okay," I said. "When we get home, we'll ask Mom and see if it's okay."

They ran into the apartment, and Michele said, "Mom, can we go to a German movie, please? Daddy will take us."

Claudia looked at me and at them and asked, "Did you eat lunch?"

Michele answered, "Yes, Daddy took us to Wienerwald. We had chicken and potatoes."

"What movie do you want to see?" Claudia asked.

Michele rattled off a title in German. Claudia looked at me again and said, "Okay. Do you know how to get to the movie house?"

I said no, so she directed me. I said, "We'll be back around four. I hope that doesn't interrupt your coffee."

She answered, "No, I planned it to be a little welcome-back coffee for you. You will still be able to see everyone when you get back."

I took the kids to the German movie. They both spoke German, and although I didn't, I had a great time watching them laugh at funny moments in a different language. I also thought about Claudia. I thought, *If I had said she could stay in Germany while I was in the advanced course, everything would be perfect between us while I was here. Then I would be gone, and she would have another ten months with her lover.* I don't know why I didn't just bring that out in the open. I guess I felt that if she knew I knew, then there would be no reason for us to stay together. Although Korea seemed good compared to now, I wanted to do all I could to stay married to Claudia.

When we got back to the apartment, the coffee was going well. Wine and mixed drinks had replaced coffee as the drink of choice, and everybody was feeling good. I apologized for being late as I greeted those I knew, and Claudia introduced me to some people I hadn't met. I mixed a rum and Coke and joined the party. The kids retired to a bedroom to play games.

Everybody started leaving around 2300, and I was glad. I was the only one who didn't smoke, and although we had the kitchen windows open, the smoky room irritated me. I also was feeling the effects of the rum and Cokes, and the effort of sitting there all that time while struggling to understand and speak German had grown tiresome. Mom had gone to bed with the kids at 2200. The last to leave was Paula, so I said good night to her and went to the bedroom to take a shower.

I was almost asleep, when I heard Claudia come in, brush her teeth, and put on her nightgown. She got into bed and asked softly, "Are you still awake?"

I was a little surprised at the soft tone of her voice. "Yes, I'm still awake," I answered.

She rolled over, put her hand on me, and pulled me toward her. I thought, *Now she's going to try sex to change my mind.* I wanted to resist but couldn't. Whatever happened, I wanted her to remember that in sex, I was good. I didn't know how good her lover was, but she probably had compared us. It was a misplaced value, and I knew that, but at the time, because of her anger at me, it was all I had. That night almost brought back the first-time feeling that had been so special for me in the past. Afterward, with the tension of the last two days eased, we both slept soundly.

She was taking a shower when I awoke. "Do you want to go to church with me?" she asked.

"Sure," I answered, thinking maybe she was giving in to going with me to Fort Sill. So after breakfast, we went to church. Worshippers packed the church. The priest conducted Mass in Latin. I, of course, understood nothing they said, but at least we were together and not fighting.

After church, we went shopping at the post exchange in Munich. We didn't talk much, but when we spoke, it was without anger. At 1500, we picked up Mom to go to a gasthaus for Sunday dinner, which was the custom in Germany. We finally got back to the apartment at 1900.

In the apartment, Claudia told the kids, "All right, take a bath, and get ready for bed." Then she said to me, "Neal, do you mind watching them? I want to go see Lilly for a couple of hours."

"Sure," I answered, wondering if Lilly was the excuse to see her lover. I took a deep breath and cautioned myself against starting an argument. As she left, she looked at me with an "I'm sorry" look on her face. I fixed a rum and Coke, feeling as lost, lonely, and betrayed as a man could possibly feel. I was glad that Marcy no longer lived across the street. It would have been an effort not to see her. Claudia had told me about Dale serving divorce papers to her.

I put the kids to bed and read each a story of their choice. I drank rum and Cokes until I felt smashed and went to bed at 2300. I didn't hear Claudia come in or go to bed, and I didn't much care.

I woke up at 0500. I thought I would get up, use the bathroom, and go back to bed, but the way I felt, I knew I wouldn't be able to go back to sleep, so I slipped into the kitchen and put on water for coffee. Then I decided I would drive to the quick shop to get a *Stars and Stripes* to read and some doughnuts to go with the coffee. When I returned, I made the coffee, poured a cup, and ate three doughnuts while reading the paper.

At 0630, I heard Claudia moving in the bedroom. She came out in her bathrobe and woke the kids for school. She said, "Good morning," as she entered the dining room.

"Good morning," I answered.

She saw the doughnuts and said, "Oh, I'm glad you bought them. I haven't had a doughnut in years."

"Help yourself," I replied, and I left to shower and shave while she got the kids ready for school.

I was shaving, when she stuck her head in the doorway and said, "I'm taking the kids to school. Be back in a few minutes."

It was Monday, and in two days, I had to buy tickets on a Davis Agency flight. I still didn't know what to do. I cleaned up the kitchen while I waited for Claudia. When she came in, I said, "Look, you have to tell me what you plan to do. Are you going with me or staying here? If you are not going, you need to tell me if you want me to help you move. You have to move out of quarters, and if you wait until the last minute, I can't help, because I'm leaving on the seventeenth."

She looked at me with anger in her eyes. "I guess we will have to get a divorce. All we do is argue anyway. I don't want to live the rest of my life arguing with you. Why can't you just let me stay here while you are in the advanced course? I can come to the States to visit you, and then when you get your next assignment, we will move there."

"Okay, Claudia, stay. I don't care anymore. I am fighting to keep us together, and you are fighting to separate us. Tell me where you want your household goods sent, so I can tell transportation. I won't argue anymore. You stay and have a happy life. It was stupid of me to think you would want to be with me. I'm finished." I grabbed my jacket and left.

I walked in the brisk morning to the entry gate to the housing area. There was a cabstand there, and I took a cab to the main Bahnhof. I watched the buildings pass by in the gloomy weather. Munich was a lovely city of old architecture blended with new architecture that originated from replacement of buildings destroyed in the war. I had no idea what I was going to do when I got to the main Bahnhof.

I got out and paid the cab driver in front of the main Bahnhof. I stood there for a few minutes, thinking, *You're here now. What are you going to do?* I decided to walk the streets I'd walked as a young and innocent soldier long ago. I started walking and, an hour later, ended up at the Hofbräuhaus.

It was 1100, and the place was already half full. I went in and found a table. The server brought me a liter of light beer and a pretzel. To this day, their pretzels remain the best pretzels on earth. I drank beer and ate pretzels while studying the early crowd of people.

I tried to identify which people were unhappy like me. It was easy to pick out the happy and unhappy couples. The happy couples showed each other the interest that I knew was missing from my life. The unhappy couples showed less interest in each other and more in other people. In the glancing looks of the women among the couples I judged unhappy, I could see an expression that said, "I would rather be with you." I missed the attention Soon In always gave me. I played this game until I was full of pretzels and beer.

I left the Hofbräuhaus wasted. I had to concentrate on walking to keep from staggering. Fortunately, I had an hour's walk in the brisk air to clear my head. I had nowhere else to go, so I took a cab back to the apartment.

Still drunk, I let myself into the apartment. Claudia was gone, which disappointed me and made me happy. I made it to the bed and fell asleep.

It was dark when I woke up. I felt like shit. I looked at my watch; it was 2030. I could hear the kids playing, and when I walked out of the bedroom, my appearance surprised Michele, Ron, and Omi. Omi, in German, asked, "Neal, where have you been?"

"I was taking a nap," I answered. Then she said something in German that I didn't fully understand. It was about Claudia going somewhere. The kids invited me to play with them, so I played Don't Get Mad until Omi announced it was time for them to go to bed.

Omi put them to bed, and I read a story to them. Omi went to bed also. There was a cot in Ron's room that she used when she stayed overnight. Before she went to bed, she got onto me for my behavior. She said a lot about Claudia and me that I didn't understand. I could detect by the tone of her voice that she was angry, but my limited German precluded me from accurately expressing my position, so I accepted what she said.

I watched German TV for a while and then took a shower and went to bed. I slept soundly and woke up thinking I was back in Korea. Claudia was still asleep, so I slipped out of bed, used the toilet, and headed for the kitchen to fix some coffee. I was on my second cup, when Claudia came into the kitchen. We gave each other a cold glance as Claudia poured herself a cup. She started getting rolls, butter, and jam out for breakfast. She set the table and placed a plate in front of me. *How long can this go on?* I thought.

I kept thinking, *Why don't I just come out and say, "Claudia, I know you are shacking up with some guy. So why don't you just say it's true that you don't want to be married to me any longer, and let's get this over with?"*

However, if I did that, I would have to live with it, and somehow, I wasn't truly ready to believe that she was unfaithful. I knew I was grasping at straws, but if she admitted it, then it would be over, and I guess down deep, I didn't want it to be over. Besides, I was as good or better as a lover than the other guy, and I suspected I was a better provider. Maybe I had a chance to turn it around.

She spoke, interrupting my thoughts. "We need to go to the commissary today. I don't have any food for dinner and the rest of the week. Plus, we need cleaning supplies to clean these quarters."

"That's fine with me," I answered. "When do you want to go?" I felt a ray of hope. She was accepting that we were moving out of quarters. "Have you decided where you want the household goods sent? I have to tell transportation tomorrow."

She looked at me with an expression of mild anger and resignation and said, "I don't care. Send them to the States. I don't need anything but the clothes for me and the kids, and I will move them to Mom's apartment on Wednesday."

So much for my optimism. Obviously, she had decided she wasn't going with me. I fought the anger rising in me and said, "Okay. But I don't need all this stuff. Why don't I see if I can put it in storage? Then, when you have a place to put it, I will tell transportation to send it to you."

"Can you do that?" she asked.

"Well, that's what I have to do anyway because I don't know where to send it in the States until I get an address at Fort Sill. So they will put it in storage and wait for an address. I'm sure they would prefer to save the transportation cost of sending it to the States."

It was time to get the kids ready for school, so she got up and ended our conversation. She took the kids to school and took Omi home while I cleaned up the kitchen. When she got back, we went to the commissary to buy food and cleaning materials. After we had the supplies in the car, I asked, "You want to have lunch at the Wienerwald?"

"Yes," she said enthusiastically. "But let's take the groceries home first." We were almost back to normal while putting the groceries away—more polite than usual, but it was a routine that we had shared many times over the last thirteen years.

We got to the Wienerwald just as the lunch crowd was thinning. After ordering and getting our drinks, I looked at her and softly said, "I love you, Claudia, and I don't want to go to the States without you. No matter what you think or feel for me, you need to know that I truly love you, and what's happening to us doesn't have to be."

She looked at me and then looked away. We sat in silence for a while. Then she said, "Neal, I just don't want to go to the States now. I don't know what my feelings are for you after all the fighting and the way we've done each other. I know I don't want a divorce, because you know I am Catholic and can't divorce. I think if I stay here while you are in the advanced course, I will be able to sort out my feelings."

I gave up then. "Okay, stay. I won't file for a divorce now. But you can't stay in quarters, because the advanced course is not an unaccompanied tour."

"I know. I will move in with Mom for now until I find something," she said in a relieved tone.

I took a deep breath and said to myself, *That's it, Neal. Be nice for the little time you have left together.* She had finally broken my heart beyond repair. Clearly, she no longer cared for me, so there was no longer any reason to try. My behavior changed in that moment. I decided I just wanted as much sex as possible before I left.

I was my best self from that moment on. That night, whether as a reward for my seeing it her way or as a way to say good-bye, we made the most passionate love we'd made in more than a year.

The next morning, she was up and had the kids ready for school when I got up. I had breakfast while she took the kids to school. When she returned, we began listing the tasks we needed to do that day. When we got to the bank account, I said, "I need to cancel the allotment to the bank. You can keep all the money in there now, and I will send you some money each month." She was not happy about that, and our newfound cooperation ended.

"Why do you need to cancel the allotment?" she asked angrily.

I tried to answer with a neutral reply. "Claudia, all the money I'm paid except a hundred dollars goes to you. I can't live on a hundred dollars a month in the States. In Korea, it was okay because I didn't need much money. But in the States, it's different. Besides, for what do you need all the money? I will send enough to take care of you and the kids. The guy you are shacking up with can provide the rest." That was the wrong choice of words to say, but her expectations of me had finally exceeded my capacity.

With a shocked look on her face, she exploded into a tirade of accusations and denunciations. I listened quietly. When she paused for a moment, I said, "What else do we need to put on our list?"

She jumped up and screamed, "Do whatever you want to!" She stormed into the bedroom. I had saved that detail for last because I knew it would end the peace between us.

I walked back to the bedroom, stuck my head in, and said, "I'm leaving now to take care of everything."

She was sitting on the bed, and when I said I was leaving, she jumped up and said, "I'm going with you."

We drove in silence to each of the offices. She waited in the car while I completed each action. I had one chore left to do when it was time to pick up the kids. We dropped by the school and picked up Michele and Ron on the way to Davis Agency to schedule my flight to the States. I got out of the car and walked around the rear of the car, past the passenger window. Claudia had rolled it down and was looking at me. It appeared she was crying. In despair, I stopped and looked at her and said, "Last chance. Make one reservation or four?"

She looked at me for what seemed like an eternity and then looked away. I turned to go, and I heard her spit out, "Make four." I kept walking, and I heard her say loudly, "Neal, make four!"

I turned, looked at her, and asked, "Are you sure?"

Looking straight ahead, she softly answered, "Yes," but the tone of the *yes* was one under duress.

I made four reservations. I knew that her agreeing to go had not changed the way she felt. She still had me caught in a web that was inescapable anytime soon. I would face more torment before our life got better.

Once Claudia accepted that she was going with me, her attitude improved slightly. We got along better and worked together to clear quarters. We cleaned Friday afternoon in preparation for our checkout inspection on Saturday. We spent Friday night sleeping on borrowed sheets with suitcases packed. We planned to drive to Frankfurt after the inspection to turn our car over to transportation for shipment to the States and spend the night in the military guesthouse.

After we got up Saturday morning, we drove to the snack bar and had breakfast. I waited at the apartment for the inspector while Claudia took the kids and borrowed sheets back to Omi. Before she left, she said, "Neal, after I drop the kids off, I am going to Lilly's to say good-bye. I should be back after that."

I watched her drive away with my heart feeling the pain of where she was going. It was 1000, and the inspector was due at 1130, so I went back over the stove and refrigerator once more while I waited. Those are the hardest items to get past the inspector. By 1200, I was beginning to worry about whether the inspector was going to make it. I could not leave until he signed my quarters clearance sheet. Finally, the phone, which was still in service, rang. It was the inspector with his excuse about why he hadn't made the 1130 appointment. He said he would be there at 1400. I reminded him of my situation, and he assured me he would be there.

I stuck a note to the apartment door, telling Claudia I had walked to the quick shop for a beer. I walked to the quick shop, bought a six-pack of Budweiser, and took it back to the apartment. Claudia was still not back. For a moment, I entertained the thought that she might have abandoned me there, but after the second beer, I realized saying good-bye sometimes takes longer than just saying good-bye.

The inspector arrived at 1400 on the dot. The inspection took about fifteen minutes, and he was signing the clearance paperwork when Claudia walked in. I was a little relieved but still feeling the sting of thinking about where she had been and what she had been doing. I gave the inspector the last three beers as he left. Claudia did the best she could to not look guilty and said, "I'm sorry I was gone so long, but Lilly wanted to have lunch together one more time. I thought the inspector was coming at 1130. What happened?"

"No problem," I said, looking at her. I don't know what she saw in my expression, but what I was saying mentally was *How can you look me in the face and lie so easily?* "The inspector was running late this morning and called to reschedule for 1400. Well, we are through here, so let's get the kids and head for Frankfurt."

It took another thirty minutes and many tears to say good-bye to Omi, but at last, we drove away in silence. I was thinking, *I have spent nine years of my life in Germany. I found happiness here, and I lost happiness here. I will never return to this place because of the bad memories it holds.*

We drove to Frankfurt and turned the car over to transportation. We spent the night in the Armed Forces Hotel and left on a Davis Agency charter flight at 1400, headed for McGuire AFB, New Jersey.

My tour in Korea was over. My trust in Claudia was gone. My integrity was questionable. I was emotionally broken and looking for some direction. The only choices I saw were to rebuild our marriage or continue on a path of destruction. As our airplane lifted off, I sighed and resolved to rebuild.

CHAPTER 5

Artillery Officer Advanced Course

A time to strive and a time to fail.

D ependents and families headed home for the Christmas holidays filled the flight to McGuire AFB. We were lucky to get seats that kept us together. The Davis Agency charter flights were cheap and, therefore, packed with as many seats as possible. Claudia and I sat across from each other in aisle seats, and Michele and Ron sat beside Claudia. We looked like a normal family flying back to the United States. However, tension and anger simmered just under the skin.

I was happy that we were together and headed to the United States. I was angry because of the conditions under which Claudia was going with me. She wasn't with me because she loved me and wanted to be with me. She had made it clear that her preference was to remain in Germany. To me, that meant she wanted to stay with her lover. I believed she felt she had to come with me or lose the life I was supporting. Sometimes, in my lowest moments, I wished I was back in Korea.

Claudia was angry, I'm sure, because I'd forced her to come with me. Somehow, she rationalized that her actions were acceptable, but we couldn't divorce because she was Catholic. What gave me hope that we could resolve our problems was that I didn't have proof of her infidelity. I wanted to believe our rift was because of the long separations, which had been close together. I could not understand how, despite it all, I loved her. Because of that, my infidelity tortured me. Something in my character was wrong, and that deeply alarmed me. How could I slip so easily from the life I'd had with Soon In back into the life I had with Claudia? Was I a fool or so weak morally that I could discard what I felt for Soon In? I could take no pride in myself. Even as I worked hard to atone for my actions by getting us back to at least the relations we'd had before I went to Korea, I did so knowing that it was not what Claudia wanted.

If I could salvage anything from the travesty my life had become, the artillery officer advanced course would provide the time to do it. The course was nine months long and would be an opportunity to take a break from the stress of military life. The army had designed the course to prepare company-grade officers for staff positions in battalions and brigades. The curriculum balanced a heavy focus on gunnery with combat planning, supply, and maintenance, set in an academic environment at Fort Sill. New subjects for me were nuclear weapons planning and employment. The instruction, scheduled over a nine-month period, provided a lot of free time for socializing and family time.

First, we had to get to Fort Sill. The flight was uneventful until we were about halfway to McGuire AFB. Most of the passengers, including me, were trying to sleep. Claudia was awake because the stress of flying kept her awake. The flight had been smooth with no turbulence, when all of a sudden, we began feeling light turbulence. That woke me up, as well as several other passengers. Claudia looked across the aisle and asked if everything was okay. I said, "Yeah, nothing to worry about."

I pulled a magazine out and started reading it. After about ten minutes, the turbulence became worse. It was jarring the aircraft in sharp slaps. I could feel Claudia looking at me for some comfort. Unfortunately, I was a little concerned. I had never experienced this form of turbulence. It felt as if it were trying to shake the aircraft apart. Knowing that Claudia was looking at me for reassurance, I continued to read the magazine as if all were well. Finally, after one violent jar that drew a response from most of the passengers, I looked at Claudia.

She was trembling and frightened. The kids were looking around her at me also. I smiled and said, "It's okay. It's just some moderate turbulence. We should be out of it soon."

Looking into her eyes, I could see that my words didn't ease her fears at all. She wasn't the only one scared now. Many passengers were looking around as if searching for somewhere to get out of the shaking aircraft. The pilot rescued the rampant emotions when he announced, "Ladies and gentlemen, I apologize for the turbulence. It appears that we have entered an area between two weather fronts and are experiencing shear turbulence. To get out of it, I have to turn ninety degrees to our course. That means we must fly toward Newfoundland. As a result, we will burn too much fuel to make it to McGuire. Therefore, we have to land in Newfoundland to refuel. I am sorry about the delay. We should be clear of this turbulence in about twenty minutes."

We could feel the aircraft bank and turn to the right. Just as the pilot had said, the turbulence began to subside after about twenty minutes. From then on, we were in light turbulence until we landed in Newfoundland. The detour to Newfoundland and refueling took three hours. The flight from Newfoundland was mostly smooth with a few patches of light turbulence.

We landed at McGuire AFB around 1900. The weather was cold and dreary. As we waited to claim our baggage and go through customs, Claudia asked with a little sarcasm, "What are we going to do now? We don't have a car. Are we going to fly to Fort Sill or catch a bus?"

"No," I replied. "Let's take a cab and rent a room at the post guesthouse. Then we can eat dinner and get a good night's sleep. Tomorrow we will take a cab to a car dealership and buy a car."

She wasn't exactly keen on that idea, but exhaustion and fussy kids stymied further conversation. We finally got all of our bags and made it through customs. Although McGuire was an air force base, civilian cabs lined up in front of the terminal as if we were in a civilian airport. We piled into one, and on the way to the guesthouse, we passed several car dealerships. One was a Ford dealership that had a big sign advertising Ford Pintos for $2,000. I pointed to it and said, "That's where we will get a car."

She wrinkled her nose and said, "I don't like Ford Pintos."

I replied, "Well, let's at least look at them in the morning."

We checked into the guesthouse and walked next door to a restaurant for dinner. While we were eating, Claudia said, "Neal, did that turbulence bother you at all? You were sitting there so calmly reading, while it terrified me. Were you just pretending?"

I looked at her and smiled. "Yes, it concerned me. I have never been in turbulence that bad. But if I had shown my fear, would that have made you feel better? I did not want to frighten you and the kids any more than you were. I figured if you saw that it did not alarm me, then maybe you would feel better."

"Well, it did help a little," she said, "but I don't think I like flying anymore." That was the first warm conversation we had had since I'd gotten back from Korea.

After bathing the kids, we finally got them to sleep. They wanted to watch TV all night. There were many more programs than there were in Germany. Claudia and I took a shower and went to bed. She drifted off to sleep quickly. It took me a little longer. I lay there remembering Soon In's warm body snuggled against mine. I looked at Claudia sleeping on the far side of the bed and longed to hold her and feel her body against me. More than that, I wanted her to feel that way about me. I understood then that the memory of Soon In would be my punishment, because Claudia would never show me the tenderness and passion she had.

The kids woke us up the next morning by turning the TV on. After breakfast, we left the kids in the room and walked to the Ford dealership. I looked at the Ford Pinto. It was a cheap hatchback big enough to hold our suitcases. Claudia did not like it, but when the dealer said that because I was an officer, I did not have to put anything down and he would discount the price to $1,800, she changed her mind. We bought a blue 1971 Ford Pinto and drove it back to the guesthouse. After we loaded the kids and suitcases, we headed west to Fort Sill.

It took two days to drive to Fort Sill, and we arrived late in the evening on the second day. It was a terrible drive. The roads were mostly snow packed, icy, or mushy from melting snow. But I was happy. I was back in the Unite States, and I was never leaving it again. I had been in the army for sixteen years and spent more than eleven of those years overseas. I was ready for a tour in my country.

When we got into Lawton, it was late. We did not feel like driving around to look for a motel, so we spent the night in the guesthouse at Fort Sill. That was cheaper anyway and near the offices I needed to visit. In the lobby of the guesthouse, I noticed a handout for incoming officers attending the FAOAC. I picked one up as we checked in. After dinner in the officers' club, I had a chance to read it. The handout said there were no quarters available for officers attending FAOAC and listed several Realtors with houses for rent in Lawton.

I did not have to sign in until January 15, so I had plenty of time to find a house. My only concern was Christmas, which was a week away. I wanted to be in a house by then so I could have Christmas with the kids. After breakfast the next morning, I started calling Realtors. I got lucky and found a house on the outskirts Lawton that was available. The Realtor agreed to meet us there at 1000 so we could look at it.

The Realtor gave me some directions to get to it, but it still took me half an hour to find it. It was a new-looking three-bedroom house at the end of a side street. It was part of a small subdivision of about forty houses. The outside of the house was well kept. When we saw the inside, Claudia and I agreed on renting it. The Realtor told us that most of people living there were military from Fort Sill. We signed for the house and paid the first month's rent. Because I was an officer, I did not have to put down a security deposit. The Realtor gave us our keys and drove away, leaving us in an empty house.

Before leaving Korea, I had asked army transportation to ship my household goods to Fort Sill. That turned out to be a wise decision on my part. We drove back to Fort Sill to the transportation office to see if my household goods were there. Again, good luck was with me. They were there, and transportation would deliver them tomorrow morning.

We got our household goods the next morning. By early afternoon, the empty house was full of our furniture. We unpacked boxes all afternoon, stopping only to eat. When we went to bed, the house was ready to live in. We were fortunate to only have a few items damaged after being shipped from Germany and sitting in storage for more than a year and a half. While we were unpacking, the couple renting the house across the street came over and introduced themselves. He was a master sergeant and an instructor. She was French. They became good friends of ours while we were there.

Once the house was up to Claudia's liking, we started getting ready for Christmas. We had to buy all-new decorations and a tree. Then we decided on presents for the kids. The weather cooperated by providing snow. It was our first Christmas together in three years. I got a permit to cut a Christmas tree on Fort Sill, so everyone was a little excited about cutting our own Christmas tree. We drove to an area set aside for cutting Christmas trees and walked around, looking for the perfect tree. We had fun doing that, except when it came to picking a tree, nobody agreed on the same tree. I finally ruled on which tree. That was the first and last time we did that. I did everything I could to make the holiday fun. Claudia tried too, but there was a contentious atmosphere between us. While we were pleasant, I'm sure the kids sensed the strain. However, overall, it was a merry Christmas.

A couple of days after Christmas, Claudia gave me some hope that we could work through our problems. I do not know if her libido took charge or if she found something in me, but that morning, we fell together in passionate love. It was like the days before I'd gone to Korea. After that, our relations began to normalize slowly. On New Year's Eve, we ate dinner at the officers' club and watched the countdown to New Year's Day on TV. It was 1972, and I prayed it would be a new year for us.

With the holidays over, I focused on preparing for my course. Part of that preparation was to see a doctor. Over the last two months, I had noticed a small protrusion on the lower left side of my groin. I was sure it was a hernia. I figured I had caused it when I picked up the heavy rocks I was using to build the barbecue pit. The little bulge didn't cause any pain, and when I was in a reclined position, it disappeared. My leave was up on January 15, but I decided to sign in early and see a doctor.

The doctor confirmed my diagnosis, and two days later, I was in surgery to repair my hernia. It was my first surgery. They gave me a spinal to deaden my groin area. When I woke up from the surgery, the nurses told me I had to lie still for six more hours before I could sit. This was to let my body replace my spinal fluid so that I would not get the headaches associated with spinals. Unfortunately for me, lying on my back for so long did not suit my anatomy.

After about two hours, I began to experience agonizing pain in my lower back. When I could no longer stand the pain, I called the nurse over. I told her my problem and said I had to turn onto my side to get off my back. She said I could not do that. I insisted I had to. She said, "All right, I will give you some painkillers."

She brought me two pills. I took the pills and waited for them to work. After about thirty minutes, my pain had only gotten worse. I called the nurse back and told her to give me something that would work, or I had to turn onto my side and get off my back. I could see she was a little frustrated with me. She said, "I just gave you some medicine for pain."

I said, "It didn't work." She left, and all I could do was watch the clock as it slowly ticked away time.

Soon she was back with her supervisor, a major. The major asked me what my problem was. I explained my pain and threw in the fact that the spinal-induced headache could not be worse than the pain I was suffering. She told the nurse to get me something, and they left.

In a couple of minutes, the nurse returned with two big pills. I took them, and five minutes later, my pain subsided to a dull but bearable ache. I tried to sleep but could not. My eyes kept opening to see what time it was. Two hours later, I had to take two more of the pills for relief.

I lay there on the gurney as the pills wore off, and the pain started increasing, but I only had five minutes longer to wait. Slowly, I watched five minutes tick away, and when the clock hit 1600, I turned onto my side. I felt immediate relief. Several minutes later, the nurse noticed me lying on my side. She walked up and said, "No one told you it was okay to turn over."

I pointed to the clock and said, "I can tell time. My six hours were up."

She walked away, and I heard her say, "What a pain in the ass."

Twenty minutes later, they moved me into a hospital room and put me on a bed. They told me that until the doctor saw me, I could only get out of bed to use the toilet. If I got out of bed, I had to be careful not to rip out the stitches. At 1700, a food server brought dinner. After eating, I had to pee, so I carefully got out of bed and went to the bathroom.

As I peed, I noticed I had little sensation in my penis. That worried me. That was a sensitive area and should not be numb. I rationalized that the numbness was from the spinal still wearing off, or God forbid, the surgeon had severed the nerves to my penis during the surgery. I was eager to see the doctor.

The doctor did not come until the following morning. I had a restless night, feeling a little worried about having no feeling in my penis. He showed up around 0900 and looked at my incision. He said it looked good and asked if I had any questions. I told him about my seemly paralyzed penis, and he laughed. He assured me the only nerves severed were surface nerves, which would grow back in a couple of weeks. I asked him when I could get out, and he said after he checked me tomorrow.

Claudia came to see me in the afternoon. She laughed when I told her about the severed nerves. I told her I would be home tomorrow. I am a funny guy when it comes to people visiting me in the hospital. I would rather they did not. I find it hard to carry on a conversation. I believe most people visit sick people because they feel they have to and not because they want to. They come to show their respect or to avoid having friends think ill of them for not visiting a sick friend. I prefer to suffer or heal alone. If close friends do not come visit me, I do not think anything less of them. I wondered if Claudia came because she loved me and was worried or because she was my wife and felt she had to.

I got out of the hospital on January 20. The doctors put me on convalescent leave for ten days. It restricted me from any lifting or exercise other than walking. The convalescent leave caused me to miss my class start date, and the school rescheduled me for the next class. Therefore, I was in a casual status until my new class started on March 6.

Casual status was fun and relaxing. I would report to the student battalion each morning at 0800. There were several of us on casual status, and each morning, the S1 would assign us details, such as writing a letter or a report, aiding an instructor in a classroom, or doing any task that called for a captain. Most of the time, there was nothing to do, so we would hang around for an hour or so and then go home. As long as the S1 could contact us, he was happy. Most of the time, the details only lasted a couple of hours, and we would have the rest of the day free.

By then, I had received notice that my Ford Capri had arrived at the Port of Houston Authority. Several other captains had cars waiting there for pickup also. As had happened in Germany, the Fort Sill flight detachment flew six of us to Houston in a U-21. I picked up the Ford Taunus and was back in Lawton around 2400. The Taunus drew attention. It was race-car orange and not sold in the United States. They didn't go on the market in the United States until 1973.

Much to my surprise, I became uncomfortable after a couple of weeks in casual status. I felt I should be doing something to earn my pay. However, the other captains convinced me that it was okay. We were just taking the comp time for all those twelve-hour days and seven-day weeks we'd worked. When I thought of it in those terms, it made sense. Besides, the students considered the advanced course a time to rest and regroup, spend time with family, and prepare for higher responsibility.

Casual status was good in one way but caused other problems. It seemed that too much time together caused Claudia and me to quarrel more often. Then there was Michele. I had hoped she would grow out of the "I want a horse" phase. She could not understand why she could not have one now. When I explained that we would only be there for nine months and then would move, she would get upset. Her response was "Why can't we stay here? Why can't we take the horse to the new place in a trailer?" I finally convinced her that no matter where we went after the advanced course, she would get her horse. That was a dangerous promise because I did not know where my next assignment would be.

I healed from my hernia operation and started my course on March 6. Claudia and I slowly settled into a routine and grew a little closer. There were two sections in my class. One was US officers, and the other was foreign officers. The one major in the class was the class leader. I was the ranking captain and in charge of the US officer section. A Brazilian LTC was in charge of the foreign section. In the section, there were ten Vietnamese, three Korean, and five South American captains, as well as five captains from several African countries.

During the course, Claudia became friends with several of my classmates' wives and the wife of the Brazilian LTC. The relaxed atmosphere of the school was conducive to social activities, so we had many parties, dances, and road trips. It turned out there were no German wives among my classmates. I was happy to see Claudia become friends with American wives. The wives had several coffees and other social functions. All in all, it was a fun time.

I had no problems with the academics. Although I had been in aviation for the last couple of years, my knowledge of gunnery and field artillery procedures was as if I had never left artillery. I had learned artillery so well during my first six years in the army that the knowledge would stay with me all my life. Staff, supply, and maintenance functions and planning were easy but troublesome because they were boring classes.

Academically, I was competing with officers who had spent their careers in artillery. They were combat veterans of Vietnam and well versed in artillery also. The major problem they had was falling back on the way they'd done things in the field. Many times, that meant they had improvised on doctrine. The instructors were teaching doctrine. Since I did not have recent experience in artillery, it was easy for me to accept what the instructors were teaching. Several of my classmates had problems accepting teachings that differed from what they'd done in their units.

The major stumbling blocks for me were planning and employment of nuclear weapons and the research paper due at the end of the course. The nuclear weapons block was difficult because it was hard. The term paper was a problem because of my lack of education. At least that was my excuse. I could write well as long as I was writing OERs, fact sheets, military letters, and simple reports. However, the term paper was equal to a thesis document and represented a large percentage of my final grade. I had no experience with writing one.

Unlike in OCS, I was competing against officers whose knowledge of artillery and staff roles was on par with mine. The rumor was that anything less than a 95 percent class grade would hurt an officer's promotion chance and future assignments. I was down to four years left in the army and hoped to make major before I retired. With that in mind, I applied myself 110 percent.

On the surface, relations between Claudia and me seemed happy and normal. However, the wrong word or comment on my part would anger her. I always asked her why she got so angry over nothing, but that only fueled her anger. Whenever we fought, a couple of days would pass before we returned to normal. On my part, the thought of her infidelity stilled bothered me. I'm not sure she felt the same about me. She had no reason to believe I had been unfaithful. Deep down, I didn't want to believe she had been unfaithful, but if she had been, I'd accepted it, and in my heart, I had forgiven her. However, I could not seem to forget it. I guess forgiveness is an action of the heart and comes easily when you love someone. But forgetting is an action of the brain and serves as a reminder that forgiveness does not resolve the lost trust. Trust is the epoxy that holds a relationship together through tough times. Without trust, there is no peace of mind, only a suspicious mind.

Still, we had some good and fun times. Each Sunday morning after breakfast, I would start my study period. Claudia would start answering her letters from Germany so she could mail them that afternoon. She always got a letter from her mom, and most of the time, she got a couple from her friends. The kids would watch TV until it was time to go to church. Claudia took them to church every Sunday morning. Instead of going with them, which I should have, I used the time alone for quality study time. When they returned, if I had finished studying, we would play games until lunch. After lunch, we would take them to a movie or to a park to play.

One Sunday morning in late April, I was studying for an exam on Monday. Claudia finished writing a couple of letters and put stamps on them. As usual, she would mail them at the post office after church. She got the kids ready and left. I finished studying and began cleaning out my notebook. I had several old notes I did not need any longer. I took the sheets of old notes to the trash can to dump them. As I started to put them in the trash can, I noticed that Claudia had torn one of her letters into little pieces before putting it in the trash can.

I thought that was unusual. She had never done that before. I had never looked at the letters she got from Germany. I asked myself why she would tear up a letter. They were in German, and I could not read them anyway. Suspicion and curiosity overcame me, and I recovered the pieces of letter from the trash can. As I gathered the pieces, I could see that they were in English.

After I had all the pieces, I spread them out on the table. I got a roll of Scotch tape and began to put the letter back together. It was a one-page letter, and it only took me about thirty minutes to restore it. I looked at the letter, and the first words I read were "My dearest darling Claudia."

I felt a terrible pain in my stomach. It was as if I had swallowed barbed wire and my stomach was trying to digest it. In disbelief, I read a strange man's love letter to my wife. The words confirmed what I'd dreaded the most. Her infidelity was true. The depth of her involvement stood out when I read, "You know I can't give you children, but I will love your children as if they were my own."

Tears came into my eyes, and I shuddered with pain I felt in my soul. The letter ended with the words "I can't wait until you are in my arms again."

I sat there stunned. I read the letter again to make sure it was real. I folded it and hid it away. I fixed a screwdriver, laid my head on the table, and sobbed. I did not know what I should do. Should I get a divorce? I didn't want a divorce. Should I accuse Claudia and have an argument? I did not want that either. My emotions seesawed between anger and hurt, and then, as always, I started to rationalize my problem.

Claudia had not done anything that I had not done. The belief that she was cheating on me had driven my indiscretion. Again, that did not justify my actions. How Claudia acted should not have guided my behavior. I had my own integrity. It should have been steadfast and unchanged by the behavior of others, including Claudia. The actions of others did not define who I was and how I acted. My character and integrity defined who I was and how I acted. I think that knowing I had failed myself disappointed me more than failing Claudia did.

After another screwdriver, I decided what I should do. I would calmly tell Claudia about my seeing the letter. I would not get angry. I would simply tell her that if she thought another man could love more deeply than I, then she should go to him. If not, then we could put this behind us and move forward. After I thought about this approach, I began to feel better. Besides, in the end, for whatever reason, she'd chosen me. She was with me now and not him.

When Claudia and the kids returned from church, I tried to be pleasant. It was hard, and I did not fully succeed in hiding my hurt. Claudia, of course, noticed my change in attitude immediately. She asked, expecting another argument, "What's wrong with you now?" As if suspecting something, she looked in the trash can. I had dumped my old notes in the can, so she didn't notice that the pieces of her torn-up letter were gone.

I did not want to argue. I did not want to discuss the letter either, so I said, "Nothing's wrong. I've got an upset stomach."

Using the upset-stomach pretense as an excuse, I did not go to the movies with Claudia and the kids. I needed time alone to think. Claudia had already said she was going to Germany after the kids got out of school. I had not wanted her to go back so soon even before I read the letter. Now I had a real problem with her going. In my mind, she was going back to see her lover. I had to deal with that idea now, and it depressed me. I knew I would have to struggle to not say something.

I had believed that when we left Germany, that was the end of it. Reading that letter five months later reopened the old wounds. When they returned from the movie, I decided that my only choice was to convince Claudia I was a better man than the one in Germany. That was going to be hard because I'd already done all I could to show Claudia how much I loved and wanted her. What more could I do?

After a couple of days, the pain in my heart subsided, and I felt normal again. I still had to discuss the letter with Claudia, but I felt I could do it calmly now. I could express myself without anger and in a mature way. I was not the first man to go through something like this.

I had to find a time when Claudia was in the proper mood and receptive to a discussion about our relations.

The time came the following Friday. We were on the way to a popular restaurant to meet friends for dinner. I started by saying, "There's something I need to tell you. I retrieved the letter from your friend in Germany that you tore up and threw in the trash, and I taped it back together."

She looked at me with an expression of shock. Before she could say anything, I continued. "You don't know how much your affair with him hurt me."

She looked down as if in shame. I said, "The part where he said he would adopt Michele and Ron and love them as if they were his own hurt the most. Your predicament is this, Claudia: he loves you, and I love you. I don't believe there is another man on this earth who will love you as deeply and completely as I do. No other man will care for you as well as I will. So you have to choose between us, because I will not settle for half of your love. That's all I've got to say about it."

She looked at me with teary eyes and said, "Neal, I'm sorry. I said good-bye to him the Saturday we left Germany. The day you found the torn-up letter, I mailed a letter to him telling him we were through and not to write anymore. That's the truth. I hope you can forgive me."

I smiled at her and said, "I've already forgiven you. It may take awhile for me to forget about it. But there's no need for us to discuss it any longer. Let's just enjoy our dinner tonight and let it be."

That was the last time we ever mentioned it. We continued as if it had never happened. I felt good about the way I'd handled the situation. I don't know what Claudia thought. She has never mentioned it again. We continued our life as husband and wife. I hoped that our union would grow stronger now that some of our anger was gone.

However, as time passed, no matter how hard I tried to believe our union was better, I could not deceive myself. Claudia always needed something I could not give her. She wanted something more exciting than married life. She was beautiful and attractive to other men. No matter how she tried to hide it, I could see she enjoyed being attractive to other men. I think then more than ever, I understood the penalty of getting married too young. She was a good mother to the kids, and she was a good wife. I could tell she was being a good wife because that was her role, and she could act it well onstage. But as the fights and arguments continued, we both began to play a role.

Unknown to me, the pain and hurt were just beginning. The anger, mistrust, hostility, infidelity, and hurt would continue for another four years. Fortunately, amid that turmoil, there would be moments of joy, happiness, and peace that were strong enough to carry us through and eventually strengthen the frail union between us.

One day I decided I would plant a garden. I called the owner and asked him if I could dig up a plot in the backyard for a garden. He said it was fine with him. The Bermuda grass would take over any plot when I left. It turned out to be one hell of a job to get the Bermuda grass out. I planned a large garden but had to settle for a ten-by-ten-foot plot because of the Bermuda grass. It was too hard with hand tools to clear it.

Claudia watched me as I struggled to clear the grass and shook her head. She did not think a garden was worth the work. The kids were optimistic. They helped and wanted to plant something. Once I got the soil ready for planting, I gave them a little area for their garden. The cucumber plants I'd grown in the back of the trailer in Daleville while attending Mohawk transition had given me a certain joy. I'd enjoyed caring for them and watching the cucumbers develop.

The little plot in the middle of a Bermuda-grass lawn was going to be my first real garden. Preparing the soil and forming the rows gave me a sense of peace. I think my battered emotions were seeking an escape. I needed a place to shed the pain and find a positive distraction from the stress of classes and life. I had not found the relief in God yet. I called on him to protect me in danger but had not realized the real peace that came from him. Maybe the peace I found in caring for my plants as they grew and matured was a step toward the peace of God. I do not know. What I do know is that I lost much of my anger at Claudia. I became more patient with her temperaments. As a result, we had fewer arguments and slowly drew a little closer together.

In June, coinciding with the kids getting out of school for the summer, we had a one-week spring break in classes. Claudia and I decided to take the kids to Disney World. On the way, we would see the Carlslbad Cave in New Mexico and the Grand Canyon. That was a fun trip, except Michele got upset at the Grand Canyon because I would not let her buy a trinket. I thought it was a waste of money. I was wrong. It meant something to her. But at Disney World, she got over her anger, and we had a great time.

We returned a week before they left for Germany. When I took Claudia and the kids to the airport for their trip to Germany, I felt I could trust her again. At least I hoped I could. I admit I had to restrain myself from making a snide comment about why she was going back. However, I did not, and perhaps that was a good step toward my healing.

They were gone for six weeks. I spent those weeks going to class, studying, and working on my paper. I had picked artillery employment in the Pacific during World War II as my subject. That was a mistake because there was little data supporting the use of artillery in the Pacific. The jungle environment of the islands where the military had fought the war did not lend itself to artillery use. As such, I struggled to write a comprehensive paper. Of course, I did not finish it then. I did a draft, put it aside until later, and completed it the week before it was due. It was not that good. I had to redo parts, and as a result, I only got an average grade.

At last, it was time for me to pick my family up at the airport. I was so happy to see them again. Much to my surprise, Claudia hugged me tightly, as if she had genuinely missed me. Of course the kids were happy to see me. They were especially glad to be back so they could watch TV. Claudia and I made love the following morning, and it was as if we were young and innocent again.

Fall came, and Michele and Ron went back to school. Claudia and I were getting along in our normal way. We enjoyed each other's company for the first time since we got to Fort Sill. The academic schedule was light, as we had finished nuclear weapons employment, the most difficult subject.

With much free time and two months left, I signed up for two college courses through the University of Oklahoma. One class, comparative economic systems, was fairly simple. The other one, business calculus, was a little difficult. But I did well, getting As in both subjects.

One day I got a note in my student box, telling me to call the DA artillery assignments officer. The DA had canceled my orders assigning me to the Third Army Flight Detachment at Fort Monroe, Virginia. The army was undergoing a major reorganization, and Third Army no longer existed. The Army Training and Doctrine Command (TRADOC) had replaced it. They no longer had a flight detachment at Fort Monroe. The major handling artillery captain assignments told me to pick a place. He would send me wherever I wanted if they had a position for me.

I would have sixteen years of service on December 3. I knew that my next assignment would probably be a terminal assignment. The war in Vietnam was winding down, reducing the flow of personnel over there. When I completed a tour at my next station, I would be too near retirement for the army to move me again, so I thought I had better pick somewhere where the duty was good and where I would enjoy my job.

As I thought about where to go, Fort Huachuca popped into my mind. It had impressed me during the six weeks I had spent in Mohawk transition. The weather was good, and I would be able to fly Mohawks and possibly become an instructor. I told the assignments major that I wanted to go to Fort Huachuca. He said okay and told me he would check the organization there to see if there was a position for an artillery captain. He told me to call him tomorrow afternoon, and he would have the information for me.

When I got home, I told Claudia about the army canceling my orders. She wanted to know what was going to happen now. I told her about my conversation with the major and how I had asked him to assign me to Fort Huachuca. Her mood quickly changed, and with fire in her eyes, she asked, "Why didn't you tell him you wanted to go to Germany? You know that's where I want to go. How can you pick that hole in the desert, when you could have gone to Germany?" She continued angrily, "You can go to Fort Huachuca! I am going back to Germany. I want you to tell the major you have changed your mind and want to go to Germany."

At first, I tried to respond calmly without anger, but the more insistent she was about not going to Fort Huachuca, the more upset I became. "Look," I said firmly, "I'm not going back to Germany—ever! You can go anytime you want to. I will find a place at Fort Huachuca for us to live. If you go to Germany, you are on your own. I told you before that I was not going to Germany. I meant it! I have spent the last ten years moving to where you wanted to live. I am going to spend my last four years in the army where I want to live."

She continued to rage, accusing me of everything she could think of or remember. I had not expected such anger and hate to come from her mouth. I knew there was nothing I could say that would appease her other than to say I would call the DA and ask for Germany. I was not going to do that, so I walked away and went out into the garage. I could hear her slamming items around and cursing me for ruining her life. The kids were due home from school in about fifteen minutes. I hoped she would regain her composure by then because I did not want the kids to suffer through another of our fights.

I walked the block to the school bus stop and met the kids. As we walked back to the house, I told them that their mom was upset at me and not at anything they had done. I wanted Michele and Ron to be prepared for the way Claudia was acting. However, when we got to the house, she had calmed down. She was mad as hell and would not speak to me, but she was not going wild, as she had before.

The next day, when I called the major, he said there was an aviation safety officer position open. It was a DA assignment, which meant I had to fill that position. I did not bother to tell Claudia. Without any mention of Fort Huachuca, it still took two weeks for her anger to subside to the point where we appeared normal again. I think speaking only when necessary is too hard when you are living together. She still was not happy. She said it was the worst thing I had ever done to her. She believed I'd done it just to get even with her. No matter how hard I tried to explain why I wanted to go to Fort Huachuca, she was not receptive. So I let it go.

The week before Thanksgiving, I went duck hunting. Fort Sill had an excellent program for hunting and fishing. It was duck season, and one of my classmates loved duck hunting, so I agreed to go with him. We went by the game management office Friday after class and got lucky. One pond was still open, so we signed up for it and signed out fifteen decoys.

We got up early Saturday morning, and I picked him up at his house. The weather was not bad, but they forecast a front to come through around 0900, so we dressed warmly and left for the pond. It was still dark when we arrived. There was a small boat by the blind, so we used it to put out the decoys. It was hard to tell how they looked in the dark. We planned on adjusting them as it got light enough to see.

Just before daylight, the wind started blowing. The temperature was about thirty degrees when the wind started. The temperature dropped dramatically from the wind chill. When it was light enough to see, the wind was blowing around thirty miles an hour. It had turned so cold that the snot running from my nose froze to my mustache. When the wind started, we could hear it splashing the water in the small pond. After an hour, all we could hear was the wind.

By the time the sky slowly got light, the temperature had dropped to twenty degrees but felt lower because of the wind chill. We wondered why we did not hear the splashing from the pond anymore. When we could finally see, we found the pond had frozen over, freezing our decoys in various poses. It started to snow then. The snowflakes were more like ice crystals driven by the wind, and we both began shaking from the cold.

We looked at each other and nodded, agreeing that it was time to get our decoys and get the hell out of there. Standing there and looking at the frozen pond, we could see that the boat was useless. One of us would have to wade out to gather the decoys. My classmate felt we should wait until the weather got better and the ice on the pond melted. He did not want to do the wading. I had signed for the decoys and did not want to take a chance on leaving them unattended. Taking a deep breath, I stepped onto the ice-covered pond.

I broke through the layer of ice and stepped into very cold water about a foot and a half deep. My legs instantly felt numb. I sloshed through the ice fifteen feet to the decoys. By then, the depth was about two feet. I pulled the decoys out of the ice and threw them onto the bank. My classmate started the car to get it warm. He put the decoys in the trunk as I threw them. As I walked back to shore, my pants froze each time I pulled them out of the water. When I stepped onto the bank, both pant legs froze from the midthighs down. They cracked as I hurried to the car to get warm. It had taken me about five minutes to get the decoys free of the ice and get back onto the bank, but by then, I was sure I had frostbitten feet. I had no feeling in them.

After about five minutes in the warm car, I began to feel my feet. The melting ice, with chunks of mud, made a mess of the floor mat. I knew the mess would anger Claudia. I would have to clean it as soon as I got home. Fortunately, I had no frostbite, and that was the last time I went duck hunting.

The second week in December, we took our final exam. It was a two-day comprehensive practical exercise. It covered every subject taught at the school. It was an open-book test, and that made it more difficult. Because of the open book, I felt obligated to look up each of my answers. That extended the time it took to complete the test. I think I would have done just as well by answering the questions I knew without looking up the answer.

When the instructors posted the final grades, mine was a disappointment. I came up in the eighty-fifth-percentile group. It was the poorest showing in my entire career. To remain competitive with my peers, I needed to be in the ninety-fifth-percentile group. I thought about it for a while and shrugged it off. I had seventeen years in the army and had no big wishes except to retire at twenty years. All I had to do was serve one more year, and that would give me a lock into retirement even if the army did not promote me.

The army had an up-or-out policy for officers. Either they promoted you, or they released you from active duty. The first time my year's group would come up for promotion to major was 1973. When it was all sorted out, I would have my eighteen-year lock-in whether the army promoted me or not. The army had promoted me to captain on December 6, 1967, two and a half years after I graduated from OCS. That was fast, but now it was catching up with me. I was a senior captain with five years in grade. The drawdown in the Vietnam War had slowed the need for officers, and therefore, the number of promotions decreased. Now my only hope for promotion was my record of performance.

All my commanders had rated me as outstanding and above my peers on all of my OERs. What was hurting me was education. I had no college degree and no artillery command time. Now the army would compare me against experienced artillery officers. I remembered what the commander in the 319th Artillery Battalion had told me when I'd left for flight school: "Get some command time in artillery." I'd had too much fun flying, so I hadn't opted for command time. Now I would suffer for those choices.

I finished with the advanced course on December 14, 1972. Unfortunately, because of my changed assignment, I received my new orders late. The earliest I could get my household goods picked up was December 26, so we spent our second Christmas in Lawton. Transportation picked up my household goods on December 26. We cleaned the house and spent the last night there. On December 27, with Claudia, Michele, and her cat in the Ford Capri, following Ron and I in the Ford Pinto, we headed west to Fort Huachuca.

We spent the first night in Abilene. The weather was cold and windy. We were all tired, grouchy, and bickering. The kids wanted tacos for dinner, and I wanted chicken. We ate tacos in the motel room. Claudia was upset because she thought I was driving too fast. Finally, exhaustion silenced the bickering, and we went to bed.

Lying in bed, waiting for sleep, I thought about the past year. I thought about what a wonderful time it could have been. But I had to face the facts. Claudia and I had squandered an opportunity to work on the problems in our marriage. I, of course, felt I had done all I could toward making it better. I felt Claudia had no interest in improving our relations. Each time I tried to get a discussion going about the way we were acting, she resisted. She would get angry and wouldn't talk. We were moving to our next station in life at the status quo. We were unhappy and unable to come together to improve our life.

We spent the second night in Deming, New Mexico. It was only two hours from Deming to Fort Huachuca. I wanted to get there while the housing and transportation offices on post were still open. I was hoping to get government quarters so we did not have to spend another night in a motel. I had no idea what the status of government quarters would be. I hoped I could find something suitable. Claudia and the kids were fighting exhaustion and were irritable. I could understand the kids' attitude but not Claudia's. She made it clear constantly that she did not want to be there but had no choice. I kept trying to be positive. I had no choice either.

CHAPTER 6

Fort Huachuca

A time to sow and a time to reap.

We left Deming, and an hour and a half later, we turned south off Interstate 10 onto Route 90. We were driving in snow-covered terrain now. Snow covered the mountains down to the three-thousand-foot level. Up ahead, I could see the Huachuca Mountains shining white in the morning sun. Where the snow had melted, dust-covered brown range grass showed. Brown mesquite trees dotted the landscape. Ron said it looked like Germany. I knew that Claudia and Michele were also in awe. It was, for the moment, a breathless beauty that only nature could produce.

We arrived in Sierra Vista at 1200 and turned into the main gate to Fort Huachuca. It had been more than two years since we were last there, and as far as I could tell, nothing had changed. We stopped at the main gate's guard building, and I got temporary passes for our cars. With Claudia following, I drove to the snack bar for lunch.

As we passed through the hospital area's collection of World War II buildings, they looked as neglected as they had been our first time there. Most of the buildings seemed empty and reflected their age. Although they'd originally been painted tan, bare wood was showing in spots where the aging paint had chipped and peeled from the walls. Everywhere we looked, we saw the decay of disused buildings. Even those in use looked barely kept. When the snow was gone, they would blend well with the brown grass and dust-covered Huachuca Mountains towering over the fort. I could picture Claudia shaking her head in disgust at how isolated we were. She was a city girl and hated small towns.

At the snack bar, we had hamburgers and french fries. I tried to make small talk about the lack of change since we were there before, but Claudia didn't seem interested in small talk. She just wanted to finish eating and find a place to live. I suggested she park the Taunus, and we'd ride in the Pinto while I arranged for quarters. She agreed, and we finished eating and headed for housing office.

When I talked to the clerk about applying for quarters, she told me I had to sign in on post officially before I could apply for quarters. I should have known that by now. Disappointed, I returned to the car, where Claudia and the kids were waiting. When I told them, Claudia's response was "What now?"

I said I was going to the United States Army Combat Surveillance and Electronic Warfare School, where I'd sign in and then sign back out on leave. I found the USACSEWS headquarters building and entered the SI's office. I explained my situation, and he let me sign in and back out on leave. He insisted on taking me around to meet the staff and commander. I couldn't say no, even though Claudia and the kids were waiting for me in the car. It took twenty minutes to do that. They were happy to have me. Army policy required the school to have an aviation safety officer because of its aviation assets. I was assigned to the position by the DA; therefore, they couldn't put me anyplace else. When I got back to the car, Claudia was angry about my taking so long. The kids were complaining about being cold. I explained what had happened, but it did little to cheer anybody up.

Moving is a pain in the ass. Most Americans don't move around like military families do. The state of having nowhere to live is distressing. It upset me that Claudia did little to help. She didn't have to do anything other than be patient and help cheer the kids up. However, as usual, I was the only one with a positive attitude. I understood Claudia's mood. She didn't want to be there, and it was her character to let me know that. I did my best to stay upbeat and take care of getting us housing.

Back at the housing office, I found out there was a one-year waiting list for three-bedroom houses. That was disappointing. Fortunately, they had temporary quarters available. I put my name on the waiting list for permanent quarters and signed for temporary quarters. The clerk gave me a set of keys and directions to the quarters. It turned out that they were in the run-down buildings we'd passed when entering Fort Huachuca.

I drove back to the snack bar so Claudia could get the Taunus. She followed me to the parking area for the temporary quarters. We parked and entered the main door with a Temporary Quarters sign.

We stepped into a hallway and entered a large family room with chairs, tables, and a TV. A young woman and two kids watching TV looked up and smiled when we entered. The room was warm and clean. The fresh paint inside contrasted with the deteriorating outside. To the left of the family room was a large fully equipped kitchen with two six-person dining tables. I looked at my diagram and saw that our bedrooms were down the left hall. I walked that way and found a door with my key number on it. I opened it and found a large bedroom with a double bed. Adjoining it was another bedroom with two single military beds.

Claudia looked around and asked, "Where is the bathroom?"

Now came the part that I knew would upset her the most. I took a breath and explained, "We have to share bathrooms and showers. The female bathroom and showers are on the other side of the family room. The men's showers and bathroom are across the hall."

She said, "Neal, you might as well get me a hotel room. I can't live like this."

The kids were deciding which bed they'd sleep in while our discussion went on. I pleaded with her to understand that it was just temporary. She should at least try it before judging it.

She calmed down, walked down to the female bathroom and showers, and checked them. When she came out, she nodded as if to say it was okay for now. The bathroom had private showers and toilets but community mirror and sinks. We checked the kitchen out and found that on our side of the kitchen, we had pots and pans, china, and silverware. We shared only the stove and the refrigerator. In the family room, whoever got there first decided what TV program to watch. After that, friendly negotiation would change channels.

We had a place to live. The one problem was Michele's cat. We had to take him to the post veterinarian and put him in quarantine for two weeks. We did that and stopped by the commissary to buy groceries. By then, it had started snowing again. We retreated to the temporary quarters to get out of the cold and snow.

We lived in temporary quarters for six weeks. We spent the first few days adjusting to the lack of privacy and timing the use of the stove to cook. Claudia impressed me with how she adjusted. Once she accepted it, she made it work. I knew in my heart that if I could get her to accept me again, we could make life work. I worked each day, so the impact of communal living was less for me.

We slept well our first night and woke up Saturday morning to a clear, cold, and sunny day. After breakfast, we drove into Sierra Vista to check the town out. We could see signs of new residential areas springing up. Building had started based on rumors that the intelligence school was moving from Fort Devens to Fort Huachuca. There was not enough housing on post to support any growth at all, so if the move happened, it would be a boom for construction in Sierra Vista. Not much else had changed.

We drove around Fort Huachuca to check out the quarters. The officer quarters were close to main post, while the NCO quarters were to the northeast of main post. The schools sat between the two areas. Claudia wanted the church schedule, so we stopped by the main chapel to get one. From there, I drove out to the airfield. Nothing had changed there since my time there before. We went by the PX and picked up some items for the kids. They would start school next week, and we wouldn't have our household goods until we moved into quarters.

I went to church with Claudia and the kids on Sunday morning. After that, Michele wanted to know when she would get her horse. I stalled a little by saying, "Let's drive out to the horse stables to see the horses." We found the stables, and Michele excitedly walked around, looking at all the horses. Her attraction to them fascinated me. It had been more than five years since she'd first asked for a horse. Her passion for one had not once subsided. I knew that soon I would have to deal with it.

That night, we ate New Year's Eve dinner in a steak restaurant. The restaurant was in an old adobe building built around 1890. It had been several businesses, including a general store, and a post office over the years and had been disused at periods. Now it was a popular steakhouse. After dinner, we drove back onto post. It had been snowing, and there was about a foot of snow on the ground. For some reason, we decided to drive to main post to see the snow.

Another of nature's beautiful moments surprised us. As we drove around the traffic circle in the center of post, we saw sixteen deer in the field by the church. Some were lying in the snow, and others were just standing there. The scene was so awesome that we drove around the circle three times to look at them. Finally, in fear of frightening them, we left.

On New Year's Day, we drove to Tucson to shop and see a movie. It was a fun day for me. The temperature in Tucson was ten degrees warmer than in Sierra Vista. We found the mall in Tucson and killed time there until it was time to go to the movie. In those days, Claudia could spend hours in stores, browsing through the clothes. Fortunately, we only had an hour to kill, so the kids didn't get too restless. After we watched the movie, *The Poseidon Adventure*, we ate dinner at Marie Callender's. It felt as if we were a happy family again.

The only problem with going to Tucson was the drive home. In the winter conditions, it took almost two hours to get back to Fort Huachuca. However, the only fine restaurants and shopping were in Tucson, so it became a weekly trip. I didn't need it, but Claudia needed to get away from the boring little town of Sierra Vista. Once we'd learned the streets and the locations of the malls and restaurants and Claudia had several new friends, I stopped going with her. She and her friends would go make a day of it. I would watch the kids.

Tuesday morning, we registered Michele and Ron for school. Since the military was still on a Christmas half-day work schedule until January 6, I decided to sign in and save some leave time. After registering the kids for school, I drove to USACSEWS headquarters and signed in. I went upstairs to the office I shared with the school's intelligence sergeant. He was off, so I started organizing my desk.

My official title was USACSEWS aviation safety officer. I also served as the school's safety officer under the supervision of the school secretary. Actually, there was a difference between the duties of the safety officer and the duties of the aviation safety officer, but as I was a senior captain, they expected me to perform both.

My first act was to collect all the safety office files and regulations. Most were current, and many were missing. I ordered all the regulations I felt I needed. I next started reading the USACSEWS SOP. I found that the school safety officer worked in coordination with the post safety officer, so

I gave him a call to introduce myself. He invited me over for a briefing on what he expected from me as safety officer. He left aviation safety to me. His only interest was ensuring we reported accidents and incidents on time.

I drove over to his office and met him and his staff. He gave me a fifteen-minute briefing laying out my responsibilities as the safety officer. That was when I realized I was undertaking a big responsibility. Safety is a major concern of commanders. Accident reports flow up the chain of command to the DA. Accidents represent some failure in a person, a procedure, training, or maintenance. Top-level commanders view the occurrence of too many accidents as a sign that a commander is lax in his supervision. That, in turn, doesn't reflect well on a commander's OER.

The commander relies on his safety officer to ensure that doesn't happen. I started my job as safety officer with some company-level experience but no experience with school safety duties. The post safety officer assured me he and his staff would provide any help I needed. He did warn me that in the past, the school had been slow in taking care of its safety needs. He had covered for them a couple times. Now, with me assigned to the position, he hoped the picture would improve. I assured him I would do my best.

I returned to my office and got out the SOP. I looked at the two-paragraph safety portion and started rewriting it. I started with the commander's responsibilities, from school level to company level and then to individual level. I was still writing at 1200, when a lieutenant colonel stuck his head in the door. It was the school secretary. He was the only one I hadn't met yet. I stood up and said, "Good morning, sir. I'm Captain Griffin, the new safety officer."

He stepped in, and we shook hands as he said, "They told me you had signed in. I didn't realize you were already at work. I see you are working on the SOP. That's good because that was one of the first tasks I was going to suggest you do. I'm glad we are on the same wavelength. I'm leaving for the afternoon since we are on a half-day schedule. You can continue working if you want to or take the afternoon off. I'm sure your family would want you with them, having just moved here. Anyway, I'll see you in the morning, and we'll go over what I expect from you."

We shook hands again, and he left, saying he was glad to have me aboard. I decided I would take his advice and go back to the temporary quarters. It probably wasn't fair to leave Claudia and the kids alone if I didn't have to.

I got there in time to eat lunch with them. After that, we drove around Sierra Vista, looking for houses. There were several houses under construction, but they were all sold. There were no existing houses for sale or for rent. We faced living in temporary quarters until permanent quarters were available.

School started the following day, and Claudia took the kids to school. I went to the office to work. I had almost finished revising the SOP, when the secretary called me into his office. He explained the school's organization and where I fit in. While army regulations fixed a direct line of communication between the safety officer and the commander, he wanted me to go through him. That was agreeable to me. He was my rater, and I wanted him to know what I did or failed to do. He pointed out that the DA required a school-trained officer to fill the aviation safety officer position. Therefore, they were sending me to the University of Southern California in Los Angeles to attend the army aviation safety officer course, starting at the end of March. It was a ninety-day course presented by the aerospace safety office. Till then, he wanted me to get current in the Mohawk. While I was doing that, he'd focus on getting the school's safety program running correctly.

I left his office with a full plate of work. Next, I drove to the airfield to visit USACSEWS aviation operations. I introduced myself to the major in charge of flight operations. He was expecting me and had already set up a flying schedule to get me current and renew my instrument ticket in the Mohawk. First, I had to get a flight physical, which he had scheduled for the following day. The next morning, he had scheduled me for ejection-seat training. After that, CW-3 Banyan, the Mohawk instructor pilot, would start flying with me. When we finished talking, he took me around and introduced me to the pilots who were not out flying students. It felt good to be back in an aviation environment. I hadn't flown in more than a year, and I was eager to get back in the air.

I talked for a while with the pilots before I left and found out that Captain Jake Benson was head of the sensor systems division in the school. I hadn't seen or spoken to him since telling him good-bye in Korea. I dropped by to see him. It surprised him when I walked into his office. We talked for about an hour, and he explained how the student flight training worked. He said as soon as I got current in the Mohawk, he would start scheduling me to fly students.

I finally made it back to my office. No sooner had I sat down than officers started dropping in and introducing themselves. It was noon before I had met everyone in the various staff offices and command group. Since we were still on half-day schedules, everybody left at noon. I was hungry and decided to go back to the quarters to eat lunch with Claudia.

She was glad to see me. With the kids in school, it was a little lonely for her. We had lunch, and she cheered up a little. However, the notion that we were going to live in temporary quarters for a long time depressed her. My news about going to school in LA at the end of March especially concerned her. I kept assuring her we would be in permanent quarters by then.

Michele and Ron rode the school bus home from school. The bus took students off post but stopped at the temporary quarters parking lot on the way. That saved us from taking them to and from school each day. They came home excited about their first day in school. Both had homework but promised to do it if they could watch TV first.

A pilot must get a physical each year, usually on his birthday, which I'd missed while in the advanced course, so I spent most of the next day getting my physical. An aviation physical is extensive. Usually done by a flight surgeon, it includes blood tests and eyes tests, such as pressure, vision, color blindness, depth perception, and field of vision. The hearing test is just as extensive. After all the supporting tests, the flight surgeon does a physical examination.

The next day, I was at the ejection-seat trainer at 0800. Including me, there were four aviators and two observers waiting there to renew our seat training. I was the fourth one to ride the seat. The instructor strapped me in the Martin-Baker trainer and stepped clear. When he yelled, "Eject!" I pulled the face curtain down and felt the Gs as the forty-millimeter shell drove me to the top of the rails. As the seat slid back down to the base, I could feel a slight pain in my neck and shoulders. I knew I would be sore for a week or so. As I climbed out of the seat, I thought, *I'm thirty-five years old. Maybe I'm too old to be doing this.*

Back at my office, I performed my first safety officer duty. I wrote a letter for the commander's signature, outlining his concern for safety and identifying some of the inspection programs his new safety officer would set up. The first program was a monthly safety inspection of occupied USACSEWS buildings. I would coordinate with training company commanders the date and time when I would inspect their buildings. The next program was to boost accident reporting. I stressed the commander's responsibility in reporting all accidents to me within twenty-four hours so I could ensure that a correct and complete accident report form went to higher headquarters. Then I referred all personnel to the revised SOP for a detailed description of safety actions and responsibilities.

I next drafted a letter on aviation safety. Aviation safety is different from personnel safety within an organization. It has special demands, such as an aviation safety meeting each month for all personnel using aircraft. My review of files found the school did not hold meetings as directed. My letter stated that I would schedule a meeting each month and report attendance in the minutes of the meeting. Attendance was compulsory for all aviators and flight personnel. I didn't know how this was going to play out. There were several old colonel and lieutenant colonel aviators in the school who might not like the idea of a captain telling them they had to attend a monthly safety meeting. But it was my job. I had to document each meeting with minutes and attendees.

After reviewing each draft letter, I gave them to the secretary for his approval before sending them to the commandant to have him sign them. After that, I went to the post's quartermaster issue point to draw my field equipment and flight equipment. I needed a flight helmet, an ejection-seat harness, flight suits, gloves, and sunglasses. It was lunchtime when I got all my equipment, so I went home for lunch.

After lunch, I took my equipment to the office to store it. I put my helmet together and adjusted it. I put my ejection-seat harness on and adjusted it. I gathered my field jacket and flight suits and took them to the tailor to have patches sewn on. Most everybody was gone when I returned to the office, so I took the rest of the day off too.

The next morning, on the way to the flight line, I stopped by the office to pick up my flight equipment. I ran into the secretary as I was leaving. He praised me for the letters and said the commandant had signed them, and copies were in distribution to the addressees. Each time an officer writes a letter for the commander's signature, he must identify a point of contact for the action the letter refers to. My name and phone number were on the letters, designating me as the POC. I shuddered a little, thinking of the phone calls I would soon be getting about the letter. But that was my job. I had been in this position before; however, I had never been so new that more than half of the officers didn't know who the hell I was.

CW-3 Banyan was waiting when I got to the flight line. We sat at his desk while he briefed me on what we were going to do that day. Even with my experience, I still had little butterflies in my stomach. Today we were going to focus on touch-and-gos for an hour. After that, we would do some upper air work.

I felt good while walking out to the Mohawk. The crew chief was standing there waiting for us. He introduced himself to me and welcomed me to Fort Huachuca. I thanked him and told him I promised to bring his aircraft back unharmed. Chief Banyan took out the checklist, and we started the preflight.

How easily I remembered each step pleased me, even though it had been more than a year since I had thought about a Mohawk. I climbed into the pilot's seat and felt a little strange. I had to adjust the seat to get the position that felt comfortable to me. Once strapped in, the chief started reading the checklist again. I was a little slow but still got everything right. I hadn't forgotten anything, thank God. When we finished the start checklist and had the engines running, I called for taxi. The tower cleared us for taxi, and I released the brakes, added power, and headed for the run-up area. My refresher training had begun.

I did touch-and-gos for the next hour. I had no problem with the takeoff and landing procedures. My control touch and reaction time were a little rusty after my layoff for a year. That was no problem because I knew those skills would come back quickly with practice, and they did.

The chief flew with me for five hours and then turned me loose for solo to get the next five hours. Policy required me to fly ten hours before he could sign me off. I divided that time between night and day flights. Once I got the ten hours, the instrument examiner, CW-3 Willy, started my instrument ticket renewal flights. After I'd had four hours of practice under the hood, he gave me my instrument flight test. I passed it with no problems, and when he signed my flight records, I was back on flying status. I was a Mohawk pilot once more.

When I wasn't flying, I was conducting safety inspections. After each inspection, I would send a written report of my findings and all corrective actions needed. Slowly, the safety profile of the school began to improve. Because I was checking regularly, commanders began checking and correcting safety deficiencies before I found and reported them. Many of my reports enabled training company commanders to force the post engineers to correct long-sought repairs immediately. Their previous requests had been given low priority, but when my inspections made them safety problems, they became the number-one priority.

My biggest problem was individual accident reports. Commanders must submit accident reports whenever a soldier has an accident, no matter the nature of the accident. Each company now had a safety NCO to prepare and send in the reports. Safety NCO was an extra duty, and many of the NCOs had critical roles, such as instructors and training developers. As such, safety was their second priority. They did it when they got to it. That forced me to stay on top of them to ensure timely reports.

I started my duties as aviation safety officer by inspecting each aviator's record. There were twenty-five aviators assigned. I made sure each record reflected that the aviator was current in terms of check ride, flight physical, quarterly flying hours, instrument ticket, and the required night flying hours. Next, I checked all past accident reports to ensure accuracy and to see if I could detect any unsafe trends. I was happy to find no reported accidents and only one incident, in which an unlatched hatch had popped open on takeoff. The organization had flown eight thousand hours without an accident, which was commendable. The only fault was that there were no minutes to support a monthly safety meeting.

I prepared a memo for the commandant's signature, scheduling one for the end of February. When the commandant got my memo, he called me in and asked if this was something new. He didn't recall signing memos directing a safety meeting. I told him regulations required it and said units must keep the minutes on file for two years. He wanted to know if the aviation folks had held any previous safety meetings. I smoothed the issue over by saying it appeared they were holding them informally. However, since I was the aviation safety officer, I would do it formally, as the regulations demanded. That kept the aviators out of trouble and got some brownie points for me. I invited him to our first meeting, and he agreed to attend. To ensure maximum attendance, I made it known that he was attending. I didn't want the commandant to surprise an aviator by asking him why he didn't attend.

I was happy with the way work was going. The only problem was with Claudia. Her being stuck in the temporary quarters without knowing anyone led to tense relations between us. She kept asking me when we were going to get out of there. Then the secretary's wife scheduled a coffee the Friday after the holidays were over. The purpose of the coffee was to introduce Claudia to the ladies and get to know each other. That saved us for a while. Claudia met several women who became friends. She began to socialize and take part in various activities. That took some pressure off me.

Still, she was unhappy that I would be in LA while she would still be in temporary quarters, so the first weekend in February, we drove to Tucson to find a house to buy. There were none in Sierra Vista. Many of the military who worked at Fort Huachuca lived in Tucson. They had a club organized, and each man donated sixty dollars a month to charter two buses. The buses departed Tucson each morning at 0500 and arrived at Fort Huachuca at 0630. They departed Fort Huachuca at 1700 and arrived at the meeting point in Tucson at 1830. If some event or schedule required someone earlier or later, that individual drove his car for that day.

I hated the idea of joining that club. I didn't want to waste three hours of my life five days a week just going to work and going home. However, I had to do something to get us out of the temporary quarters. We were tired of living under those conditions. That weekend, we found a three-bedroom house in Tucson that we liked. It was close to the bus pickup and not far from the center of Tucson. We got the paperwork and told the agent we would be back next weekend to close the deal.

Tuesday morning, Claudia called me. Excited, she told me to call the housing office. They had a set of quarters available if I wanted them. They needed to know my decision soon. I hung up and immediately called housing. The clerk explained that a three-bedroom house was available in the area that mixed senior NCOs and officers. The officers ahead of me had turned it down, so I was next on the list. I told them I wanted it but wanted to at least look at it. The clerk said he would send someone to the quarters if I could meet the housing agent in fifteen minutes. I said yes, and he gave me the address. I called Claudia and told her I would pick her up in five minutes to look at the quarters.

When we got to the address, the housing agent was waiting for us. From the outside, the quarters looked okay. They were freshly painted, and a small fenced-in patio was in the front of the house. Inside, we found a large family room, a large kitchen with a breakfast bar and dining room, a breakfast nook, a laundry room, a large master bedroom with a bathroom and shower, two smaller bedrooms, and a bathroom and shower in the hallway. The freshly painted walls made the house look new, even though it was ten years old. The location was the only reason the officers ahead of me had rejected it.

I looked at Claudia and asked if we wanted it. She said yes. I told the agent I would take it. He got out the inventory list and paperwork. We inventoried the property in the house, and an hour later, I signed for it. Just like that, we had a house, which saved us from living in Tucson. Now I had to get my household goods shipped and moved in. That would be a pain in the ass for me. Claudia would want everything put just so and then would change her mind two or three times. But there was a reward in the end: I would only make one more move in the army. That would be when I retired.

Our quarters sat in an ideal spot. We could look out the window and watch Michele and Ron walk to school. A warrant officer lived on our left. The house on our right was empty while engineers renovated it. A captain lived across the street from us. We could walk, if necessary, to the PX. It was a five-minute drive to my office. We had a large but poorly landscaped yard. The army didn't waste much money on landscaping yards. However, Claudia and I were happy to have it. I was glad I didn't have to commute from Tucson every day.

Slowly, we settled into a routine. In the middle of March, the USACSEWS women's club had a tea to welcome all the new women. At the meeting, they had several activities for the women to join. Claudia and her friend signed up for tennis. When she came home and told me about it, I laughed. I had never seen her do anything athletic in nature, so I doubted she would stay with tennis, but I had to go with her to buy some balls, a racket, and a tennis outfit.

She surprised me. Not only did she stick with tennis, but she became good at it. She became so dedicated to it that I bought her a membership to the local tennis club for her birthday in 1977. She would play tennis until the 1990s. She won many ribbons and trophies. She finally had to quit because problems with her feet made it too painful to play.

By now, she had met several German wives. She started inviting them to coffee on Saturday afternoons. During the week, along with playing tennis, she enjoyed lying in the sun. Like all Germans, she wanted a tan. I was happy that she was meeting people and socializing. The happier she was, the better we got along. However, no matter how well we got along, I always sensed a longing in her for something I couldn't provide.

I guess in all honesty, I was jealous of her. I couldn't help but notice that when we were out, she still flirted. I would never say anything, but it ate at me. She was beautiful and attractive to men, and she knew that. Our arguments were always over minor issues we disagreed about. However, I suspected the real cause was my subconscious objection to the way I felt she treated me.

By the middle of March, I was flying students. Jake would schedule me to fly a class of TOs. I enjoyed that. Each class contained three enlisted students. They had to plan and fly three SLAR, three IR, and three camera flights. Most of the training flights were at night, and it was a pleasure to fly in the clear skies of Arizona. I could see for miles and concentrate on instruction and not on dealing with weather problems, as I had in Korea. I managed to complete one class before it was time for me to go to school in LA.

I did my safety officer duties during the day and flew students at night. I concentrated on completing all my safety tasks before I left. I wanted to attend school without worrying about my responsibilities at Fort Huachuca. I coordinated my absence with the post safety officer, and because of the effort I had put into the program in support of him, he agreed to handle issues for me while I was gone.

My plan was to drive to Los Angeles in the Ford Capri. Claudia would use the Pinto while I was gone. The program manager for the aviation safety officer course sent me a welcome packet two weeks before I left. It had all the information I needed on housing, personnel support, and academic events while I was there. Since there was no housing available, it provided a list of apartments and hotels within the local area that rented to students attending USC. I didn't know there was a small military base, Fort McArthur, in LA, where I had to sign in. The personnel office there would provide all financial and personnel support for me.

Claudia helped me pack my suitcase the night before I left. I was joking about how she was eager to get rid of me, but I don't think that was exactly true. She just wanted me to look good and didn't trust my choice of clothes. We had a pleasant evening. I discussed all she could do if she needed help. She worried about helping the kids with homework. I assured her that she could. Michele, of course, was pressing for her horse. She harbored anger at me because I kept making excuses for not buying her one. It wasn't so bad now, because Huachuca Riding Club rented horses, and each weekend, I could take her to the stables to rent a horse for her to ride. That appeased her for now, but I knew the day was coming when I would have to buy her a horse.

I left early the next morning. Interstate 10 made the drive easy, because once on it, I could take it all the way to LA. The only problem was in Phoenix. They had not completed the interstate through Phoenix, and I had to take detours for about thirty miles, which added an extra hour to the trip. I found Fort MacArthur in San Pedro, about twenty miles south of LA, around 1700. I signed in and rented a room for the night in the guesthouse.

That night, I looked through the housing information. I saw that there were some short-term-lease apartments available in Torrance. Torrance was a little suburb about ten miles from USC. I decided I would drive there tomorrow to see if I could rent an apartment. I hoped Claudia and the kids would come after school was out at the end of May.

When I got to the apartment complex, I found a furnished three-bedroom apartment for $500 a month. That was about right, because I was getting thirty-six dollars a day per diem. The apartment was on the second floor and was nice. There was a swimming pool in the complex. I didn't know it at the time, but there were also horse stables adjoining the complex, where folks from the surrounding area boarded their horses.

After I checked into the apartment, I drove to the USC campus and registered for my course. I received a large packet containing information on the course and classes. Also included were rules for conduct on the

USC campus. There were instructions to keep a low profile because of continuing antimilitary sentiment on campus because of the Vietnam War. I fought back a twinge of anger when I read that. A captain in the US Army had to keep a low profile in his country because of a bunch of immature kids.

On the way back to the apartment, I stopped at a supermarket and bought some food and cleaning supplies. I missed Claudia while doing that. At Fort Huachuca, we went to the commissary together to shop. It was afternoon when I made it back to the apartment. Kids were home from school and were playing in the small playground near the pool. Many of the older kids were in the pool area. Seeing all the activity, I decided it would be a good idea for me to start exercising again.

After I brought my supplies into the apartment and put them away, I changed into some shorts and tennis shoes. I jogged out to the street and started running. The apartment complex was large, so I decided I would run around the complex for starters. When I later drove the distance, it turned out to be just more than two miles. Back in the apartment, I did some push-ups and sit-ups to complete my exercise. I figured that would be a good workout for each day.

After I showered and ate a bowl of chili, I sat down with a beer and opened my student packet. The first paper I looked at was the course outline. As I read the list of subjects crammed into the one-semester period, I thought, *Wow*. The courses—aviation investigation, aviation accident prevention, aeronautical engineering, aviation psychology, biomedical traits, and communications and aviation management—were worth eighteen credit hours and caused me to shake my head. No one would voluntarily take this many tough subjects in one semester. Only the army would sign officers up for such a heavy academic load and expect them to do well.

I looked at the subjects and thought, *I am going to have to bust my ass to get through this.* Then I told myself to calm down. I already knew a lot about prevention. I certainly knew aviation communications and management. Only four subjects would be new, and I could probably handle those with some hard study. My mood changed a little. I didn't feel as threatened by the course. I would just have to apply myself. I had done it before. I could do it now.

According to the class schedule, our first hour covered the usual introduction, administrative needs, class attendance, and conduct. After that, we started right in on the first subject: accident prevention. I found a parking authorization card in the packet. Because of the limited parking, each car parked in the class area needed an authorization card in the window. That was all the data on the course. The rest of the information listed local sights to visit, recreation areas, and shopping areas.

After thumbing through advertisements, I put the packet away. I called Claudia to let her know I'd made it okay and to see how she was doing. Everything was fine. The weather was terrible, cold and snowy. I told her I would call every couple nights or so. I gave her the number at the school so she could get a hold of me if she had an emergency. After we hung up, I got my clothes ready. I watched an hour of TV, set my alarm clock, and went to bed.

The next morning, at the introduction, the course manager provided us a list of attendees and their addresses and phone numbers. He then introduced our instructors, who all had impressive credentials. Experienced pilots all had doctorate degrees and were professionals in the fields they taught. Most importantly, they were down to earth and able to mix humor with instruction. After each instructor said a few words about his subject, we took a break. After the break, we started our first classes on accident prevention and communications.

When I read through the list of attendees, I saw that two of them lived in the same apartment complex I was in. At the break, we got together and agreed to carpool each day. Since they had their families with them, I volunteered to drive each day. That worked out well. They chipped in for gas, and we enjoyed each other's company during the drive.

While we started with accident prevention and communications, we were soon into each of the other subjects. The objective of a safety program is accident prevention. Each of the other subjects was an integral part of an accident prevention program. Experts examine accidents to find out the causes, so those in charge can correct the problems and prevent future accidents. Examining an airplane accident involves expertise in several fields. Aeronautical engineers look for structural and mechanical faults. Medical and psychological experts look for human failures and causes. When the accident investigation team gathers and examines all the results, they must communicate their findings to all involved. Aviation management must incorporate the lessons learned into their daily routine to ensure the same accident doesn't reoccur.

Despite all the efforts and science applied to prevent accidents, there are no new accidents. Every new accident has already occurred sometime in the past. As one of the instructors would fondly say, "Despite the best efforts of men and mice, some little genie will always come by and piss on the pillows of science."

The first tool we each had to buy, if we didn't already have one, was a calculator with trigonometry and square root functions. Those little gadgets, which are so common and cheap today, were just entering the market in 1973. They also were expensive. Instead of a calculator, we could use a slide rule, which was much cheaper. Like half of the class, I bought a slide rule at the school store. It had been years since I'd used a slide rule, so it took me a couple hours of practice to relearn its use. A calculator might have been easier, but the slide rule was just as accurate.

Although the academic load was heavy and I needed at least three hours of study and reading each night, it was one of the most enjoyable courses I have ever attended. The instructors were great. The syllabus divided subjects between classroom lectures and practical exercises. As an example, several exercises consisted of going to a crash site and conducting a crash-site investigation. The instructors organized us into teams, and we competed against one another for the best investigation results.

Even in the psychology classes, we had practical exercises. In one exercise, we watched a ten-minute film with no sound. The film showed a couple having dinner in a restaurant. They engaged in conversation, and then the man started looking at a lovely woman at another table. His constant gaze at her appeared to upset his companion, who got up and appeared to say something angrily at the man. She left, and the man rose, went to the other woman, and spoke to her. He joined her at her table, and the film ended.

Our task was to write a description of what was taking place in the film. The purpose of the exercise was to show that when questioning eye witnesses to an accident, you have to be careful of what they describe. What they think they saw might not be correct. Because of personal experiences, people impose on what they see a sense of what they expect to see. As an example, a two-engine aircraft crashed on an approach two hundred meters from the runway. When investigators asked several witnesses who'd seen the airplane approaching the airfield if both engines were running. Three witnesses, all with experience in aviation, stated that both engines were working. That stumped the investigators because they found one of the engines seven miles from the airfield. It had fallen from the airplane and was a primary cause of the crash. Yet three witnesses considered to be experts did not notice that an engine was missing from the aircraft as they watched it crash. The reason they didn't see the engine missing was because their experience and knowledge led them to expect to see two engines on a twin-engine aircraft. Thus, psychologically, they saw two engines.

We fell victim to the same psychological phenomenon as we watched the film. All of us described a married man flirting with another woman while with his wife. She got upset and stormed out of the restaurant. Without sound, that was what it looked like to us, because that was what we expected. It was the same old story. However, when replayed with sound, the film was about a producer having dinner with his wife and discussing his problem of finding a woman to play a particular role in a film. He saw the blonde woman and told his wife that she might be suitable for the part. The wife told him to go speak to the woman about the part. She would go home to release the babysitter. When the instructor replayed the film without sound, we saw how facial expressions and animated movement can fool you into seeing what you expect to see.

The psychology course was the most difficult of the courses. However, the instructor said he would make it easy for us. In our first class, he gave us two pages containing two hundred questions. He said the answers to those questions were what he wanted us to take from his class. We looked at the questions. There were multiple-choice, true-or-false, fill-in-the-answer, and essay questions. He then smiled and said fifty of those questions would be on the final test. On the surface, that made the course easy. I mean, how could knowing the questions on the final test not make a course easy? Believe me, I hit the books every night, trying to get the answers to all the questions. It took me until two nights before the final test to finish answering the questions. Then I had to spend another couple hours each night studying the answers so I could remember them. That was the instructor's final example of how life is not always as it appears. Having a copy of the questions to the final test and ninety days to learn the answers seemed like a dream come true. In the end, it was a nightmare.

The days flew by because of the thoroughly interesting subjects and the hard study needed each night. Each night, as soon as I got home, I would eat and start studying. I got up early in the morning and did my run and exercise. On the weekends, I got up and, after breakfast, studied for two hours. After that, I explored the area.

I found that Redondo Beach was only four miles from my apartment. I would drive down to the beach and watch the anglers fish on the pier. It had been a long time since I'd been fishing. The way my life now differed from the way I'd grown up was almost shocking. I was two different men, because the life of my teens still lay just below the surface of my skin.

By the third weekend, I missed Claudia so much that I decided to drive home for the weekend. It was an eight-hour drive if all went well. I reasoned that if I left around 1500, I would make Sierra Vista by 2300. It turned out that classes were over at 1500 that Friday, so I called Claudia and told her to expect me. I told my carpool buddies that after school, I was driving straight to Sierra Vista, so one of them would have to drive to school that day.

After school, I wasted no time in hitting the road. I made it to Sierra Vista at 2330. Claudia had gone to bed by the time I got there, so I slipped into bed without waking her. I spent a wonderful Saturday and half a day Sunday with my family. It was a refreshing break from the constant study. I left for LA at noon on Sunday to give myself extra time if I had problems. I was back in my apartment at 2100.

I made that trip one more time before June. On June 1, the kids were out of school, so that weekend, I picked Claudia and the kids up and brought them to LA to stay until I completed my course. It was pleasant to be back together as a family. Claudia and the kids respected my study-time needs, and I spent all my free time doing what they wanted.

Each day while I was in school, they stayed by the pool. The kids swam and played on the playground. Claudia was happy because she could lie in the sun. She became friends with a woman who came to the pool each day with her kids. This woman lived in the apartments and was familiar with the LA area. She started taking Claudia shopping with her, which Claudia enjoyed.

One day, after they visited a beauty salon and got their hair fixed, she took Claudia to Schwab's Drugstore. Schwab's was famous for its old-style ice cream counter and deli. It was also a hangout of several movie stars. They were hoping to see some while they were there. Sure enough, Shelley Winters and several friends came in and had ice cream. When Shelley left, she stopped by Claudia's table and told Claudia that she loved her hairstyle and color.

That made Claudia's day. She was excited that evening as she told me about it. I had to agree with Shelly. Claudia's hair color was different. It wasn't her natural brunette color. She had a slight reddish tint to it, which highlighted her beautiful face.

About a week later, her friend's husband got four tickets to *The Tonight Show Starring Johnny Carson*. The four of us went to dinner and then to the Johnny Carson show. I thought it was a fun show, but Claudia wasn't impressed. It was late when the show started, and she was sleepy. She didn't understand many of the jokes, so it was a little boring for her.

Michele found out there was a horse stable in the rear of the apartment complex. During the day, she would walk to the stable to watch the horses. She made friends with one of the young girls who had horses stabled there. The girl had two horses, and she let Michele ride one. In turn, Michele helped clean the horses and stalls.

Three days before I completed my course, I came home and found Claudia upset. Michele and her girlfriend were there, and Michele was crying and holding her arm tucked into her chest. Claudia didn't know what to do. Michele couldn't move her arm because it hurt so badly. Her girlfriend kept saying she was sorry. I asked Michele what had happened, and she said she had fallen off the horse. I finally got her to let me look at her arm.

The arm didn't look broken. There was no swelling or any sign of a break. I pulled her blouse back, looked at her shoulder, and saw the problem. She had broken her collarbone. I told Claudia that we had to take her to the emergency room to get the bone set. Michele didn't want to go. She wanted to wait until we got back to Fort Huachuca. I told her girlfriend that Michele was okay. It was just a broken collarbone.

Claudia got Ron, I got Michele into the car, and we drove to a hospital about a mile from the apartments. On the way, I said, "All right, Michele, what happened?"

I sensed that Michele and her friend had not been truthful with the story that Michele had fallen off the horse. She was a good rider, so something else must have happened. Finally, Michele told me they were racing, and her horse turned suddenly. She wasn't expecting it, and she fell sideways off the horse. She said proudly and in pain, "Dad, I was winning too."

Her friend's dad had given his permission for Michele to ride the horse but had warned them not to race or do anything other than ride. That was why her friend had kept saying she was sorry. Michele said later that she was the one who'd suggested they race.

Ron and I were in the emergency waiting room when Michele's friend and father came in. Claudia had gone with Michele and the doctor. The father came up, introduced himself, and apologized for what had happened. He told me he would pay the medical bill. I told him no. I was in the military, and the army would pay for it. His anguish and insistence that he pay for everything made me feel that he worried about my suing him. I told him to relax. "Kids are kids, and when they love horses, they are going to do stuff that will hurt them. I don't blame you or your daughter for anything. Michele was just as responsible for what happened as anybody. It was just an accident." He seemed a little relieved by my words but insisted on giving me his business card and asked me to call him if there was any way he could help. I thanked him and told him we were fine.

He asked if he could wait with me and see Michele. I said of course. About thirty minutes later, Michele and Claudia returned. Her shoulder was in a cast, and her arm was in a sling. Claudia said the doctor had confirmed it was a broken collarbone. Her friend's father said he was sorry about her injury. Michele told him it was her fault. She had fallen off the horse. I was glad there were no serious injuries. It was late, and I had two final tests the following day, so I got everybody in the car and left.

I graduated from the army's aviation safety officer course with an A-. I had the fourth-highest grade in the class. I was proud of my accomplishment. It had been a tough semester, and my grade showed me that I could excel academically in any future college course.

My lease ended at the end of the month, so I decided to stay for a couple of days and take the kids to Disneyland before returning to Fort Huachuca. We had a great time despite Michele's cast. After spending a day at Disneyland, Claudia and I cleaned the apartment, said good-bye to friends, and headed back to Fort Huachuca.

Much had happened while I was away. First, we had a new neighbor. A sergeant major had moved in next door to us. He had a wife and three kids. He was Czechoslovakian, and his wife was Yugoslavian. He had slipped across the Iron Curtain during the Czech uprising in 1956. Later, he'd joined the army and met his wife while stationed in Germany. They both spoke their native languages, German, and English. We became good friends and shared common interests. His wife and Claudia became good friends and still are today, forty years later.

The army moved all tactical military intelligence training to Fort Huachuca. The army merged USACSEWS's mission into military intelligence to create the US Army Intelligence Center and School (USAICS) and retired USACSEWS. USAICS was organized under the new TRADOC model, with a director of doctrine and training, a director of combat development, a director of maintenance and logistics, a director of training evaluation, a school secretary's office, and a command group. The commander was now a brigadier general, and each director was a colonel. They moved my position into the purview of the director of maintenance and logistics.

In the move, the intelligence basic officer course, intelligence advanced course, and all the enlisted MOS courses except EW and signals intelligence left Fort Devens came to Fort Huachuca. EW and signals intelligence training remained at Fort Devens.

When I reported to duty, I found my desk and files moved to a small building that housed the director of maintenance and logistics. I reported to the director, a short, gruff colonel who always had a cigar lit or unlit in his mouth. He turned out to be an excellent boss.

Also occupying the small building were the deputy director, a lieutenant colonel, the director's secretary, a budget analyst civilian and his assistant, and an attractive young blonde woman. She was new to her job and inexperienced. She was the wife of a captain in the army communications command, the other command on post.

Her boss, a civilian GS-13, enjoyed giving her reports and papers to prepare, knowing she wasn't sure what to do. I would watch her struggle to try to gather the data and prepare a memo or fact sheet in the proper format. I felt sorry for her, so I started helping her, and from that, we became good friends. The problem, of course, was the difficulty of a man and a woman just being friends. She was twenty-four years old, and as time went by and she became more knowledgeable in her job, our relations began to change.

The creation of USAICS almost tripled my duties as safety officer. I had more old building to inspect and more accident reports to coordinate. I also had to write a monthly safety memo for the commander's signature. That was the first time I'd had to write for a general officer, and of course, it stressed me a little. I invited the commander to each monthly aviation safety meeting, so my presentation had to be good. Some lieutenant colonels and majors complained about attending the meetings, but since I had the memo announcing the meeting signed by the commander, they reluctantly came.

A week after we got back from LA, I drove Claudia and the kids back to LA. Claudia and the kids were going back to Germany for four weeks while the kids were still out of school, and their Davis Agency charter flight left from the LA airport. This time, she planned on bringing her mom back to stay with us. We spent the night in LA, and after they boarded the plane Sunday morning, I drove back to Fort Huachuca.

While they were gone, I settled into my new office and expanded job. Jake scheduled me for more and more student training flights. That was a relief because safety officer duties were boring. Most of the student flying was at night, and since Claudia was gone, I didn't complain about the night flights.

Because of my effort to cross-train a TO in Korea, I felt I had a vested interest in training the TOs. I wanted it done right and enjoyed working with young soldiers. Each student had to plan and conduct three IR, three SLAR, and three camera flights. Once they'd completed the training flights, they planned a final flight that served as a graded test. Usually, one pilot flew the training flights, and another conducted the test flight.

On each flight, the student gave the pilot flight directions and altitude to get to their target. Once there, the student ran the particular sensor and directed the pilot on where to fly to cover the target area. The pilot was responsible for reviewing the plan and ensuring the accuracy of the plan. During the training flights, the pilot corrected any errors the student made and critiqued each leg of the flight. In addition, the pilot was responsible for showing the student how to fly the aircraft on autopilot. That way, if the pilot became disabled, the student could get the aircraft over friendly terrain. There, he could eject the pilot, and then he could eject. The key to this procedure working was the student staying oriented. He had to know which way to turn the aircraft toward safety. During their mission planning, the instructor gave the student a mission order depicting the enemy's and friendly forces' locations. The student used that information to plan his mission and fix where friendly forces were with his targets.

On the student's first flight, I would teach him how to turn on the autopilot found on the panel between our seats. Then I would let the student practice flying the aircraft with the autopilot. Flying the OV-1 on autopilot was easy. All the student had to do was turn the autopilot on and use the hand knob to turn, descend, or climb. If you wanted to turn left, you moved the knob left, and you moved it right to go right. You moved it forward to descend and back to climb. I taught the student not to change altitudes unless it was necessary. Changing altitudes required matching power changes. If the student tried to climb, he could stall the aircraft. If he descended, he could gain too much airspeed and aggravate controlling the aircraft with the knob. I showed my students how to make minor descents and climbs without using power changes.

After I had given my students enough time to fly with autopilot, I started interjecting an emergency. During the mission, without warning, I would put the aircraft into a steep turn or a dive, followed by a turn in another direction to confuse the student. Then I would announce that antiaircraft fire had hit the aircraft and wounded the pilot, leaving him unconscious. Then I would take my hands off the controls and watch the student's reaction.

The first time I did this, each student reacted the same: with a moment of confusion. Then the students would reach for the control knob without turning the autopilot on. When they couldn't get the aircraft straight and level, they would remember to turn the autopilot on. They would then get the aircraft straight and level but continue flying in the same direction in which I was flying the aircraft. I would let them fly for a minute or two and them ask them where they were going.

They, of course, said, "Toward friendly forces." Then I would ask which direction the friendly area was from the point where the antiaircraft fire had hit the aircraft. After they answered, I would ask them to check the compass and tell me what direction we were flying. That was when they would realize they were going in the wrong direction. Often, they were hesitant to make a turn until I encouraged them to. Once we were flying in the right direction, I had them explain what they were going to do next.

By then, they had settled down and could explain what they would do. I wanted them to tell me they would broadcast on Guard frequency and report the emergency. Next, they would point the aircraft toward an uninhabited area and eject me first and then themselves. After we discussed those actions, I would take control of the aircraft and continue the training mission.

Each mission was different. An SLAR mission consisted of an altitude high enough to clear ground obstacles, a start point, and an end point. When I was training TOs, the TO did all the planning, and the pilot checked his work. On an actual mission, the pilot and TO plan the mission together, as I'd experienced in Korea. Once the aircraft was airborne, the TO directed the pilot to the start point. That trained the TO in navigation and terrain recognition. At the start point, the TO turned the SLAR on and checked the fixed-target and moving-target screen to ensure he was getting results.

On an IR mission, the target was usually a road segment. The pilot usually flies an IR mission at low level at night to get maximum effectiveness from the IR. The student plans the route till the start of the IR leg and identifies it on the ground to the pilot. The pilot then descends to the altitude for the mission and flies over the road until the student reports the end point. The student turns the IR on at the start point and off at the end point. Flying IR missions at night makes navigation difficult. Good mission planning is essential for an IR mission.

Camera missions are similar to IR flights. The target might be an area or a point target, such as the village in Korea. The student plans the altitude necessary for getting the best photo of the target. Planning includes the route to and from the target. If the target is an area target, the student must plan the heading and turns to cover the area. The pilot and TO plan a day or night camera mission, depending on the tactical situation. Sometimes they combine a camera mission with an IR mission, depending on the target.

The school used the same flight routes and targets for each student class. After a while, I knew all the target locations and routes by memory. That made flying students much easier and allowed me to focus on training the students and less on flying the aircraft.

At the end of August, it was time for me to drive to LA to pick up Claudia, Mom, and the kids. I had planned on driving in the Ford Capri, which was a small car, but my next-door neighbor convinced me I should take his big Dodge instead. He said it would be better for Mom because of the room it provided. The only problem was that it had no air conditioner. However, since I was driving back at night in the cool air, I wouldn't need air-conditioning. I was hesitant about doing it, but in the end, I accepted his offer, mostly because I didn't want to offend him by refusing his generosity.

Early Saturday morning, I left Fort Huachuca in his big Dodge, headed for Los Angeles International Airport. I decided to take I-10 to I-8 and go to San Diego and then up to LA. The map showed that would be the shortest route. The car was running fine, but I had all four windows open to keep the temperature bearable. It was 110 degrees outside as I crossed the southern Arizona desert on I-8.

About fifty miles east of Yuma, I heard a pop and watched the engine temperature start to climb. I pulled off to the side of I-8 and shut the engine off. I was in the middle of nowhere. It was hot, and there was no shade anywhere. I opened the hood of the Dodge, and as I'd suspected, the fan belt had busted. There was only one town on the hundreds of miles of interstate between Casa Grande and Yuma. I had passed it twenty miles ago. The traffic on I-8 in those days was sparse to nonexistent, and after sitting there in the heat for twenty minutes without one car passing, I decided I had to do something.

I remembered passing what looked like a junkyard about a mile back. I could see the sun reflecting off a tin roof, so I started walking toward it. I prayed that it was open, because it represented the only chance I had for help. It took me fifteen minutes to get to it. I was soaking wet with sweat in the 110-degree heat. I had to climb over the four-string barbed-wire fence that formed a barrier to the interstate. I cut myself on the barbs.

I walked up to the large shed-like building, which was open on one side. Two men were working on stripping parts off an old wreck they had pulled under the shed. I startled them when I said hello to get their attention. They looked at me, and one, with surprise in his voice, asked, "How in the hell did you get here?"

I could understand their amazement. This was the only building in sight in any direction, and you could easily see twenty miles in any direction. When I explained my problem to them, both thought I was lucky to have broken down where I had. I told them I needed a fan belt for a 1968 Dodge. They said they had one, but they would have to take it off an old wreck.

While I waited in the ninety-degree shade of the shed, they walked into the acre of wrecked cars. In about ten minutes, they came back with a fan belt. They only charged me eighteen dollars for the belt, which was expensive but cheap in my circumstances. Then I left my driver's license with them to guarantee I would bring back the crescent wrench and pair of pliers I borrowed.

I climbed back over the fence and trekked through the heat back to the Dodge. I didn't know if I would be able to replace the fan belt. Thank God, I had no trouble loosening the generator's bolts and moving it so that I had enough slack to put the belt over the pulleys. I got greasy and dirty from the work, but I got it done. By then, the radiator had cooled enough for me to take the cap off. As expected, when I got the cap off, coolant spewed out. It looked as if I'd lost more than half of the coolant. Now I had another problem: I needed water to replace what I had lost, or at least enough to get to the next service station.

I hiked back to the junkyard and recovered my driver's license. I asked them if I could have some water. They said yes, if I had something to put it in. All they had were gas cans, and they didn't want water in them. One guy said there might be some milk cartons in the trash can. I dug through the trash can and found a one-quart and a one-pint milk carton. I filled them up with water and climbed back over the fence.

When I got back to the car, I realized I was thirsty. I had perspired a great deal while walking back and forth between the junkyard and the car. Fixing the fan belt also had drained my body. It occurred to me that I needed to get to a service station soon. I poured the water into the radiator. It didn't fill it enough for me to see water. I told myself that it had to be enough, because I was starting to feel the effects of heat exhaustion.

I started the car and watched the engine temperature gauge. It climbed to normal. I pulled back on the interstate. Fifteen miles later, I reached an intersection with an Exxon service station. By then, I had to pee. Plus, I was sweaty, dirty, and greasy. I pulled in by the restrooms and parked.

The door to one of the restrooms was partly open. I could see a Men sign, so I entered and locked the door. I thought it was strange that there was no urinal, but in my state, I didn't pay any attention. I peed and washed my face and arms. I dried and walked out. There, standing in line, were four women. I looked at the door I had just come out of and gasped at the sign on the door: Women. I shook my head and said sorry. They looked at me with anger as I hurried to my car. When I'd entered the restroom, I'd been in such a rush that I didn't notice that the partly open door hid the first two letters of the sign.

I filled my radiator up and bought three large bottles of water. I hurriedly started the car and drove away. In my peripheral vision, I could see the women pointing to me as they told their husbands what had happened.

The three bottles of water barely quenched my thirst. Despite my having all the windows down in the car, all that blew in was 110-degree air. I filled up in Yuma and bought more water. Sweat soaked my clothes and made my skin greasy from body oil. I felt dirty and was beginning to tire from the constant heat, even though the hot wind blowing through the car was dry. In the heat, my progress across the desert seemed slow.

At last, I reached the Julian, Laguna, and Cuyamaca mountain ranges east of San Diego. I started the slow drive up from below sea level to five thousand feet. It took ten minutes to reach the crest of the mountain range and feel the comfort of cooler air. It was about eighty-five degrees, but compared to the 110, I felt as if I had turned on an air conditioner.

About fifty miles east of San Diego, I-8 ended, and I detoured onto the one-lane highway leading into San Diego. That portion of I-8 was still under construction. My progress slowed to fifty miles an hour and sometimes slower the closer I got to San Diego, and the traffic increased.

I had not counted on the delays, because the map showed I-8 continuing all the way to San Diego.

It was late afternoon when I got past San Diego and headed north to LA. I was back on an interstate now and making better time. Around 1900, I was on the outskirts of LA and about twenty miles from LAX, so I started looking for a motel. I found a Holiday Inn and checked in. On the way up from San Diego, I could think only of having a cold beer and some Kentucky Fried Chicken. As soon as I got my shaving kit in the motel room, I drove to KFC and bought an eight-pack of chicken. Then I stopped at a convenience store and bought two cold quarts of Budweiser beer.

Back in the motel room, I ate six pieces of the chicken and drank one of the beers. After that, I felt almost human again. I tried to watch TV, but I felt so grimy that I had to take a shower. Besides, the beer and chicken were making me sleepy. I didn't want to go to bed too early, because Claudia's plane wasn't due to arrive until 1200. I didn't want to hang around the airport waiting all morning. If I went to bed late, I would sleep late, which was better than waiting in the airport.

I couldn't stand the way I felt any longer, so I gave in and took a shower. That spoiled my plan. The hot shower and half of the second beer put me to sleep. I woke up the next morning at 0700. The TV was still on, and for a second or two, I thought I had just drifted off to sleep. However, I could see daylight through the window. It had been dark when I'd checked in. I tried to sleep some more, but my effort was in vain. I got up, shaved, and headed for breakfast.

I got to the airport at about 1000, which wasn't bad. Those were the days before there was so much security, so I bought a paper and walked to Claudia's arrival gate. After I read the paper, I thought about Claudia. I was happy to have her back home, but I wondered who she had seen while she was in Germany. That caused the old pang of hurt and suspicion to rise. I dealt with my thoughts for a while and then took a walk around the airport. I watched men and women greet their wives, husbands, girlfriends, and boyfriends at several gates. The love they expressed in their greetings made me wonder if they had to deal with the same memories and hurt that I bore. It was hard to tell. I knew that when I greeted Claudia, I would hold her and kiss her, and to someone watching us, ours would seem like the happiest of relationships. But that wasn't the case. It was what it was.

At last, I saw my family walking up the airplane exit. Claudia was helping Mom. She saw me and waved. I could see her tell the kids, and I watched them look for me. Then we were all together, hugging one another and making small talk. Claudia looked beautiful. Mom was telling me hello, and I was trying to tell her I was happy to see her again. The kids were telling me about the flight as we moved toward the baggage claim.

While I waited for their bags, they went to the restroom. When they returned, Claudia said they were hungry, so we needed to eat something before we left. We had lunch in an airport diner. Our talk centered on the flight, and I told them about driving the Dodge. Claudia thought the Dodge was a bad idea because it had no air conditioner. I agreed with her but tried focusing on the positives: the room in the car and the fact that we would be driving through the desert at night, when it should be cool.

After lunch, we loaded the bags into the car and headed south to San Diego. I explained why I was going that way. Claudia thought it was a good idea because she wanted to see San Diego. It was a beautiful drive along the coast to San Diego. I hadn't paid much attention on the drive up. I'd been too miserable and just wanted to get to LA. Now it was different; the temperature was in the seventies, which was comfortable, and everybody enjoyed the drive.

When we got through San Diego and made it to the crest of the mountains east of San Diego, it was 2000. It was still cool, and everybody was napping except me. We started down the winding descent to the desert, and it started to get warmer. When we reached the desert floor, it was a hundred degrees, even though it was 2100. The heat woke everyone up, and the complaints started.

I couldn't blame them. I was miserable too. By midnight, it had probably cooled to ninety degrees. It was a bad decision to take the Dodge. I felt bad for Mom. She was in no way familiar with such heat. She told Claudia that she didn't think she could breathe in such hot, dry air. We suffered in some silence and a little cussing over the next four hours. Everybody was relieved but in a bad mood when I pulled into our driveway at our quarters on Fort Huachuca. It was 0400 before everyone went to bed. I got a couple hours of sleep before I had to get up and go to work.

I didn't know it at the time, but our relationship was going to take a dive. While I was happy to see Mom, after a while, I felt she polarized

Claudia against me. Maybe it wasn't true, but it was the way I felt. She provided a ready babysitter and made it easy for Claudia and me to attend the many parties and events that were common in those days. However, she always took sides with Claudia during our arguments. I would gladly accept blame for half of the arguments but not all of them. Yet to Mom, I was the culprit in all of them. Still, Claudia and I struggled on and had some excellent days. The problem was that the bad days began to outnumber the good days. I began to feel the pressure and stress of being unhappy at home and trying to give an outstanding performance at work.

Michele was beginning to revolt because I hadn't bought her a horse. What she didn't know was that each time I talked to Claudia about buying one, Claudia didn't want to. Finally, around the middle of September, we drove down to the Sierra Vista stables to look at a horse advertised for sale.

We met the family who owned the horse at the stables. They took us to their stable and showed us a blue appaloosa. The horse was friendly and came running up to the fence when she saw us. Michele fell in love immediately. She looked at me and said, "Dad, I want her."

Claudia said, "Let's talk about it." Mom was saying she didn't think Michele was old enough to have a horse.

We left the appaloosa and looked at another horse for sale. Michele said she wanted the appaloosa. The people who owned the appaloosa had gathered around their car, so I said, "Let's go talk to them again."

What happened next was funny. We were standing around in a circle, discussing the appaloosa and the price they were asking. The owners were telling us what a good horse she was, when out of nowhere, the horse stuck her head into the circle as if she were joining the conversation. I laughed in amazement. To me, that was an omen. The owner said, "By the way, she is a very smart horse. She knows a dozen ways to get out of a stall. She can pick locks and crawl under or jump over fences. You have to lock her stall securely."

I said, "Okay, Michele, she's your horse," and she jumped up and down with joy, thanking me. I arranged to have the owners haul her on post to the Buffalo Corral stables for me. They agreed, and I told them I would let them know when I had a stall ready. I paid them $800 for the appaloosa. They were kind enough to throw in the tack, which saved me another $400.

We left the stables and drove on post to Buffalo Corral stables. I leased a stall for the appaloosa. The manager told me I had to have a vet check the horse before I could keep her on post. I also would have to join the riding club. I joined the riding club, but since it was Saturday, I would have to wait till Monday to arrange for a vet to check Michele's new horse.

I took Claudia, her mom, and Ron home. They had had enough of standing out in the hot and dusty air. They had seen and smelled enough horses for that day. Michele and I returned to the stables to inspect our stall and see what we needed to secure the appaloosa in it. I could see I had to repair the lock and replace two of the two-by-eight rails. We drove downtown to the lumberyard, and I bought the two-by-eights and a heavy lock. I had to put the boards inside the Pinto and let them stick out the rear with a red flag on them. I took our material to the stables and unloaded it. Then I had to go to the PX to buy a hammer, a saw, tape, a square, a screwdriver set, a wrench set, and some nails. I needed those tools anyway.

When I had the rail fixed and the lock installed, it was 1700. Michele was eager to help me and kept making a verbal list of the stuff she was going to do to dress up her stall. I said the first thing she needed was a name for her horse. She said, "I already have a name. It's going to be Blue." I congratulated her on her choice of a name. It was a perfect name for a blue appaloosa.

By Wednesday, the vet had checked Blue, and she was pacing nervously in her new stall at the Buffalo Corral stables. Michele was proud and couldn't wait to get to the stables to start riding Blue and teaching her tricks. She painted Blue's name on a board to put on her gate. The minute she got home from school and did her homework, she was asking Claudia to drive her to the stables. Claudia had something else to complain about now. She didn't join me in sharing Michele's joy of owning a horse. To Claudia, the horse was an inconvenience that she blamed on me.

Blue turned out to be a gentle but powerful horse. She took to Michele, and Michele became an exceptional rider and equestrian. She matured by caring for Blue. Though devoted to Michele, Blue was still an imp of a horse. At least once a week, she figured out how to get out of the stall. I would get a call to come catch her and put her back in her stall. I got into the habit each day of pretending to leave the stable with Michele. We drove a little ways off so Blue couldn't see us and stopped. We would watch Blue for a few minutes to see what she would do. Several times, I discovered how she was getting out of the stall by watching what she did when she thought we were gone. I finally got the stall secured so that she couldn't get out.

Claudia would take Michele to the corral each day after school, and I would pick her up when I got home from work. After Michele started forming friendships with other horse owners, she found rides to and from the corral with them. That took some of the strain off us and eased some of Claudia's complaints.

My days became routine. I conducted inspections during the morning and prepared reports in the afternoon. It was easy work. There were no big challenges. Meanwhile, Claudia met several German wives and spent her time going to coffees, playing tennis, and sunning herself.

Our relations became routine too. We would argue and give each other the silent treatment for a week, make up and laugh for a week, and then fight again. No matter what I did, I couldn't please her enough to create a constant and loving relationship. I know the kids were tired of our fighting, and I was too. I began to feel I would be happier out of our marriage.

After we bought Blue, Claudia wanted a new car. She didn't like the Pinto and wanted to trade it in for something new. We saw some advertisements for new Chevrolets at a dealership in Tucson, so one weekend, we drove to Tucson to check out the Chevrolets. We ended up buying a Chevrolet Monte Carlo. It was a beauty, and of course, it became Claudia's car. I kept the Ford Capri as my car.

I don't know why, but during that period, women became attracted to me. Several of Claudia's friends openly flirted with me. I don't know if Claudia noticed it and chose to ignore it. I never gave her a reason to distrust me. At the office, the budget analysis clerk and I became closer. She was attractive and young and clearly had feelings for me. I found comfort in her smile and friendly conversation during the times when Claudia and I were fighting. I looked forward to seeing her each day and spent as much time in the office as I could to be near her.

Michele had started riding in gymkhanas each Saturday. I was there each morning, supporting her. I convinced Claudia that she should also go to show support for Michele. Michele and Blue placed in or won almost each gymkhana in her class. Blue loved to run and compete. I told the clerk about the gymkhanas and invited her to come watch them.

One Saturday, Claudia, Ron, and I were watching the gymkhana, when the clerk showed up with her daughter. I introduced her to Claudia and Ron, and she joined us to watch the gymkhana. After Michele rode in her event, Claudia wanted to leave, so we said good-bye and left. On the way home, Claudia was a little upset about the clerk. She halfway accused me of having something going on. I convinced her that the clerk only worked in my office, but secretly, I felt good about her coming because she wanted to. I took it to mean she'd come to see me as much as the gymkhana.

As time passed, I became more resentful of the way Claudia treated me. However, nothing I said changed her attitude. I slowly got the notion that she had tired of me also. I believe she stayed only because of the kids and her belief that as a Catholic, she couldn't divorce. So we continued to muddle through living. Thank God there were some good times between us. They were just enough to hold us together.

Thanksgiving came, and we had dinner at the mess hall with the troops. It was the second time Mom had eaten in an army mess hall. Impressed by the decorated mess hall, she couldn't get over how many choices of food there were. We had fun that day. Maybe it was the season, but after Thanksgiving, in the days before Christmas, Claudia and I had an uncommon peaceful period. It was enough to give me hope that she was changing.

We had a wonderful Christmas. The weather provided snow, and the two weeks of half-day duty provided time for us to spend together. I started playing tennis with Claudia. She was into it, and to be honest, she beat me more than I could beat her. On days when the courts were clear of snow, we played tennis. It felt as if we were a normal family.

New Year's Eve turned life upside down. Everybody was getting together to celebrate New Year's at a club in Sierra Vista. Mom was going with us. The next-door neighbors were going, and several couples Claudia knew were going to be there. Michele was old enough to babysit. I was looking forward to a great time.

When we got to the club, the others were already there. Claudia introduced me to the three couples who sat opposite us at our table. All the women were German and equally attractive. Their husbands were NCOs, none of whom I knew. The drinks flowed, and we were having a good party. The band was a local band, and they were good. We were all dancing and having a good time. Claudia was stunning in her party dress, and I couldn't keep my eyes off her.

The club served a small meal around 2100. That slowed the dancing down and started some conversations. After the meal, the band started up again, and so did the dancing. Around 2300, the drinks and dancing began to take a toll. There was less dancing and more sitting and talking.

At one point, Claudia was dancing with someone, and I was sitting at the table. The couple in front of me was talking, and I joined in. The conversation somehow turned to the centerfold in *Playboy* magazine. They wanted my opinion of her. I replied that I didn't read *Playboy*. I preferred the magazine *Bon Appétit*. It was noisy, so we were leaning toward each other so that we could hear over the din. She was attractive and had flirtatious eyes. Out of the blue, she asked me how I felt about open marriages. At the time, I didn't know what an open marriage was.

She was explaining an open marriage, when Claudia sat back down. Claudia didn't join the conversation but listened. When the wife finished explaining an open marriage, I said I didn't have an opinion. Maybe it was right for some people, but I was sure it wouldn't work for other people. She nonchalantly said she and her husband had an open marriage. I looked at him, and he nodded to confirm it. She went on to explain how it had made their marriage stronger.

I could hear an invitation in her voice. She was suggesting Claudia and I try it. Before I could answer her, someone asked Claudia to dance, and she got up and left. "Well," I answered, "I would have to be unhappy and not in love with my wife to engage in an open marriage." That chilled her flirtation with me. I told her, "I'm very much in love with my wife and like what I have. I don't need anything else." She seemed disappointed that I had turned her down. I was a little stunned at how blatantly she had propositioned me with her husband sitting there.

Our conversation died then, and she turned to one of the other couples. When Claudia returned from dancing, she was obviously angry with me. When I asked her what was wrong, she only said, "You know what." I guess she knew about the couple's open marriage arrangement. I couldn't understand why she was angry with me for talking about it.

The wife saw that Claudia was upset at me and said in German, "Don't worry, Claudia; he only has eyes for you."

That didn't appease Claudia. She was cold and distant for the rest of the night. When the countdown to New Year's rang in the new year, she turned her head when I went to kiss her. She shook my hand and frowned when she said, "Happy New Year." This angered me. I had done nothing but talk to her friends. We were all feeling the effects of the many drinks we had consumed. That might have incited more anger.

When we got home, Claudia was yelling at me in a rage. By then, I was just as angry as she was. I was angry at her anger at me. I saw that it was getting out of hand. She was calling me names with her face twisted in pure hatred. She got in my face and, out of control, slapped me. Much to my surprise and hers, I slapped her back. That was the first and only time I ever struck Claudia. She charged back at me, and all I could do was hold her hands to keep her from clawing my eyes out. The kids were awake now and screaming. Mom had a hold of Claudia, trying to pull her away. At the same time, she was saying how terrible I was to have hit Claudia.

Our fighting alarmed our next-door neighbors. One neighbor, Leslie, came over to see if we were okay. By then, Mom had pulled Claudia away, still crying and cussing me. I told Leslie that everything was okay. Claudia had drunk too much and was a little upset at me. Claudia started yelling that I had hit her. Leslie looked as if he had gotten into a position he didn't want to be in and looked at me. I said, "She slapped me, and I slapped her back. That's all that happened."

He said, "Okay," and he left. Claudia went with Mom and the kids to the bedroom. I sat down in a chair to wait until everyone was in bed.

I was in disbelief at how fast a fun evening had turned into pure hell. I couldn't understand Claudia's anger. During the fight, she had accused me of talking about sex with her friend and wanting to sleep with her. I'd kept telling her that her friend was talking about sex, not me, but nothing I said changed her mind. The violence of her reaction had a devastating effect on me.

I had seen her face twisted in hatred as she verbally and physically attacked me. I had never seen that before. I knew she held much pent-up anger just under her skin. I'd never believed it was as bad as I saw that night. I broke that night. I psychologically accepted that she didn't love me.

I even had empathy for her. She must have spent every day feeling stuck in a relationship she hated. In a way, I could understand how it all came to a head and why she had to vent that anger.

I was crying now. My optimism that everything would work out had shattered. I no longer could believe that. I was crying because my love for her didn't matter. I was going to suffer because of that love. I would keep trying and hoping for the best but would not believe it was going to happen. There was no way I could see to change her feelings toward me. I remembered Dale's warning not to live the life he had for many years.

I slept on the couch that night. When the noise of Claudia banging pots and pans in the kitchen woke me up, I got up, went into the bedroom, got in bed, and went back to sleep. An hour later, I woke and couldn't go back to sleep. I got up, showered, shaved, and walked into the kitchen to get something to eat. I could tell everyone was mad at me. No one said good morning or even looked at me. I fixed some toast, cereal, and coffee and ate in silence. I thought it was wrong of Claudia to make the kids think that what had happened last night was my fault. I wouldn't have done that to her. But that was the way she was, and I knew she would never change.

After breakfast, I drove to the office. I was on leave, but I hoped the clerk would be there. I knew she was on leave too, but I still hoped she would come in. She wasn't there, so I talked with the XO for a while and did some paperwork. I was just killing time to delay returning home. After a couple of hours, I left and went home. What should have been a happy time was another miserable day.

The Christmas and New Year's holidays ended the first Monday after Near Year's, and everybody went back to work full-time. By then, relations had improved a little between us. We were speaking and civil to each other. I was happy to see the clerk again, and she seemed happy to see me. I was glad to be at work for eight or nine hours each day. The less I saw of Claudia, the lower the odds of us fighting.

As I always did after one of our fights, I began to rethink the way I was acting. I didn't want this coldness between us. I wanted the exact opposite of the way we were behaving. As always, her beauty and our enormous libidos overcame the rift between us, and we were lovers again. The anger of our fight was forgotten for a while, and we were close again. However, I felt the same pressure I had as a kid when my father came home and I looked for some sign he was drinking again. Each day, I looked for some sign that Claudia and I were on the verge of another argument.

The operations officer for the maintenance aviation division, when reviewing my flights records, noticed that I was rotary-wing qualified. Since he needed helicopter pilots, he asked me if I wanted to check out in the UH-1, the Huey. I, of course, said yes, and I started my transition.

The process was a repeat of the phases I'd gone through in rotary-wing transition, except it was on the Huey. I learned the preflight checks and start-up procedures. Then I learned to hover and taxi. Once I could do that, we started takeoffs and landings. The Huey was much larger than the OH-13 or the OH-58, but the principles of flying it were the same. It took a couple of hours for me to learn to hover in it. I still knew the technique for hovering but lacked the control touch. Control touch is the one constant in flying. The techniques remain the same, but you lose the control touch when not flying a certain aircraft every day.

I struggled with my subconscious impulse to round out on landings. You don't round out to land a helicopter. You lower the collective, put a little back pressure on the cyclic, and let the helicopter settle to the ground. Of course, you have to use pedal as the collective is lowered to keep the nose straight. After ten hours, I could hover, taxi, land, and take off safely. I wobbled a lot, but that would go away as my control touch became smoother.

As I became skilled in those maneuvers, we started emergency procedures, such as autorotation, hydraulics-off landings, and lost-tail-rotor procedures. Autorotation was the same as a normal landing, except you had one shot at setting it down, so it had to be right. It took me several tries before I made one successful autorotation. On a no-hydraulics landing, you have to bring the aircraft in flat and fast, set it down on the skids, and let it slide to a stop. We only practiced a couple of them, because the maneuver grinds up the skids.

Once I was skilled with emergencies, I started advanced flight maneuvers, such as landing on slopes. There were several helipads located on Fort Huachuca. One pad was about two hundred meters from the building I worked in. It was a raised pad with long slopes on its sides. It was a perfect spot to practice slope landings. I spent an hour practicing landing on the side of the pad. To do that, I'd slowly touch down the uphill skid and slowly lower the downhill skid. Holding the Huey in that position takes increased pitch and plenty of power. It also makes a hell of a lot of noise.

I didn't realize how much noise we were making until the next morning in the office. Everybody started telling me about the helicopter that had been landing and hovering around the landing pad. It had made so much noise that it had shaken the whole building. They'd thought the windows were going to break. I laughed and explained that I'd been flying the helicopter and making the noise. I said it was the only approved pad to practice slope landings. I promised we wouldn't do it again except for when I took my check ride. I would have to prove to the instructor that I could successfully land on a slope.

After I had twenty hours of transition training, I took my check ride. As usual, I had checkrideitis but managed to pass. After that, I started instrument training. I flew the Huey another ten hours under the hood, doing all approaches. I joked about how unsteady the Huey was when flying on instruments. The unsteadiness was because of the winds and convection that constantly bounced it around. It was work to fly a Huey on instruments. I couldn't wait to take my check ride and get what I considered torture over with. Flying a Mohawk on instruments was like riding in a comfortable Cadillac after riding a bicycle. However, overall, I enjoyed flying the Huey and was proud of my dual rating.

Under an agreement with the FAA, the intelligence center and school provided search and rescue, or SAR, and support for the western region of the United States. The Mohawk's infrared and cameras provide a unique capability when searching for downed aircraft. The infrared system can detect and film a difference of a half degree in temperature. The temperature of the metal in a downed aircraft is always different from the material around it. For instance, the tail of an aircraft protruding from a snowbank would be a couple of degrees warmer than the snow. The infrared system would easily detect that difference. The IR film would show the tail section sticking out of the snow. The system also marks the time, latitude, and longitude on each frame of imagery. That makes it easy for an imagery interpreter to find the tail section's location.

The vertical camera provides a similar capability in SAR missions. The Mohawk can film a large area surrounding the suspected location of a downed aircraft. Then imagery analysts can study closely the imagery for any sign of the aircraft. The camera will see objects that aircraft flying visual surveillance often miss. One of our pilots flying an SAR in Montana took imagery of a large remote area. There had been several visual flights over the area with no luck. When the imagery analyst studied the imagery, he found a Help sign the survivors had placed on the ground, which led to their rescue. In addition, he found the wrecks of three other planes that had been missing for several years.

I had just completed my Huey transition, when the deputy director called me into his office. He told me to get my equipment and some clothing for a week and report to the airfield. The sheriff of San Bernardino County, California, had asked for SAR help in finding an aircraft down in the Big Bear Lake area. I would meet the sheriff there at the Big Bear Airport. The flight section was getting a Mohawk ready. SSG Mabry would be my TO. Major Bing, the Maintainance Aviation Director(MAD), and Specialist Five Moore were already on the way.

Filled with excitement, I drove home to get some underwear and my shaving kit. I was also a little uneasy. This would be my first mission other than training students. I told myself it was okay. I was doing something different from anything I had done before. It was normal to be a little concerned about how I would do. Claudia wanted to know why I was home so early.

I explained what I was going to do and said I didn't know when I would be back. I guessed the mission would last anywhere from several days to a week. She wanted to know what had happened to the plane. I told her I didn't know other than that it had disappeared off radar late yesterday afternoon. No one had seen it or heard from it since.

SSG Mabry was waiting for me when I got to the airfield. He squeezed our bags into the IR equipment bay while I went to see the operations officer and file a flight plan. The operations officer had a map of Big Bear Lake for me and gave me the FM frequency to contact the sheriff on when I got close to Big Bear. After talking to him, I filed a VFR plan direct to Big Bear Airport. Airport data showed that the runway had medium-intensity runway lights (MIRL) and a two-light precision approach path indicator system (PAPI) that provided a four-degree approach slope to each runway end. The runway altitude was 6,752 feet with standard nonprecision markings on each end.

I plotted the heading from Fort Huachuca to the airport and calculated the distance. Based on the en route winds, I adjusted my heading and came up with a two-and-a-half-hour flight. The weather forecast for the area called for intermittent snow showers with a ceiling of two thousand feet and four miles of visibility. That seemed acceptable, but I planned a heading to an alternate field in case the weather at the airfield was so bad I could not land.

After takeoff, I climbed to six thousand feet and turned to my heading. I put the Mohawk on autopilot and unfolded my map. I noted checkpoints on the map that I could use to check the accuracy of my heading. The brown desert floor was featureless except for the dry washes and streambeds. Snow covered the small mountain ranges above the four-thousand-foot level. The farther west we traveled, the more snow covered the ground in patches.

My heading of 310 degrees took us south of Tucson and Phoenix. The smog obscured a clear view of the cities in the dry air. Slowly, the terrain started to change, and I could see mountains ahead. The tops were higher than we were, so I climbed to ten thousand feet. We put on our oxygen masks to check them in case we had to go higher. My time en route told me the mountains were the ones around Big Bear.

When Big Bear Lake came into view, we started looking for the airport. Snow covered the area as far as we could see, making it difficult to see the airport. Then, from a distance, we saw the medium-intensity runway lights, and the runway came into view. I called the tower for landing, and the tower cleared me for a straight-in approach. I did the prelanding check and started descending. I called the sheriff's operations center and told them we were approaching the airport for landing. The operator told us that someone would meet us at the parking apron.

I reported short final, and the tower cleared me for landing. As I was rolling out, the tower directed me to a parking apron that was for SAR support aircraft. Approaching the apron, I saw a civilian directing me to a parking spot. I parked the Mohawk, and we climbed out into the cold air.

The individual who parked us asked if we needed fuel, and I said yes. A deputy sheriff drove up and introduced himself. He said the deputy sheriff in charge of the SAR was waiting at the operations center to brief me. I told SSG Mabry to stay with the aircraft while they refueled. The deputy said he would drop me off and come back to get SSG Mabry.

I followed the deputy into the SAR operations center. There were several people sitting around a table, talking to another deputy. Three other men were standing by a big map of the area. The deputy greeted me, and I introduced myself. He expressed gratitude for my being there and introduced me to the people sitting at the table. They were family members of the two men aboard the twin-engine Beechcraft last heard from in the Big Bear Lake area.

The deputy told me that Major Bing and his TO were flying an IR mission over the area where traffic control radar had last seen the aircraft. The aircraft had been en route to Big Bear Airport, when it had disappeared from the radar screen. Heavy snow had been falling in the area at the time. As we spoke, we moved to the large map of the area. He pointed out the area that Major Bing was searching with IR. He told me that since yesterday, five Civil Air Patrol (CAP) aircraft had flown visual reconnaissance over the area without any luck. The snowstorm had dumped more than sixteen inches of snow over the area, blanketing the entire area and hiding any sign of a crash. In addition, the mountainous terrain and altitude made it difficult for the Civil Air Patrol planes to do a good search of the area. Because of that, they had called for our support in hopes that our sensors would find the crash site.

The family members gathered around the map to hear what I had to say. I told him I did not want to dash hopes, but if snow covered the site and the aircraft, IR would not detect it. If, on the other hand, some part of the aircraft was bare, then the IR would detect it. Because of the snow cover, the vertical camera might provide a better chance of finding the site. The advantage of the camera was that if snow covered a protruding section of the aircraft, a picture would show that. The infrared film would not detail it if there was no temperature deviation between it and the surrounding area.

I continued by recommending that I film the area with the vertical camera on top of the IR. While we were waiting for the readout of the film, I would fly a visual search of the area, since the terrain and altitude wouldn't affect me. If the weather warmed some, it might melt some snow and expose parts of the aircraft. If that happened, then I could make another IR run over the area. Everybody was enthusiastic about what I was saying. I secretly hoped we could find the aircraft in time to save any survivors, but looking at the terrain and knowing that the snow was sixteen feet deep in places and deeper in gullies, I was not sure we would find anything.

Just as I finished speaking, Major Bing called the SAR operations. He wanted to know if I was there yet. The deputy said yes, and he asked to speak to me. I took the mike, and he told me he was en route to March AFB to drop off the film for processing. After that, he was returning to Fort Huachuca. I was to stay on station and provide all support until the sheriff released me. I told him, "Roger." SSG Mabry arrived, and I introduced him to everybody.

The deputy asked me what I recommended we do now. I said, "SSG Mabry and I are going to plan a camera mission over the area. It's getting dark outside, and because of the terrain, I'd prefer to fly it in the morning, in daylight." He agreed. He said that would give the analyst at March AFB time to analyze the IR film. He said after we finished our planning, he would take us to a hotel room he had arranged for us. The hotel had a restaurant, and we could eat there.

It took us an hour to plan our photo mission. Constantly changing terrain complicated the task of photographing the area. The area varied in altitude from one to two thousand feet, which meant we would have to change altitude constantly to use the maximum ability of our vertical camera. That meant we had to have good weather to fly the mission safely. In addition, it would take all of our film to cover such a large area. We checked the weather before we left for the hotel. The forecast was more of the same: intermittent snow showers with a cloud deck at ten thousand feet and visibility of six miles. If it held, that would be good enough for us to complete the mission.

After dinner at the hotel, we sat in the bar and had a drink with the deputy, CAP pilots, and family members of the missing men. The CAP pilots were different ages and were interested in our Mohawk. That topic dominated the conversation, but out of it came a discussion of our abilities and the likelihood of success. Our presence gave the family members some hope. They made it clear that if we did not find them, they appreciated our being there and lending help. That inspired SSG Mabry and me to do everything possible to find them. After one drink, we left for bed.

It was snowing the next morning and was cold. After we had breakfast and got to the airfield, the snow stopped, and the sun was out. We had to delay taking off until it warmed enough to clear the ice from our wings. Around 1000, we took off and headed to our start point. We had eighteen legs to fly, and some of the legs were more than twelve miles. On some legs, we had to fly at one altitude, stop filming, and do a 360-degree turn while climbing to a higher altitude. At the end of the turn, we would be on the heading we'd started on. SSG Mabry would turn the camera back on at the point at which he'd stopped it for the turn, and we would continue filming the leg. We had to do that several times while either climbing or descending to a lower altitude.

It was hard work and took concentration to stay on our plan, but we were driven by the knowledge that we were trying to save two lives. I prayed that somewhere below us, our camera caught the image of the downed plane. We used up our camera film in an hour and forty-five minutes, but we managed to cover the area. I called SAR operations and told them I was going to March AFB to drop the film off and would be back in a couple of hours. I landed at March, and SSG Mabry removed the film and gave it to the IE team that met us. While ground attendance men refueled the Mohawk, we had lunch.

By the time we got back to Big Bear Airport, the weather had warmed. All around the airport, snow was melting. The deputy took us back to the SAR operations tent to wait for the imagery readout results.

An hour later, we received some partial results that showed no sign of an aircraft or remains of one. The analysts would continue their study of the photos, but I had a hunch that the snow had blanketed any wreckage that was easily discernable. The news disappointed everybody. We reviewed the extent of the search area for the possibility of expanding it. The deputy didn't think that would be necessary. The flight path was mostly over populated areas, and someone would have noticed the crash by now. That was why they'd focused the search on the remote area surrounding Big Bear Lake. However, just to make sure, CAP pilots would search the flight path leading into the remote area.

I told the deputy that I wanted to do an IR mission. It had warmed up enough to melt snow in the area. Maybe some part of the downed aircraft would be visible. He agreed, so SSG Mabry and I planned an IR flight over the same route we had used for the photo mission. This time, we reversed the flight path to get a different perspective. We waited until the hottest part of the afternoon to fly the mission. That allowed the maximum melt of snow. After we finished the mission, we delivered the IR film to March AFB, refueled, and returned to Big Bear Airport.

It was night when we got back. The landing approach into the airport was from the west, and I was descending over snow-covered mountains that glistened in the dim moonlight. The scene reminded me of Korea and its snow-covered mountains. Back on the ground, all we could do was wait for the readout of the IR imagery.

While we were waiting in the SAR operations building, Sheriff Bland came in. He thanked us and the CAP pilots for our support. He said we could return to Fort Huachuca in the morning. We had done the best we could. We could do nothing other than hope the film readouts would produce something. I told the sheriff that I had four hours of fuel. Since it only took two hours to get to Fort Huachuca, I would do a visual search for an hour before leaving. The Mohawk was a visual reconnaissance and surveillance aircraft also. We might get lucky and find something. He agreed to that. The family and friends of the two missing men thanked us again before we left for the hotel.

The next morning, SSG Mabry and I flew the area for an hour, searching for any sign of a downed aircraft. All we saw was snow. Even the trees were hard to make out because of the snow on them. The wind blowing across the mountains caused turbulence, and the Mohawk bounced around. I felt admiration for the CAP pilots who flew visual search missions in their light aircraft. If the turbulence bounced our big Mohawk around, it must have given them big problems. After an hour without seeing anything, I turned the Mohawk east on a heading for Fort Huachuca. I called SAR operations and told them I had nothing to report and wished them good luck.

We got back to Fort Huachuca around 1600. I filled out the logbook and went to our operations to talk to Major Bing. I briefed him on what I had done. He told me the sheriff's office had called him to report that analysts had found two wrecked aircraft in the imagery I'd taken.

Unfortunately, they were old crashes that had never been found. But at least the sheriff could close the records on them. He'd thanked Major Bing again for our support.

I drove back to my office, feeling good that we had done something. I was disappointed that we hadn't found the aircraft they were looking for. Everybody said, "Welcome back," when I walked in. I smiled and said it was good to be back. I looked at the budget clerk. She was smiling happily at me. Her expression showed a look of pride in me. I felt a tingle of longing as I smiled back at her. The colonel came out of his office and interrupted our silent exchange of emotions. He wanted me to brief him on the mission. By the time we finished talking, everyone had left, and the office was empty. There was a little folded yellow Post-it stuck to my desk. I opened it and read, "Missed you."

When I got home, everybody was eating dinner. Claudia said hello and got me a plate. She asked why I had not called her to let her know I was coming back. I told her I'd had no way of knowing exactly when I would return. I tried to tell her about the mission and how beautiful Big Bear was, and she listened politely but showed little real interest. I asked how things had been there and listened to her tell me what she had done. As she spoke, I felt a vast sense of disappointment. She had shown no expression of love or joy that I was back. I compared her response to the joyful smile and little note left by the clerk. I could see how wide the rift between us was growing.

For the rest of the evening, I helped the kids with homework. Claudia had cleaned the kitchen and was on the phone with one of her friends. Mom watched TV. Michele told me about the gymkhana on Saturday. She said she had to wash and comb Blue tomorrow so she would look like a champion. Claudia finished talking on the phone and told me she and her friend were going to Tucson tomorrow. She was having a coffee on Saturday and wanted me to buy some food for it. Also, she wanted some German wine for the coffee. I asked her if she was going to the gymkhana, and she said no.

When the kids finished their homework, I played a game with them until it was time for them to go to bed. Claudia was asleep in front of the TV. Mom said good night and went to bed with the kids. I fixed a gin and tonic and watched the news. Claudia woke up, said she was going to bed, and left. I sat there trying to untangle my emotions.

I had spent the last three days doing something worthwhile, something I wanted to share with the one I loved. I interpreted Claudia's lack of interest in what I had done as lack of interest in me. I was dying, frustrated by trying to earn a token of warmth and love from her. Words from Hank Williams's song "Cold, Cold Heart" kept coming into my mind: "What can I do to change your mind and melt your cold, cold heart?"

As always, I thought that maybe the problem was me. Was I expecting too much? Were other couples this distant and casual, or was it just us? My feelings for the clerk were starting to worry me. I wanted those feelings to be for Claudia. Finally, I turned the TV off and took a shower. I got into bed with a beautiful woman. She was snoring gently as I sighed and drifted off to sleep.

I awoke about forty minutes before we normally got up. I lay there for a few minutes and then got up and used the bathroom. That woke Claudia up, and she got up and went to the bathroom. I expected her to return to bed, and then we would make love, as we usually did. However, I heard the shower turn on, and disappointed, I rolled over and tried to sleep some more. She came out of the bathroom to get some underwear and said, "I'm going to take a shower, okay?"

I could not hide the disappointment in voice when I answered, "Sure, go ahead."

I do not know if that was what she wanted or not, but she spat, "You sure seem pissed this morning. It must be because something did not go your way."

She was right. It was. Now we were in a familiar fight again. I knew not to say anything else, so I remained silent as she waited for my reply. After a few seconds, she went back into the bathroom. I managed to drift off to sleep for a few minutes until she woke me up by getting dressed. From the look on her face, I could tell she was ready for a fight, so I kept quiet.

She asked me what I wanted for breakfast, and I said, "Bacon and eggs."

She left for the kitchen, and I got up to shave and face another day in my own private hell. We spoke little during breakfast. Most of the attention was on getting the kids ready for school. I told her to be careful driving as I left for the office.

Work was my refuge from my personal problems. I enjoyed the friendly atmosphere of the office. I had the company of individuals who respected me and appreciated my contribution to our mission. I had the beautiful clerk to look at and think about. I had safety inspections to conduct and reports to prepare. All of this was an escape from the reality of my family life. It was, in retrospect, a mistake to find an escape to avoid dealing with my personal life, but at the time, it was convenient.

The colonel called me in after he came back from staff call to discuss a potential problem. He told me the army had directed combat support company to take an army training test (ATT). The company provided combined arms orientation training for the officers attending the basic and advanced courses. The company had a 105-millimeter towed artillery platoon with four howitzers assigned. The platoon was a reduced version of a 105 battery.

The problem lay with the artillery personnel assigned to the company. They had not had MOS training in more than a year. That meant the army didn't consider them combat ready. Even though they only displayed the use of artillery units in a school environment in the army, they had to be combat ready. The only way they could gain that status was to take and pass an ATT. The USIACS commander directed range control personnel to open the east range so the artillery platoon could start live fire training in preparation for the ATT.

The east range was a large, sprawling area separated from the main post. Located east of State Route 90 and Huachuca City and bordering Sierra Vista on the north and State Route 81 on the south, it extended east to the San Pedro River. Fenced and posted as federal land with no trespassing, the army had not used it for live firing since World War II. The relative isolation and size of the area made it a prize camping and hunting area. The range control office granted access to all who applied for a pass to keep some control. However, over the years, civilians unaware of the use policy merely opened the gate and entered to camp and hunt. The range control office also became lax in enforcing the no-trespassing policy. Therefore, no one had any idea how many people were camping on the range.

The colonel realized that we faced a safety problem in opening the range to live firing. He called me in to ask my advice. I laid out the safety precautions I saw as a safety officer and an artillery officer. First, I told him we needed to close the range and secure all gates with locks. Next, we needed to sweep the range and clear all personnel from the range. We needed to post in the local papers and Tucson papers that the range was closed and that live firing would begin soon. Then we needed to develop range fans to define the safe firing area. These firing fans would ensure that no rounds fell anywhere near Sierra Vista or Huachuca City. Next, I would ensure that the platoon commander was current on procedures for live firing and that the commander appointed a qualified range safety officer for each firing exercise. The range safety officer had to understand how to prepare maximum and minimum ranges, left and right deflection limits, and site to mass for each firing site.

After listening to my advice, he asked me to write up the requirements in a memo for the commander's signature. I did that, and he took it to the commander for his signature. The commander was hesitant to sign it, because he thought these were routine procedures that the support company commander would handle without a memo from him. The colonel returned and told me of the commander's decision. It disappointed me, and I told the colonel that I would not trust the support company to handle the procedures without outside checks. He told me to watch their effort and let him know what I thought.

Oh well, I thought. I had done my job as safety officer. The commander had taken my counsel and decided, so I put it out of my mind until later, when the unit announced it was ready to start live firing exercises. It was Friday afternoon, and people were leaving early. The clerk and I were flirting with each other. I wondered if she was sincere or just flirting for the fun of it. She always had an invitation in her smile and look. She left at 1615. She had to pick her daughter up at the nursery.

After she left, I thought about going home. This was the first time in my army career that I'd had a job with no pressure or stress. There were no tough inspections to prepare for or ATTs to prepare for and take. It was a good job. I worked eight hours a day unless I was flying, which I did not consider work. It was a dream job until I had to go home. I never knew what I would have to contend with at home, but it did not involve the happiness I found at work.

When I got home, Claudia was still gone. Mom had fixed dinner. Michele wanted me to take her to the corral so she could get Blue ready for the gymkhana. After we ate, I took Michele to the corral. Ron came with us, and we helped Michele wash and groom Blue. I did some work on the rails. Blue was trying to break them in two so she could get out. This was a constant battle with her.

It was dark when we got back to the house. Claudia was still not home. I began to worry a little about her. When I put the kids to bed at 2100, Mom went to bed too. As she did, she said something in German about Claudia being gone so long. I did not fully understand what she said. I went to bed at 2200, and Claudia still was not home.

I could not go to sleep while worrying about her, so I was awake to hear the car pull into the carport at 0100. When she got to the door, I heard Mom say something to her. Mom sounded angry. Claudia opened our bedroom door and quietly entered. I pretended I was asleep as she undressed and brushed her teeth. There was nothing I could say, since she would turn whatever I said into an argument. I fought the urge to speak and finally went to sleep.

I woke lying against her. Her body aroused me. I got up, went to the bathroom, and got back into bed. She did the same. I put my arms around her, and she responded. We had wonderful sex. That was my fix. The passion of our sex held me as a slave to her treatment of me. Our relations were wonderful for the next few days. She would say in the next argument that I was only nice when I got what I wanted. I could see how she would say that. There was always peace after sex. However, it was only because I was more tolerant of her abusive treatment. I could not understand why the beauty of our sex did not make her want to improve our relations, as it did for me.

The weekend turned out pleasant. I took Michele and Ron to the gymkhana while Claudia and her mom got ready for her coffee. When we returned, there were several German wives at the house. The coffee and the cake that Claudia had baked served as lunch. After that, she asked me to open some wine. I opened some wine, put out some snacks, and joined the party. Michele and Ron watched TV. It was a pleasant afternoon. The only problem was the cigarette smoke that filled the dining room. Claudia and the other women smoked. I did not, but at the time, I could not get Claudia to quit.

By 1800, everyone was feeling the wine, and the coffee ended. I was glad. It was time to fix food for the kids. By then, Claudia was tipsy, so Mom and I did most of the cleanup and cooking. By 1930, Claudia was asleep on the couch. If Claudia did not host a coffee, one of the other women would. Then Claudia would come in tipsy. Mom and I would have dinner waiting. Sometimes we would eat by ourselves because Claudia stayed out so late. That slowly became a Saturday routine.

The routine differed when we were fighting, which was most of the time. I would take my reel and rod and go fishing in one of the ponds on post, which the game management folks stocked with trout. I would find a spot in the sun and sit against the bank. The limit was five trout, and it was usually easy to catch them. Sometimes it was so peaceful sitting in the sun out of the wind that after I caught my limit, I would not bait my hook. I would just sit there and let my mind wander. Several times, I drifted off to sleep. When it neared dinnertime, I would go home and clean the trout. Even if we were fighting, Claudia enjoyed the fried trout I fixed.

One morning the second week in February, the colonel called me on the intercom. He told me he was sending me on another SAR mission. Yesterday afternoon, a Beech Baron had taken off from Eagle County Regional Airport in Colorado, and two minutes later, it had lost communication with the tower. The pilot's destination was Denver. A husband, wife, and two kids were aboard. Major Bing had talked by telephone with the sheriff heading the SAR and explained what our sensors could do in support of the SAR. They were waiting for me at the Eagle County airport. The MAD was getting a Mohawk ready, and the training department would provide a TO. I said, "Okay, sir," and stood up. The intercom was loud, and the clerk had heard what the colonel told me. She looked at me with a frown that said, "I do not want you to be gone." I smiled and shrugged as if I had no choice. She smiled, and with her lips, she made a kissing sign as if she were kissing me good-bye. She looked away quickly as if surprised by what she had done.

That surprised me, as did the reaction I felt. The impulse to hold her in my arms and kiss her was overpowering. I put my hat on, and as I walked out the door, she looked at me. I smiled and lifted my hand in a small wave. I wanted to simulate kissing her, but everybody was wishing me good luck, so I just said thanks and left. I thought about her gesture all the way home to pick up my shaving kit. I was feeling an urge that I did not know what to do about. I did not want to be unfaithful to Claudia again, but our constant fighting was driving me toward not caring anymore.

I told Claudia about my mission as I picked up my shaving kit. She was angry with me about something, so she just looked at me. Then she asked when I would be back. I said the mission should not take longer than a couple of days. She said okay and turned back to what she was doing. I told myself to put our problems out of my mind. I had to concentrate on the mission. Too many aviation accidents happen because of mentally engrossed aviators with personal problems. That was not going to happen to me.

I got to the airfield as quickly as I could. SSG Mabry was my TO again. He was good, and I trusted his counsel. While he checked the sensors, I filed a VFR flight plan direct to Eagle County. My time en route was about two hours and forty minutes. Eagle County is located in a narrow valley surrounded by eight- to eleven-thousand-foot mountains. That meant we would be working at some high altitudes. The weather forecast was for a layer of clouds at twelve thousand feet and ten- to twenty-knot wind, which meant turbulence over the mountains.

During preflight, I checked our oxygen system. We would need it when we got there, since we would be operating at altitudes above ten thousand feet. Before I left, I checked with Major Bing to see if he had any more information about the mission. He did not but said his description of the IR capability had impressed the sheriff and his team. It had given them hope of quickly finding the downed aircraft.

The colonel had given me the mission at 0900, and I took off, headed for Eagle County Regional Airport, at 1030. The airport was located about 150 miles west of Denver and about five miles east of the little town of Eagle. It was in a valley formed by the Eagle River along US 6, between Grand Junction and Vail. An hour and a half after takeoff, I could see the mountains of Colorado. I was at ten thousand feet, and the mountains appeared higher than I was. A thick blanket of snow covered them. As the weather forecast had said, there was a layer of clouds hanging over the tops of the mountains.

Thirty minutes from my destination, I was over high mountains. To clear the tops, I climbed to eleven thousand feet, and we put on our oxygen masks. The Mohawk was bouncing around in the turbulence, and I could see why. The wind was blowing so hard that I could see the snow blowing off the peaks. Fortunately, on my flight path, I did not see any mountains that appeared higher than me, but to my left and right, I could see plenty of mountains that were higher. Visibility was good, only limited by the terrain.

We were both looking ahead for the airport now. According to my time, I should have been over it. I was starting to get a little nervous, when we saw the valley and the river. The terrain dropped off sharply on either side of the valley. Based on the winds, I figured I was east of the airport. I looked to the west and saw it about six miles west of my position.

I started a turn toward the airfield and called the tower. "Eagle tower, this is Army 743, six miles east of runway for landing."

"Army 743, this is Eagle tower. Cleared for a straight-in approach to runway twenty-five. Altimeter 31.07. Winds from two hundred forty at ten knots. Report set up on final."

"Eagle tower, this is Army 743. Roger."

I rolled out of my turn on the runway heading and pulled off power to and extended my speed boards to lose altitude. Runway elevation was 6,500 feet, and I needed to lose 3,300 feet pretty fast. At 7,700 feet, I retracted my speed boards and added power. I was about two miles from the runway, so I reported on final.

The tower cleared me to land and told me to contact ground control after touchdown. As I neared the end of the runway, I could see a group of airplanes parked off to the side of the main apron. I suspected that was where they parked the CAP aircraft. I saw a group of people walk out of a tent near the aircraft. They were watching me land. SSG Mabry commented that they had probably never seen a Mohawk before. Then he added jokingly, "You'd better make a good landing, not your usual crash." He did not have to tell me that, because I was concentrating on making a perfect landing.

The ten-knot wind was almost down the runway, so it caused no problems. I put in a little aileron and rudder to impress my viewers. The Mohawk settled softly onto the runway, and I reversed the engines to slow down. SSG Mabry had entered the ground control frequency, and I called ground control for taxi instructions. They directed me to the apron where the civilian aircraft were parked. A ground maintenance individual guided me into a parking spot.

I shut the engines down, and we climbed out of the Mohawk. An individual left the group of civilians who were watching us and approached the aircraft. He introduced himself as a deputy sheriff in charge of the SAR effort. He said to follow him, and he would brief us on the situation. SSG Mabry said he would take care of refueling and told the ground maintenance guy we needed JP-4.

I followed the deputy sheriff to the tent that served as the operations center for the SAR. The people watching me land had gone back inside and were waiting for us. Inside, the sheriff introduced me to the people assembled there. There were several CAP pilots, but most of the people were family members, including the brother and father of the downed pilot and the mother and father of the wife, and several friends. I could see the concern on their faces. They were wealthy people. The brother of the pilot of the missing aircraft was a lawyer involved in government.

He was the one who spoke to me. "Captain Griffin, I spoke on the telephone with Major Bing, and he assured us the IR sensor could find my brother's aircraft. The CAP searches have not found anything. There was snow yesterday, and it may have covered the aircraft. Tell me how the IR sensor can find the aircraft."

I felt a little uneasy now. The attitude of the brother and others suggested they believed I would find the aircraft without any problem. I directed my comments to the group. "First, let me explain how the infrared sensor works. As the sensor scans the area below the aircraft, it detects and measures the temperature of objects in the area. It develops an IR negative based on deviations of half a degree in temperature. As an example, if I fly over a car sitting in the snow, the car will be warmer or colder than the snow. Because everything around it is snow and is the same temperature, the car appears as a car on the negative because of the different temperatures. That's true of everything. The sensor captures plant life, rocks, roads, houses, and people because of the temperature differences. If any part of the downed aircraft is sticking out of the snow, the IR sensor will detect it. That's because the part sticking out of the snow will have a different temperature than the snow or anything around it. But if snow covers the aircraft completely, the IR sensor will not detect it, because there is no temperature difference."

That brought an instant angry reaction from the brother. "But, Captain, the major assured me the IR sensor would find it even if snow covered it. Now you say you cannot find it if it's buried in snow. Are you saying your major was misleading me?"

I could hear the other family members muttering in anger and disappointment. The anger the brother was directing at me caught me off guard. "Sir, I'm sure Major Bing did not tell you the IR sensor would find the aircraft even if snow covered it. There must have been a misunderstanding."

The brother cut me off, cussing. "You damn people cannot get your act together. I'm going to call some experts who know how IR works. I want whoever is lying reprimanded." With that, he stormed out of the tent, followed by the rest of the family members.

I looked at SSG Mabry, and he looked pissed as hell. I was about to tell him, "Let's go back to Fort Huachuca," when the sheriff spoke. "Captain Griffin, I can't excuse his actions, but please understand that they have gone without sleep since the aircraft went missing. Whatever Major Bing told him got their hopes up. I understand IR and know what you said is the truth. I will keep them away from the area while you and SSG Mabry are present. I still need you to look for the aircraft. You provide the only real chance of finding it in these conditions. This afternoon, the temperature has been a couple of degrees above freezing. There might be a chance that melting snow revealed some part of the aircraft and that the IR will detect it. I personally believe it went down in one of the gullies or crevices. There's twenty- to thirty-foot snow in those places."

I said, "Okay, that's what I came to do. Brief me on the circumstances of the aircraft's disappearance."

The deputy moved over to the map tacked to a board sitting on an easel. As SSG Mabry and I gathered around the map, the CAP pilots moved in with us. The deputy began by identifying the pilot and his passengers. H said, "Yesterday they filed a flight plan for a 0900 departure to Denver. The ground crew servicing the Beechcraft watched the pilot load several large bags into the rear of the aircraft. Based on their knowledge of the Beechcraft, they felt he exceeded gross weight limits with the number of bags and the four people aboard. The active runway was runway twenty-five, which meant the pilot had to do a climbing right turn to intercept the airway to Denver. The tower cleared the aircraft for takeoff, watched the pilot climb out for a minute or two, and then watched him start a right turn. They turned their attention to another aircraft for a minute and lost sight of the Beechcraft. They tried to call the pilot but got no answer. They contacted Denver control to see if the pilot had contacted them. Denver had no contract with the aircraft. Denver tried for several minutes to reach the aircraft by radio without success.

"The pilot's ETA to Denver was an hour and forty-five minutes. They kept trying to make radio contact, as did Denver control. After the ETA passed with no aircraft, the tower declared an emergency and reported the aircraft missing. That's about the extent of what's known about the flight.

"When the tower told the sheriff's office, he launched an SAR. CAP pilots flew five SAR missions that afternoon, searching for the aircraft. He notified the family of the downed pilot, and they arrived late evening. By then, ground crews on skimobiles were out searching for any sign of wreckage. They searched most of the night while the family waited in the tent for any news. CAP pilots flew more missions as soon as it got light enough to fly. Meantime, the sheriff's department called Fort Huachuca, seeking SAR support. The brother wanted a number to contact somebody at Fort Huachuca to discuss what they could do in support of the SAR. That's when he got Major Bing's number. He called Major Bing and got the information about using IR to find the aircraft. I'm not sure what Major Bing told him, but after the call, he was enthusiastic about your arrival and help. Of course, you know what happened when you talked to him."

I asked the deputy if he knew how much flying time the pilot had in the Beechcraft. He told me the brother had told him that his brother had about two hundred hours. He'd said his brother was a good pilot, and he was confident in his flying skills. I asked if the pilot had been eager to get to Denver. The deputy said he thought so. They were going there to a family get-together.

Based on what the sheriff told me, I began to form a picture of the pilot. The safety officer course at USC was paying off now. I could see the profile of a pilot overconfident in his skills and determined to get to Denver. He was flying an aircraft that was possibly over its maximum operating weight. At these altitudes, the aircraft would be almost at its maximum performance capability. I remembered many similar case studies from the safety officer course with pilots who had similar profiles. The outcome had always been catastrophic.

I asked the CAP pilots if any were familiar with the Beechcraft's takeoff speed and rate of climb. Two said yes; they had several hundred hours in the Beechcraft. The climb-out speed was 110 knots, and the rate of climb at that speed was about four hundred to five hundred feet per minute. I asked them what being overweight at these altitudes would do to the performance. They replied that the pilot would have to reduce the rate of climb in order to maintain a safe climbing airspeed. They all agreed that the pilot would have been in trouble by taking off overweight at these altitudes. His best bet would have been to fly the valley west until he reached a safe altitude and then turn east to intercept the airway to Denver.

Based on the information the sheriff and the CAP pilots gave, I decided I would fly an IR search and, after that, a camera search. The air force imagery interpretation school at Lowry AFB in Denver was providing analyst support. After I completed my missions, I would fly to Denver to drop the film off for analysis. I would spend the night at Lowry AFB and return to Eagle in the morning.

The search area was small because of the mountains. The CAP pilots had thoroughly searched the valley. Since the pilot of the missing aircraft had planned to intercept the airway to Denver, that narrowed the area in which we should find him. If he'd followed his planned route, he would have taken off and climbed to an altitude at which he thought it was safe to turn toward Denver. That was easy to plot because the tower had had him in sight for a couple of minutes. SSG Mabry and I drew a line at a right angle to the flight path at what we figured was the estimated distance he would have traveled before starting his 180-degree turn. That represented our western boundary. We extended that line five miles past the airway, heading to Denver. At the five-mile point, we drew a line east parallel to the airway heading. That line formed our northern boundary. We did the same for our southern boundary. A line running north and south at Vail formed our box.

That box was our search area. It was ten miles wide and ten miles long and consisted mostly of mountainous terrain. Some of the mountains on the north side were more than ten thousand feet tall. The ones on the south ranged from seven thousand to nine thousand feet.

While we were planning our mission, the brother and family returned to the tent. The brother apologized for his earlier anger. He had checked with other IR experts and found that what I had told him was true. As we left the tent, he asked us to please do everything we could to find the aircraft. I assured him that we would.

I took off and climbed to eleven thousand feet. I turned to our northern leg, and we began the IR search. At some points along the leg, I was only five hundred feet above the mountaintops. The wind was blowing plumes of snow off the mountaintops and creating a turbulence that buffeted the Mohawk. I told myself, *The pilot never made it this far north. He could not have climbed high enough to clear these mountains.* I descended five hundred feet for each of the succeeding legs as the mountaintops got lower and lower.

On the last leg, we reversed our flight path and turned on the camera. By reversing our flight path, I felt we would get a different image of the mountains we were flying over. At each end of the camera run, I would bank south and climb to the next altitude. No matter how powerful the Mohawk engines were, I knew never to try to outclimb the terrain.

Flying over this area for the second time convinced me the pilot had done just that. He had taken off overloaded and started a climbing right turn to intercept the Denver airway. He'd quickly seen that the terrain was rising faster than he was climbing. He'd applied full power and kept pulling the nose up until he stalled and went straight into one of the gullies. He'd probably augured straight in, and that was why we could not see any broken trees or terrain scars to point to a crash site. That was my opinion of what had happened. Of course, I could not tell anybody, because there was no proof that had happened. It was a gut feeling based on the little experience I had.

When I finished the camera search, I called SAR operations and told them I was going to Lowry AFB to drop off the imagery. I would return in the morning. I climbed to the base of the clouds at twelve thousand feet and called Denver approach for a vector to Lowry AFB. They gave me a heading and cleared me to fourteen thousand feet. I reported at fourteen thousand feet and turned on the autopilot. I was doing an IFR approach, so I got out my approach plates for Lowry AFB. After about forty-five minutes, Denver approach handed me off to Lowry approach. They cleared me for a GCA into Lowry, and twenty minutes later, I was parking the Mohawk.

The sheriff had arranged for Lowry imagery intelligence instructors to pick up the IR and camera imagery. They arrived while we were refueling the Mohawk. SSG Mabry removed the film from the instrument bay and gave it to the instructors. They dropped us off at base ops, and I closed my flight plan. We got a ride from base ops to the officer and NCO billets.

After checking in, we met in the mess hall annex to eat. As we ate, I asked SSG Mabry what he thought about the search. He was blunt: "We are wasting our time, sir. I believe he stalled the aircraft and crashed shortly after takeoff. The aircraft is in one of those gullies buried under ten feet of snow."

I told him I agreed.

I was back at Eagle by 1015 the following morning. The weather was the clearest it had been since we'd arrived. The sheriff's deputy told us the imagery instructors had looked at the imagery overnight. They'd found nothing. That explained the disappointed looks on the faces of the family members. The brother approached me and asked if there was anything else I could do.

I said, "Yes, I want to try something. Based on what I've seen while flying over the area and the estimated weight of the aircraft when it took off, I have a theory about what might have happened. Let me try to copy the flight path of your brother when he took off. I will try to do it under his conditions if I can. It might provide a better idea of where to concentrate the ground search."

I started the Mohawk and taxied to runway twenty-five. I had identified on the map where the tower had last seen the aircraft before turning their attention to another aircraft. At that point, or shortly after, the Beechcraft had disappeared, and the tower had lost radio contact with it. I was going to take off and maintain slow flight at the Beechcraft's projected speed on the climb out. When I reached that point, I would start a 180-degree climbing turn to intersect the Denver airway.

By copying those parameters, I would get a feel for what had occurred. After I took off, I kept fifteen degrees of flaps down and my gear down to stay at 110 knots, which mirrored the Beechcraft's speed and shape. I tried to climb at four hundred feet for a minute. It took almost full power for me to do that. When I reached two minutes, I looked down and saw that I was just about at the spot on the ground where the tower had last seen the aircraft. I started a 180-degree climbing turn. I had to lower the nose to maintain my airspeed. It took me about thirty seconds to realize that in this configuration, I was not going to clear the mountains in my path. I immediately raised my gear and applied full power, and the airspeed quickly jumped to 140 knots. I pulled back on the nose and climbed at six hundred feet per minute to clear the rising mountains. For a moment, the position in which I'd almost found myself shocked me.

After I had safe airspeed and altitude, I raised my flaps and circled back over the path I had flown. I searched the terrain below as I descended toward the airfield. It consisted of an array of snow-covered trees and gullies. There were no roads in the two-square-mile area, and the land didn't look level enough for snowcats to search the area. Reports from the area said the snow was between twelve and twenty feet deep. I saw no scar or sign that an aircraft had crashed in the area. However, the moment of panic I'd felt when I realized I could not outclimb the rising terrain using the Beechcraft power settings convinced me that this was the area in which the aircraft had gone down.

I returned to Eagle and landed. The sheriff's deputy, family members, and CP pilots were waiting for me in the operations tent. I looked at them and felt their pain. "Okay," I said, "based on what I just did, I believe the most probable location of the aircraft is in an area about two miles off the west end of the runway. I would focus the search from that point on a line no more than five miles to the north. Because I could not safely fly the Beechcraft's configuration, I believe the pilot found himself in a climbing turn, trying to outclimb the rising terrain, and stalled. He must have gone straight in not to leave any sign of impact."

I pointed to the location on the map that I was referring to. The sheriff's deputy slowly shook his head and said, "If he went down in there, we are not going to find them until spring, when the snow melts. That area is impossible to search except from the air. We have flown it a dozen times, looking for some sign of the aircraft, and you have run IR and camera with no success."

He looked at the family members and said, "We will search another day. After that, we will change our status to recovery. We will have to wait until the snow is clear before we continue our search."

The family members nodded in agreement and disappointment. The sheriff's deputy thanked me for my help and released me. I gave him my phone number and asked him to call me when they found the aircraft. I said that knowing its location would help us in future support to SAR missions. He promised he would, and we said good-bye to the group.

I filed a VFR flight plan for Fort Huachuca, and fifteen minutes later, SSG Mabry and I were on our way home. The wind was still whipping the snow off the mountaintops in plumes. I had the Mohawk on autopilot, and as it rolled and bounced in the turbulence, I looked out at the mirror on the fuselage. I could see my reflection in it. My sunscreen visor was down, and with my oxygen mask on, I looked like an astronaut. I studied the reflection and thought, *Is that you, Neal Griffin? Is that the shy boy who was always chosen next to last in sandlot football?* It had been a long journey for Neal Griffin to see his reflection in his Mohawk side mirrors at eleven thousand feet over the snow-covered mountains of Colorado.

It had been a long journey in miles and in life. I could see myself in high school and recalled the day I'd boarded the train for basic training. *What a rookie.* I'd had no idea what lay ahead. I'd had no idea that I would be going to jump school, Special Forces, OCS, and flight school. I'd had no idea of the joy and disappointment I would suffer or the sweat and tears I would shed along the way. Now I had every reason to be proud of my accomplishments, and I was. But I knew that my accomplishments had not come from my talent and education. My accomplishments were God's gift to me. My failures belonged to me. Sadly, at that point, the failures tormented my life and overshadowed the gifts God had given me. The reflection was that of another man. It couldn't be me.

SSG Mabry interrupted my traveling mind. "Sir, let's descend so we can get rid of these oxygen masks."

I looked down and saw that we were out of the mountains. I turned the autopilot off, reduced power, and lowered the nose. I leveled off at eight thousand feet, and we took the masks off. I looked back at my side mirror and said good-bye to the image of someone who could not be me. I checked some ground reference points and corrected my heading. I knew we should be landing in about an hour. I thought about what I was going home to. Who was I most excited about seeing?

I parked the Mohawk on the apron in front of our hangar at 1515. After I completed entries in the logbook, I walked upstairs to the operations room. I put my equipment down and walked to Major Bing's office. His secretary told me he was not in. He was clearing, and she did not expect him back. I asked her what had happened, and she said all she knew was that the army had transferred him, and he was leaving immediately. Nobody knew what was going on.

I returned to operations and spoke to the operations sergeant. He did not know why Major Bing had departed so quickly. Major Marshall, the operations officer, had left for the day, and the rest of the pilots were flying students. I decided I would ask the deputy director when I got back to the office. I did not want to bring a problem to the attention of the command without first talking to Major Bing, but I wanted to clear up the misinformation the brother of the missing pilot said he had gotten from Major Bing. It was Friday afternoon, and when I got to the office, everybody had left except the deputy director.

I knocked on his door and walked into his office. I debriefed him on the mission and expressed my concern about the brother's misunderstanding of the IR sensor's ability. He told me in confidence that the commander had relieved Major Bing and reassigned him because of several similar incidents. My incident was not the first time he had misled someone about the sensors on the Mohawk. Either he was ignorant of the capabilities, or he was deliberately misleading people. He said not to worry about it. The brother had called the director and complained about Major Bing. He had also complimented me on my effort to find his brother's aircraft.

I left the office feeling better about the SAR mission. As it turned out, that was the last time I flew an SAR mission in the Mohawk. When I got home, Mom and the kids were eating dinner. Claudia was in Tucson, as usual. I ate dinner with the kids and Mom. Michele told me the corral needed fixing again. Blue had kicked a rail and broken it. Michele had tied a rope as a temporary fix. I complimented her on her initiative and told her I would fix it in the morning.

After dinner, I took a shower. I helped the kids with their homework, and we played a game until they went to bed. Mom drank a rum and Coke and watched TV until the kids went to bed. She followed them to bed, leaving me sitting in front of the TV and wondering what the hell Claudia was doing. It would have been wonderful if she had been home so I could talk about the mission with her. It was hard to believe she could spend all day and half the night walking through the malls, shopping. I was asleep when she came in. I woke up momentarily, but exhausted, I went right back to sleep.

When I woke up the next morning and went to the bathroom, my movement woke her up. I climbed back in bed as she went to the bathroom. She got back in bed, and we made love. Her orgasm was strong and wild with mine. Lying there in the afterglow, I again struggled to understand how our sex could be so good and our marriage so difficult. I hoped the closeness of our morning union would carry us through the day and weekend. It did, and we had a great weekend together. I wanted to ask why she was getting home so late from Tucson, but I avoided the subject. I'm sure it would have spoiled the mood for the weekend.

She started her period Monday, precipitated by her PMS. The fighting and anger began again. There was nothing I could do that would please her, so I resolved myself to another period of anger and fights. Talk about life on a roller coaster.

I was glad to leave for work and escape the madness at home. The budget clerk beamed when I walked into the office and smiled at her. She was genuinely happy to see me. I had a bunch of actions waiting for my attention. The director came in from the Monday morning staff call and told me to come into his office. *Oh shit,* I thought. *What have I done now?*

He looked at me and smiled. He motioned to a chair and said, "Sit down, Neal. Just like you warned the commander, it happened. The combat support company posted warning signs last week on all the gates to the east range, announcing live artillery firing would start this morning. The company commander considered that satisfactory to clear people off the range. Well, they fired the first two rounds this morning at daylight, and to their surprise, eight trucks with campers came streaming out of the impact area. They were damn lucky they didn't kill anyone. Now the USAICS commander has ordered a ceasefire until we assure him the range is clear. When he announced that at the staff call, he nodded at me as if to say, 'We told him so.' Now I want you to set up a procedure to ensure the range is clear each time the battery schedules live firing."

I smiled as I replied, "Sir, I think the solution is easy. First, send out some trucks to scour the range from the ground. At the same time, I will fly a Huey and search it from the air. That should fine anyone left on the range who didn't notice the firing this morning. To ensure the range is clear each time the battery plans on firing, we'll schedule an overflight of the range to ensure it's still clear. While that's taking place, we'll have the engineers repair and beef up the gates so no one can get past them."

"That's what I had in mind," he said. "You schedule a flight now, and I'll tell the school S3 to get some vehicles out to search for any remaining campers. Let me know after you have overflown the range and it looks clear."

I went to my desk and looked at the clerk. She had an "Is everything okay?" look on her face. I winked at her and picked up my phone. I dialed the flight operations office and scheduled a Huey for a range reconnaissance flight. I explained to the operations officer what had happened and told him that this would become a standard mission before each live firing exercise. He said he would have a Huey waiting when I got to the airfield.

The clerk brought a memo to my desk for me to check. She asked what had happened, and I explained. As I checked her memo, she stood beside me and leaned over to read with me. I could smell her perfume and feel the heat from her body. I fought the urge to put my arm around her and pull her close. Her memo was perfect and didn't need my scrutiny. I knew she was having me check it just to get near me, because as I read the memo, I could see in my peripheral vision that see was looking at my face. I finished reading the memo and looked up at her. Had we been alone, the attraction was so strong that I would have kissed her. I knew she would have kissed me back.

I had to break this off because it was obvious to anyone watching us what was happening. "The memo looks good," I said as I handed it to her and broke the spell. She said thanks and walked back to her desk. I got my flight helmet and left for the airfield.

That exchange of raw emotions was a relief from the fighting with Claudia. It also gave me courage to think that maybe I could live without Claudia. I could find love again. For some reason, the affair in Korea had not given me the confidence that I was getting with the budget clerk. The problem was that I didn't want to replace love with an affair. My exchange with the clerk convinced me that I didn't have to fight with Claudia for the rest of my life. I could leave if I wanted to. After all, Claudia had wanted to stay in Germany after I returned from Korea. She'd had a guy she was shacking up with and known she could go on without me. Maybe the clerk was providing me the strength to end what had become an unhappy marriage.

CW-2 Carson and I flew the range recon mission. We found two more campers on the far east side of the range. We circled over their location while the ground vehicles moved slowly to our position. There were several people in the group below. They watched us, wondering what we were doing. We watched the ground team reach their location, and we turned to finish our recon. After we finished the recon and returned to the airfield, I called the director and told him the range was clear as soon as the two campers cleared the gates. The good part about the incident was that it raised the respect for me as a safety officer. It also gave the director something of substance to put on my OER.

I went home for lunch before returning to the office. Claudia was sullen and indifferent as I explained what I had done. I knew PMS was likely to blame, but it still angered me. I went back to the office, tired of the anger between us. I was mad at myself for taking the abuse from Claudia and accepting it. I knew I was slowly giving in to my infatuation with the budget clerk.

One day the clerk came in visibly upset. After a while, she came over to my desk and sat down. I could see she had been crying, so I asked what was wrong. She softly told me she was having a problem with her husband. She was sure he was having an affair with a friend of hers. They all hung around in the same group, and he'd even kissed the other woman in front of her and the woman's husband. They'd said they were just kidding around, but she believed it was more than that. She said it had been going on since she'd started working eight months ago. Her husband had not wanted her to work to begin with and had been upset when she'd taken the civil service job.

She'd finally confronted him about his carrying on with their friend. That had led to an argument, and she'd told him to go on and have sex with her. He'd replied that he would if she felt that way. Angry, she'd said, "I will make it easy for you. I will invite her over, and when she gets here, I will leave for two hours." He had not believed her, so she'd called her friend over, and when the friend had arrived, she'd told them to do whatever they wanted to, because she was leaving. She had not thought her friend would stay, but she had, and as far as she knew, they'd had sex. Her friend had been gone when she got back. Angrily, she'd asked her husband, "How was it?"

He'd replied, "Great. Thanks for setting it up."

She had said, "I don't care anymore." She had cared and had believed he would not do it.

Her words floored me as they flowed from her mouth. It was as if a dam had broken, and she was letting all her pent-up feelings pour out. I now had a better understanding of why she was coming on to me. She was either getting even or leaning on me for the help she needed in getting through these troubles, but I think she let her emotions go too far, because I could see desire in her eyes when she looked at me sometimes. I knew it was there, because I had it in my eyes when I looked at her.

I took a consoling position during her meltdown to me. She was sincerely hurting about her marriage breaking up. I was not able to do much consoling, because her boss called her in for a meeting. She left, and they were in a meeting for two hours. Meanwhile, I had some safety inspections to conduct, so I left also.

I thought about what she had told me. It surprised me that other couples might be having marital problems. For so long, I had believed I was the only with problems.

It was 1630 when I returned to the office. The clerk was ready to leave. I saw her husband pull into the parking lot as I walked into the office. He was tall and handsome and the commander of one of the signal companies in the signal battalion. He was better looking than I was. On her way out, she stopped by my desk and whispered, "Can you meet tonight? I need to talk to you."

I said, "Sure, how about on Tank Hill at 1900?"

She replied, "I will be there," and she left.

Tank Hill was at the base of the Huachuca Mountains and overlooked the fort. Its name came from the fact that the fort's water tank was located there. Because it provided such a scenic view of the fort and the San Pedro Valley, the engineers had built a large parking area with picnic tables around the edges. It was a popular spot for having picnics and just viewing the area. We could meet there, and no one would question our parked cars.

I got home and told Claudia that I had to go back to work after dinner. I felt strange lying to her. I did not like the idea of lying and slipping around. I left the house at 1830 and took the street that I took to work. I circled and drove to Tank Hill and parked. It was dark, and the lights across the fort and valley were beautiful. There was one other car parked at the far end of the parking area.

About five minutes till seven, I could see the lights of a car coming up the hill. I had a little knot in my stomach. I had no idea what was going to take place when she got there. The car pulled in beside mine, and she motioned for me to get into her car. I got out, walked around to the passenger side, and got in.

She looked at me and said, "Thanks for meeting me. I can't stay long. I just wanted to finish our conversation from this afternoon. I don't know what to do about my husband. He accuses me of being cold and unloving. I have never refused him sex until lately. Were you faithful to your wife while you were in Vietnam?"

I said yes, and she continued. "He told me that he used to get hand jobs from the women. He didn't consider that being unfaithful to me. Why would he tell me something like that? Other wives might consider that grounds for divorce. I was angry, but I got over it. I'd hate to divorce him and hurt our daughter. But then I think I could do that. I can work and support myself. I can make it on my own. What do you think I should do?"

I looked at her and said, "You are asking the wrong person. I can't advise you. When I look at you, I get an overwhelming desire to hold you and make love to you. I see the longing in your eyes when you look at me. It would be a mistake to give in to that want in these circumstances. If we did, we would only hurt our spouses and, in the end, hurt ourselves. I'm trembling right now with desire for you. I can't advise you other than to say maybe you and your husband can go to marriage counseling together. Make sure what you end up doing is really, truly what you want to do and what you would do whether I was in the picture or not."

She looked at me for a minute or two. She was beautiful in the dim light of the stars. Then she softly spoke. "I've got to go. Thanks for talking with me. Do one favor for me. Kiss me."

I slowly leaned across the seat and kissed her. Her lips parted, and the kiss became passionate and tender. We slowly moved away from each other. She nodded as if she were affirming some question she had and said, "I've got to go now."

I got out of her car and watched her back out. She looked at me, smiled, and drove off. I stood there watching her lights go down the hill as my passion passed. I had opened Pandora's box. It would be hard to shut it now.

I was not ready to go home, so I dropped by the officers' club and drank a beer. CW-2 Carson came in and joined me. We moved to a table and ordered a pitcher of beer. A couple more aviators joined us, and we had a party. I was drunk when I got home at 2300. Claudia was waiting for me. She wanted to know what I'd been doing. I told her, "After I finished working, I went to the club to have a beer. I met Matt and a couple other aviators there, and we partied." That did not suit her, and an argument resulted. She accused me of everything under the sun. She was still angry about events that had happened years ago, and she brought them up. Finally, Mom came out of her room and scolded us. She said she'd had enough of our fighting and was going back to Germany. That ended the fight, and I slept on the couch.

I woke up with a hangover. I shaved and fixed myself some cereal. When I got to the office, I had two messages on my desk. I looked at the budget clerk. She was on the phone but smiled at me. I stared at her for a couple of seconds, remembering the thrill of the kiss. She turned back to her conservation, and I looked at my messages.

The first one was to call Jake. I dialed his number, and he answered. I said, "Hi, Jake. This is Neal. I got a message to call you."

He replied, "Yeah, you want to go fishing in Mexico this weekend?"

"I don't know," I answered. "Tell me about it."

He said, "There are three of us going so far. We fish for bass in Obregon. It's a containment lake about twenty kilometers from Guaymas. They rent cabins for twenty dollars a night. I pull my boat, and we troll the lake for bass. The fishing is out of this world. We are going to leave Thursday and come back Monday. All you have to do is take a three-day leave."

Jake's invitation was a godsend for me. I needed a break from the turmoil I was in. Besides, I had not been fishing in years other than sitting on the little ponds on post, fishing for trout. "Count me in," I told Jake. "What fishing gear do I need, and what do I need to bring?"

"You need a rod and reel, of course, and some deep-diving lures. You don't have to bring anything this time except your personal stuff. I'll get all the food we need. My boss is going, and he will bring cooking equipment. We'll divide the cost four ways. I'll pick you up at your house Thursday morning at 0600. You can use your military ID to cross the border and get a visa. Come by my office, and I will show you the best lure to buy."

I got up from my desk and went to the deputy's office. I told him I wanted a three-day leave. I was going to Mexico to go fishing. He said he would take care of it. I told him I was going to see Captain Benson and would be back in about thirty minutes.

Jake showed me several lures. He said the best ones were deep-diving Bombers. I had never heard of those lures. He also showed me some deep-diving Rapalas, and I knew what to buy then. We talked some more about the trip, and he showed me pictures from previous trips. He said they tried to go every two months. I left his office, excited about going fishing. I knew it would give me some time to think and take stock of my emotions and life. I knew I couldn't keep on going the way I was.

The director's secretary typed my leave. She and the budget clerk were friends, and she told the clerk that I was going to Mexico. When I got back to my desk, the clerk came over and said she wanted to go too. I said, "You don't how bad I want you to go."

She laughed and pouted, saying, "I will miss you. It's no fun here without you." Her expression became seductive, and she said softly as she left, "I knew you would be a good kisser."

Her comment made me feel like a teenager again. At the same time, I realized something. She was leading me on! I knew I would have never initiated an effort to seduce her. That was both a weakness and strength on my part. I was too shy and timid to ever take the first step. However, when I recognized that she was leading me, I had the confidence to follow.

Claudia was upset that I was going fishing and had not discussed it with her first. I pointed out that I'd told her as soon as I got home. Her counter was that I had already decided I was going. I could not understand why she would not want me to go. All we would do was fight if I were at home. I think her concern was about my spending money on fishing. However, she did pick out clothes for me to wear on the trip. She did not want me taking my best clothes fishing. Then, as some sign of amends, she got up early and fixed breakfast for me. We sat quietly while eating it. She was beautiful, and I knew the passion of which she was capable. I knew I loved her deeply, but the explosive anger she held in check just under her skin was dulling that love. I was tiring of my efforts to love her, endure her constant wrath, and still perform well at work. Maybe my going fishing would serve as some form of therapy for us. We needed therapy, especially me, before I went past a point of no return.

Jake blew his horn at 0600, and I grabbed my bag and fishing equipment. Claudia had looked out the window and opened the door for me. She was standing at the door, so I put my bag down and put my arm around her to kiss her good-bye. She kissed me with a frown on her face, but she kissed me nevertheless. I picked up my bag and piled into Jake's camper, and we were off.

It took a little more than eight hours to drive the 326 miles to Guaymas. Highway 15 was a one-lane major artery south from Nogales to Guaymas. It was in disrepair, and traffic was heavy. The terrain was high Sonoran Desert all the way. It was hot and dusty, with only one town, Hermosillo, which was halfway to Guaymas. This was my first trip through the area. Over the next thirty years, I would drive down Highway 15 many times to fish the inland lakes and the Sea of Cortez.

Finally, we reached Obregon. Obregon was the third and largest lake formed by dams across the Yaqui River. The Yaqui River flowed south from Aqua Pieta on the US border with Douglas, Arizona. The Germans had built the dams prior to World War II. There was a rumor that they'd planned on basing seaplanes on the lakes, possibly to attack the United States. The lakes provided water for irrigation but had become prime fishing destinations for largemouth bass.

Obregon was the only lake with cabins for rent. A Mexican American had recognized the potential and secured the rights to lake property. He'd built six cabins around the lake, and he rented them mostly to Americans who traveled there to fish. Many Americans fished there. Besides those occupying the cabins, there were always several fishing camps set up around the lake.

It was an exciting weekend for me. I had a break from the pressure and stress of fighting with Claudia. It also gave me time to think about the budget clerk and what was developing between us. Each day, we trolled the lake early in the morning and in the afternoons. We caught loads of big bass. It surprised me that we could catch largemouth bass by trolling. In Florida, I had always fished for them using live bait. Officers also are soldiers, and when soldiers get together, it's always fun. In the evenings, after fishing, we played poker, which I loved. I was doing all the things I enjoyed and had not done for years. It was fun to spend time with my old friend from Korea. I hated to see the trip end.

We hauled a cooler packed with fish back to Fort Huachuca. I took enough for one meal. I did not know how Claudia, her mom, and the kids would like fresh bass. I did not want to waste any if they did not care for it. Claudia somewhat welcomed me home when I walked into the house. She was pleasant and listened to my description of the trip. I fried the bass fillets that night, and Claudia fixed German potato salad, which is a good combination with fried fish. Everybody loved it, even the kids.

The next morning, Claudia came into my arms, and there was peace for several days. My constant hope that the peace would last affected my conduct at the office. I tried to avert flirting with the clerk. It was hard because she was seductive in her expressions to me. As always, the peace at home ended.

The argument that ended the peace was so fierce that Mom demanded we book her a flight back to Germany. That was another thing Claudia claimed she hated me for. We booked her a flight out of Phoenix, and that weekend, we drove her to the airport. The anger in Claudia did not subside after that. She told me she wished it was me leaving and not her mom. She said she hated me for bringing her to this horrible place instead of going back to Germany. She accused me of doing it on purpose to punish her. I heard about every perceived wrong I had done to her. As I listened to her ranting, the anger swelled in me until I thought I would explode.

I had done everything possible as a husband to meet her demands and make her life happy. If she did not see that now, she never would. My seeking the assignment there was for me. It was the first time in sixteen years of service that I had asked for an assignment to a place I wanted to go. In that moment, I decided I would move out and into a place in Sierra Vista. Maybe a separation would help us find a better way.

That night, I sat down and drafted a letter to the artillery branch, requesting a transfer to Vietnam. I left it on the table to think it over before completing it to mail. While I was at work, Claudia read it, put it in an envelope, and mailed it. When I found out she had done that, I was outraged. It was a sloppily written draft, and she had sent it to the office that managed my career. The embarrassment it would cause me when they read it didn't seem to bother her. I got home from work the second week of March with my mind made up. I told her I was through fighting. I was going to find a place downtown to live. I would move out as soon as I had a place. She looked at me as if she did not believe it. Then she said, "Well, maybe you should." The next day, I found a trailer for rent in one of the trailer parks on the outskirts of town. I told her I would move over the weekend.

Friday night, she said she wanted to take me to dinner so we could talk. She was a little shocked at what I had done. We went to a popular Mexican restaurant that we both liked. It was a nice dinner. She was pleasant and told me that she did not want me to move out. She did not want a divorce. She wanted to be part of my life forever. She felt we could work out our problems. She seemed honestly hurt and sincere about not wanting me to move. Her soft pleading almost changed my mind. She seemed genuinely repentant. However, all I could say was "I am sorry that it has come to this." I knew I had to carry through with my plans to move, even though I found it painful because of how it was hurting her. I loved Claudia beyond belief, but us staying together and fighting the way we did was not healthy. All I could say to console her was "I'm sorry."

She finally accepted that I was moving. Then we started talking about how we'd handle the money and the quarters. She wanted to know what we would tell the kids. I said we'd tell them we were going to separate for a while so we could learn to stop fighting. They would understand that because they were also tired of our fighting. She cried a little as we discussed what we would do. I told her we would keep the bank account. I would only take $500 a month for myself. The rest would be hers. I would give her my phone number at the trailer so she could reach me in case of an emergency. She could always reach me on my work phone. When we had answered all our questions, we slowly left and returned home.

When we got home, we told the kids what I was going to do. They were upset, but we convinced them that I would not be gone forever. Of course, we did not know that to be true. They were still upset about it and went to bed crying.

The next morning, I loaded my clothes and stereo into the Capri and told Claudia I would be back for the rest as soon as I unloaded those items. She was now angry that I was going to move out. I ignored her angry words and said I did not want to fight. It took two trips to get all the clothes and equipment I needed. I spent the rest of the day arranging the trailer.

The trailer was comfortable. It had two bedrooms. One was a large main bedroom, and I needed only sheets and towels before I was ready to live there. After I had all my stuff put away, I went to the store and bought some food and beer.

That night, I sat there watching TV and thinking, *What the hell have I done?* I would have to tell my boss on Monday. The army always had to have a reliable means of contacting personnel who lived off post, so I had to give them my new address and phone number. There was going to be some embarrassment in telling the people I worked for that my wife and I had separated.

It was a long weekend. There was little for me to do. Sunday night, I went to the club and met Matt at the bar. He was a bachelor and lived in the BOQ. I guess the bar was like his living room. We were on our second beer, when a crowd of people came in and took a table. The budget clerk and her husband were part of the group.

I watched her in the bar mirror as she talked. She had not noticed me when they'd entered the bar. After about fifteen minutes, she looked up, and our eyes met in the mirror. She half smiled as she recognized me. We held our gaze for a few seconds before she turned back to the conversation at the table. From then on, we exchanged glances.

By 2200, I had drunk all the beer I wanted. Matt was ready to go, so we stood up and paid our bill. I took one last look at her. She was watching me. I raised my hand and waved good-bye. I could feel her watching me as I followed Matt out of the bar. The beer helped me sleep that night.

I was up early the next morning. I had to fix my breakfast after I shaved. There was no one to do it for me. I was off to a good start.

I got to the office just as the staff major general was opening it. We talked for a few minutes, and I gave him my new address and phone number. I went to my desk and threw myself at the work waiting for me. I felt refreshed somehow. My mind seemed clearer, and I cleared up several old actions before everybody else arrived. I felt like a schoolboy seeing his girlfriend when the budget clerk arrived.

She walked in the door that took her by my desk to hers. She smiled at me all the way to her desk. She was radiant. Her blues eyes sparkled and appeared full of mystery as she told me hi. She left the slight scent of her perfume as she passed my desk. I had a quick fantasy of holding her in my arms. I presumed the kiss that night in the Tank Hill parking lot had been an invitation, but I was too shy or unsure how to answer her invitation. As soon as she got to her desk and took her coat off, her boss called her into his office. That interrupted the exchange of looks between us. I had an inspection to do, so I took that opportunity to leave.

I spent all morning inspecting all the training battalions' facilities for safety violations. It was a monthly requirement. I found several violations not yet corrected since the last inspection. The commanders needed engineer support to correct them, and despite their emergency requests, the engineers had not responded. I took a copy of the requests to the post safety officer to lay the responsibility on him. When we'd finished discussing the issues and corrective actions, it was lunchtime.

I grabbed a hamburger and took it with me back to the office. I hoped everyone but the budget clerk had left for lunch by then. The office was empty except for the clerk and the colonel's secretary. Both usually brought lunch and ate it in the office. The clerk had pulled her chair up to the secretary's desk, and they were talking as they ate lunch. They both looked at me and smiled when I walked in the door. I told them hi as I walked to my desk and sat down.

The clerk picked up her lunch, pulled her chair to my desk, and sat down. She knew about my moving into the trailer. She said she was sorry that my wife and I had separated. I tried to shake it off by being noncommittal about it. I said I was sorry too, but the conditions between us had become so hostile that I had no other choice. I changed the subject to her relationship with her husband by asking if things had improved with them.

She said no. They argued constantly. She was open in discussing her problem. She said, "He accuses me of being cold and indifferent in sex. I told him he was right. I said, 'I have sex with you so we do not fight and not because I want to or feel any desire for you.' Then he got up and slammed the door, leaving the house. Last night, when you saw us, that was the first time we had been out in two weeks. I only went because our friends were going. You surprised me by being there. I wanted so much to go over to talk to you, but that would have been awkward, and I did not want to cause any fights." Then she said, "I've got to go to Tucson Saturday. Do you want to go with me?"

I thought about it for a few seconds and said yes. She said, "Let's meet here at 1000, and you can drive my car. I have to buy some clothes, and after that, we can have lunch."

We had just settled our plans, when the director and deputy returned, followed by the rest of the staff. That ended our talk, and we went back to work. I finished several inspection reports and wrote the aviation safety meeting memo for the commander's signature. The budget clerk's boss took her with him to a budget meeting with the USAICS budget officer. Jake called and wanted to know if I wanted to go fishing at the end of the month. I said of course. We talked for a while, and I asked him to schedule me for some student flights. He said he would when the next class started.

Matt called at 1500 and asked me to fly an unattended ground surveillance sensor (UAGSS) mission with him. I quickly said yes and told the deputy where I was going. I got my helmet and headed for the airfield. Marines primarily used UAGSS in avenues of approach, on flanks, and in areas where friendly forces had limited visibility by dropping them from helicopters. The intelligence officer would choose an area where he wanted sensors emplaced. The UAGSS section would load a helicopter with sensors and drop them in a pattern in the earmarked area or areas. The weight of each sensor would bury it on impact, leaving only the small antenna visible. The sensors could detect foot or vehicular traffic and broadcast that data back to a recording station. The data gave units early warning of movement toward their position.

Matt was waiting for me when I got to the airfield. I climbed into the pilot's seat and started the Huey. We flew to the east range to a dirt airstrip. The instructors and students were waiting at the end of the runway. I brought the Huey to a hover and taxied over to their location. The two big marine sergeants loaded thirty sensors and three students aboard the Huey.

Once they were aboard and strapped in, I took off and climbed to five hundred feet. Each student would practice dropping ten sensors. The target area was along the dirt landing strip, which they were using to simulate a road. Ideally, a student drops the sensors so they form a line, with sensors about fifty feet apart. That spacing is hard to get right, especially with the Huey moving along at eighty knots. Each student, strapped in a harness, stands on the skids to drop the sensor. He has to work fast to achieve the fifty-foot spacing. A reluctance to stand on the skids while dropping the sensor deters some students.

Once each student had dropped his ten sensors, I would land the Huey at the dirt strip, and the students would recover their sensors. The instructors would measure the spacing and critique the students on their performance. The critiques were funny, especially when a student didn't get out on the skid far enough to drop the sensors correctly. The instructors threatened to throw the students out if they didn't do it properly.

Matt and I spent an hour flying students. It was fun for me because I was using a Huey to do a mission instead of a training flight. It was after 1630 when we landed the Huey at the airfield. When I got to the office, everybody was gone, and it was closed, so I headed to the club to get something to eat.

The days passed slowly. The idea of going to Tucson with the clerk intrigued me. It felt like a safe date. It was in the middle of the day, and she would have her daughter with her. On the other hand, each day, when I returned to the trailer, I waited for the phone to ring. Deep down, I hoped Claudia would call, if for nothing more than curiosity. There were no calls.

On Saturday, I met the clerk, as we had planned. We spent a pleasant afternoon in Tucson. Her daughter was a pleasure to be around. She had bright blue eyes and blonde hair. She was just as beautiful as her mother. During lunch, I learned about the clerk and her high school years. She hadn't gone to college. She'd met her husband in her senior year, and they'd married after she graduated. It occurred to me that her unhappiness was a result of marrying too young. I was positive that was the underlying cause of Claudia's unhappiness and anger. When we got back to Fort Huachuca and my car, I kissed her good-bye. She looked at me with what seemed like a promise in her eyes as she drove away.

I started flying students the following Monday, so I did not spend much time in the office. Taking a three-student class through the airborne portion of their training was a three-day project. I dropped by the office for a few minutes just to check my inbox and see the clerk. Wednesday night, I flew the final training flights and debriefed my students.

In an office environment, there is a continual flow of correspondence. At the directorate level, it's even heavier than in lower-echelon offices. Most of it has an action with a suspense date attached to it. In my three-day absence, my inbox had slowly filled with actions. As a result, on Thursday, I spent the day writing letters, memos, and fact sheets for various subjects. Not all of them were on safety. The director assigned suspenses to his officers for various actions. By afternoon, I had completed most of my suspenses and could spend some time talking with the clerk. To others, it appeared we were talking about the project she was working on. We were to a certain extent, but at the same time, we were talking between the lines. Our little huddle ended when the director called me into his office to discuss one of the letters I had prepared for him.

We finished long after the civilians had left for the day. I went home and opened a can of chili for dinner. I'd been eating plenty of chili lately and chasing it with beer. I finished eating and washed the dishes. There was nothing on TV, so I decided to take a shower and shave. By doing that, I could sleep late the next morning.

I finished all of that and was deciding what to do with the stack of framed awards lying on my coffee table, when someone knocked on the door. I wondered who it could be. I thought it was Matt, wanting me to go bar hopping with him. I opened the door, and my heart skipped a beat. The clerk stood there. She smiled and asked, "Can I come in?"

Nights like that only happen in fictional novels usually, but they also happen in real life sometimes. They create memories that no one forgets. Maybe they are not meant to be forgotten. Maybe they happen to help troubled people make it through the night.

The next morning in the office, I looked at the clerk differently. Maybe it was a look of love. I'm not sure. I am sure she looked at me in the same way. We were now in forbidden territory. I convinced myself that I did not care. I wanted to be free of Claudia and the disaster our marriage had become. I think the clerk felt the same way about her marriage.

By the middle of April, I was sure I was in love with the clerk. She told me the army was reassigning her husband to Fort Monroe in three months. She was moving into an apartment downtown in expectation of staying there. It had been a month since I had moved out, and still, I had heard nothing from Claudia. I had called the kids several times to talk with them. Whenever Michele had gymkhanas, I went to watch. Despite the relief I felt in my life now, I still had a deep, stabbing wish to see Claudia.

The Monday before my birthday, I received a letter from the deputy sheriff who'd coordinated the SAR at Eagle, Colorado. He had promised to let me know if and where they found the Beechcraft. He said I had been right in my prediction of where the crash had occurred. They'd found the aircraft in a gulley two miles off the end of the runway and a mile and three quarters north. It appeared the pilot had stalled the aircraft and crashed nose first into the gulley. At the time, the gulley had had at least twenty-five feet of snow in it. The aircraft had gone straight in through twenty-foot trees, burying itself in the snow. The straight-in angle hadn't downed any trees or created crash marks on the terrain. The snow on the trees must have fallen into the hole after the aircraft, covering all traces of the aircraft. He thanked me again for my help in searching for it.

In April, I got my annual flight physical. Aviators must get one each year in the month of their birthday. A flight physical is an extensive examination. Tests for depth perception, color blindness, peripheral vision, pressures, and sight are part of the vision exam. I passed it with flying colors. My vision was twenty-ten in my left eye and twenty-fifteen in my right eye. You couldn't ask for better vision than that.

However, something with my vision had been bothering me for several years. When I combed the hair on the left side of my head, I noticed that my left eye tracked downward toward my shoulder while my right focused on my comb. I never experienced any pain or headaches, and since I always passed my flight physical, I never gave it any thought. My reasoning was that if something was wrong, it would show up in my physical. Therefore, I continued to ignore it.

I had a habit of reading the paper each morning with breakfast. One of my first tasks after I moved into the trailer was to start delivery of the *Tucson Star*. On Wednesday morning, my thirty-sixth birthday, I read that enemy forces had ambushed an accident investigation team in Vietnam, killing all team members: seven American soldiers and four South Vietnamese soldiers. The article explained that the attack violated an agreement with North Vietnam. Under that agreement, accident investigation teams could conduct investigations unharmed as long as they were unarmed.

The team was unarmed and investigating an accident near the Laotian border. Negotiations were under way in Paris to end the war. One of the early agreements was to allow the United States to investigate the hundreds of missing aircraft that had crashed in remote areas. The teams would be unarmed and protected by ARVN soldiers. Obviously, that agreement had not worked in this case. On the other hand, teams had completed many investigations without incident. The United States would continue these investigations until the late nineties.

About two hours after I got to the office, the intercom on my phone rang. I answered it, and the deputy director said there was a major from the artillery officer branch on line one.

I picked it up and answered, "Captain Griffin speaking, sir."

A major who identified himself as an artillery assignment officer at the Pentagon in DC said, "Captain Griffin, I see you have asked for an overseas assignment. I have one, but because you have so much overseas duty already, you have to volunteer for it. There are only thirty qualified artillery captains in the army, and you are the most qualified for the mission. It's a team leader position for an accident investigation team in Vietnam. If you accept the assignment, you will have to leave within a week for some training at Fort Lewis. What say you?"

My first thought was that they had the draft letter Claudia had mailed. The article in the paper that I'd read that morning explained the need for a new team and leader. Had this offer arrived six weeks ago, I would have jumped at it. Even now, the hair on the nape of my neck stood up when I thought about it. My new relations stymied my decision. If I accepted, it would no doubt be the end of Claudia and me. I did not know how it would affect my relations with the clerk. I had to give this mission some careful thought before I decided. I replied, "Sir, this is not a decision you make on a moment's notice. How much time do I have to decide?"

He said, "I understand. I need your answer by Friday. That's as long as I can wait before assigning another officer to the position."

I said, "Thanks, sir. You'll have my answer by Friday."

I hung the phone up and looked at the clerk. She was looking at me with a "What's up?" expression. The deputy director walked over and asked, "What was that about?"

I explained it to him loudly enough that the whole office could hear. As I finished speaking, I looked at the clerk. She was pouting. The deputy director turned to return to his office and said, "Think about it, Neal. That's a dangerous place, and your ass is exposed while examining accidents without the means to defend yourself."

I told him I was going to give the decision some hard thought. I looked at the clerk and smiled. Her smile said, "I can make you turn the offer down."

Before she left for the day, she told me she was taking tomorrow off. She was moving into her new apartment. I asked if I could help, and she said no. Her husband was helping her move. He was not happy about her moving and was trying to convince her not to. Before she left, she gave me a birthday card. I opened the card and read, "A big tiger will eat you, but a little pussy will never harm you." A picture of a tiger was on the top of the card, and a picture of a cat was on the bottom.

That evening, I considered the pros and cons of accepting the team leader assignment. It was an opportunity to apply my safety office training and leadership skills in a combat setting. There was no question that the job would be challenging and dangerous. A successful performance would be a plus for my career, especially since I was coming up for promotion to major in October. It might compensate for my lack of a college degree.

On the other hand, I thought going into isolated sites without weapons for team defense was reckless.

Then there were the personal costs associated with taking the assignment. Accepting the job would without a doubt be the end of Claudia and me. I might have already ended our marriage by moving out. That left the future I might have with the clerk. Leaving now without solidifying our relationship would end it. I would be thirty-six years old and alone. The idea of that had a sobering effect on me. The one sure fact I knew about myself was that I could not live alone. Knowing my shyness and social skills, I had little confidence that I would forge new relationships this late in my life. The fact that the clerk had made the advances that had led me into an affair with her proved to me that I lacked the confidence needed to do it on my own. My fear of rejection and embarrassment would hold me back unless someone aggressively led me. I was afraid of starting over at my age. What I had was not perfect, but it was better than nothing.

In the end, the fear of losing what I had left of my personal life made me decide to turn down the assignment. My involvement with the clerk influenced my decision. It also, in the end, saved my marriage. Without that involvement, I would have accepted the assignment. I called the major the next morning and told him thanks but said I would have to decline the offer.

That weekend, I went fishing with Jake again. It was the end of April, and the weather was beautiful, with temperatures in the high eighties. In Obregon, it was downright hot. The cabins did not have air-conditioning, so there was no way to escape the heat until late at night. Nevertheless, we caught bass and had fun.

However, something was happening to me. I was thinking more about Claudia and less about the clerk. I had not filed for a divorce. I guess that in my mind, she and I were just separated for a while until Claudia came to her senses. I had no idea if she had become involved with another man. She was beautiful and could have any man she wanted. I felt a little jealously, and I did not want to.

Back in the office, my routine continued. The clerk was glad to see me. She invited me to come to her apartment that night. It seemed as if I were in limbo. I was waiting for something to happen instead of making something happen.

I parked in her apartment complex's parking lot at 1900. It was dusk, but there was still enough visibility left to see. As I parked and got out of my car, I saw another car pull into the parking lot. As I walked toward the stairs to the clerk's apartment, I heard the car's engine rev, and wheels squealed as the car pulled out of the parking lot. I caught a glimpse of the driver, and he looked a lot like the clerk's husband. When the clerk let me in, I told her what I'd seen and asked her if her husband knew about me. She said he did. "But don't worry. He has nothing to say about who I see."

Ten minutes after my arrival, the phone rang. I looked at her and said, "That's your husband." She talked to him, and in a few minutes, she was crying. I don't know what he was telling her, but it upset her. Finally, she hung up and composed herself, but the incident hung over us and cooled the passion between us.

Jake had scheduled me to fly a new class of TOs the next day. That tied me up for three days, and I saw little of the clerk during that time. When I was back in the office, she said, "I need to talk to you when possible." After everybody left for lunch, I asked her what was going on. She said that her husband had cleared quarters and needed a place to stay. She had agreed to let him stay at the apartment. She insisted that did not change things with us. She said, "Let's go to your trailer, and I will show you that nothing has changed."

She followed me to my trailer and did her best to convince me that she still wanted me. Despite that, I felt that somehow, we had lost something. It was if we were actors who had lost interest in their roles and whose performance had become unbelievable. It was hard for me to accept her husband living with her and nothing happening between them.

Back at the office, no one could tell that our relations had chilled. We still smiled and talked. However, I started finding tasks that would keep me out of the office. I did inspections and then did them again. I flew every mission I could. I started going out with Matt every night. I tried to party away the sense that I had lost everything. I started to regret turning down the team leader assignment.

May came, and the mesquite trees started sprouting. That was a sure sign that winter was over. The warm weather brought back memories of better times. The results of the major's promotion board held in March were out. I could not find my name on the promotion list, which meant they had passed me over. A week later, I received a letter from the Department of the Army, confirming my nonelection to major. The letter also explained that if the next promotion board in February of 1975 didn't promote me, I would have to leave the army. While I was optimistic that they would promote me, I did not worry about having to leave the army. I would have more than eighteen years of service. That gave me a lock in, and I could continue to serve and retire as a captain.

The army did not promote Jake either. Not getting promoted was a bigger concern to him than to me. He only had fifteen years of service. If the army failed to promote him, he had to leave the army. His main problem was his branch. He was an infantry officer and never had served in an infantry company or had command of a company. The infantry did not think much of aviators who did not have branch experience as a commander. I had talked to him about that in Korea and recommended he apply for ground duty to get some infantry command time. However, he did not think it was necessary because of his time as commander of the Sixth Aviation Platoon. Another big factor affecting promotions was the downsizing of the army after Vietnam. There were fewer majors needed as the army shrank. All we could do now was wait for the results of the next promotion board.

I had not spent any time with the clerk since the day she'd come to the trailer to convince me that nothing had changed by her husband staying with her at her apartment. We had tried to find some time, but something always popped up. Besides, I had a feeling the infatuation we felt had dampened. On a Tuesday morning in the second week of May, my phone rang.

I answered it, and Claudia said, "Hi. It's me. How are you?"

"I'm fine," I answered. "How are you?"

"I'm okay," she said. "I've been meaning to call you to wish you a happy birthday. I just decided today I would do it, even though it's three weeks late."

I felt a sudden rush of desire and longing. "Well, thank you. That was sweet of you to remember my birthday." Then I heard myself saying, "Listen, if you are not busy tonight, let's go to dinner."

There was a moment of silence, and then she said, "I'm not busy, and I would love to go to dinner."

I said, "Okay, I will pick you up at 1800. Is that okay?"

She replied, "Yes, I'll be ready."

I felt like a teenager going on his first date on Tuesday evening. I parked in front of our quarters and rang the doorbell. Claudia answered the door. She was beautiful. She smiled at me and said, "Come on in. I need to put on some lipstick, and you can say hello to the kids."

I walked into the living room, where Michele and Ron were watching TV. I smiled at them and said, "Hey, guys, how are you?"

They looked at me, and Ron came over and hugged me. Michele just said, "Hi."

I told them how good it was to see them again, but I could tell that what I had done had hurt them. I felt terrible. I remembered my childhood and how my father had hurt me with his alcoholism. I had hurt my kids for a different reason. That did not matter. Hurt is hurt, whatever the reason. I was trying to engage them in a conversation, when Claudia said, "I'm ready."

The kids both looked at me as if to ask, "Are you coming back?"

Claudia gave Michele instructions about going to bed. She was babysitting Ron. She babysat for other couples and was dependable. I walked over and kissed her. Then I hugged Ron and said, "Good night."

We went to the Mexican restaurant where we had eaten before I moved out. We ordered, and when our drinks arrived, we started a small-talk conversation. As we waited for our meal, Claudia asked me what I planned to do. I had been gone for two months, and I had not filed for divorce. She told me she had hired a lawyer and was waiting for me to do something.

I told her I did not know what I wanted to do. It was true. I had avoided taking any action other than moving out. I had left everything in limbo. Now, sitting across the table from her, I questioned why I had moved out. I could feel the love and want for her that I had suppressed to a point. It would not go away. I think it had robbed me of the ability to take any step beyond moving out. Again, I had waited for her to proceed. Just as I needed the clerk to lead me on, I needed Claudia to end our marriage.

She asked me in a serious tone, "Are you seeing someone? My lawyer tells me that based on his experience, you would not have moved out unless there was someone else."

I delayed my answer by asking her if she was seeing someone. She shook her head as if that were a stupid question and said, "Of course not."

I knew then that I had to lie. My brain told me that I could save our marriage if wanted to. If I told her the truth, that would end it. Even though she believed I was seeing someone, unless I confirmed it, she could give me the benefit of the doubt. She would be able to swallow her pride and take me back. So I told her no.

She responded with a sad smile and said, "It does not matter, does it?"

I was working on a reply, when our food came. By then, I had drunk two beers, and she was on her third glass of wine. Our conversation became friendlier as we ate. We talked about music and the kids. After dinner, we moved to the bar area and had another round of drinks. I asked her to dance. We moved together on the small dance floor.

It was a thrill to hold her again. I could not believe the desire that raged through me. I think I felt it in her too. After several dances, she said it was time to go.

Like a teenager on a first date, I walked her to the door. She opened the door, and I thanked her again for a wonderful evening. She looked at me and said, "Come on in for a while." I followed her in.

We made it as far as the kitchen table. She turned, and I was standing in front of her. I reached out to her, and she came forward into my arms. Our passion erupted, and the table was as far as we got. The sex was wild and urgent, just as scenes in a dozen movies have depicted it. When it was over, we stood there holding each other for a few minutes. Then she said, "I guess we should go to bed."

I kissed her softly and said, "I would love to, but I've got to go to work in the morning. I don't have anything here. I would have to go to my trailer to shave and dress. It would be better if I go now."

"You are right," she replied.

I kissed her again, and she let me out. I drove home feeling as if I were floating on air. What had just happened was worth every argument we'd ever had. I knew then that I was moving back into quarters. I had been foolish to think I could ever leave her. The one concession from her I wanted was for her to ask me to move back. I needed to believe that she wanted me back and that tonight was not just a response to her libido.

A week went by, and I did not hear from her. Then, on May 25, the director called me into his office. The deputy was standing there also. The director said, "Neal, you have done a great job as safety officer, but now I need you in another job. You are the ranking captain aviator in the school. Major Marshall has just put in his retirement papers and is going on a thirty-day leave. That leaves the aviation maintenance division without a chief. I'm putting you in the position, effective immediately. Pack your bags, and report to the airfield. I want you to keep the aviation safety officer duties. I will appoint another school safety officer to replace you. Do you have any questions?"

I stood there looking at him for a few seconds before saying, "No, sir, not now."

"All right," he said. "You'd best get to your new job."

I thanked him and returned to my desk. I took a deep breath. I'd just been put in a lieutenant colonel's position. I looked at the clerk, who was looking at me. She came over to my desk and asked what that was about. I told her the director had put me in charge of the maintenance aviation division. I was moving to the airfield. She congratulated me and told me to call her as soon as I got into my new office, so she would have a number to reach me.

I told her I would and sat down at my desk. I had two actions to take care of before I could go. It took me an hour to coordinate the actions and complete the memos. I gave the drafts to the secretary and told her to give them to the deputy when she finished typing them. I grabbed my flight equipment and aviation safety officer records and files.

I stopped at the door and looked across the office. I smiled and said, "It's been fun. I'll see you when I come for staff call." Everybody waved good-bye, and I walked out the door.

I was in a little bit of shock as I drove to the airfield. I was taking a lieutenant colonel job. I had butterflies in my stomach as I parked my car in the parking spot marked "Chief, MAD." Thank God I had just enough swagger to feel competent that I could do the job. I knew the mission, and my experience as XO of the Fifty-Fifth Aviation Company in Korea told me I could manage the personnel. This job was a hell of a lot better than safety officer.

I walked up the stairs to the MAD offices. The first office area was flight operations. The flight operations area consisted of a dispatch counter and two desks for the clerks. Behind the counter was a flight operations board with all the aircraft and their statuses listed on it. Across from the dispatch counter was a room with four desks. The instructor pilots and standardization instructor pilots occupied that room. In line with that office was the operations officer's office. A hallway ran between those offices and the dispatch to the rear entrance to the chief's office.

The MAD chief's office consisted of three smaller offices. The first office on entering the room was the secretary's office. Facing the secretary's room on the right was the staff major general's office. On the left was my new office. For someone used to doing all his own work, having a staff to aid me suggested I would be so busy that I needed a secretary to answer the phone for me, schedule my meetings, and prepare my correspondence. Plus, I had a staff major general to help me with personnel problems and general management of MAD operations.

It had been a week since I had been in operations, and when I walked in, the operations sergeant said, "Hey, Captain Griffin, good to have you aboard."

From his greeting, I knew that everybody knew I was taking charge. The civilian clerk was new and was on the phone, calling in a flight plan, so I stuck my head into the SIP and IP room to say hello. All three staff members were sitting there and greeted me with a "Welcome aboard." I continued down the hall to the MAD office.

I walked in, and my secretary stood up and introduced herself. The staff major general walked out of his office and greeted me. He opened the door to my office, and I walked in and put my flight equipment down. He sat down, and I asked him to give me a brief review of the operation and any hot issues.

It took him about twenty minutes to go over our maintenance and supply functions. He said there were no hot issues at the moment. The constant problem was keeping the Mohawks flying. Personnel-wise, we were short on officers. We had the three WOs in the standardization section, one captain, and a maintenance WO. The Tables of Distrubution and Allowance (TDA) assigned all the aviators to the Department of Training and Doctrine. We were short a major for the operations officer position and a captain for the assistant operations officer position. On the enlisted side, we were short three crew chiefs and four mechanics.

After he finished, I told him I wanted to go downstairs to meet the supply and maintenance people. I already knew the operations personnel, except for the new clerk. We walked downstairs and across the hangar to the supply and maintenance offices. He introduced me to the five supply civilian clerks. I made the mistake of asking them if they had any problems I should know about. They gave me an earful. I finally stopped them by saying, "I'm too new right now to understand your problems. Let me have a few days to orient myself, and then we will address the issues you have surfaced."

Next, I met the maintenance people. The maintenance officer was a young captain who was full of initiative. The WO was a W-4 with years of experience. I left with the impression my maintenance section was in good hands. Before I left, I told them I would start an equipment inventory tomorrow so I could sign for all the equipment. The maintenance section had the most equipment and would be a challenge to inventory.

After that, I walked around the hangar and watched the work on two Mohawks and one Huey. I had done this before during safety inspections. The men working on the aircraft were a good group of mechanics. It was obvious they were following all the prescribed procedures. After I walked around the hangar, checking its condition, I returned to my office.

As I passed by the standardization section room, I stuck my head in the door. I looked at my Mohawk SIP, Larry, and said, "You're the acting operations officer until I can get one assigned."

He looked up and replied, "Sir, I don't want to be operations officer."

I smiled at him and said, "Yeah, I know. But you are going to have to do something to earn your W-3 pay."

He shook his head and mumbled, "Okay, sir, got it."

I spent the rest of the day reviewing the SOP and the files of past actions and problems. Around 1600, the budget clerk called. My secretary buzzed me on the intercom and said, "Sir, you have a call from a woman on line one."

I picked up my phone, wondering who it was. When I said, "Captain Griffin speaking," she said in a sexy voice, "Hello, Captain Griffin. I thought I would call you to see how you were doing. I miss not seeing or talking to you."

It was pleasant to hear her voice. I was several hours into a new job that had put me out of my comfort zone. It was soothing to hear a voice from that comfort zone. I hoped she would tell me that she would come see me that night, but she did not. We talked for about twenty minutes until she said her husband was there to pick her up. I hung up feeling a little let down. I needed someone—not to share my pending problems with but to let me relax in a place where problems did not exist.

When I hung up the phone, my secretary stuck her head in the door and said if I did not need her any longer, she was leaving. After almost a year and a half, I hadn't gotten used to the civilian workforce leaving at 1615. I told her to go. I didn't need her. The military worked till 1700 unless some project or action required working past 1700. There were no fixed hours for the military. I could work all day and fly students for four hours at night. However, civilians reported for work at 0730 and left at 1615.

I continued studying the list of responsibilities I had as MAD chief. At 1710, the staff major general stuck his head in the door and said he was leaving. Then I was alone in a big office. I didn't hear any sounds coming from the operations area, so I assumed they were all gone too. There were no flights scheduled for that night, so there was no reason for anyone to be there.

I leaned back in my chair and looked around my office. Charts on the wall were reminders of problems with aircraft maintenance, supply issues, and budgeting shortfalls. These were offset by the projected student load and flying-hour demands. In a nutshell, my job was to make the budget, aircraft availability, and supplies meet the projected flying-hour program. It seemed simple enough. I had experience in each area. It didn't appear that it took a lieutenant colonel to handle the job. I was sure I could.

The only problem I faced was being a captain and dealing with the lieutenant colonels and higher-ranking officers. They were in charge of agencies that I would go to in order to receive budgetary support, get maintenance and supply priorities resolved, and balance post support needs. My ace in the hole was the Director of Logistics (DLOG). I worked for him, and since I had proven my ability to him as a safety officer, he would support me when I needed it. He was a crusty colonel and enjoyed a good confrontation. Feeling the weight of the responsibility I was taking on, I turned the light off in my office and headed for my trailer.

When I got to the trailer, I did not feel like preparing something to eat. I decided to chance calling Claudia. She might go out to dinner with me. She answered the phone, and after we greeted each other, I asked her if she wanted to go to dinner. She said she had just fixed dinner but would feed the kids and meet me for dinner. I felt a surge of excitement when she said yes. I told her where to meet me at 1830. After I hung up, I took a shower and shaved. I again had the emotions of a teenager going on his first date as I dressed.

We met at the old steakhouse where we'd eaten New Year's Eve dinner when we'd first arrived there. I don't know why I picked that restaurant. I think the memory of our first meal there on the eve of a new year was symbolic of what could be a new start for us. I got there ahead of her and watched as she parked and got out of her car. I had watched her do that many times and in many places in the world. Most of those times had been joyous occasions for me. That night was equally joyous, but I felt a poignant regret for where I had let our relations go.

She walked up to me, and I took her hand and looked at her. "Wow," I said in greeting her. "You look fabulous."

She smiled and said, "Thank you," as we entered the restaurant.

I was eager to tell her about my new assignment. I waited until we had ordered and then asked her how she was doing. She told me about the kids and some minor problems she had in the house. It was small talk, but there was little more she would say under the conditions. Then she told me she had tried to call me at the office, but they'd told her I had moved to another office. That was something I wanted to hear. She had made an effort to contact me.

"Didn't they give you my new number?" I asked.

She said, "Yes, but when I called it, a woman answered and said you were out of the office. So I said I would call back later. But then I got busy, and it was after 1700, and I figured you wouldn't be there. Then you called me. Why did they move you?"

I told her about my new job. As I told her, I was looking for some sign of her pride in me for taking a lieutenant colonel's job. I desperately wanted her approval. There we were, separated and in limbo over divorce, and I was still looking for her approval. After I finished explaining my responsibilities, she said congratulations. She went on to say, "You have always done a good job. I think you will do well there, and they should promote you."

I told her I agreed with her and thanked her for noticing. Our drinks arrived, and we shifted subjects to the kids. Talking about them intensified my longing for a normal life again. I was reluctant to swallow my pride and ask her if I could move back in, but that was what I wanted to do. I wanted her to swallow her pride and ask me to move back.

After we finished eating, she said she wanted to see my trailer. I said, "Okay, but it's not much." She followed me to the trailer park and parked beside me. We went in, and I took her on a tour. When we got to the bedroom, she stopped and looked at me. We came together in passion.

Later, while lying in bed and talking, we heard someone banging on a door. Claudia thought it was my door, but I said, "No one knows where I live, so it must be another trailer."

After a couple more bangs, she said, "Get up, and see who it is." I got up and went to the door, but before I opened it, I heard a car start and drive away. I opened the door, and there was no one there. I went back to bed and told her it was nobody. She replied in a noncommittal way, "You sure it wasn't your girlfriend?"

I looked at her and regretted my involvement with the clerk. It had happened because I needed a crutch to help me leave Claudia. All I wanted now was to get back with Claudia and forget everything else. "I don't have a girlfriend," I told her. "Look, I want to move back in with you and the kids. Do you want me to?"

She lay there in silence for several minutes. My heart was about to burst. Suppose she said no.

Then she said, "Neal, you moved out. I didn't want you to. If you move back in, are you going to move out every time we have an argument? If that's the case, then no, I don't want you to move in."

"I'm sorry for doing that," I replied. "No, I will never move out again."

"Then move back in if you want to," she said. "Don't you think it's embarrassing the way we are acting?"

I said, "Yes, but I don't care. We will get over it."

I moved back into my quarters the following Saturday. It had been three months, and a lot had happened. When I moved back in, I expected a great improvement in our relations. Sadly, it did not happen. Claudia did not change the way she treated me. The difference was that I held my anger much better and avoided arguments with her. In a way, that made our relations seem better. However, I still felt rejected most of the time. I sucked it up because I knew I would never leave her again. I was living out one of those old country songs in which the woman runs over the man, but his love for her makes him endure the hurt she causes him.

A week after I moved back in, I had to fly students on their night flights. However, after I flew one student, the weather turned bad, and we postponed the remaining flights. When I got home, Claudia was gone. I asked the kids where she was, and they said she'd gone to the officers' club.

She had said nothing about going to the club. It appeared she had expected me to be gone until 2400 while flying students and had decided to go to the club. I wondered, *Why did she not mention it to me, and why did she go?* I had no problem with her going to the club to see friends. However, her going the way she had gave the appearance of slipping out, and that angered me. I dressed and went to the club to check on her.

When I got to the club, I went into the bar. I saw a large group of people sitting around two tables. I recognized several of her friends and several of the officers they were sitting with. The women were sitting between the males as if they had split up into couples. The group did not notice me as I stood in the entrance to the bar. They were laughing and having a good time.

I stood there for a minute or two, debating how I should handle the situation. My anger and disbelief that she would do something like this so soon after I moved back in overcome me. I walked up to the table, and she looked up at me in surprise. The conversation at the table went silent when the group recognized me. I looked at Claudia and said harshly, "I think it's time you come home now."

After I said that, I gave the group a hard look and walked out. I was raging inside and fought to get myself under control before I got home. When I walked into the house, Michele asked me if I had found Mom. I said, "Yes, she was at the club with a bunch of people." The way I said it must have upset her. She and Ron were happy that I had moved back in.

They did not want anything to cause me to move out again. They did not understand that I had vowed never to do that again.

I walked back to the bedroom and undressed to take a shower. I'd just gotten out of the shower, when Claudia came in. She was pissed. She tore into me for embarrassing her in front of her friends. I let her rage for a few minutes until she quieted. I looked at her and said, "How do you think I feel going to the club and finding my wife sitting with another man?"

She said, "I wasn't sitting with another man! That's just the way we sat down so we could talk."

I was calm now; the damage was done. The belief that life would be better between us evaporated into reality. I asked, "Why didn't you tell me you were going to the club tonight?"

She looked at me with clenched teeth and said, "Because I knew how you would have reacted. If you had been here, I would've gone with you."

"Just think about how it looks, Claudia," I replied. "You slip out to go to the club. Those guys you were sitting with are single. They know you are married. You show up alone, and they see you as someone running around on her husband. I know most of those guys, and I have to work with them. How do you think I will feel now each time I meet one of them? How do you think I will feel when he looks at me and thinks you are screwing around on me? If you did that while I was gone, I'd have no complaint. But I'm not gone now. I think you should at least try to help me get our marriage on the right track again. I am doing the best I can. But I won't let you screw over me and not say something about it."

She walked out of the bedroom while I dressed. She came back and asked, "Where is Michele?"

I answered, "I don't know. She was here when I came back here to take a shower."

Claudia asked Ron where Michele was.

He said, "She was crying and left."

I asked him if he knew where she was going. He said, "No, she just got up and left."

Claudia got mad again and blamed me for Michele being gone. She claimed I must have done something to cause Michele to leave. I told her, "When I got back, Michele asked me if I'd found you. I told her you were with a bunch of people at the club."

Worry tempered her anger now. "You need to go find her."

I was a little worried too. "The most probable place she went is the stables," I said. "I'll drive down to the stables and see if she's there."

I drove halfway and saw her walking along the road. I stopped the car and told her to get in. She was mad and hurt and wouldn't answer me or get in the car. She just kept walking. I told her to get in and said I would take her to the stables. She stopped and looked at me. Then she slowly got in the car. I asked her if she knew the stables were closed now. She said yes, of course, but she wanted to see Blue.

I drove her to the stables as she softly sobbed. The gate to the road was locked, so we had to stop there. I looked at her and said, "Honey, I'm sorry that your mother and I fight and, in doing so, hurt you. But you don't have to worry about us parting. I moved out once, but I give you my promise now that I will never do that again. I love you and Ron too much to ever do that again. I love your mother too. It doesn't seem like it to you based on the way we fight all the time, but it's true. I will do my best never to fight with her again and hurt you and Ron."

I knew the pain she was feeling. I had felt it too many times for too many years as a kid when my father came home drunk. Now I was doing it to my kids. That sobered me and put a powerful incentive behind my promise not to argue with Claudia. I could accept her anger and accusations for the sake of my kids. We sat there for a few more minutes. Then Michele said she was ready to go home.

After that night, relations improved between Claudia and me. They were mainly superficial improvements. She was still quick to anger over nothing, but I restrained my responses, and no major fights occurred. I kept telling myself that the days when she was pleasant and loving outweighed the angry days. We went to many parties at her German friends' homes. Something that helped us get closer was playing tennis.

As I've said, she loved to play tennis. I bought myself a racket and started playing with her. We played on the weekends and in the evenings after dinner. She was good and relished beating me each time we played. Of course, when I won, she didn't handle it well. However, I didn't win often, which preserved the good time we had. I was proud of how well she could play and told her often. She reminded me of how skeptical I'd been when she'd first started.

Even though life appeared normal between us, I still had a nagging feeling that she wasn't that faithful to me. Her actions, innocently or intentionally, gave me the impression that she was trying to make up for what she'd missed by getting married so young. Her infidelity in Germany had proven she was capable of cheating. She still went out with her friends and took a weekly trip to Tucson. It was hard to believe she shopped all day and into the night. She still flirted with other men in my presence. Other than that, she never did anything overtly to leave me with my negative feelings. I often thought it was my infidelity that tortured me. It probably was, and I deserved it. Much of the way I felt had to do with my poor self-esteem too. Still, I wanted more than anything in the world to feel as if I could trust her. I loved her and wanted to spend the rest of my life with her. I probably could have benefited from some sessions with a therapist, but I could live with what we had, so I accepted it.

The first two days as MAD chief, I focused on inventorying equipment. It took two full days to account for the $400 million worth of aircraft, vehicles, tools, and buildings I signed for. There was some minor equipment missing, but that was not my responsibility. Major Bing would have to account for it.

After I completed the inventory, I began to enjoy my new position. The work was not that hard at all. I had to ensure our maintenance scheduled provided aircraft to support training. For that, I had a maintenance officer. I had to ensure all aviators keep current. For that, I had the operations officer. He made sure all aviators took their flight physicals, met instrument flying and night flying requirements, and passed their standardization checks. The most difficult task was coordinating our budgetary needs.

There were two budgetary programs I had input to. One was the school budget, which provided my operational funds. The other was the post budgetary process. Since we were a tenant under the post command, I had to defend my post support requirements. The largest budget expense came from the fire and rescue personnel and equipment stationed at the airfield. Their sole responsibility was to the airfield. I was the largest aviation unit on the airfield and flew more hours than the other two units combined, so a larger portion of the fire and rescue budget was to support my mission.

A week after I took over as chief of MAD, the post budget office had its meeting to resolve the budget for the following fiscal year. The army was facing budget cuts because of the war in Vietnam winding down. Two areas the post was looking at to make cuts at the airfield were fire and rescue and air traffic controllers. The airfield commander left it up to me to defend the fire and rescue requirements.

The deputy post commander, a lieutenant colonel, recommended cutting the fire and rescue at the airfield by half. By his calculations, that would save the post $300,000. The post fire department would provide support as needed to make up the difference. His reason was that there had been no emergencies needing fire and rescue support over the last eighteen months. Therefore, we could move that support to the post fire department. They could respond within fifteen minutes to any emergency at the airfield.

When he recommended that, he looked at me. It got quiet at the meeting. My first thought was *This guy is either kidding, or he's a complete idiot.* Everyone was looking at me, waiting for my response. I composed myself and worked out a response that would be respectful of his rank yet let him know how stupid his recommendation was.

I said, "Sir, on the surface, that sounds like a valid recommendation. But if we examine it, we can see that it's based on the wrong assumption. First, the fire and rescue unit base their staffing and equipment needs on army calculations for an airfield our size, the complexity of the aircraft based at the airfield, and the number of flights in and out of the airfield. This staffing is not based on the number of emergencies but rather on what it takes to respond to a potentially catastrophic event. You see, no one plans an emergency involving an aircraft, just like no one plans a fire on post. But the resources must be available when one occurs.

"The fire and rescue unit at the airfield is specially trained and equipped to handle aviation accidents and, in our case, accidents involving aircraft with ejection seats. I assure you that a catastrophic accident would be well beyond the help of fire and rescue if it's not waiting on the ground for the aircraft declaring an emergency. How about a 'What if?' situation? Suppose post fire personnel are on a post fire. Will you pull them off that fire and send them to the airfield? The record of no emergencies that you use to support your rationale is due to a strong safety program.

"I have four aircraft flying tonight. They will fly student training missions until around 2400. Any one of them at any time could declare an emergency that would dispose of your statistic. If they did make an emergency landing and needed an immediate fire and rescue response and the fire and rescue personnel were on the way from main post, who would accept responsibility for loss of life or aircraft? I believe it would be ludicrous to cut the fire and rescue support at the airfield based on the reasons you propose. Aviation emergencies are unpredictable. Fire and rescue assets are there in the event of an emergency. The number of emergencies has nothing to do with allocation of fire and rescue assets. Therefore, I recommend we find some other way to make more-intelligent cuts."

I was trembling when I finished. The lieutenant colonel was a little red in the face. I don't know if it was from rage or embarrassment. After all, a captain had just implied that his recommendation was laughable. He mumbled something about moving on and revisiting the recommendation later. When I returned to my office, I called the Director of Logistics (DOL) deputy and briefed him on what had happened. I wanted my boss to hear about my confrontation from me and not from the deputy post commander. I was happy to see that post cut no airfield fire and rescue assets from the budget. Several of the fire and rescue personnel called me to say thanks after hearing about the budget meeting. Of course, I had a hard time with the lieutenant colonel during later meetings. However, I never backed away from my responsibility because of a difference in rank. I never heard another word about it.

Summer came in a blaze of heat. Claudia was planning on going to Germany for six weeks as soon as the kids got out of school. They flew out of Phoenix on June 22. Now, with everything else, I had a horse to take care of each day. Time passed slowly with Claudia gone, but something was different this time. She wrote me two letters. They were sweet and seemed to say she missed me. On the other hand, the clerk called me each afternoon just before she got off work. We would talk for ten or fifteen minutes. There was a longing in her conversation, but I never accepted the invitation.

In the middle of July, she called and told me her husband was leaving for his new assignment, and she was going with him. I had suspected she would, and in a way, I was glad. The fire that had raged between us had cooled, and I wanted everything to work out with Claudia. The Friday afternoon of that week, the DOL office had a farewell party for her. She wanted me to come, but when she said her husband was going to be there, I declined. The next Monday, she called and asked me to meet her in the parking lot at 1600. She said she had something to tell me. I met her, and she got out of her car and into mine. She said, "I want to tell you that I will always love you. I want to say good-bye because we are leaving in the morning." With that, she leaned over and kissed me. It was a long kiss, and when it ended, she said, "Good-bye. I hope I see you again someday." She got out of my car and into hers, waved, and drove away. I never saw her again.

I volunteered for as many flights as possible while Claudia and the kids were gone. Work helped the time pass and, in a way, kept me out of trouble. In July, we had some maintenance problems with our Mohawks. There were two classes in session, and one of our good birds developed an oil leak. Usually, an oil leak would ground an aircraft until maintenance corrected the problem. I had the SIP fly the aircraft for an hour, and we measured the amount oil of lost during the hour. It turned out the engine lost about half a quart of oil. It was safe to fly the Mohawk with two quarts low. The problem with this particular aircraft was the leak, and we had no way to tell if it would suddenly get worse.

While we were wrestling with the oil-leak problem, the logistics deputy called me. Obviously, the director of training had called the logistics deputy and expressed concern that we were not going to have enough aircraft to support student training. The deputy wanted to know what the story was. I explained that we had two planes down for hundred-hour PMs. Two were down for engine replacements. I had one that was leaking oil. The maintenance officer had taken it out of commission. I had checked the rate of oil leak and believed we could fly it for an hour at a time with no danger. I overrode the maintenance officer's decision with instructions to fly it for one hour at a time. Each time it landed, the crew chief would check the oil level and add more oil if necessary. That would allow us to support the training. Of course, I was pushing post maintenance to get the work on my other aircraft completed.

He told me I was taking a chance on the aircraft leaking oil. I agreed but pointed out that I had no alternative if I wanted to support training. He retorted that either way, it could reflect on my OER if anything went wrong. That angered me a little. It brought back memories of the operations officer in the Thirty-Fourth Signal Battalion during the IG and CMI in Germany. I replied that I understood the possible effect it could have but would rather perform the mission and not worry about how it would affect my OER. I think he detected the dislike in my tone over being threatened with my OER. He ended with "Good luck," and he hung up.

We completed the training without incident. I got all of my birds out of maintenance, and we were healthy again. I told the maintenance officer that I wanted better maintenance scheduling so we never had four aircraft down for maintenance. He was a little miffed about that because he always did a good job, and having four aircraft down was unusual. I recognized that. I just wanted to prevent him from becoming complacent.

Although I was the boss, it was difficult for me to find time to fly. There always seemed to be a meeting I had to attend or some other problem that needed my attention. The easiest way for me to meet my minimums was at night. One day I scheduled myself for a night cross-country training flight to March AFB in California. Flight time there was an hour and forty-five minutes. I planned on landing, refueling, and flying back to Fort Huachuca. That would give me three and a half hours of night cross-country, which met my quarterly night-flight requirements. One of the TOs needed flight time, so he was glad to fly with me.

The flight to March AFB was routine. The weather was clear with unlimited visibility. There's little habitation between Phoenix and March. It's mostly desert with small settlements here and there. The lights from the little settlements sparkled like diamonds in the dark night. About fifty miles from March Air Force Base, Los Angeles flight control handed me off to March AFB approach control for a ground control approach landing.

The March controller vectored me to final approach. I was descending two miles from touchdown, when the controller suddenly told me to cancel the landing. The airfield was closed. They directed me to turn left before reaching the runway. I immediately applied power and leveled off. Then the controller told me to climb to five thousand feet and go to an alternate airfield. As I started climbing, I could see B-52 bombers taxiing for takeoff. The DA had launched a practice nuclear attack during my approach. The B-52s had a limited time to get airborne. That gave them priority.

I hadn't planned on this happening. I'd planned to refuel and go back to Fort Huachuca. The weather was clear all across the west, and there was no need to plan for an alternate, but I had to land somewhere to refuel. I could not make it back to Huachuca without refueling. I did a quick check of my map and saw that San Diego was the closest airfield. I asked March traffic control to give me a vector to San Diego. They cleared me to ten thousand feet on a heading of 180 and directed me to call LA Center and refile my flight plan.

I contacted LA Center, reported my position, and asked for clearance to the San Diego airport. They approved my request and gave me a new heading of two hundred degrees. When I reported on two hundred, they told me to contact San Diego approach for landing instructions. I contacted San Diego approach and reported my position. They cleared me for an ILS approach into San Diego. A couple of minutes later, they gave me a vector to the San Diego outer marker.

I turned to that heading while I quickly thumbed through my approach templates to find the San Diego ILS approach. I was sweating now. I had to review the approach and set the radios on the right frequency. At the same time, approach control was giving me vectors to the outer marker and instructions to start my descent. I could see the lights of San Diego off to my left and knew I would be on the outer marker soon.

I finally got my radios tuned. I could see the course marker moving on my flight director. I was at the outer-marker altitude when approach cleared me for an ILS approach and told me to report outer marker. I turned inbound to intercept the course marker and saw that I was above the glide slope. I lowered the nose to lose altitude and crossed the outer marker. I reported outer marker and did my landing check. I was on course and on glide slope finally.

I thought the approach was a little dangerous. As I crossed the middle marker, there were skyscrapers on either side of the approach course. The runway lights were a blur in the center of a sea of lights from traffic around the airport and from the skyscrapers. The weather was clear for my approach, so I had visibility of the runway during the whole approach. I shuddered, thinking about what it would be like to make this approach in bad weather with no visibility. There was no room for error. The skyscrapers seemed close and ominous.

I landed and refueled within twenty minutes. The flight back to Fort Huachuca was uneventful, but the memory of that approach and landing still gives me goose bumps. I don't know whether it's a lack of confidence in my instrument landing ability or some other fear that I don't understand, but either way, I never filed a flight into San Diego again. I have never flown into San Diego on a civilian flight and don't ever plan to do so.

On August 12, a week before Claudia and the kids returned, the DOL staff major general called and said the director wanted to see me in his office. He had no idea what it was about. I figured he knew but did not want to tell me. All the way to the DOL, I wondered what had I done or not done for him to call me to his office. That was always the case with me. Even though I knew my work was usually beyond reproach, getting called into the boss's office always produced the same emotion.

I walked into the DOL building and smiled at the director's secretary. She smiled at me and rang the director on the intercom. He answered, and she said, "Captain Griffin is here." Then she said, "Okay, go on in; he's waiting for you."

I knocked on his doorjamb and heard him say, "Come on in, Captain Griffin."

I walked in and said, "Good morning, sir."

I saw a major sitting in one of the chairs around the director's coffee table. The director replied, "Good morning, Captain Griffin. Thanks for coming." He looked at me and said, "Captain Griffin, meet Major Turner. Major Turner just signed in, and because of his rank, he will take over your job as chief of MAD." He looked at Major Turner and said, "Major Turner, this is Captain Griffin. He has been the chief of MAD for the past three months and has done an outstanding job."

The director continued as we shook hands and exchanged greetings. "Captain Griffin, you are the new operations officer. Take Major Turner with you, and show him around. I'm sorry that you only got a chance to serve as chief of MAD for three months. I hate to jerk you around, but I have to put the ranking officer in charge. I think the operations job is just as important, and I know you will do a great job there." That ended our session.

Major Turner followed me to the airfield. When we walked into the operations office, I introduced him to everybody, announcing that he was the new MAD chief and I was the new operations officer. I led him into the chief's office and introduced him to the secretary and staff major general. We went into his office, and I briefed him on all the current actions and potential problems. He was a personable officer, and I liked him as soon as I met him.

When I finished briefing him, he apologized for taking my job. He told me he had been in Alaska and had hoped to stay there for another three years. However, USAICS had asked for a lieutenant colonel to fill the MAD chief's job. They'd sent him. I appreciated his sincerity and told him it was no problem; I did not like the job anyway. I preferred the operations officer job because that was where all the action was. He pointed to the master parachutist wings under my aviator wings and asked, "How many jumps do you have?"

He wore parachutist wings under his aviator wings. I replied, "Ninety-nine jumps, sir."

He appeared astonished. "Why didn't you make one more jump and make it an even hundred?"

"Well, sir," I said, "I had to leave for flight school and never got the chance."

"Oh, that's too bad. You could have been a century jumper."

"I'll tell you what I'll do, sir. One of these days, when everything is right, I'll eject from a Mohawk and count that as my hundredth jump."

"No, you don't have to do that," he replied, laughing.

By then, I figured it was time to leave and let him orient himself. I picked up my gear and told him to call me if he had any questions on what I had done. He said he would, and I walked out to the operations officer's desk. Major Turner was a great person to work for. We went on to become good friends and stayed good friends after we both retired.

The W-3 whom I'd made temporary operations officer had already moved his stuff out. I hung my ejection-seat harness and helmet up and sat down. I sat there for a minute or two, looking around. What I'd said about there being more action as operations officer was true. I preferred this job. There was more and closer interaction with the aviators and operational staff. I would talk with my fishing friends at the Directorate of Training (DOT) on a regular basis as they scheduled training flights. I didn't have to deal with dumb lieutenant colonels each day. This was a position in my comfort zone, and I was happy to be in it.

After about five minutes, the civilian aviation flight records clerk, Kathy, knocked on my door. I smiled and asked her to come in. She said she wanted to welcome me as the new boss and see if I wanted a cup of coffee. I said thank you and yes to the coffee. When she said, "I'll bring you one," I said, "No, I will get it myself." I never took to having someone wait on me. I followed her out to the coffee urn and poured myself a cup of coffee. I asked her who managed the coffee fund, and she said the operations sergeant did.

The flight operations section was staffed with a sergeant and two civilians. As I said, Kathy was the flight records clerk. She maintained aviator flight records and assisted with flight operations as needed. The sergeant and another civilian did the aviation operations tasks. They scheduled flights and aviators for each flight, maintained control, and tracked USAICS aircraft operating in the local area. We had an agreement with Libby Airfield operations that we would keep control of our aircraft when flying training missions in the local area. My pilots did not have to file a flight plan under that agreement, which simplified student training. My operations section provided that service during training flights. Kathy assisted the sergeant from 0730 to 1615. The other civilian clerk came in at 1500 and worked till 2300.

Just as I had as the chief of MAD, I first read the SOP and all the regulations about USAICS flight operations. That took a couple of days, but after that, I had a good feel for my responsibilities. I found that little effort had been put into keeping the SOP and regulations current. That was a by-product of not having major inspections during the year. In fact, I found no record of any inspection of the operations branch by a higher headquarters. The saying that a unit does well what the commander checks is never truer than in school environments. There was no one in USAICS qualified to inspect MAD. The post's aviation operations branch had the know-how to inspect my operations, but no one had asked them to. That was going to change under my watch.

After I had familiarized myself with the job, I called everyone into my office. My staff consisted of three WO pilots, the operations sergeant, and the two civilians. They all listened as I explained my philosophy. I opened by saying, "I am privileged to be here. I'm probably the easiest person in the world to work for. I like to work hard and play hard." I looked at Matt. "Matt can confirm that. However, I demand we do our work every day. At day's end, I expect each of us to go home confident that if a major inspection was scheduled for the next morning, we would ace it. I do not accept anything less than that."

I continued, "From what I can see, we don't have much work. We do most of our work, such as flight operations and check rides, as needed. But what we do have is a major record-keeping job. It is time consuming to care for the flight records of thirty-two aviators. It takes time to enter flight hours, night hours, weather requirements, and standardization checks and keep flight records current. We have to project flying hours for aviator training and currency. That projection supports our budget input. Overall, not much work for us. The purpose in me telling you what you already know is to let you know that I want to go home each day knowing we are ready for inspection. That means we do our job every day, and when done, then we can play."

I looked at Kathy. "There are some new tasks I want you to do. Each month, I want you to send out a memorandum listing all the aviators and how they stand on meeting yearly currency demands. I want you to prepare it for my signature. First off, we need to get Major Turner current, so schedule his refresher training and standardization ride. Schedule him for early morning flights before his daily schedule can interrupt his training. Standardization section, you guys take care of that. My office is always open, and I am available to help you anytime. Do you have any questions of me?"

With that meeting, I started my new job as operations officer. It took three weeks to get the records updated and to set up the work ethic that I wanted. Meanwhile, Claudia and the kids returned from Germany. My move to operations officer surprised her. Her concern was that I had done something wrong. She understood when I explained that a major had replaced me.

Once I had my expectations met, my job became fun. I had no major problems and much free time. I could fly as many missions as I wanted. I could go fishing in Mexico. That had not been possible as the chief of MAD. Some little problem had always popped up that precluded me from going. Jake had stopped pulling his boat to Obregon. Instead, we would go deep-sea fishing in Guaymas.

Jake found a motel and RV campground located on a peninsula south of Guaymas Bay. A Mexican captain named Jesus chartered his boat from the site. We would call him to charter the boat for Saturday and Sunday and then reserve rooms at the motel for Friday through Sunday. Since we did not have to pull a boat, we could drive down in our cars on Friday and drive back on Monday. Sometimes Jake would take his camper down. Two of us would sleep in it, and two would sleep in the motel room.

The boat was an old wooden boat with a diesel engine. It had a small galley and provided all the fishing equipment for four people. Captain Jesus was at least eighty-five years old, but he had two younger crewmembers. Captain Jesus had been fishing in those waters for many years and always took us where we could catch fish. We trolled for cero mackerel most of the time. It was fun, and we caught loads of fish.

Claudia still got upset when I went fishing. She would never say why. She just got upset. I had to leave under that mantle each time. I had to deal with my anger or let it spoil my trip. I wished she could one time say, "Have a good time, Neal." But she never did. However, when I got back, everything would be okay between us.

Fall arrived, and the kids were back in school. By October, all the grass that had been so green and beautiful had turned brown. It hadn't rained in three weeks, and the land and streams had dried out. It was still hot and dusty. The fine red dust blown by the constant wind permeated and coated everything. The landscape was brown and dead looking. It would remain that way until the rains came again next June.

Jake called me and said he had some aviators coming in for the OV-1D qualification course. There were two captains and a colonel. He wanted me to fly the colonel on the area orientation flight. The colonel was en route to Vietnam to command the Mohawk unit there. For those types of classes, we gave high-ranking officers, such as the colonel, preferential treatment. I agreed to fly the colonel on his area orientation flight, and Jake said he would have the colonel call me to schedule the flight.

The next morning, the colonel called and asked if we could do the flight that evening at 1800. I told him that was fine and said I would meet him at the flight line. He arrived at 1800, and we shook hands as

I introduced myself. I did the preflight as he called out items from the checklist. In the cockpit, he impressed me with his knowledge of the Mohawk system. We taxied to the run-up area, and five minutes later, we were airborne.

As usual, I turned south over the east edge of the Huachuca Mountains and flew to the border. I pointed out the landmarks and the border as it ran east toward the Mule Mountains and Nacho. I continued past Bisbee and pointed out the open pit mine. We continued to the end of our local area, ten miles east of Douglas. I took him north from there to Willcox and the Willcox Playa. At Willcox, I turned west toward Tucson. I identified each of the major geographic and man-made features to use as guides. It was starting to get dark. I turned south of Tucson and flew south down I-17 to Nogales. At Nogales, I turned east and flew over the Huachuca Mountains to our starting point.

The colonel was attentive and asked several questions about the local area. At our starting point, I flew to Cloud Nine Trailer Park and pointed it out. It was the trailer park I'd stayed in during my separation. It also was the contact point for Libby AAF when approaching from the east. From there, I flew northwest to the intersection of Highway 80 and Highway 90. Then I turned west to Apache Pass and pointed it out. Apache Pass was the contact point when approaching from the west.

That ended the orientation flight, so I called the tower. "Libby tower, this is Mohawk 691. Apache Pass for landing."

"Roger, Mohawk 691. Cleared for a straight-in to runway eleven. Altimeter 29.01. Winds one hundred sixty at thirty-five knots, gusting to forty-five knots. Would you prefer runway eighteen based on the winds?"

"Negative, Libby," I replied. "Runway eleven is okay."

"Roger, Mohawk 691. I've got you in sight. Report short final for runway eleven."

"This is Mohawk 691. Report short final," I answered.

We completed the prelanding and landing. The Mohawk was bouncing around from the wind. I could tell the colonel was a little nervous by the way he kept fidgeting in his seat. It was a stiff wind but nothing the Mohawk could not handle in the hands of a skilled pilot. However, the colonel didn't know how skilled I was at crosswind landings. The Bird Dog had taught me how to make a crosswind landing. The night Jake had checked me out in Korea in a forty-five-knot crosswind had taught me how to make one in the Mohawk, but the colonel did not know that.

"Libby tower, Mohawk 691 is short final for runway eleven."

"Roger, Mohawk 691. You're cleared to land. Winds now thirty-five knots, steady at one hundred sixty, occasionally gusting to forty-five."

"Roger, Libby tower. Mohawk 691 cleared to land."

When I got over the threshold, I took my crab out and put in right aileron. When my nose lined up on the centerline, I put in left rudder to hold the Mohawk on the centerline. With the right wing down, the Mohawk slowly settled toward the runway. With the help of a thirty-five-knot wind, my ground speed was way below normal touchdown speed. When I reached my roundout attitude, I raised the nose while adjusting aileron and rudder to hold me straight down the centerline. My right gear touched softly down on the runway. I slowly took out the right aileron and lowered the left wing. I felt the left gear touch softly down. Both main gears were on the runway, and we were rolling straight down the centerline. I felt the nose getting heavy, so I lowered the nose gear onto the centerline. My ground speed was so slow that I didn't have to reverse engines to slow down. I had just made a perfect textbook crosswind landing. That I'd done it in a big Mohawk made it even more impressive.

The colonel looked at me and said, "Damn, that was a beautiful landing, Captain Griffin."

I told him thanks as I got clearance to taxi. Inside, I was a little proud of myself too. I knew the colonel would remember Captain Griffin whenever the subject of crosswind landings came up. I parked the Mohawk on the apron, and we got out. I asked him if he had any questions of me, and he said no. Then he congratulated me on a fine orientation ride and left. I completed the logbook while the crew chief tied the aircraft down and pinned the seats.

The next couple of months were good for me. I was having fun at work, and Claudia and I were getting along well for some reason. Her interest in tennis and our playing together worked to create a bond between us. We had a couple of tiffs but nothing major. The kids were doing well in school. As we approached Thanksgiving, I could actually say I was happy. As with all the times before, I had become the resident expert in my job. My superiors respected me and never questioned my judgment and decisions.

After Thanksgiving, TRADOC headquarters told USAICS that they would conduct an IG and CMI of the unit the second week of December. An aviation team from Fort Rucker would be part of the TRADOC team and inspect aviation operations. Once again, my instincts and work ethic were right on the money. While the rest of the USAICS worked day and night to catch up on the work that they should have done daily, my people continued the normal routine.

The inspection team spent three hours inspecting my records and flying-hour program. They found no discrepancies. They cited my branch among the best in TRADOC. We received a plaque for our safety record of more than fourteen thousand hours with no reportable incident. I couldn't claim responsibility for the entire fourteen thousand since we had only flown five thousand hours since my assignment as aviation safety officer. I was proud of my people and the job they had done.

The following week began the Christmas holidays. The training department released students from training so they could spend Christmas with their families. All permanent party personnel began a half-day work schedule. I was supposed to schedule work so that everybody got half a day off each day. That meant half of my people would work in the morning and half in the afternoon. That didn't make sense to me, so I scheduled my people to work one day on and one day off. Everyone loved that schedule, and it ensured the office was staffed during duty hours. I usually came in every day and worked till noon. That way, I could handle any major problems that might come up.

There were no student training flights. Most flights were for aviators catching up on their minimum flight-hour requirements. It was easy to keep their records updated, so we spent most of our time playing cards and answering the phone. Spades was our favorite game. Kathy and I played as a team and became good.

Once again, Claudia and I celebrated New Year's at a party, this time at a friend's house. The couple who'd engaged me in a conversation about open marriages was there. I was careful this time not to get into any serious conversations with them. I did not want a repeat of the previous New Year's. We had a good time, and for the first time, I felt that the prospects for the new year were looking good for Claudia and me.

However, I noticed something about two of her friends. They seemed unhappy and often, I thought, cold to their husbands. When I danced with them, they seemed to hold me a little tighter than necessary. As the drinks were flowing, I credited their behavior to the alcohol and the mood of the party. Because of my problems with Claudia, I had developed a sense of when a woman was hitting on me. I had noticed that most of those who came on to me were her friends. Because of that, I guessed they probably knew of the troubles Claudia and I had. Or they knew something about Claudia that made them believe they could tempt me. However, what they did not know was how much I loved Claudia. She drew me to her like a moth to a flame, and to describe me as only having eyes for her was accurate.

In January, deer season opened on Fort Huachuca. White-tailed and mule deer were plentiful on Fort Huachuca. The white-tailed deer were smaller and found in the higher altitudes. The mule deer were much larger and found at lower altitudes. In preparation for deer hunting, I had bought a Springfield .308-caliber rifle with scope. Jake and my fishing buddies had made plans to hunt together. On the first morning, we signed into our area before daylight.

We had done a recon of the area earlier and picked positions to hunt from. The positions were about a quarter of a mile apart and provided a good view of the area. As quietly as possible, we moved in the dark to our positions to await daylight. This was the first time I had been hunting since Fort Stewart, Georgia. I had hunted throughout my teens to supply food for my family and considered myself an excellent hunter. As I eagerly waited for daylight, I did not know I was about to find something out about myself that I would have never thought possible.

It was cold and got colder just before the sun came up. I was cold and trying to remain still as the sun slowly gave enough light to see across my area. As I scanned my area, I looked along a dry streambed, and to my surprise, I saw a big buck standing by a mesquite. He stood about 150 meters from my position. It was an easy shot, especially with a scope. He was standing and looking around as I slowly raised my rifle and put the crosshairs on his chest.

I stared at him through my scope as I prepared to squeeze the trigger. He was magnificent. He stood there looking proud and beautiful. I took a deep breath and held it as I started to squeeze the trigger. I was trembling—but not from the excitement that a hunter about to make a kill has. I was trembling from the thought that I was about to kill a magnificent animal that I did not want to kill. I asked myself why I was doing this. I did not need the deer for food. I would not kill an animal for a trophy. The image of the Vietcong messenger I'd shot from the backseat of the Bird Dog appeared in my mind. Regret flooded through me, and tears rolled out of my eyes.

I took my finger off the trigger and slipped the safety on. I could not kill that deer. It was not that I was unable to kill him. I did not want to kill him for any reason. Life was too precious. All life was precious, not just human life. In the Bible, in Genesis, God told Adam that he gave humans dominion over the animals on earth. That was a grave responsibility. I had no right to take the life of that deer just because it was hunting season. I had killed enough. I could never take another animal's life.

When I resolved not to ever kill an animal again, I felt better. I watched the big buck move slightly as something alarmed him. He looked toward Jake's location and suddenly, with a graceful bound, disappeared down the dry creek bed and out of sight. The sun was up now, and I could hear an occasional shot from some hunter. I had not realized how long I had watched the buck with my scope. I said a little prayer for his safety.

I saw Jake a couple hundred meters off, walking toward my position. He was huffing and puffing from trekking across the rough desert terrain. As he walked up to me, he called out, "Neal, didn't you see that big buck out in front of you? Why didn't you shoot him?"

"I saw him, Jake. But he was standing behind the mesquite tree. I was afraid if I fired with him behind the mesquite, the limbs might deflect the round. I kept waiting for him to step out into the open, but something spooked him, and he took off."

That explanation appeased Jake. After that, we started walking to see if we could scare up a deer. When we met back at the truck and no one had killed a deer, I felt relief. Over the next two years, I went hunting many times, but I never fired my rifle. I spent most of the time watching the deer through my scope and marveling at their grace and beauty. I spent my time looking for rock formations that might contain gold. I never found any, but it was fun just the same. Years later, I gave my rifle, which had never killed an animal, to my son. He never used it to hunt.

One Friday afternoon in early February, Matt came into my office. He said, "Hey, sir, I've got a problem. Captain Brown wants to schedule a Huey for this weekend. He said it was for a training flight because he's too busy during duty hours to get away for flying. He wants me to fly with him. He's listed four passengers and said he wants to practice high-altitude landings on Miller Peak and Carr. You need to call him and listen to what he actually wants to do."

I called Captain Brown's office, and he answered the phone. "Captain Brown, this is Captain Griffin. I'm calling about the Huey you want to schedule for Saturday. What flight training are you planning?"

He paused for a moment. "I want to practice some high-altitude landings. After that, I want Matt to drop me and my passengers off on Miller Peak. There's a reported eight feet of snow on Miller. It is the southernmost mountain with snow in the United States. I want to ski down it and try to get into *The Guinness Book of Records*. Matt can fly the Huey while one of my passengers takes pictures of us skiing down the mountain. Then he can pick us up when we get to the bottom and return to the airfield."

My mouth fell open as I listened. When he finished, I bluntly said, "No. No way will I approve a Huey for that purpose. I can think of a dozen things that can go wrong and what the accident report would reflect. That's just the beginning. The investigation into the misuse of government equipment would be equally entertaining. If you want to ski down Miller Peak, then hike up it, but there'll be no helicopter ride."

He pleaded with me to approve the Huey. He said they would climb it, but the snow was too deep. His pleas fell on my deaf ears. No way would I risk one of my helicopters on a fool stunt like that. I finally told him to go see the CG and said that if the CG told me to do it, I would. We hung up with him pissed at me. Matt was laughing at our conversation and said, "Thanks, boss."

Spring finally arrived with one last winter storm in April that froze all the newly budded trees. One of Claudia's and my friends was visiting us from Germany. Her name was Paula, and she was the mother of one of Claudia's childhood playmates. Paula had taken a liking to Claudia.

As Claudia had grown into an adult, they'd remained friends. After we'd married, she'd become my friend by our marriage. She was a nice woman, and we have remained friends till this day.

Her first visit to the States was that April for two weeks. When I knew she was coming, I created an itinerary to entertain her. The first item on the itinerary was visiting the Grand Canyon and Las Vegas. We left for the Grand Canyon the day before that last winter storm hit. After seeing the canyon, I planned on driving to Las Vegas. I had reservations for two nights and tickets to one of the dinner shows. When we got to Flagstaff, it was dark and snowing. We spent the night in a hotel and drove to the Grand Canyon the next morning. It was disappointing to stand on the rim of the Grand Canyon and see nothing. A thick layer of clouds covered the canyon, blocking any view of sights. I said, "Paula, look out there and imagine the biggest hole you can think of, and that's the Grand Canyon."

We left the canyon, disappointed. Paula had come so far to see it. It should have been one of the highlights of her trip. When we got Las Vegas, the weather had cleared, and the sun was shining. We spent two nights there and had a wonderful time. Back in Arizona, we spent the rest of her stay visiting the local historic sites. I enjoyed her visit. I told Claudia to tell all her friends to come visit. I would gladly show them the attractions of the Southwest.

When I got back to work, the talk was about the army's decision to open aviator training and the technical observer's MOS to females. That caused an issue with my warrant officers. It led to a big discussion among us about the fitness of female army pilots. My WOs had the opinion that they would never be able to trust a female helicopter pilot, let alone a fixed-wing one. I thought they were exhibiting male chauvinism, and I pointed that out. They did not agree. Matt said, "Suppose I was giving a female a check ride in a Mohawk, and she screwed a maneuver up. What would I do if she started crying when I counseled her?"

I knew why he asked me that question. We had been inserting basic course lieutenants as part of their tactical assault training. Before the exercise, Matt and I briefed the lieutenants on exiting the Huey once we touched down. We carefully showed the eight lieutenants, three of which were female, how to exit the Huey. In training and in combat, troops must exit forward and to the sides. They must never exit to the rear of the hovering helicopter. There have been many soldiers killed by exiting to the rear and running into the moving tail rotor.

Confident that we had made that clear to the young lieutenants, we loaded them aboard the Huey. After a fifteen-minute flight, we simulated a combat assault onto an LZ. When we touched down, the lieutenant in charge exited, leading the rest of the students. Four exited to the left of the Huey, and four exited to the right. Shocked, we watched the last student on the right run straight toward the rear of the Huey. She cleared the tail rotor by five feet.

Normally, we would have pulled pitch the moment the last troop was out of the Huey, but Matt said, "Set her down, sir." I set the Huey back down firmly on its skids. Matt unbuckled, exited the Huey, and ran to the lieutenant who had exited to the rear. She was in a prone position, simulating combat. Matt threw his flight helmet onto the ground, grabbed her, and pulled her to her feet.

I watched as he reprimanded her for running to the rear instead of the forty-five-degree angle from the Huey, as we'd instructed her to do. He was animated and chewing her out. Suddenly, he made an exasperated gesture and shook his head. He picked up his helmet and left the lieutenant standing at attention as he returned to the Huey. He put his helmet on, climbed into the aircraft commander's seat, and said disgustedly, "Let's go."

I pulled pitch and moved forward until I had transitional lift and started climbing away from the LZ. As I turned to go back to Libby for our next set of students, I asked him what had happened. He looked at me with an expression of disgust and said, "She started crying. How in the hell can we go to war with lieutenants who cry when they are being chewed out? What are they going to do in combat when life goes to hell—cry? The army is making a mistake if they put females in combat units."

We flew two more insertions that morning. The students exited the Huey correctly. However, Matt would not change his mind about females in the army. I tried to point out that everybody made mistakes once in a while, and hopefully, the lieutenant had learned her lesson. Matt said he understood that, but that was not his problem. The emotional traits of females concerned him the most.

He repeated his original question about what to do if counseling a female pilot for screwing up on a Mohawk check ride. I thought for a few seconds before I answered. "I don't know, Matt. But what I know is this: for a female to get through flight school, she will have to do more—and do it better—than any man. Here's why. Men will be the instructors. Because of their bias, they will require female students to perform better than men. Females will have to prove themselves much more than you or I ever had to do. I believe that those who do get through flight school will be better pilots at that stage than you or I were when we graduated.

"I think if I were counseling a student and she started crying, I would ignore it. As a young lieutenant but a seasoned soldier, I was chewed out to the extent that I had tears in my eyes. But the tears were not from the ass chewing. They were from my disappointment in myself. I was hurt that I had screwed up and that somebody had to point it out. Maybe your lieutenant was responding the same way. I don't know. I only hope that as the army modernizes itself and corrects the lessons learned from Vietnam, our training produces the best, whether they are female or male."

Matt had listened to my spiel, but I was not sure he bought it 100 percent. "I hope you're right, sir. But I tell you, if I were to get on a commercial Boeing 707 and see that the pilot was a female, I would worry for the whole flight."

Work ended our conversation. Later, as I thought about Matt's parting statement regarding a female pilot in the cockpit, I could not honestly say how I would feel. I knew that it would be tough for a woman to get there, and if she did, she would be a damn fine pilot.

We got our first batch of female students for TO training shortly after our discussion. I flew them on their IR night missions. It relieved me to find that they did really well. In fact, overall, they were better than most male students I had flown. They were attentive, had thoroughly planned their missions, and stayed oriented in the air. When I simulated antiaircraft fire striking the aircraft and disabling me, they responded quickly and accurately. The only fault they had was in loading the sensor equipment into the sensor bay.

The sensor package for the IR system weighs about fifty pounds. To load it, the TO picks it up and bends over to slide it into the bay and secure it. The male TOs have difficulty doing it. The female students rarely have the upper body strength to perform the task smoothly. They end up meshing fingers and tearing fingernails. I noticed that they overcame this problem by flirting with the instructors and getting them to help. I made it clear to the class and the instructors that if the female students could not load the IR sensor by themselves, then I would fail them.

That ended the problem. They struggled but loaded it correctly on their final exam flights. For what it's worth, my assessment of females in the military is that they can do the job if commanders and supervisors demand they perform it. Females quickly learn that they can slyly solicit help from their male peers and get it, but females wishing to make the military a career should begin to develop their upper body strength at a young age. Lack of upper body strength is the fault that will more than likely disqualify them from a certain MOS.

One of the subjects discussed during my safety officer course at USC was man-machine interface. It was clear to me that the ejection-seat harness designed for men was not suitable for females. The way the harness crossed their breasts could injure their breasts during an ejection. I encouraged them to address that fact on their end of the course critique sheets. At the same time, I put in a recommendation to the USAASO (United States Army Aeronautical Services Office) at Fort Rucker, identifying the problem and recommending that the military redesign harnesses used by females. I never heard any more about it. During the rest of my time in the army, females continued to use the same harnesses men used.

In May, Claudia booked reservations to Germany for eight weeks. She, Michele, and Ron would leave after the kids got out of school. I did not want her to stay that long, but I did not make much of an objection. Our relations were good, and I did not want her going to Germany mad at me. I still felt the pain of betrayal each time she went to Germany. Although we got along okay, she still displayed behavior that made me distrust her. I had learned to accept her behavior because there was never any proof that she was being unfaithful. In the end, I would dismiss my concerns as immaturity on my part for not letting the past go. After all, I was the guilty one.

Around May 1, I received a letter from the DA, telling me I had not been selected for promotion to major. The letter told me that normally, the army would have ended my service, but since I had more than eighteen years of service, I could remain on active duty until I completed my twenty years. It was a blow to my ego. I had been an outstanding enlisted man and officer. At the time, there was controversy over how the promotion boards determined whom to promote. The army was selecting officers with regular army commissions over reserve officers, who often had better performance records and were better qualified. That was army policy. The army considered officers with RA commissions to be career officers. Officers with reserve commissions were not. The army permitted them to serve on active duty based on the needs of the army.

The army did not promote Jake and gave him one month to close out his records and leave the service. I felt sorry for him. Fortunately, the army allowed officers who had been NCOs before their commission to apply for retention as NCOs. Jake applied for retention as a staff sergeant, and the army approved his request. Next, he applied for flight controller school and was accepted. He made sergeant first class and completed his twenty years in the army as an army flight controller.

About a month after all the passed-over letters went out, I read about a captain who had started a class action suit against the army. He was asking all captains whom the army had passed over who felt their OERs did not justify that to join his class action suit. I filled out a form and mailed it to him. I knew my record was better than those of half of the captains whom the army had promoted.

My job as operations officer was fun and free of stress. It soon took my mind off not making major. Unless I was flying, I went to work at 0700 and went home at 1700. That started to cause a problem. I had too much free time. I was not taking college courses at night. Then it occurred to me that I missed the stress I had become used to in other assignments. To compensate for that stress, I decided I needed a hobby. One day I read in the weekly bulletin that the arts and crafts shop on post was offering silversmith classes. The two-hour classes were on Tuesdays and Thursdays. They covered lapidary, casting, and jewelry making. The cost was thirty dollars for eight classes. I signed up for the classes, and a new world opened for me.

The classes were interesting and challenging. I quickly found out that I had a knack for lapidary and jewelry making. Over time, I saw that I had an artistic ability I'd never known about. I could design and make rings, bracelets, and necklaces that were beautiful and sold as fast as I produced them. I did not make the traditional Indian jewelry that was the big rage at the time. My designs were modern but made with silver, gold, turquoise, malachite, azurite, and red coral.

The popularity of Indian jewelry created a huge demand for turquoise, malachite, azurite, and red coral. Except for the red coral, these minerals were all associated with copper. Because of the number of copper mines in Arizona, they were plentiful. Most of the minerals were of good quality in the beginning, but the demand soon caused low-grade minerals to appear. Red coral was already expensive. Jewel-quality red coral came from the Mediterranean Sea, off the coast of Italy. Divers had to go deep to get it, which added to the cost. The demand for it became so high that diving began to destroy the coral reefs, so Italy banned the harvest of it. That doubled and tripled the price and made it against the law to sell or buy it.

When I first started, I bought my materials at the arts and crafts store. It so happened that Kathy loved Indian jewelry, and when she could, she got her husband to take her to the old mine sites, where she would look through the tailings for turquoise. We talked about that often during lunch while playing cards. One day she talked about an old Tiffany turquoise mine. That was unusual because most of the turquoise was a by-product of copper mining. The Tiffany mine turquoise was of such fine grade that Tiffany matched it with gold to produce contemporary jewelry.

One day Matt, Kathy, and I agreed to meet on Saturday morning to drive out to Gleason to look for the mine. Gleason, or what remained of it, was an old ghost town. It had been a copper mining town at the turn of the century, but by 1920, the price of copper had become so cheap that it was not profitable anymore, so the town had died and soon become rubble as people took away anything of use. It was located on an old dirt road about ten miles east of Tombstone, Arizona. Other than Tombstone, there was nothing but an occasional isolated cattle ranch for miles after that.

We met that Saturday morning and piled into Matt's truck for the drive. It took about an hour to get to the ruins at Gleason. From there, Kathy directed us to the site of the old Tiffany mine. After about fifteen minutes, we found the dead-end dirt road leading to the small hill where the shaft was located. We parked, walked about fifty meters up and around the hill, and found the tailings scattered away from the mine's shaft.

We first explored the shaft. It went straight in for about forty yards and was cluttered with debris and old cans. After seeing no sign of turquoise in the shaft, we started looking through the tailings. We walked around staring at the ground for an hour before I found a large hunk of partially buried turquoise. I happened to see a little spot of blue, and when I uncovered it, I found the piece. What made the Tiffany turquoise valuable was that it developed in quartz. It was hard compared to other turquoise. Finding that small piece of rock had a marked effect on me. From that day on, I spent every weekend I could get away exploring mines and searching tailings for turquoise, malachite, and azurite with which to make my jewelry.

That day was also the beginning of a new tradition. After several hours of searching for turquoise under a blazing sun, we stopped in Tombstone for beer and lunch. Of all the old western towns, Tombstone is my favorite place. Most of the attractions are the same buildings built in the late 1800s during the boom days of Tombstone. The Crystal Palace Saloon has not changed since it was built. Before it burned down, Johnny Ringo's was where we gathered after our trek through the desert looking for stones. Often, there would be eight or nine of us in the group. I always tried to get Claudia to go, but she never would. I took the kids several times. Kathy took her three kids several times. It was a fun outing that provided exercise, the excitement of treasure hunting, and the fun of enjoying cold beer and snacks.

I made my first necklace from a piece of the Tiffany turquoise. It was a teardrop-shaped piece in silver, and I was proud of it. Claudia seemed pleased and wore it once or twice. However, she was not a fan of turquoise and silver. It has been in her jewelry box since then. She does not wear it, but she will not part with it. I guess that means something.

My jewelry making brought me pleasure and gave me something of which to be proud. One could find me in the arts and crafts shop several nights a week after I started. Claudia did not care about my being gone. I enjoyed the comradery with the other artists working on their creations. We helped each other and learned from each other. The hobby became therapeutic for me and took my mind off many of the pains I felt while Claudia was in Germany.

Claudia and the kids left for Germany the first week in June. I decided that while they were in Germany, I would take a couple weeks of leave to visit my mother and father in Florida. I left early in the morning on July

1 and drove straight through to my mother's house in Jacksonville Beach. It was 2,010 miles from my quarters on post to her house. It took me a day and a half, but I was young then. I did not want to spend money on a motel room; that was my real reason for driving straight through.

I had a great time in Florida. It was the first time I had seen my family since I'd gotten out of Vietnam and stopped by for a few days before going to Germany. I went fishing with my brother and his friends. My friend Bobby was working overseas at the time, so I did not get to see him. It had been more than fifteen years since I'd last seen him. I went to church with my mother, which pleased her. I knew by then that I was her favorite child. She was proud to introduce me to her friends in church.

I tried to spend time with my dad. He was doing light cabinetwork between drunks. He was getting old, and it was hard for him to do heavy work. The edge of the porch roof had been leaking, and a couple of rafters had rotted. I fixed them for him. I found that his drinking did not affect me the way it had when I was a kid. I felt sorry for him and the way he had wasted his life. I understood a lot more about alcoholism now. I believed that he probably wished he had done better but could not overcome the devils that tortured him. I would never know what those devils were. The brief conversation we'd had after I returned from Vietnam had given me a little insight into his wants and needs, but I never had enough conversations to understand my father, and that would become one of my biggest regrets. It later became one of the impetuses for my writing the journal of my life in the army.

The monsoons, or summer rains, hit Arizona at the end of June. The heat and humidity produce thunderstorms almost every afternoon. Almost overnight, the desert and mountains change from a dusty brown to a vivid green. The landscape's beauty is breathtaking. The monsoons were active during the two weeks I was in Florida. The range grass, forced to grow and produce seeds in the short growing season, shot up almost waist high. I was due a check ride when I returned from Florida, so I had the SIP give it to me on my first day back.

The ride was uneventful. I completed all the maneuvers and emergency procedures correctly. As we advanced through the sequence of maneuvers, we worked our way up near Willcox Playa. With my concentration on flying the aircraft and performing the check ride maneuvers, I hadn't been paying much attention to my ground location. I knew the area like the back of my hand and could look at the terrain and immediately orient myself. At the end of the ride, the SIP told me to put my head between my knees. I put my head between my knees, and he took control of the Mohawk.

He did a series of maneuvers to disorient me to the attitude of the aircraft. After several maneuvers, he gave me control. I immediately raised my head and checked my airspeed and attitude indicator. I was in a steep right turn and near stall speed. I simultaneously applied max power, lowered the nose, and leveled the wings. Within ten seconds, I had recovered to normal flight. He said, "Good. Take us home."

I said, "Roger," and looked out of the aircraft to get my bearings. What I saw surprised me. Everything was so green and looked so different that I did not recognize one landmark. I was lost. I quickly looked at my compass heading. I was flying northwest. That was wrong. I turned south, hoping I would see something I recognized. The SIP saw my confusion and said, "You are heading to Douglas."

I was instantly aware of my position when he said that. I turned smoothly toward Fort Huachuca and said, "Thanks. I was totally lost. Everything is so green that I did not recognize a thing."

I was not really lost. I would have flown on a 180-degree heading until I recognized some landmark. I would have quickly recognized one of the towns since the green color wouldn't disguise them. On the course I was flying, I would have seen Bisbee and Douglas in a couple of minutes. That would have been all it took to confirm my location.

Claudia and the kids got back from Germany just before the kids started school again. I was happy to see them again. While there was pain while she was gone, there was joy when she returned. We were super nice to one another, as if to make up for the time apart. Michele was glad to return to her horse and horseback riding. She made it clear that she did not want to go to Germany again. She was fourteen going on twenty and entering the terrible teenager phase.

After a couple of weeks, we were back into our normal routine. Claudia played tennis each day with her friends. Some nights, when I did not go to the craft shop, we would play tennis under lights. On Fridays, she went to Tucson with two or three friends, and on Sundays, she either hosted a coffee or went to a friend's house for one. Once every couple of weeks, we would go to a party at someone's house. It was our social routine.

We continued to squabble for no clear reason. I tried to follow other couples while we were out to see if they acted the way we did, but in public, people are normally on their best behavior. I wanted to have a loving relationship that was anger free. I would look in the mirror, take the blame for our spats, and then try to make up with her. She always took the position that I made up just to have sex. Nothing I said or did would change her mind.

I started reading books on marital relations. I genuinely wanted to fix the problems between us. I looked for our situation in each book I read. One theme was a common thought in each book: the notion that when couples fight, it is not typically about the issue that started the fight. It's usually about some unresolved hurt or issue that is held inside until vented over some unrelated issue. The most common subject couples argue over is money. However, once the argument begins, it changes into one over anger that has nothing to do with money. That's what troubled me about us. I would get mad about something trivial, and before I knew it, I was in a full-blown fight about something I did not understand. The way she would bring up events from the past that had nothing to do with what we were arguing about made sense after reading those books.

I never brought up past events that had hurt me. I prided myself on the fact that once I forgave a hurt, it was over. It might linger in my mind, but I would never bring it up again. The one act I had not forgiven her for was the way she continued to make me feel she was being unfaithful. The distrust came from the friends she associated with more than anything else, such as Marcy Smith, who had influenced her enough to get her to move Atlanta, Georgia. I didn't like the all-day shopping trips she went on to Tucson with shady girlfriends whom I knew. Sometimes she would spend a week in El Paso with another shady girlfriend. That girlfriend's husband had been in the army and stationed at Fort Huachuca. We had been friends with them until he found out she was running around on him, and they'd divorced. He'd moved to Tucson, and she'd moved to El Paso.

I am sure that what she believed I had done weighed heavily on her mind, but when we were together, I tried never to do something that would cause her to distrust me. When we were at parties, I was by her side and gave her my maximum attention. I had read that trust was sacred between couples. Once destroyed, it could never return. I did not believe that. I knew I loved Claudia so much that if we ever fixed our relationship, there was no way I would ever cheat on her again. It was not in my soul.

That summer, the army announced that Israel was buying several Mohawks. Part of the agreement was for us to train the TOs. A group of Israeli officers arrived at the end of September to start training on the different sensors. I flew three of the officers on IR training missions.

Their demand for preciseness on each mission impressed me. They selected their targets and planned the mission. I noticed that each target was well out of our local area. That meant long flights between each target. During each flight, the ability of the student to keep me on the exact heading to the target impressed me. They all closely checked the time and ground tract on the map. Periodically, they gave me commands to turn left or right half a degree. Since my compass only measured to the degree, I would touch the rudder to make the course adjustment. Sometimes they would have me adjust airspeed. I would make the corrections, and at the same time, I wondered why they insisted on such detail.

We flew precisely over the target at the estimated time, which was impressive. No US students ever found the target that accurately. Their navigational skills were awesome. Since they were foreign students, we kept a professional relationship during the entire time we trained them. At the end of the training, they threw a big party for us to express their gratitude.

At the party, I could speak to my students and praise them on their navigational skills. That was when I found out that they were also F-4 navigators. I found that their serious approach to training and their skills were essential to Israel's survival. Israel was a nation of four million people. Surrounding them were more than ninety million people who wanted nothing more than to destroy them. To defend Israel, they might have to attack targets hundreds of miles from their borders. Pinpoint navigation was essential to get to the target and back. As such, when they trained, they prepared for that mission. I gained a new respect for the people of Israel after that night. It was a great party. While the Israeli officers trained hard, they partied hard too.

The United States Army Security Agency and Test Evaluation Center, located at Fort Huachuca, had been running some airborne tests of emerging electrical systems. Fort Rucker adapted two Mohawks for them to use as the aerial platform. In October, they finished the tests. Because of the extensive electronic adjustments to the aircraft, it was too expensive to refit them for their original missions. Fort Rucker decided they would mothball one at Davis-Monthan AFB in Tucson. They wanted the other one flown back to Fort Rucker. It was an easy adjustment to put dual sticks in it and use it for student training.

The USASATEC did not have pilots assigned, so I had to put one of my pilots on TDY with them to support their tests. The other pilot was on TDY also, and after the test, he returned to his unit. USASATEC asked MAD to fly the Mohawk back to Fort Rucker; they would pay for the TDY costs.

All my pilots were flying training missions, so I decided I would fly the aircraft to Fort Rucker. I scheduled a major in the combat development directorate to be my copilot. He needed flight time to keep his currency and flight pay. It was hard for him to get away from his desk job to fly. At least that was his excuse. We planned on him flying to Fort Sill, Oklahoma, on the first leg. We would refuel and spend the night there. The following day, I would fly all the way to Rucker.

Two days before I was going to leave, my phone rang. I answered it, and the caller identified himself as Captain Brown, aide to the CG of Fort Rucker. After he verified I was the pilot flying the Mohawk to Fort Rucker, he told me the CG wanted me to load the instrument bay with cases of Coors beer. He said the CG would repay me for the cost of the beer. I asked him why it would not be easier to buy it there. That was when I found out that at the time, they did not sell Coors beer east of the Mississippi River.

The day before we left, I bought eight cases of Coors and loaded them into the Mohawk electronics bay. I guess you could say I was using an army aircraft to bootleg beer. However, I could not tell the CG that I would not do it. That would be akin to committing professional suicide. When we took off, we barely had room to put our small bags in the bay because of the beer.

As planned, we landed at Fort Sill, refueled, and spent the night. It was fun to fly cross-country again. We filed an IFR flight plan, but the weather was clear all the way to Fort Sill and forecast to be clear at Rucker also. As planned, the major flew the leg to Fort Sill, so I flew the leg to

Rucker. When we got over Mississippi, we started running into towing cumulus. The flight got bumpy as we busted through the clouds. I told the major that I hoped the turbulence did not shake the beer up too much. We started running into rain about eighty miles west of Fort Rucker, and approach control began vectoring us around thunderstorms. After several vectors, they turned me onto a GCA. I busted out of the clouds at the middle marker and landed.

As I rolled out, ground control told me to follow the truck at the end of the runway. The truck guided us across the airfield to a mostly deserted apron. There, two staff cars were waiting. When we got out of the Mohawk, a captain walked up and asked if I was Captain Griffin.

I said yes, and he said he was Captain Brown. "Do you have the CG's stuff?" he asked.

"Yes," I answered. "There are eight cases in the equipment bay."

"Great," he responded as he motioned for one of the staff cars to pull over by the Mohawk. "How much does the CG owe you?" he asked as he motioned for the driver to load the beer into the trunk of the staff car.

I pulled out my receipt for the beer and handed it to him. He looked at it and said, "Man, that's cheap," and he counted out thirty-six dollars. He continued, "Captain, the CG really appreciates what you have done. He has provided his staff car and driver for your use. He will take you wherever you want to go. I presume you are flying back to Fort Huachuca in the morning. Let him know what time to take you to the airport in Dothan. If there is anything else you need, give me a call at this number." He gave me a card with his name and phone number on it. That was the way general aides were—all business and to the point. He got into the staff car with the beer. We got into the other staff car.

We flew out of Dothan the next morning on American Airlines. After a two-hour layover in Dallas, we made it to Tucson midafternoon. We had to wait an hour for the Fort Huachuca shuttle bus, and we finally made it home. That night, I smiled to myself. Now, along with pimp, I could also call myself a bootlegger.

My main passion now was making jewelry. On the weekends, Claudia would play tennis, while my friends and I would explore for minerals. At least two or three times a week, I hit the crafts shop after dinner and worked on my creations until it closed at 2200. The only coral available was orange coral, which was expensive when you bought it at craft shops. It was not the same as red coral and lacked the beauty red coral had when mixed with deep blue turquoise. One day in September, Kathy told me that someone she knew had a bunch of red coral for sale. I told her I wanted to buy some, so she said she would arrange for me to meet the guy selling it.

About a week later, she told me the guy would meet us at a rest stop on the outskirts of Benson. Benson was a small town about twenty miles from Sierra Vista. That night, I met Kathy at the hangar, and we drove to Benson. We pulled into the rest stop and stopped beside the only car there. It was dark and a little scary. I was thinking, *Suppose this is a setup to rob us.* Before we got out, I asked Kathy if she was sure this was a safe deal. She said an old friend had vouched for the guy we were meeting. We had to meet like this because it was illegal to sell red coral from the Mediterranean.

We got out of the car and walked to the other car. The guy asked who we were, and when we identified ourselves, he got out of his car. He opened the trunk of his car and revealed several bags of red coral and turquoise. I picked a small bag of coral that cost me $160. It was worth it. From what I bought, I could cut and polish more than a hundred cabs.

Two or three bracelets with red coral and turquoise would sell for more than $200, so the trip and the money I paid for the red coral were well worth it.

About the middle of October, Staff Sergeant Willis called. He was the husband of one of Claudia's German girlfriends. He wanted to know if I still made Indian jewelry. I said I did. He told me that his wife's birthday was in a week, and he had no idea what to get her. He wanted to know how much I would charge to make her a bracelet and a ring. I thought for a minute and then asked him how much he wanted to pay and said I would make a bracelet and ring for that amount. He had been looking for something around a hundred dollars. I said, "Okay, get me the ring size, and I will make it." I felt bad charging him that much, because we knew each other, but what I would make him would be worth a hell of a lot more than a hundred dollars.

His wife was a close friend of Claudia's. She was an attractive blonde. Of all of Claudia's girlfriends, she appeared the most honest and sincere. She always came to Claudia's coffees and was one of the last to leave. She went to Tucson with Claudia often. She was always at the parties but most of the time without her husband. She did not come on to other men, as the rest did. Another detail about her that struck me was an occasional sadness in her eyes at times.

Staff Sergeant Willis dropped by my office the next day with one of her rings. I told him I could size it and make the ring the same size. He seemed relieved that I was making her the jewelry. It was as if he had gotten out of a bind.

I started to work on the bracelet and ring that night. I cut and polished four turquoise and four red coral cabs. Then I shaped a bracelet out of a solid piece of one-inch-wide silver stock. I annealed and shaped it until I had a formed and balanced bracelet. The next night, I prepared the bezels for each cab and soldered them onto the bracelet. After that, I made twelve silver beads—two the size of the stones, then two smaller ones, and so on until I had six for each side of the bracelet. I soldered them on each side of the bracelet in descending size. On the third night, I carefully mounted the cabs into the bezels. I alternated one turquoise and one red coral. After they were all mounted, I examined the piece for any flaws. The instructor stopped by several times to look at what I was doing. He complimented me on my work and wanted to know if I wanted to enter it in a crafts show coming up in two weeks. I told him no, as I had already sold it. He asked how much I had sold it for, and when I told him, he shook his head. He told me I was selling my art too cheap. The bracelet was worth three times that.

After he left, I went to the buffers and spent an hour polishing the bracelet. After I finished shining it, I used some liver of sulfur to create a patina effect around the mounted stones. After that, my bracelet was a beautiful piece of jewelry.

The following night, I cut a quarter-inch-wide piece of solid silver stock to make the ring. I sized the ring Staff Sergeant Willis had given me and cut the silver band to that length. Again, I annealed, shaped, and filed until the ring was the exact size of the sample ring. I used hard silver solder to solder it together. Next, I cut and polished two turquoise cabs and one red coral cab. I prepared the bezels and soldered them to the band using a soft solder. I mounted the stones and polished the ring. Again, I carefully used liver of sulfur to create a patina around the stones. When I finished, I set the ring beside the bracelet to see if I had achieved a matching bracelet and ring. The combination was perfect. It was the best work I had ever done. I placed the pieces in a box with cotton to give to Staff Sergeant Willis.

I had taken unusual care while making the set. For some reason, I'd felt compelled to make it the best quality possible. I was proud of the finished product. It proved to me that I could take orders for jewelry and satisfy the customer. I hoped Staff Sergeant Willis's wife liked it.

I called Staff Sergeant Willis and told him the jewelry was ready. He came to my office, and I handed him the box. He opened it and lifted the bracelet out to look at it. As he looked at it, he said, "Wow, this is beautiful. Are you sure a hundred dollars is enough?"

I said, "Yes, that's all."

He handed me the money and said, "Thanks again," and he left.

Kathy had looked at the bracelet and ring when I brought them into the office. She shook her head, saying, "That jewelry is worth much more than a hundred dollars."

The day after Staff Sergeant Willis's wife's birthday, my phone rang. I answered it, and it was Staff Sergeant Willis's wife. She said, "Neal, I got your number from Claudia. I hope you don't mind me calling you. But I had to tell you how much I love the bracelet and ring. My husband told me you made them for me. Because you made them, they will always be special, and I will treasure them forever. Thank you so much."

I replied, "It was my pleasure. I hoped you would like them."

She said, "I do, more than you can imagine. I'll let you go now. I hope I see you at the next coffee."

"You will," I answered, and she hung up. Her call pleased me. Her gratitude was genuine. It made me wonder why I thought I sensed a little sadness in her. There was something more than gratitude in her tone, but I did not think any more of it. I hoped her happiness over the bracelet and ring would make Claudia a little proud of me and my artistic skill. She never seemed excited about the jewelry I made, even though she liked the money I made from selling it.

Claudia had a coffee the next Sunday afternoon. Several of her friends came, including Staff Sergeant Willis's wife. She was wearing the bracelet and ring. Everybody was complimenting her bracelet and ring. She looked at me with a sensuous smile and said, "Neal made them." That resulted in my getting several compliments.

It was a fun afternoon with coffee and bear claws, followed by chips and dip and several bottles of wine. Over Claudia's insistence that we keep partying, everybody started leaving around 1800, except Staff Sergeant Willis's wife. She stayed, and we kept drinking wine and eating snacks. She was drinking wine as if she were trying to get rid of the blues. Around 2000, I noticed that she was starting to get a little tipsy, so I suggested that Claudia make some coffee. However, she wanted wine. Around 2100, her husband called to see if she was coming home.

That triggered an angry response from her. In a slurred and loud voice, she told her husband she was not coming home. She was staying with Neal. Claudia and I were a little tipsy, but we had not drunk half the wine she had, so we took her comment to be the alcohol talking. Out of character, she sat down in my lap. She put her arms around me and, in a drunken and pleading voice, said, "Can I stay with you?"

Claudia laughed and said, "No. We are going to take you home now." Claudia looked at me and said, "Come on, Neal; we need to take her home. She's had way too much to drink."

I agreed. I was a little unsure of what Claudia was thinking. I tried to get up, but she would not get out of my lap. She kept saying, "I don't want to go home. I want to stay here."

I said, "You can't stay here. Your husband is waiting for you to come home."

That got a fiery response from her. "I don't want to go to him. I hate him. I want to stay here."

I could see that she was about to pass out, so I told Claudia to open the car door. I would carry her out to the car. I managed to lean forward in my chair and rise, picking her up with me. She put her arms around my neck kept moaning, "I don't want to go home. I want to stay with you." I made it to the car and got her in the backseat. I held her while Claudia drove us to her quarters.

She was still resisting when I picked her up and carried her to the door. Staff Sergeant Willis heard the commotion and opened the door for us. When she saw him, she turned to me and wrapped her arms around me, saying, "I don't want you. I want to stay with Neal."

Staff Sergeant Willis helped me get her into the house and onto a couch. He apologized for her behavior. He told us that he had never seen her like this. I apologized for letting her drink too much. She was lying on the couch, almost asleep and still mumbling that she did not want to go home. Staff Sergeant Willis walked us to the door. He told us that she would be okay in morning after she slept if off.

I drove home. Claudia was talking about how drunk her friend was. I asked her if Staff Sergeant Willis and his wife were having problems. She told me she did not know. Her friend had never mentioned any problems. I chalked her behavior up to the alcohol, but I could not deny the reaction I'd had to her sitting my lap and hugging me. It was an intense arousal. I'd wanted to put my arms around her and hold her closer to my body. I honestly did not know what would have happened if we had been alone. I chalked that up to the moment and the alcohol I had consumed. I cautioned myself about my reactions. If I loved Claudia, I should not have the sexual reaction I'd had. I never said anything to Claudia about it.

Her friend called her the next day to apologize. She said she'd drunk so much that she could not remember how she'd gotten home. Claudia told her what had happened. I do not think Claudia mentioned the way she'd sat in my lap or what she'd said. Anyway, the next time I saw her friend, she did not apologize to me. She just smiled and held her arm up to show me she was wearing the bracelet and ring.

It was the end of October 1975, and I was about a year from retirement. I started thinking about what I would do after I retired. It was a little like when I'd graduated from high school. I honestly did not know what I wanted to do. I had two choices to consider: I could apply for a pilot position with one of the airlines—my multiengine experience and commercial license were big factors in my favor—or I could apply for a job with the National Transportation Safety Board (NTSB) as an accident investigator. My training at USC would help me get into that field. But I did not know what I wanted to do.

After lunch, I went to the latrine. Before returning to my office, I combed my hair. For the first time, I got the impression that my left eyeball was protruding slightly. While I had noticed my left eye tracking downward as I combed the left side of my head, the protruding was something new. I felt my eye with my fingers, but everything seemed normal. I dismissed it as lazy eye muscles and returned to my office.

I did not think anything else about my eyeball until the following week. It was November 4, and I was about to make a discovery that would change my life forever. I noticed that as I looked down, I could see part of my face that I did not remember seeing before. I shut my left eye and looked down but did not see that part of my face. I shut my right eye and repeated the process. I could see part of my face with my left eye.

That got my attention. I thought maybe my left eye was protruding, so I took a pencil and placed it over my right eye. It formed a bridge between my forehead and cheekbone. I tried the same thing on my left eye, and to my surprise, I could not make a bridge. My left eye stuck out too far. I repeated the process several times but got the same results each time. Now I was convinced that my left eye was protruding.

I called Kathy into my office. I looked at her and said, "Kathy, take a look at my eyes. Look closely, and tell me if you think my left eyeball may be protruding from the socket."

She walked up to me, studied my eyes for a few seconds, and then said, "Yes, Neal. I think your left eye is sticking out farther than your right eye."

"I thought so," I said. "It's been like that for a while. It just dawned on me today that it was actually protruding."

She shook her head and told me I needed to get it checked. I told her I had taken my flight physical six months ago, and everything was fine with my vision. If there had been a problem, the flight surgeon would have detected it when he examined my eyes.

Then she said something that alarmed me, because I had not thought of it: "Neal, it could be a tumor pushing your eye out. You need to get it checked!"

Now I was a little concerned. I had never entertained the idea of a tumor pushing my eye out. I realized then that I had to have an optometrist check my eye. I looked at the Fort Huachuca organization chart and found the number of the optometry department at the hospital. I called, and a nurse answered. I asked to speak with a doctor, and she asked why, so I had to explain my problem to her. She listened and then said, "You'd better come in so we can see what you are talking about. There's a doctor in the clinic now, so get here as quickly as you can."

I hung up, got my cap, and told Kathy I was going to see the doctor. When I got to the hospital, I went to the optometry clinic and walked in. The nurse I had spoken with was behind the counter. I told her I was Captain Griffin. She told me to follow her and led me down a hallway to the doctor's office.

She told the doctor that I was Captain Griffin. He looked at me and said, "I understand that you think your eye is bulging out. Tell me why you think that."

He listened as I explained how I had noticed my eye tracking downward over the years. I told him about passing the flight physical eye exams. Then I explained what I had done with the pencil to check my eye.

When I finished, he said, "Huh," and he directed me to take a seat in the examination chair. I sat down, and he began to examine my eyes. He looked at me from different angles. He asked me if I ever had headaches or pain in my left eye. When I said, "Never," he shook his head as if it were hard to believe. Then he took a pencil and tried to bridge my left eye. I watched him nod his as if agreeing with me. After checking my eyes for about fifteen minutes, he walked back to his desk and sat down.

He looked at me and said, "I've never seen anything like this. Your left eye is definitely protruding a centimeter or so. You say you have never had any pain associated with your eye. I cannot find anything wrong with your vision. Your eye looks healthy inside. I do not know what the problem is, but something is pushing your eye outward. I need to get you to a hospital with more capability than we have here. You have three choices. You can go to the naval hospital in San Diego, the army hospital in San Antonio, or the air force hospital in Denver. I do not recommend the naval hospital. Naval doctors are notoriously bad. Brooke Army Hospital in San Antonio is a teaching hospital. That's where I recommend you go."

He looked at me, waiting for an answer. I replied, "Okay, I'll take Brooke Army Hospital. When do you want me to leave?"

He made some notes on my records and said, "I want you on the medevac flight out of Fort Huachuca in the morning."

The urgency in his voice frightened me a bit. I was not prepared to leave that fast. I was concerned. Before, I had been curious about what was causing the eye to protrude. Now, from his tone, I had the impression I was facing something dangerous to my health. "What do you think the problem is with my eye, Doctor?" I asked.

He looked at me and said, "I don't know. It could be for several reasons, some bad and some not so bad. We need to get you to a place where they can find out what's wrong. Be at the airfield at 0800 in the morning. The air force medevac stops by here. I will make all the arrangements to get you on it and admitted to Brooke Army Hospital."

I left the clinic in a depressed state of mind. I drove to the airfield and explained my condition to Major Turner. He was astonished and asked me all about my eye. After I explained everything, he told me not to worry. He thought if it was something bad, I would have felt some pain occasionally. He told me not to worry about anything and to go on home. He would call everybody and explain what was happening.

I drove home, trying to think of a way to tell Claudia so that she would not worry. Then, feeling sorry for myself, I thought, *Why worry about that? She never worries about me anyway.*

When I walked in, she was surprised. She responded in the usual way: "What are you doing home?"

The way she asked that always amused me. I replied in my usual way: "Because I live here."

She shook her head, expressing her dislike of my response. "I mean why are you home early?"

I got a beer out of the refrigerator and told her what had happened. She listened with an expression of disbelief. When I finished, she asked, "Is it serious?"

I tried to downplay my concern so as not to alarm her. "I don't know, honey. The doctor said it's probably not something life threatening because of the long time I have noticed it."

She looked hurt. "You never told me about a problem with your eye. What else are you keeping from me?"

I assured her there was nothing else wrong with me. I explained that I'd never mentioned my eye to her because I'd never thought there was anything wrong with it. "It was only after Kathy broached the subject of a tumor that I decided to have the doctor check it. He could not figure out what was causing the problem. That is why he is sending me to Brooke AH. The doctors there are the leading experts in the army on eye problems."

I turned the conversation to the issues she would have to take care of while I was gone. Since I did not know how long I would be gone, there were several bills she would have to pay. She never failed to astound me. She got upset because she would have to do this. It was as if she thought I was leaving just so she would have to take care of the tasks I normally did. It upset me a little that paying some bills worried her more than my condition. Fortunately, we did not start a fight over my having to go to the hospital.

I had trouble sleeping that night. I could not keep my mind off the object behind my eye. It had to be a tumor. What else would push the eyeball out of its socket? The good news was the length of time I had noticed that my eye was tracking wrong. It had been at least six or seven years, maybe more, since I first had noticed the problem. The doctor had said that meant that whatever was causing it was growing slowly. That was a positive sign since cancerous growth is usually fairly rapid. I left the house the next morning feeling apprehensive about what fate awaited me.

I boarded the AF medevac that morning with two other soldiers. The plane had made a round-robin from San Antonio to Anchorage and down the west coast, picking up patients. Fort Huachuca was its last stop before returning to San Antonio. The aircraft was almost full of patients. Several were on stretchers. Most appeared badly injured or seriously sick. I felt a little silly explaining why I was going to Brooke Army Hospital. A bulging eye that had perfect vision and caused no pain did not seem serious.

The medevac landed at Lackland AFB around 1100. An army bus picked up the walking passengers, while ambulances picked up the ones on stretchers. The bus took us to an admission center. It took about fifteen minutes for the technicians to complete the paperwork, put an ID band on my arm, and admit me to Brooke. When he completed that, he directed me to ward C on the second floor.

Ward C was a male-only ward. It was a large room with two bays and several private rooms. A huge latrine and shower were located between the two bays. The nurses' station was near the latrine. I took my medical folder to the nurses' station and gave it to the captain at the counter. She looked at it and at me. She placed my records on a clipboard and made some notes. When she finished that, she looked at me and asked if I had a medium waist. I said yes, and she opened a metal cabinet and took out a dark blue robe and two light blue pajama bottoms and tops. She handed them to me and told me to follow her.

She led me into one of the bays to an army cot. The cot was identical to every army cot I had seen before. A rolled mattress sat at the end of the cot. On top of the mattress were two sheets and two wool blankets, folded neatly. On top of those was a pillow, and on top of the pillow was a pillowcase, folded neatly. She pointed to the cot and said, "That's your bunk. Stay in or on it or in the bay. You can leave the bay to use the latrine or go downstairs to the mess hall. If you want to go anywhere else, you will have to sign out at the nurses' station."

She told me to put my pajamas on and make up my bed. The robe and pajamas were standard wear for the ward and mess hall. A nurse would be by in a few minutes to take my vitals and start my chart. The wall locker at the rear of the cot was for my use. She recommended I get a lock for it. She asked me if I had any questions, and when I said no, she gave me a small booklet. She told me to read it. It was the SOP for the ward. There were no exceptions to it. With that, she left. She was a cute captain with a no-nonsense attitude. I decided my challenge would be to get her to smile before I left.

I looked around the bay. There were fifteen cots lined up in army fashion. Six of them had patients on them. The two individuals occupying the cots to my right gave me sloppy salutes when I looked at them. Both said, "Welcome aboard, Captain."

I smiled, shrugged, and replied, "Glad to be here."

They walked over and introduced themselves. I made my bed while they explained why they were there. Both had cancer. One had cancer of the throat, and the other one had cancer of the esophagus. They had been there for a couple of weeks, undergoing examinations. The one with throat cancer had just started radiation treatment. The one with cancer of the esophagus was waiting for surgery. The doctors were trying to figure out a way for him to eat with his esophagus gone. Again, I felt silly explaining my bulging eye. They had serious problems, while I was healthy except for my eye, which could be nothing.

A nurse pulling a medical cart interrupted our conversation. She told me to go change into my pajamas and robe. She had to take my vitals. I went to the latrine and changed. I lay on my cot while she took my blood pressure, temperature, and heart rate. When she looked at my blood pressure, she said, "Wow, with pressure like that, you are going to live forever."

I asked her what it was, and she told me 68 over 105. She asked if I felt faint. I told her no and asked why. She said, "You have such a slow heart rate. It's much lower than average." I told her I had exercised all my life, and doctors had diagnosed me with bradycardia. She made a note on my chart about that. While a good sign, my low blood pressure became a pain in the ass. The nurses took vitals every four hours. Each time they took my blood pressure, it was so low that they would take it again to make sure the reading was correct. In the middle of the night, that became irritating.

I walked down to the mess hall with my two new bay friends. The food was delicious, and there was plenty of it. I quickly realized that if I ate three meals a day the size of the one I had at lunch, I would quickly get fat, so I started a PT program. I would walk down the long hallway to ward B and back to the stairs. That was about two hundred yards. Then I would climb the stairs four stories to the top and back down to the hallway. It took me thirty minutes to do that five times. I figured if I did that once a day, I could keep my weight under control. It worked, because I did not gain a pound during my stay at Brooke.

After lunch, I lay in my bunk, wondering when I would see a doctor and find out what was wrong with me. Finally, around 1600, a major stopped by and introduced himself. He was the ophthalmologist and eye surgeon assigned to my case. He told me he would examine me in the morning. That was good news. I expected a quick resolution of the problem with my eye. Sadly, I was going to be disappointed.

Then next morning, a technician wheeled me through the hallways in a wheelchair to the optometry clinic and rolled me into an examination room. After about fifteen minutes, my doctor entered the room. He greeted me and started reading my medical file. When finished, he said, "All right, let's take a look at your eye." He did a complete examination of my eye, and when he'd finished, he looked at me and said, "I don't see anything wrong."

He started asking me questions about my eye: How long had I noticed the problem? Did it ever hurt, or did I ever have headaches? These were questions I had answered several times. Then he asked if I had ever injured my eye. I told him no, except in high school, when a player in a football game had kicked me in the forehead. I'd had to get stitches for a cut above my eyebrow.

After the question-and-answer session, he called a technician in and told him to prepare me for a sonogram of my eye. The technician glued a rubber sheet around my eye, forming a cup. Then he filled the small cup formed by the rubber sheet with water. The doctor moved the sonogram instrument over my eye for several minutes as we watched the screen for any sign of an object or tumor. There was nothing.

The doctor turned the sonogram off and looked at me. "There's nothing in your socket or eyeball as far as I can tell. Frankly, the sonogram can only show us a foreign object and not a tumor. This afternoon, I am going to have some x-rays taken of the left side of your head. I hope we will be able to see something in the x-rays."

That afternoon, the technician wheeled me to the x-ray lab. I tried to get him to let me walk, but he would not. Hospital protocol required me to be taken to all appointments on a gurney or in a wheelchair. I felt foolish, but I did not argue. When the technician had finished the x-rays, he wheeled me back to the examination room. The doctor was waiting for us. He put the x-rays on a reading light and studied them for a few minutes. He shook his head and frowned in disappointment.

He turned to me and said, "There's nothing there that I can see. But the only way we would see a tumor on an x-ray would be because the tumor had eaten into or eroded a bone. We would see the damage to the bone. In your case, there is no damage to any of the bone surrounding the eye socket. That means we are at square one again. I'm going to study the possible courses of action now. When I come up with something, we will try it. I want you to have your thyroid checked tomorrow. I'll see you the following day."

When I got back to the ward, everyone wanted to know how it had gone. All I could tell them was "So far, they have not found anything that would cause my problem." I told them they were checking my thyroid tomorrow.

The one with throat cancer said to look on the bright side. "No news, in this case, is good news." I agreed with him, but on the other hand, I wanted to know what was wrong and what the potential result might be.

The next morning, a technician picked me up with a gurney and wheeled me to the radiology lab. There, I drank some radioactive fluid that would allow the x-ray to see my thyroid work. It turned out that it was normal. They wheeled me back to the ward.

That afternoon, my doctor dropped by and asked if I would mind taking part in a medical review program. I said no. He said, "Good. On Saturday, we'll take you to an examination room. We have invited all the optometrists and ophthalmologists in San Antonio to exam you and discuss your case. It's like an open house, except you will be on display. We hope we can get some ideas or suggestions that will help us diagnose your problem."

The following morning, I sat in an examination chair for about four hours. A parade of doctors examined my eye. They asked me a myriad of questions about whether I had headaches or pain in the eye. My better-than-perfect vision and the absence of headaches and pain in my bulging eye puzzled them. Finally, it was over, and my doctor thanked me and said he would see me Monday morning.

That afternoon, I lay in my bunk, feeling frustrated. I had been there for a week and knew almost no more than I had the day I'd gotten there. I did know the cause of my problem was not a foreign object or my thyroid. That was something. I also was lonely. I decided to call Claudia to tell her the news and find out how she and the kids were doing. I got out of bed and walked to the nurses' station. They had two phones labeled for patient use. Of course, it was difficult to have a private conversation standing at the nurses' station.

Claudia was happy that they hadn't found anything seriously wrong with me. She wanted to know how long I would be there. I told her I did not know. I hoped they would find the problem soon so I could get back before Thanksgiving. She said she hoped so too. She told me my office had called and wanted to know how I was doing. They wanted my phone number so they could call to check on me. The director of logistics had called them to find out how I was doing, so they had to keep him informed about my condition and status. I told her to give them my number and tell them that they had not found anything so far and that there was no word on how long I would be there.

The weekend was long and boring. The highlights were going to the mess hall to eat and my exercise period. On Saturday afternoon, a Red Cross representative came by, pulling a cart with books. I signed for a couple so I would have something to read. I read, slept, ate, exercised, and started the process again. What upset me the most was my good health. I was not sick but was confined to a ward of seriously ill people. I was self-conscious about that. It was hard to feel at ease during our conversations.

Monday started another week of frustration. The doctor repeated all the tests with the same results. The doctors were just as frustrated as I was. The one point they all agreed on was that the problem was not a malignant tumor. At least they were pretty sure because of the mass's slow growth based on my reports. However, its continued growth would eventually destroy my sight in that eye. Furthermore, there was a possibility that it could turn malignant. Their inability to diagnose my problem stymied them. On top of that, I found out that I would be unable to go home for Thanksgiving.

Because of my unique status, the army cut orders temporarily assigning me to Brooke AH. Medical leave was not allowed. I could take a pass, but Fort Huachuca was beyond the distance limitations for a pass. That pissed me off. I was not sick. I was in good physical condition, and if I had not brought attention to my eye, I would have still been at home and at work. Now I was stuck in the dismal ward of a hospital for God knew how long. Claudia was upset that I could not come home for Thanksgiving. She seemed angry with me for not being able to come home. In retrospect, I don't think she was angry, but the way she expressed her disappointment came across to me as anger. She wanted to know when they were going to find out what was wrong with my eye, but all I could tell her was that I did not know.

It was actually Kathy who cheered me up. She called every two or three days. We would talk for fifteen or twenty minutes. She encouraged me to be patient. They would find something eventually. She would fill me in on what was going on in USAICS, plus all the latest rumors. Major Turner called once a week to check on me. He reminded me that hospitals were for sick people, and if I was not sick, I should think about coming back to work. I had to laugh at that suggestion. I would have to go AWOL to go back to work.

The weeks dragged by with no developments on my eye. Every Saturday, I underwent the show-and-tell period with all the eye doctors in San Antonio. I think they even flew a few in from out of town to examine the captain with the bulging eye. However, the collective wisdom of all the doctors who examined me was not enough to diagnose the cause of my bulging eye.

One day, out of boredom, I wrote a note that said, "Help me, please. I am being held against my will." I remembered reading about a similar joke. That afternoon, when the Red Cross volunteer came by with her books, I slipped the note into her hand. She looked at me, and I put a finger over my lips, signaling her to be silent. I looked around as if to make sure no one had seen me give her the note. Then I waved her away. She had a startled expression on her face. The note in her hand and the desperate look on my face obviously confused her. She walked away without reading the note. She looked back once at me and disappeared toward the nurses' station.

I was lying in my bed, waiting for the response. I heard the static the loudspeaker made when someone turned it on. Then a stern voice boomed, "Captain Griffin, report immediately to the nurses' station."

I walked up to the nurses' station, trying to suppress a smile. The major in charge looked at me and, in a firm voice, said, "Very funny, Captain Griffin."

I could see the note I had written in her hand as she continued to chew my ass out for conduct unbecoming of an officer. I kept saying, "Yes, ma'am," as I agreed with her. I could see the cute captain pretending to look at some records with a big smile on her face. I had known I would make her smile. Finally, the major ran out of words or steam and tossed her head with a short laugh. "Look," she said, "you do not have to hang around this ward every night. You can sign out on pass and go wherever you want to. You just have to be available during the day. The doctors are working hard to find out what's wrong with your eye."

She was right. I could sign out on pass, and I knew that. But what would be the purpose of going on pass? I was not the type to sit in a bar and drink. I had no reason to go shopping. What other reasons would I have to go on pass other than just to get out of the hospital? However, the major's little talk caused me to think about taking a pass. I could take a bus downtown and stroll along the River Walk. That might be fun on a warm day. The weather in San Antonio during November and December is unpredictable. One day it's hot, and the next it's cold.

I did eventually start going out on pass. My positive outlook dimmed as time passed without the doctors finding out what was wrong with my eye. Once I started going on pass, I began to enjoy going downtown to the mall or the River Walk. Usually, on the way back, I would stop at the officers' club to drink a couple beers and play the jukebox. I seldom saw more than four or five officers in the club. I could sit and enjoy my beers and music without having to engage in a conversation. A couple of beers were all that was necessary to help me sleep. Sleeping at night had become a problem because of naps I would take while hanging around the ward.

By the second week in December, there were still no results. I was beginning to think I would spend Christmas there, when the doctors got a break. They managed to schedule me for a new imaging x-ray called a computer-aided tomography scan, or CAT scan. At the time, there were only four of the machines in the United States. Fortunately for me, Methodist Hospital in San Antonio had one. The CAT scan provided three-dimensional imagery of the region around my eye and inside my skull. It would enable the doctors to see what was causing my eye to bulge.

For the first time since the standard tests had failed to discover my problem, I had hope that at last, we would know something. Of course, that did not mean it would be good news, but by then, I just wanted to know what was wrong, treat it, and get back to my life. With hope mingled with the fear of impending bad news, I prepared for the CAT scan.

An army ambulance took me to Methodist Hospital on a gurney. They rolled me into the CAT scan room and transferred me to the table section of the CAT scan. I felt like an idiot during the whole process. I could have caught a taxi to the hospital like any healthy person. The ambulance ride made me feel foolish. The technicians carefully placed me on the table. They fixed my head on a precise spot and braced it. I would have to hold that position without moving for fifty minutes.

When they had me prepared for the procedure, they retreated behind a lead curtain. The machine hummed to life, and the table I was lying on began to move forward into a tubelike area. I could see my head slowly pass through a spinning sensor of some type. I shut my eyes and focused on not moving. Time passed slowly as I moved into the tube and back out of the tube. Finally, my head was out of the tube, and the scan was over. As usual, I had to lie there while a radiologist checked the imagery to ensure they had everything. Then it was back on the gurney, into the ambulance, and to the ward.

I had to wait until the next morning to find out the results. Emotionally, the wait was like many of the exams I had taken in flight school or OCS. I hoped I'd done well, but I was not sure what well was in this case. I pretty much knew that the issue had to be a tumor or growth of some type. I just had to hope that it was not malignant.

After breakfast the next morning, the cute nurse walked up to my bunk. I stood up and said good morning. She smiled and said, "Good morning to you. Dr. Cook wants to speak to you in his office. Do you remember how to get to it?"

This was it. I was going to find out my fate. I smiled at her and answered, "Yes, I will never forget how to get to it as long as I am on a gurney. No gurney this morning?"

She shook her head and said, "Nope, you can walk." Teasingly, she continued, "The walk will do you good."

She turned and left. She had been working around thousands of patients. Probably just as many had tried to hit on her. I have always liked to think that had I tried, I would have been successful. There was something in the way she used her eyes when we spoke. She looked back once and smiled before disappearing out of sight. I put on my robe and headed up the stairs to the corridor leading to Dr. Cook's office.

Dr. Cook was sitting in an exam room, waiting for me. He told me to come in and have a seat. He looked at me and said, "I have some good news and some bad news. Which do you want first?"

That is never a good choice to hear from your doctor, but it was better than hearing only "I have some bad news." My heart was racing, and I felt as if I were trembling. I looked at my hand to make sure it was steady. Whatever the news was, I wanted to take it calmly and bravely. I replied, "I'll take the good news first."

"Well," he said, "the good news is that the cause of your eye bulging is a hemangioma. A hemangioma is a mass of blood vessels and capillaries that bundle into a tumor-like formation. It's benign. Because it is normal body tissue, we couldn't see it with standard procedures. The bad news is that it's situated around the optic nerve, within the muscle cone of your eye. Over time, fatty tissue has formed, and vessels and capillaries have grown. The eye socket is a precisely machined space to hold your eye. Any growth within has no room to expand except to push your eye out of the socket. Therefore, you can see how that has happened to you. There are many hemangiomas all over your body doing no harm. The problem in your case is its location. Unfortunately, it formed inside the muscle cone and in the eye socket."

He paused to let that information sink in. I felt much better in knowing that I did not face some form of cancer. He continued, "The question now is what to do about it. Do we watch it and wait on any decision, or do we look at removing it surgically? So far, it has not caused you any pain, but as it continues to grow, it will cause pain. Now would be the time to remove it, because the smaller it is, the less damage there will be to the eye from the surgery. Why don't you think about it and let me know tomorrow what you want to do? Do you have any questions?"

I said, "Yes. How will surgery affect my vision? If it's around the optic nerve, won't that cause damage to my eyesight?"

He answered, "In all honesty, there will be some damage to the optic nerve. I can't promise there won't be. I just can't say how much damage. The problem is that the larger it gets, the more damage we can expect. That's why now is better than later."

I looked at him, hoping for some reassurance, but he just looked at me. I knew the decision was up to me. He had done all he could for now. I told him I would think about it and come see him in the morning.

I spent the rest of that day mentally going over my choices. I was a year away from retirement. Would it be better to do the surgery now while I was still in the army or wait? Finally, that night, I decided I would have the surgery. I prayed to God for his blessing. During my prayer, I found myself wondering why God should hear me. I only went to him when I needed his help. I did not honor him in what I did or failed to do. Now I was frightened and calling on him once again to forgive me and protect me. I could look back over my life and see the many times he had protected me and given me the intelligence to succeed. I prayed he wouldn't run out of patience with me.

The next morning, before I told Dr. Cook my decision, I asked him what he would do if he were me. He said he would have the surgery now. I nodded, agreeing, and said, "That's what I want." He asked me if I was sure. I said yes. I had committed myself. I had to trust God and Dr. Cook that I would come out of surgery as good as I had gone into it.

Dr. Cook had already told me there would be some damage to the optic nerve. I was optimistic that it would be little and not be a cause to ground me from flying. He went on to explain how the surgery would go. They would saw a triangular piece of bone out of the side of my head and approach the eye from there. I immediately had second thoughts about the surgery when he told me that. The idea of someone sawing into my skull shocked me. I felt a wave of weakness come over me, and I had a sensation that I would faint. I took a deep breath and slowly let it out. I felt a little stronger after that, and slowly, the sensation of fainting left. What scared me was the sawing part. However, I managed to convince myself that it was just the idea that was frightening and not the procedure.

Controlling my emotions was one of my strengths. I managed to shake off the image of my skull with a piece of bone removed. By then, Dr. Cook was explaining that anytime you mess with the optic nerve, there is a chance of damaging it. Like the spine, the optic nerve cannot repair itself after trauma. Their focus during the surgery would be on removing the hemangioma with minimal damage to the optic nerve. He then explained that they needed to do one more procedure before the surgery.

He had scheduled me for a venogram of the eye region in the morning. He explained that a venogram is an x-ray test that takes pictures of the blood flow through the veins in a certain area. During the procedure, the radiologist injects dye into the veins, and as blood flows, the x-ray can make an image of it. While the CAT scan gave them a picture of the hemangioma mass, a venogram would detail each blood vessel and how the vessels formed the mass. It seemed like a simple procedure that would be important in helping the surgeons.

The next morning, they wheeled me into the x-ray room on a gurney. The radiologist came up to the gurney, introduced himself, and explained what he was going to do. First, he had to ask me some questions. The questions were the usual ones about previous injuries, illnesses, and allergies. When I told him I was allergic to shrimp, he seemed alarmed about it. He asked me if I was allergic to iodine. I told him I did not know for sure. I told him I could eat all seafood except shrimp. He told me he had to check that out with an allergist before he did the venogram. The dye used in the venogram contains iodine. Iodine is what most people allergic to shrimp are really allergic to. He left me lying on the gurney in the hallway.

I lay there for about an hour before a technician stopped by and asked if I was okay. I told him yes and asked if he knew how much longer it was going to be. He said he did not know. The radiologist was still checking the danger to me from the iodine. With that, he left. Another hour went by, and just like the time I was in recovery from the hernia operation, my back started to hurt. I was turning and twisting in every possible way to ease the pain. I knew the only way to ease it was to stand up and get off my back.

Finally, the pain was so bad that I sat up on the gurney. That was equally uncomfortable, but it eased the pain little. It was not much, but it was just enough so that I could bear it for a while longer. The hallway was empty, and I had not seen anyone since the technician more than two hours ago, which added to my frustration and discomfort. Just when I decided I'd had enough and was going to climb off of the gurney, I heard voices.

I could see the radiologist and another doctor coming down the hallway. When they got to the gurney, the radiologist said, "I'm sorry that took so long, Captain Griffin, but we have to be sure the venogram is not going to cause you any problems. Dr. Able is with me. He's an allergist and will help me during the venogram."

He rolled me into the x-ray room and said, "This is how we're going to do it. I'm going to insert a needle into the large vein over your right eye. It feeds the blood to your left eye. When I'm ready to take the x-rays, I will inject dye into that vein. I want you to apply pressure on the artery below your left jaw just before I insert the dye. While you hold pressure there, I will insert the dye and take a series of x-rays. First, I need to position the x-ray machine."

He moved the x-ray arm over my head. I had to lie on my right side with the x-ray plate under the side of my head. He positioned it and told me to hold still. I felt him insert the needle into the vein in my forehead. That was not at all painful. Then he told me to put pressure on the arteries.

When he was satisfied that I had pressure on the arteries, he told me he was injecting the dye and said I needed to keep the pressure and hold still until he told me to relax.

When he injected the dye, I was not ready for the intense pressure and pain I felt. I flinched, and he said, "Oh yeah, I forgot to tell you about the pain. It won't be for long. Now, hold everything until I tell you to relax."

I could hear the x-ray machine clicking as I struggled to remain still. The pain in and around my eye was almost unbearable on top of the pain in my back. At last, I heard him say, "Relax." I released the pressure on the arteries and tried to move my back without moving my body position. He told me to hold still until he checked the film.

About five minutes later, he returned and told me we had to get some more shots. He repositioned me, and we repeated the process. The pain was just as bad as it had been the first time. It seemed like an eternity before he said to relax.

Again, I waited for his return. He was gone a little longer this time, but when he returned, he said, "That's it. We got what we need." I pleaded with him to let me off the gurney so I could walk back to the ward. He would not do that, but he let me stand up for a few minutes before the technician wheeled me back to the ward.

I felt beaten from the pain in my eye and back. I got up and took a shower before I went to lunch. After lunch, I did my PT walk. When I got back to the ward, I found a note lying on my bed. It said to give Dr. Cook a call. I walked to the nurses' station and called him.

He told me, "The venogram was exactly what we needed to plan the details of the surgery, and I have scheduled the surgery for the seventh of January. I am going to put you on convalescent leave beginning tomorrow, the fifteenth of December. The nurses will prepare your leave papers. I want you back on the second of January. Do you have any questions?"

I answered with a resounding "No, sir." I was jubilant. I was off for two weeks. It seemed as if I had been there forever. At last, I was going home. All I had to do was find a ride to Fort Huachuca.

I called Claudia and told her the good news. She wanted to know when I would be home. I told her I did not know exactly. I was going to try to get a hop. If that did not work, I was going to buy a ticket and fly commercially. She encouraged me to get a hop because she did not want to spend the money for an airline ticket. I told her I would try, but I wanted to get home the fastest way I could. After she hung up, I felt joyous that she was as excited about my coming home as I was.

I ended up having to buy an airline ticket. I got to Tucson in the afternoon and managed to catch the Fort Huachuca shuttle bus. When I walked into the house, Claudia and the kids were eating supper. Michele and Ron ran to hug me and ask if I was okay. Claudia said, "Hi. Welcome home." I joined them for dinner, and the time at Brooke AH seemed far away. Again, it amazed me that in just a few hours, someone's life can changed radically. I'm not talking about a tragic or disastrous event that changes life. I'm talking about being someplace, living a different life, and then, in just a matter of hours, moving from that world back to a world where you have a familiar life. My many assignments that had me in Vietnam one day and the United States the next day or Korea one day and Germany the next day always made me aware of that tempo in life.

I went to the office the next day to say hello and report my status. I had to explain the cause of my eye bulging and my surgery several times. I had many well-wishers, but none were as caring as Kathy. She felt responsible because she had urged me to have my eye checked out. She had called me every week to see how I was doing. Claudia had called me twice.

I had become good friends with Kathy and her husband, Pete. During the last summer, he had decided to build a swimming pool. He'd dug the pit for the pool and put the plumbing in. Then Matt, some of Pete's friends, and I had gathered at their house for a weekend pool party. We'd laid the blocks to form the walls that weekend. During the week, Pete had poured the floor of the pool. The next weekend, we'd plastered the walls of the pool and prepared the forms for the walkway around the pool. During the week, Pete had poured the walkway. One weekend later, we'd had a big party and swum in the pool.

Kathy and I, by working together, had become close. It was difficult for me to preserve the supervisor-to-worker relationship, but I did not let the friendship affect my professional duties. However, Kathy was going past what her duties required. On nights when I flew students, she stayed until I'd completed the last flight. Before Jake left, he would bring his camper to the flight line. He would use the operations FM radio from his camper and control flights from there. During ground time, while we exchanged students, he provided coffee and treats that Kathy brought.

I enjoyed the attention. I got from her what I was missing at home. She appreciated me and took pride in what I did. She always had a smile and an encouraging word. However, all of this attention was not without cost. Pete and Kathy began to have marital problems. I began to feel I was the cause of the problems. I enjoyed going mineral hunting on the weekends, and so did Kathy. Pete did not have any interest in that, so he never went. Claudia did not have any interest, and she did not go. Kathy, Matt, my next-door neighbor and his wife, and I usually went. We stopped by Johnny Ringo's on the way home to drink beer and dance. We had fun; there was no denying that. Sometimes I got the feeling Kathy was asking for more, but I was over the budget clerk and wanted no more involvement with anyone other than Claudia.

Claudia and I were soon in the Christmas bustle. Claudia was writing many Christmas cards to Germany. We had presents to buy and a Christmas tree to decorate. Since I was present, I had the operations section plan and put on a potluck Christmas party for the MAD personnel. Claudia and her girlfriend came to it. Her girlfriend wore the bracelet and ring I'd made for her. I circulated among my men and the civilians at the party. Each time I looked at Claudia's friend, she was looking at me. So was Kathy. Talk about being the wrong person at the wrong time.

In the noise of the many conversations echoing through the hangar, my mind wandered. I was talking but in a robotic sense because my thoughts were adrift. I was thirty-seven years old, and for some reason, I had become attractive to women. Was that true, or was I just imagining it? Until I'd left Korea, I'd never felt attractive to anyone. Now I kept asking myself, *Why this attraction?* It was coming at a time when I really did not want it. I just wanted Claudia's attraction. Before I'd gone to Korea, no one had seemed attracted to me in the least. There had to be something new that I was projecting to cause women to find me interesting. I thought the answer was twofold. First, Claudia was so beautiful that other women found me desirable because anybody married to her had to have some appeal. Second, Claudia treated me badly. Her friends knew that either by their observations or Claudia's conduct. They must have believed I would welcome the attention of another woman.

I was keenly aware that I had lost my moral compass between Korea and now. I was struggling to find it and get back on an honorable course. I believed that my eye problem was God's way of calling attention to where I was. It was a nudge for me to clean up my act. I had become a person who did what I often warned Claudia about. I'd let the actions of someone else dictate who I was. I had let Claudia's conduct become the excuse for my bad behavior as a man and a husband. That was a flimsy excuse because I knew I was responsible for what I did or failed to do.

Now the temptation was before me again. I could detect the offers in the smiles of two attractive women. On the surface, they were friend-to-friend smiles, but below the surface, they promised much more. Claudia interrupted my trance. "Neal, we're leaving now. I'll see you at home."

I looked at them and said, "Thanks for coming. I hope you enjoyed the party."

Claudia's friend smiled and replied, "It was fun. Thanks for inviting me."

I watched them walk out of the hangar. One of the TOs asked me if I wanted to play spades. I said sure and joined him as his partner in a game of spades.

I ended the party around 1800. By then, most of the people had left. It took us half an hour to clean the hangar and put everything away. When I got home, Claudia's friend was still there. She had drunk quite a bit, but when she saw me, she laughed and said there'd be no repeat of the last time. She stayed for one last drink, and Claudia drove her home.

The days passed quickly. With each day, I became more apprehensive about my coming surgery. I kept telling myself to trust in God and the doctors. The idea of them sawing my skull open worried me the most. Claudia fixed a nice roast for Christmas dinner, and the weather cooperated, providing almost a foot of snow.

We went to one of Claudia's friends' houses for a New Year's Eve party. It was fun. I drank a lot. I danced a lot. I danced with Claudia and with her friend. Again, her husband did not attend the party. During a slow dance, she pulled me tightly against her and squeezed my hand for the whole dance. It was late, and no one was watching the dancers any longer. I tried not to notice her body against me. When the dance was over and we pulled away, I squeezed her hand to recognize her actions. She whispered a thank-you as we walked back to our seats.

I caught the air force medevac on January 2 and was back at Brooke AH that afternoon. My bunk was just as I had left it. One of my bunkmates was gone. They had transferred him to another hospital. There were several new patients suffering from various cancers. Matt was right: a hospital is for sick people, and no one should stay in one if he or she can help it. The ward nurses were all smiles as they welcomed me back. I marveled again at how fast location can change life. The night before, I'd slept in a warm bed with my beautiful wife. Now, just hours later, I was in a drab hospital ward with strangers joined together in illness.

The evening meal on January 5 provided my last food and water before surgery. On January 6, Dr. Cook examined me again to make sure there were no changes in my health. By then, I was hungry. He had sympathy for me but only allowed me to drink a glass of water and nothing else.

The morning of January 7, a technician with a gurney arrived at 0700. He wheeled me down a new corridor to a door marked "Surgery." Inside, he wheeled me to an area where they transferred me to a different gurney. There were several doctors and nurses in the room. A man in a surgical suit came to my gurney and introduced himself. He said he was my anesthetist. He asked me some questions about my weight and allergies. He asked me to describe why I was there, just to make sure he had the right patient and right procedure. Then he inserted a shunt into a vein in my arm and taped it down.

Dr. Cook walked up in surgical dress and asked me if I was ready. I said yes, and he motioned for a nurse to push me into a room marked "Operating Room." The anesthetist followed us into the room. They rolled me up to a table under some bright lights and transferred me to the table. Several people in surgical gowns and masks gathered around the table. The anesthetist said, "Okay, Captain Griffin, I'm going to inject something to make you sleep. I want you to start counting backward from one hundred."

I said, "Okay," and I started counting. I convinced myself I would make it to at least ninety; however, the world went dark at ninety-six. My next sensation was a terrible urge to pee. My eyes were shut, and I was in some dark place with the urge to pee. I tried to say something but could not form words, so I started moaning as loudly as I could.

I sensed a figure beside me and heard a distant voice ask, "Are you okay?"

"Pee," I mumbled. "Pee."

The voice, a little clearer now, asked, "You have to pee?"

"Yes," I mumbled with urgency.

"Okay," the voice said. "I'm putting a bedpan under you."

I felt hands lift me, and something cold slid under me. The voice said, "Okay, go ahead." I could tell now that it was a female voice.

I was still semiconscious. I tried to pee. No matter how hard I tried, I could not make myself pee while lying down. Even though my bladder felt as if it were going to burst, I could not pee. I tried to speak again, but all I could do was moan. The female voice asked, "What's wrong?"

I tried to open my eyes to see, but they would not open. I struggled to form words but managed to say, "I can't pee lying down. I've got to stand up, please."

I heard the female voice tell someone, "He can't pee lying down." Then she spoke to me again. "Okay, we are going to stand you up and hold a container for you to pee in. But you are going to have to hold your penis."

I was conscious enough to think that was funny. I tried to laugh but made some strange noise and replied, "I'll hold it."

I could feel hands turning me to the side of the gurney so my feet hung down. The strong hands eased me to my feet, and I felt my robe pulled to the side. I could feel two people holding me erect. Then the female voice said, "Okay, I'm holding a container. Go ahead and pee."

I moved my hand and found my penis. I could not see where I was peeing. I just let it go into the dark. After a minute or two, the voice said, "Wow, you did have to pee."

Finally, my bladder felt empty, and I muttered, "I'm finished. Thanks. I'm sorry to be a problem."

As the arms returned me to the prone position back on the gurney, the voice said softly, "You're no trouble. That's why we are here."

As soon as I was prone, I started drifting into darkness again. I asked the darkness as it descended, "Why did I have to pee? I've had nothing to drink in over twenty-four hours."

The urge to pee woke me again. I tried to speak, but again, all I could do was moan. I was groggy. The familiar voice asked, "What's wrong?"

"I've got to pee again," I mumbled.

The voice said, "Okay, wait a minute till I get my partner and a container."

A couple of minutes later, I heard her say, "Okay, you know the routine. We are going to stand you up now."

I felt them move me to the upright position. When she told me to go ahead, I tried to open my eyes. I managed to get the right eye slightly open enough to see what I was doing. This time, when I finished, I looked at the two nurses holding me. They wore captain bars on their white smocks. I tried to smile and, still slurring my words, said, "I'm finished. Thanks again. Next time, I'll stand myself. I don't know why I have to pee so much. I haven't had anything to drink in days."

As they put me back on the gurney, one said, "No, you will stand when we say you can. We will keep standing you up as long as necessary. The reason you have to pee is because of the saline solution we're pumping into you."

Now it made sense. I drifted back into darkness. I don't know how long I was out, but it wasn't the urge to pee that woke me. I was sick to my stomach and had to throw up. My gagging and heaving as I tried to rise attracted a nurse. It was a different nurse. She helped me sit up and put a container under my mouth. I heaved up bile for a few minutes until the sickness passed. She left a new container on my nightstand and told me to use it when I felt I had to heave.

I lay back down. I could see now out of my right eye. I couldn't open my left eye, which was bandaged anyway. I wasn't drowsy like before. I looked around and saw that I was in an intensive care unit. I saw the nurse returning to my gurney. She asked me how I felt.

I said, "Okay for now." She took my blood pressure and temperature. I noticed that I was hungry and thirsty. I asked her if I could have something to eat and drink. She brought me two crackers and a small cup of apple juice. She told me to be ready to heave it up. Five minutes after I consumed it, I threw it up.

That became the routine for the next four hours. I threw up about every thirty minutes. After about four hours, whatever was making me feel nauseated left me. By then, it was morning, and I felt better.

About 0800, Dr. Cook came by to see me. He examined me and asked how I was doing. I described my bout of nausea. He told me he'd expected that. It was also a bad sign. Historically, it signaled damage to the optic nerve. He removed the bandages on my left eye as he explained what they'd done during surgery.

"A plastic surgeon aided in removing and replacing the bone from the temple area of the left eye. His purpose was to ensure no scars would show. He removed a triangular piece of bone to provide access to the tumor. The hemangioma was the size of a small egg and found around the optic nerve inside the muscle cone. They had to peel the tumor from around the optic nerve like peeling an orange. I needed three pints of blood during the operation. They removed the hemangioma and closed the site. The plastic surgeon sewed your eyelids together to protect your eyeball during healing. I will remove the stitches in a week, and we will be able to judge how much, if any, vision you lost. I can promise you there will be some vision lost. I hope it's minimal, but we've got to expect it." He asked me if I had any questions. I asked when they would move me back to the ward.

He told me that as soon as I could hold down food, they would take me back to the ward. After he left, the nurses brought me some pills for pain. Frankly, I had little pain, considering the extent of the invasive surgery. The only discomfort I felt was the nausea.

The bouts of nausea became less frequent by the afternoon. The nurses let me walk to the latrine now. They walked with me to steady me if I needed it. I asked for food, and they brought me a small serving of mashed potatoes, some green beans, and a little piece of chicken breast. I ate it and had no problem holding it down. They kept me there that night and rolled me back to the ward early the next morning.

After I got back on my cot, my ward buddies gathered around to find out what had happened. I explained the surgery the way Dr. Cook had explained it to me. They congratulated me on the mass not being cancerous. I thanked them and wished them the best for their upcoming surgeries. The nurses brought me breakfast, lunch, and dinner that day. The cute captain brought some pain pills each time she came to take my vitals. I refused them because the pain was not bad enough.

About midmorning, I had to go to the bathroom. I got up and, with a little wobble, shuffled to the latrine. The sight of my eye shocked me. It was swollen. It was black and blue, and small pieces of dried blood clung to the stitches holding my lids together. The place where they had cut open my skull was still bandaged, so I could not see what it looked like. I looked grotesque. A nurse had told me that I had to go to the mess hall for meals tomorrow. Looking at my eye, I did not think that was a good idea. I would ruin breakfast for people with weak stomachs. I mentioned this to the nurse, but it did not concern her. She told me there were patients who looked a lot worse than I did eating in the mess hall.

That evening, Claudia called to see how I was doing. After that, Kathy called. After Kathy called, the aide for the commanding general of USAICS called. The general got on the line and wished me a speedy recovery. We chatted for a minute or two. He asked about my family and if they needed anything. I thanked him and said they were fine. He ended by telling me to call him personally if I needed anything. I thanked him, and he hung up.

Back in my bunk, I reflected on his call. He did not know me well, but I was one of his officers, and he was the commander. He did what good commanders do: he made sure that I was well and that my family was taken care of. You cannot ask for more than that. The next day, I received a get-well card signed by most of the MAD personnel. It was a usual gesture, but it still made me feel good that they were thinking of me. All of this attention made me glad that I had the surgery in San Antonio. I guess it was selfish of me to be thankful that no one could come visit me, but as I said before, I prefer no visitors while I'm in the hospital.

At first, I was self-conscious when I entered the mess hall to eat. I really did not look good. My eye was swollen, with my eyelids stitched together. It was black and blue and seemed dirty since I could not wash it. However, I did not gross anybody out, so I soon got over being self-conscious. The doctor had warned me about doing anything strenuous. He worried I'd rip out stitches, so I did not do my PT while the stitches were still in.

A week later, the swelling was gone, and the doctor removed my stitches. It was similar to a scene in a movie in which a doctor removes the bandages while everybody waits to see if the patient can see again. In my case, he was removing stitches from my eyelids. The suspense was the same, though. After the stitches were out, the doctor flushed out my eye to clear the lubricant they'd applied to it before they'd stitched my eyelids together.

Because of my optimistic nature, I expected to see as soon as my eye was clean. It shocked me to find I had no vision except a small cat eye of sight that was diplopic. I could see no more than half of a man's face with twenty-ninety clarity. The little bit I saw was up and to my left. The doctor examined my eye and tried to hide his disappointment. He told me the trauma to the optic nerve had caused it to atrophy. He was sorry and disappointed, but whenever there is trauma to the optic nerve, there will be damage. I asked if my vision would improve in time. He said maybe a little, but he did not expect it would improve much.

Just like that, my life as I had known it was gone. I could no longer fly unless the army would give me a waiver. I would not be able to get a job as a pilot with an airline. Those were just the immediate impacts that I could think of. I had no idea how many other changes I faced.

When he'd finished with my eye, he took the bandage off the side of my head. He cleaned the stitches and bandaged my eye. He told me it looked good. They would remove the stitches in a couple more days. He told me to continue taking it easy and said he would see me in a couple of days. I could see that he was genuinely upset over the loss of my eyesight. I later learned that he was Mormon and a caring man. I did not in any way regret having him do the surgery. He was an instructor at the army medical school and one of the best-qualified eye doctors in the army.

All my ward mates were as disappointed as I was over the loss of vision in my left eye. I was discovering something else about the little vision I had. Because it was diplopic, the double vision caused my eyes to feel strained as the muscles tried to focus them. The little vision I had in the left eye was not enough for my brain to focus it with the right eye. Plus, after several hours in the sun, I would feel eyestrain of a different sort. My left eye wouldn't dilate fully. When the pupil in my right eye dilated, the pupil in my left eye remained the same. I felt a constant strain from the dual effect of diplopia and the pupil not dilating. That was something I had to learn to live with, or I'd have to have my left eye removed. One doctor said he could fix the issue by killing the little vision I had left. In the end, I decided to live with the discomfort.

One other immediate impact was the lack of depth perception. I had grown somewhat used to it while my eye was bandaged. Now it was a permanent condition. I was okay at distances beyond twenty feet. Twenty feet is the range where both eyes center vision into one image. I had the same depth perception as anyone at twenty feet or greater. However, distances twenty feet or closer caused me problems. I could not catch a ball or any object tossed to me. Half the time, when I reached to shake hands, I would miss the other person's hand. I had to overcome hundreds of little habits like that. My life had changed, but I was fortunate because I still had vision in one eye.

I called Claudia that evening and told her the bad news. She was sympathetic but worried about how it would affect my army career. I told her that it did not change anything, except I would no longer be on flight status and draw flight pay. However, I planned on applying for an exception to the policy that grounded me. I knew of several one-eyed pilots on active duty. She wanted to know when I was coming home. I told her I did not know yet. We ended our conversation with her asking me to let her know as soon as possible.

That night, I lay in bed, pondering my future. I had to retire by next December. That was less than a year away. What was I going to do then? The employment opportunities in the Fort Huachuca and Sierra Vista area were slim. Most people worked for the government on post. The jobs in Sierra Vista were mostly service-type jobs that paid little. I would have to wait six months before I could apply for a civil service job on post. I could use my GI Bill benefits and go to college. That and the little unemployment benefits I had coming would provide enough until I could take a job on post.

However, I had another alternative. I had been reading advertisements for managers needed at Red Lobster restaurants. The Red Lobster seafood restaurants were popular and expanding. An individual would apply and, if accepted, attend a food manager course provide by Red Lobster. After the person graduated, Red Lobster would assign the individual to an assistant manager position at one of their restaurants. The only problem was the individual had no choice of location. The demand for managers was coming from new restaurants in remote locations, such as Montana and Wyoming. I knew that Claudia would not go with me to some small town in Montana.

What kept my morale up was my belief that God had always taken care of me. He would do it now. I just had to find out what he had in mind. I figured something would develop over the next nine months. I took an optimistic view again. God had given man two eyes for a reason.

If something happened to one, he still had the other one. Looking around my ward, I saw men much worse off than I. They faced death, while my concern was what to do when I retired.

The next morning, I received get-well cards from the commanding general of USAICS and from MAD. That was a nice gesture, and it prompted the nurses to say, "You must be an important captain for the CG to send you a get-well card."

I played the game and replied smugly, "Yes, I am."

With the cards came a set of orders. In disbelief, I read,

> Captain Wimberly N. Griffin is hereby reassigned to personnel company, Brook AH, Fort Sam Houston, Texas, with a reporting date of January 31, 1976. The individual will be medically retired under the provisions of army regulation 40-63, paragraph 7-23, and atrophy of the optic nerve. Individual is authorized movement of family and household goods.

I was in shock and pissed. My immediate thought was *I do not want them to medically retire me, especially not now. This must be some mistake.* With the orders in my hand, I walked to the director of optometry's office and knocked on the door. I heard someone say, "Come in," and I entered. A colonel sat behind the desk. He had the same name as the officer who had signed my orders.

I saluted and reported. "Sir, Captain Griffin. I do not have an appointment to see you, but I just got these orders assigning me to Fort Sam Houston for medical retirement. Sir, I do not want a medical retirement. I want to serve out the rest of my time and retire in November. Besides, my family—and everything else—is at Fort Huachuca. I would have to move here and then move back to Fort Huachuca. That does not make good sense."

He put his hand up for me to calm down. He reached into his outbox and pulled a set of records from it. I could see they were my records. He opened the records, looked at them for a few seconds, and then looked at me. "Captain Griffin, you have atrophy of the optic nerve. The army requires us to medically retire you. There's no choice about it."

"I understand, sir," I replied, "but there must be some way I can appeal that decision."

"Not according to the regulations," he said, shaking his head.

I knew it was useless to continue talking to the colonel. He was not going to change his mind, so I politely said, "Thank you, sir." I saluted and left.

I walked back to the ward, desperately trying to figure out a way to get the orders changed. I decided that first I needed to read the army regulation used as an authority to retire me. I put on some civilian clothes and signed out on pass to visit the personnel company.

I caught the post bus to the personnel company. After telling the first clerk what I wanted, he led me to a small room with a bookcase of regulations and told me to help myself. I found the volume with AR 40-63 in it. I turned to the paragraph quoted in my orders and started reading. I read it quickly, and it shocked me to read that the army must medically retire or discharge personnel with atrophy of the optic nerve, depending on their status. I sat back in disbelief.

After sitting there in anger with no means to unload it, I decided to reread the paragraph. This time, the key terms popped out. The paragraph said personnel with atrophy of the optic nerve subsequent to disease would be medically retired or discharged. I was elated. That was not my case. My atrophy was following surgery, not disease. I carefully read the entire regulation to make sure there was no requirement to retire me as a result of surgery. There was not. It was clear that the stipulation was only for disease. I asked the clerk to make me a copy of the page covering atrophy of the optic nerve following disease, and he made me two copies.

I caught the bus back to the ward. This time, I called the colonel's office to schedule a meeting. I did not want to anger him by busting in without an appointment. He agreed to see me the following morning at 0800. That night, I read the paragraph on atrophy of the optic nerve until I had every fact memorized. I had to convince him not to medically retire me.

I knocked on his door the next morning precisely at 0800. He said to come in. I entered, and in my best military form, I stepped before his desk and reported to him. He returned my salute and asked what I wanted. I stood at parade rest as I spoke. "Sir, you are retiring me because of the atrophy to the optic nerve in my left eye, citing AR 40-63 as the authority for it. I have carefully read the AR. It states the army must retire a patient for atrophy of the optic nerve subsequent to disease. My medical records state that my atrophy is subsequent to surgery. Therefore, I do not have to be retired. I respectfully ask that I not be retired. There is nothing preventing me from doing my job with vision in one eye. I wish to get back to that job as soon as possible."

He looked at me with what appeared to be anger and frustration. "Let me see your copy of the paragraph," he said as he pointed to the papers I held. I handed it to him. He read it slowly. Then he leaned back in his chair and said, "Look, Captain, we are trying to help you. By our medically retiring you, your retirement pay will be tax free for the rest of your life. That's a big savings if you live another thirty years. But if you do not want that, then I am not going to force it on you."

Before he asked me, I said forcefully, "I do not want it, sir."

He nodded and said, "Okay, Captain, these orders will be rescinded. As soon as it is possible, we will discharge you back to active duty. Now, get out of my office."

I saluted him and said, "Thank you, sir." I did an about-face and marched out of his office. I waited until I was outside to pump my fist and say, "Yeah!"

I felt damn good while walking back to the ward. All my ward buddies were happy about my win against bureaucracy. Thinking about my position, I decided that God had put me in this situation for two reasons. The first reason was to teach me to never again blindly trust doctors. Once we knew what the issue was, I could have continued with a bulging eye for years or at least until it started causing me problems. The second reason was to teach me to examine events and not just accept them because the army said so. I figured God had closed the doors in my future that needed vision in two eyes. If he'd done that, then he'd certainly opened doors that I had not considered. Now I had to find those doors.

Ten days after my surgery, the doctors removed the stitches from the side of my head. You could not see the scar from the incision. The plastic surgeon had made the incision in a wrinkle line to hide its existence. That had worked better than the rest of the procedure. To this day, there's no sign that doctors removed a piece of my skull and put it back. The doctor warned me not to bump or injure the site where they'd removed the piece of bone. It would take several weeks for the bone to heal fully. Then he told me they were putting me on convalescent leave for two weeks. After that, I could go back to work.

At last, it seemed my life was back to normal. I checked the AF medevac flights and found there was one stopping in Phoenix the following day. I got a seat on it. All I had to do now was get to Fort Huachuca. I called my operations branch and talked to Kathy. They were happy I was coming home. I told her to see if one of the Mohawk pilots needed some cross-country training and schedule a flight to Phoenix to get me. I would be there at 1800. I called Claudia next to tell her when I would be home. The phone rang and rang with no answer. There were no answering machines yet, so I could not leave a message. I decided I would either surprise her or chance being surprised.

I could hardly sleep that night. I kept waking up and checking my watch. Finally, I fell into a sound sleep around 0400 and overslept. The nurse roused me out of my sleep as she made her rounds. I took a shower and shaved. I dressed and had breakfast. Then I had to wait for the 1500 shuttle bus to take me to the airfield. There's nothing more boring than hanging around a hospital ward.

I had cleared my bed and put the sheets in the laundry bin, so I waited in the lounge room. I was just about to leave, when the loudspeaker announced that I had a call at the nurses' station. It was Claudia, calling to see how I was doing. When I told her I would be home around 2000, she was suddenly upset. She asked why I had not let her know I was coming home. I told her I'd just found out yesterday afternoon, and when I'd called, no one had answered the phone. I told her I'd called again that morning, and no one had answered. She hesitated and then told me she was visiting her friend in El Paso for the weekend. The kids had two days off because of a teachers' workshop, so she'd decided to drive to El Paso on Wednesday afternoon.

That made me angry and, I guess, jealous. I'd expected her to be home. She knew I would be coming home anytime. Then she asked me if I minded her staying for the weekend. I told her I would really appreciate her being home when I got there. She fired back that she did not see why she had to be home just because I was coming home. In anger, I told her I did not give a damn what she did, and I slammed the phone down. No sooner had the phone quit shaking in the cradle than it rang again. Thinking it was Claudia, I answered it.

It was Kathy. She wanted to tell me that one of the IPs would pick me up in Phoenix. I thanked her, and she said she bet Claudia was glad I was coming home. Mad, without thinking, I said, "I don't think so. She's in El Paso, visiting friends for a week." Kathy said she was sorry to hear that. I told her I had to leave now to catch the bus for the airfield.

We hung up, and I grabbed my bag and walked out to catch the bus. I could hear the phone ringing as I started down the stairs. I was heartbroken and wondering what or who was in El Paso that interested Claudia more than me. I had thought we were doing better in our relations, but I could see now that she was the same Claudia. At the one time in my life when I needed reassurance and support, I got only indifference and the same betrayal. Such was my mood as I headed back to Fort Huachuca and my uncertain future.

Randy, one of my WOs, was waiting for me in the private pilots' lounge when I got to Phoenix. We filed an instrument flight plan to Libby AAF. He helped me load my bag, and we climbed into the Mohawk. It was one of the training Mohawks with dual sticks. He asked me if I wanted to fly it back. I said yes and took the controls. I was at the controls of an aircraft that I had so much experience in that I could fly it skillfully under any conditions. However, now the lack of depth perception caused me to fumble around as I reached for the various control knobs. They were not where I saw them. I managed to fly the aircraft, but I knew I was not the same. Over time, I would develop visual cues to aid me in overcoming the effects of having no depth perception, but first, I would do some stumbling and fumbling.

The flight to Libby took an hour and a half. Randy filled me in on what was happening at the office. There were no major problems, only the usual personality conflicts between the pilots assigned as instructors in the training department and our pilots. Both groups felt they were the experts. One major event was coming up: the aviation company of the Georgia National Guard was coming to Fort Huachuca for summer camp. They would bring eight of their Mohawks with them. The advanced party would be there next week to coordinate their stay and use of the airfield.

As we passed Tucson, we canceled our IR flight plan and turned directly toward Apache Pass. I called the tower for landing instructions over Apache Pass, and the tower cleared me for a straight-in approach. I did the prelanding checks and made a normal approach. When we got on short final, I told Randy to get on the controls with me in case my roundout was too high or going to be too late. Theoretically, depth perception would not affect me on landing. A pilot looks down the runway at distances greater than twenty feet for his sight picture to round out. However, I wanted to make sure I did not screw up and damage the aircraft. It turned out to be a safe landing. It was not a great landing, but considering it was my first one in two months, it was not bad. It turned out to be my last flight in the Mohawk.

It was 2000 and after duty hours. MAD was closed, except a crew chief was waiting for us. After we filled out the logbook, Randy gave me a ride home. I got out of his car, thanked him, and watched as he drove off. Seeing Claudia's car parked in the carport surprised me. I thought, *What the hell is she doing back*?

I walked in through the kitchen door. Claudia was sitting on the couch, watching TV. She had an angry scowl on her face. All I could think to say was "What the hell are you doing here? I thought you were in El Paso."

She said, "I was."

"Damn," I replied, "you must have driven pretty fast. I just spoke to you four hours ago."

Before she could answer, the phone rang. I answered it. It was Kathy. I said sweetly, "Hi, Kathy."

She said, "You're home. Listen, why don't you meet us down at the Hillbilly Club? We'll celebrate you coming home."

The volume on the phone was loud, and I was sure Claudia could hear what she said. I told her I could not make it. Claudia was home, and I was exhausted. She tried to talk me into coming, but I thanked her for caring and said we would have a party later. I looked at Claudia; she was looking at me. I could see the anger in her face. She asked bitterly, "Is that your girlfriend wanting to see you?"

I did not want to have a fight. It dumbfounded me to see her there. I'd expected her to be in El Paso. I answered her without rancor. "No. It was just Kathy. A group of my friends are at the Hillbilly Club. They wanted me to come make it a welcome-back party. They did not know you were here."

She seemed puzzled. "Why did they think I wasn't here?"

"Well, when you hung up, the phone rang, and it was Kathy, checking on me," I explained. "She wanted to know if I wanted her to call you to let you know I was coming home. I told her not to bother, because you were in El Paso."

She looked away as if embarrassed that Kathy knew she'd been in El Paso. She was still upset that she'd had to come home. I was curious why she'd come back, so I asked, "Why didn't you stay in El Paso?"

She said, "How could I stay and enjoy myself? You threatened me by telling me I could do whatever I wanted and then hanging up on me."

I cautioned myself not to argue, so I tried to answer with no anger. "All I meant was that you could stay or come home. I did not care. If you are angry, it's because you feel guilty about something. I do not want to argue tonight. I'm tired. I'm glad to be home and able to sleep in my own bed tonight. I'm going to take a shower and sleep in that bed."

With that, I carried my bag into the bedroom and left her siting on the couch. I unpacked my bag and put the dirty clothes in the washing machine. I took a shower and went to bed. I was not upset. I told myself it was stupid for me to expect anything more from Claudia. It would have been nice for her to ask how I felt or say, "I'm glad you are okay," or do anything that showed she was a little concerned about me. However, all I got was her anger because I'd disturbed her visit with her friend.

The kids were already asleep when I got home, so I did not see them until the next morning. They were glad to see me and wanted to know what had happened. I told them about the surgery. They gasped when I told them the doctors had cut a hole in my head. I could tell they were worried that something bad was wrong with me. I was careful to put them at ease about anything being seriously wrong. I told them the bad part was that I could not play catch with them again, because I had no depth perception and could not catch the ball. They did not understand how that would affect me, so I told them that when they got home from school, I would show them.

Claudia had gotten up before me, and she fixed breakfast while I shaved and talked with Michele and Ron. As we ate, I noticed something different in her behavior. There was no hostility toward me. There was no adoration either. She just seemed resolved to be pleasant. I still felt the effects of anger and did not want to give in to peace so easily. I felt wronged by the way she had treated me. I wanted to feel her attention, appreciation, and happiness that I had escaped something life threatening. However, the people with whom I worked gave me the welcome I'd expected from her.

The roller coaster of our life continued. Two days later, all was normal between us. I wanted her love so desperately that I could not stay mad long. As a result, the unresolved issues built up in me. I had to deal with those issues emotionally and still work to keep us happy. I swallowed a lot of pride in those days just to keep my family together. I took it easy, as the doctors had instructed me to do. My thin scar soon totally disappeared into the wrinkle line.

As I healed, I prayed I would regain some vision in my left eye. I struggled to overcome the lack of depth perception but was thankful that I was not struggling with total blindness. The first time I pulled the car into a parking spot, I had to slam on the brakes. I had no idea how close or how far I was from the other cars. I stumbled a lot on curves and steps. It took me about six months to notice that I had developed other visual cues to help me. Of course, I had to relearn how to hit a tennis ball.

It took awhile, but I developed enough new cues to play tennis. Claudia loved it because she could beat me easily. My only problem was returning a ball if it got too close to my body. If it stayed at arm's length to either side of me, I could judge its location more accurately and return it, but when I got in a position where the ball came directly toward me, I had problems hitting it. The other problem was the aching in my eyes caused by the left eye not dilating. That strained my right eye to the point where I tried to wear a patch on the left eye. The patch caused a pressure headache after a while, so I had to find something else. The only choice I had other than killing the little vision I had was to black out the left lens of my glasses. That helped a little, but enough light leaked around my left lens to still cause a tension headache after a while.

I spent most of my convalescent leave at the craft shop. That was where my lack of depth perception affected me the most. Placing tiny pieces of solder in place was trying. I had to redo work because of my failure to line it up accurately. The time I took to prepare a piece of jewelry doubled.

However, I learned to be patient, correct my mistakes, and keep working. It was therapy for my ego and my soul. I enjoyed the feeling of success as other amateur craftsmen admired my work.

I returned to duty feeling rested and recovered. As expected, there was a pile of paperwork waiting for my attention. Catching up on reports and answering correspondence consumed my first two days. Among the correspondence was my request to the Department of the Army to remain on flight status. I filed it even though I did not expect the army to approve it. The army was drawing down and did not need the aviators it had on duty. But I figured it was worth a shot.

The advanced party of the aviation unit from the Georgia National Guard arrived three days after I returned to work. The SIP for the unit, a lieutenant, scheduled a meeting with me to coordinate their operations with MAD. He asked of us fuel support and second-echelon maintenance of their aircraft if one went down. They had their own training exercise planned, using the local area. I offered him the use of my operations section to support his flying, but he turned down the offer. They were going to set up a field site. We coordinated the FM frequencies they would use for command and control of their exercise.

I recommended he use my FM frequencies for emergencies. Our knowledge of the area would be helpful to a pilot in an emergency. I explained that my policy was for a pilot with an emergency to declare it first with ATC and the tower. Then he should contact my operations for advice and help. I could evaluate the problem and help the pilot decide how to handle it. He declined the offer, saying he preferred to handle it through his channels. I told him to stay in touch and let me know if he needed any help as their training proceeded.

A week later, the entire unit arrived. They used the apron on the west end of the field to park their aircraft and set up GP tents to house the personnel. A week passed without incident. They were flying several missions a day and caused no conflict with our student training.

On the following Wednesday at 1000, Kathy came into my office. In an agitated voice, she said, "Captain Griffin, the tower just called. A Mohawk has just crashed on the east range. They want to know if it's one of our aircraft!"

I jumped up and walked to the operations board to make sure. I knew we did not have a bird up, but I wanted to make sure. I looked at my board and saw that it was clean. It had to be a National Guard aircraft. I picked up the phone and told the tower operator that it was not one of our aircraft. If it was a Mohawk, it was one of the National Guard Mohawks. He thanked me and hung up. I picked up our hotline to the National Guard flight operations tent. The sergeant who answered confirmed that a training aircraft had crashed, but that was all he knew.

I could hear sirens now. I walked out of the hangar and joined a crowd of soldiers watching emergency vehicles race down the road toward the east range. It's amazing how fast word of a downed aircraft gets around. I also could see a plume of black smoke rising from the brush. I returned to my office, and since Major Turner was at a meeting, I called the director of logistics and advised him of the situation. He asked me to confirm it was not one of our Mohawks. I assured him it was not.

At 1200, the airfield commander called me. Aviation command had cut orders making him OIC for investigating the accident. He was preparing orders for me to be the lead investigator because of my training. He wanted to meet with me at 1230 in his office. I grabbed a quick bite at the snack truck and walked to the airfield commander's office.

Two captains, a lieutenant, and the flight surgeon were in his office when I got there. He told us that we were the accident investigation team for the crash that had occurred at 0945. He told me I would lead the investigation because I was a school-trained aviation safety officer. He looked at me and said, "What do you want to do first?"

I told him that first, I wanted to know what had happened. He said all he knew right now was that an SIP had been giving a pilot an instrument check ride. He'd shut down one engine to simulate an emergency and could not restart the engine. For some reason, he could not maintain altitude and a safe airspeed on the remaining engine. He'd called the tower over Huachuca City and declared an emergency. The tower had asked him his position, altitude, and fuel status. The pilot had reported he was over Huachuca City at 5,200 feet on a single engine and unable to keep altitude. The tower had cleared him for a straight-in to runway eighteen and asked why he could not maintain altitude. The pilot had responded that he did not know. He'd had to descend at two hundred feet per minute to maintain safe single-engine airspeed. He'd said they had been unable to restart the left engine.

The tower had asked the pilot if he had jettisoned his fuel tanks. The pilot had mumbled, "Oh," and then reported that he had now, but it had not helped. The tower had told the pilot that if he could not make the runway, he should point the aircraft east and eject. The last transmission the tower had heard was hard to understand but sounded like "Eject, Jack!" The report from the emergency personnel on the scene said there were no survivors.

The airfield commander looked at me and asked, "What is our course of action?"

I replied, "First, sir, we need to put some security on the site. We need to keep everybody away from the crash scene until we can complete our inspection of the site."

He called the post commander's office and asked for twenty-four-hour security around the site. After he did that, we got in two jeeps and drove to the crash site. When we got there, two MPs were providing security. The airfield commander told them that post security would relieve them shortly.

I stood for a few minutes, studying the crash site and the wreckage. From what I could see, it appeared the Mohawk had impacted the ground inverted at a shallow angle. Impact must have been at a slow rate of speed, because the impact scar was only about 120 feet long. The aircraft had caught fire on impact or after impact. It appeared fire had destroyed most of the aircraft. I could see both engines, which appeared to be in good shape. The cockpit was crushed and showed fire damage. I could see the remains of the pilot in his seat. All that remained was the trunk of his body. Either the crash had destroyed the rest of his body, or the fire had burned it up. His trunk showed extreme fire damage. The fire had burned about a two-acre area around the crash site before the emergency personnel put it out.

The aircraft had been flying at about 160 degrees when it impacted. I looked to the east and saw the ejection seat. It was lying against the side of a small hill about two hundred feet from the fuselage. I walked over to the seat. Still strapped in the seat and slumped over, the lieutenant looked as if he were sleeping. There was no blood visible. The only sign there was a problem was his color. His face was gray. One arm hung at his side, and the other one lay across his lap.

The parachute, while fully deployed from the ejection seat, was not open. There were no ground scars to show that the seat had touched the ground. The signs were around the seat. It must have slammed into the small hill where it sat.

The rest of the team joined me in front of the ejection seat. They were looking at me as if to say, "What do we do?" I realized why I was in charge. I was the only one who had any clue about what to do. I took charge of the investigation. I told one of the members to get a pad and start a to-scale diagram of the crash site. I said, "Identify and mark every piece of wreckage and its location around the fuselage." I told the flight surgeon to take charge of the bodies after the coroner arrived and released them. I asked the airfield commander if he would gather the flight records of the two pilots from the National Guard unit and get copies of the tower and aircraft communications available for us to listen to. I also asked him to get us a camera so we could take pictures of the site. He left in his jeep to do that.

I had the other member of the team help me measure the ground scar and the propeller strikes. When an aircraft crashes and the engine is still running, the propeller will still be turning. If the angle of impact is shallow enough, the propeller will strike the ground several times before the aircraft impacts the ground. By finding the propeller marks and measuring the distance between marks, one can calculate the speed of the aircraft and the rpm of the propeller. This enables an investigator to decide the status of the engine at impact.

After we completed that, I examined the engines. The left engine had one blade damaged from the impact. The blades were in the feather position. It was obvious that engine was not functioning at impact. The blades on the right engine were mangled from striking the ground, so we knew they were spinning at impact.

Next, we examined the fuse panel and control switches. From what we could see, the Mohawk had inverted and wiped out the cockpit. However, the fire had not destroyed the fuse panel, and the impact had left most of the control switches intact. One reason for checking the fuse panel was to see if any fuses had popped or been pulled by one of the pilots. Sometimes an SIP, when giving a check ride, will shut down an engine by pulling a fuse. I also wanted to know the settings of the instrument and engine switches. It is possible the impact will dislocate switches or knock them out of an original setting, but knowing the possible arrangement of the switches and controls helps confirm other findings.

It took us all that afternoon and the next morning to complete our examination of the crash site. When we finished, I had sketches, pictures, and a description of the entire scene to scale. I also had the maintenance people recover the engines and ship them to Tobyhanna Maintenance Depot. Tobyhanna had the ability to examine an engine and find out if there was a problem with it. It provided this service support for all army accident investigations.

A week later, we got the report on the engines from Tobyhanna. The number-two engine, the right engine, had been operating at full power at impact. The number-one engine, the left engine, was in good shape. After Tobyhanna repaired the minor damage, it started and ran without problems. They found no problems with the engine other than the damage caused at impact.

The afternoon after we got the Tobyhanna report, we gathered in the airfield commander's conference room. We made copies of all the information we had gathered. While the rest of the team reviewed what we had collected so far, I went to the National Guard's operations tent. I wanted to discuss the nature of the flight that morning and to review their safety program and status of aviator training. The lieutenant, their SIP, had been giving the pilot an instrument check ride. The lieutenant was a full-time employee of the aviation company. He was a GS-9 in civil service, and when on active duty, he was a lieutenant. The pilot was a reservist on active duty for this training period. He was a pilot for a major airline and had more than twenty thousand flying hours.

I took copies of minutes from their safety meeting files, which dated back a year. I found that they had had several incidents in the past two years but not in the last eight months. After that, I went to the maintenance shop and reviewed the maintenance records for the downed aircraft. I found something interesting about the aircraft. Several times, pilots had written it up for being unable to maintain altitude and safe single-engine speed. When a pilot tried to hold altitude when flying on a single engine, the airspeed would bleed off until it was necessary to either restart the off engine or descend to maintain safe airspeed. The maintenance personnel had checked the aircraft many times but could find no reason for the problem. I made copies of those write-ups to take back with me.

We met again the next morning in the airfield commander's conference room. By then, only I and another captain were left on the team. I did not need the rest of the team until we met to review all of our findings and work out the cause of the accident. Our first action was to interview all the pilots from the National Guard company. We directed our questions to get an assessment of the morale of the unit and to identify any undue command pressure on their operations. Because of the answers to our questions, we began to see a unit with low morale brought about by command pressure.

Command pressure appeared to be the underlying problem. It might have been a cause in the deaths of the two pilots. In prior years, the unit had had a poor accident record. They'd experienced a chain of accidents that had damaged several aircraft. The commander had addressed the problem with a memorandum threatening to fire the next permanent party pilot who had an accident and get rid of any National Guard pilot involved in an accident. After finding out about the memo, I got a copy of it.

Pilots should not have to pilot an aircraft under the threat of losing their jobs or positions if they have a problem that causes damage to an aircraft. Airplanes are complicated pieces of machinery and subject to break at any time. The pilot is seldom at fault for an engine or system failure. Commanders can question his handling of the emergency and identify training deficiencies. The problem is that command pressure often has a negative effect on how a pilot handles an emergency. In this case, it might have caused the deaths of two pilots.

After interviewing the pilots, we spent the afternoon listening to the tower tapes. By listening to the conversation between the lieutenant and the tower, we could re-create the sequence of events leading up to the crash. The sequence began with the Mohawk in a holding pattern over the Tombstone intersection at nine thousand feet. The lieutenant called the tower and asked for a practice instrument approach to Libby. Libby cleared him for a VOR approach to runway thirty. The lieutenant then directed the pilot flying the aircraft to conduct an instrument approach into Libby AAF. The Tombstone intersection is on an airway between Tucson and El Paso. It's located about thirty miles north of Libby AAF. The pilot simulated calling Libby for an approach, and when the lieutenant controlling the flight cleared him, he left the holding pattern on a course to Libby.

When the lieutenant reported to Libby that they had left the Tombstone intersection, the tower cleared them to descend to and maintain eight thousand feet. They started the descent on a VOR radial to Libby. During the descent, the lieutenant gave the pilot an engine-failure emergency by shutting down the left engine. The pilot reported doing that to the tower.

The flight continued normally until they reached eight thousand feet. By then, they were approaching Huachuca City. The lieutenant reported eight thousand feet, and although it was not on the tapes, he must have told the pilot to restart the number-one engine. The engine would not start. They tried again, and still, it would not start. The lieutenant took control of the aircraft at that point and reported to the tower that they had an emergency. He reported the left engine out and the inability to maintain safe single-engine airspeed without descending to compensate.

The tower affirmed the emergency and cleared him to land on runway twenty-one. The tower asked for altitude and fuel quantity. The lieutenant reported he was now at 5,600 feet with a full amount of fuel. The tower asked him to maintain 5,600 feet, and the lieutenant reported they could not do that. To keep the aircraft flying, he had to descend at a rate of four hundred feet per minute. The tower then asked him if he had released his drop tanks in an effort to lighten the weight of the aircraft. The lieutenant said no and then reported he had jettisoned the drop tanks. The tower asked if that helped. The lieutenant reported, "Negative." The tower asked him for position and altitude. The lieutenant reported, "Five miles north of Libby and southeast of Huachuca City at fifty-one hundred feet." The tower reminded him that runway elevation was 4,670 feet. That was the last transmission except for "Eject, Jack!" The tower tried to make contact, saw the black smoke rising from the east range, and launched an emergency response. At the same time, people around Huachuca City started calling to report that an airplane had crashed on the east range.

We listened to the tapes at least six times to make sure we transcribed them correctly. There was one dispute among us, regarding the exclamation of "Eject, Jack!" Some of the tower personnel and two on the accident investigation team were not sure that what they heard was "Eject, Jack!" The words sounded like something else to them. We played the tapes slowly to improve the sound but still had dissension among the listeners.

I heard "Eject, Jack!" I'm not sure if I was biased by the fact that "Eject, Jack!" fit the expected dialogue in the situation. In my mind, having seen the accident site, I could form a picture of what had occurred seconds before the aircraft impacted.

After listening to the tapes and reviewing all the documentation we had gathered, I told the team we needed to draft our conclusion about what had happened. I asked each of them to study all the data we had collected and be prepared to draft a written report. I suggested we vocalize it first, and then I would take notes and commit them to a written report. We would all review the report and change it if necessary. Once it satisfied us, we would provide it to the airfield commander for his approval and signature. After he signed it, we would forward it to the Army Board for Aviation Accident Research at Fort Rucker. That would end our responsibility if they accepted it.

The following is my summary of the formal report:

> The SIP and pilot were on a routine instrument training flight. The pilot was under the hood in a holding pattern. The SIP cleared the pilot to leave holding and perform a VOR approach to Libby AAF. The tower cleared the pilot to descend to eight thousand feet. That was roughly 2,400 feet AGL at their position. During the descent, the SIP introduced an engine failure by shutting down the left engine.
>
> When they reached eight thousand feet, the pilot tried to restart the left engine without success. They tried two more times to restart, and for reasons unknown, the engine would not start. At that point, the SIP took the controls and declared an emergency. (At that point, unless they could start the engine, they could not make the

airfield. The terrain in the San Pedro Valley rises to the south. The aircraft was at its highest altitude above the terrain at that point. As it flew south toward Libby, it was descending as the terrain rose to meet it.)

Normally, Mohawks perform well on a single engine. However, this particular aircraft had a history of being unable to maintain altitude and safe single-engine airspeed when flying on a single engine. In each case, pilots reported they had to descend to maintain safe airspeed. Maintenance personnel had checked the aircraft several times but could not find the cause.

The SIP requested a straight-in approach to Libby. The tower approved his request and asked for normal reports of altitude and fuel available. The SIP reported he had to descend at four hundred feet per minute to maintain safe airspeed. The tower asked if he had jettisoned his drop tanks. He had not but did so immediately. However, that did not help. The tower asked for his location, and the SIP reported that they were over Huachuca City. The next transmission the tower heard sounded like a garbled "Eject, Jack!"

After the tower was no longer able to contact the aircraft, it began emergency procedures already discussed.

Based on all our knowledge and a review of all documents, we believe the final sequence of events occurred as follows. After last reporting his position over Huachuca City, the SIP realized he was not going to make the airfield. He had full power on the right engine, trying to maintain altitude. This meant he was applying full right aileron and left rudder to hold the aircraft straight and level. At two hundred feet AGL, the SIP decided to eject. This was two hundred feet below minimum safe-ejection altitude for the ejection seat. Based on the wreckage and ground location of the SIP and ejection seat, he told the pilot to eject, thus the "Eject, Jack!"

The SIP then released the controls and pulled the ejection handle between his legs. For some reason, the pilot failed to eject. When the SIP released the aileron and rudder controls to pull his ejection-seat handle, the aircraft immediately rolled to the left from the torque of the right engine at full power. It appears the aircraft was in an attitude with the left wing pointing to the ground as the SIP's ejection seat cleared the aircraft. In that form, the seat traveled parallel to the ground until it contacted the side of the hill about two hundred feet from the aircraft. The G forces on impact killed the SIP.

The aircraft continued to roll and struck the ground inverted at a shallow angle. The propeller strikes point to a fifteen- to twenty-degree angle. The impact sheared the top half of the cockpit and part of the fuselage until the aircraft stopped. The pilot died as the cockpit impacted the ground. The resulting fire destroyed most of the fuselage and a major portion of each wing.

The accident investigation team believes the cause of the accident was pilot error coupled with an unknown or phantom mechanical problem that existed with the aircraft. The SIP was in error to give a single-engine emergency in an aircraft known to have problems in maintaining safe single-engine airspeed without descending to compensate for loss of power in one engine. Knowing the nature of the aircraft, the SIP should have introduced the single-engine emergency in the traffic pattern or within proximity of the runway to ensure landing under the conditions that occurred. The team also feels that command pressure influenced the pilot's decision to eject beyond the point for a safe ejection. The commander's memo threatening to dismiss or relieve from duty the next pilot who damaged an aircraft might have influenced the pilots to try to save the aircraft way past what was prudent.

I'm proud to say the Army Board for Aviation Accident Research accepted the report. Not only did they accept it, but also, they sent a letter to the airfield commander, commending him and his team on their investigation. The accident investigation report was among the best ever received. I like to take credit for making it a good report. My time in the safety officer course at USC paid off in this case.

I regret not demanding that the lieutenant accept my offer to follow his flights on my FM frequency. Had I known of his emergency at the beginning, I believe both of them would still be alive. Because of my familiarity with the area, I would have quickly recognized that at the rate he was descending, he would not make the airfield. I would have ordered him to point the aircraft east and eject while he had a safe altitude to do so. He, of course, could have chosen not to accept my order, but my order making me responsible might have overcome any command pressure he felt to save the aircraft.

After the challenge of the accident investigation, my job became boring. I could not fly until the army resolved my application to remain on flight status. I could fly as a passenger, but we did not fly passengers. My pilots supported me by asking me to be copilot in the Huey. They trusted my piloting skill and had no qualms about flying with me. However, true to my nature, I would not allow it. I would not let another pilot fly with me as copilot, because it would violate official regulations. I held myself to the same high standards I demanded of others.

I guess that subconsciously, I was feeling stress. Consciously, I thought I was doing okay. A week after I completed the accident investigation report, Claudia and I got into an argument for some reason. The argument evolved into an angry fight. Finally, frustrated by anger I did not understand and despairing over the course my life had taken, I said I'd had enough and stormed out of the house. I did not know where I was going. I just wanted to go somewhere that would take my mind off the way I felt.

I ended up at the Hillbilly Club. It was Friday night, and they had a live band playing. Couples crowded the dance floor. I got a drink at the bar and walked to the tables surrounding the dance floor. Most of the tables had drinks sitting on them, which meant they belonged to the couples dancing. A Korean girl sat at one table, nursing a drink and watching the dancers. There were no other glasses sitting on the table, so I walked up to her table.

She looked up at me. She was young and attractive. I asked, "May I sit here?"

She smiled, nodded, and said, "Please."

I sat down in a chair across from her. I asked her if she was there with someone, and she said no. I asked her name and told her mine. She seemed happy about my sitting down with her. The band started another song, and I asked her if she wanted to dance. We danced a slow dance, and she moved in against my body. I was trying to decide if she was single or a prostitute working the bars. After the dance, we returned to our table in silence.

I was about to ask her if she was married, when I noticed someone standing to my right side, close to the table. I looked up, and there, looking into my eyes, was Claudia's friend. My first reaction was that she had found me with another woman, and how was I going to explain it? I stood up and smiled. "Hi," I said with genuine pleasure at seeing her but not sure why she was there. I asked, "Is Frank here with you?"

She said, "No, I was looking for you."

"Why were you looking for me?" I asked.

She looked at the Korean girl, who looked puzzled. I looked at her and said, "My wife."

She replied, "Oh," and with disappointment on her face, she looked back at the dancers.

Claudia's friend said, "Let's go somewhere we can talk. It's noisy in here."

I said, "Sure," and I led her to a couple of seats at the far end of the bar. It was not that quiet, but at least we could speak at a normal level.

We sat down, and I asked her if she wanted a drink. She said yes, and I ordered her a Tom Collins. After the bartender brought the drink, I asked her how she'd known I was there.

She said, "I called Claudia to talk and found out that you two had argued. Claudia told me that you stormed out of the house. I knew you liked the Hillbilly Club, so I figured that is where you would go. After we hung up, I drove here."

I smiled at her and said, "My question should have been why you wanted to find me."

She looked at me with piercing blue eyes. The expression on her face told me she was about to say something that would affect our relationship. She looked down and then back at me before she spoke. "Neal, I have loved you almost from the first time we met. I think you must know by my actions that I feel something more for you than just that you are the husband of my friend. I almost said it the time I got so drunk you had to carry me home. I no longer have any love for my husband. You are not to blame for that. Our problems started on our wedding night. I found out that he was bisexual. That devastated me, but I have tried to make our marriage work. But I gave up long ago."

I was stunned at what she was saying. I had sensed that she felt some attraction to me. Honestly, I felt an attraction to her. But I would never again start an affair, no matter how bad my personal problems were. She had tears in her eyes as she continued. "I have watched the devotion and love you show Claudia despite the many problems between you. Claudia has told me about the arguments you get into. The way you treat her has finally convinced me that I have to end my marriage. I had hoped that somehow you would fall in love with me. But I know that won't happen, because no matter how bad Claudia treats you, you will only love her. Her other friend always describes you as only having eyes for Claudia."

She paused and drank her Tom Collins. She motioned that she wanted another one. I ordered her one and a beer for me. I looked at her, not knowing what to say. I finally said, "I'm truly sorry. I am attracted to you. But I have made the mistake before of thinking I was in love with someone else. It turned out that it was more lust than love. I have vowed that I would never hurt Claudia or some other woman who was expecting more than just sex. I do love Claudia, and I can't deny that."

I was at a loss as to what else to say. She took my hand and looked at me. She spoke again. "I know that. I don't want just an affair. But I can no longer stay here, wanting you and knowing that it won't happen. That's why I wanted to find you tonight. I wanted to tell you how I feel and see how you reacted to it. It's obvious now that we will never be together. But I wanted you to know that you could have had me."

She paused again, as if she hoped I would express a desire for her. My silence was loud. She continued, "I have made up my mind to return to Germany. My son and I are leaving next week. You are the only one I have told so far, so please keep it a secret. I will apply for a divorce in Germany and see what life will bring me there."

I could hear the resolve in her tone. It was the first time I had seen her so sure of herself. She finished her drink and said, "There's something else I want to say to you, Neal. I am a little bitter in saying this, because I love you. I think I could have made you the happiest man in the world. I think you are a good man. But I can see that your devotion to Claudia has blinded you. The sad part is, Claudia doesn't know what she has and certainly doesn't deserve you. I know a side of Claudia that you don't know, and I think you should know it. She's always flirting with other men, and I think she is a little crazy. She has you, but she is still wild, as if she's single. When she goes to Tucson, she always stops at the Holiday Inn lounge for drinks. She says that's the best place to pick up men. She said in Germany, she and her cousin always went to the hotel bars. The men there are usually businessmen with money. They are only there on business, and they have a room for sex. That's why I stopped going to Tucson with her. Neal, you deserve better than Claudia. You have to get over your love for her, or she has to change. I'm leaving now, so this is my good-bye."

Her words stunned me.

She slid off the barstool. She put her arm around my neck and kissed me. She looked at me as if she felt sorry for me. Then she turned and walked out of the club. I sat there like a fool, mentally staggered by what she had told me about Claudia. I felt as if my heart had stopped beating. I had enough to deal with, and now this. I hurt so much that I didn't even feel anger.

I tried to tell myself not to believe her, because she was angry over my rejection and wanted to hurt me. However, I knew she was telling the truth. A long time ago in Germany, I'd asked Claudia where she went when she went out with her cousin. She'd told me they went to fancy hotel bars because they were nicer than the bars full of drunken GIs. They could talk

690

and enjoy the music. That had seemed believable to me, and I'd accepted it. I would have never thought it was for the reason her friend had just told me.

I signaled the bartender for another beer. The hurt started to turn to rage as I realized how stupid I had been. Then the real pain started when I realized there was nothing I could do but accept my lot. I was thirty-seven years old and would soon retire. I had personally sacrificed so much to keep my family together. I did not have the will to put the effort I had spent into a new life and family. I would have to suck up what I had just learned and go on with the life I was living. I now realized what Dale had tried to tell me that day at the Munich airport. I admired him for having the courage to get out of his prison.

I was starting to feel the effects of the three beers, and I ordered another one. I could see how country music and beer were good partners with broken love. *What should I do? Go see if I can find that Korean woman or go home?* I did not want the Korean woman. I wanted to go home to a loving wife I trusted. I had an involuntary sob, and tears flooded my eyes.

As it always was with me, the more I thought about a problem, the more any rage I felt would give way to rationale. Nothing had changed between Claudia and me because of what her friend had told me. I just had not known that Claudia was doing that. We were still married, and we had good times. As a matter of fact, the last four or five months had been really good. Our argument that night had been more my fault than Claudia's. I also had noticed lately that she did not go to Tucson as often as she used to. When she did go, she was home by around 1800 and not 0100 in the morning. Maybe our relations were getting better, and I just had not noticed it.

I finished the beer and decided I'd better go home before I was too drunk to drive. By then, I had rationalized that there was no reason to tell Claudia what her friend had said about her. What good would it do? We would fight, and Claudia would deny it. In a few days, the anger would pass, and we would be friends again. I tried to remember how Claudia had acted when returning from a late night in Tucson. I did not remember her acting any differently. Many times, we had made love the next morning. Where did that leave me? I did not want to believe it was true, so I accepted as truth that she went to bars but never went with a man to a room. When

I got home, she was still up, watching TV. She looked at me and looked away with anger. Then she asked where I had been. She seemed contrite, which surprised me. I told her I had been to the Hillbilly Club. She turned back to the TV without commenting. Her friend left for Germany the following Wednesday. I guess she never told Claudia about our meeting at the Hillbilly Club or what she had told me, nor did I ever mention my meeting with her friend.

Within two days, we were over the fight that had driven me to the Hillbilly Club. I reached a startling conclusion during those two days. My behavior was a lot like my father's habit of going on a drunken bender for a week and then sobering up and acting normal for another two weeks. That had given my siblings and I the hope that he would not go on a drunk again. But he always did. I realized that each time Claudia and I got into a fight, instead of making up right away, I would harbor a grudge in anger for a week. However, I did not want to do that. I did it to show Claudia I did not care—but I did care. As I had in dealing with my father's behavior, Claudia waited out my anger. Looking in the mirror one morning, I told myself I had to stop that. I was the one, more than Claudia, responsible for the problems between us. I did not notice it at the time, but we were slowly healing the rift between us. We were getting along better, and we were fighting less now than we had over the last five years.

Bad news comes in bundles occasionally. At least it did for me. That week, I received a letter from the DA. They denied my application to remain on flying status as an exception to policy. Attached to the letter were orders officially grounding me at the end of March. Soon after that, the FAA canceled my commercial pilot's license. In the letter, they said I could take a flight test with an examiner and get a private pilot's license if I wanted. I never did. I had not expected the DA to approve my application, but I had hoped they might. Now it was fact: I was no longer an army aviator. I had lost something I had worked hard and sweated to earn. It was a bitter blow to the way I read my book of life. I had to turn a page and face an uncertain future.

I expected that next, they would move me from the operations officer job. That would have been a final blow to my ego. However, no one even mentioned moving me. I do not know if it was because of my performance or because of the shortage of officers resulting from the drawdown in Vietnam. Whatever the case, I held the position until I retired.

April came, and I turned thirty-eight years old. My attitude had changed a little. I had to decide what I was going to do after I retired. As in the months before my graduation from high school, I had no idea what to do. I tried to enlist the kids and Claudia in helping me decide, but Claudia was not much help. She did not want to move back to Florida. The kids were adamant that they were not going to move from Sierra Vista. Both of them told me that this was the only home they knew. I had taken them from homes and friends and dragged them around the world many times. This time, they were not going to go with me. I would counter by asking them where they would stay. I tried to make them understand that I would have to go where I could work, but at their age, they did not understand that that was the deciding factor.

Claudia was planning her yearly summer visit to Germany. She was leaving as soon as Ron got out of school. This time, Michele did not want to go, and Claudia had agreed to let her stay. I was happy about that because it meant I did not have to take care of her horse for six weeks. She was sixteen, and we had taught her to drive. She got her driver's license that March, which was a big help because she could drive herself to the stables. The only problem was that she had become a pain in the ass. She was at the age where she resented my guidance and rebelled at anything I wanted of her. She was still respectful but felt she knew everything, so while I enjoyed her being home, she felt I was an intrusion on her life.

Despite her rebellious moods, I admired and loved her very much. She was bright in school. Although she spoke perfect German, she took French as her language elective. Most students in her shoes would have taken German. She had always been a responsible kid. Kathy told me a friend of hers who ran a gas station was looking for someone to do his books at the end of the month. I suggested Michele. I asked Michele if she wanted to do it, and she said yes. The owner showed her how to do the job the first month, and that was all the instruction she needed. From then on, at the end of each month, she picked up all the owner's receipts, sales, and bills and did his bookkeeping. For that, she earned fifteen dollars. It was not much, but the experience was invaluable.

By the end of April, the weather turned hot and dry. It was spring, and with the drawdown in Vietnam, we received fewer and fewer students. That meant budget and personnel cuts. Everything slowed down, and my job became even more boring. Several times, I considered asking for a transfer to the MI instructor pool, but I always decided that since I was retiring, I would just stick it out.

I still kept my high standards and resisted fixing something that was not broken just for a good OER. That's a trend among officers. They try to do something each new rating period to show improvement over the last period. Most of the time, they fix something that was not broke to begin with, the reason being that it's easier to fix something that's not broken than to fix something that is broken. That, in my view, is what politicians do. They fix policy that is working, because it's too hard to fix the broken problems in the United States. By my observations, a new commander will always try to fix something in his new unit that did not need fixing. It is his way of taking charge of success and making it his own.

As we faced budget cuts, I had to reduce the flying hours each quarter. I had to concentrate on giving the assigned pilots enough hours to preserve their minimums. Now, instead of meeting minimums while flying students, I had to schedule training flights.

One day a captain asked if he could fly two hours on a Wednesday afternoon. He was an instructor and did not have any classes to teach on Wednesday afternoon. I always helped instructors, because budget cuts had also reduced their numbers and when they were scheduled to be on the platform, they had to be present. I approved his request for a two-hour training flight. He said he planned on doing a cross-country and some touch-and-gos. Per his flight plan, he took off at 1400 with a TO who also needed flight time for pay.

I was at my desk, reviewing records, when Kathy stuck her head in the door. She told me there was a park ranger on the telephone who wanted to speak with the officer in charge of the Mohawks. I picked up the phone and said, "Captain Griffin speaking."

The voice on the phone said, "I'm a park ranger for Patagonia Lake and National Forest. I have a problem I need to discuss with you. One of your Mohawks buzzed the lake four times about fifteen minutes ago. That's against FAA regulations. There was a crowd of people at the lake, and he was so low that he frightened some of them, and they registered a complaint with me. I would prefer not to put in a formal complaint with the army if we can work it out to ensure it never happens again."

I was flabbergasted. I could not believe what he was telling me, so I asked him, "Sir, are you sure it was a Mohawk?"

He described a Mohawk to me and then told me the tail number. It was a Mohawk, and it was one of mine. I told the ranger it was one of my aircraft and asked him for the exact times the pilot had buzzed the lake. He gave me the details, and I thanked him for not making a formal complaint. He said it was paperwork he would like to avoid, and if we could work it out, he would accept that. I assured him I would take care of it and report to him what I had done. That satisfied him, and we hung up.

I walked out to the operations desk and looked at the flight board. The tail number matched the number on the Mohawk the captain was flying. I told Kathy to tell the captain when he returned to see me. Then I told Major Turner what had happened. He wanted to know what I was going to do. I told him I had to talk to the captain first before I decided. He said okay and told me that whatever I decided, he would back me.

About thirty minutes later, I heard a Mohawk engine whine on the parking apron. Several minutes later, I heard Kathy tell the captain I wanted to talk to him. He knocked on my door, and I told him to come in and shut the door. He had a surprised look on his face as he shut the door.

I told him to sit down, and I asked him if he was aware of his rights under Article 32 of the military code. He said yes and wanted to know what this was about. I told him that a Patagonia park ranger had filed a complaint about a Mohawk buzzing the lake. I said, "The tail number matched the number of the aircraft you were flying."

His face turned red when I told him that. Before he could speak, I continued. "You know it's a violation of my SOP, army regulations, and FAA policy to buzz a public place for any reason, right?"

He looked shaken at what I'd said. "Why don't you tell me what hell you were doing and why?" I said angrily.

"Well, my mother and father are visiting us, and with my wife and kids, they were spending the day at the lake. I was just showing them what a Mohawk could do. I did not realize I was breaking any laws."

It was déjà vu, except instead of a lieutenant almost destroying a Mohawk in Korea, it was a captain doing something stupid. I was cold now with anger. "Well, Captain, you at least knew that it violated my SOP. I have your initials recognizing that the SOP forbade low-level flight except for student IR and camera training. You have put me and, more importantly, the commander of USAICS in an embarrassing situation. I have to take action to ensure the park ranger it will not happen again, or he will file a formal complaint through channels to the army. If he does, the report will come from the army to the commander of USAICS and then down through channels to me."

I could see the captain was beginning to resent the way I was talking to him. "According to the park ranger, you made four passes over the lake, scaring the hell out of the people there. On one pass, you were so low and close to the camping area that your prop blast blew several tents down. You risked destroying a two-million-dollar aircraft and injuring the people on the ground and the TO in the aircraft with you. Statistically, almost twenty-one percent of army aviation accidents are the result of stupid stunts such as yours."

He was uncomfortable at this point. I paused to think, and then I asked, "What do you think you deserve for your unprofessional behavior?"

He looked at me defiantly and responded, "You just chewed me out. I don't think I deserve anything more than that. I didn't injure anyone or damage any equipment. I didn't do anything that a hundred pilots haven't done. My only problem is that you caught me doing it. I think the ass chewing is plenty."

I knew the ass chewing would not satisfy the park ranger. We would have bigger problems if the people at the lake got word that the only action taken against the pilot who'd scared the shit out of them was an ass chewing. I was sure someone among them would contact their representative over the incident. I would have if I were one of them. The park ranger had taken a chance by letting me take care of the incident. He could be in hot water for not making a formal complaint.

I looked at the captain and, letting my anger show, said, "I don't think you understand, Captain. What you did far exceeds the ass-chewing-and-forget-it solution. I intend to write a letter of reprimand for the signature of the director of logistics. I will ask that it become a part of your official record. My first consideration was to ask for an Article 15, but that would get the attention of the CG, and I'm hoping to keep this incident at the directorate level. At the same time, I hope the letter of reprimand and its resulting impact on your career will be enough for the park ranger."

He shook his head in anger and asked if I was finished with him. I said yes and told him he could leave. He turned and stormed out the door, slamming it behind him. I took out my writing pad and started drafting the letter of reprimand.

A couple of minutes passed, and I heard a knock on the door. I said, "Come in," and Kathy opened the door and looked at me. The walls to my office were thin, and I had raised my voice during my conversation with the captain. I could tell she and everyone else had overheard our conversation.

The expression on her face was as if she were looking at a stranger. She had never seen or heard me rebuke someone as harshly as I had the captain. She did not know what to say until I smiled at her. She shook her head and said, "I hope to hell I never do anything to get you that mad."

Two of my WOs stuck their heads in the door. They did not say anything. They just gave me a thumbs-up. I completed the draft reprimanding the captain for poor judgment, unprofessional conduct, and endangerment of personnel and military equipment. I included a statement that the letter would be part of his record during his assignment at USAICS.

When I had the draft completed to my satisfaction, I took it to Major Turner. He read it and asked if I was sure I wanted to ruin the captain's career. I said, "Not particularly, but I'm sure I do not want him in the army if he believes he can do what he did and get away with it." I expressed my fear to Major Turner that if we did not take this incident seriously, then the park ranger would file a formal report. He agreed and took the draft to the director for his approval and signature.

The next day, I drove to the lake and gave a copy of the signed letter to the park ranger. After he read the letter, he felt that it remedied the problem. I thanked him again and left. That was the last I ever heard from him.

However, the captain paid an extreme price for his misconduct. The commander did not recommend him for promotion on the next DA promotion board. As a result, the army released him from service. I do not know if the letter of reprimand had any impact on that. The captain never said anything to me about what had happened, but before his family left the area, his wife talked to me on the phone and called me about every dirty name I knew and a few I did not know for getting him kicked out of the army. I felt bad about what had happened, but I knew that if he had done something stupid again and killed someone, I would have felt worse.

A few days before Claudia left for Germany with Ron, I saw an advertisement for new houses for sale in Sierra Vista. I would have to move from government quarters after I retired, so it dawned on me that it would be better to move before I retired. I convinced Claudia of that, so we decided to look at the newly built houses before she left. The price of the houses ranged from $35,000 to $40,000. We looked at four models and found a three-bedroom, two-bath 1,560-square-foot model that we both loved. What's more, one was under construction, and the builder would complete it in about four weeks.

I started the paperwork to buy it right away. I needed Claudia to help pick out the paint colors, rugs, and kitchen tile. We managed to complete the task before she left. We financed the house through the VA, so there was no down payment needed, and two weeks after she left for Germany, I closed on the house and signed the loan papers. Two weeks later, the house was ready, and I did the final inspection and accepted the keys. Claudia and I were home buyers for the first time in our marriage.

In August, I decided to move from quarters into my new house. I started packing our belongings into boxes. It took me a week to pack everything. I rented a truck and, with the help of my neighbor, moved everything into my house on Steppe Street in Sierra Vista. I knew where to put furniture and beds, but I left some items in the boxes for Claudia's help. Like all new houses, our house had no landscaping except for the few bushes the contractor had planted. Both the front yard and backyard were dirt.

I knew Claudia would not accept dirt, so I started planning my landscape. She and Ron got back at the end of August, before I started work on the landscape. I kidded her about her staying gone until I got us moved and cleared quarters. She said she was just smart. As I'd suspected, her next words were "I want a fence, and I want this dirt covered with grass."

I decided I would first build the fence. I had never built a fence before, so I bought a book about fence construction and read it. I had a natural talent for construction work; plus, building a fence is the bottom end of construction and requires little skill. The only help I needed was with digging the postholes. Claudia had become close friends with an American woman. They played tennis together every day, so her friend volunteered her husband to help me.

They came over one Saturday to barbecue and dig postholes. I had to rent a posthole digger to dig the postholes. Arizona soil is hard and filled with rocks. Without a digger, it would have taken me weeks to dig the holes. I had carefully laid out the fence and marked the location of each post. When they arrived, we started on the holes.

A five-horsepower engine runs the auger that digs the holes. To use the digger, two men hold the digger vertically over the spot for the hole and let the auger dig. I had no problems until the auger hit a rock, and then it slowed as it pushed against the rock. That transferred the torque to the two people holding the digger.

It turned out that the husband helping me was not in good physical shape. Each time we hit a big rock and the torque reversed, it overpowered him, and he would stumble. That put all of the horsepower on me, and I wasn't strong enough to keep the five-horsepower engine from turning me. The result was that it took us all day to dig forty holes, and by then, he was so exhausted he could hardly stand. We took showers and did the barbecue.

He volunteered to help me set the posts and build the fence, but I declined. I told him I could do the rest by myself at my leisure. If I needed his help, I would call him. I never called him, and I think he was grateful for that. I set the posts in one weekend, but it took me two weekends to nail the rails and cedar panels. I loved working on the fence, and as I finished each eight-foot section, I would stop to admire it. It took 320 feet of fence to enclose my backyard. I was proud of the fence, and Claudia's compliments on how nice it looked made me feel good.

Landscaping my yard became my passion. I could hardly wait until the weekends to start another project. Before I finished, I had extended the little four-by-six-foot slab that had come with the house to a twenty-four-by-sixteen-foot patio. I laid slump block and built arches on the sides and the end of the patio. Then I put the roof on. I added a room on the west side of the house. I covered the front with rocks, which was the preferred ground cover. It was attractive and saved water. I won the Sierra Vista House of the Month award one time for my landscaping design and use of shrubbery.

Before I knew it, November arrived. I received a letter from the DA, telling me that as a reserve officer, I had to leave active duty at the end of November. I had the choice of retiring or not retiring; I could continue to work for the army without pay. I took the letter to personnel and told them to retire me. I had avoided thinking about what I would do after retirement, but the letter made it clear that it was time for me to start seriously planning my retirement. I decided I would stay in Sierra Vista because of the kids. I would apply for my VA benefits and get a college degree. I would apply for a civil service position on post. In fact, the main employers in the area were the military organizations on post. I would have to wait six months before I could go to work for the government, but I figured I could make it with my retirement, VA, and unemployment benefits. I started counting the days till retirement with that plan in mind.

Around the middle of November, I received orders promoting me to major, effective the middle of January 1976. That was a help since I got eleven months of back pay as a major. Of course, I had to take off my captain's bars and sew gold oak leaves on my uniforms. I had to buy a new dress hat with field-grade mesh on the visor. I did it with pride, and Claudia was proud to see me wearing the rank of major. She had been with me from PFC to staff sergeant to major. I think I had a little vanity in me, because each time I looked in the mirror, I had to grin with pride at the oak leaves on my collar.

I waited until after the Thanksgiving holiday to start clearing post and ending my official responsibilities. I wrote all the OERs on my officers and NCOs. I inventoried my property, and Major Turner signed for it. He did not have a replacement for me, so he planned on assuming my duties. I returned all of my field equipment and flight equipment. As part of retirement, I had to undergo a medical examination. The dentist checked my teeth and replaced one crown, and on November 29, I finished clearing post.

The thirtieth fell on a Friday. At the end of each month, the post held an end-of-month parade and awards ceremony. At the ceremony, the USAICS commander presented decorations and awards to the receiving soldiers. At 0900 on November 30, I stood in ranks with eight other men who were receiving awards that day. As Claudia watched from the grandstands, the USAICS commander presented me with the Meritorious Service Medal for outstanding service to the army, culminating with my assignment as operations officer of MAD. That was it—my last official act as an officer and soldier in the army. As I stood there waiting for the troops to pass in review, I thought of the hundreds of times I had stood or marched on a parade field. Now it was over. All I had to do was go by the personnel office to sign out.

I met Claudia after the ceremony, and we drove to the personnel office. She waited in the car while I went to sign out. The personnel officer gave me my personal records, and then we reviewed my DD Form 214, my report of separation from active duty. I signed it, and he made several copies for me. We shook hands, and I was officially out of the army. I had an inactive reserve obligation until I was sixty, but that would only affect me in a mobilization for war.

I walked to the car, where Claudia was waiting. As we drove home, I thought about what I still wanted to do. I wanted to go to the hangar to tell everyone good-bye, but Claudia asked me to drop her off first. I did not say anything to Claudia, but I was a little disappointed that no one had thrown a retirement party for me.

I walked through the hangar, shaking hands and saying good-bye. The odor of JP-4 exhaust and the sounds of aircraft engines were familiar and comfortable. I hated for it to end. I did not tell Matt or Kathy good-bye, because we would still meet on the weekends. Major Turner told me that everybody was getting together tomorrow in Tombstone for lunch, and he wanted Claudia and me to come. I told him I did not know what Claudia had planned, but we would try to make it.

I got into my car and slowly looked at the parked aircraft and the buildings. I nodded as if affirming something that I felt. Maybe it was regret or anticipation. It was some vague sensation that came over me for a few seconds. For the first time in twenty years, I was in charge of my life. I was thirty-eight years old and still young.

EPILOGUE

Claudia and I went to Tombstone for lunch. It turned out that the get-together was a surprise retirement party. Major Turner had arranged for the Tombstone Vigilantes to hang me (a mock hanging, of course). The Tombstone Vigilantes dress in the attire of the 1880's act out old western events at parties and other social activities. It was one of those parties that you remember until you die. Plus, Tombstone was and still is my favorite town.

I started college, and six months after I retired, I took a temporary position as an imagery analysis instructor in the Directorate of Training and Doctrine (DOTD), USAICS. I taught imagery interpretation, photogrammetry, and target recognition for about a year. Then the director moved me to another section to develop training for new intelligence systems.

Six months after I started working in the training development section, funds ran out for temporary employees, and I was terminated. Two of the sergeants with whom I worked were amateur entrepreneurs, and they asked me to open a fence construction company with them. I did, and we opened the Third Rail Fence Company Inc. I was president of the company for a year and a half. We were successful, but I was working twelve-hour days six days a week to get the company going. Claudia was unhappy about that. Her reason surprised me: she wanted me home with her on the weekends and holidays.

I was still going to Cochise College at night. A friend who was the chief of the doctrine development branch in DOTD and I were taking the same class. He was short three writers in his branch and had funds to hire them. He wanted me to apply for a position. My job would be to research and write field manuals providing doctrine, tactics, and techniques for military intelligence combat operations. So after twenty years of struggling with the task of writing while in the army, I resigned from the fence company, sold my stocks, and accepted his offer. I couldn't believe I was taking a writing job after my poor writing skills had haunted my military career.

Twenty years later, I was a GS-13 and chief of the doctrine division. I supervised a writing branch and an editing and production branch. I was recognized army wide for my expert knowledge of military intelligence doctrine, tactics, and techniques. During those years, Michele and Ron matured into outstanding adults. They are both happily married and successful and are a joy to Claudia and me.

Despite the comment of "Not recommended for higher education" on my final high school report card, I graduated from the University of Arizona in 1987 with a grade point average of 3.67 and a bachelor of science degree in business administration.

Claudia and I remained in Sierra Vista for another twenty-eight years. By the end of 1977, a new Neal and Claudia had evolved. It was as if the previous ten years didn't exist. I often wonder how we survived those years of our discontent. Today we are happy, deeply in love, and totally devoted to one another. On our next anniversary in 2015, we will mark fifty-six years of marriage.

I once told a dear friend that because of my conduct, I had failed in my marriage. My friend responded, "No, when you've been happily married for more than fifty years, that's not failure. That indeed is success."

I know that many reading this memoir will want to judge Claudia and me by what they read. That's fair. But for those who know us now, I hope you will judge us by who we are today.

The one thing I know is that on my own, I could not have accomplished what I have done. Only by God's grace and mercy, for reasons yet unknown to me, have I come so far. For that, I praise and humbly thank him each day.

My first mission in Viet Nam-coastal
reconnaissance with naval Observer.

Me displaying the equipment that I take with me on a
reconnaissance mission, Qui Nhon, Viet Nam, 1967.

Returning from a mission. The red and blue books are maps
with my sighting annotated. Qui Nhon, Viet Nam, 1967.

Me in front of Beaver. Germany, 1968.

Mohawk parked on apron on Yoido Island.

Me standing by a Mohawk on Yoido Island, 1971.

At my job at XO, April 1971.

Me flying Mohawk over Arizona, 1975.

Fishing in the Sea of Cortez, 1975.